Zukunft der Hochschulbildung - Future Higher Education

Hochschulbildung befindet sich weltweit in einem dramatischen Umbruch. Studienanfängerquoten von über 70 Prozent innerhalb der nächsten 15 Jahre in den Industrieländern sowie eine drastisch steigende Nachfrage in den Entwicklungs- und Schwellenländern markieren einen neuen Stellenwert und eine gewandelte Funktion der Hochschulbildung in Gesellschaften des postmodernen Zeitalters. Zur gleichen Zeit steigen die Anforderungen an Hochschulen, ihre Absolventinnen und Absolventen darauf vorzubereiten, eine globale und digitalisierte Welt von morgen zu gestalten. Die Rolle die der Hochschulbildung für die Umsetzung der Ziele für nachhaltige Entwicklung (Sustainable Development Goals) zukommt, spricht eine deutliche Sprache: Ohne eine inhaltliche und organisatorisch erneuerte Hochschule der Zukunft werden gesellschaftliche Problemlagen wie sie etwa mit dem Klimawandel verbunden sind, Herausforderungen der zukünftig noch zunehmenden Migration, Konflikte, die durch populistische Gesellschafts- und Politikentwürfe entstehen und die damit verbundenen Frage nach der Zukunft der Demokratie, nicht zu lösen sein. Die Entwicklung eines erneuerten gesellschaftlichen Konsenses über die Rolle der Hochschulbildung der Zukunft erfordert es, Foren und Kanäle zu schaffen, in denen die Frage der Hochschulbildung der Zukunft diskutiert werden kann. Die Reihe „Zukunft der Hochschulbildung" hat zum Ziel, Beiträge aus der ganzen Breite der wissenschaftlichen und gesellschaftspolitischen Themen aufzugreifen und damit die Entwicklung von tragfähigen Konzepten für die Zukunft der Hochschulbildung zu unterstützen.

Die Themen der Reihe spannen sich von tiefgehenden Gesellschaftsanalysen, der Bedeutung des Wissenschaftssystems und Hochschulbildungssystems in der Gesellschaft der Zukunft bis hin zu Fragen des zukünftigen Hochschulmanagements. Dabei werden empirische Studien aber auch grundlegende Ansätze zu Hochschulinnovationsthemen fokussiert, auch zu Detailthemen, wie bspw. alternativen Studienformen, Mikrozertifikaten, der digitalen Transformation, Blockchain für die Hochschule und anderen Themen.

Ulf-Daniel Ehlers · Laura Eigbrecht
Editors

Creating the University of the Future

A Global View on Future Skills and Future Higher Education

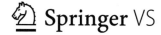

Editors
Ulf-Daniel Ehlers
Forschungsgruppe NextEducation
@ Fakultät Wirtschaft, DHBW Karlsruhe
Karlsruhe, Germany

Laura Eigbrecht
Forschungsgruppe NextEducation
@ Fakultät Wirtschaft, DHBW Karlsruhe
Karlsruhe, Germany

ISSN 2662-5768 ISSN 2662-5776 (electronic)
Zukunft der Hochschulbildung – Future Higher Education
ISBN 978-3-658-42947-8 ISBN 978-3-658-42948-5 (eBook)
https://doi.org/10.1007/978-3-658-42948-5

© The Editor(s) (if applicable) and The Author(s) 2024 "This book is an open access publication."

Open Access This book is licensed under the terms of the Creative Commons Attribution 4.0 International License (http://creativecommons.org/licenses/by/4.0/), which permits use, sharing, adaptation, distribution and reproduction in any medium or format, as long as you give appropriate credit to the original author(s) and the source, provide a link to the Creative Commons license and indicate if changes were made.
The images or other third party material in this book are included in the book's Creative Commons license, unless indicated otherwise in a credit line to the material. If material is not included in the book's Creative Commons license and your intended use is not permitted by statutory regulation or exceeds the permitted use, you will need to obtain permission directly from the copyright holder.
The use of general descriptive names, registered names, trademarks, service marks, etc. in this publication does not imply, even in the absence of a specific statement, that such names are exempt from the relevant protective laws and regulations and therefore free for general use.
The publisher, the authors, and the editors are safe to assume that the advice and information in this book are believed to be true and accurate at the date of publication. Neither the publisher nor the authors or the editors give a warranty, expressed or implied, with respect to the material contained herein or for any errors or omissions that may have been made. The publisher remains neutral with regard to jurisdictional claims in published maps and institutional affiliations.

This Springer VS imprint is published by the registered company Springer Fachmedien Wiesbaden GmbH, part of Springer Nature.
The registered company address is: Abraham-Lincoln-Str. 46, 65189 Wiesbaden, Germany

Paper in this product is recyclable.

In a world without future, each parting of friends is a death. In a world without future, each loneliness is final. In a world without future, each laugh is the last laugh. In a world without future, beyond the present lies nothingness, and people cling to the present as if hanging from a cliff.

Alan Lightman

Foreword by Andreas Schleicher

I am honored to contribute a preface to this important book, "Creating the University of the Future", edited by Ulf-Daniel Ehlers and Laura Eigbrecht. The volume appears at the right time as the world continues to change at an unprecedented pace. More than ever before, it is essential that higher education around the world evolves to ensure that students are equipped with the Future Skills they need to lead happy lives, succeed in their professional careers and better contribute to societies living in peace together. This requires a bold and visionary approach to higher education, one that prioritizes Future Skills, promotes development of learner agency, and prepares students for the challenges of the future.

The idea to have a fixed curriculum which is then transmitted to students is really an idea of the past. The idea of the future is one where educators become creative designers of innovative learning environments, where the curriculum is seen as a product of co-creation, where learners and educators decide together what content is relevant in this moment for that purpose, and in what way it can be approached. The kind of things that are easy to teach and maybe easy to test are precisely the things that are now easy to digitize, to automate. We must ask: what makes us human? How do we complement, not substitute the artificial intelligence we created in our computers? Learning is no longer about being taught, but about developing a compass, the navigation tools to find your own way in a world that is increasingly complex, volatile, ambiguous. Our capacity to navigate ambiguity, in the moment of crisis, is perhaps the most important one to have.

At the OECD, we are committed to provide support to national and institutional policy-makers to create visions for future learning and thus also the University of the Future. This book is a valuable contribution to this effort, bringing together experts from around the world to share their insights, examples, and experiences on this important topic. The editors, Ulf-Daniel Ehlers and Laura Eigbrecht, have done an excellent job in curating a range of perspectives and approaches from a truly global perspective. Their mission has been to take stock of the current discussion on Future Skills development in higher education and thus support the process of establishing a global common understanding of Future Skills for future higher education. Due to the diverse range of higher education institutions contributing their experiences and expertise, the book offers a comprehensive overview of the current state of play of Future Skills in higher education and related challenges.

In a global panorama, the selected contributions are presenting experiences of including Future Skills into higher education programs both in the field of teaching and learning as well as on an institutional and even a more conceptual, international, policy-related level. All contributions share a common understanding and aim at guaranteeing that students are equipped with the Future Skills they need to succeed in an ever-changing world. The University of the Future must be flexible and allow students to learn at their own pace and in collaboration. It must focus on learner agency and ensure that students are prepared for the challenges of the future.

Most importantly, a Future Skills culture on all levels should be promoted, and this should be done in a similar way as future learning should take place: driven by optimism, respective of present and future challenges, and facing these in transformative processes of co-creation, of openness and of developing new visions together.

In conclusion, I want to extend my sincere gratitude to Ulf-Daniel Ehlers and Laura Eigbrecht for bringing together this valuable collection of perspectives and experiences, and to all the contributors for sharing their insights and expertise. I am confident that "Creating the University of the Future" will be an invaluable resource for university leaders, teachers, and students alike, and will inspire them to embrace the opportunities and challenges of the future.

Andreas Schleicher
Director of Education and Skills at the OECD

Paris
October 2023

Editors' Preface

The book in front of you is a truly global collaboration. After almost 10 years of research on Future Skills for higher education and a growing interest from the entire higher education sector, we wanted to go global and find out how Future Skills are discussed in higher education in other parts of the world. We termed our project the "Global Future Skills" project and reached out to colleagues and institutions from all over the world, spreading the call for contributions to six continents. The resonance was overwhelming and while contributions kept coming in, we started to understand that Future Skills are much more than just a mode of studying and learning in higher education. The concept is having a much deeper impact and touches the fundamental structures and beliefs of higher education institutions all around the world. It is going deeper and touches the fundamentals of our institutional constitutions. "Creating the University of the Future" as title of our project came to us naturally when all contributions and chapters, ideas and charts were on the table and we took charge of the enormous power of innovation and reform which came through between the lines of the Future Skills concepts from colleagues who agreed to contribute.

While we kept adding more chapters to the book, it became apparent that any Future Skills Turn in higher education would demand for more than some small reforms but rather implies a new culture in higher education. To capture some of these visions on future higher education and learning, we reached out to some of the most prominent visionary pioneers and led a series of fascinating conversations which we decided to include as a special and authentic conversation format into the book. We are very thankful to all colleagues who agreed to engage in an in-depth conversation to explain their view on new learning and next-mode higher education.

The publication in its entirety shows: The world is changing at a pace never before seen in history. Rapid advancements in technology, globalization, and shifting demographics are reshaping the world we live in. The skills that were once considered essential for success are becoming obsolete, and new skills are emerging in their place. In this book, we explore the Future Skills that will be essential for individuals to thrive in the future, and how universities can adapt to equip students with the skills they need to succeed.

The university has long been a bastion of learning and knowledge creation. However, universities must evolve to meet the changing needs of students and the workforce. Traditional models of education are no longer sufficient in preparing students for the challenges and opportunities of the future. As such, we need a new vision for the future university, one that is adaptive, innovative, and focused on developing the skills that will be essential for creating a sustainable future world worth living in.

Creating the University of the Future is a call to action for universities to rethink their approach to education. We believe that universities have a critical role to play in shaping the future of work, of societies living together in peace and preparing students for the challenges ahead. This book provides a roadmap for universities to develop the skills that will be essential for success in the future. It draws on the latest research and presents insights from experts across a range of fields to identify the key skills that will be most valuable in the future.

Creating the University of the Future is a must-read for anyone interested in the future of higher education and work. It provides a comprehensive overview of the skills that will be essential for success in the future, and a roadmap for higher education institutions to adapt and thrive in this changing landscape. We hope that this book will inspire higher education institutions to embrace innovation, collaborate with employers and policy-makers, and create a brighter future for their students and the world.

On a last note we would like to thank all authors and co-authors, and last but not least, a special thanks to a wonderful team which supported us with all practicalities and details in the publication process—especially Daniella Pauly Jensen, Josefine Schaeffer, Emily Rauch and Silke Huber for reviewing, supporting and working out the graphical work and all logistics needed.

Editors' Preface XI

Finally, let us express a very special learning: Creating a book like this is a professional but also a very personal journey of meeting new colleagues and creating a social network in which collaborators become good friends. Thank you! You will all stay with us on our journey to creating the future university.

Karlsruhe, Germany
in October 2023

Ulf-Daniel Ehlers
Laura Eigbrecht

What Can You Expect from this Book?

Creating the University of the Future—A Global View on Future Skills and Future Higher Education is a book about the role of higher education institutions in a world which is changing faster than ever before. Never has it been more urgent to actively shape the global transformation we are facing in order to create the best possible future, and never has there been a greater imperative for students to learn the necessary skills—Future Skills—for this. Their promotion is currently one of the most debated challenges for higher education institutions all over the world.

This book presents visionary higher and tertiary education programs aiming at Future Skills for their graduates. It compiles contributions from more than 50 authors who are engaged in global intergovernmental organizations such as UNESCO and OECD involved in research and policy-making as well as from higher and tertiary education institutions from different countries and continents.

With the challenges ahead, the book calls for the "Future Skills Turn" on a global level to become reality and demands for rethinking our current educational systems and realities. This volume aims at increasing visibility for existing and emerging innovative teaching and learning practices for educational professionals, while informing educational leaders about the newest Future Skills strategies, and inspiring all educational stakeholders on their journey towards future-ready higher education.

The publication is structured into five distinct sections which are shortly summarized below.

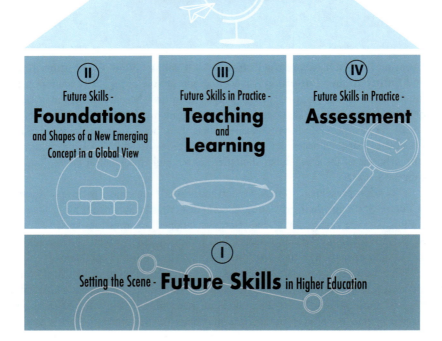

Part I: Setting the Scene—Future Skills in Higher Education

Part I focuses on introducing the concept and relevance of Future Skills and giving an overview to the reader by introducing the different contributions. The terminology and a working definition for meaning, scope and context of what "Future Skills" as a concept refers to will be elaborated, and the Future Skills concept as developed by Ehlers (2020) is introduced. Additionally, insight into

What Can You Expect from this Book? XV

a range of existing Future Skills frameworks in form of a meta-analysis is presented and discussed. In the section's final chapter, the editors summarize success factors for implementing Future Skills into higher education based on recommendations from all contributing authors.

Part II: Future Skills—Foundations and Shapes of a New Emerging Concept in a Global View

Part II focuses on discussing basic Future Skills concepts and approaches in (global) higher education. The section is composed of a number of Future Skills conversations which were conducted to capture current forefront thinking on Future Skills in higher education, amongst them leading authorities in the field, like Andreas Schleicher (OECD) and Tom Wambeke (ITCILO). Global experts like Tony Bates (Tony Bates Associates Ltd.), Wolfgang Stark (University of Duisburg-Essen) and Francesc Pedró (UNESCO IESALC) each give insights into the important determinants of changing higher education towards Future Skills. The section is concluded by a contribution on a new theory of change for higher education based on a global empirical study.

Part III: Future Skills in Practice—Teaching and Learning

Part III provides a deep dive into higher education practices in different countries and institutions through insight into teaching and learning Future Skills. A Future Skills expert-talk with Angela Duckworth (Character Lab) will lead the way, followed by selected examples of Future Skills-ready higher and tertiary education on a larger scale such as the 42 Coding Schools or the approach of Team Academy.

Part IV: Future Skills in Practice—Assessment

Part IV focuses on the important and hotly debated theme of assessment of Future Skills in higher education. After an introduction to different Future Skills assessment methods and practices, the contributions present a wide range of self-evaluation approaches, formative assessment concepts and teaching-learning integrated "assessment as learning" approaches, as well as the role of concepts such as micro-credentials for validating and recognizing Future Skills.

Part V: Future Skills in Higher Education—The Wider View

Part V widens the perspective and presents selected national and international Future Skills initiatives and approaches. All initiatives aim at making society and lifelong learning future-proof and are integrating educational policy and higher education practices. Here, Singapore's Future Skills approach is described from two perspectives, followed by examples from the Japanese and European context and an inspirational outlook from New Zealand on the concept of creating a Universal Learning Community for Future Skills.

Contents

Part I Setting the Scene – Future Skills in Higher Education

1 Creating the University of the Future: A Global Panorama on Future Skills.. 3
Ulf-Daniel Ehlers and Laura Eigbrecht

2 Towards a Future Skills Framework for Higher Education........ 21
Ulf-Daniel Ehlers

3 The Practice of Future Skills Learning: An Assessment of Approaches, Conditions and Success Factors................... 61
Laura Eigbrecht and Ulf-Daniel Ehlers

Part II Future Skills – Foundations and Shapes of a New Emerging Concept in a Global View

4 "I've Learnt Everything I Know from the World."............... 75
Ulf-Daniel Ehlers and Laura Eigbrecht

5 Future Skills—Back into the Future? Emerging Trends in Educational Innovation in Higher Education.................. 93
Francesc Pedró

6 Teaching the Skills Needed for the Future...................... 123
Tony Bates

7 Future Universities as Activating Resonance Spaces. New Roles in Society—Innovative Approaches.................. 139
Wolfgang Stark

XVII

8	**Building a Creative Ecosystem of Intentional Serendipity**	161

Ulf-Daniel Ehlers and Laura Eigbrecht

9 Beyond Future Skills in Higher Education: A New Theory of Change ... 175

Eglis Chacón, Emma Harden-Wolfson, Luz Gamarra Caballero, Bosen Lily Liu and Dana Abdrasheva

Part III Future Skills in Practice – Teaching and Learning

10 "If You Really Want to Change the World, the Smartest Way to do so is Through Education" ... 201

Ulf-Daniel Ehlers and Laura Eigbrecht

11 Team Academy: Future Skills and the Future of Learning ... 215

Michael P. Vogel

12 Education for Future Skills Development: Cognitive, Collaborative and Ethical Skills ... 241

Carmen Păunescu and Mary McDonnell-Naughton

13 The World Citizen School Model. Learning Philosophy and Learning System for Global, Socially Innovative and Value-Based Future Learning ... 261

Michael Wihlenda

14 Learning Design for Future Skills Development in Small State Contexts ... 283

Sandhya Gunness, Karen Ferreira-Meyers and Thanasis Daradoumis

15 Boosting Future Skills in Higher Education. Lessons Learned from Funding Programs, Networking, Establishing Standards & Curricular Integration ... 313

Felix Suessenbach, Judith Koeritz, Andreas Wormland and Henning Koch

16 May the Code Be with You: The 42 Learning Model in Germany ... 335

Ulf-Daniel Ehlers and Laura Eigbrecht

17 Interdisciplinary Project to Build Teaching Skills: A Pedagogical Approach ... 351

Mônica Cristina Garbin and Edison Trombeta de Oliveira

Contents XIX

18 Changemaking on Campus 369
Judit Costa

19 The "University of the Future" of the Philippines: The Case of University of the Philippines Open University's Master of Public Management Program 373
Juvy Lizette M. Gervacio

20 Using Real-World Problems and Project-Based Learning for Future Skill Development: An Approach to Connect Higher Education Students and Society Through User-Centered Design... 393
André Luiz Maciel Santana and Roseli de Deus Lopes

Part IV   Future Skills in Practice – Assessment

21 Assessment of Future Skills Learning: Changing Futures in Higher Education 421
Nicole Geier and Ulf-Daniel Ehlers

22 Active Learning and Integrated Assessment: Minerva's Approach to Teaching Future Skills 437
Megan K. Gahl, Abha Ahuja, Raquel H. Ribeiro, Maia Averett and James Genone

23 Developing a More Granular and Equitable Approach to the Learner-Earner Journey. The Role of Badging, Micro-Credentials and Twenty-first Century Skills Within Higher Education to Enable Future Workforce Development 457
Grame Barty, Naomi Boyer, Alexandros Chrysikos, Margo Griffith, Kevin House, Tara Laughlin, Ebba Ossiannilsson, Rupert Ward and Holly Zanville

24 Formative Assessment of 21st Century Skills................. 489
Tobias Seidl

25 The State of Skills: A Global View from Burning Glass Institute and Wiley 509
Ulf-Daniel Ehlers and Laura Eigbrecht

Part V Future Skills in Higher Education – The Wider View

26 Future-Skilling the Workforce: SkillsFuture Movement in Singapore 515
Soon-Joo Gog, Edwin Tan and Kelsie Tan

27 Anticipating the Future: Continuing Education at the National University of Singapore 529
Miriam J. Green, Christalle Tay and Ye-Her Wu

28 Aiming to Build Future Skills for Society 5.0: Educational DX (Digital Transformation) of University Education in Japan 549
Keiko Ikeda

29 Future Skill Needs for IT Professionals—an Empirical Study 569
Marina Brunner and Ulf-Daniel Ehlers

30 Future Higher Education in New Zealand: Creating a Universal Learning Community for Future Skills 589
Stephen Marshall

Editors and Contributors

About the Editors

Ulf-Daniel Ehlers Ulf is the founder and director of NextEducation, an international boutique-research institute currently hosting the largest project base on Future Skills research activities in Europe. Ulf is a learning innovation expert, founder of mindful-leaders.net, serial entrepreneur, and Professor for Educational Management and Lifelong Learning at the Baden-Wuerttemberg Cooperative State University in Karlsruhe. From 2011–2017, he held the position of Vice-President at the same university and has been responsible for Quality and Academic Affairs. He also held positions as Associate Professor of University Duisburg-Essen (Germany), Professor for Technology-Enhanced Learning of University Augsburg (Germany) and Associate Professor of the Graduate School for Management and Technology of the University of Maryland University College (USA). Ulf has delivered keynotes and spoken to audiences in more than 45 countries. He is author of more than 18 books and 300 scholarly articles with over 7000 academic citations. Ulf is a trained coach, facilitator, and expert for mindful communication, and holds degrees in English Language, Social Sciences, and Education Sciences from the University of Bielefeld, where he finished his Ph.D. with honors in the field of Technology-Enhanced Learning in 2003. He was awarded his habilitation in 2008 from the University of Duisburg-Essen. His writings on Quality in Education are internationally awarded.

Laura Eigbrecht is an academic researcher at the Baden-Wuerttemberg Cooperative State University (DHBW Karlsruhe) at the Chair of Educational Management and Lifelong Learning. As a doctoral candidate at TU Dresden, she conducts research in the field of transformative and participatory Future Skills in Higher Education. Her further research interests include future higher education, Education for Sustainable Development, community engagement in higher education, student participation and inclusion, and transformative education. After her binational Bachelor's degree in European Media and Culture at Bauhaus-Universität Weimar (GER) and Université Lumière Lyon 2 (F) and her Master's degree in Children's and Youth Media at Universität Erfurt (GER) and Tilburg University (NL), she worked at KiKA (German public children TV channel) as well as in teaching and consulting in the field of migration, language, and education. She continues to produce podcasts and radio contributions on topics such as the future of higher education and sustainability.

Contributors

Dana Abdrasheva MSc Korkyt Ata Kyzylorda University, Kyzylorda, Kazakhstan

Abha Ahuja Academic Director at Minerva Project/Associate Professor of Natural Sciences at Minerva University, Miverva Project/Minerva University, San Francisco, USA

Editors and Contributors

Maia Averett Senior Academic Program Manager at Minerva Project/Professor of Computational Sciences at Minerva University/Professor of Mathematics at Mills College, Miverva Project/Minerva University/Mills College, San Francisco, USA

Grame Barty Co-Leader ICoBC Global Workforce Development Working Group/Head of Issuing Authorities, ICoBC/Credshare, Neutral Bay, Australia

Dr. Tony Bates Research Associate at Contact North, Tony Bates Associates Ltd./Contact North, Ontario, Canada

Dr. Naomi Boyer Executive Director, Education Design Lab, Washington, DC, USA

Marina Brunner Chair of Innovation and Technology Management, Karlsruhe Institute of Technology, Karlsruhe, Germany

Luz Gamarra Caballero MPSP Newcastle University, Newcastle, Australia

Eglis Chacón MSc Boston College, Chestnut Hill, USA

Dr. Alexandros Chrysikos BSc Senior Lecturer and Researcher in Computing Science (Cyber Security), London Metropolitan University, London, UK

Judit Costa Partner, Ashoka Deutschland gGmbH, Berlin, Germany

Thanasis Daradoumis PhD Professor in the Department of Computer Science, Multimedia and Telecommunications, Open University of Catalonia, Barcelona, Spain; Professor in the Department of Cultural Technology and Communication, University of Aegean, Mytilini, Greece

Roseli de Deus Lopes Associate Professor, Universidade de São Paulo (USP), São Paulo, Brazil

Edison Trombeta de Oliveira Adjunct Professor I, University of Sorocaba, Sorocaba, Brazil

Ulf-Daniel Ehlers Professor for Educational Management and Lifelong Learning, Business Faculty, DHBW Karlsruhe, Karlsruhe, Germany

Laura Eigbrecht Educational Management and Lifelong Learning, Business Faculty, DHBW Karlsruhe, Karlsruhe, Germany

Prof. Karen Ferreira-Meyers Associate Professor and Coordinator of Linguistics and Modern Languages at the Institute of Distance Education, University of Eswatini, Kwaluseni, Eswatini

Megan K. Gahl Senior Director of Curriculum and Pedagogy at Minerva Project/Professor of Natural Sciences at Minerva University, Minerva Project/Minerva University, San Francisco, USA

Mônica Cristina Garbin Professor in the area Methodology and Distance Education, Virtual University of the State of São Paulo, São Paulo, Brazil

Nicole Geier Educational Management, Institute for Pedagogy, Carl von Ossietzky University Oldenburg, Oldenburg, Germany

James Genone Managing Director of Higher Education Innovation at Minerva Project/Professor of Social Sciences at Minerva University, Minerva Project/Minerva University, San Francisco, USA

Juvy Lizette M. Gervacio Assistant Professor, Master of Public Management Program, University of the Philippines Open University, Quezon City, Philippines

Dr. Soon-Joo Gog SkillsFuture Singapore, Singapore, Singapore

Miriam J. Green Principal Policy Analyst in the Office of the Provost, National University of Singapore, Singapore, Singapore

Margo Griffith Edalex Pty Ltd, Hobart, Australia

Sandhya Gunness Senior Lecturer at the Centre for Innovative and Lifelong Learning, University of Mauritius, Ebène, Mauritius

Emma Harden-Wolfson McGill University, Montreal, Canada

Dr. Kevin House Education Futures Architect, Education in Motion, Singapore, Singapore

Keiko Ikeda Professor in the Division of International Affairs, Kansai University, Osaka, Japan

Dr. Henning Koch Program Manager, Stifterverband, Berlin, Germany

Judith Koeritz Program Manager, Stifterverband, Berlin, Germany

Dr. Tara Laughlin Education Designer, Micro-Credentialing Project Manager, Education Design Lab, Washington, DC, USA

Bosen Lily Liu MSc UNESCO International Institute for Higher Education in Latin America and the Caribbean, Caracas, Venezuela

Editors and Contributors

Stephen Marshall Director of Centre for Academic Development, Victoria University of Wellington, Wellington, New Zealand

Mary McDonnell-Naughton PhD Senior Lecturer, Technological University of the Shannon, Athlone, Ireland

Ebba Ossiannilsson Professor and Research Fellow, Victoria University of Wellington, Wellington, New Zealand

Francesc Pedró UNESCO Institute for Higher Education in Latin America and the Caribbean, Caracas, Venezuela

Carmen Păunescu PhD Professor, Bucharest University of Economic Studies, Bucharest, Romania

Raquel H. Ribeiro Senior Manager of Partner Programs at Minerva Project/ Associate Professor of Computational Sciences at Minerva University, Minerva Project/Minerva University, San Francisco, USA

André Luiz Maciel Santana Professor, Insper Institute of Education and Research, São Paulo, Brazil

Prof. Dr. Tobias Seidl Professor for Academic Key Competences at the Faculty of Information and Communication, Stuttgart Media University, Stuttgart, Germany

Dr. phil. Wolfgang Stark Organizational and Community Psychology; Organizational Development Laboratory and Center for Societal Learning and Social Responsibility, University of Duisburg-Essen, Essen, Germany

Dr. Felix Suessenbach Researcher, Stifterverband, Berlin, Germany

Edwin Tan SkillsFuture Singapore, Singapore, Singapore

Kelsie Tan SkillsFuture Singapore, Singapore, Singapore

Christalle Tay Equal Dreams, Singapore, Singapore

Michael P. Vogel Professor of Entrepreneurship Education; Founder and Director of Team Academy Program, Bremerhaven University of Applied Sciences, Bremerhaven, Germany

Rupert Ward Director of Strategic Partnerships & 21st Century Skills Working Group Co-Lead/Professor of Learning Innovation and Associate Dean, ICoBC/ University of Huddersfield, Berlin, Germany

Dr. Michael Wihlenda Founder, World Citizen School, Tübingen, Germany

Andreas Wormland Program Manager, Stifterverband, Essen, Germany

Ye-Her Wu Advisor at the Futures Office and Associate Dean of SCALE-Global, National University of Singapore, Singapore, Singapore

Dr. Holly Zanville Executive Committee of the ICoBC/Research Professor and Co-Director of the Program Skills, Credentials & Workforce Policy (GWU), ICoBC/George Washington University, Washington, DC, USA

List of Abbreviations

ADB	Asian Development Bank
AI	Artificial Intelligence
ALSET	The Institute for Applied Learning Sciences and Educational Technology
ATC21S	Assessment and Teaching of 21st Century Skills
AYCL	All-You-Can-Learn
BA	Bachelor of Arts
BHEF	Business Higher Education Forum
BSc	Bachelor of Science
CBR	Community-Based Research
CCP	Campus-Community Partnerships
CDE	College of Design and Engineering
CDO	Chief Digital Officer
CEO	Chief Executive Officer
CET	Continuing Education and Training
CFA	Chartered Financial Analyst
CFO	Chief Financial Officer
CHRO	Chief Human Resource Officer
CHS	College of Humanities and Science
CLLC	Community Learning for Local Change
CSL	Community Service Learning
CSO	Chief Strategy Officer
CSTI	The Council for Science, Technology and Innovation
CV	Community Service Learning
DEIJ	Diversity, Equity, Inclusion and Justice

DHBW	Duale Hochschule Baden-Württemberg (Baden-Wuerttemberg Cooperative State University)
DIRK Dual	Digitales Reflexionstool zur Kompetenzentwicklung im dualen Studium
DLE	Data Literacy Education
DX	Digital Transformation
DYOM	Design Your Own Module
ECPA	European Community Psychology Association
ECT	European Credit Transfer
EQF	European Qualification Framework
ESBD	Entrepreneurship and Sustainable Business Development
ESCO	The European Skills, Competences, Qualifications, and Occupations
ESG	Environmental, Social and Governance
EU	European Union
FEC	Future Economy Council
FGD	Focus group discussion
GCSE	General Certificate of Secondary Education
GDP	Gross Domestic Product
GER	German
GIF	Gründung, Innovation, Führung (Venture, Creation, Innovation, Leadership)
GII	Global Innovation Index
GSC	Global Smart Classroom
GTP	Graduate Trainee Programs
HC	Habits of Mind and Foundational Concepts
HCD	Human-Centered Design
HE	Higher education
HEI	Higher Education Institution
HEQCO	Higher Education Quality Council of Ontario
HOTS	Higher Order Thinking Skills
HR	Human Resources
HRDC	Human Resources Development Council
HSBC	Hongkong and Shanghai Banking Corporation
IAL	Institute for Adult Learning
IB	International Baccalaureate
IBE	International Bureau of Education
ICL	Institutes of Continuous Learning

ICoBC	International Council on Badges and Credentials
ICT	Information and communication technologies
IDB	Interamerican Development Bank
IDE	Institute of Distance Education
IEEE	Institute of Electrical and Electronics Engineers
IESALC	International Institute for Higher Education in Latin America and the Caribbean
IHL	Institutes of Higher Learning
IIGE	Institute for Innovative Global Education
ILO	International Labor Organization
IoT	Internet of Things
IP	Interdisciplinary Project
4IR	4th Industrial Revolution
ITCILO	International Training Centre of the International Labor Organization
ITM	Industry Transformation Map
ITO	Industry Training Organizations
ITP	Institutes of Technology and Polytechnics
IWF	Institute for Working Futures
JSA	Jobs-Skills Analyst
JSI	Jobs-Skills Insights
KIT	Karlsruhe Institute of Technology
KSAVE	Knowledge, Skills, Attitude, Values, Ethics
LOC	Learning Orchestra Canvas
LOTS	Lower-Order Thinking Skills
MBA	Master of Business Administration
MBIE	Ministry of Business, Innovation and Employment
METI	Ministry of Economy, Trade and Industry
MEXT	Ministry of Education, Culture, Sports, Science and Technology
ML	Machine Learning
MOOC	Massive Open Online Courses
MP	Minerva Project
MPM	Master of Public Management
MSc	Masters of Science
MTC	Mastery Transcript Consortium
MU	Minerva University
MVP	Minimum Viable Products
NACE	National Centre of Excellence for Workplace Learning
NFT	Non-Fungible Tokens

NGO	Non-Governmental Organization
NUS	National University of Singapore
ODeL	Open and Distance E-learning
OECD	Organization for Economic Co-operation and Development
OER	Open Educational Resources
PBEL	Place-Based Entrepreneurial Learning
PBL	Problem-Based Learning
PISA	Program for International Student Assessment
PMET	Professionals, managers, executives, and technicians
PSA	Philippine Statistics Authority
PTE	Private tertiary education organization
SADC	Southern African Development Community
SCALE	School of Continuing and Lifelong Education
SDGs	Sustainable Development Goals
SDPs	Skills Development Partners
SEA:ME	Software Engineering Automotive & Mobility Ecosystem
SFQBs	SkillsFuture Queen Bees
SIE-T	Social Innovation Education Toolbox
SME	Small and medium enterprises
SPSS	Statistical Package for Social Sciences
SSG	SkillsFuture Singapore Agency
STEAM	Science, Technology, Engineering, Arts, Mathematics
STEM	Science, Technology, Engineering and Mathematics
STREAM	Science, Technology, Relationships, Engineering, Arts, Mathematics
SUNY	State University of New York
THE	Times Higher Education
TM	Talent Management
TRAQOM	Training Quality and Outcomes Measurement
TVET	Technical and Vocational Education and Training
UN	United Nations
UNESCO	United Nations Educational Scientific and Cultural Organization
UNESWA	University of Eswatini
UNICAMP	University of Campinas
UNICEF	United Nations International Children's Emergency Fund
UP	University of the Philippines
UPOU	University of the Philippines Open University
US	United States
USA	United States of America

USP	Universidade de São Paulo
VIA	Values in Action
VLE	Virtual Learning Environment
VR	Virtual Reality
VUCA	Volatility, uncertainty, complexity, and ambiguity
VUSSC	Virtual University for Small States of the Commonwealth
WDARF	The Workforce Development Applied Research Fund
WDC	Workforce Development Council
WEF	World Economic Forum
WHEC	World Higher Education Conference
WICHE	Western Interstate Commission for Higher Education

List of Figures

Fig. 1.1	Future Skills overview according to three main dimensions (Ehlers, 2020)	6
Fig. 1.2	Future Skills Triple Helix Model (Ehlers, 2020, created by Alina Timofte)	8
Fig. 1.3	Ten Seconds of Change for Higher Education (Ehlers, 2020)	9
Fig. 1.4	Map of contributing authors to this volume	12
Fig. 2.1	Search term frequency in comparison (Google trends search from January 2023)	25
Fig. 2.2	The Future Skills concept within an action competence framework (Ehlers, 2020, p. 54)	30
Fig. 2.3	Future Skill-Profiles Overview (Ehlers, 2020)	31
Fig. 2.4	Illustration of qualitative analysis and mapping of terms (Ehlers, 2022)	41
Fig. 4.1	ANDREAS SCHLEICHER	76
Fig. 6.1	Required sequence of courses for Bachelor of Computer Sciences, Dalhousie University, Canada	131
Fig. 6.2	Examples of the learning outcomes/skills required before beginning a course, and on completion of a course	132
Fig. 7.1	Actors Represented in Community Service Learning. (Adapted from Ruda et al., 2015)	145
Fig. 7.2	Quintuple Helix Innovation. (Adapted from Carayannis & Campbell, 2012)	149
Fig. 7.3	Matrix of Systems Learning and Leadership. (Adapted from Scharmer, 2019)	152
Fig. 7.4	Results from "Universities of the Future"—Wolfgang Stark, 2022	153

Fig. 8.1	Tom Wambeke	162
Fig. 9.1	Pathways to 2050 and beyond (UNESCO IESALC, 2021a, p. 39)	180
Fig. 9.2	Vision of the futures of higher education based on the expert and public consultations (UNESCO IESALC)	181
Fig. 9.3	Future skills and beyond: Theory of change (UNESCO IESALC)	182
Fig. 9.4	Frequency of elements in the theory of change (UNESCO IESALC)	185
Fig. 10.1	Angela Duckworth	202
Fig. 11.1	GIF Competence Diamond. (Own representation)	221
Fig. 11.2	Flipping the curriculum (Holmes et al., 2019, p. 28)	225
Fig. 11.3	Pedagogical cornerstones of the Team Academy. (Own representation)	228
Fig. 11.4	Typical evolution of team companies. (Own representation)	229
Fig. 12.1	Future Skills conceptualization	244
Fig. 12.2	Learning Method Design	248
Fig. 13.1	Member initiatives of the World Citizen School—Status 12/2022	263
Fig. 13.2	World Citizen School Education	269
Fig. 13.3	Learning spiral: "Learning journey of the individual (I) in social contexts (We)"	269
Fig. 13.4	Learning system based on the impact logic of the Learning Orchestra Canvas	271
Fig. 13.5	Learning Orchestra Canvas	275
Fig. 14.1	Global Innovation Index showing strengths and weaknesses for Mauritius (Dutta et al., 2021)	286
Fig. 14.2	Technology Infrastructure 2016–2018. (Modified from Krönke, 2020)	288
Fig. 14.3	The integration of societal and scientific praxis in transdisciplinary research. Reprinted with permission from Jahn et al. (2012, p. 8)	293
Fig. 14.4	Main competencies to be developed during the Transdisciplinary Skills and Competencies Module for 1st-year students	296
Fig. 15.1	Illustration of the Future Skills 2021 framework containing 21 competencies across 4 skill dimensions: classic, transformative, digital, and technological	317

Fig. 15.2	Illustration of the Future Skills for Openness framework containing 20 competencies across 3 dimensions: tool set, skill set, and mindset	319
Fig. 16.1	Max Senges	336
Fig. 16.2	Bloom's taxonomy (Xristina Ia, 2012)	345
Fig. 16.3	Confucius (work by Kanō Sansetsu, AMorozov, 2021)	347
Fig. 17.1	The phases of the Interdisciplinary Project	356
Fig. 19.1	Perceptions of Students on the 17 Competencies Based on Future Skills	387
Fig. 20.1	Double-Diamond Process and Point of View Definition	400
Fig. 20.2	Real-World Problems Solving Program, an Adaptation of Startup Garage Innovation	402
Fig. 20.3	General topics suggested by the instructor	403
Fig. 20.4	Decision Chart	407
Fig. 20.5	Effort and Impact Points	407
Fig. 20.6	A wearable that helps seniors with Alzheimer's in their daily tasks	408
Fig. 20.7	Motorcycle Support for a mechanic shop with constrained space	409
Fig. 20.8	User Story template—prioritizing team effort and story value (user point of view)	409
Fig. 21.1	Relationship of assessment and learning in the concepts assessment of learning, assessment for learning, and assessment as learning (in close accordance with Yan & Boud, 2022, p. 15)	424
Fig. 21.2	Types of integration of portfolio and student self-assessment concepts in degree programmes	429
Fig. 22.1	Example student view of a single Learning Outcome (LO) in the Outcome Index in Forum, Minerva Project's proprietary learning platform. A student can track all assessments of a single LO across courses in the Outcome Index, can view where the LO was introduced, and see an average across all scores	446
Fig. 22.2	Learning Outcomes (LOs) are scaffolded throughout the Minerva curriculum to promote knowledge transfer. Future Skills oriented LOs are typically introduced in the first-year courses. Students apply these LOs in upper year courses in the context of their chosen disciplines. At MU students apply these skills in fourth year capstone projects	448

Fig. 23.1	Mastery Transcript Representation by MTC (2023)	466
Fig. 23.2	Credential Ecosystem (own representation by Kevin House)	467
Fig. 23.3	Education Design Lab twenty-first Century Skills Framework Representing Nine Digital Micro-credentials and 27 Sub-Competencies (Education Design Lab, 2023)	477
Fig. 25.1	Top non-tech jobs requiring AI/ML by share of skill demands (own representation by the Burning Glass Institute, the Business-Higher Education Forum, and Wiley)	511
Fig. 26.1	Skills identification to skills progression cycle (own representation)	518
Fig. 27.1	Multiple pathways for undergraduates (NUS College of Humanities & Sciences, 2021)	533
Fig. 27.2	Multiple pathways for undergraduates (NUS College of Humanities & Sciences, 2021)	534
Fig. 27.3	Example of possible DYOM development timeline provided by Dr. Andi Sudjana Putra	539
Fig. 28.1	Evolution of Societies up to Society 5.0 (Keidanren, 2016)	551
Fig. 28.2	Global Smart Classroom (GSC) at Kansai University	556
Fig. 28.3	Japan Virtual Campus (University of Tsukuba, 2023)	561
Fig. 28.4	Direction of Reformation for corporate strategy for human capital (adopted from METI, 2020)	562
Fig. 28.5	Necessary change in a community of employment practices (Adopted by METI, 2020)	563
Fig. 29.1	List of skills for future IT professionals (Brunner & Ehlers, 2021)	573
Fig. 29.2	Future skills profiles (Ehlers, 2022)	575
Fig. 29.3	Overview of the answers to the importance of the individual future skills (Brunner & Ehlers, 2021)	578
Fig. 29.4	Assessments of Importance of different Skill Sets (Brunner & Ehlers, 2021)	579
Fig. 29.5	Skill profiles per role for IT professionals (Brunner & Ehlers, 2021)	580
Fig. 29.6	Importance of transversal skills for different roles of IT professionals (Brunner & Ehlers, 2021)	581
Fig. 30.1	Mass and universal education skills frameworks	603

List of Tables

Table 2.1	Future Skills competence fields and profiles in overview (Ehlers, 2020)	32
Table 2.2	Methods in Future Skills Studies (Ehlers, 2022)	39
Table 2.3	Comparative analysis of existing Future Skills models (translated from Ehlers, 2022)	43
Table 2.4	Media Competence Dimensions according to Baacke et al. (1991).	49
Table 2.5	Comparative Overview of Digital Future Skills (Ehlers, 2022)	50
Table 3.1	Recommendations for promoting Future Skills in higher education	67
Table 5.1	Summary of existing empirical evidence on the learning gains and estimated costs of some innovations in higher education	115
Table 11.1	GIF Competence Matrix	222
Table 14.1	Mapping the Delors Report (1996) to Future Graduate Skills	296
Table 14.2	Table of Learning activities for the Transdisciplinary Skills and Competencies Module	297
Table 15.1	Selection of Future Skills from the Future Skills 2021 framework relevant to the Stifterverband's programs: Entrepreneurial Skills (ES), Data Literacy Education (DLE) and Curriculum 4.0.nrw (C4)	318
Table 15.2	Selection of Future Skills from Future Skills for Openness frameworks relevant to the Stifterverband's programs: Entrepreneurial Skills (ES), Data Literacy Education (DLE) and Curriculum 4.0.nrw (C4)	320

XXXVII

Table 15.3	Number of obstacles and supporting factors in eleven clusters during the process of including Future Skills into the curricula in the Curriculum 4.0.nrw program	329
Table 17.1	Interdisciplinary Project Skills	360
Table 19.1	Description of the Reimagined Assessment. *Source*: Gervacio (2022)	384
Table 19.2	Profile of the Research Participants	385
Table 20.1	Skills expected in Industry 4.0—employer's point of view (left) and academic papers point of view (right).	398
Table 20.2	Problem Definition Protocol: four dimensions of a problem. . .	404
Table 20.3	Outstanding Projects in 2020	413
Table 22.1	Learning Outcome (LO) examples from four core competencies and example sub-competencies (Appendix A, Kosslyn & Nelson, 2017)	441
Table 22.2	Example rubrics for the Learning Outcome #biasidentification . . .	445
Table 23.1	Examples of Definitions of Micro-credentials	469
Table 24.1	Operational definitions of creativity and innovation in the KSAVE model (Binkley et al., 2012, p. 38)	494
Table 24.2	Layout of the key competence modules	495
Table 24.3	Levels of reflection according to Bräuer (2014, p. 17–71)	501
Table 29.1	Research Flow and Data Collection (Brunner & Ehlers, 2021) . . .	577

Part I
Setting the Scene – Future Skills in Higher Education

Part I focusses on introducing the concept and relevance of Future Skills and giving an overview to the reader by introducing the different contributions. The Future Skills concept according to Ehlers (2020) as well as a meta-model integrating several Future Skills frameworks are presented. In a final chapter the editors give a short synopsis of success factors for implementing Future Skills into higher education based on recommendations from all contributing authors.

Part I

Future Skills in Higher Education -
The Wider View

Future Skills -
Foundations
and Shapes of a New Emerging
Concept in a Global View

Ⅲ
Future Skills in Practice -
Teaching
and
Learning

Future Skills in Practice -
Assessment

Ⅰ
Setting the Scene - **Future Skills** in Higher Education

Creating the University of the Future: A Global Panorama on Future Skills

1

Ulf-Daniel Ehlers and Laura Eigbrecht

Abstract

The challenge of promoting Future Skills is one of the currently most debated ones for higher education institutions all over the world. In this chapter, the editors provide a conceptual basis for the contributed chapters as well as an overview of the sections and contributions of this book. The concept and relevance of Future Skills for Higher Education on a global scale is addressed, followed by an outline of how future universities could look like and which trends will shape this future. Followed by this, the five sections of the Creating the University of the Future book are introduced with short summaries of the chapters and the perspectives they contribute to discussing, promoting and reimagining Future Skills learning in higher education.

U.-D. Ehlers
Professor for Educational Management and Lifelong Learning, Business Faculty, DHBW Karlsruhe, Karlsruhe, Germany
e-mail: ulf-daniel.ehlers@dhbw-karlsruhe.de

L. Eigbrecht (✉)
Educational Management and Lifelong Learning, Business Faculty, DHBW Karlsruhe, Karlsruhe, Germany
e-mail: laura.eigbrecht@dhbw-karlsruhe.de

© The Author(s) 2024
U.-D. Ehlers and L. Eigbrecht (eds.), *Creating the University of the Future*, Zukunft der Hochschulbildung - Future Higher Education,
https://doi.org/10.1007/978-3-658-42948-5_1

1.1 Introduction

In a world which is changing faster than ever before, it has never been more urgent to actively shape this global transformation in order to create the best possible future. Today's students need to learn the necessary skills for this—Future Skills. The challenge of promoting them is one of the currently most debated ones for higher education institutions all over the world.

Future Skills are skills which enable students to collectively impact societal transformation in order to create more sustainable futures. In other words, we define Future Skills as competences that enable individuals to solve complex problems in a self-organized manner and to act (successfully) in highly emergent contexts. They are based on cognitive, motivational, volitional, and social resources, are value-based, and can be acquired in a learning process (Ehlers, 2020, p. 53). In the public discussion on higher education concepts, they have meanwhile contributed to a decisive change, which we refer to here as the Future Skills Turn (Ehlers, 2020, 2022). The Future Skills concept we follow is based on educational research, comprises 17 skills profiles, and represents a strong alternative vision of higher education. It integrates a variety of Future Skills frameworks and approaches into one comprehensive model, as will be shown in Chap. 2.

The starting point for the enormous concept that is Future Skills is the diagnosis that current concepts of higher education do not confront the pressing challenges of our societies with convincing concepts for the future (Hippler, 2016; Kummert, 2017)—neither the sustainable design of our environment nor the related social or economic challenges. Global challenges are exacerbated by a constantly accelerating globalization process and ever faster digital progress. In this situation of digital acceleration, the characteristic feature is that of uncertainty and the inescapable necessity is that of creative responsibility (Ehlers, 2020). It is the responsibility of all of us to make the best of the possibilities and to find ways to deal with this uncertain future. This is about nothing more and nothing less than the preservation of our planet and our livelihoods.

The institution of higher education is faced with the challenge of reinventing itself—at a time when it is undergoing an enormous growth process and a rate of 70% higher education students of one age cohort or more is predicted in most nations by the year 2050 (Ehlers, 2020). Higher education institutions must address the question: which Future Skills will the graduates of tomorrow need, and how can they support them in acquiring them? Future Skills are first and foremost an educational concept—therefore it is necessary to describe them in terms of educational approaches and root them in existing educational theories. In earlier works, we have done this by creating the so-called Future Skills

Triple Helix Model, which was developed within the framework of the Next-Skills study (Ehlers, 2020). The NextSkills study has used a multilevel and multi-method research design including desk research, document analysis, expert evaluations, open half-structured qualitative interviews, and Delphi surveys. The aim was to create an inventory of skills needs for the future and analyze and cluster it to so-called Future Skills profiles. A second research phase was then looking at integrating the findings from the first phase with a body of existing concepts and theories. The findings have been further developed with research and teaching experiences for Future Skills promotion in different higher education teaching and learning settings and initiatives.

In the last five years—since 2017 with the publication of the first (explicit) Future Skills study in Germany—the interest in Future Skills for the field of academic education has multiplied and recast the discussion about key competences and other related concepts, such as 21st Century Skills, Graduate Attributes, or soft skills. It draws on a history of discussing competences and skills, starting with soft skills and key competencies, and now integrating transformative, sustainability, and global citizenship skills. There are different perspectives to the discussion, closer to employability matters, individual development, or community and society-oriented approaches. There are many reasons for this, which lie in societal megatrends such as digitalization, demographic change, and the development of an educational society (Ehlers, 2020). These challenges being not limited to regional or national context, the skills needed to master them should also be discussed from a broad perspective and across countries and educational contexts.

They lead to an increasing importance of Future Skills as precisely those abilities that allow individuals to possess and/or regain the ability to shape their own lives and social contexts in a world of constant change and in future emergent—i.e., unpredictable—and rapidly changing situations of demand. In terms and concept, Future Skills can be distinguished from those competencies that are not particularly future-oriented. The concept of emergence serves as a differentiating dimension between current or previous competence requirements and those that are relevant to the future. In particular, those contexts of action that exhibit highly emergent developments of life, work, organizational and business processes require Future Skills to cope with the needs. Emergence thus defines the dividing line that separates previous, or traditional, areas of work from future areas of work. Since this boundary is not clearly schematic but fluid, and many organizations are undergoing transformation processes in which weakly emergent work contexts are evolving into highly emergent work contexts, the need for Future Skills is also an evolving domain rather than a binary state of either/or.

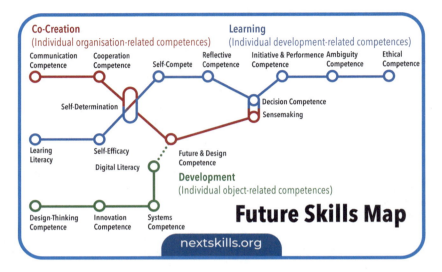

Fig. 1.1 Future Skills overview according to three main dimensions (Ehlers, 2020)

Based on the in-depth interviews and the assessment of experts surveyed worldwide, 17 Future Skills profiles (see Fig. 1.1 for an overview)[1] were constructed that are of particular importance for future university graduates. Each profile consists of a bundle of individual competences, so-called reference competences. Future Skills profiles are clusters of future-relevant skills. The various Future Skills profiles can be assigned to three dimensions: those Future Skills that relate to one's own development (learning—individual development-related), the development of specific solutions (development—individual object-related) and to joint development in social systems (co-creation—individual organization-related).

---

[1] Full comprehensive Future Skills descriptions can be accessed in Chap. 2, and also in Ehlers (2020).

1 Creating the University of the Future …

Professionals—i.e., acting persons—can develop Future Skills in relation to themselves (subject-related), in relation to dealing with a task, topic, or object (object-related), or in relation to the organizational environment, i.e., the social system (world-related). A relation with three poles emerges, each pole being in relation to the other. With respect to actions in highly emergent contexts, all three poles and their relation to each other are always determinant in every action. Because of the close interconnectedness of all three poles and their interrelated integration, we refer to this concept as the Future Skills Triple Helix model. The resulting concept is suitable for the formal description of actions in highly emergent contexts.

The classification criterion for Future Skills profiles is the target of relation:

- relation of an individual to themselves in the present, past or future (subject or time dimension—learning),
- relation of an individual to a certain object (object dimension—development) or
- relationship of an individual to a person or a group in the world (social dimension—co-creation).

All three dimensions are in turn interrelated and influence each other. The three dimensions thus form the Future Skills Triple Helix model (Fig. 1.2), in which the three skill dimensions interact in concrete actions. They enable a better understanding of the factors that make up future action skills.

While there seems to be a common understanding of the relevance of promoting Future Skills with learners, students, graduates, citizens, there is a certain responsibility of higher education in promoting these if they want to stay relevant and fulfill the requirements of today's and tomorrow's societies. The challenge of promoting Future Skills is one of the currently most debated challenges for higher education institutions all over the world. With this initiative, we aim at facilitating the discussion, of connecting actors, researchers, stakeholders, and all involved in this important undertaking. We want to make visible what is already there and want to inspire to envision what could be there—this is the starting point of our Global Future Skills initiative.

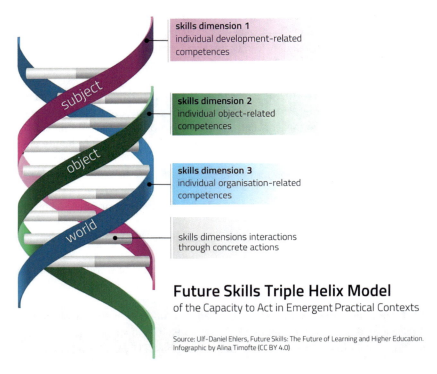

Fig. 1.2 Future Skills Triple Helix Model (Ehlers, 2020, created by Alina Timofte)

1.2 Ten Drivers for a Future University

Ehlers (2020) summarized ten drivers (Fig. 1.3) which are influencing the shape and future outlines of a Next University model and which our Future Skills considerations need to be reflective of.

1—Digital Transformation: Digitization is a powerful development for universities. A wide range of publications bear witness to this. However, the current discussion about university strategies shows that digital transformation is not an end in itself. It is becoming apparent that fewer and fewer universities are adopting a *digital* strategy, and more and more are moving towards understanding digitization as a means of strategically rethinking or sharpening their own university profile. The result is then a strategy for *higher education in a digital world*, but not a strategy for digitization.

1 Creating the University of the Future ...

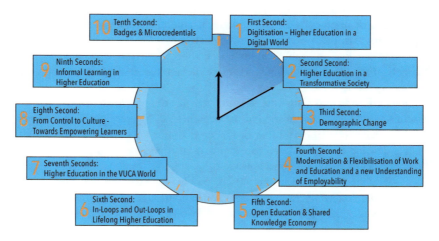

Fig. 1.3 Ten Seconds of Change for Higher Education (Ehlers, 2020)

2—(Media) Transformation Society: the development of the media has always led to fundamental social upheavals in historical terms. According to Dirk Baecker (2018), we can analyze that we live on the verge of a "next society" with largely changed communication possibilities and rules. The question that arises is: how can universities prepare their students and graduates for the next society (Baecker, 2018)?

3—Demographic Change: Schofer and Meyer (2005) use university statistics to show that university expansion has been an accelerating process in all advanced countries of the world since the middle of the twentieth century at the latest, but that it is taking place at different speeds. A university participation rate well above the 50% mark will therefore have to be expected everywhere (Baethge et al., 2015; Teichler, 2013).

4—Modernization & Flexibilization of Education and Occupation Systems: three developments can be observed: 1) The labor market is evolving from a *professional system of work* to a *technical system of work* (Lisop, 1997). 2) A development from *lifetime employment* to *lifetime employability* can be observed (Beck et al., 2014) as well as a development 3) from a *professional* employee to a *company-based* labor entrepreneur (Voß & Pongratz, 1998). Beck (1986) also speaks here of a new culture of *self-evidence*.

5—Open Education & Shared Knowledge Economy: while universities mostly see themselves as the sole producers, administrators and mediators of scientific progress, more and more new models are emerging to make knowledge, scientific results, data, publications and learning materials available. Based on models of the Sharing Economy, the question is asked how a Shared Knowledge Economy can look like.

6—In-Loops and Out-Loops: learning will no longer take place in the sole, exclusive model of qualification at the beginning of a career phase, but learning will increasingly also have to be an academic lifelong activity, as career requirements develop ever faster, and career phases also present themselves as lifelong evolving changing professional episodes.

7—Higher Education in the VUCA[2] world: both the ability to continuously adapt to the constantly changing environments through learning and the ability to successfully deal with uncertainties are two key future challenges for higher education.

8—From a Control Illusion to an Enabling Logic: we know that competence-oriented teaching and learning works especially well in environments structured according to socio-constructivist principles. They are didactic models that go beyond pure factual knowledge and problem-solving and penetrate the field of creative self-developed and self-responsible innovation.

9—Informal Learning: universities usually concentrate on the formal teaching and study aspects when designing their teaching–learning scenarios. This involves, for example, using digital media to support the transfer of knowledge. The entire area of informal learning is neglected. However, informal learning is the area where most learning processes have been proven to take place.

10—Alternative Certifications & Micro-Credentials: micro-credentials, badges, nanodegrees and Micro-Masters have been on everyone's lips for some time now. The underlying idea and concept of academic education, made possible by micro-credentials and micro-qualifications, is to enable lifelong informal documentation of education, lifelong documentation of academic education, in which informal and formal elements, modules, and learning experiences are interwoven through accredited or non-accredited, certified or uncertified, modules into an academic educational biography.

---

[2] The VUCA world is characterized by Volatility, Uncertainty, Complexity und Ambiguity.

The increased participation in academic education and the increasing digitization of higher education have a mutually reinforcing effect on the organization and design of studies, teaching, and research. A new diversity and decoupled processes are the result and trigger a noticeable creative pressure towards individualization and the lifelong need for academic education. Universities will have to undergo fundamental changes in the way they organize their studies. More students, new target groups, and an unprecedented diversity of target groups, who need to be valued and supported in personalized study situations, are coming to the universities. To this end, the function of higher education institutions with regard to social integration and the social dimension of studying in an academic educational society is becoming increasingly important. In conjunction with this, the concept of lifelong learning is gaining in importance for universities. Many interconnected changes in university teaching and organization are set in motion like a domino effect when this initial shift occurs. There is, for example, the concept of micro-credentials, alternative certification systems that enable learners to organize their own portfolio of qualifications and competences digitally and in a more self-determined way and require higher education institutions to professionalize their systems of recognition and credit. Digitization enables the flexibilization of space and time structures and greater transparency of all study-related information systems over the entire study life cycle. In a digital world, we are experiencing a decreasing importance of knowledge transfer and an increasing need for guidance, support, and coaching in a more diverse world of studies. In addition, the decoupling of processes of teaching, testing, and certification of competences plays an increasingly important role. Based on the changed framework conditions in an educational society and the pressure for change that affects academic qualification processes, new requirements for a modern, further developed higher education model arise for higher education institutions.

1.3 The Global Future Skills Initiative: What Can You Expect?

While there seems to be a newly established consensus on the responsibility of higher education in taking students' Future Skills development into account, questions remain on how to do so on all levels of teaching and learning—on the policy or macro level, on the institutional or meso level, and on the micro level, meaning in the classroom.

However, in our research, we noticed how many approaches already point to a direction where skills development is central and that many institutions, actors,

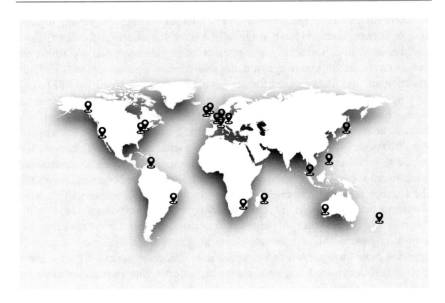

Fig. 1.4 Map of contributing authors to this volume

and stakeholders involved in (higher) education have already started to pave the way for Future Skills development—piloting, trying out, developing programs. While there seems to be no uniform, one-fits-all solution for promoting Future Skills in higher education worldwide, there is a search and experiencing going on in many regions, institutions, settings by sharing ideas, approaches, feedback and co-developing a vision for future-proof higher education—which we noticed in many exchanges on our Future Skills research, in workshops and conferences. We also noticed a rising interest in concrete, hands-on examples of how to promote Future Skills in higher education.

From this, the idea of the Global Future Skills initiative was born—with the goal of increasing visibility of existing and emerging practices and approaches and contributing to new visions, networks, and exchanges by moving visionary Future Skills practices forward. Two methods were used to put this plan into realization: to compile peer-reviewed contributions for a book publication and to do interviews with experts in the field to be released both in the book and in a podcast series.

In this publication, you will find contributions by more than 50 authors from more than 15 countries from all continents except Antarctica and more than 20 different institutions. The map of contributing authors (Fig. 1.4) will give a short glimpse to the geographical variety of the submissions—followed by an overview of the chapters.

1.4 Preview of Book Sections and Chapters

We will start with a foundational introduction to the theme of Future Skills in **Part I—Setting the Scene—Future Skills in Higher Education** in an opening chapter.

In the chapter **Towards a Future Skills Framework for Higher Education**, based on a qualitative meta-analysis of 13 studies and publications on Future Skills, **Ulf-Daniel Ehlers** will give an insight and analysis into the existing research and discourse on Future Skills, with a specific analysis of Digital Competences in Future Skills concepts. He proposes a framework encompassing 17 skill profiles which are able to serve as a conceptual model for Future Skills approaches. On basis of its 17 skill profiles, other existing Future Skills models can be categorized and compared with each other.

Laura Eigbrecht and **Ulf-Daniel Ehlers** will follow up with the chapter **The Practice of Future Skills Learning: An Assessment of Approaches, Conditions and Success Factors,** analyzing the Future Skills definitions of our contributing authors. As we asked our submitting authors not only to base their submissions on a specific definition and/or concept of Future Skills, but also to add some practical recommendations for Future Skills promotion based on their approaches and experiences, we will also provide an analysis in this chapter, concluding in an outlook for a Future Skills vision for higher education and its conditions for success.

We will go one step further with **Part II—Future Skills—Foundations and Shapes of a New Emerging Concept in a Global View** and discuss basic concepts and outlines concerning Future Skills in (global) higher education.

For the opening chapter, **OECD's Andreas Schleicher** will share his thoughts and experiences on Future Skills in a **Future Skills Conversation. "I've learnt everything I know from the world"**—this is how he refers to his expertise in education from experts and professionals from all over the world—but it is also something to keep in mind concerning Future Skills learning. Not only will Andreas Schleicher share his personal learning pathway, but also his thoughts on the future of education and skills—which should aim at collective agency and integration of teaching, learning and assessment, but not exactly at equipping everybody with the same skill set.

Focusing more closely on higher education, **Francesc Pedró** from the **UNESCO International Institute for Higher Education in Latin America and the Caribbean (IESALC)**, in his chapter called **Future Skills—Back into the Future? Emerging Trends in Educational Innovation in Higher Education**, will describe these trends from an international or even global perspective. While there is a strong discourse on teaching and learning settings going on, lectures are still the most widely used teaching strategy, with a classic university model persisting. However, new Future Skills demands are driving educational innovation—with the main innovation domains in instructional content and design, processes, and technology. Pedró describes the tension between innovation and the classic university model and proposes strategies on how to overcome this.

Tony Bates is taking the challenges of digital technology for skills needs into account in his chapter called **Teaching the Skills Needed for the Future**. While technology is influencing and changing all domains of our everyday lives, teachers and instructors are facing the challenges of equipping learners with the skills needed to master this change. The chapter explores the skills that will be needed, and ways in which such skills can be developed—those being critically important for the students' quality of life, be it in universities or vocational education. The good news is: there are many opportunities to develop intellectual and practical skills for work and life activities in a digital age, without corrupting the values or standards of academia.

Future Skills are a subject touching the discussion of the role of universities in society—a discussion that **Wolfgang Stark** is having a closer look at in his chapter **Future Universities as Activating Resonance Spaces. New Roles in Society—Innovative Approaches.** Drawn from many debates and explorations with diverse higher education stakeholders, he conceives universities as an Active Resonance Space going beyond business matters, addressing future societal challenges. With the concept of service learning as a participative and empowering approach, a future-ready institutionalization of transformative learning and teaching can take place, with a close link between universities and civil society.

In another **Future Skills Conversation, ITCILO's Tom Wambeke** is proposing, for Future Skills-ready education, **Building a Creative Ecosystem of Intentional Serendipity**. He will give insights into how Future Skills are closely linked to improvisation and how we need to become human chameleons for mastering today's and tomorrow's complex problems. He proposes a whole mindset switch which is needed for making Future Skills learning a reality: new roles for teachers and learners, a new sensitivity for lifelong learning opportunities, and the courage to come up with radically different solutions.

Even widening the perspective, **Eglis Chacón, Emma Harden-Wolfson, Luz Gamarra Caballero, Bosen Lily Liu** and **Dana Abdrasheva** from the **UNESCO International Institute for Higher Education in Latin America and the Caribbean (IESALC)** propose **A New Theory of Change** in their chapter **Beyond Future Skills in Higher Education: A New Theory of Change.** It is based on a survey conducted by the institute which gives a global perspective by reaching respondents from nearly 100 countries. The approach helps to identify

Future Skills needs for today's students and future generations, but also the accelerators for promoting them and the goals this transformation of individuals, institutions and society should lead to.

After presenting these general debates underlying the discourse on Future Skills, we will have a closer look at Future Skills in practice in section III and IV, starting with **Part III—Future Skills in Practice—Teaching and Learning.**

A Future Skills Conversation with psychologist **Angela Duckworth** from **Character Lab** leads into the next section: **"If you really want to change the world, the smartest way to do so is through education"**. Angela Duckworth talks about character and strengths of mind, will and heart—and emphasizes the importance of other persons to support personal development for growing up well. Initiative, independence, curiosity, and science—these are some of the concepts which will be discussed as important when teaching and learning Future Skills.

But how to put this into practice? A first example is provided by **Michael P. Vogel** from Germany. In his chapter **Team Academy: Future Skills and the Future of Learning**, he introduces Team Academy's innovative higher education model and its first application in Germany for Future Skills development, based on entrepreneurship education and combining educational approaches such as team coaching and real-life action learning. While introducing this model into an existing institutional context might seem radical, the chapter inspires us by showing it is possible, that higher education is already changing—and that *Why* might be more important for the first steps than *How*.

Carmen Păunescu (Romania) and **Mary McDonnell-Naughton (Ireland)** develop a specific Future Skills set and focus on how it can be promoted in different higher education programs. In the chapter **Education for Future Skills Development: Cognitive, Collaborative and Ethical Skills**, they explain how individuals' reflective practice and critical thinking can be supported. Entrepreneurship education and nursing ethics education serve as case studies to show how different disciplines, institutional contexts and curricula can be explored and enhanced through Problem-Based Learning to support students' Future Skills learning—and how ethics education should be an integral part of this across disciplines.

Michael Wihlenda, founder of the **World Citizen School** at the **Weltethos Institute** of the **German University of Tübingen**, presents to us **The World Citizen School Model. Learning Philosophy and Learning System for Global, Socially Innovative and Value-Based Future Learning**. This approach started as an extracurricular network for civically engaged student initiatives and developed into a holistic learning system with student engagement and social innovation at its core. It emphasizes on Future Skills as a societal benefit—or, in other words, to conceive Future Skills learning as transformative learning.

Future Skills learning must also be reflective of one's individual, cultural, and societal contexts and this is a perspective taken by **Sandhya Gunness, Karen Ferreira-Meyers** and **Thanasis Daradoumis** in their chapter called **Learning Design for Future Skills Development in Small State Contexts**. Here, the small Southern African states of Mauritius and Eswatini and the **Universities of Mauritius** and **Eswatini** are in focus for capacity building for future challenges—with a high need for graduates' Future Skills development. Values such as community, resilience, sustainability, and tolerance serve as an orientation framework and moral compass for Future Skills development and teachers' and learners' perspectives are explored in order to identify Future Skills needs and approaches for promoting them.

In a different approach and setting, the German initiative **Stifterverband** contributes to Future Skills education in German higher education with research, frameworks, and funding programs. In the chapter **Boosting Future Skills in Higher Education: Lessons Learned from Funding Programs, Networking, Establishing Standards & Curricular Integration**, **Felix Süßenbach, Judith Koeritz, Andreas Wormland** and **Henning Koch** present a Future Skills framework and programs, focusing amongst others on entrepreneurship education and data literacy, to underline higher education's responsibility in promoting students' Future Skills.

While these programs aim at integrating Future Skills education into existing institutional contexts, **42 Coding Schools** are taking a different approach to education. In a **Future Skills Conversation** entitled **May the Code Be with You: The 42 Learning Model in Germany**, **Max Senges** from German 42 schools in Wolfsburg and Berlin discusses the educational approach of the schools and how they contribute to their students' Future Skills learning in a very specific way—with skills profiles such as coding literacy, planetary thinking and life entrepreneurship.

In their chapter **Interdisciplinary Project to Build Teaching Skills: A Pedagogical Approach**, **Mônica Cristina Garbin** and **Édison Trombeta de Oliveira** from the **Virtual University of the State of São Paulo** introduce an educational approach based on Project-Based Learning and Human-Centered Design, integrating theory and practice and aimed at promoting students' Future Skills such as problem-solving and collaboration. They accentuate the potential of inter- and multidisciplinarity and promote the integration of theory and practice for students' Future Skills development.

Ashoka's **Judit Costa** gives an insight into Ashoka's approaches to **Changemaking on Campus**. When discussing Future Skills, we aim at students and graduates not only reacting to, but designing and co-creating change. With different programs and the tagline "Everyone a changemaker", Ashoka aims at building a community of changemakers with a responsibility towards society across universities and countries.

How could the University of the Future look like, promoting students' Future Skills? This is what **Juvy Lizette M. Gervacio** is discussing in the chapter entitled **The "University of the Future" of the Philippines: The Case of University of the Philippines Open University's Master of Public Management Program.** Here, she focusses on the potential of distance education programs in promoting students' Future Skills, with Public Management students at the core of her research, and makes a strong point for digital learning settings to make learners collaborate and reflect on their self-efficacy and challenges of emergent futures, affecting their work and Future Skills requirements.

Roseli de Deus Lopes and **André Luiz Maciel Santana** from **Universidade de São Paulo** contribute a chapter on **Using Real-World Problems and Project-Based Learning for Future Skill Development: An Approach to Connect Higher Education Students and Society Through User-Centered Design.** They discuss Future Skills from an engineering perspective, with an educational setting promoting Future Skills learning through User-Centered Design and incorporating real-world problems into a Computer Engineering course. Based on this case study, they reflect on the great potential of real-world problems in promoting Future Skills learning.

Part IV—Future Skills in Practice—Assessment focuses on Future Skills assessment and validation.

Nicole Geier and **Ulf-Daniel Ehlers** propose an approach which shows how student self-assessments can be integrated into learning and teaching practices at higher education institutions in order to promote Future Skills learning and assessment. The chapter **Assessment of Future Skills Learning: Changing Futures in Higher Education** reflects on assessment practices and a paradigm shift towards *assessment as learning* which is taking place, presenting a new vision of skills assessment and an example of integration into the whole student life-cycle.

With a well-established concept, **Megan K. Gahl, Abha Ahuja, Raquel H. Ribeiro, Maia Averett** and **James Genone** lead us into the subject of assessing Future Skills with their chapter **Active Learning and Integrated Assessment. Minerva's Approach to Teaching Future Skills**. They report on the **Minerva** Project's large expertise in transformational education programs for promoting Future Skills, working with a learning taxonomy relating Future Skills to Learning Outcomes, introducing, assessing, and reinforcing them throughout a study program. One learning: alignment is key.

The approaches presented by **Grame Barty, Naomi Boyer, Alexandros Chrysikos, Margo Griffith, Kevin House, Tara Laughlin, Ebba Ossiannilsson, Rupert Ward** and **Holly Zanville** focus on micro-credentials and badges as alternative credentialing approaches: **Developing a More Granular and Equitable Approach to the Learner-Earner Journey: The Role of Badging, Micro-Credentials and 21st Century Skills within Higher Education to Enable Future Workforce Development.** The authors propose different ways to align Future Skills needs and higher education courses by introducing more granular learning supported by badges, micro-credentials and alternative credentials and personalizing Future Skills learning in a lifelong learning context.

Tobias Seidl from the German **Hochschule der Medien** presents a specific learning and assessment model adopted and integrated at the institution's faculty of Information and Communication in his chapter **Formative Assessment of 21st Century Skills**. This approach to Future Skills learning has integrated key competence modules in all BA study programs with a formative assessment approach supporting students' individual learning journeys.

The State of Skills: A Global View from Burning Glass Institute and Wiley presents insights into how skills needs can be explored and assessed. Emerging skill sets have been identified for the "State of Skills" report in order to discuss how learners can be prepared for new challenges and Future Skills needs.

Part V—Future Skills in Higher Education—The Wider View is dealing with national and international Future Skills initiatives and approaches in making society and lifelong learning future-proof.

Soon-Joo Gog, Edwin Tan and **Kelsie Tan** from the **SkillsFuture Singapore** Agency share their experience in developing Future Skills on a national level in **Future-Skilling the Workforce: SkillsFuture Movement in Singapore**. In Singapore, Future Skills are strongly promoted both in the initial education system and in lifelong learning, with an ecosystem aligning skills needs and training opportunities—tightly connected to the goal of an inclusive and prosperous society.

Part of that ecosystem is the **National University of Singapore**, and in their chapter **Anticipating the Future: Continuing Education at the National University of Singapore**, **Miriam J. Green, Christalle Tay** and **Ye-Her Wu** let us zoom into Future Skills education in the domain of continuing education. They describe their contribution to Singapore's Future Skills strategy, collaborating with government and industry—and not only taking students into account, but also university staff and graduates as lifelong learners.

The discussion on Future Skills is aligned with the objective to transform society into a Society 5.0 in Japan. **Keiko Ikeda** of **Kansai University** shares these discussions and their meaning for Future Skills development in her chapter **Aiming to**

Build Future Skills for Society 5.0: Educational DX (Digital Transformation) of University Education in Japan. Future Skills development, curriculum transformation, digital transformation and the internationalization of university are presented as drivers for promoting and working towards Society 5.0 in collaboration with multi-stakeholder groups.

The chapter **Future Skill Needs for IT Professionals—An Empirical Study** by **Marina Brunner** and **Ulf-Daniel Ehlers** presents a large-scale quantitative survey on Future Skills for IT professionals, analyzing data from 16 European member states.

In the final chapter, **Stephen Marshall** from the **Victoria University of Wellington** presents a chapter on **Future Higher Education in New Zealand: Creating a Universal Learning Community for Future Skills.** While exploring the national context of New Zealand for Future Skills development and education, he looks beyond existing approaches by proposing the Universal Learning Community, linking individuals, institutions, employers, and communities for the common goal of creating a shared Future Skills vision.

References

Baecker, D. (2018). *4.0 oder Die Lücke die der Rechner lässt.* Merve.

Baethge, M., Cordes, A., Donk, A., Kerst, C., Wespel, J., Wieck, M., et al. (2015). *Bildung und Qualifikation als Grundlage der technologischen Leistungsfähigkeit Deutschlands 2015* (Studien zum deutschen Innovationssystem 1–2015). https://www.uni-heidelberg. de/md/journal/2015/05/studis_01_2015_tlf.pdf.

Beck, U. (1986). *Die Risikogesellschaft.* Suhrkamp.

Beck, U., Giddens, A., & Lash, S. (2014). *Reflexive Modernisierung: Eine Kontroverse* (6th ed.). Suhrkamp.

Ehlers, U.-D. (2020). *Future skills: The future of learning and higher education.*

Ehlers, U.-D. (2022). *Future skills—The future of higher education and the future of learning: 17 skills profiles for the future of higher education.* https://next-education.org/wp-content/uploads/2022/08/Future-Skills-Report-Eng_V9.pdf.

Hippler, H. (2016). *Wozu (noch) Geisteswissenschaften?* https://rotary.de/bildung/wozu-noch-geisteswissenschaften-a-8984.html.

Kummert, T. (2017). *Endlich einer, der nicht nur Formeln anwenden kann.* https://www. sueddeutsche.de/karriere/arbeitsmarkt-endlich-einer-der-nicht-nur-formeln-anwenden-kann-1.3623308.

Lisop, I. (1997). Subjektbildung als Basis: Zum Umgang mit didaktischer Unbestimmtheit. *DIE Zeitschrift für Erwachsenenbildung* (4), 35.

Schofer, E., & Meyer, J. W. (2005). The worldwide expansion of higher education in the twentieth century. *American Sociological Review, 70*(6), 898–920.

Teichler, U. (2013). Hochschulexpansion – Auf dem Weg zur hochqualifizierten Gesellschaft? In T. Schultz & K. Hurrelmann (Eds.), *Die Akademiker-Gesellschaft: Müssen in Zukunft alle studieren?* (pp. 30–41). Beltz Verlagsgruppe.

Voß, G. G., & Pongratz, H. J. (1998). Der Arbeitskraftunternehmer – Eine neue Grundform der Ware Arbeitskraft? *Kölner Zeitschrift Für Soziologie Und Sozialpsychologie, 50*(1), 131–158.

Prof. Dr. phil. habil. Ulf-Daniel Ehlers is an internationally renowned Professor for Educational Management and Lifelong Learning at the Baden-Wuerttemberg Cooperative State University (DHBW) Karlsruhe which he headed as Vice-President between 2011 and 2017.

Laura Eigbrecht is principle investigator, teacher and doctoral student at the Baden-Wuerttemberg Cooperative State University (DHBW) Karlsruhe and holds degrees in European Media and Culture and Media Pedagogy.

Open Access This chapter is licensed under the terms of the Creative Commons Attribution 4.0 International License (http://creativecommons.org/licenses/by/4.0/), which permits use, sharing, adaptation, distribution and reproduction in any medium or format, as long as you give appropriate credit to the original author(s) and the source, provide a link to the Creative Commons license and indicate if changes were made.

The images or other third party material in this chapter are included in the chapter's Creative Commons license, unless indicated otherwise in a credit line to the material. If material is not included in the chapter's Creative Commons license and your intended use is not permitted by statutory regulation or exceeds the permitted use, you will need to obtain permission directly from the copyright holder.

Towards a Future Skills Framework for Higher Education

2

Ulf-Daniel Ehlers

Abstract

Skills are the ability and capacity to act and be able to use one's knowledge in a responsible way to achieve a goal. Future Skills are an emerging concept based on the theory of competence and action, which form a holistic concept, involving the mobilization of knowledge, skills, attitudes, and values to meet complex demands. The NextSkills study distinguishes between three different types of skills: learning and growth skills which refer to an individual's development process, design and innovation skills which refer to an individual's capacity to deal with a certain object, task, or assignment in a new, creative way, and co-creation skills which refer to an individual's way to productively shape their social environment and relation to the world.

As trends such as globalization and advances in artificial intelligence change the demands of the labor market and transform societies and everyday life, people need to rely even more on their uniquely (so far) human capacity for creativity, responsibility, and the ability to "learn to learn" throughout their lives. Social and emotional skills, such as empathy, self-awareness, respect for others, and the ability to communicate, are becoming more important as our lives become more ethnically, culturally, and linguistically diverse. This chapter summarizes the

---

U.-D. Ehlers (✉)
Professor for Educational Management and Lifelong Learning, Business Faculty,
DHBW Karlsruhe, Karlsruhe, Germany
e-mail: ulf-daniel.ehlers@dhbw-karlsruhe.de

© The Author(s) 2024
U.-D. Ehlers and L. Eigbrecht (eds.), *Creating the University of the Future*, Zukunft der Hochschulbildung - Future Higher Education,
https://doi.org/10.1007/978-3-658-42948-5_2

skills models provided by the NextSkills study and shows how the categories for Future Skills developed in the study can be used to compare other Future Skill approaches. It gives an overview of 13 Future Skills studies and analyses the role digital literacies play within these studies.

2.1 Introduction: Future Skills as Guiding Principles for Future Higher Education

With the increasing flexibility of biographies, the responsibility of individuals to develop individual competence strategies for their own lives is growing. Professional and private spheres of life are becoming increasingly blurred and intertwined. In terms of education, we can diagnose a real "drift to self-organization" (Ehlers, 2020, p. 122). This is characterized by a de-standardization of educational pathways, in which the fit between informal and formal educational opportunities and professional and private requirements must more and more be prioritized by the students themselves and translated into *individual learning and action strategies* that are increasingly aimed at acquiring "Future Skills". Higher Education Institutions across the globe are faced with the challenge of responding to this.

Future Skills are competences of a specific nature (Agentur Q, 2021; Ehlers, 2020). For example, if the task is to develop a solution to a new problem, often the ability to approach the problem from different perspectives, the flexibility and openness to accept several pathways to a solution, and interdisciplinarity are important. In a major study conducted between 2017 and 2020, called the NextSkills study (Ehlers, 2020), we decided to introduce labels for these competence areas and combine several competences into one "Future Skill" profile—in this case with the label "design-thinking competence" (Ehlers, 2020). If, for example, another area involves dealing with increasingly networked, often multiple, unclear, and complex organizational roles and contexts at work—or also privately when, e.g. operating in very widely differentiated patchwork and elective family constellations—skills such as dealing with ambiguity, acting in uncertain situations, and dealing with heterogeneity are important. These skills are also combined into one label in the NextSkills study, called "ambiguity competence". We termed these labels *Future Skills Profiles* in the NextSkills study (Ehlers, 2020); the study lists 17 such Future Skills Profiles.

In the last five years—since 2017 with the publication of the first (explicit) Future Skills study—the interest in Future Skills for the field of academic education has multiplied and is reshaping the discussion about key competences.

2 Towards a Future Skills Framework for Higher Education

The reasons are diverse and predominantly lie in societal megatrends such as digitalization, demographic change, and the development of an educational society (Ehlers, 2020). They lead to an increasing importance of Future Skills as precisely those abilities that allow individuals either to shape or to regain the ability to shape their own lives and individual social contexts in a world of constant change and in future emergent—i.e., unpredictable—and rapidly changing situations. "Future Skills" are therefore about those competencies that are of particular importance for the ability to act in such future situations, which, due to their rapid changes, repeatedly produce new, complex problem situations, for which preparation through education and training in a traditional sense (knowledge transfer in a preparational mode) is no longer effective. Numerous Future Skills studies are now available.[1] However, they are very heterogeneous both in their understanding of what Future Skills are and in the methodological design used to identify them. One example is the formulation of "virtual leadership" as well as "leadership skills" in one and the same study (Dettmers & Jochmann, 2021) and "adapting leadership culture" (Hays & ibe, 2017) as well as "leadership skills" (Agentur Q, 2021) in other studies—it remains unclear whether these are referring to the same meaning or in what way, if any, they are nuanced differently. Also, the approaches and the terms used are often not based in education theory and thus are not easily transferable to any learning design.

Another challenge is that so far, there is no conceptual framework for Future Skills available. Therefore, the different approaches cannot be compared easily. This refers both to the terminology used for individual Future Skills as well as to a comparative presentation of the scope of the respective approaches. The result is a design vacuum regarding support processes and the associated changes in learning culture, both in universities and other educational settings or places of learning, such as the workplace or for continuing education. Where can teachers and learners find orientation and how can they be supported in understanding how the terms and concepts of one approach relate to those of another?

This describes the problem addressed in this article: the variety of approaches and concepts currently available is not easily comparable. The scope of approaches and studies is not transparent and thus not accessible for orientation in the field of higher education. Therefore, we develop a conceptual framework which allows a comparison of Future Skills approaches and test it with the Future

---

[1] An overview of currently published studies and approaches on Future Skills is constantly updated at https://nextskills.org/fs-metaanalyse/.

Skills approaches available in the German-speaking area since 2016. We will base the conceptual framework on the NextSkills study which will be explained and will use its categories to classify the Future Skills listed in the selected approaches.

The chapter is making five steps: first, a brief overview of the **conceptual genesis of the term Future Skills** is provided (Sect. 2.2). This is followed by a brief summary of the state of research on Future Skills with regard to its implementation in higher education (Sect. 2.3). In Sect. 2.4, the research design used to identify the 17 Future Skills profiles of the NextSkills study is described. In addition, the understanding of competences and the internal structure of the NextSkills model are presented. In a final section—Sect. 2.5—the Future Skills lists of the 12 existing Future Skills studies in German-speaking countries since 2016 are analyzed and matched according to the 17 profiles.

2.2 State of Play for Future Skills in Higher Education: A Term with a Short History but an Enormous Career

Research and practice on *Future Skills* for higher education are booming. The different conceptualizations and understandings that are emerging in the related discussion can be roughly divided into two discussion streams. On the one hand, there is a general discussion of, first, vocational and then, later on, also specific higher education-related concepts set in a field of tension between a primarily "mimetic" (based on learning as imitation) and a "transformative" (based on learning as transformation and change) paradigm. The latter, which in Germany found its origin in 1974 with Dieter Mertens and his concept of key qualifications ("Schlüsselqualifikationen"), today is still followed internationally with continuing intensity in research works on *graduate attributes*. On the other hand— emerging since the 2000s—there is the discussion on the topic of *Future Skills* or 21st Century Skills.

The increasing relevance is reflected in the sharp rise in the number of publications on the topic over the last 15 years (see Fig. 2.1 and Ehlers, 2020 for more details).

2 Towards a Future Skills Framework for Higher Education

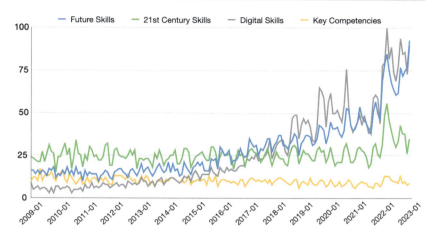

Fig. 2.1 Search term frequency in comparison (Google trends search from January 2023)

In the background of the debate on Future Skills there is an ongoing discourse about employability, which has put the discussion about the educational function of higher education on the agenda of higher education policy, especially since the Bologna reform in Europe in the mid-nineties of last century.[2] While popular with policy, employability as a concept is discussed quite controversially amongst educational professionals. Alesi and Teichler (2013, p. 35) conclude that the term "employability" is unfortunate in several respects, as it primarily addresses the "exchange dimension" (income, position, etc.), whereas the Bologna Process is primarily concerned with the "use dimension" of higher education (autonomy, etc.) and the dimension of employment would be only a supplement (Schubarth & Speck, 2014). After its introduction in 1974 through Mertens, the term "key competences" has established itself as main concept since the 1990s (Enderle et al., 2021). Conceptually, Future Skills is based on a broad understanding of competences and often relates to a specific selection of competences, usually summarized in frameworks, many of them analyzed in this chapter.

---

[2] For more information on the Bologna Process in Europe please refer to https://education.ec.europa.eu/education-levels/higher-education/inclusive-and-connected-higher-education/bologna-process.

2.2.1 Concept

From a conceptual point of view, Future Skills represent a selection of action competences that are important for the future (Ehlers, 2020). These, in turn, are defined as "dispositions for action" that are based on knowledge, enabled by abilities, and are motivated by values and attitudes (Heyse & Erpenbeck, 2009). Following these theoretical foundations, Future Skills can be defined as competences that enable individuals to solve complex problems in a self-organized manner in highly demanding contexts (see Sect. 2.3 for a more detailed definition). The starting point for the enormous career of the concept of Future Skills is the diagnosis that current concepts of higher education do not confront the pressing challenges of our societies with convincing concepts for the future (Hippler, 2016; Kummert, 2017)—neither the sustainable design of our environment nor the related social or economic challenges.

2.2.2 Research

The importance of Future Skills can be stated in Germany specifically for the field of university graduates (Ehlers, 2020; Enderle et al., 2021; Huber, 2016, p. 106, 2019, p. 157; Wild et al., 2018, p. 274) as well as for professional development (Agentur Q, 2021; Dettmers & Jochmann, 2021; Stifterverband & McKinsey, 2018), also internationally (Ashoka Deutschland & McKinsey, 2018; McKinsey Global Institute, 2017; OECD, 2018; World Economic Forum, 2020). Currently, there are 13 Future Skills studies for the German-speaking area since 2016 and at least 37 international studies. As a more general trend, Future Skills concepts include digital competences but place a stronger emphasis on more transversal competences. There are only few and non-systematic data on the current state of implementation of Future Skills in higher education. The reasons for lack of implementation data can be attributed to the complex nature of measuring Future Skills (e.g., creativity or ethical competence) and to the low level of maturity of the young and still developing empirical research in the field.

Despite insufficient measurement methods, the international research literature describes in detail, and with only a few discrepancies, that universities are not sufficiently geared to Future Skills. In the U.S. literature, the gap between skills demanded by the labor market and those taught in higher education institutions is supported by a number of empirical studies (Aasheim et al., 2009; Cox et al., 2013; Daud et al., 2011; Finch et al., 2013; Koppi et al., 2009) which identified that employers placed the most importance on "soft skills"—academic reputation was ranked as least important. Rigby et al. (2009, p. 8) also speak of an "implementation gap" in this context, while Osmani et al. (2015, p. 367) refer to it as a "broad mismatch". According to Tran (2015), university graduates are poorly prepared for "Life Skills" because curricula are often outdated or irrelevant. Accordingly, it can be stated that there is a general deficit in the curricula of universities to align them with the promotion of competences that are particularly relevant to Future Skills.

2.2.3 Meaning

The terminology for Future Skills has been subject to a conceptually differentiated development within the last 20 years. In Germany, they have developed from "key qualifications" in the field of vocational training (Mertens, 1974) to "key competencies" also for higher education. This took place through an intensive debate within the 1990s to further concepts around core and key skills, which Echterhoff (2014) traces in detail. In an international research review, Treleaven and Voola (2008) list eleven different terms and approaches from different authors: key skills, key competences, transferable skills, graduate attributes, employability skills (Curtis & McKenzie, 2001), soft skills (Freeman et al., 2008; Precision Consultancy, 2007); graduate capabilities (Bowden et al., 2000); generic graduate attributes (Bowden et al., 2000; Ginns & Barrie, 2004); professional skills, personal transferable skills (Drummond et al., 1998); generic competences (Treleaven & Voola, 2008; Tuning Project, 2008). Rigby et al. (2009) summarize these synonymously used terms under the umbrella term "graduate skills". They define these as skills that are not only relevant for professional development, but above all focus on personal development and the holistic education of the individual to become an engaged member of society (Rigby et al., 2009, p. 4).

A meta-analysis of more than 50 existing approaches to Future Skills by Ehlers (2020) shows that they usually consist of skills lists which are evaluated as important and meaningful. However, the approaches are mostly not based on sound competence-theoretical approaches (Clanchy & Ballard, 1995; Ehlers, 2020; Ginns & Barrie, 2004; Sin & Reid, 2005). Moreover, there is no empirical or conceptual modeling that would allow to critically classify the models in terms of their substance and scope. From the perspective of educational science, the character of arbitrariness can be stated for many of the approaches.

This paper aims at closing this currently existing orientation gap. For this purpose, a categorical framework is constructed, by means of which existing approaches can be divided into larger and well-defined fields of competence.

2.3 Which Future Skills Are Relevant for Future Higher Education: the NextSkills Study

The state of play shows that Future Skills are highly relevant for the future of higher education institutions, both curricular-wise and strategically for enabling them to shape attractive programs for students. In order to find a starting point for curricular integration and for strategic initiatives, institutions and educational professionals need to answer the question: which is a suitable Future Skills framework for their purposes? However, currently there is no universal framework to compare Future Skills studies and the skills listed in them.

The NextSkills study (Ehlers, 2020; Ehlers & Kellermann, 2019) provides Future Skills profiles which can serve as a categorical framework for the first time. It was developed from an extensive inventory of future relevant skills, which were collected from in-depth interviews and grouped into thematic fields, so-called Future Skills profiles. The Future Skills profiles contain a number of so-called "reference competences". The profiles serve as a reference framework which enables comparing the skill lists of existing Future Skills approaches. The following section will describe the methodological design used to develop the 17 Future Skills profiles, elaborate on the underlying theoretical foundation used, and describe each Future Skills profile in detail.

> **Research Methodology of the NextSkills Study**
> The research study NextSkills was conducted between 2017 and 2020. It aimed to analyze which skills are needed for a productive and proactive design of future life and work from the perspective of organizations and their members. In addition, the study analyzes requirements for higher education institutions. To this end, Future Skills profiles were identified in a multi-step research process using a multi-method design. In a first step, so-called Future Organizations were identified through a criteria-led landscape analysis which served as the empirical field. The selection process took place in 2015 as part of a competition in which over 8,500 partner organizations were contacted and given the opportunity to submit their

> HR development concepts. 124 organizations took part in the competition and were evaluated in a criteria-supported expert rating by 15 experts. 17 organizations were finally included in an in-depth interview study between December 2016 and June 2017. Participants in the interviews were the staff responsible for the *Future Organizations*. 20 participants took part in 17 in-depth interviews, resulting in approximately 700 min of qualitative interview material. An inventory of Future Skill descriptions was extracted from the material, as well as skill constructs and clusters. In order to further refine and validate the qualitatively acquired results, a Delphi study was conducted with an international panel of experts. The Delphi study included two rounds of consensual expert participation. Fifty-three international experts from different organizations and institutions were invited to participate in the study. The studies resulted in 17 Future Skills profiles.

Based on the in-depth interviews and the consultation of experts in a Delphi study (Ehlers & Kellermann, 2019), 17 skill profiles representing competences were constructed. Each profile contains a few sub-competences—so-called "reference competences". The fact that Future Skills can be defined, described, and differentiated into a system of profiles and reference competences evokes the question of a systems change in higher education in which the focus is no longer on a system of *preparation through knowledge transfer*, but rather on viewing education as a process of supporting development of dispositions for action and readiness to deal with complex, unknown future problem situations through reflection, values, and attitudes. This in turn leads to rethinking curricula to focus on support of learner agency and learning assessment; to move from a view of "assessment of learning" to understanding "assessment as learning" (Ehlers et al., 2022). In a foundational publication on Future Skills, we define Future Skills as follows:

> **Definition:** Future Skills are competences that allow individuals to solve complex problems in contexts characterized through a high degree of emergence in a self-organized way and enable them to act (successfully). They are based on cognitive, motivational, volitional, and social resources, are value-based, and can be acquired in a learning process (Ehlers, 2020, p. 53).

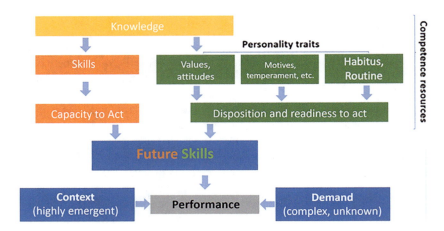

Fig. 2.2 The Future Skills concept within an action competence framework (Ehlers, 2020, p. 54)

Competence theory focusses on the way individuals are able to act and thus go beyond what they know. The ability and disposition to act successfully in an unknown future situation is at the center of competence research. Future Skills are such competences which are needed to enable successful action in specific circumstances and contexts of action, which we refer to as "emergent contexts". The ability to act or, as competence theory frames it, to "perform", is generally based on three decisive components, described in Fig. 2.2:

1. Knowledge, as an enabler for action,
2. Skills, building the capacity to act and
3. Values, motives, and habitus, forming the disposition to act.

Capacity and disposition then lead to any action performed by an individual. In cases where individuals act without the security of prior experience because of a permanently shifting environment, which makes it difficult to rely on prior experiences, Future Skills are in demand. We base the characterization of such contexts on the concept of autopoiesis from Maturana & Varela (1980), later on adapted by Luhmann (1976) to organizational theory, and thus speak of contexts and systems as emergent.

Future Skills, therefore, are not just any competences. Future Skills can be distinguished from those competences that are not particularly future-oriented. The

2 Towards a Future Skills Framework for Higher Education

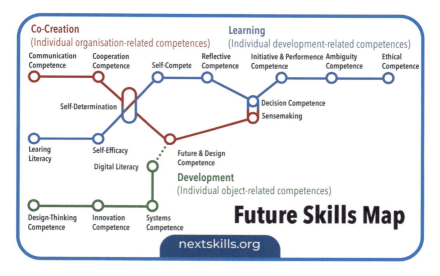

Fig. 2.3 Future Skill-Profiles Overview (Ehlers, 2020)

concept of emergence—explained before and in more detail in Ehlers (2020)—serves as a differentiating dimension between any standard competences and those competences that are particularly relevant to the future. Those contexts of action that exhibit highly emergent developments in life, work, organizational, and business processes require Future Skills to cope with the requirements. Emergence thus defines the dividing line that separates traditional and future work areas. Since this boundary is not clearly schematic, but rather fluid, and many organizations are in transformation processes in which work environments evolve into highly emergent work contexts quickly, the need for Future Skills is also an evolving area and not a binary state of either/or.

Emergence versus *submergence* is thus an important basic distinction for explaining the meaning of Future Skills (Ehlers, 2020). Future Skills profiles can be divided into three fields, which are shown in Fig. 2.3 as three subway lines of the Future Skills Map. This division follows the so-called "Triple Helix Model" by Ehlers (2020). It is based on the insight that the skills required to cope with the demands of action can be structured according to three interacting dimensions:

Table 2.1 Future Skills competence fields and profiles in overview (Ehlers, 2020)

Future Skills-Profiles	Reference competence(s)	Short description
Learning—Subject development-related competences		
Learning literacy	• Self-directed learning • Metacognitive skills	Learning literacy is the ability and willingness to learn in a self-directed and self-initiated fashion. It also entails metacognitive skills
Self-efficacy	• Self-confidence	Self-efficacy as a Future Skills Profile refers to the belief and one's (self)confidence to be able to master the tasks at hand relying on one's own abilities and taking over responsibility for one's decisions
Self-determination	• Autonomy	Self-determination as a Future Skill describes an individual's ability to act productively within the field of tension between external structure and self-organization, and to create room for self-development and autonomy, so that they can meet their own needs in freedom and self-organization
Self-competence	• Self-management • Self-organization competence • Self-regulation • Cognitive load management • Self-responsibility	Self-competence as a Future Skill is the ability to develop one's own personal and professional capabilities largely independently of external influences. This includes other skills such as independent self-motivation and planning, but also the ability to set goals, time management, organization, learning aptitude and success control through feedback. In addition, cognitive load management and a high degree of personal responsibility

(continued)

2 Towards a Future Skills Framework for Higher Education

33

Table 2.1 (continued)

Future Skills-Profiles	Reference competence(s)	Short description
Reflective competence	• Critical thinking • Self-reflection competence	Reflective competence as a Future Skill includes the willingness and ability to reflect, i.e. the ability to question oneself and others for the purpose of constructive further development, as well as to recognize underlying systems of behavior, thought and values and to assess their consequences for actions and decisions holistically
Decision competence	• Responsibility-taking	Decision competence is the ability to seize decisions and to evaluate different alternatives against each other, as well as making a final decision and taking over the responsibility for it
Initiative and performance competence	• (intrinsic) Motivation • Self-motivation • Motivation capability • Initiative-taking • Need/motivation for achievement • Engagement • Persistence • Goal-orientation	Initiative and performance competence refers to an individual's ability to motivate themselves as well as to his/her wish of contributing to achievement. Persistence and goal-orientation form the motivational basis for performance. A positive self-concept also plays an important role as it serves to attribute success and failure in such a way that the performance motivation does not decrease
Ambiguity competence	• Dealing with uncertainty • Dealing with heterogeneity • Ability to act in different roles	Ambiguity competence refers to an individual's ability to recognize, understand, and finally productively handle ambiguity, heterogeneity, and uncertainty, as well as to act in different roles

(continued)

Table 2.1 (continued)

Future Skills-Profiles	Reference competence(s)	Short description
Ethical Competence		Ethical competence comprises the ability to perceive a situation or situation as ethically relevant, including its conceptual, empirical and contextual consideration (perceive), the ability to formulate relevant prescriptive premises together with the evaluation of their relevance, their weight, their justification, their binding nature and their conditions of application (evaluate) and the ability to form judgements and check their logical consistency, their conditions of use and their alternatives (judge)
Development—Object-related competences		
Design-thinking competence	• Flexibility and openness • Versatility • Ability to shift perspectives • Interdisciplinarity	The Future Skill Profile Design-thinking competence comprises the ability to use concrete methods to carry out creative development processes open-endedly with regard to given problems and topics and to involve all stakeholders in a joint problem and solution design process
Innovation competence	• Creativity • Innovative thinking • Willingness to experiment	Innovation competence as a Future Skill Profile includes the willingness to promote innovation as an integral part of any organizational object, topic and process and the ability to contribute to the organization as an innovation ecosystem

(continued)

2 Towards a Future Skills Framework for Higher Education

Table 2.1 (continued)

Future Skills-Profiles	Reference competence(s)	Short description
System competence	• Systems-thinking • Knowledge about knowledge structures • Navigation competence within knowledge structures • Networked thinking • Analytical competence • Synergy creation • Application competence • Problem-solving • Adaptability	Systems competence as a Future Skill is the ability to recognize and understand complex personal-psychological, social, and technical (organizational) systems as well as their mutual influences and to be able to design and/or accompany coordinated planning and implementation processes for new initiatives in the system
Digital literacy	• Media literacy • Information literacy	Digital literacy is the ability and disposition to use digital media, to develop them in a productive and creative way, the capacity to critically reflect on its usage and the impact media have on society and work, both for private and professional contexts, as well as the understanding of the potentials and limits of digital media and their effects
Co-Creation—Organization-related competences		
Sensemaking	• Meaning creation • Value orientation	The Future Skill Profile Sensemaking comprises the willingness and ability to construct meaning and understanding from the rapidly changing structures of meaning within future work and life contexts, to further develop existing structures of meaning or to promote the creation of new ones where they have been lost

(continued)

Table 2.1 (continued)

Future Skills-Profiles	Reference competence(s)	Short description
Future and design competence	• Willingness to change • Ability to continuously improve • Future mindset • Courage for the unknown • Readiness for development • Ability to challenge oneself	Future and design competence is the ability to master the current situation with courage for the new, willingness to change and forward thinking, to develop situations into other new and previously unknown visions of the future and to approach these creatively
Cooperation competence	• Social intelligence • Team-working ability • Leader as a coach • Intercultural competence (organizational culture) • Counselling competence	Cooperation competence is the ability to cooperate and collaborate in (intercultural) teams either in face-to-face or digitally aided interactions within or between organizations with the purpose of transforming differences into commonalities. Social intelligence, openness, and advisory skills play a key role for this competence
Communication competence	• Language proficiency • Presentation competence • Capacity for dialogue • Communication readiness • Consensus orientation • Openness towards criticism	Communication competence as a Future Skill entails not only language skills, but also discourse, dialogue, and strategic communication aspects, which—taken together—serve the individual to communicate successfully and in accordance with the respective situation and context, in view and empathy of her/his own and others' needs

1. Competences for learning and personal development: Individual development-related Future Skills that relate to the ability to develop oneself as a person, referred to here as individual development-related competences
2. Future Skills that relate to the creative development of solutions and the handling of subjects and work objects, work tasks and problems, referred to as individual object-related competences
3. Future Skills that relate to the social, organizational, and institutional environment in the sense of co-creation (Scharmer, 2009), referred to here as individual organization-related competences.

The individual Future Skills named by the respondents can be conceptually located within this three-dimensional action space (Fig. 2.3).

Table 2.1 provides an overview of the individual Future Skills profiles, the associated reference competences, and the descriptions of the competency fields.

In the next section we are going to analyze further Future Skills studies and then compare them. For the comparative analysis we will use the 17 Future Skills profiles as analytical categories. In a qualitative analysis approach, we will attempt to categorize all skills listed in the approaches examined and summarize them within the 17 Future Skills profiles.

2.4 Comparing Different Future Skills Approaches: Insights from a Future Skills Landscape Study

2.4.1 Comparison of Future Skills Research Methods

The following sections provides insights into, and analysis of research methods of 13 different Future Skills studies which were conducted between 2016 and 2022. They differ in focus, methodology, and orientation. For example, studies such as the D21 Digital Index (Initiative D21 e.V., 2021) are more focused on digitization, digital and media competences, or digital skills. A Stifterverband and McKinsey (2018) study also focused on digital skills, but included transversal Future Skills and, in an updated version of its framework (Stifterverband & McKinsey, 2021), so-called transformative skills as well.

In terms of methodology, Future Skills studies usually employ forecasting methods to determine Future Skills requirements (Wagemann et al., 2021). In earlier writings, we have analyzed comprehensively the methods used to study skill demands (Ehlers & Bonaudo, 2021). Table 2.2 provides an overview of the research methods used. Most of the approaches use several methods, however only three of the studies use qualitative methods. Due to the possibility of approaching open research questions in open analysis processes of qualitative material, specifically inductive qualitative analysis is suitable for modeling future unknown competence requirements. Often, exploratory qualitative interviews, Delphi surveys, or focus group methods are used. All other studies use rather confirmatory quantitative approaches, which are based on already existing hypotheses and operationalize already known competence descriptions from, e.g., job advertisements. The example of the study by Agentur Q (2021) shows particularly well how a big data and machine learning-based analysis of current job advertisements is used to identify those competences that are currently particularly important in certain industries. While these methods can be empirically quite easily operationalized—and large amounts of data can be processed, especially with the help of machine learning methods—they tend to limit the research field to already known skills requirements that carry relevance already today and extrapolate them into the future. If, on the other hand, the objective is to go beyond the requirements already known today and already defined in job advertisements to determine what the contours of future forms of life and work and their competence requirements might look like, this can be done better by means of open and qualitative procedures such as expert, learner, or employee interviews or other qualitative methods such as data collection via focus groups or Delphi studies and subsequent inductive construct-forming data evaluation procedures. This is especially true for assessments of scenarios that lie in a more distant future.

A dimension of analysis which has not been considered in the comparative analysis of research methodologies is that of competence understandings and educational theoretical foundations underlying the approaches. They vary from modelling competences as a list of terms found in job portals (Agentur Q, 2021) to approaches grounded in competence theory (Ehlers, 2020). While all of the studies refer to Future Skills, their heterogeneity and different focus results into very different concepts and terms for the phenomenon of Future Skills. Differently named Future Skills therefore often refer to actually similar competences. For example, the Future Skill "ability to change perspective" is also referred to as "flexibility and openness" or labelled as "design-thinking competence"—as is the case in the NextSkills study. The "ability to deal with increasingly networked, often unclear and complex organizational roles" is also included in some of the studies, labelled differently. In the NextSkills study, this competence is summarized with the label "ambiguity competence".

2 Towards a Future Skills Framework for Higher Education

Table 2.2 Methods in Future Skills Studies (Ehlers, 2022)

		Quantitative Methods			Qualitative Methods				
		Expert Survey	Stakeholder Survey Company	Stakeholder Survey Learners/Citizens	Expert Interview	Focus Group	Delphi	Job Advertisement analysis	Literature Review
1	Ehlers 2020			(X)	X		X		X
2	Graf et. al. 2020						X		X
3	Stifterverband McKinsey 2018/21		X		X	X			
4	Handelsblatt 2021							X	X
5	Strametz 2020								X
6	Agentur Q 2021	**X**						X	
7	TH Nürnberg 2017	**X**		X					X
8	Step-stone/Kien-baum 2021		X						
9	GDI/ Jacobs Foundation 2020	**X**							X
10	Sinus-Institut 2020			X					

(continued)

Table 2.2 (continued)

		Quantitative Methods			Qualitative Methods				
		Expert Survey	Stake-holder Survey Com-pany	Stake-holder Survey Learn-ers/Cit-izens	Expert Inter-view	Focus Group	Delphi	Job Adver-tise-ment analysis	Lit-erature Review
11	Hays 2017			X					
12	ZiviZ 2020			X					X
13	bitkom 2017		X						

2.4.2 Meta-Analysis and Comparison of Skills

In this section we present a meta-analysis of different Future Skills studies. The meta-analysis is based on the method of qualitative meta-analysis of Schnepf and Groeben (2019). Here, we view qualitative meta-analysis as a systematic summary of empirical studies using qualitative content analysis. We view this approach as superior to presenting a 'narrative overview article', or conducting a meta-synthesis—especially in a field of research like Future Skills, because approaches are diverse and often not well operationalized.

The meta-analysis categorizes a body of 252 skills derived from 12 Future Skills studies by means of a categorial framework built from the NextSkills study. This framework contains the 17 different Future Skills profiles. In order to create a possibility to compare the lists of skills contained in each of the 17 approaches, such a framework was necessary. In the first step we created a long inventory listing all 252 skills from the 12 Future Skills approaches in question. We then assessed the suitability to use the 17 Future Skills profiles from the NextSkills study as comparison categories. In order to assess their suitability, we performed a structured qualitative analysis of the body of skills attempting to allocate them into one of the 17 categories of the framework.

It became clear that the framework had to be broad enough to summarize as many differently nuanced skills labels as possible, and at the same time needed to be differentiated enough to adequately discriminate different competence clusters from one another. Analyzing and allocating the skills listed in the 12 Future Skills

2 Towards a Future Skills Framework for Higher Education

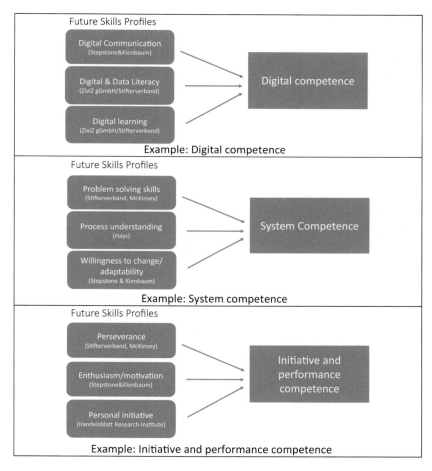

Fig. 2.4 Illustration of qualitative analysis and mapping of terms (Ehlers, 2022)

approaches was an act of qualitative content analysis leading to the final result that all 252 skills contained in the 12 reference studies have been analytically allocated into one of the 17 Future Skills categories. It proved helpful that each of the 17 analysis categories of the NextSkills study was explicitly defined (see Tab. 1.1 and Ehlers, 2020 for more detail). The analysis was performed by a team of two researchers using communicative validation to increase intercoder reliability (Mayring, 2008). Figure 2.4 illustrates the process of qualitative mapping of terms.

From the body of 13 studies, a skill inventory has been created. In a series of steps, the skills from the different approaches which were included into the qualitative meta-analysis were analyzed. Duplications have been omitted and multi-dimensional formulations expanded (skill items which contained two or more skills in one skill formulation).

The result presented in Table 2.3 shows how the 252 competences were allocated to the 17 analysis profiles. Apart from the numbers of items allocated to the analysis categories, Table 2.3 also shows the so-called "allocation quota". The "allocation quota" states the ratio of skills which, during the research process, we were able to actually allocate to the comparison categories (see Table 2.3). The analysis reveals that for all skill sets analyzed, the "allocation quota" was 100%, which means that we were able to allocate all Future Skills items from the inventory of Future Skills. In conclusion, the skill profiles of the NextSkills study are able to serve as a general framework model—at least for the approaches investigated in this meta-analysis. They are sufficiently precise and, on the other hand, are broad enough to cover all the areas addressed in the Future Skills approaches examined.

An analysis of the frequency of skills within the respective Future Skills profiles reveals an accumulation in the following areas[3]:

1. self-competence (10 mentions) and learning literacy (8 mentions) in the subject development-related dimension.
2. digital literacy (9 mentions) and design-thinking competence (8 mentions) in the object-related dimension
3. cooperation competence (12 mentions) and communication competence (9 mentions) in the organization-related dimension.

The Future Skills profiles self-determination (1) and ethical competence (3) are those with the fewest mentions among the approaches examined.

2.4.3 Analyzing "the Digital Dimension" within Future Skills

In this section, we are going to analyze what we call "the digital dimension" within Future Skills approaches. Because of the huge impact digital transformation has on

---

[3] The table includes the Future Skills framework by Stifterverband & McKinsey from 2018 as well as the updated and enhanced version from 2021. The Future Skills profiles listed in both versions are counted as one mention in the following section.

Table 2.3 Comparative analysis of existing Future Skills models (translated from Ehlers, 2022)

	Future Skills Profile Next Skills Study	Current Future Skills Studies												
		Graf et al. 2020	Stifterverband McKinsey 2021	Handelsblatt 2021	Strametz 2020	Agentur Q 2021	TH Nürnberg 2017	Stepstone/ Kienbaum 2021	Stifterverband McKinsey 2018	GDI/ Jacobs Foundation 2020	Sinus-Institut 2020	Hays 2017	ZiviZ 2020	bitkom 2017	Matches TOT
	Number of competences	*22*	*21*	*52*	*5*	*33*	*16*	*35*	*18*	*3*	*6*	*23*	*11*	*7*	*252*
	Allocation quota	*100%*	*100%*	*100%*	*100%*	*100%*	*100%*	*100%*	*100%*	*100%*	*100%*	*100%*	*100%*	*100%*	
Nr.	Subject development-related competences														
1	Learning literacy	x	x	x			x	x	x	x		x	x		9
2	Self-efficacy	x			x		x			x	x				5
3	Self-determination	x													1

(continued)

Table 2.3 (continued)

	Future Skills Profile Next Skills Study	Current Future Skills Studies												
		Graf et al. 2020	Stifterverband McKinsey 2021	Handelsblatt 2021	Strametz 2020	Agentur Q 2021	TH Nürnberg 2017	Stepstone/ Kienbaum 2021	Stifterverband McKinsey 2018	GDI/ Jacobs Foundation 2020	SinusInstitut 2020	Hays 2017	ZiviZ 2020	bitkom 2017	Matches TOT
4	Self-competence	x	x	x		x	x	x	x	x	x	x	x		11
5	Reflective competence	x	x	x	x		x		x	x	x			x		9
6	Decision competence	x			x	x	x	x*			x	x				7
7	Initiative and performance competence	x	x	x	x	x		x	x				x			8
8	Ambiguity competence	x	x			x	x	x				x				6
9	Ethical competence		x	x	x											3

(continued)

Table 2.3 (continued)

Future Skills Profile Next Skills Study	Current Future Skills Studies													
	Graf et al. 2020	Stifterverband McKinsey 2021	Handelsblatt 2021	Strametz 2020	Agentur Q 2021	TH Nürnberg 2017	Stepstone/ Kienbaum 2021	Stifterverband McKinsey 2018	GDI/ Jacobs Foundation 2020	Sinus-Institut 2020	Hays 2017	ZiviZ 2020	bitkom 2017	Matches TOT
Object-related competences														
10 Design-thinking competence	x*	x	x	x	(x)		x	x		x		x		9
11 Innovation competence		x		x	x	x		x	x					6
12 Systems competence	x		x	x	(x)	x	x							6
13 Digital literacy	x	x	x	x	x	x***	x	x		x		x	x	10
Organisation-related competences														

(continued)

Table 2.3 (continued)

	Future Skills Profile Next Skills Study	Current Future Skills Studies													
		Graf et al. 2020	Stif- terver- band McK- insey 2021	Han- dels- blatt 2021	Strametz 2020	Agen- tur Q 2021	TH Nürn- berg 2017	Step- stone/ Kien- baum 2021	Stif- terver- band McK- insey 2018	GDI/ Jacobs Foun- dation 2020	Sinus- Institut 2020	Hays 2017	ZiviZ 2020	bitkom 2017	Matches TOT
14	Sensemak- ing		x	x	x	x			x	x		x			7
15	Future and design compe- tence		x	x	x		x	x		x		x			7
16	Coopera- tion com- petence	x	x	x	x	(x)	x	x**	x	x	x	x	x	x	13
17	Communi- cation com- petence	x	x	x	x	x		x	x	x	x	x			10
	TOT	13	13	12	12	11	11	11	10	9	8	8	7	2	

*risk-taking, ** virtual cooperation, *** specifically for artificial intelligence* our lives and work environments, digital literacy is often used synonymously with Future Skills. Our analysis shows that this general impression can be indeed found in research in the fact that from a quantitative point of view, digital-related skills play an important role within Future Skills approaches: 95 of 252 skills listed in our inventory are digital skills. However, a closer look into them also shows that there is a bias within the digital skills explored in the Future Skills approaches. Mostly, they relate to knowledge about "the digital" or usage of digital tools; creativity-related and reflexive analytical skills are underrepresented.

In five of the 12 studies examined, digital Future Skills form a strong focal point. All 95 skills which were found within the analyzed Future Skills approaches were in a first step allocated into one category—the analysis category called "digital literacy". However, since digital competences are of particular importance in many approaches, an additional, qualitative analysis has been conducted for these competences. The aim was to find out what they are focusing on. As an analysis framework, a well introduced and simple model for media literacy by Dieter Baacke et al. (1991) was employed. It contains four dimensions to characterize different aspects of digital action and capacity: media analysis, media knowledge, media usage, and media design (Baacke et al., 1991). The approach differentiates between dimensions of capabilities such as using media and digital tools for different purposes, expressing oneself by creating content in digital environments, and developing own digital environments, but also goes beyond usage and content creation into more analytical and creative dimensions. "Media analysis" is thus referring to analytical-reflexive and critical ways to think about, analyze, and use digital technology. The dimension "media design" means to go beyond the currently existing and invent, create, and design media and digital technology, respectively using digital technology to invent and create solutions. The four competence dimensions are also briefly described in Table 2.4.

For the analysis process of the 12 studies examined, a basic inventory was drawn up containing all 95 digital skills that had been summarized in the category of "digital literacy" in the first step of the analysis described above. It must be noted that in most of the digital competences included in the studies currently available, it is noticeable that no clear definition is given for the digital skills listed (e.g., "cyber security" as a Future Skill is not further defined). For this reason, a multi-step approach was used for the analysis: In a first step, those competences were assigned to the four dimensions and sub-dimensions of the media competence model that could be clearly allocated in terms of content. In the second step, those competences were assigned for which there were no direct equivalents in the media competence dimensions. This was the case, for example, because they do not relate to a skill but in their formulation rather describe a thematic field which for example was the case for "cybersecurity". It remains unclear if, with this wording of the skill, capacity for development of cybersecurity solutions are referred to, or management, or maybe architecture skills to design a system. We therefore had to take a decision to frame them into an action-related skill concept. This was done through an application perspective. These respective skill concepts were framed as "application and implementation of concepts in the respective subject area". The thematic keyword "cybersecurity" therefore was interpreted as "application and implementation of concepts in the topic area of cybersecurity" and therefore assigned to category C1 (media use, receptive).

This analysis process finally made it possible to allocate all 95 digital Future Skills to the four dimension and subdimensions.

Table 2.5 shows the result.

The analysis shows a clear bias. "The digital" dimension in the Future Skills approaches analyzed is leaning heavily toward using digital media and knowledge about digital technologies. We found an over-proportionally strong occupation of the media use dimension within the digitally related Future Skills. Almost half of these skills fall into this area (42 out of 95). The dimension of media literacy is also strong, with a total of 23 out of 95 mentions. The focus here is on instrumental skills (18 mentions). Thus, in the present Future Skills approaches, digital competences which refer to receptive and interactive usage competences as well as knowledge about media (informative subdimension) and instrumental-qualificatory usage are most pronounced.

In contrast, reflexive-ethical aspects, and the ability to analyze the social consequences of digital transformation, which are contained in the dimension of media criticism, are underrepresented. In total, only 15 of the 95 items fall into the three subdimensions of media criticism: ethical (4), reflexive (3) and analytical (8). This paints a picture of skills approaches that are primarily focused on use and application and implementation (dimensions B & C), while a more reflexive view on digital capabilities is rather weakly contained in the Future Skills approaches analyzed. Only Stifterverband (2021), Ehlers (2020) and Agentur Q (2021) explicitly mention ethical digital skills at all.

2 Towards a Future Skills Framework for Higher Education

Table 2.4 Media Competence Dimensions according to Baacke et al. (1991)

A	Media analysis	Critical analysis of the content of media
A1	Analytical	Adequate comprehension of social processes
A2	Reflexive	Relate what has been analyzed to oneself and one's actions
A3	Ethical	Clarification of the analysis and reflection on social responsibility
B	Media knowledge	Knowledge about media and media systems
B1	Informative	Knowledge of processes and structures, e.g. how journalists work
B2	Instrumental-Qualificatory	Knowledge about the operation or technical handling
C	Media usage	Apply media and use interactive offers
C1	Receptive, apply	Program usage skills, reception
C2	Interactive, offer	Interactive action—beyond receptive-perceptive use
D	Media design	Innovative, creative, aesthetic changes & developments
D1	Innovative	Changes and further development of the media system
D2	Creative	New, creative, aesthetic innovations

Finally, the fourth dimension, creative media design, turned out to be most weakly represented. The skills contained here are those which represent the capacity to invent and create, design innovative digital solutions, think beyond the existing state of the art, and go beyond what is currently thinkable. It is also about employing digitally suggested concepts in order to be able to innovatively develop new creative solutions to previously unknown problems. This dimension also covers the field of creation in an aesthetical sense. The sub-dimension creative media design (D2) is the most weakly represented of all, with only two mentions. Innovative media design (D1) is slightly more pronounced, with a total of 11 mentions.

Overall, it is quite astonishing that this dimension is only weakly represented in the Future Skills studies. It is this capacity which is needed in emergent life and work environments which are impregnated and influenced through digital developments, tools, and frameworks. In such environments, the ability to find new ways to sustain procedures and structure how we live and work together seems indispensable. Thus, the lack of elaboration of this dimension within existing approaches to the future of skills can be understood as a desiderate and gap which needs future work to close it.

Table 2.5 Comparative Overview of Digital Future Skills (Ehlers, 2022)

Media Competence Dimensions and Subdimensions	Future Skills Approaches												
	Description	Ehlers 2020	Graf et al. 2020	Stifterverband McKinsey 2021	Handelsblatt 2021	Agentur Q 2021	TH Nürnberg 2017	Stepstone/ Kienbaum 2021	Stifterverband McKinsey 2018	Sinus-Institut 2020	ZiviZ 2020	bitkom 2017	Matches TOT
Media Analysis	Critical examination of the content of media												
Analytical	Adequate comprehension of social processes	1			4					1	1	1	8
Reflexive	Relate what has been analyzed to oneself and one's actions	1			1			1					3

(continued)

Table 2.5 (continued)

Media Competence Dimensions and Subdimensions	Future Skills Approaches												
	Description	Ehlers 2020	Graf et al. 2020	Stifterverband McKinsey 2021	Handelsblatt 2021	Agentur Q 2021	TH Nürnberg 2017	Stepstone/ Kienbaum 2021	Stifterverband McKinsey 2018	Sinus-Institut 2020	ZiviZ 2020	bitkom 2017	Matches TOT
Ethical	Clarification of the analysis and reflexion on social responsibility	1		1		1			1				4
Media knowledge	Knowledge about media and media systems												

(continued)

Table 2.5 (continued)

Media Competence Dimensions and Subdimensions	Future Skills Approaches												
	Description	Ehlers 2020	Graf et al. 2020	Stifterverband McKinsey 2021	Handelsblatt 2021	Agentur Q 2021	TH Nürnberg 2017	Stepstone/ Kienbaum 2021	Stifterverband McKinsey 2018	Sinus-Institut 2020	ZiviZ 2020	bitkom 2017	Matches TOT
Informative	Knowledge of processs and structures, e.g. how journalists work	1			2			1				1	5
Instrumental-qualificational	Knowledge about the operation or technical handling	1	1	2	3	2	1	1	3	1	2	1	18

(continued)

Table 2.5 (continued)

Media Competence Dimensions and Subdimensions	Future Skills Approaches											
	Description	Ehlers 2020	Graf et al. 2020	Stifterverband McKinsey 2021	Handelsblatt 2021	Agentur Q 2021	TH Nürnberg 2017	Stepstone/Kienbaum 2021	Stifterverband McKinsey 2018	Sinus-Institut 2020	ZiviZ 2020	bitkom 2017	Matches TOT
Media usage	Apply media and use interactive offers												
Receptive, apply	Program usage skills, reception	1	1	3	3	2	3	1	3		1	3	21
Interactive, offer	Interactive action—beyond receptive-perceptive use	1	1	1	5	1	2	3	3		3	1	21

(continued)

Table 2.5 (continued)

Media Competence Dimensions and Subdimensions	Future Skills Approaches												
	Description	Ehlers 2020	Graf et al. 2020	Stifterverband McKinsey 2021	Handelsblatt 2021	Agentur Q 2021	TH Nürnberg 2017	Stepstone/ Kienbaum 2021	Stifterverband McKinsey 2018	Sinus-Institut 2020	ZiviZ 2020	bitkom 2017	Matches TOT
Media Design	Innovative, creative, aesthetic changes and developments												
Innovative	Changes and further development of the media system	1		3	3		1	1	2				11
Creative	New, creative, aesthetic innovations	1			1								2

A conclusion can therefore not neglect the fact that contemporary Future Skills approaches are treating digital literacies in a biased way. With the exceptions mentioned, we conclude that skills which relate to creative, socially reflective, and ethically sound approaches to an uncertain digital future are under-represented in Future Skills approaches. Those relating to use and application of existing digital concepts and tools on the other hand are strongly elaborated. Further development of digitally related Future Skills within the existing Future Skills approaches is therefore necessary, both structurally (to which dimensions of competence do the competences belong?) and in terms of content (to which dispositions for action are the competences directed?).

2.5 Conclusion

Current Future Skills studies and concepts can be described with the NextSkills model, which contains 17 profiles that form a framework concept for Future Skills. By dividing Future Skills into three dimensions of action—subjective, individual development-related skills; objective, task- and topic-related skills; social, world/organization-related skills—the NextSkills approach also goes beyond a static model of pure skills enumeration and definition.

The contribution takes place at the transition point of a concept change. Previous concepts such as 21st Century Skills or Sustainability Competences, which were used to describe key competences or transversal skills, are replaced by the concept of Future Skills. However, this term is not a conceptually rigid and unambiguously dimensioned term, but rather a collective category of such key competences, which are compiled as lists of different types and now stand for future competency concepts, or "Future Skills".

The article presents the studies on this topic published in German-speaking countries within the last five years and analyzes them in their respective conceptual depth and definitional strength. In addition, a framework model is proposed, which can be used to classify all existing approaches. The classification into the categories or profiles of the NextSkills approach used for this purpose allows a complete assignment of all 252 Future Skills.

The meta-analysis makes it possible to draw the following conclusions about the status of current Future Skills research:

1. **Heterogeneous and evolving field:** The term used in all the approaches under review is "Future Skill". However, it does not denote a clearly delineated and well-defined concept of skills, but rather describes a variety of key points and

ideas about what skills people would need to possess in order to positively shape the future of their respective organizations or lives. In some cases, the respective approaches only mention topics or topic words instead of competences.

2. **Many approaches without a clear theoretical foundation for action:** Future Skills is an "emerging concept" for which there are only a few approaches to date with a theoretical foundation for action. The NextSkills study proposes such an action-theoretical foundation. The approach of action competence, which makes it possible to describe Future Skills as a set of selected action competences, is a path that can be consolidated in the future. Some of the concepts mentioned contain references or descriptions of the understanding of action competence in their respective publications. Overall, it could be cautiously formulated that Future Skills each represent a specific selection of action competences.

3. **Harmonization of the available approaches is possible via a category model:** The framework model presented here for Future Skills with 17 profiles is suitable for assigning the large number of different Future Skills and thus making them comparable. An analysis of the frequency of mentions within the respective Future Skills profiles reveals a clustering in the following areas:
   - self-competence (10 mentions) and learning literacy (8 mentions) in the subject develpent-related dimension.
   - digital literacy (9 mentions) and design-thinking competence (8 mentions) in the object-related dimension
   - cooperation competence (12 mentions) and communication competence (9 mentions) in the organization-related dimension.
   - The Future Skills Profiles self-determination (1) and ethical competence (3) are those with the fewest mentions within the approaches examined.

4. **Ideas about digitally related competences within Future Skills concepts are diverse:** The analysis paid particular attention to digitally related Future Skills. Digital or technical skills will undoubtedly be an important Future Skills ingredient, but many of the Future Skills approaches examined lag behind existing comprehensive digital skills models in terms of concept breadth and depth. The analysis shows a wide range of more than 93 digital skill mentions, which are predominantly located in the area of use and conceptual knowledge about digitization, but not to the same extent in the critical reflection of the consequences of digitization or the creative redevelopment of digital work and life ecosystems.

5. **Education as a point of reference:** Almost all contributions on the topic of Future Skills lack a clear (educational) theoretical foundation of what con-

stitutes competence or competence acquisition, which makes its use for educational processes difficult, arbitrary, or impossible. At present, only the approach we have developed (Ehlers, 2020) has an explicit theoretical foundation. Many of the topics or competences listed as Future Skills are identified without underlying personality and learning theories and refer exclusively to the cognitive domain.

All in all, Future Skills are a very dynamically developing concept that is suitable for promoting a new negotiation about future educational goals between universities, the labor market and society. The NextSkills framework can serve as a frame of reference.

References

Aasheim, C. L., Williams, S., & Butler, E. S. (2009). Knowledge and skill requirements for IT graduates. *Journal of Computer Information Systems, 49*(3), 48–53. https://doi.org/1 0.1080/08874417.2009.11645323.

Agentur Q (2021). *Future Skills: Welche Kompetenzen für den Standort Baden-Württemberg heute und in Zukunft erfolgskritisch sind.* https://www.bw.igm.de/news/meldung. html?id=101055.

Alesi, B., & Teichler, U. (2013). Akademisierung von Bildung und Beruf. Ein kontroverser Diskurs in Deutschland. In E. Severing, & U. Teichler (Eds.), *Akademisierung der Berufswelt?* (pp. 19–39). Bertelsmann.

Ashoka Deutschland, & McKinsey (2018). *The skilling challenge: How to equip employees for the era of automation and digitization – And how models and mindsets of social entrepreneurs can guide us.* https://www.ashoka.org/de-de/files/2018theskillingchalleng eashokamckinseypdf.

Baacke, D., Frank, G., & Radde, M. (1991). *Medienwelten – Medienorte: Jugend und Medien in Nordrhein-Westfalen.* Westdeutscher Verl.

Bowden, J., Hart, G., King, B., Trigwell, K., & Watts, O. (2000). *Generic capabilities of ATN university graduates.*

Clanchy, J., & Ballard, B. (1995). Generic skills in the context of higher education. *Higher Education Research & Development, 14*(2), 155–166. https://doi. org/10.1080/0729436950140202.

Cox, A. M., Al Daoud, M., & Rudd, S. (2013). Information Management graduates' accounts of their employability: A case study from the University of Sheffield. *Education for Information, 30*(1–2), 41–61. https://doi.org/10.3233/EFI-130929.

Curtis, D. D., & McKenzie, P. (2001). *Employability skills for Australian industry: Literature review and framework development.* https://www.voced.edu.au/content/ ngv%3A33428.

Daud, S., Abidin, N., Mazuin Sapuan, N., & Rajadurai, J. (2011). Enhancing university business curriculum using an importance-performance approach. *Inter-*

national Journal of Educational Management, 25(6), 545–569. https://doi. org/10.1108/09513541111159059.

Dettmers, S., & Jochmann, W. (2021). *Future skills—Future learning*. https://media.kienbaum.com/wp-content/uploads/sites/13/2021/06/Kienbaum-StepStone-Studie_2021_WEB.pdf. Accessed 1 Dec 2021.

Drummond, I., Nixon, I., & Wiltshire, J. (1998). Personal transferable skills in higher education: The problems of implementing good practice. *Quality Assurance in Education, 6*(1), 19–27. https://doi.org/10.1108/09684889810200359.

Echterhoff, N. (2014). *Schlüsselkompetenzen – ,Schlüssel' für die Arbeitswelt des 21*. Universität Duisburg-Essen, Diss., 2014. Universitätsbibliothek Duisburg-Essen.

Ehlers, U.-D. (2020). *Future skills: The future of learning and higher education.*

Ehlers, U.-D. (2022). *Future skills compared: On the construction of a general framework model for future competencies in academic education.* https://nextskills.org/wp-content/uploads/2022/07/2022-06-15-Future-Skills-Bildungsforschung_final_Vs_2ENG.pdf.

Ehlers, U.-D., & Bonaudo, P. (2021). *Research methodology to gather labour market intelligence and identify skills mismatches.* https://next-education.org/wp-content/uploads/2023/01/CHAISE-WP2_D2.1.1_Research-Methodology-to-gather-labour-market-intelligence-and-identify-skills-mismatches_v3.pdf.

Ehlers, U.-D., Geier, N., & Eigbrecht, L. (2022). *Changing futures in higher education: Assessment of future skills learning.* https://next-education.org/wp-content/uploads/2022/06/2022-06-07-Report-Self-Assessment-Version17-final.pdf.

Ehlers, U.-D., & Kellermann, S. A. (2019). *Future skills—The future of learning and higher education: Results of the international future skills Delphi survey.*

Enderle, S., Lehner, A., & Kunz, A. M. (2021). *Das Schlüsselqualifikationsangebot an deutschen Universitäten: Empirische Befunde.* Beltz.

Finch, D. J., Hamilton, L. K., Baldwin, R., & Zehner, M. (2013). An exploratory study of factors affecting undergraduate employability. *Education + Training, 55*(7), 681–704. https://doi.org/10.1108/ET-07-2012-0077.

Freeman, M., Hancock, P., Simpson, L., & Sykes, C. (2008). *Business as usual: A collaborative and inclusive investigation of existing resources, strengths, gaps and challenges to be addressed for sustainability in teaching and learning in Australian university business faculties* (ABDC Scoping Report).

Ginns, P., & Barrie, S. (2004). Reliability of single-item ratings of quality in higher education: A replication. *Psychological Reports, 95*(7), 1023–1030. https://doi.org/10.2466/PR0.95.7.1023-1030.

Hays, & ibe (2017). *HR-Report 2017: Schwerpunkt Kompetenzen für eine digitale Welt.* https://www.hays.de/documents/10192/118775/Hays-Studie-HR-Report-2017.pdf/3df94932-63ca-4706-830b-583c107c098e. Accessed 1 Dec 2021.

Heyse, V., & Erpenbeck, J. (2009). *Kompetenztraining: Informations- und Trainingsprogramme* (2nd ed.). Schäffer-Poeschel.

Hippler, H. (2016). *Wozu (noch) Geisteswissenschaften?* https://rotary.de/bildung/wozu-noch-geisteswissenschaften-a-8984.html.

Huber, L. (2016). „Studium Generale" oder „Schlüsselqualifikationen"?: Ein Orientierungsversuch im Feld der Hochschulbildung. In U. Konnertz & S. Mühleisen (Eds.), *Bildung und Schlüsselqualifikationen: Zur Rolle der Schlüsselqualifikationen an den Universitäten* (pp. 101–122). Lang.

2 Towards a Future Skills Framework for Higher Education

Huber, L. (2019). „Bildung durch Wissenschaft" als Qualität des Studiums. *Das Hochschulwesen, 67*(6), 154–159.

Initiative D21 e. V. (2021). *D21-Digital-Index 2021/2022: Jährliches Lagebild zur Digitalen Gesellschaft.* https://initiatived21.de/app/uploads/2022/02/d21-digital-index-2021_2022.pdf.

Koppi, T., Sheard, J., Naghdy, F., Chicharo, J. F., Edwards, S. L., Brookes, W., et al. (2009). What our ICT graduates really need from us: A perspective from the workplace. *Proceedings of the Eleventh Australasian Conference on Computing Education, 95*, 101–110.

Kummert, T. (2017). *Endlich einer, der nicht nur Formeln anwenden kann.* https://www.sueddeutsche.de/karriere/arbeitsmarkt-endlich-einer-der-nicht-nur-formeln-anwenden-kann-1.3623308.

Luhmann, N. (1976). The future cannot begin: Temporal structures in modern society. *Social Research: An International Quarterly, 43*, 130–152.

Maturana, H. R., & Varela, F. J. (1980). *Autopoiesis and cognition: The realization of the living* (1st ed.). Springer.

Mayring, P. (2008). *Qualitative Inhaltsanalyse: Grundlagen und Techniken* (10th ed.). Beltz.

McKinsey Global Institute. (2017). *Jobs lost, jobs gained: Workforce transitions in a time of automation.* https://www.mckinsey.com/featured-insights/future-of-work/jobs-lost-jobs-gained-what-the-future-of-work-will-mean-for-jobs-skills-and-wages.

Mertens, D. (1974). Schlüsselqualifikationen. Thesen zur Schulung für eine moderne Gesellschaft. *Mitteilungen aus der Arbeitsmarkt- und Berufsforschung, 7*(1), 36–43.

OECD. (2018). *The future of education and skills: Education 2030.* https://www.oecd.org/education/2030/E2030%20Position%20Paper%20(05.04.2018).pdf.

Osmani, M., Weerakkody, V., Hindi, N. M., Al-Esmail, R., Eldabi, T., Kapoor, K., et al. (2015). Identifying the trends and impact of graduate attributes on employability: A literature review. *Tertiary Education and Management, 21*(4), 367–379. https://doi.org/10.1080/13583883.2015.1114139.

Precision Consultancy. (2007). *Graduate employability skills: Prepared for the business, industry and higher education collaboration council.* https://core.ac.uk/download/pdf/30688676.pdf.

Rigby, B., Wood, L., Clark-Murphy, M., Daly, A., Dixon, P., Kavamah, M., et al. (2009). *Review of graduate skills: Critical thinking, teamwork, ethical practice and sustainability.*

Scharmer, C. O. (2009). *Theory U: Leading from the futures as it emerges.* Berrett-Koehler; McGraw-Hill.

Schnepf, J., & Groeben, N. (2019). Qualitative Metaanalyse mithilfe computergestützter qualitativer Inhaltsanalyse – Am Beispiel von Lokale-Agenda-21-Prozessen. Forum Qualitative Sozialforschung/Forum: Qualitative Social Research, Vol 20, No 3 (2019): Qualitative Content Analysis I. Advance online publication. https://doi.org/10.17169/FQS-20.3.3313.

Schubarth, W., & Speck, K. (2014). *Employability und Praxisbezüge im wissenschaftlichen Studium.* https://www.hrk-nexus.de/fileadmin/redaktion/hrk-nexus/07-Downloads/07-02-Publikationen/Fachgutachten_Employability-Praxisbezuege.pdf.

Sin, S., & Reid, A. (2005). Developing generic skills in accounting: Resourcing and reflecting on trans-disciplinary research and insights. *Annual Conference for the Association for Research in Education,* 1–22.

Stifterverband, & McKinsey (2018). *Future Skills: Welche Kompetenzen in Deutschland fehlen.* https://www.stifterverband.org/medien/future-skills-welche-kompetenzen-in-deutschland-fehlen.

Stifterverband, & McKinsey (2021). *Future Skills 2021: 21 Kompetenzen für eine Welt im Wandel* (Diskussionspapier). https://www.stifterverband.org/medien/future-skills-welche-kompetenzen-in-deutschland-fehlen.

Tran, T. T. (2015). Is graduate employability the 'whole-of-higher-education-issue'? *Journal of Education and Work, 28*(3), 207–227. https://doi.org/10.1080/13639080.2014.900167.

Treleaven, L., & Voola, R. (2008). Integrating the development of graduate attributes through constructive alignment. *Journal of Marketing Education, 30*(2), 160–173. https://doi.org/10.1177/0273475308319352.

Tuning Project (2008). *Reference points for the design and delivery of degree programmes in business.* http://tuningacademy.org/wp-content/uploads/2014/02/RefBusiness_EU_EN.pdf.

Wagemann, C., Goerres, A., & Siewert, M. B. (Eds.). (2021). *Handbuch Methoden der Politikwissenschaft.* Springer VS.

Wild, S., Deuer, E., & Pohlenz, P. (2018). Studienerfolgsverständnis von hauptamtlichen Lehrkräften im Studienbereich Wirtschaft der Dualen Hochschule Baden-Württemberg (DHBW) – Ein Typisierungsversuch. *Zeitschrift Für Evaluation, 17*(2), 269–287.

World Economic Forum. (2020). *The future of jobs report 2020.* http://www3.weforum.org/docs/WEF_Future_of_Jobs_2020.pdf.

Prof. Dr. phil. habil. Ulf-Daniel Ehlers is an internationally renowned Professor for Educational Management and Lifelong Learning at the Baden-Wuerttemberg Cooperative State University (DHBW) Karlsruhe which he headed as Vice-President between 2011 and 2017.

Open Access This chapter is licensed under the terms of the Creative Commons Attribution 4.0 International License (http://creativecommons.org/licenses/by/4.0/), which permits use, sharing, adaptation, distribution and reproduction in any medium or format, as long as you give appropriate credit to the original author(s) and the source, provide a link to the Creative Commons license and indicate if changes were made.

The images or other third party material in this chapter are included in the chapter's Creative Commons license, unless indicated otherwise in a credit line to the material. If material is not included in the chapter's Creative Commons license and your intended use is not permitted by statutory regulation or exceeds the permitted use, you will need to obtain permission directly from the copyright holder.

The Practice of Future Skills Learning: An Assessment of Approaches, Conditions and Success Factors

3

Laura Eigbrecht and Ulf-Daniel Ehlers

> **Abstract**
>
> The edited volume "Creating the University of the Future" is a body of evidence that Future Skills are viewed as a possibility to fill the gap between demands for skills and competences and the current state of provision in higher education. The provided experiences, practices and implementation concepts from educational professionals in the field provide an opportunity to analyze and synthesize the perspectives and experiences around Future Skills and their implementation in higher education institutions. Authors were asked to elaborate on their specific definition of the concept of Future Skills and to provide recommendations for promoting Future Skills in higher education in practice based on their experiences. Building on this, the chapter provides a panoramic view of places and institutions, analyzes the provided Future Skills definitions and synthesizes the practice recommendations given in order to close with an outlook for a Future Skills vision for higher education and its conditions for success.

L. Eigbrecht (✉)
Educational Management and Lifelong Learning, Business Faculty, DHBW Karlsruhe, Karlsruhe, Germany
e-mail: laura.eigbrecht@dhbw-karlsruhe.de

U.-D. Ehlers
Professor for Educational Management and Lifelong Learning, Business Faculty, DHBW Karlsruhe, Karlsruhe, Germany
e-mail: ulf-daniel.ehlers@dhbw-karlsruhe.de

© The Author(s) 2024
U.-D. Ehlers and L. Eigbrecht (eds.), *Creating the University of the Future*, Zukunft der Hochschulbildung - Future Higher Education,
https://doi.org/10.1007/978-3-658-42948-5_3

3.1 Introduction

"Future Skills development" is a term like "quality education": much sought after, equally difficult to achieve, not tangible but immediately noticeable if absent. By gathering different Future Skills approaches, we aim to make more visible and manifest the logic of the still young concept and the mechanics of putting it into practice in higher education. In the previous chapters of this "Creating the University of the Future" publication, we've introduced the concept, have discussed this emerging Global Future Skills initiative, have presented the different contributions published in this volume, and have summarized the results of a meta-analysis of Future Skills studies and approaches. The book is a body of evidence that Future Skills are viewed as a possibility to fill the gap between demands for skills and competences and the current state of provision in higher education. It is a body of experience, practices and implementation concepts from educational professionals in the field. These provide a unique opportunity to us which we are valorizing in this chapter: an analysis and synopsis of the perspectives and experiences around Future Skills and their implementation in higher education institutions.

We've asked the authors to elaborate on their specific definition of the concept of Future Skills and to provide recommendations for promoting Future Skills in higher education in practice, based on their experiences. This chapter shall provide an analysis and synthesis of these elements: we will start with a panoramic view of places and institutions (Sect. 3.2), analyze the Future Skills definitions provided (Sect. 3.3), and finally synthesize the practice recommendations given (Sect. 3.4) before concluding in Sect. 3.5 with an outlook for a Future Skills vision for higher education and its conditions for success. The analyses are based on an inductive, content-structuring qualitative content analysis (Kuckartz, 2018) conducted with the software MAXQDA applied to the text passages identified which a) provide a Future Skills definition or concept and b) provide recommendations based on the authors' experiences in promoting Future Skills in higher education.

3.2 Panorama of Contributions: Places and Institutions

The future is complex. To deal with it in a productive and active way, Future Skills are necessary. There is a multitude of challenges graduates are facing today—and as multifaceted as these challenges are, so are the approaches of dealing with the importance of Future Skills in higher education. One way to deal with this complexity is to allow a multitude of perspectives on the subject of Future Skills in Future (Higher) Education. Some may be more labor-market-oriented, while others follow a broader understanding of employability or focus more on citizenship.

However, the multitude of perspectives to be discovered when venturing into Future Skills research and practice is even greater. In this volume, we compile contributions from authors who are engaged in transnational, multinational or even global international organizations involved in research and policy-making, such as the IESALC (International Institute for Higher Education in Latin America and the Caribbean) of UNESCO based in Caracas, Venezuela, the OECD, based in Paris, France, and the ITCILO, the International Training Centre of the International Labor Organization, based in Torino, Italy. Another internationally focused perspective comes from the ICoBC, the International Council on Badges and Credentials, based in Berlin, Germany. We present contributions from Skills-Future Singapore, a national government agency, from Tony Bates, who is related to Contact North, a Canadian regional network (Ontario's Education & Training Network), from the Stifterverband with a specific German focus on higher education strategy and policy-making, from Ashoka, an international organization involved in regional and local contexts worldwide, and from The Burning Glass Institute with Wiley as an international publisher. The volume naturally brings many higher education institutions from different countries and continents together, public and private, centralized or with different locations—from countries as diverse as New Zealand and Japan, Romania and Ireland, Singapore and Brazil, the Philippines and Germany, the USA and Mauritius, Eswatini and UK.

3.3 Future Skills Definitions

There also is a certain diversity of Future Skills definitions present in this book, starting from the editors' approach based on our own research. While working with the contributors, we asked them to reflect on the definitions and approaches underlying their Future Skills projects and programs reported in the book. It is thanks to this work that we are able to see the shapes and coordinates of the emerging concept of Future Skills currently evolving in higher education around the world.

The definition introduced by Ehlers (2020, p. 53) is as follows:

> Future Skills are competences that allow individuals to solve complex problems in highly emergent contexts of action in a self-organized way and enable them to act (successfully). They are based on cognitive, motivational, volitional and social resources, are value-based and can be acquired in a learning process.

Several authors decided to base their chapter on this precise definition or refer to it such as Barty et al., Wihlenda and Garbin & Oliveira. While the concept of Future Skills is often named synonymously to other **terms**, we find references to soft skills (Bates), 21st Century Skills (Wihlenda; Barty et al.; Seidl), key competencies (Seidl) and an analogy of character and Future Skills (Duckworth).

Definitions also refer to different **(target) groups** such as learners (Pedró), individuals and people (Gervacio; Süßenbach et al.; Paunescu & McDonnell-Naughton; Vogel; Bates; Ehlers) or even young people (Wihlenda). Relating to the specific outline and the context of the Global Future Skills initiative, students and graduates (Ikeda; Seidl; Gahl et al.; Senges; Wihlenda; Chacón et al.; Stark) or, more precisely, engineering students (Deus Lopes & Santana), are named in several definitions. But what comes after graduation? Here, individuals are conceived as employees (Paunescu & McDonnell-Naughton) or citizens (Gunness et al.). Stark's definition also takes faculty or staff into account in his Future Skills concept.

This is closely related to the **context** to which the proposed definition or approach refers to. Most often, the industry, employers, or the world of work are named here (Gog et al.; Seidl; Gahl et al.; Deus Lopes & Santana; Senges; Süßenbach et al.; Wihlenda; Paunescu & McDonnell-Naughton; Vogel; Stark; Bates; Pedró), but society as a context is also often referred to (Ikeda; Marshall; Seidl; Deus Lopes & Santana; Vogel; Stark) or even global society and citizenship (Wihlenda). Moreover, Future Skills matter for life more generally (Duckworth; Pedró) and are needed in a changing world (Gahl et al.), for individuals (Senges; Barty et al.) and collectively (Gunness et al.; Vogel). We see here that in all cases, higher education with a focus on Future Skills goes beyond the walls of university buildings.

The definitions are more or less concrete, precise and clear, sometimes agile, and sometimes include a sound **theoretical framing**, such as in the cases of Seidl, Barty et al., Gervacio, Süßenbach et al., Ehlers and Garbin & Oliveira. A clear **timeframe** to which the future refers is rarely provided. Süßenbach et al. look five years into the future while other concepts refer to a more general future

3 The Practice of Future Skills Learning ...

(Gog et al., Seidl, Pedró, Ehlers) or to future and present time both (Ikeda; Vogel; Schleicher; Paunescu & McDonnell-Naughton; Seidl).

Future Skills definitions and approaches also can be analyzed and differentiated according to the **aim** or **mission** promoted in the approach—and there is a great variety to be named. In a most basic approach, Future Skills are simply needed to survive (Ikeda) in the twenty-first century (Wambeke) or a rapidly changing economic and technological environment (Bates). More closely study-related, they are needed to master one's studies (Seidl). In very active approaches, they help to act (Ehlers), transform (Stark), innovate (Wambeke), to shape (Senges) and lead change (Ikeda). Challenges and problems shall be solved (Ehlers) or addressed (Gunness et al.; Pedró) and goals pursued (Vogel). There is also the question to compete (Wihlenda) or be successful as an individual (Gahl et al.; Gervacio) and of thriving (Gunness et al.) and empowering (Süßenbach et al.).

While there is a certain variety in Future Skills definitions and the related target groups, contexts and goals, all authors share the belief that their promotion matters in higher education, a belief they base their practices and argumentations on. Authors were also asked to share practical recommendations for promoting Future Skills which are summarized in the following section in order to identify conditions of success for promoting Future Skills in Higher Education.

3.4 Practice Recommendations

Practice recommendations are always context-dependent. They represent a certain procedure which has been found suitable for the very context of its implementation. In order to analyze these experiences, we have tried to decontextualize the recommendations and find overarching principles of successful implementation of Future Skills. The process of decontextualization was possible through employing an inductive, content-structuring qualitative content analysis.[1] In this process, three main categories were determined, these being a) the target group the recommendations refer to, b) the focus and c) the level. They shall shortly be presented and summarized in order to synthesize some principal conditions of success.

---

[1] Authors were asked to contribute practice recommendations in form of adding a special section ("Info box") as part of their chapters: "Future Skills in Practice: Our Recommendations".

a) Which target groups are important to include when implementing Future Skills concepts?

The three **target groups** mostly referred to are closely related to the higher education focus of this publication—these are the **learners** (e.g. Gog et al.; Süßenbach et al.; Gunness et al.) or individuals (Gog et al.; Marshall), **teachers**, faculty, and researchers (e.g. Marshall; Seidl; Wihlenda; Vogel) as well as **institutions** or institutional leaders (e.g. Marshall; Gog et al.; Gervacio; Süßenbach et al.; Chacón et al.). Government and policymakers are also addressed by Gog et al., taking Singapore's national context into account, and by Chacón et al., adopting a transnational or global perspective in discussing Future Skills. Future Skills needs are also related to society as a whole (Gunness et al.; Süßenbach et al.; Gog et al.; Marshall), relating individuals to societies and making Future Skills a possible matter of social cohesion. Also related to the higher education context, student engagement centers (Wihlenda; Chacón et al.), startup schools (Wihlenda) and student support teams (Chacón et al.) are addressed in the authors' recommendations. A preliminary conclusion can be drawn: Future Skills implementation in higher education demands for a whole system approach. It is not just a matter of a single target group—such as learners or teachers—but can and should be supported through multiple stakeholders in the educational context: learners, education professionals, institutional leaders, as well as policymakers.

b) What is the focus and direction of Future Skills implementation in higher education?

The data on Future Skills practices gathered in this book shows a variety of aims, values, and missions of Future Skills development:

- Social cohesion and sustainability (Gunness et al.) and inclusivity (Gog et al.; Gunness et al.)
- Economy-focused approaches refer to the labor market, economic growth, or industry and argue for closing existing skills gaps (Gog et al.; Barty et al.; Süßenbach et al.; Deus Lopes & Santana)
- On an individual level, Future Skills are seen as a means for people to realize their fullest potential (Gog et al.) and for lifelong learning (Barty et al.)
- A transversal issue woven like a thread through many of the experiences provided is related to a much-needed change in higher education, such as a cultural change (Süßenbach et al.), a more general restructuring of higher education (Barty et al.; Süßenbach et al.; Chacón et al.) and a change and integration of Future Skills into higher education curricula (e.g. Brunner & Ehlers; Seidl; Deus Lopes & Santana; Gervacio).

3 The Practice of Future Skills Learning ... 67

In summary, we find that Future Skills development in higher education is a strong value-driven and normative discourse which is generally aiming at empowering individuals, providing space for individual meaningful learning, and boosting self-responsibility and autonomy of individuals on their pathway through their lifelong learning journey. In order for this to come true, change requirements are articulated for higher education.

c) Which level is addressed in recommendations for Future Skills implementation?
The recommendations discussed address higher education as a whole; on the micro level of teaching and learning in classrooms and beyond, the meso or institutional level, and the macro or policy level. They are summarized in Table 3.1 and can be accessed more closely in the individual chapters of the book.

Table 3.1 Recommendations for promoting Future Skills in higher education

Level	Recommendation
Micro: teaching and learning in the classroom	• Follow a **learner-centered** approach: empowerment and ownership, becoming self-directed learners, individualizing one's learning pathway, co-designing learning environments and pathways with students (Gunness; Paunescu & McDonnell-Naughton; Vogel; Chacón et al.; Barty et al.)
	• Adapt **teaching and assessment** approaches: active and applied methodologies such as Project and Problem-Based Learning, participatory and transdisciplinary approaches (Wihlenda; Garbin & Oliveira; Chacón et al.), assessment as a strategy for Future skills learning considering constructive alignment as a principle (Brunner et al.; Gervacio; Chacón et al.; Seidl)
	• Integrate Future Skills into **curricula** and redesign courses accordingly (Deus Lopes & Santana; Süßenbach et al.)
	• Reach out **beyond the classroom** in teaching and learning settings: external partner organizations, communities, real-life contexts, student initiatives as learning spaces (Chacón et al.; Vogel; Paunescu & McDonnell-Naughton; Wihlenda; Marshall)
	• Support the learning process with **digital media** and digital or hybrid settings (Gervacio; Garbin & Oliveira; Paunescu & McDonnell-Naughton)
	• Engage students in **research** (Chacón et al.)
	• Promote student **reflection** in teaching and learning settings (Paunescu & McDonnell-Naughton)
	• Support students in **developing their own Future Skills learning needs** and pathway in their chosen study program as student support staff (Chacón et al.)

(continued)

Table 3.1 (continued)

Level	Recommendation
Meso: institutional level	• Address the integration of Future Skills as a project with a **holistic change** process (Seidl; Chacón et al.)
	• Train **teachers** in Future Skills teaching and learning (Brunner & Ehlers; Garbin & Oliveira) and rethink or reconsider their role more as that of coaches (Vogel)
	• Promote **reforms** concerning Future Skills, e.g., by integrating the Sustainable Development Goals into the institutional strategy (Chacón et al.; Gervacio)
	• Consider approaches of **granularizing** learning with micro-credentials, badges, etc. (Gervacio; Barty et al.)
	• Envision the institution as a **lifelong learning** university (Gervacio)
	• Address **student governance** structures and students to advocate for Future Skills learning in all courses, promote **student engagement** learning opportunities, and incite cross-institutional learning opportunities (Chacón et al.; Wihlenda)
	• **Lobby** for considering Future Skills in higher education and form **coalitions** (Seidl; Gervacio; Garbin & Oliveira; Süßenbach et al.)
	• Make stakeholders **aware**/conscious of the relevance of Future Skills and thus **promote cultural change** (Süßenbach et al.; Deus Lopes & Santana)
	• Connect with other educational stakeholders to form powerful **Future Skills coalitions** and to promote reforms in the ecosystem (Gog et al.; Chacón et al.; Süßenbach et al.)
	• Discuss and promote a **shared understanding** of Future Skills, supported by orientation frameworks or supporting documents (Seidl; Süßenbach et al.; Gunness et al.)
	• Consider **context, values,** and moral understandings when discussing Future Skills (Marshall; Gunness et al.)
	• Start with **trying out** new things while staying **flexible** about results and methods (Vogel)
Macro: policy level	• Play an **active role** as government in the skills ecosystem on an economic level in **coordinating skills demand and supply** with other stakeholders (Gog et al.)
	• Consider Future Skills in higher education **development plans** on the policy level (Chacón et al.)

3.5 Conclusion: Conditions of Success for Promoting Future Skills in Higher Education

Based on the qualitative analysis made from all contributions in this book, we are able to derive some general and some more specific recommendations and success factors. The first set of recommendations can be understood as factors which need to be considered in order for Future Skills to gain relevance and in order to shape a Future Skills environment and ecosystem within the higher education context:

- Faculty Development: ensuring that faculty members are equipped to promote Future Skills learning, through training and support, can improve the quality of the provided educational experiences.
- Relevance to labor market demand: aligning education programs with Future Skills that are in high industry demand helps to ensure the relevance and practicality of the educational experiences provided.
- Interdisciplinary Approach: problems do not know disciplines and their solution always demands multidimensional and interdisciplinary approaches. Incorporating Future Skills across multiple disciplines can help students develop a holistic understanding of the subject.
- Experiential Learning: Providing students with opportunities to apply their knowledge through projects, internships, and other hands-on experiences can increase their motivation and enhance their learning.
- Flexibility and Adaptability: With the rapid pace of technological change, it is important for education programs to be flexible and adaptable to changing demands and needs.

In addition, we also found the clear need for change in higher education. Future Skills approaches demand new perspectives on our current educational systems. This reform agenda needs a sound approach to manage this transformation towards changing cultures in higher education. The authors provided recommendations on important factors which need to be considered in these change processes.

From this analysis, we can dare to synthesize and formulate some conditions for success for promoting Future Skills in Higher Education—aimed at everyone who is taking some steps towards future higher education.

For successfully promoting a **Future Skills culture in higher education,** it is necessary to:

- Form coalitions, exchange practices and approaches, inspire and share. A transformation on many levels is needed, but every step counts—and connecting can inspire, energize, and empower.
- Involve all educational stakeholders in the process—(lifelong) learners, teachers, institutional leaders, civil society, the world of work, politics—while considering that seemingly fixed roles can and have to change: learners will become designers and experts, teachers will become coaches, learning will become more participatory and individualized, knowledge will become more personal and decentralized as a basis to build Future Skills upon, and digital tools and environments will facilitate these processes. This will, however, possibly need some more guidance and counseling in order to support learners to navigate through their own learning pathways and become ever more autonomous learners in this process.
- Reflect on existing learning, teaching, and assessment practices and how these are included in curricula: they can successfully contribute to Future Skills learning once this process is considered holistically and reflection on Future Skills development is incited. Not everything has to be reinvented.
- Be open and flexible and start with small steps instead of perfectionism: many steps are needed on all levels, but every step in the right direction will contribute to deepen a much-needed Future Skills culture in higher education.
- Not consider higher education institutions as enclosed but as open spaces and connect them to society while offering real-life and meaningful learning and engagement opportunities supporting learners' transformative learning journeys—and involve students or lifelong learners in participatory processes in co-designing the future of these institutions.
- Discuss Future Skills in a competence-oriented way, putting learners, their personal and social wellbeing first and go beyond purely functional Future Skills approaches. This also means that we should not consider Future Skills learning as an isolated experience characterized by concurrence but connect learners and make them support each other in their learning journeys—and accentuate Future Skills for connecting and cooperating, as tomorrow's challenges cannot be solved by disconnected individuals, but only by diverse and inclusive teams.
- Not fear discussing values and normative assumptions in determining the Future Skills that matter for a certain vision of a future. Values and motivation are an important component of Future Skills, so these should be debated and made transparent—without everyone having to agree on these, but being aware of them.

References

Ehlers, U.-D. (2020). *Future skills: The future of learning and higher education.*
Kuckartz, U. (2018). *Qualitative Inhaltsanalyse: Methoden, Praxis, Computerunterstützung* (4th ed.). Beltz Juventa.

Laura Eigbrecht is principle investigator, teacher and doctoral student at the Baden-Wuerttemberg Cooperative State University (DHBW) Karlsruhe and holds degrees in European Media and Culture and Media Pedagogy.

Prof. Dr. phil. habil. Ulf-Daniel Ehlers is an internationally renowned Professor for Educational Management and Lifelong Learning at the Baden-Wuerttemberg Cooperative State University (DHBW) Karlsruhe which he headed as Vice-President between 2011 and 2017.

Open Access This chapter is licensed under the terms of the Creative Commons Attribution 4.0 International License (http://creativecommons.org/licenses/by/4.0/), which permits use, sharing, adaptation, distribution and reproduction in any medium or format, as long as you give appropriate credit to the original author(s) and the source, provide a link to the Creative Commons license and indicate if changes were made.

The images or other third party material in this chapter are included in the chapter's Creative Commons license, unless indicated otherwise in a credit line to the material. If material is not included in the chapter's Creative Commons license and your intended use is not permitted by statutory regulation or exceeds the permitted use, you will need to obtain permission directly from the copyright holder.

Part II
Future Skills – Foundations and Shapes of a New Emerging Concept in a Global View

Part II focusses on discussing basic concepts and outlines concerning Future Skills in (global) higher education. For this, several Future Skills conversations were conducted with leading authorities of the field, like Andreas Schleicher (OECD) and Tom Wambeke (ITCILO). With Tony Bates, Wolfgang Stark and Francesc Pedró (UNESCO IESALC) further experts add their specific expertise to the book, followed by a new theory of change for higher education based on a global empirical study.

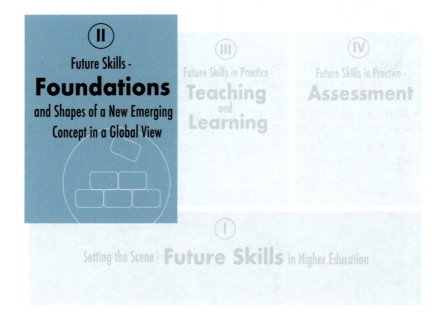

"I've Learnt Everything I Know from the World."

4

A Future Skills Conversation with Andreas Schleicher

Ulf-Daniel Ehlers and Laura Eigbrecht

> **Abstract**
>
> Andreas Schleicher (Fig. 4.1) is Director for Education and Skills at the OECD. He initiated and oversees the Programme for International Student Assessment (PISA) and other international instruments that have created a global platform for policymakers, researchers, and educators across nations and cultures to innovate and transform educational policies and practices—and that have stimulated discussion on competence needs of today's and future learners. In this conversation, we focus on Andreas Schleicher's pathway to working with Future Skills as well as on future educational concepts for promoting them.

Ulf-Daniel Ehlers: We would like to dive into the conversation with a personal question: can you remember what could be called a Future Skills moment or an anecdote from your life where you thought 'I went to school, I went to university, but in this moment, what really helped me, that was my Future Skill'?

U.-D. Ehlers
Professor for Educational Management and Lifelong Learning, Business Faculty, DHBW Karlsruhe, Karlsruhe, Germany
e-mail: ulf-daniel.ehlers@dhbw-karlsruhe.de

L. Eigbrecht (✉)
Educational Management and Lifelong Learning, Business Faculty, DHBW Karlsruhe, Karlsruhe, Germany
e-mail: laura.eigbrecht@dhbw-karlsruhe.de

© The Author(s) 2024
U.-D. Ehlers and L. Eigbrecht (eds.), *Creating the University of the Future*, Zukunft der Hochschulbildung - Future Higher Education,
https://doi.org/10.1007/978-3-658-42948-5_4

Fig. 4.1 ANDREAS SCHLEICHER

Andreas Schleicher: Yes, absolutely. I was in Thailand and lost my way. It was after school and I had to navigate in an environment that was completely unknown to me. It took me four hours to find my way back to the hotel, but I learnt suddenly that what I remembered from the past was at that moment not what would help me to find my future.

Ehlers: I have a similar story from when I lost my way one evening in Brussels. The saying I kept from that is: you have to lose yourself to find yourself—and this has been a guiding orientation.

Laura Eigbrecht: You're a very well-known expert for education. What made you this expert? How come that you're burning for education and that you really wanted to work in the field of education?

Schleicher: I actually originally focused on science. I studied Physics; my first job was in the field of medical industry. Then I had to do my military service and I set it to civil service—and they sent me to a school with disadvantaged learners. It was a fascinating environment for me. At first a difficult experience—I encountered people who I had not really met in my daily life before, but it was absolutely intriguing. The first thing that came to me really was that many of these students would have been perfectly normal if they had lived in an environment that had been more conducive to learning and to their social and emotional development—many of them came from really difficult families. I thought: we can really make a difference as educators. These almost two years changed my outlook on life and also what I wanted to do and achieve in life.

About my expertise in education: I've learnt everything I know from the world. I had the fortune of working in and with over 80 countries on design and development; I followed public policy, ministers of education, educators over the years and that's really where I learnt everything I know.

Eigbrecht: I see the idea to have a global outlook in order to analyze where we are in right now, to see different ways to approach it. Was there a moment of irritation where you thought: maybe this system is not working so well, the educational system of Germany, for example?

Schleicher: Yes, in fact! I think you learn about yourself best when you look at other systems, other people, other approaches. You understand the idea of language the moment you learn a foreign language. Before, you don't think about it, you take it for granted; you think that every object has one way to express it. Suddenly you learn a foreign language and you can see the world through different lenses, perspectives, appreciate different ways of thinking, different kinds of approaches—that's really what enriched my thinking. I started to think about the German education system first when I learnt about other education systems. I could see the strengths of the system in integrating the world of work and the world of learning in the system of vocational education. But I also learnt about the weaknesses—the fact that the system very early on in the lives of people makes not well-founded judgements about what people are good at and not so good at. It doesn't leave people enough room to develop their own identity, their own kind of aspirations.

I learnt through comparisons, through contrasts and with an open mind. I do believe that learning will become increasingly important, because we've seen through the pandemic that the future will always surprise us. Future Skills are not about a specific skill set that we can define today and that will be valid forever—they are about our capacity to be open to alternative futures, to be receptive to how the evolution of labor demand, of skill demand really evolves and then to find creative responses to this. This really is the challenge of our times. We cannot learn that much from the past, because in a pandemic, the past was not a very good guide to what we should be doing. But we can learn by looking outwards to how other people, other institutions are responding to those kinds of challenges. If you are in higher education, you suddenly ask yourself: what is your value proposition? Some people say: we just do remote learning, we just do online courses. But people don't go to university to consume online content; they go to university to meet a great professor, to work with researchers in a laboratory, they want to experience campus life—and suddenly that's out of the picture. So what are we there for? Who are we? What are the kinds of knowledge, skills, attitudes and values we want to develop? How do we do that? These questions really are the ones that help us find our future.

Ehlers: You were telling us about your own biographical learning pathway which brought you where you are today—I love this kind of story. I think that many people have stories like that to share while it is so hard to form them into a concept. And it shows that what really matters is individual—taking the initiative and going forward, making experiences and distilling out of these experiences what matters. But it is so difficult to put this idea into a curriculum.

> *"For me, the idea that there should be a study curriculum, and then we transmit it, is an idea of the past."*

Schleicher: For me, the idea that there should be a study curriculum, and then we transmit it, is an idea of the past. The idea of the future is that we have educators who become creative designers of innovative learning environments and that the curriculum is the product of co-creation where you have learners and educators work together on what content is relevant in this moment for that purpose. The kind of things that are easy to teach and maybe easy to test are precisely the things that are now easy to digitize, to automate. We have to ask ourselves: what makes us human? How do we complement, not substitute the artificial intelligence we created in our computers? Learning is no longer about teaching you something, but about giving you the compass, the navigation tools to find your own way in a world that is increasingly complex, volatile, ambiguous. Our capacity to navigate ambiguity, in this moment of crisis, was perhaps the most important thing to have. The reaction of education systems to shut down everything the moment things were difficult shows how helpless we were, rather than to think: we need to do things differently. We were only able to switch things off—and I think that's often a reaction when you lack that capacity to navigate an ambiguous situation.

4 "I've Learnt Everything I Know from the World."

Ehlers: I was once talking to an old, long-term, very high-esteemed professor of competence research. He had developed a very differentiated view on competencies—action competencies, social competencies, personal competencies, subject-matter competencies, etc. In the end of that conversation, he said: In all my research, what we also found out is what really matters and makes people active and makes them engaged, that's what I like to call activity competence or initiative, people just taking things into their hands, going forward and starting to learn, making experiences. With all these competencies which we can map out— what is also becoming apparent is that self-organization and being creative and initiating are increasingly more important. Would that also be your understanding of important Future Skills?

Schleicher: Absolutely—that is what I would call agency—and a competency is an enabler for that agency. The key is: are you capable to mobilize your cognitive, social and emotional resources to do something? It matters what you know—it matters what you can do with what you know. But ultimately, success is about putting that into action—that agency is really important. But agency is not just an individual kind of attribute—what's equally important is co-agency or collective agency. We learn and do things in dialogue; the sum of people is bigger than the sum of its parts. I think that agency, co-agency, collective agency are really the ultimate tests of competency. If you just accumulate competencies but you cannot put that into action, you will not be very impactful in this world.

> *"But agency is not just an individual kind of attribute—what's equally important is co-agency or collective agency."*

Eigbrecht: We've seen in our research that there are many people discussing Future Skills. We see very different ideas about Future Skills in these debates— ideas about: why do we need these Future Skills and what's the world that we are working towards? So what is your idea and conceptualization of Future Skills?

Schleicher: I look at a triangle where knowledge is the foundation. I look at the capacity of people to use that knowledge; the skills dimension. But then the third part is really the values and attitudes that help us navigate. You want a great engineer—but you actually want an ethical engineer, an engineer who knows how to use his or her knowledge for the better, someone who can use and apply their knowledge creatively, with knowledge, skills, values and attitudes as enablers for agency, co-agency, collective agency. That's really how I look at the future. You could say that everything that is static will lose its relevance for humans—

because that's what you can digitize. So our human capacity will be that navigator: can you live with yourself? Can you live with people who are different from you? Can you live with the planet? Can you see the future as much as you see the present, make the right choices? Climate change is a good example—can we think beyond our immediate horizon, see the longer term and translate that future into our present? I don't see artificial intelligence as a magic power—it's just a great amplifier and an amazing accelerator. But it will amplify good human skills and good human knowledge in the same way it amplifies poor human judgement and skills. I think that's really where we should focus our energy when we think about the future—think really carefully about what will differentiate us from technologies that we created.

Ehlers: One thing we found when we did research on Future Skills all over the world is that there are actually at least two different discussion strands to it: One has to do with employability, to turn employability into a 'digital employability'. How can we equip citizens of a country with suitable digital skills along their lifelong learning journey so they can perform in their jobs? Some countries like Japan, Singapore, Canada have national Future Skills initiatives which are looking into this kind of upskilling of citizens. But then there is another kind of understanding, often found in higher education, which is a more emancipatory understanding of Future Skills. It is relating Future Skills to questions like: how can we live together, co-create together, shape the future of our societies in a way that it is just, sustainable and peaceful? So we are wondering: where is it leading, this discussion on Future Skills? Is it necessary to bring these debates together or how will they evolve? What is your outlook on this debate?

Schleicher: I agree to your observation that there are more narrow and wider views. My own outlook on this has evolved over the last decades. I would have given a lot of importance to these employability aspects when I started my career, because in those days, we had a fairly clear picture of the future. We could educate people for jobs, we knew what employment looked like—we learned for a job. Today, learning is the job—learning has become the work. What really matters now is not what specialist you are, but if you have that capacity to become a specialist in a new field that nobody else has discovered in a short period of time. Employability becomes harder and harder to grasp and if we focus too much on it, we educate people for our past, not for their future. In the past, you could genuinely rely on what older people could tell you. They knew the world—and they could help you find your way through it. Today, when you meet older people, you never know if what they tell you is timeless wisdom or just outdated. When

4 "I've Learnt Everything I Know from the World."

I went to school, literacy was about decoding text—very carefully curated books, I could trust that information to be true because many people had validated it. Today, young people look things up on Google and find 100,000 answers to their question—they have to construct knowledge, not just extract knowledge. What is going to become increasingly important is your capacity to learn, but also to be willing and able to unlearn and relearn when the context changes.

"Employability becomes harder and harder to grasp and if we focus too much on it, we educate people for our past, not for their future."

Ehlers: Connected to that, if you think about initiatives like PISA for example, which are very important for national policy-making not just in the OECD countries, but all around the world—how do you think you could weave this kind of idea more into the assessments so that they become a stimulus for shaping the education systems for the future we just discussed on the national level?

Schleicher: This is a really interesting question. On the one hand, I think what is technologically possible in the field of assessment has enormously evolved. When I started with PISA, we couldn't dream of assessing something like empathy or curiosity—today we can. Where the difficulty often lies is connecting that with the reality of educators—I learned my lesson with that in 2015. When we started PISA, we focused on things like individual problem-solving—we know how to assess these things. In 2015, we told ourselves: the most important problems you don't solve on your own, but by collaborating with other people—so we assessed collaborative problem-solving skills in PISA. But when we tried to bring that message back to teachers, educators and governments, teachers said: It's so interesting, but it's not in our curriculum and it's not really my job. And policy-makers said: Very nice, but you better learn that in the workplace—in school, you have to build the foundations. One of the biggest mistakes I think we made in the field of education over the last few hundred years is to divorce learning and assessment. We ask people to pile up years and years of knowledge and then one day we call them back and say: now tell me everything!—in a very constraint, contrived environment. That frames how we learn, and that's why collaboration doesn't really play out in the world of learning. What we need to do better is to integrate learning and assessment so they become two sides of the same coin; and the cognitive, social and emotional aspects of learning need to play an equally important role.

"One of the biggest mistakes I think we made in the field of education over the last few hundred years is to divorce learning and assessment."

Ehlers: I agree! But also something teachers and schools still have difficult times with.

Schleicher: In a way, maybe a thousand years ago, we did better than we do today. A thousand years ago, learning was all about apprenticeship—you learned from and with other people, you learned by experience, you learned by doing. When you made a mistake, it had probably real consequences for you, because you didn't learn somewhere in a classroom. Today, even when we do project-based learning in schools, at the end of the lesson the teacher throws all products into the bin because they serve no purpose.

I think we have to really find that kind of learning where assessment and learning are entirely integrated. But the difficulty really is to have results that we can translate back into having learners learn better, teachers teach better and education institutions becoming more effective. This year, we are going into the field with a really interesting PISA assessment of creative thinking skills. But I'm afraid of the same story, that everyone will say: oh, how nice and how interesting! But what does it mean for me in my classroom? Building these bridges, reintegrating assessment, learning and teaching—that is the challenge that we have in front of us. Educators see themselves too often in a knowledge transmission function rather than as designers of innovative learning environments, the ones who really frame the ideas—and I think we need to work on that. On the other hand, I believe it's crucially important that we advance the field of assessment itself—you can only change and improve what you can somehow make visible. If you teach in very advanced ways but you only measure in very reductionist ways, the latter will always win.

> *"Building these bridges, reintegrating assessment, learning and teaching—that is the challenge that we have in front of us."*

Eigbrecht: When working with our students we try to use all kinds of Future Skill pedagogies like problem solving and project-based teaching or working on basis of real practice. But still we feel everyday that it is difficult to land this idea in the institution. In our teaching in higher education, we think we know why it is important to work with Future Skills, but we wonder: how can we show and showcase it—how can we not convince students, but how can we have them have that experience that Future Skills matter? And how can we inspire other teachers for Future Skills? Because in the field of higher education, we need to have everybody on board. Do you have recommendations for strategies on changing higher education that work?

4 "I've Learnt Everything I Know from the World."

Schleicher: We have probably seen a lot more change and progress in early childhood education and schools than in the university sector when it comes to new ways of teaching and learning, cross-disciplinary learning, project-based learning, to the integration of the world of learning and the world of work.

In a way, the university sector has remained the most conservative part of that ecosystem and I believe that in a way what makes the higher education sector so resistant to change is the success to bundle three things: owning the content, managing the delivery and basically being the accreditor—having the monopoly over deciding what a success in education is. It will take some time until higher education loses that monopoly, but you'll see micro-credentials and other forms of recognizing learning, and I think at that point, higher education will become more open to focus on a broader skill set. We already see today that young people graduating from universities are having difficulties to find a good job. At the same time, employers say: we cannot find people with the skills we need. That gap is not narrowing but widening and higher education needs to be more aware of the evolution of the world and what it means for the knowledge, skills, attitudes and values of people, with the social and emotional side playing an increasingly important role.

Ehlers: I would like to reflect on my own institution: we work in a university which combines practice experience and study phases in a very structured model. On the one hand, we know that this kind of combining real experience with reflection is the only true way to really develop competencies and agency. On the other hand, since we have formed this kind of education process into a standard institutional guideline, we are dictating it to students which not always take up on it in a way of self-motivated learning. When we ask students to inspire through telling their stories, ownership starts to unfold and students are starting to listen and to inspire each other. And I think this kind of self-learning is what we really need to be attentive to—this individual development and progress is so important.

Schleicher: I very much agree. The key really is to give learners true ownership over what they learn and how they learn, when they learn and where they learn over their life cycle. But that ownership really needs to be genuine, that one can feel to be in control of this process—that this is about me developing myself and not learning for a course. Where you do that, you will get a very different kind of outcome. I believe that future places of work are future places of learning. In a way, maybe a workplace will become more like a university and a university more like a workplace. We might see people going back and forth between different stages in their lives to not learn for their current job but learn for what they want to do in their future and maybe learn things that relate to nothing practical. My idea has always been that people should do two degrees in their lives—one thing you have a real passion for, something that really interests you, where you think you can really become good at, and then something else where you can make a living of. Maybe you will find bridges between those two things that are completely unforeseen later in your life. I think that ownership over the learning agenda is really important—and I think good education institutions are also good at that. That also means that educators need to become much more like mentors, coaches and facilitators, evaluators and social workers and psychologists—people who understand who you are and who you want to become and can accompany you on that journey.

Eigbrecht: What you are saying also shows that a paradigm shift on many levels needs to be set in motion in higher education. A change of the big picture is in front of us. Sometimes I feel that we begin to see here and there some progress already—maybe slower in higher education than in other domains. How would you say has the debate around Future Skills and about higher education evolved in the past years and what do you think is the role of the pandemic in it?

Schleicher: Of course the pandemic had a devastating effect—it has dramatically amplified almost any form of inequality in our education systems. If you were able to learn on your own, if you had access to great resources, an ecosystem that was supportive—maybe this period has been liberating and exciting for people. But if you used to be spoon-fed by your professors or teachers, if you had maybe no motivation to learn on your own, you were left badly behind.

But at the same time, what the pandemic has done is really put the locus of control at the frontline—it made educators really creative designers. It also made people more aware that learning is not a transaction business. If you were a great instructor, you were out of business that moment. Only when you could really reach your students, you could build that connection without having them under control in the classroom or the lecture hall—and I think teachers understood that message. What I see happening is that many learners go back to their professors and say: In this moment, I learned to learn independently. I learned to set my own learning goals, to structure my own learning processes, to discipline myself. I can see many educators who go back to their institutions and say: I did become a creative designer, I learned new things on my own, I created new tools with my colleagues. I built a good kind of team around me—and I want to work differently.

I think that momentum will remain, so learning will be different. Certainly, technology has become not just an instrument to conserve existing practice, but to truly transform it. The last years have been a turning point, at least an opportunity for that.

Eigbrecht: Not just in our own university but also during the Europe-wide podcasts which we did with students during the pandemic they voiced two issues: a *big hope* that things get back to normal and they can meet back on campus and be socially active. But also *a fear* that things *will* go back to normal and nothing will have changed, no modern, flexible and digital study opportunities any longer. How do you think we can move on post-pandemically and use the learning gains for the creation of a new form of higher education?

Schleicher: I think that the future will always be surprising us on this, and I think this moment of crisis is just one element on this pathway that will put into question the status quo. I believe educational institutions that will not fundamentally adapt are going to lose their relevance. The big challenge for us is not the inefficiency of education—even if we can talk about this as well—but that education loses its purpose and its relevance, and young people see that. Many employers at the high end of skill distribution do not longer look just at universities, but they found their own ways to facilitate learning, and you can see more and more alternatives of learning. We should not underestimate the number of people who discovered during the pandemic that things can be done differently and that there are other people thinking about the same kind of questions. Before, innovation was very isolated—and education has always been very insular, people looking inside the classroom, inside the institution. Now you can see people looking more outward—to the next educator, to the next institution, to the next education system. And I think that will remain—and where it doesn't, where education goes back to normal, you're going to see institutions very quickly lose in relevance. This monopolistic culture that we really have—we have mostly provider-oriented education in the higher education space—is not going to be sustainable.

Ehlers: The things that you are saying are resonating with me, because in our group, our thinking, our tradition, we are also very much driving this reform agenda for higher education. I am convinced that the way forward is again a bridge-building exercise—as it has been also in the past. As the futures of higher education are probably largely determined by the expectations of their members—students, teachers, external stakeholders—we need to work to build trust for the futures we desire and need to create a dialogue in order to console the existing expectations. Bridges between those who are now expecting to go back to the old normal and those who expect to create a new normal after the pandemic—and who feel slowed down, hindered, unable to move forward and to promote opening up education, and focus on learning and not on teaching. So I wonder—in your experience: what are possible future pathways? Are there international models for this and what are the mechanisms behind them?

Schleicher: I think the look outwards always makes you optimistic. I can't say there is one system which has figured everything out, but you can see: wherever you find a problem, you see others who are very much advanced and addressing that issue. Looking at educators' careers, one of the big problems we still have in Germany is to believe that you put educators into a kind of very good and long training program, then you put them into a classroom, and they are going to be successful for the rest of their lives. That's outdated—but we can see alternatives. Lifelong learning of educators has become a reality where the training of educators no longer just happens in universities, but in schools and in learning communities. In Germany, teachers are well-paid and still not enough people want to become a teacher—because the work is financially attractive and intellectually unattractive. In other countries, they maybe pay a little bit less, but they give people a work environment where you can grow (in) your career, where you work with interesting people, where you have more responsibility, where you have more time to spend with the learners. That's what makes me optimistic: the world is an amazing laboratory of ideas, we just have to look at it more carefully. The same is true for the higher education space. As an extreme alternative—in Singapore's Future Skills program, they turned things around. They basically said: we're no longer giving the money to universities to decide what they are going to offer to students—we are going to give to every person a credit when they are born and they decide what to learn, where to learn, what mode of learning is relevant for them, and then they build their own education pathways. Suddenly you have young people say: I don't just do my Bachelor, my Master, my PhD—I do my Bachelor, then I work for some years, then I go back to upgrade my skills. You can change these models, and that's really what makes me hopeful. You do not need to reinvent everything, you can today look at the different alternatives, how they play out and with what success and then create your own approach in your own context. Success is not about copying and pasting solutions from other places, but about what works in what context and how can you reconfigure these ideas, spaces, people, technologies and time in a way that actually works well in your own situation.

> *"As an extreme alternative—in Singapore's Future Skills program, they turned things around. They basically said: we're no longer giving the money to universities to decide what they are going to offer to students—we are going to give to every person a credit when they are born and they decide what to learn, where to learn, what mode of learning is relevant for them, and then they build their own education pathways."*

Ehlers: In our Future Skills Lab (next-education.org) we've just developed a method called "Personal Development with Future Skills". In that we are working with students along their own boundaries of personal development and the development of individual learning pathways. By reflecting on their own, they learn how to become professional learners. The feedback we get, especially from experienced students, is very positive. They even say that this had been the first time for them to learn about Future Skills, reflecting their learning, ethics, decision taking, and so on. The stories which you are sharing made it very clear that we need a different way to think about education: more as a flexible, value-based, enabling and individual pathway and not as a predefined collective exercise in which the curriculum is perceived as a restraining must, limiting my possibilities to learn rather than opening up a pathway for my own as a student.

I would like to turn to another issue which is also very much on my heart: the issue of equality in education. All the educational reform ideas, our Future Skills approach for example, how can they become an opportunity for all, serve the agenda for just and equal opportunities and not just become reality for a chosen few privileged? During the pandemic times, we could see the disparities growing between those who could cope with the changing opportunities and structures, and the others, who have been really left behind. When we are now pushing the Future Skills agenda in higher education I wonder: how can we avoid disparities between those who are learning in environments where they can acquire them and who understand how to do that, who are having these skills to self-develop—and then the others, those who do not? How can we envision an inclusive future in that regard?

> *"You could say: in the past, democracy was about the right to be equal—today, democracy is about the right to be different."*

Schleicher: You point to one of the biggest challenges ahead of us—the challenge of opportunity. But I think that's not just in learning—it's a huge shift in our societies. You could say: in the past, democracy was about the right to be equal—today, democracy is about the right to be different. And I think the same is true for learning. Our learning systems have to understand people's identities and individual capabilities and then find the right methods of learning. To me, that's where the biggest potential of technology is: technology is becoming very good at understanding how people learn differently—it can figure out what makes you interested, where you're bored, where you're good at or where you're struggling. This way, we can give people tailored learning opportunities and combine these with educators—educators who have that human capacity to understand who you are and who you want to become and will invest in you. The biggest misconception is that you provide everybody with the same learning opportunities and then will get equitable outcomes. It works when it is about the transmission of very basic facts and figures—it just doesn't work when it is about advanced skills. Elite institutions have understood that—if you go to elite private institutions today, they are exactly focusing on those capabilities, on those human skills.

When you do your first job interview, that's when you find out: they're not just looking at your grades, your knowledge, they are looking at how you interact with people, how you manage yourself. And I think that education systems have to become much more nuanced and responsive to the individual capabilities of people—which also means to accept that people have different talents and that success is really multidimensional. We need to give up this notion that everybody arrives at the same skill set.

> *"The biggest misconception is that you provide everybody with the same learning opportunities and then will get equitable outcomes."*

Eigbrecht: One related question comes to mind: Future Skills development is demanding and more complex—more than learning facts. Looking at our research results we can see that while students today have a greater awareness of the importance of Future Skills, they also feel a rising pressure. It is not enough anymore to learn facts but also about personal development. They feel: I want to succeed in life, it's my own responsibility, not just in class but all the time. The rise of self-organization which we describe in our research is opening new avenues but is also putting stress on students. This often *is* described by students as pressure that also evokes mental health crises, et cetera. What's your perception on how to encourage students to Future Skills learning in a positive way which is not a way to put more pressure on individuals?

Schleicher: I think the pressure felt is actually real. In a fast-changing world, our mental capacity to adapt is stretched. As humans, we are designed to keep the world in balance—we struggle when living in an unbalanced world. I think that is what puts enormous strain on young people, but the answer to this cannot be to make the world easier to make it easier for people to adapt. That would be utopian. The answer only can be to help students become more resilient, more actively capable to address these kinds of anxieties, to build stronger agency, a self-concept that is adaptive to future realities. A friend of mine who also works in education, Amanda Ripley, told me her own story. She was studying in a university in Canada, in a very demanding kind of program, and really struggling. One day she said: I'm going to give up, this is just too much for me, I cannot cope with this. She had a Chinese roommate who got up in the morning every day, worked, got to sleep early, seemed calm and managed everything, got good grades. She asked that roommate: I don't know what I can do. I'm going to give up, I will not succeed. And the roommate told her: I can really see how you struggle, you must be under enormous pressure—and this is the first time you experience this. You know, I experienced this from first grade.

I think we often create a very artificial reality for people in education—a reality where we say we know what you need to learn, and this is what we're going to test in the exam—a reality that is predictable. And then suddenly people find themselves in a different world when they get to university, or even after. I think this cognitive, social and emotional resilience is something we need to make a much bigger effort for—because we live in this time of accelerations, and there's no end of this in sight. Our human capacity to thrive in this imbalanced, volatile world is going to be hugely important, and that is something that, from the earliest days in our lives, we need to pay more attention to.

Ehlers: Thank you for this story! Another thing I wanted to ask you is: when the OECD published their Future of Education and Skills 2030 concept, what was the reaction? Because this is also all about Future Skills. What was the reaction of your member states, of institutions and policy-makers?

Schleicher: This was one of the most interesting experiences for me. When I proposed that project to our member countries six years ago, their reaction was extremely negative. Curriculum is the holy grail—this is something that we do in our member states, we don't want anyone to deal with that from the outside. Then we started with the work. We brought together students, educators, people from philanthropy, civil society, public policy to work on the OECD Learning Compass 2030—and you could suddenly see that governments became more and more interested in it. It became a rapidly growing community—I don't think we have done anything that had a greater impact. In terms of change, I would actually say that this has been more impactful than our work on PISA.

To give you an example: last year we assessed social and emotional skills of people and the Koreans saw that there were 15-year-olds who were less creative than 10-year-olds. Think about it for a moment—if I would tell you your students do worse in mathematics at age 15 than at age 10, you would think that there was something terribly wrong going on in our school system. I actually met the Korean deputy prime minister to talk about this. She told me: for days, I couldn't think of anything else. And then they started to look at this learning compass and to think about it: how can we actually frame our education narrative? We are so extremely successful academically, but we miss out on some of those other elements. What can we learn from that—can we work with it? It really created a movement in the country, and you can see how society is taking up that message. Educators are looking at that learning compass as something that can help them—so I think it's that kind of tools we are lacking. In education, we have piles and piles of curricula that spell out the mechanics of learning and content—but we never ask ourselves about purpose. What are the Future Skills we want to teach? We teach people how to calculate an exponential function—but we don't teach them the idea, the nature of that exponential function. And that is what you need to understand when you want to work on climate change or on a pandemic. I wish we had more processes in our societies where educators across borders, across subject area fields work together to ask themselves that question of purpose.

Ehlers: I think it is important to understand that Future Skills demand a different type of learning which is different from teaching and testing unconnected knowledge chunks but that we rather need a well-connected curriculum which is designing education around purpose and mission. Tools like the Future Skills approach (nextskills.org) or the OECD Learning Compass[1] help to create a narrative around purpose, around the future capabilities which we would like to stimulate and support in students' learning. These tools are in a way functioning and serving as a counterpart to the curricular approach in order to unleash individual development—and they are carrying the Future Skills idea that there is much more to learn than the knowledge in the curriculum.

---

[1] https://www.oecd.org/education/2030-project/teaching-and-learning/learning/learning-compass-2030/

4 "I've Learnt Everything I Know from the World."

Schleicher: What we often do in the field of education when we talk about Future Skills is that we hide in the comfortable world of the things that we can easily define. If you look at our education systems, the big questions in our life do not appear: love, death, why we are here on this earth. Those are the questions that move us all, but we do not articulate them in education—because they are the ones which go beyond the easily definable. I think that question of purpose will be increasingly important in education—to help people find meaning in life.

Eigbrecht: Talking of purpose: I would like to ask you about your vision of education and higher education in the next ten, twenty years. How would you wish for it to be? What's your ideal future education like?

Schleicher: Probably think less about education, think more about learning, think more about personal development. We will see higher education at any stage and in any part of our lives in some ways, less visible as institutions and places, more visible as an activity, more something that accompanies me rather than where I go to. And I think that working and learning will become very closely intertwined—as something that gives people inspiration and helps people find new meanings, new fields, new interests in their lives. Once again, we no longer learn for a job, but the job becomes our capacity, our willingness to learn—and learning environments should become responsive to these different needs of people.

Prof. Dr. phil. habil. Ulf-Daniel Ehlers is an internationally renowned Professor for Educational Management and Lifelong Learning at the Baden-Wuerttemberg Cooperative State University (DHBW) Karlsruhe which he headed as Vice-President between 2011 and 2017.

Laura Eigbrecht is principle investigator, teacher and doctoral student at the Baden-Wuerttemberg Cooperative State University (DHBW) Karlsruhe and holds degrees in European Media and Culture and Media Pedagogy.

Open Access This chapter is licensed under the terms of the Creative Commons Attribution 4.0 International License (http://creativecommons.org/licenses/by/4.0/), which permits use, sharing, adaptation, distribution and reproduction in any medium or format, as long as you give appropriate credit to the original author(s) and the source, provide a link to the Creative Commons license and indicate if changes were made.

The images or other third party material in this chapter are included in the chapter's Creative Commons license, unless indicated otherwise in a credit line to the material. If material is not included in the chapter's Creative Commons license and your intended use is not permitted by statutory regulation or exceeds the permitted use, you will need to obtain permission directly from the copyright holder.

Future Skills—Back into the Future? Emerging Trends in Educational Innovation in Higher Education

5

Francesc Pedró

> **Abstract**
>
> This chapter begins by revisiting the concept of educational innovation in the context of higher education. It then examines why, for the first time, there is such a broad social consensus on the need to promote educational innovation and why so many higher education institutions are making such an effort to jump on the innovation bandwagon. Second, it discusses some patterns of development that demonstrate that, despite the appearance that the problem that educational innovations should tackle is well-defined, there is no one solution, and efforts are being directed in numerous and diverse avenues. Thirdly, the chapter addresses several of the risks accompanying the growing emphasis on innovation, notably in terms of equality, assessment, and innovation fatigue. Finally, it offers several public policy pathways to facilitate the convergence of discourse and practice toward systemic innovation.

F. Pedró (✉)
UNESCO Institute for Higher Education in Latin America and the Caribbean,
Caracas, Venezuela
e-mail: f.pedro@unesco.org

© The Author(s) 2024
U.-D. Ehlers and L. Eigbrecht (eds.), *Creating the University of the Future*, Zukunft der Hochschulbildung - Future Higher Education,
https://doi.org/10.1007/978-3-658-42948-5_5

5.1   Introduction

Since the end of the nineteenth century, there have been recurrent calls to reconsider the predominant model of higher education provision given its inadequacies to changing social and economic demands and expectations. Particularly during the pandemic, newspaper pieces, television broadcasts, and a great deal of social media chatter have been showing a growing agreement on the importance of changing the paradigm that is still globally predominant—and most likely will continue to be so when the appearance of radical transformation caused by the epidemic begins to fade. The idea that, if we had not inherited higher education as it is, our current views about education would drive us to construct a vastly different system is already a certainty (Drucker, 1998). Against this context, educational innovation in higher education develops as an investigation geared specifically at redesigning provision and delivery modes.

Many discussions about teaching and higher education assume that the reality of today's classrooms is populated with highly innovative methods. However, it is difficult to find empirical evidence about how teaching is happening in university classrooms. Two examples show that the most widely used teaching method, lecturing, is hardly in line with the rhetoric of innovation that often populates the discourses about higher education. The first example comes from an examination of the main teaching strategies used in business administration programs in more than 200 European universities. In that domain, where the development of practical skills and competencies in management is so important, it is difficult to understand why the most widely used method is still lecturing, as opposed to problem-solving or the work on case studies (Leon, 2016)—while good lecturing can be inspiring and convincing, it is not appropriate for the development of skills that promote agency and self-regulation whereas a hands-on approach could be far more suitable. A second example comes from the analysis of the evolution of teaching strategies in economics programs in US colleges and universities over the last two decades (Asarta et al., 2021). Again, the expectations are disappointed by facts: the most widely used teaching strategy is lecturing. Furthermore, the examination of the evolution of teaching strategies over the past two decades shows that lecturing has remained the top method increasingly supported by computer-based presentations. The latter has increased at a pace that doubles the rate of increase of strategies that could be easily linked to more interactive or student-centered strategies such as cooperative learning or discussions among students.

Research insistently reminds us that, from the beginning of the nineteenth century, educational innovations have been constant, almost overwhelming at times, yet despite this, formal higher education continues to resemble itself globally because the underlying model is universal (Meyer et al., 1992, 1997). Some analysts have

5 Future Skills—Back into the Future? Emerging Trends ...

gone as far as to claim that, despite all, higher education has changed progressively in its internal structure, the configuration of procedures, and use of technology. Still, it does not appear that the universal model of higher education has undergone a major shift (Elmore, 2004). In a way, the paradox is that the more things have changed on the surface of higher education institutions, the stronger the classic universal model has become (Sarason, 1996).

5.2 Conceptualizing Future Skills

Intuitively, the concept of Future Skills refers to the skills that would best equip learners to address the life and work challenges that are likely to be faced by them in the near future, based on our current assumptions. Implicitly, the concept of Future Skills is an assertion of the mismatch between labor markets, projected or actual, and the current educational provision. Therefore, it fully adheres to the assumption that the global economy is undergoing fast transformation due to technical, demographic, environmental, and geopolitical factors (Ehlers, 2020). This transformation will unavoidably alter the character of labor, bringing new possibilities and risks. It is already doing so as the mismatch can already be seen in the unaddressed expectations of companies, particularly those operating in the digital economy or in areas where technology requires new profiles and skill sets.

The conversation about Future Skills has been particularly salient in postsecondary education, notably in technical and vocational training and higher education, given that their outputs are critical in a knowledge economy (Bowles et al., 2019; Ehlers, 2022). The link between labor market needs and Future Skills can easily be seen in a growing importance that this conversation has gained in international for a promoted by economic organizations such as the World Economic Forum (WEF) or the OECD (OECD, 2018). They have contributed enormously to raising awareness that technology and digitalization will strongly impact future employment. To deal with this, some governments have generated strategies, programs, and dedicated units to deal with Future Skills, such as in Canada, England, Japan, and South Korea. In addition to the technical knowledge and experience required for jobs in the digital economy, companies also seek professionals with certain transversal skills, such as creativity, critical thinking, leadership, and emotional intelligence. Those skills benefit companies from perspectives that are also essential for their businesses.

However, the numerous frameworks discussing Future Skills utilize hundreds of phrases to refer to such skills and competences, impeding the debate about education's future (Kotsiou et al., 2022). One of the most widely quoted comes from the WEF. The WEF estimates that by 2025 some 85 million jobs may disappear due to automation resulting from technological advances, so its experts believe that the best skills for workers in 2025 will be intrinsically human and impossible to replicate in a machine (World Economic Forum, 2022). Thus, critical thinking and problem-solving top the list of skills employers believe will be crucial for professionals in 2025. Other skills on this list include active learning; creativity, originality, and initiative; analytical thinking; leadership and social influence; technology use and control; technology design and programming; resilience, stress tolerance, and flexibility; and reasoning and the ability to shape ideas and concepts. This list openly supports that the mismatch that fuels the discussion about of Future Skills goes beyond economic and labor considerations, as social transformations also require new personal and social skills. However, it remains to be seen whether these skills are sufficiently well developed in the current educational provision. Investment in three foundational social institutions—education, healthcare, and care—would re-start the engine of social mobility across economies, fill unmet demand for healthcare and childcare, increase the quality of education systems and ultimately drive growth (World Economic Forum, 2022).

The concept has also been criticized because the common lists of Future Skills often include some that have to do with personal abilities that, although trainable, are not acquired in a few months. Sometimes not even in years, such as critical thinking, creativity, leadership, the ability to shape ideas and concepts, or technology development and design. In fact, for many of them, in addition to a long learning process, it is also necessary to have a certain innate facility to develop them, as in the cases of leadership or creativity. Then, the question is how far the current learning arrangements provide conducive environments not only for flourishing these skills but, even more so, to avoid their cancellation or suppression after years of traditional educational provision that may kill creativity, for instance (Robinson, 2010). For decades, traditional education promoted a different set of skills, possibly more in line with the needs of industrial societies and economies, thus far from today's needs.

In sum, the concept of Future Skills openly supports the claim that today's educational provision does not address the skill development needs of current and future workers and citizens well, either because they are not aligned with labor market demands or social requirements. In this conversation, the future, although elusive and nebulous, serves as a significant orientation for predicting future positive changes, progress, and accomplishments, and thus drive educational reform and innovation (Hall et al., 2022).

5.3 Conceptualizing Educational Innovation

It is challenging to get a consensus on the concept of educational innovation. In general, innovation is defined as the act of creating and disseminating new tools, practices, organizational systems, or technologies (Foray & Raffo, 2012); therefore, innovation can be equated with the concept of development and contrasted with that of research along a continuum linking research and development. However, innovation differs from development in that the latter focuses on the generation of practice-oriented knowledge. In contrast, innovation results from applying this knowledge to a new product, service, method, or technology (Godin et al., 2021). In this context, the success of innovation would be measured by market adoption; in other words, total success would translate into universal generalization, which would paradoxically lead to the loss of the innovative character that this new product, service, technique, or technology would have had at its inception.

In complex organizations such as higher education institutions, several factors might lead to the acceptance of innovation or its avoidance. From an economic perspective, for an innovation to become ubiquitous, the cost–benefit equation must have a positive balance, i.e., the overall expenses and efforts necessary to embrace the innovation must be compensated by a bigger benefit (Rinkinen & Harmaakorpi, 2018). It is a matter of innovating to increase the company's overall efficiency or steer the firm toward new goods or services. The higher education industry is reluctant to accept the abovementioned approach for several reasons. On the one hand, there is a denial of any notion of education that includes measuring effort and outcomes. For instance, in certain higher education systems, instructors' work appears to be significantly impacted by reductive quantification techniques to make their work more accountable (Hardy, 2021). On the other hand, the higher education sector lacks the formalized elements of standardization that exist in other sectors, such as the health sector: much of the knowledge upon which instructors base their professional practice belongs to the domain of the tacit, and socially constructed practice, and is not subject to the same levels of protocolization that are evident, for instance, in an industrial production process or the prescription of medical treatments (Hardy, 2020; Murnane & Nelson, 1984). In the higher education sector, more so than in others, innovation is frequently equated with a change in any of the elements that comprise the essence of the traditional education model. Its success is not measured in terms of widespread adoption based on its greater effectiveness in promoting better learning or learning of a different nature, but rather in terms of the satisfaction of the actors who have made it possible—in particular, its promotors.

Throughout this chapter, however, educational innovation is defined as a dynamic change that adds value to the processes occurring in a higher education institution (both pedagogical and organizational) and that results in improved student learning outcomes or educational stakeholder satisfaction, or both (OECD, 2009). Furthermore, this definition includes the operational stipulation that only changes in procedures that result in demonstrable gains, particularly in learning, qualify as educational innovations. In so doing, the definition acknowledges the possibility of changes without demonstrable effects or even bad impacts, i.e., changes that do not result in genuine innovations.

5.4 The Imperative for Educational Innovation

The term "university" evokes a remarkably similar image throughout the world, which has its roots in economic rationality that, particularly with the expansion of demand around fifty years ago, seeks to solve the equation of how to provide the benefits of higher education to the greatest number of students at the lowest possible cost, with also clear political implications. However, as stated by Martin Trow over fifty years ago, the university as we know it looks to be only a common-sense answer to the dilemma of providing higher education to the masses (Berger & Luckmann, 1966). Accordingly, the conventional model of higher education provision prioritizes organizational formulae and teaching procedures that optimize the transmission of content or instruction.

The massive financial effort necessary for the massification of higher education might be quickly recouped by the benefits of having a workforce prepared to function as competent management in a manufacturing and industrial environment and, subsequently, in a services world (Tye, 2000). Indeed, the logic of higher education massification is based on the principles that all students should learn the same thing, at the same pace and in the same sequence, and that differences in results are due to the different innate abilities of students and their varying levels of effort; consequently, the best performers are selected to continue studying and will eventually be rewarded with higher-paying jobs, as befits a meritocratic regime. The latter summarizes the reasoning for the traditional paradigm of higher education, which is still in use today.

There is no shortage of literature regarding teaching and higher education, for instance, opposing the traditional learner to the 21st-century learner, saying we are becoming far more active and oriented towards problem-solving (Crisol-Moya et al., 2020; Wilson, 2018). However, innovation is more than a pedagogical imperative. Four drivers have been pushing the quest for more innovative teaching strategies in higher education even before the pandemic.

The first driver is the concept of skills development as a result of a growing trend toward ensuring that higher education programs respond to the needs of the labor market. While there have been many discussions about the exaggerated role that the skills seem to be playing now in the development of teaching strategies and the design of higher education programs, employers expect graduate profiles that not only master the corresponding subject but have well-developed skills in areas such as problem-solving, teamwork, communication or critical thinking (Succi & Canovi, 2020). The issue here is that the traditional approach to higher education is still discipline-led and study programs seem not to consider the need to foster the development of such transversal skills enough. This confidence on skills development assumes that the development of the new economy requires, more than graduates with content knowledge, competent, highly skilled knowledge workers. They will know how to apply content to problem-solving, work in teams in multilingual and multicultural contexts, have a critical sense, know how to communicate, and, above all, are creative to generate, through their work, new knowledge and spur innovations (Barrichello et al., 2020; Heckman & Kautz, 2014). In conclusion, a societal consensus has developed around the notion that it is not enough for higher education to teach content; it must also support the development of transversal and transferable abilities. As a result of the inadequacy of the old education model, it is vital to investigate, via innovation, alternative models that are more adapted to these modern needs, which all indications suggest will increase in the future (Biasi et al., 2021).

The second driver is essentially the demographic and social dimensions of the economic changes, which translate into the need to learn to coexist in increasingly socially, culturally, and linguistically varied and complicated circumstances. In this new environment, classrooms in higher education must explore modes of social interaction and shared learning in which diversity is recognized and appreciated (Schröder & Krüger, 2019) and where Future Skills are promoted. Again, this necessitates that both the organization of the provision of higher education and the processes underlying it provide environments where these learning-focused activities may occur, which is difficult within traditional pedagogical institutions. Moreover, the phenomenon of the diversification of student academic profiles that comes with the massification of higher education can be seen as a corollary. While new populations have been attracted to higher education with different age profiles, the point is that with the massification of higher education, the range of academic profiles among students has been widening. A higher education system that caters only to 10 or 15% of a student cohort can assume that only the cream, that is, the most academically oriented students will be on board. Although many will contest this assumption, the truth is that when higher education systems cater to the majority of a student cohort, as happens to be the case in OECD countries where the net access rates to higher education are already around 70%, inevitably, academic profiles among students will diversify, and with this the needs will also expand in terms of pedagogical strategies if university programs are designed to promote success and not simply to select the most academically endured students. There is some evidence showing that the more students are accepted into higher education, the more diverse their profiles become, and inevitably, as a result also of social changes, the less academically engaged they are, arguably because the provision of higher education is less meaningful for them, not because of their own limitations. An indication of these changes comes from a recent study that compared the average weekly study hours of US college students in 1960 and in 2010 (Babcock & Marks, 2011). In short, over two generations, the percentage of weekly study hours has been cut by half; in other words, today's students span half the number of weekly hours their grandparents devoted to studying.

The third reason is the recognition of the mismatch between the techniques of communication and work within higher education classrooms and in the real world outside of these institutions. While the trend toward increased use of technology in the classroom, and beyond it, was already apparent well before the pandemic started, there has been a change in attitudes towards digitalization on the site of both teachers and students as a result of the massive experiment that the pandemic has represented when it comes to technology use for teaching and learning. Both teachers and students seem to be far more optimistic about the possibilities of virtual learning as well as hybridization or the potential of digital materials than they were before the pandemic, with the only exception of online proctoring, which is well accepted by students and not so much by teachers according to the latest data available (Johnson et al., 2021). The external demand on universities and instructors to incorporate technology and, incidentally, to adapt their teaching methods, was noticeable well before the pandemic. During the pandemic, technology-supported teaching, under the form of emergency remote education, was the only strategy to ensure pedagogical continuity during closures. Rather than innovating teaching, technology was used to reproduce traditional forms of lecturing under a remote modality. It remains to be seen how much of the cumulated experience on technology-supported higher education by teachers and students alike translates into durable and sustained changes in pedagogy or in the whole student experience. Empirical research has demonstrated that the costs of technology integration are not justified until considerable changes are made to the organization and processes of teaching and learning due to technological advancements (Comi et al., 2016). Thus, technology represents an innovation potential, but its presence alone does not necessarily ensure innovation.

The fourth driver is the need to improve the productivity of higher education. Although many voices would not accept the use of the term, the fact is that many higher education systems worldwide have been suffering from low graduation rates. In some European countries such as Spain or Italy, only 6 out of 10 new entrants in higher education will graduate at some point. In countries such as the Republic of Korea or the United States, where the majority of high school graduates get access to higher education, graduation rates are even lower, down to four out of every ten new entrants. While the causes of dropping out can be very diverse, ditching strategies and lack of significance of what students are meant to learn in higher education can be very powerful drivers for abandonment. This driver can be related to the international pressure that stems from the needs of increasingly globalized economies that rely heavily on science and technology as drivers of innovation and competitiveness, to focus the attention on the capacity of their higher education systems to produce the skills that must feed these economies and generate the virtuous circle of R&D on which knowledge economies are founded.

In conclusion, these four external factors (the demand for high-level skills, social and demographic changes, technological changes, and international competition) explain in large part why there is a growing social consensus globally on the need to promote innovation, which translates into an imperative (Marklund et al., 2009), also in higher education work (Bates, 2012). To these external elements must be added the internal dynamics of higher education institutions, which explains why this social consensus applauds and encourages teachers' innovative initiatives.

5.5 Emerging Trends

While many essays provide hints about new pedagogies (Carbonell, 2015), that make a personal synthesis of innovation experiences (Bona, 2016), or that criticize the lack of disruptive innovations in education (Christensen et al., 2008), there is no inventory or international observatory of educational innovation in higher education that provides a clear picture of what the emerging global trends are. Governments and higher education institutions alike frequently struggle to find innovations inside their systems, evaluate their impacts (even for inventions they have funded), and contribute to their spread when there is evidence of their value. There are, however, signs (e.g., Delphi-based research) that education innovations in higher education can be organized along three important axes: innovations in instructional content and design, process innovations, and technology-supported innovations, all of them having important organizational implications. The three axes are analyzed below.

5.5.1 Innovations in Instructional Content and Design

The first axis is curricular. It should be the most important because it defines the expectations for the entire higher education experience. However, since the control of degrees continues to be centralized in many countries, particularly by quality assurance agencies, universities have fewer opportunities to innovate in this area. In nations where the curriculum is open and allows for substantial variability across higher education programs and institutions, such as in North America, or when it is specified in terms of standards to be attained after each cycle, such as in Southern Europe, curricular innovations are more likely to occur. However, governments and quality assurance organizations approach these developments with extreme caution.

In general, curricula determined by teaching loads of different disciplines or courses are being replaced by flexible formulae that emphasize transversal axes and the development of Future Skills. According to Pietarinen et al. (2017), the belief underlying these curricular changes is that eliminating topics is a requirement for learning centered on developing competencies. For many years, the concept of competencies was contrasted with that of content to emphasize that teaching could not solely focus on information transmission and its corollary, memorization; consequently, the need to develop innovative teaching methods centered on how to help students forge their competencies was emphasized. Due to the misunderstanding caused by a grasp of constructivist ideas, content was eventually vilified (Nordin & Sundberg, 2016). Nevertheless, the successful development of useful skills and competencies also needs the transfer of content, which is ultimately the substance on which competencies work.

Innovations in the curriculum that aim to foster the development of competencies extend beyond the standard university fields. For example, although we speak of mathematical, linguistic, and scientific competencies, there is a growing emphasis on so-called transversal competencies, such as the so-called 4 Cs in the Anglo-Saxon world (communication, critical thinking, collaboration, and creativity) (Partnership for 21st Century Skills, 2016) or 21st century competencies, or Future Skills. Their instruction has been highly suggested globally, especially in Europe, as was the case with the European 2020 Strategy's priorities. Even though everyone seems to understand what they are intuitively, there is still no universal definition. However, even more than the emphasis on competencies linked to different disciplines, these others increase the difficulty of teaching and put the validity of curricular disciplinary models in jeopardy (Neubert et al., 2015).

5 Future Skills—Back into the Future? Emerging Trends …

This trend translates into a shift from designing study programs based on the content to be taught to a reference to the objectives that the students should achieve in terms of skills and competencies at the end of the courses. The percentage of European universities using an objective-centered approach in study programs has increased dramatically in just five years, which is already the preferred approach to program design in that region (Sursock, 2015). Setting objectives quite often equates with a competency-based approach to program design where the most important element is making explicit what the students should be able to do, often regarding a clearly defined assessment framework using rubrics. In other words, with this competency-based approach also comes a different understanding of how the student learning assessment should work. The critique of this approach comes more from an ideological perspective that is convinced that the role of higher education should not be linked to the development of skills and competencies but rather focus on the generation of critical minds in line with the classical liberal programs. Whether all competencies used to define study programs should be related to labor market needs or can go beyond that is a matter of open discussion worldwide.

The emphasis on skills development has given rise to two new phenomena: the corporate university and micro-credentials. Both are distinctive forms to respond to the requirement of high-level skills development in a more efficient way than traditional universities have been doing in the past. The corporate university can be defined as a model of higher education provision designed by corporations to suit their own needs and, by extension, to the needs of other corporations and firms. It is also a form of engagement of the private sector in higher education that in deregulated contexts can easily evolve as a more cost-efficient model than traditional public universities (Aronowitz & Giroux, 2000). Micro-credentials emerged along similar lines as an attempt to provide cost-effective credentials in response to labor market needs, particularly in technology-related fields, following intensive, short-duration training (Hunt et al., 2020). Micro-credentials are becoming increasingly popular also in traditional universities and are no longer the patrimony of corporate universities.

5.5.2 Process Innovations

The second axis of innovation is the diversity and richness of teaching and learning activities. This axis highlights two main innovation directions: Project-Based Learning (PBL) (English & Kitsantas, 2013) and the personalization of learning. Both PBL and personalization hold a lot of potential for the development of

Future Skills—the former because it creates an appropriate real-like context and the latter because it is the only way by which the learner can receive formative assessment individually.

Internationally, PBL, also known as problem-based learning (English & Kitsantas, 2013), appears to be developing as the new methodological paradigm in higher education. However, the emphasis on developing skills and competencies necessitates a pedagogical framework in which student engagement is both the vehicle and the desired end; after all, competencies are created via action, or "learning by doing" as Dewey defined it in 1916. It is no surprise that the bet for objective-setting and competency development-oriented study programs translates into innovative teaching strategies that would certainly be much more useful in that respect than lecturing. If one of these new strategies seems to be gaining ground, that is for sure Problem-Based Learning, or Project-Based Learning, depending on the context (Gallagher & Savage, 2020). Inevitably for the development of practical skills and competencies such as problem-solving or critical thinking, there is no better way than confronting students with real problems or projects that, on the other hand, can also promote the interdisciplinary approaches that are also so valuable in the eyes of today's companies in knowledge economies. A survey in the United States showed some years ago that the percentage of undergraduate programs requiring project-based learning is nowadays the majority; in approximately 1/4 of these programs all the students are required to embark on PBL (Hart Associates, 2016).

PBL may take a variety of forms, but its most important characteristics are quite straightforward (Barron & Darling-Hammond, 2008):

- Students learn through confronting real-world obstacles or problems that they must answer through a project;
- they have increased autonomy to manage and direct their learning activities;
- teachers assist them throughout the process, supporting investigation and reflection; and eventually,
- typically, students produce projects in groups or at least in pairs.

Thus, PBL provides a chance for cooperative learning and, consequently, the development of collaboration skills in a social setting that values difference and solidarity via different groups.

The second trend of process innovations is distinct but not necessarily contradictory: learning personalization or customization. The supporting belief is that improving the results of a class group requires, paradoxically, paying more attention to those students who, throughout the learning process, encounter more obstacles, either because of their starting conditions or simply because, at some point, they may need a specific reinforcement that only individualized attention, through tutoring, or in a small group, can resolve in time (Maguire et al., 2013).

Personalization has had several iterations (Prain et al., 2013). The more recent wave, heavily enhanced during the pandemic, was enabled by the increasing use of technology-supported platforms. The use of platforms has made it possible not only for each student to progress at her own pace and with resources that adapt to her interests or needs but also for teachers to monitor each student's learning path individually. But, again, it must be emphasized that innovation along these lines is only conceivable if the contractual arrangements associated to the teaching load foresee freeing up the required time and resources.

5.5.3 Innovations in Technology

The third axis is technological, which is the axis most linked with education innovation in recent years, to the point that innovation and technology are sometimes mistaken for synonyms when they are not. As a result of technologically supported educational innovation, many experiments have been conducted to exploit the potential of digital devices, services, and applications, either to optimize known processes or to enable entirely new ones in teaching and educational administration and management. The growth of this association between technology and innovation is largely attributable to the contribution of the technology providers. All companies in the sector, from hardware makers to services and content providers, ensure that appropriate technologies are available in classrooms. They do so not simply to market their products but also to promote their image of what a university in the twenty-first century should be. In other instances, with some sort of messianism, they have assumed a prescriptive role without considering the actual demands and instructional priorities recognized in higher education classrooms, causing rejection (Williamson, 2017). They correctly assert that universities cannot stay ignorant of technological progress. But not everyone would agree that no one is in a better position than the industry to prescribe how higher education should utilize technology to achieve its goals.

Technology is nothing more than a window of opportunity. Unfortunately, innovative technology uses in the classroom do not always lead to developing innovative methodologies, as they can also facilitate consolidating the traditional pedagogical model. Consequently, it is not surprising that it can be challenging to separate the wheat from the chaff (Falck et al., 2015). On the other hand, certain innovations in content (such as the emphasis on transversal competencies) and, especially, in processes (both in PBL and in the personalization of learning) can benefit from the support provided by technology.

Nevertheless, combining all the experimental avenues that technology-supported educational innovation is pursuing is extremely challenging. In this regard, Cuban's distinction between first- and second-order pedagogical changes established decades ago is extremely helpful, as it clarifies the true added value of technology in education (Cuban, 1988).

A first-order change happens when the inclusion of new technology enables improving and enhancing processes without substantially altering them. An example of first-order change is the replacement of traditional blackboards in classrooms with digital whiteboards, whose practical advantages and resultant increased efficiency are obvious. However, using digital whiteboards does not always result in a revolution in teaching but the technologization of well-established content-transmission processes. The same could be said about the increasing use of e-learning platforms such as Zoom or Teams or digital teaching resources: even open educational resources are not, in and of themselves, an educational innovation because their use does not necessarily imply a pedagogical change, regardless of the technical benefits, cost savings, or values that their use or sharing entails (Wiley et al., 2014a, b).

A second-order change happens when methods are significantly transformed, allowing for executing different tasks with distinct rewards. The clearest example is the so-called "flipped classroom," in which students access information outside of class hours, freeing up classroom time for activities other than content transmission or entirely virtual school instruction (Lo & Hew, 2017). The flipped classroom concept, which was first created for teaching science, is fast expanding throughout the globe and has quickly extended from secondary to higher education.

The distinction between first and second-order relates to the magnitude of the changes: although first-order adjustments cannot significantly alter processes, second-order changes can fundamentally do so. First-order technological changes are not innovations, but second-order technological changes are. Indeed, pedagogical techniques appear to have produced much better outcomes, particularly when attempting to shift from a content-centered teaching model to one that emphasizes developing skills and competencies, provided the pedagogical design includes second-order adjustments. However, the necessary pedagogical transformation can only be implemented if the full potential of technology is harnessed. A growing body of empirical research identifies the conditions in which educational strategies supported by technology can yield much better outcomes than those that do not substantially use technology (Arias Ortiz & Cristia, 2014).

Including technology is only an opportunity for instructional innovation that may or may not be utilized. And secondly, improvements facilitated by technology only qualify as educational innovations when technology is employed for at least one of the following purposes (Pedró, 2016):

1. student's active engagement;
2. cooperative education;
3. quick feedback to student activity; or
4. forging relationships with the world beyond the classroom.

Following the pandemic hybridization, that is the use of technology-based solutions to enhance the learning experience of students in the classroom or beyond lectures, has emerged as a promising avenue. The reference to hybridization comes from the fact that this approach would maximize the opportunities of face-to-face learning with the possibilities offered by synchronous and asynchronous teaching, particularly through dedicated e-learning platforms. Again, there is evidence that this trend existed well before the pandemic, and in the post-pandemic higher education landscape, student preferred teaching methods are now pointing to their expectation of increased use of more digital resources and materials, even in face-to-face instruction. Moreover, many students seem to be willing to follow some of their courses online even if they are in a residential campus. It all comes down to flexibility, a motto that business schools, in particular, have already adopted during the pandemic and plan to elaborate on increased flexible approaches to ensure that connectivity's benefits translate into adaptability in different student contexts (Avent & Richardson, 2022). A good example of the possibilities of hybridization is the flipped classroom, whose success depends on several factors, including student engagement (O'Flaherty & Phillips, 2015; Sosa Díaz et al., 2021).

The pandemic made distance higher education compulsory for all students. Institutions and faculty consistently developed their capacities to transition from emergency responses, most of the time generated without any prior experience of distance education, to more mature approaches to distance higher education that involved more sophisticated use of e-learning platforms and applications and more refined instructional designs. It is not easy to see at this point whether distance education for undergraduate students is going to be on the rise in the coming years. However, there is certitude about the fact that when it comes to post-graduate education, particularly in the case of professionals, distance education will become the preferred approach by students because of the flexibility and increased quality of the student experience (Miller et al., 2021). Massive Open

Online Courses or MOOCs generated a true hype and are entering now in a more mature status where well-established universities are the real players. If coupled with micro-credentials, MOOCs can become a new channel for the delivery of higher education particularly to graduated professionals seeking for quick and reliable ways of upscaling their skills (Goglio, 2019). With or without MOOCs, there are already several countries where students in distance undergraduate programs will soon become the majority, such as Brazil (Red Indices, 2021). Interestingly, in the United States, where the demand for distance higher education programs was declining well before the pandemic, it seems now to be on the rise according to the latest data (Cheslock & Jaquette, 2022).

Some of the pioneers in learning sciences research are also pioneers in investigating how technology might help transform instructional designs. These relationships are not coincidental. As scientists have come to a better understanding of the fundamental characteristics of learning, they have realized that the structure and resources of traditional classrooms often provide little support for effective learning. In contrast, when used to promote second-order changes, technology can enable teaching methods that are much better suited to how students learn.

Technology will continue to evolve and create new opportunities, some of which are only now being explored. Considering the potential of virtual reality, artificial intelligence, or the application of Big Data and learning analytics is sufficient to conclude that these windows of opportunity will expand dramatically in the future. However, this does not imply that new technology opportunities will always result in second-order modifications and, consequently, genuine innovations (Selwyn, 2015). UNESCO has frequently emphasized the need for improving digital teaching abilities as a means to dispel this common misconception (UNESCO, 2011).

5.6 Organizational Consequences

Innovations in content, processes, and technologies, when they affect an institution as a whole and not just a course, a program, or a single instructor, necessitate significant organizational changes. Unfortunately, some of the most common organizational adjustments target the old paradigm based on the premise of one instructor per course. Thus, for instance, the objective is to make the parameters for the configuration of class groups more flexible, both in terms of the number of students and their respective instructor assignments, as well as the duration of classes, which have been transformed into work sessions, paving the way for block-teaching. This can lead to times during the day when a relatively large group of students, equivalent to two or three traditional class groups, can be left under the supervision of a single instructor to engage in a low-demand activity, such as watching a video, in exchange for the opportunity to work in much smaller groups, each with its instructor.

Herein lies the significance of instructional leadership in higher education. In this context, leadership should be understood as a particular way of managing human resources at the department or school level that makes it possible to generate significant work priorities for educational improvement that the entire faculty also share; to direct the work of the department or school by these priorities, making the appropriate decisions; and, finally, to review the progress of the team by these priorities, and to evaluate their performance (Fowler & Walter, 2020). Therefore, there must be leadership in a department or school with a cohesive team, but this leadership should not always be mirrored in a single individual who would acquire all decision-making authority. International forums insistently refer to distributed or networked leadership, specifically to indicate that it should be exercised from different levels, personal and group, and to avoid placing all expectations and responsibilities on the leader at the center (Vuori, 2019).

At first look, this conceptual shift may appear to be the product of a transitory trend, such as the preference for the word leadership over coordination. Nevertheless, the reference to leadership suggests a paradigm shift: instead of supervising compliance with regulations external to the department or school and internally coordinating the actions derived from their mandatory compliance as traditionally deans and department chairs do, the reference to leadership includes an important nuance: the capacity to manage, motivate, and professionally develop human teams, while facilitating the economic and material conditions necessary for them to carry out their teaching responsibilities. Thus, there is a shift from a paradigm centered on the absence of regulations and standards in a context of full autonomy and freedom to teach by the individual, tenured professors, to one characterized by an emphasis on leading teams to execute a project in which research and innovation will inevitably play a central role.

Research has demonstrated that pedagogical leadership is essential for the formation of effective teaching teams and their ongoing motivation, as well as for fostering an institutional learning climate and environment that enables, guides, and acknowledges innovation efforts to enhance learning. In addition, research has revealed, not unexpectedly, a correlation between the quality of educational leadership and the quality of student learning (Leithwood & Jantzi, 2005; Smith, 2008).

5.7 Risks

At first look, the fact that there is currently a favorable social environment for educational innovation and multiple projects is encouraging. Nonetheless, the innovation imperative must confront some hazards. These dangers are associated with the system's fairness, the evaluation of the effects of innovations, and teacher professional burnout.

In terms of equity, there is a paradox in which institutions or programs that work in highly complex contexts or serve a large number of diverse, vulnerable, or first-generation higher education students, which should receive more resources to enable significant innovations, are in a worse position to innovate unless the system considers them a true priority in this regard, which is not the case everywhere. It is not just a problem of acquiring additional resources to innovate but also having the best conditions to find the time to innovate (Raffo, 2014). High rates of faculty turnover in complex contexts and their lower average levels of experience and qualifications make it challenging to cultivate an environment conducive to innovation in institutions serving vulnerable or at-risk students. Moreover, it should come as no surprise that the frequency of innovative programs is lower in these contexts (Wilcox et al., 2017).

Second, the innovation imperative does not appear to have yet made the essential shift in the educational paradigm consistent with the requirement for systems to progress toward more social justice. The pedagogical discourse on innovation is not explicitly concerned with equity but focuses on fostering change that emphasizes achieving greater learning gains. Today, innovation is required most in equity, but the literature on that is scarce. For example, little effort is made to correlate innovations with reducing student dropouts or improving student achievement (Nichols, 2022) compared to the growing body of research that advocates for using learning analytics and artificial intelligence for that same purpose (Perrotta, 2021). When innovation is restricted to adopting technology-supported activities, the discussion regarding equitable implications focuses nearly solely on access and connectivity. In addition, inclusion often clashes with innovation since, to compete for middle-class students, some higher education institutions promote creative approaches above inclusive ones and sell them as their "institutional brand" (Baena et al., 2020). In developing contexts, where innovation in the provision of higher education is frequently equated with some forms of privatization (Lumadi, 2020; Verger et al., 2018), equity discussions rarely challenge the implications of alternative or innovative instructional strategies and instead focus on the neoliberal policy principles upon which the corresponding regulatory arrangements are based. In other words, the innovation rhetoric is more frequently associated with the need to disrupt the system than with the necessity of a fairer higher education provision from a social justice perspective.

The gap between innovation and equity discourses in higher education significantly influences the lack of desire and capacity for innovative initiatives to demonstrate their impact on enhancing learning outcomes. Innovators seem to be persuaded that national and (almost nonexistent) international assessments in higher education are incapable of quantifying the benefits of new models. This belief stems from a degree of ignorance regarding these assessments, which are erroneously charged with the original sin of evaluating only several indicators of public prestige, often associated with fundraising or research impact, and not the degree of development of the complex and transversal competencies, such as teamwork or problem solving, that the innovations seek to promote (Solomon & Lewin, 2016). Therefore, the argument arises that the innovations' intended outcomes cannot be evaluated using existing methods.

Thus, the second paradox is that the innovation imperative is acknowledged, but any attempt to analyze its consequences is denied so as not to distort the process; in other words, it is as if it were a question of continually inventing, but without regard for its results (Carrier, 2017). Higher education sector seems to take innovation as if it were just another buzzword but does not appear to have acquired the significance that innovation has had for decades in both the private business sector and the provision of public services (Sandamas, 2005). Indeed, in this larger context, innovation appears to be "the design and implementation of new procedures, products, services, and methods of delivering (public services) that result in significant advances in efficiency, effectiveness, or end quality" (Mulgan & Albury, 2003, p. 23).

Contrarily, educational innovation could be defined as a dynamic change that adds value to the processes that take place in an educational institution (in both the pedagogical and organizational fields), and that translates into improvements in student learning outcomes or the satisfaction of educational stakeholders, or both (OECD, 2010). This definition includes the operational nuance that only changes in procedures that result in demonstrable gains, particularly in learning, qualify as educational innovations. This entails acknowledging the presence of first-order changes without demonstrable effects or even bad impacts, i.e., changes that do not result in genuine innovations. However, the moral commitment that higher education institutions and instructors have to provide a learning environment that optimizes opportunities and contributes to its enhancement by relying on current knowledge and creating new evidence is disregarded by deliberately engaging in blind innovation (Bryk et al., 2015). Therefore, genuine educational innovations must utilize empirical research to establish their efficacy (Coburn et al., 2016). On the other hand, an innovation that cannot demonstrate the improvements it produces is merely a change whose effects are unknown and, in the worst case, chaotic or haphazard management of resources that could put student learning at risk.

Finally, higher education leaders should pay attention to innovation fatigue among teachers (Hargreaves & Shirley, 2009). This multidimensional phenomenon stems either from an overwhelming external need for change (e.g., expressed in continual changes in program prescriptions or internal restrictions) or from the incapacity of innovation to win the uphill struggle for sustainability. Ultimately, this exhaustion reflects the mismatch between rising expectations for innovation and the actual organizational, professional, and resource capacity of higher education institutions and faculty (Coburn et al., 2016). The result of external pressure that is not accompanied by mechanisms of recognition and support for the efforts that instructors make can be a resistant attitude that is determined to maintain the fundamentals of the traditional higher education model because, quite simply, it is more comfortable than the uncertainty of a continuous and not necessarily recognized effort.

5.8 Concluding Remarks: Towards Systemic Innovation

This examination of emerging trends suggests that, except for technological developments, innovations in content and methodologies and their organizational implications cannot be considered new in the strictest sense. It is possible to find precedents for each of the elements that currently dominate the landscape of innovation in higher education in a substantial portion of the progressive education initiatives of the 19th and early twentieth centuries: peer learning (Girard, 1835), the active method (Marion, 1888), project-based learning (Kilpatrick, 1918), interest centers (Decroly, 1907), and individualized teaching (Dewey, 1916).

Two conclusions can be drawn from the fact that the same innovations have persisted for over a century. On the one hand, the traditional model of higher education is solid and has served its purpose so well thus far that it is difficult to replace it (Darling-Hammond, 2010). Nevertheless, on the other hand, innovations continue along the same lines as they did a century ago, likely because they are the ones that make the most sense. They persist because we don't have the collective resources, financial, political, or cultural, to change them. Think about the model of how education is delivered through school: based on a nineteenth century factory model and unfit for purpose, often seriously questioned but remaining unchanged. The same can be said for higher education. However, whereas in the twentieth century, they did so due to the ideological conviction of their promoters, in the spirit of social reformism, they make more sense today because they are more in tune with the new demands of the economic and social context than the traditional higher education model.

Two different rationalities coincide in the imperative of educational innovation: the first seeks to respond to the needs derived from the new economy and an increasingly globalized and technology-dependent society; the second seeks to dignify the student as an actively and socially learning subject, placing her at the center of the learning process. Although contextual conditions change very rapidly, the broad global avenues of educational innovation appear consistent across the globe and, except for technology-related innovations, have been regarded as open and explored options for more than a century. If they are now receiving a more favorable social response and seem to be progressively adapted to previously unheard-of levels, it is because they meet the requirements of a new emergent social consensus on what and how to study in higher education.

To transform this impetus into a reforming force, we must consider how to disseminate not only the phenomenology of innovations (describing what they are like) but also their effects through empirical evaluations (demonstrating their added value); we must emphasize that innovations promote equity and improve educational opportunities for the most disadvantaged and vulnerable students in higher education; and, in short, we must be able to distinguish between the phenomenology of innovations and their effects.

Unfortunately, not every higher education institution is positioned to be innovative, and not every policy climate, both at the national and institutional levels, is favorable to educational innovation. In addition, research on educational innovations over the past few decades helps to identify the crucial variables that make an educational environment conducive to sustained innovation and that speak primarily to the capacity of educational institutions to absorb new ideas (Zahra & George, 2002). Institutional policies may help in promoting by, for example, incentivizing the establishment of educational leadership models that stimulate innovation (Knapp et al., 2014), or enhancing the stability of faculty, hence lowering their turnover.

In the health sector, a field with many parallels to education, remarks such as those just expressed would not be novel (Willingham, 2012): can anybody conceive of an advance in medical procedures or the prescribing of pharmaceuticals that would not be founded on comprehensive evaluation studies of their effects? More work is likely required in the higher education sector to bring the world of empirical evidence, with all its limitations, closer to classroom teaching practice so that the imperative of innovation does not seek change for its own sake but rather promotes change because it enhances students' learning opportunities. If this were to be accomplished, the higher education sector would have more tools to foster systemic innovation as opposed to spawning idiosyncratic breakthroughs that are, in the end, little more than summer flowers.

On the few occasions this has been carried out rigorously, the findings gained have been encouraging. For instance, comprehensive research by the U.S. National Academy of Sciences revealed the effectiveness of active approaches in developing scientific, engineering, and mathematics learning abilities (Freeman et al., 2014). More recently, another experimental investigation has revealed irrefutable proof that project-based learning improves learning outcomes (Duke et al., 2021). Of course, it could be argued that this is not new, as evidence accumulated even through research reviews long ago indicated this (Thomas, 2000). Unfortunately, evidence appears to be available only in restricted, specialized academic circuits where practitioners are rarely present, and no great effort is made to reach them—not to mention the lack of incentives for faculty to spend much effort on improving their teaching.

The most important question when talking about innovations in higher education is whether they work or not. Unfortunately, the pedagogical discourse about educational innovation is not very prone to the empirical assessment of results. However, the existing evidence, while scarce, points to some interesting facts. The attached Table 5.1 summarizes the existing evidence on assessing the results of the innovative trends.

The evidence on learning gains has been supplemented with reference to the cost estimate because what would be the point of promoting innovations that cannot be sustained over time because of the high cost they represent. In short, except the change in the orientation of study programs from content-based to competency-oriented, the three other innovative trends tend to have higher costs than traditional teaching and learning methods in higher education, spanning from two times to up to five times—and this increase comes as a result of the much-needed interaction that seems to be key for student success. Other than this, PBL seems to be worth the effort, given the benefits for learning results and student satisfaction. More mixed is the evidence about hybridization or distance education as it all comes down to one recurring problem, technology per se does not make a difference: what makes the difference is the teaching strategy.

The first implication is that educational innovation and empirical research must be brought closer together (Pedró, 2015). It is a process that necessitates policies supporting this reconciliation and promoting real empirical research for

5 Future Skills—Back into the Future? Emerging Trends ...

Table 5.1 Summary of existing empirical evidence on the learning gains and estimated costs of some innovations in higher education (Source: own representation)

Innovation	Evidence on learning gains	Cost estimates
Objective vs. Content	Nonexistent, but strong on cultural change	Marginal
PBL	• Enhances deep learning (ES = 0.11) (Dolmans et al., 2016) • Superior when it comes to long-term retention, skill development and satisfaction of students and teachers (Strobel & van Barneveld, 2009)	3 times traditional
Hybridization	Superior if used for PBL (ES = 0.5), better student engagement (Fukuzawa & Boyd, 2016)	2 times traditional
Distance education	No significant difference (phenomenon) but interaction is critical for retention and gains (Martin et al., 2022; Zhao et al., 2005)	3–5 times traditional, depending on degree of interaction

teaching improvement in higher education. It explains with evidence the added value of the many innovation avenues and the elements that define their relevance and effect. However, it also requires policies that provide faculty members who wish to innovate with the tools of empirical research and the professional skills that allow them to translate evidence into improved teaching practices (Bryk et al., 2015).

There is a pending agenda for higher education institutions and teachers. There is no shortage of empirical evidence about what works, with many dedicated academic journals. Unfortunately, these journals seem to serve more the interests of academics working on teaching and learning from various perspectives rather than the professional interests of teachers themselves. There is probably a need to introduce a new culture that promotes that faculty with teaching responsibilities understand the importance of accepting that they need to undergo a professional development process because being an excellent researcher does not equate to becoming an acceptable teacher. A passionate researcher can be an excellent role model. However, even the most experienced academic could benefit from a better understanding of the scientific laws that govern learning and from joining forces with other colleagues to learn in a collegial community about what works in teaching in higher education and why and how to translate that research-based knowledge into better practices. Educational innovation needs to move from the current stage of blind testing into a more scientific approach for those expected to promote a scientific approach to problem-solving, precisely.

Today, the word "higher education" or "university" evokes the same mental image everywhere in the world: that of a structure with classrooms where students await their professor's lecturing. Moreover, there is a wide societal belief that this old model no longer serves the interests and demands of the twenty-first century. However, the fact is that we are still unsure of the mental picture of higher education that will replace the one that still populates our minds. This likely explains why there are so many parallel paths of innovation, none of which have ever produced an alternative image with sufficient strength to be universally accepted. Twenty-five years have passed since Sarason (1996) said that it was time to replace intuitions and reasoning as much as possible with reliable, usable, and pertinent data. Only when we have substantial evidence on the many avenues of educational innovation will we be able to jointly determine what higher education in the twenty-first century should be like and make it a reality for every student. We are already late.

References

Arias Ortiz, E., & Cristia, J. (2014). *El BID y la tecnología para mejorar el aprendizaje: ¿cómo promover programas efectivos?* Banco Interamericano de Desarrollo.

Aronowitz, S., & Giroux, H. A. (2000). The corporate university and the politics of education. *The Educational Forum, 64*(4), 332–339. https://doi.org/10.1080/00131720008984778.

Asarta, C. J., Chambers, R. G., & Harter, C. (2021). Teaching methods in undergraduate introductory economics courses: Results from a sixth national quinquennial survey. *The American Economist, 66*(1), 18–28.

Avent, C., & Richardson, L. (2022). Analyzing distance learning during COVID-19 to innovate future course delivery. *Business Education Innovation Journal, 13*(13), 158.

Babcock, P., & Marks, M. (2011). The falling time cost of college: Evidence from half a century of time use data. *Review of Economics and Statistics, 93*(2), 468–478.

Baena, S., Collet-Sabé, J., Garcia-Molsosa, M., & Manzano, M. (2020). More innovation, less inclusion? Debates and discussions regarding the intersectionality of innovation and inclusion in the Catalan school system: a position paper. *International Journal of Inclusive Education,* 1–13.

Barrichello, A., Morano, R. S., Feldmann, P. R., & Jacomossi, R. R. (2020). The importance of education in the context of innovation and competitiveness of nations. *International Journal of Education Economics and Development, 11*(2), 204–224.

Barron, B., & Darling-Hammond, L. (2008). *Teaching for meaningful learning: A review of research on inquiry-based and cooperative learning.* Edutopia.

Bates, S. M. (2012). *The social innovation imperative: Create winning products, services, and programs that solve society's most pressing challenges.* McGraw-Hill.

Berger, P. L., & Luckmann, T. (1966). *The social construction of reality. A treatise in the sociology of knowledge.* Penguin Books.

Biasi, B., Deming, D. J., & Moser, P. (2021). *Education and innovation.*

Bona, C. (2016). *Las escuelas que cambian el mundo.* Plaza & Janés.

Bowles, M., Bowes, N., & Wilson, P. (2019). Future-proof human capabilities: Raising the future employability of graduates. *International Journal of Business and Social Science, 10*(11), 18–29.

Bryk, A. S., Gomez, L. M., Grunow, A., & LeMahieu, P. G. (2015). *Learning to improve: How America's schools can get better at getting better.* Harvard Education Press.

Carbonell, J. (2015). *Pedagogías del siglo XXI: Alternativas para la innovación educativa.* Octaedro.

Carrier, N. (2017). How educational ideas catch on: The promotion of popular education innovations and the role of evidence. *Educational Research, 59*(2), 228–240. https://doi.org/10.1080/00131881.2017.1310418.

Cheslock, J. J., & Jaquette, O. (2022). Concentrated or fragmented? The U.S. Market for online higher education. *Research in Higher Education, 63*(1), 33–59. https://doi.org/10.1007/s11162-021-09639-7.

Christensen, C. M., Horn, M. B., & Johnson, C. W. (2008). *Disrupting class. How disruptive innovation will change the way the world learns.* McGraw Hill.

Coburn, C. E., Hill, H. C., & Spillane, J. P. (2016). Alignment and accountability in policy design and implementation: The Common Core State Standards and implementation research. *Educational Researcher, 45*(4), 243–251.

Comi, S., Argentin, G., Gui, M., Origo, F., & Pagani, L. (2016). *Is it the way they use it?* Economics of Education Review. Advance online publication. https://doi.org/10.1016/j.econedurev.2016.11.007.

Crisol-Moya, E., Romero-López, M. A., & Caurcel-Cara, M. J. (2020). Active methodologies in higher education: Perception and opinion as evaluated by professors and their students in the teaching-learning process. *Frontiers in Psychology, 11,* 1703.

Cuban, L. (1988). *The managerial imperative and the practice of leadership in schools.* State Universtiy of New York.

Darling-Hammond, L. (2010). *The flat world and education. How America's commitment to equity Will determine our future.* Teachers College Press.

Decroly, O. (1907). *Le programme d'une école dans la vie.* Fondation Ovide Decroly-Centre d'Études decrolyennes.

Dewey, J. (1916). *Democracy and education: An introduction to the philosophy of education.* Macmillan

Dolmans, D. H., Loyens, S. M. M., Marcq, H., & Gijbels, D. (2016). Deep and surface learning in problem-based learning: A review of the literature. *Advances in Health Sciences Education, 21*(5), 1087–1112.

Drucker, P. F. (1998). The discipline of innovation. *Harvard Business Review, 76*(6), 149–157.

Duke, N. K., Halvorsen, A.-L., Strachan, S. L., Kim, J., & Konstantopoulos, S. (2021). Putting PjBL to the test: The impact of project-based learning on second graders' social studies and literacy learning and motivation in low-ses school settings. *American Educational Research Journal, 58*(1), 160–200. https://doi.org/10.3102/0002831220929638.

Ehlers, U.-D. (2020). *Future skills: The future of learning and higher education.*

Ehlers, U.-D. (2022). Future skills as new currency for the world of tomorrow. In R. Sharpe, S. Bennett, & T. Varga-Atkins (Eds.), *Handbook of digital higher education* (pp. 84–98). Elgar.

Elmore, R. F. (2004). *School reform from the inside out: Policy, practice, and performance.* Harvard Education Press.

English, M. C., & Kitsantas, A. (2013). Supporting student self-regulated learning in problem-and project-based learning. *Interdisciplinary Journal of Problem-Based Learning, 7*(2), 6.

Falck, O., Mang, C., & Woessmann, L. (2015). Virtually no effect? Different uses of classroom computers and their effect on student achievement. *CESifo Working Paper Series* (5266).

Foray, D., & Raffo, J. (2012). *Business-driven innovation: Is it making a difference in education? An analysis of educational patents* (OECD Education Working Papers 84).

Fowler, C. S., & Walter, S. (2020). Instructional leadership: New responsibilities for a new reality. *College & Research Libraries News, 64*(7), 465–468.

Freeman, S., Eddy, S. L., McDonough, M., Smith, M. K., Okoroafor, N., Jordt, H., et al. (2014). Active learning increases student performance in science, engineering, and mathematics. *Proceedings of the National Academy of Sciences, 111*(23), 8410–8415.

Fukuzawa, S., & Boyd, C. (2016). Student engagement in a large classroom: Using technology to generate a hybridized problem-based learning experience in a large first year undergraduate class. *Canadian Journal for the Scholarship of Teaching and Learning, 7*(1), 7.

Gallagher, S. E., & Savage, T. (2020). Challenge-based learning in higher education: an exploratory literature review. *Teaching in Higher Education,* 1–23.

Girard, J.-B. (1835). *Des moyens de stimuler l'activité dans les écoles.* Actes de la Société suisse d'utilité publique.

Godin, B., Gaglio, G., & Vinck, D. (2021). *Handbook on alternative theories of innovation.* Elgar.

Goglio, V. (2019). *The landscape of MOOCs and higher education in Europe and the USA.* European MOOCs Stakeholders Summit, 2019.

Hall, T., Wegerif, R., Loper, S., Ní Chróinín, D., & O'Brien, E. (2022). Digital education futures: Design for doing education differently. *Irish Educational Studies, 41*(1), 1–4. https://doi.org/10.1080/03323315.2021.2022072.

Hardy, I. (2020). *School reform in an Era of standardization: Authentic accountabilities.* Routledge.

Hardy, I. (2021). The quandary of quantification: Data, numbers and teachers' learning. *Journal of Education Policy, 36*(1), 44–63.

Hargreaves, A., & Shirley, D. L. (2009). *The fourth way: The inspiring future for educational change*. Corwin Press.

Hart Associates. (2016). *Trends in learning outcomes assessment*. Key Findings from a Survey among Administrators at AAC&U Member Institutions.

Heckman, J. J., & Kautz, T. (2014). Fostering and measuring skills. In J. J. Heckman, J. E. Humphries, & T. Kautz (Eds.), *The myth of achievement tests. The GED and the role of character in American life* (pp. 25–86). The University of Chicago Press.

Hunt, T., Carter, R., Zhang, L., & Yang, S. (2020). Micro-credentials: The potential of personalized professional development. *Development and Learning in Organizations: An International Journal, 34*(2), 33–35. https://doi.org/10.1108/DLO-09-2019-0215.

Johnson, N., Seaman, J., & Veletsianos, G. (2021). *Teaching during a pandemic: Spring transition, fall continuation, Winter evaluation*. https://www.bayviewanalytics.com/reports/teachingduringapandemic.pdf.

Kilpatrick, W. H. (1918). The project method. *Teachers College Record, 19*(4), 1–5.

Knapp, M. S., Copland, M. A., Honig, M. I., Plecki, M. L., & Portin, B. S. (2014). Practicing and supporting learning-focused leadership in schools and districts. *Learning-focused leadership in action: Improving instruction in schools and districts,* 181–210

Kotsiou, A., Fajardo-Tovar, D. D., Cowhitt, T., Major, L., & Wegerif, R. (2022). A scoping review of Future Skills frameworks. *Irish Educational Studies, 41*(1), 171–186. https://doi.org/10.1080/03323315.2021.2022522.

Leithwood, K., & Jantzi, D. (2005). *How leadership influences student learning*. The Wallace Foundation.

Leon, R.-D. (2016). The development of the future european knowledge workers. An academic perspective. *Management Dynamics in the Knowledge Economy, 4*(3), 339–356.

Lo, C. K., & Hew, K. F. (2017). A critical review of flipped classroom challenges in K-12 education: Possible solutions and recommendations for future research. *Research and Practice in Technology Enhanced Learning, 12*(1), 4.

Lumadi, M. W. (2020). School finance reform for curriculum innovation: An equity prospect. *South African Journal of Education, 40*(4).

Maguire, M., Ball, S. J., & Braun, A. (2013). What ever happened to…? Personalised learning as a case of policy dissipation. *Journal of Education Policy, 28*(3), 322–338.

Marion, H. (1888). La méthode active. *Revue pédagogique* (1), 1–19

Marklund, G., Vonortas, N. S., & Wessner, C. W. (2009). *Innovation imperative: National innovation strategies in the global economy*. Elgar.

Martin, F., Sun, T., Westine, C., & Ritzhaupt, A. (2022). Examining research on the impact of distance and online learning: A second-order meta-analysis study. *Educational Research Review,* 100438

Meyer, J. W., Kamens, D., & Benavot, A. (1992). *School knowledge for the masses*. Falmer Press.

Meyer, J. W., Boli, J., Thomas, G. M., & Ramirez, F. O. (1997). World society and the nation-state. *American Journal of Sociology, 103*(1), 144–181.

Miller, A. N., Sellnow, D. D., & Strawser, M. G. (2021). Pandemic pedagogy challenges and opportunities: Instruction communication in remote, HyFlex and BlendFlex courses. *Communication Education, 70*(2), 202–204. https://doi.org/10.1080/03634523.2020.1857418.

Mulgan, G., & Albury, D. (2003). *Innovation in the public sector*. Strategy Unit, UK Cabinet Office.

Murnane, R. J., & Nelson, R. R. (1984). Production and innovation when techniques are tacit. The case of education. *Journal of Economic Behaviour and Organization* (5), 353–373.

Neubert, J., Mainert, J., Kretzschmar, A., & Greiff, S. (2015). The assessment of 21st century skills in industrial and organizational psychology: Complex and collaborative problem solving. *Industrial and Organizational Psychology, 8*(2), 238–268.

Nichols, T. P. (2022). *Building the innovation school: Infrastructures for equity in today's classrooms*. Teachers College Press.

Nordin, A., & Sundberg, D. (2016). Travelling concepts in national curriculum policy-making: The example of competencies. *European Educational Research Journal, 15*(3), 314–328.

OECD. (2009). *Evaluating and rewarding the quality of teachers: International practices*. OECD.

OECD. (2010). *Inspired by technology, driven by pedagogy: A systemic approach to technology-based school innovations* (1st ed.). OECD.

OECD. (2018). *The future of education and skills: Education 2030*. https://www.oecd.org/education/2030/E2030%20Position%20Paper%20(05.04.2018).pdf.

O'Flaherty, J., & Phillips, C. (2015). The use of flipped classrooms in higher education: A scoping review. *The Internet and Higher Education, 25*, 85–95.

Partnership for 21st Century Skills. (2016). *Framework for 21st century learning*.

Pedró, F. (2015). Las políticas de investigación e innovación en educación: una perspectiva supranacional. *Bordón Revista de Pedagogía*, 39–56.

Pedró, F. (2016). *Tecnologías para la transformación de la educación*. Fundación Santillana.

Perrotta, C. (2021). Programming the platform university: Learning analytics and predictive infrastructures in higher education. *Research in Education, 109*(1), 53–71. https://doi.org/10.1177/0034523720965623.

Pietarinen, J., Pyhältö, K., & Soini, T. (2017). Large-scale curriculum reform in Finland–exploring the interrelation between implementation strategy, the function of the reform, and curriculum coherence. *The Curriculum Journal, 28*(1), 22–40.

Prain, V., Cox, P., Deed, C., Dorman, J., Edwards, D., Farrelly, C., et al. (2013). Personalised learning: Lessons to be learnt. *British Educational Research Journal, 39*(4), 654–676. https://doi.org/10.1080/01411926.2012.669747.

Raffo, C. (2014). *Improving educational equity in urban contexts*. Routledge.

Red Indices (2021). *Panorama de la educación superior en Iberoamérica a través de la Red Indices* (Papeles del Observatorio 22). Buenos Aires.

Rinkinen, S., & Harmaakorpi, V. (2018). The business ecosystem concept in innovation policy context: Building a conceptual framework. *Innovation: the European journal of social science research, 31*(3), 333–349.

Robinson, K. (2010). *The element: How finding your passion changes everything*. Penguin Books.

Sandamas, C. (2005). Innovation in public services: Literature review. *Innovation Forum* (April), 1–20.

Sarason, S. B. (1996). *Revisiting "the culture of the school and the problem of change."* Teachers College Press.

Schröder, A., & Krüger, D. (2019). Social innovation as a driver for new educational practices: Modernising, repairing and transforming the education system. *Sustainability, 11*(4), 1070.

Selwyn, N. (2015). Technology and education—Why it's crucial to be critical. In S. Bulfin, N. F. Johnson, & C. Bigum (Eds.), *Critical perspectives on technology and education* (pp. 245–255). Palgrave Macmillan.

Smith, L. (2008). *Schools that change: Evidence-based improvement and effective change leadership.* Corwin Press.

Solomon, Y., & Lewin, C. (2016). Measuring 'progress': Performativity as both driver and constraint in school innovation. *Journal of Education Policy, 31*(2), 226–238. https://doi.org/10.1080/02680939.2015.1062147.

Sosa Díaz, M. J., Guerra Antequera, J., & Cerezo Pizarro, M. (2021). Flipped classroom in the context of higher education: Learning, satisfaction and interaction. *Education Sciences, 11*(8), 416.

Strobel, J., & van Barneveld, A. (2009). When is PBL more effective? A meta-synthesis of meta-analyses comparing PBL to conventional classrooms. *Interdisciplinary Journal of Problem-Based Learning, 3*(1), 44–58.

Succi, C., & Canovi, M. (2020). Soft skills to enhance graduate employability: Comparing students and employers' perceptions. *Studies in Higher Education, 45*(9), 1834–1847.

Sursock, A. (2015). *Trends 2015: Learning and teaching in European universities* (EUA Reports 2015). https://eua.eu/downloads/publications/trends%202015%20learning%20and%20teaching%20in%20european%20universities.pdf.

Thomas, J. W. (2000). *A review of research on project based learning.* Autodesk Foundation.

Tye, B. B. (2000). *Hard truths: Uncovering the deep structure of schooling.* Teachers College Press.

UNESCO (2011). *Transforming education: The power of ICT policies.* Unesco.

Verger, A., Zancajo, A., & Fontdevila, C. (2018). Experimenting with educational development: International actors and the promotion of private schooling in vulnerable contexts. In G. Steiner-Khamsi & A. Draxler (Eds.), *The state, business and education* (pp. 16–38). Elgar.

Vuori, J. (2019). Distributed leadership in the construction of a new higher education campus and community. *Educational Management Administration & Leadership, 47*(2), 224–240.

Wilcox, K. C., Lawson, H. A., & Angelis, J. I. (Eds.) (2017). *Innovation in odds-beating schools: Exemplars for getting better at getting better.*

Wilcox, K. C., Lawson, H. A., & Angelis, J. I. (2017). Schools as innovation-ready learning organizations. In K. C. Wilcox, H. A. Lawson, & J. I. Angelis (Eds.), *Innovation in odds-beating schools: Exemplars for getting better at getting better* (pp. 1–18).

Wiley, D., Bliss, T. J., & McEwen, M. (Eds.). (2014a). *Handbook of research on educational communications and technology.* Springer.

Wiley, D., Bliss, T. J., & McEwen, M. (2014b). Open educational resources: A review of the literature. In D. Wiley, T. J. Bliss, & M. McEwen (Eds.), *Handbook of research on educational communications and technology* (pp. 781–789). Springer.

Williamson, B. (2017). Educating Silicon Valley: Corporate education reform and the reproduction of the techno-economic revolution. *Review of Education, Pedagogy, and Cultural Studies, 39*(3), 265–288.

Willingham, D. T. (2012). *When can you trust the experts? How to tell good science from bad in education.* Jossey-Bass.

Wilson, J. L. (2018). *Student learning in higher education: A Halsted press book.* Routledge.

World Economic Forum (2022). *Jobs of tomorrow: The triple returns of social jobs in the economic recovery.* Geneva.

Zahra, S. A., & George, G. (2002). Absorptive capacity: A review, reconceptualization, and extension. *Academy of Management Review, 27*(2), 185–203.

Zhao, Y., Lei, J., Yan, B., Lai, C., & Tan, S. (2005). What makes the difference? A practical analysis of research on the effectiveness of distance education. *Teachers College Record, 107*(8), 1836–1884.

Francesc Pedró is the director of the UNESCO International Institute for Higher Education in Latin America and the Caribbean. He is professor of education policy at the Pompeu Fabra University (Barcelona) and has worked as senior policy analyst at the OECD Centre for Educational Research and Innovation and at UNESCO as chief of education policy. He has published widely in education policy, higher education, and education technology.

Open Access This chapter is licensed under the terms of the Creative Commons Attribution 4.0 International License (http://creativecommons.org/licenses/by/4.0/), which permits use, sharing, adaptation, distribution and reproduction in any medium or format, as long as you give appropriate credit to the original author(s) and the source, provide a link to the Creative Commons license and indicate if changes were made.

The images or other third party material in this chapter are included in the chapter's Creative Commons license, unless indicated otherwise in a credit line to the material. If material is not included in the chapter's Creative Commons license and your intended use is not permitted by statutory regulation or exceeds the permitted use, you will need to obtain permission directly from the copyright holder.

Teaching the Skills Needed for the Future

6

Tony Bates

Abstract

Technology is leading to massive changes in the economy, in the way we communicate and relate to each other, and increasingly in the way we learn. Teachers and instructors are faced with a massive challenge of change. There are many opportunities in even the most academic courses to develop intellectual and practical skills that will carry over into work and life activities in a digital age, without corrupting the values or standards of academia. Even in vocational courses, students need opportunities to practice intellectual or conceptual skills such as problem-solving, communication skills, and collaborative learning. The chapter explores the skills that will be needed, and ways in which such skills can be developed. It approaches questions such as how we can ensure that we are developing the kinds of graduates from our courses and programs that are fit for an increasingly volatile, uncertain, complex, and ambiguous future as well as how we can teach or help students develop the skills they will need in the twenty-first century.

T. Bates (✉)
Research Associate at Contact North,
Tony Bates Associates Ltd./Contact North, Ontario, Canada
e-mail: tony.bates@ubc.ca

© The Author(s) 2024
U.-D. Ehlers and L. Eigbrecht (eds.), *Creating the University of the Future*, Zukunft der Hochschulbildung - Future Higher Education,
https://doi.org/10.1007/978-3-658-42948-5_6

6.1 Introduction

In a digital age, we are surrounded, indeed, immersed, in technology. Furthermore, the rate of technological change shows no sign of slowing down. Technology is leading to massive changes in the economy, in the way we communicate and relate to each other, and increasingly in the way we learn.

Economically, competitive advantage goes increasingly to those companies and industries that can leverage gains in knowledge (OECD, 2013). Indeed, knowledge workers often create their own jobs, starting up companies to provide new services or products that did not exist before they graduated.

From a teaching perspective, the biggest impact is likely to be on technical and vocational instructors and students, where the knowledge component of formerly mainly manual skills is expanding rapidly. Particularly in the trades' areas, plumbers, welders, electricians, car mechanics and other trade-related workers are needing to be problem-solvers, IT specialists and increasingly self-employed business people, as well as having the manual skills associated with their profession.

Artificial intelligence (AI) is another development that is already affecting the workforce. Routine work, whether clerical or manual, is being increasingly replaced by automation. Although all kinds of jobs are likely to be affected by increased automation and applications of AI, those in the workforce with lower levels of education are likely to be the most impacted. Those with higher levels of education are likely to have a better chance of finding work that machines cannot do as well—or even creating new work for themselves.

Thus, teachers and instructors are faced with a massive challenge of change. How can we ensure that we are developing the kinds of graduates from our courses and programs that are fit for an increasingly volatile, uncertain, complex, and ambiguous future? In particular, how can we teach or help students develop the skills they will need in the twenty-first century? This chapter explores the skills that will be needed, and ways in which such skills can be developed.

6.2 The Skills Needed in a Digital Age

Learning involves two strongly inter-linked but different components: content and skills. Content (often called knowledge) includes facts, ideas, principles, evidence, and descriptions of processes or procedures ('knowing'). Skills include understanding, analyzing, evaluating, applying: 'doing' (Kassema, 2019). Both are essential components of learning. Skills can be both cognitive (for example, critical thinking) or emotional (for example, motivation).

6 Teaching the Skills Needed for the Future

I use the terms 'skills' and 'competencies' in somewhat different ways. Competencies are defined as a combination of knowledge, skills and attitudes applied appropriately to a context in order to achieve a desired outcome. Competencies (or competences in Europe) usually require a relative short course in duration and are specific to certain tasks (often but not necessarily defined by employers). Unlike competencies, many 'high-level' soft skills such as critical thinking are cumulative and do not have a clear endpoint. They are not necessarily tied to an immediate task.

My distinction between competence and skill is not hard and fast and there is in reality considerable overlap—a skill may require the building of several competencies—but in essence the difference is that competencies are specific and short-term whereas skills are more general and longer lasting. Individuals need these higher-level intellectual or soft skills to survive in a rapidly changing economic and technological environment, whereas a competency can easily become out of date as jobs change.

Soft skills need to be developed over a program (indeed a lifetime) rather than in a single course. Novak Djokovic kept winning at tennis not because he continued to get faster and stronger than younger players, but because he continued to hone his skills (including strategy and will-power) to a level that compensated for his diminishing strength and speed.

Most instructors and teachers are well trained in content and have a deep understanding of the subject areas in which they are teaching. Expertise in skills development though is another matter. The issue here is not so much that instructors do not help students develop skills—they do—but whether these intellectual skills match the needs of knowledge-based workers, and whether enough emphasis is given to skills development within the curriculum.

How do we then identify how to build critical thinking skills, for example from first year through to graduation in a particular discipline? How does the development of skills in later stages build on work done earlier in a program?

These are some of the questions I seek to address in this chapter.

6.2.1 The Needs of a Digital Society

Prediction is always risky, but usually the big trends in the future can already be seen in the present. The future will merely magnify these current conditions, or current conditions will result in a transformation that we can see coming but is not here yet. Examples are many:

- The Internet of Things where almost everything is digitally connected
- Autonomous vehicles and transportation

- Massive amounts of data about our personal lives being collected and analyzed to anticipate/predict/influence our future behavior
- Automation replacing and/or transforming human work and leisure
- State agencies and/or commercial oligopolies controlling access to and use of data
- Lack of transparency, corruption of messaging, and magnification of these distortions, in digital communications.

One thing is clear. We can either as individuals throw up our hands and leave all these developments to either state or commercial entities to manage in their own interests, or we can try to prepare ourselves so that we can influence or even control how these developments are managed, for the greater good.

This is what is meant when talking about developing twenty-first century or Future Skills, or preparing for a digital society, although in many ways the future has already arrived. We have a responsibility for ensuring our students are educated sufficiently so that they understand these issues and have the means by which to address them. This is a responsibility of every educator because it affects all areas of knowledge.

For instance, the science professor needs to instill in her students an ability to identify reliable and unreliable sources of scientific data, and an ability to apply that knowledge in ethical ways that benefit mankind. This is a particularly important responsibility for those teaching computer sciences. We need to teach about the dangers of unintended or unknown consequences of artificial intelligence applications and of automated analyses of mass data, potential biases in algorithms, and the need to audit and adjust automated procedures to avoid unforeseen but harmful consequences before they do damage.

Digital (rather than purely online) learning has a critical role to play, because in order to develop these skills our students' learning itself needs to be digitally embedded. Only by mastering technology can we control it.

6.2.2 What Skills?

The skills required in a knowledge society include the following (The Conference Board of Canada, 2014):

- *Communications skills*: as well as the traditional communication skills of reading, speaking and writing coherently and clearly, we need to add social media communication skills. These might include the ability to create a short You-

Tube video to capture the demonstration of a process or to make a sales pitch, the ability to reach out through the Internet to a wide community of people with one's ideas, to receive and incorporate feedback, to share information appropriately, to identify trends and ideas from elsewhere.

- *The ability to learn independently*: this means taking responsibility for working out what you need to know, and where to find that knowledge. This is an ongoing process in knowledge-based work because the knowledge base is constantly changing. Incidentally, this not necessarily academic knowledge, although that too is changing; it could be learning about new equipment, new ways of doing things, or learning who are the people you need to know to get the job done.

- *Ethics and Responsibility:* these are required to build trust (particularly important in informal social networks), but also because generally ethical and responsible behavior is in the long run more effective in a world where there are many different players, and a greater degree of reliance on others to accomplish one's own goals.

- *Teamwork and flexibility*: although many knowledge workers work independently or in very small companies, they depend heavily on collaboration and the sharing of knowledge with others in related but independent organizations. In small companies, it is essential that all employees work closely together, share the same vision for a company and help each other out. In particular, knowledge workers need to know how to work collaboratively, virtually and at a distance, with colleagues, clients and partners. The 'pooling' of collective knowledge, problem-solving and implementation requires good teamwork and flexibility in taking on tasks or solving problems that may be outside a narrow job definition but necessary for success.

- *Thinking skills* (critical thinking, problem-solving, creativity, originality, strategizing, for example): of all the skills needed in a knowledge-based society, these are the most important. Businesses increasingly depend on the creation of new products, new services, and new processes to keep down costs and increase competitiveness. Also, it is not just in the higher management positions that these skills are required. Trades people in particular are increasingly having to be problem-solvers rather than following standard processes, which tend to become automated. Anyone dealing with the public in a service function must identify needs and find appropriate solutions. Universities in particular have always prided themselves on teaching such intellectual skills, but the move to larger classes and more information transmission, especially at the undergraduate level, undermines this assumption.

- *Digital skills:* most knowledge-based activities depend heavily on the use of technology. However, the key issue is that these skills need to be embedded within the knowledge domain in which the activity takes place. This means, for instance, real estate agents knowing how to use geographical information systems to identify sales trends and prices in different geographical locations, welders knowing how to use computers to control robots examining and repairing pipes, radiologists knowing how to use new technologies that 'read' and analyze MRI scans. Thus, the use of digital technology needs to be integrated with and evaluated through the knowledge-base of the subject area.
- *Knowledge management:* this is perhaps the most over-arching of all the skills. Knowledge is not only rapidly changing with new research, new developments, and rapid dissemination of ideas and practices over the Internet, but the sources of information are increasing, with a great deal of variability in the reliability or validity of the information. Thus, the knowledge that an engineer learns at university can quickly become obsolete. There is so much information now in the health area that it is impossible for a medical student to master all drug treatments, medical procedures, and emerging science such as genetic engineering, even within an eight-year program. Thus, knowledge management is the key skill in a knowledge-based society: how to find, evaluate, analyze, apply, and disseminate information, within a particular context. Above all students need to know how to validate or challenge sources of information. Effective knowledge management is a skill that all graduates will need to employ long after graduation.

In 2018, the Royal Bank of Canada issued a report, called 'Humans Wanted'. This was based on an analysis of big data derived from job postings over a 12-month period on LinkedIn, in which the actual skills being requested by employers were identified and analyzed, and from which an analysis of the demand for different types of labor was conducted.

The report argued that there will be plenty of jobs in the future, but they will require different skills from those generally required at the present. In particular, many of the new skills needed will be what are perhaps confusingly called soft skills, such as attentive listening, critical thinking, digital fluency, active learning, etc. (confusing, because these 'soft skills' are often as difficult to cultivate as 'hard skills', and many of these skills, such as critical thinking, are not new but will become increasingly important). These are future skills that automation and AI cannot easily replicate or replace but which will be needed in the new digital economy.

6 Teaching the Skills Needed for the Future 129

Two of the main conclusions from the Royal Bank report were as follows:

- Canada's education system, training programs and labor market initiatives are inadequately designed to help Canadian youth navigate this new skills economy.
- Canadian employers are generally not prepared, through hiring, training, or retraining, to recruit and develop the skills needed to make their organizations more competitive in a digital economy.

6.2.3 Skills and Learning Outcomes

The Royal Bank of Canada and other studies highlight that it is becoming increasingly important to define learning outcomes in terms of skills acquisition. Such studies identify some of the issues around developing the knowledge and skills that students will need to succeed, not just in the workforce, but in life generally in the last three quarters of this century. However, such reports have barely touched the tip of this particular iceberg. Few studies have attempted to suggest how students can develop these skills or what instructors need to do to help students develop such skills.

When developing curricula, in terms of deciding not only what but also how to teach, we need to ask the following questions:

(a) Are programs clearly identifying the learning outcomes expected from a program of study?
(b) Do these learning outcomes sufficiently take into account skills as well as content/topics?
(c) Are these learning outcomes relevant for a digital society?

In other words, we have a major pedagogical challenge in several parts:

- Identifying the most important soft skills that students will need
- Identifying the best way to teach such soft skills
- Assessing students' ability in soft skills
- Identifying the extent to which soft skills are generalizable.

The key point here is that content and skills are tightly related but as much attention needs to be given to skills development as to content acquisition to ensure that learners graduate with the necessary knowledge and skills for a digital age.

6.2.4 Education and the Labor Market

However, there is a real danger in tying university, college, and school programs too closely to immediate labor market needs. Labor market demand can shift very rapidly and, in particular, in a knowledge-based society, it is impossible to judge what kinds of work, business or trades will emerge in the future.

The focus on the skills needed in a digital age raises questions about the purpose of universities in particular, but also schools and vocational colleges to some extent. Is their purpose to provide ready-skilled employees for the workforce? Is it really the job of historians or physicists to teach skills such as attentive listening, time management or social perceptiveness?

Certainly, the rapid expansion in higher education is largely driven by government, employers and parents wanting a workforce that is employable, competitive and if possible affluent. Indeed, preparing professional workers has always been one role for universities, which have a long tradition of training for the church, law, and much later, government administration. The goal for education now should be to ensure that as well as a deep understanding of the content and core values of a subject discipline, students can also develop skills that enable them to apply such knowledge in appropriate contexts.

Secondly, focusing on the skills required for a knowledge-based society (often referred to as twenty-first century skills) merely reinforces the kind of learning, especially the development of intellectual skills, for which universities have taken great pride in the past. Indeed, in this kind of labor market, it is critical to serve the learning needs of the individual rather than specific companies or employment sectors. To survive in the current labor market, learners need to be flexible and adaptable, and should be able to work just as much for themselves as for corporations that increasingly have a very short operational life. The challenge then is not re-purposing education but making sure it meets that purpose more effectively.

Thirdly, enabling students to live well and to feel some measure of control in a technology-rich society is surely the responsibility of every educator. For instance, all students, whatever their discipline, need to know how to find, evaluate, analyze, and apply information within their specific subject discipline. With so much content of varying quality now available at one's fingertips, such skills are essential for a healthy society.

Thus, in some cases it is a language issue: instructors may be achieving some of these 'twenty-first century skills' such as critical thinking within the requirements of a specific discipline without using this terminology (for example, 'compare and contrast…' is a critical thinking activity).

6 Teaching the Skills Needed for the Future

However, the Higher Education Quality Council of Ontario (HEQCO) published a report in 2018 that claimed to be one of the first major attempts to measure employment-related skills in university and college students on a large scale (Weingarten et al., 2018). HEQCO used a test designed to evaluate students' ability to analyze evidence, understand implications and consequences, and develop valid arguments.

The HEQCO study found that high-level soft skills are hard to measure and probably need to be defined and communicated more clearly and purposefully by instructors. In particular, development of such skills needs to be considered at a program level so instructors can define what level of skill they expect of students when they arrive, and to what level that skill has been increased or improved by the end of a course or program.

A good example of this is from the Faculty of Computer Science at Dalhousie University in Canada. The department developed a chart (Fig. 6.1 below) showing the inter-relatedness between specific learning outcomes, course content, and course and learning outcome sequencing, so that each instructor understood what level of skills and outcomes students would have from previous courses, and could identify what levels of skills they were passing on when students left their course (Fig. 6.2 below). One result of this was to move the theory courses from the fourth year to the first year, as this helped students in the later stages of the program.

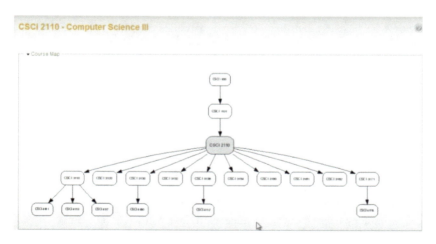

Fig. 6.1 Required sequence of courses for Bachelor of Computer Sciences, Dalhousie University, Canada

Fig. 6.2 Examples of the learning outcomes/skills required before beginning a course, and on completion of a course

Focusing on twenty-first century or future skills does not challenge, in any way, core disciplinary values or make universities or colleges merely preparatory schools for business, but they do ensure that students leave with skills that prepare them well for living in a very challenging age.

6.2.5 Rethinking Teaching and Learning

These are essentially curriculum and pedagogical issues. It means rethinking not only the curriculum and how we teach it, but also the role that technology can play in developing such skills. How can technology increase empathy and understanding (for example, through creating virtual environments or simulations where students play the role of others)? How can technology be used to provide scenarios that enable skills development and testing in a safe environment? How can technology be used to enable students to solve real world problems?

There are a million possible answers to such questions, and they need to be answered by instructors and teachers—and by learners—with deep understanding of their subject matter. But subject knowledge alone is not enough if we are to

6 Teaching the Skills Needed for the Future 133

make the last three quarters of the twenty-first century a time when all people can thrive and feel free.

6.3 Teaching Future Skills in a Digital Age

Although skills such as critical thinking, problem-solving and creative thinking have always been valued in higher education, the identification and development of such skills is often implicit and almost accidental, as if students will somehow pick up these skills from observing faculty themselves demonstrating such skills or through some form of osmosis resulting from the study of content.

It is of course somewhat artificial to separate content from skills because content is the fuel that drives the development of intellectual skills. The aim here is not to downplay the importance of content, but to ensure that skills development receives as much focus and attention from instructors, and that we approach intellectual skills development in the same rigorous and explicit way as apprentices are trained in manual skills.

6.3.1 Developing Skills

What methods of teaching are most likely to develop soft skills? In fact, we can learn a lot from research about skills and skill development (Fallows & Steven, 2000; Fischer, 1980):

- Skills development is relatively context-specific. In other words, skills need to be embedded within a knowledge domain. For example, problem-solving in medicine is different from problem-solving in business. First of all, of course, the content base used to solve problems is different. Less well understood, though, is that somewhat different processes and approaches are used to solve problems in these domains (for instance, decision-making in medicine tends to be more deductive, business more intuitive; medicine is more risk averse, business is more likely to accept a solution that will contain a higher element of risk or uncertainty). Embedding skills within a particular context such as a subject discipline is perhaps the biggest challenge for educational institutions in a digital age. How well does an ability to think critically about English literature transfer to other areas of critical thinking, such as political analysis or assessing the behavior of a workplace colleague? In many cases, some elements of these soft skills do transfer well but other parts are more context specific. More attention needs to be paid to what is known about the transfer of skills, based on research, and to ensuring this evidence affects the way we teach.

- Learners need practice—often a good deal of practice—to reach mastery and consistency in a particular skill.
- Skills are often best learned in relatively small steps, with 'jumps' increasing as mastery is approached.
- Learners need feedback on a regular basis to learn skills quickly and effectively; immediate feedback is usually better than late feedback;
- Although skills can be learned by trial and error without the intervention of a teacher, coach, or technology, skills development can be greatly enhanced or speeded up with appropriate interventions, which means adopting appropriate teaching methods and technologies for skills development.
- Although *content* can be transmitted equally effectively through a wide range of media, *skills development* is much more tied to specific teaching approaches and technologies (discussed in more detail in Sect. 6.3. below, and Bates, 2022).

What are the implications of this for not only teaching methods, but also curriculum design? It is worth remembering that unlike competencies, many 'high-level' soft skills such as critical thinking are cumulative and do not have a clear endpoint.

6.3.2 Setting Goals for Skills Development

Thus, a critical step is to be explicit about what skills a particular course or program is trying to develop, and to define these goals in such a way that they can be implemented and assessed. In other words, it is not enough to say that a course aims to develop critical thinking, but to state clearly what this would look like in the context of the particular course or content area, in ways that are clear to students. In particular, skills should be defined in such a way that they can be assessed, and students should be aware of the criteria or rubrics that will be used for assessment.

6.3.3 Thinking Activities

These include activities that enable students to practice a range of skills, such as critical thinking, problem-solving, and decision-making. A skill is not binary, in the sense that you either have it or you don't. There is a tendency to talk about skills and competencies in terms of novice, intermediate, expert, and master but, in reality, skills require constant practice and application and there is, at least with regard to intellectual skills, no final destination. With practice and experience, for instance, our critical thinking skills should be much better at 65 than at 25 (although some might call that 'wisdom').

A major challenge over a full program is to ensure a steady progression in the level of a skill, so, for instance, a student's critical thinking skills are better when they graduate than when they started the program. This means identifying what level of skill they have before entering a course, as well as measuring it when they leave. So, it is critically important when designing a course or program to design activities that require students to develop, practice and apply thinking skills on a continuous basis, preferably in a way that starts with small steps and leads eventually to larger ones.

There are many ways in which intellectual skills can be developed and assessed, such as written assignments, project work, and focused discussion, but these thinking activities need to be designed, then implemented, on a consistent basis by the instructor.

6.3.4 Practical Activities

It is a given in vocational programs that students need lots of practical activities to develop their manual skills. This, though, is equally true for intellectual skills. Students need to be able to demonstrate where they are along the road to mastery, get feedback on it, and retry as a result. This means doing work that enables them to practice specific skills.

There are many ways that this can be done. To give just one example, students would be asked to cover and understand the essential content in the first three weeks, do research in a group, develop an agreed project report, in the form of an e-portfolio, share it with other students and the instructor for comments, feedback and assessment, and present their report orally and online. Ideally, they will have the opportunity to carry over many of these skills into other courses where the skills can be further refined and developed. Thus, with skills development, a longer-term horizon than a single course will be necessary, so integrated program as well as course planning is important.

6.3.5 Discussion as a Tool for Developing Intellectual Skills

Discussion is a very important tool for developing thinking skills. However, not any kind of discussion. Academic knowledge requires a different kind of thinking to everyday thinking. It usually requires students to see the world differently, in terms of underlying principles, abstractions and ideas (Laurillard, 2002).

Thus, discussion needs to be carefully managed by the instructor, so that it focuses on the development of skills in thinking that are integral to the area of study. This requires the instructor to plan, structure and support discussion within the class, keeping the discussions in focus, and providing opportunities to demonstrate how experts in the field approach topics under discussion, and comparing students' efforts.

6.3.6 Measuring Skills

Another challenge is measuring skills. I was once questioned by a colleague when I said my students were learning to think critically.

'How do you know?' he said.

My answer was: 'I know it when I see it in their assessments.'

'But how will your students know what you are looking for if you can't describe it in advance?'.

The HEQCO study mentioned earlier found that final-year students had somewhat higher scores in literacy and numeracy than their first-year counterparts, although there was considerable variation among programs, but little difference between the test scores of incoming and graduating students in critical-thinking abilities, although critical thinking ability too showed considerable variation among programs.

There are a number of possible criticisms of this study. One of the challenges that the HEQCO study faced was finding valid and reliable ways to assess soft skills. The first study measured literacy, numeracy and problem-solving abilities of adults using everyday scenarios. But why assess these skills outside the knowledge domains in which they were taught, given the importance of context? Were the measurements sensitive enough to really discriminate differences in skill development over time?

Nevertheless, it is worrying that HEQCO found that after four years of post-secondary study there was no noticeable difference in critical thinking skills.

6 Teaching the Skills Needed for the Future

Is this because this is not being well taught, or because the tests used were not valid? Any attempt to identify learning outcomes involving skills requires consideration from the beginning of how these skills can validly be assessed. Instructors should not complain about HEQCO's assessment methods if they cannot justify their own methods of identifying and assessing skills.

6.4 In Conclusion

There are many opportunities in even the most academic courses to develop intellectual and practical skills that will carry over into work and life activities in a digital age, without corrupting the values or standards of academia. Even in vocational courses, students need opportunities to practice intellectual or conceptual skills such as problem-solving, communication skills, and collaborative learning. However, this will not happen merely through the delivery of content. Instructors need to think carefully about:

- exactly what skills their students need to develop;
- how these skills fit with the nature of the subject matter;
- the kind of activities that will allow students to develop and improve their intellectual skills;
- how to give feedback and to assess those skills, within the time and resources available.

This is a very brief discussion of how and why skills development should be an integral part of any learning environment. However, effectively developing the skills needed in a digital age is critically important, not only for the economy, but also for the quality of life of our students.

Acknowledgements This is an edited version of Chap. 1 of *Teaching in a Digital Age*, by the same author.

References

Bates, T. (2022). *Teaching in a digital age: Guidelines for designing teaching and learning* (3rd ed.). Tony Bates Associates Ltd. https://pressbooks.bccampus.ca/teachinginadigitalagev3m/.

Fallows, S. J., & Steven, C. (2000). *Integrating key skills in higher education: Employability, transferable skills, and learning for life*. Kogan Page; Stylus Publishing Inc.

Fischer, K. W. (1980). A theory of cognitive development: The control and construction of hierarchies of skills. *Psychological Review, 87*(6), 477–531. https://doi.org/10.1037/0033-295X.87.6.477.

Kassema, J. J. (2019). Knowledge and skills: What do we know about it. *Humanities Education eJournal, 3*(6). https://doi.org/10.2139/ssrn.3381008.

Laurillard, D. (2002). *Rethinking university teaching: A conversational framework for the effective use of learning technologies* (2nd ed.). Routledge.

OECD. (2013). *OECD skills Outlook 2013: First results from the survey of adult skills*. OECD Publishing.

Royal Bank of Canada. (2018). Humans wanted: How Canadian youth can thrive in the age of disruption. Toronto. https://www.rbc.com/dms/enterprise/futurelaunch/_assets-custom/pdf/RBC-Future-Skills-Report-FINAL-Singles.pdf.

The Conference Board of Canada. (2014). Employability skills 2000+. https://ciel.viu.ca/sites/default/files/esp2000.pdf.

Weingarten, H. P., Brumwell, S., Chatoor, K., & Hudak, L. (2018). Measuring essential skills of postsecondary students: Final report of the essential adult skills initiative. Toronto. https://heqco.ca/wp-content/uploads/2020/02/FIXED_English_Formatted_EASI-Final-Report2.pdf.

Dr. Tony Bates is a private consultant specializing in online and distance learning. He was until recently Senior Advisor to the G. Raymond Chang School of Continuing Education at Ryerson University, and is a Research Associate at Contact North, both in Ontario, Canada.

Open Access This chapter is licensed under the terms of the Creative Commons Attribution 4.0 International License (http://creativecommons.org/licenses/by/4.0/), which permits use, sharing, adaptation, distribution and reproduction in any medium or format, as long as you give appropriate credit to the original author(s) and the source, provide a link to the Creative Commons license and indicate if changes were made.

The images or other third party material in this chapter are included in the chapter's Creative Commons license, unless indicated otherwise in a credit line to the material. If material is not included in the chapter's Creative Commons license and your intended use is not permitted by statutory regulation or exceeds the permitted use, you will need to obtain permission directly from the copyright holder.

Future Universities as Activating Resonance Spaces. New Roles in Society—Innovative Approaches

7

Wolfgang Stark

> **Abstract**
>
> This paper draws on more than five years of intensive debates and explorations with a large number of active and engaged citizens and scholars, teachers, students, staff and university leaders. It will sketch emerging pictures and patterns of the new role of universities as an Activating Resonance Space addressing future societal challenges—beyond teaching and research focused on an industrialized and business-driven world. Based on more than 15 years of engagement in community service learning as a participative and empowering approach of Project-Based Learning and teaching, the paper proposes important steps toward an institutionalization of transformative learning and teaching, which will address current and future societal challenges.

W. Stark (✉)
Organizational and Community Psychology; Organizational Development Laboratory and Center for Societal Learning and Social Responsibility, University of Duisburg-Essen, Essen, Germany
e-mail: wolfgang.stark@steinbeis-isl.de

© The Author(s) 2024
U.-D. Ehlers and L. Eigbrecht (eds.), *Creating the University of the Future*, Zukunft der Hochschulbildung - Future Higher Education,
https://doi.org/10.1007/978-3-658-42948-5_7

7.1 Changing Paradigms

Traditionally, higher education has been defined by the type of knowledge one had acquired—i.e., what you officially have been credited for (Bachelor/Master). According to this model, universities[1] educate highly specialized and excellent professionals and scientists/scholars.

The value of universities still is measured by the amount of explicit knowledge supposedly gained, by the amount of external funding spent, and by a scientific impact factor—which is measured by the number of citations in relevant scientific journals. What if universities of the future would need to go beyond just academic excellence? Should a "scientific impact factor" be supplemented by a "societal impact factor" (Håkansson, 2005; Smith, 2001; Weber et al., 2015), which measures the results of a university by the positive effects it has on the common good and civil society?

Universities today are challenged by new conditions and requirements based on basic changes both in technology and society: specialization and technological excellence may not be sufficient any more to address the growing complexity and challenges we are experiencing in our world. Therefore, in the future, educational success of Higher Education will have to be measured by how flexibly graduates can adapt to constantly changing environments and new requirements. For the twenty-first century and the future global challenges of an interconnected and increasingly complex world, we need a new understanding of learning: parallel to effective academic knowledge transfer and application, we need to foster the skills and competences of both students and faculty/staff of universities, how to address societal challenges and how to transform business, communities, and our societies for our common future. Hence, universities need to educate and establish joint learning spaces for a constant re-orientation and re-invention, both on individual, group, and institutional levels.

Frameworks and conditions for successful action in professional domains, everyday life and organizations have changed significantly: not only in the last 2 years of global pandemics, but for 10–15 years already. Thinking in terms of certainties, cause-effect relationships, input–output categories is no longer sufficient as the main school of thought, especially for people who act responsibly. We are moving into a "post-linear" age that demands new skills from societal actors: to

---

[1] In this paper, we use the term "universities" as a generic term for all subtypes of Higher Education Institutions, which may be different depending on country or region (research universities, academic universities, universities of applied sciences, specialized universities or colleges for art, music, dance…).

deal creatively with uncertainty (Stark et al., 2017), but also to identify and use opportunities and potentials for a new "world of resonant relationships" among actors, referring to researchers like Hartmut Rosa (2018) and Bruno Latour (2005, 2021).

A large part of the leaders in business and society have been, and still are, educated based on the model of "cause-and-effect" and "input–output", which is also paramount in an industrial world. Hence, their patterns of decision-making have a high impact on the future of our rapidly changing global civil society, but do not fit anymore with the complex challenges we are facing today and in the future.

As we are entering a "post-linear age", both managers and employees in our business world or social institutions, and politicians and active citizens will need to be characterized by a high level of self-reliance and collaborative competence. We all need to acquire skills to act both professionally and responsibly under conditions of high uncertainty. They do not deny imponderables in order to pretend confidence—they name and analyze imponderables in order to ask deeper questions. They do not restrict complex realities to supposedly secure, basic facts. Instead, they will be able to develop a comprehensive picture of a complex situation and ways to act responsibly in uncertainty. They will clarify personal considerations and priorities; act as opponents of "no alternatives" and as advocates of a conscious decision-making for one of several alternatives. They will name spheres of interest and channels of influence on decisions and thus complete the full picture of a decision-making situation.

However, parallel to our predominant idea of leadership, higher education today still, and largely, follows an idea of linearity and predictability; input–output relations. Therefore, the need for a higher education that cuts across disciplines and prepares students for ambiguity and non-linearity, supporting differentiated and complex thinking and action, becomes all the more evident. As future responsible leaders, leading networks, and groups to influence the "post-linear age" will be significantly shaped by the cultures and academic narratives of our universities, the core of a future university therefore rather should be transdisciplinary: "thinking outside of the box", deeper learning from errors, encouraging experimentation, and foster a culture of critical and productive questioning. To promote a true "culture of deeper learning" (Reimers, 2021) within and between civil society, business, and our societal institutions, we need to develop personalities and identities of future generations and leaders by reinforcing social and societal responsibility and a sense of community (Heidbrink & Hirsch, 2006).

In higher education strategy development, we have been experiencing a strange discrepancy since I have entered the university system as a teacher and researcher some 25 years ago. We are stuck between:

- An uplifting demand and debate for reform, which sees universities as an intellectual and future-oriented basis for technical and social innovations for the demands of future global and networked civil societies (Mittelstraß, 2003)
- The actual structural changes, which tend to be short-tempered, adapting to political and economic interests and demands and bowing to the administration of quantitative measures and qualitative shortages instead of actively and creatively shaping them.

Therefore, the question remains of how to rethink higher education and universities in addition to and beyond digitalization. The first steps of developing our universities for "resonating" toward societal challenges have been made by establishing Campus-Community Partnerships between universities and civil society.

7.2   Campus-Community Partnerships

Universities and Higher Education Institutions (HEI), since the 1970s, have become increasingly business-oriented. This is why universities sometimes can be viewed as being designed according to the industrial model (Robinson & Robinson, 2022).[2] Growing awareness and competition toward global sustainability in the last 10 years promoted new strategies, unique selling propositions, and clear mission statements beyond excellence in research, as well as an expansion of university cooperation and funding options.

The concept of "Campus-Community Partnerships" is associated with a number of approaches toward the transformation of Higher Education: Community Service Learning (CSL), Community-Based Research (CBR), Community Co-Creation, University Civic Engagement, Social Entrepreneurship, Community Outreach, Engaged Universities and more.

Campus-Community Partnerships (CCP) (Stark et al., 2014) become relevant to higher education strategies, because they go beyond opening up a traditional "academic ivory-tower"; they also go beyond "university-business-relationships" which seemed to be prevalent for decades. In many universities, CCPs are part of HEI's mission statement, they can help to raise the profile of universities and, as a program, address fundamental questions of university development.

---

[2] A remarkable RSA Animate-video on a Ken Robinson TED-Talk shows the essence of this debate: https://youtu.be/zDZFcDGpL4U.

Campus-Community Partnerships integrate different formats in which universities (*campus*) and civil society actors (*community*) work on (practical or research) problems of the community for mutual (operational) benefit and act jointly in the process of working on them (*partnership*). Principles of CCP, like

1. Orientation towards the common good,
2. Generation of immediate or operational benefits for all participants, and
3. Collaborative process design at eye level,

distinguish Campus-Community Partnerships from other approaches focusing on collaboration between science and business.

Community Service Learning (CSL) (Aramburuzabala Higuera et al., 2019) has clear methodological similarities to Problem-Based Learning, Project Learning and Research-Based Learning. Programmatically, however, only CSL intends to focus on the common good and is therefore understood as a form of Campus-Community Partnership. Research projects often collaborate with organizations outside the university, including non-profit organizations. However, these organizations generally are *objects of* research and are researched without being involved. *Community-Based Research*, on the other hand, aims to include the legitimate interests of the university and the community partner in the research process, with regard to the research results and, if applicable, their utilization. *Voluntary engagement*, even if initiated and mediated by the university, usually focuses predominantly on the aspect of the common good. To be considered a Campus-Community Partnership in the above sense, it needs to be systematically linked to academic teaching/learning settings. A *Training Workshop* for executives of a company by the university can become a Campus-Community Partnership if, for example, a local school is involved as a participant and beneficiary.

The examples suggest added values that can be expected when existing practices are changed with Campus-Community Partnership principles in mind; in this respect, we see these principles as a prerequisite for harnessing all potentials for both universities and (civil) society.

7.3 Community Service Learning

Especially for the side of universities as primary initiators of Campus-Community Partnerships, a broader context is also central, which Ramaley's (2000) view of Community Service Learning illustrates:

> "Service learning can be viewed as a form of pedagogy designed to enhance learning and promote civic responsibility as well as one of a set of strategies to link the capacity of a college or a university to the needs of society" (Ramaley, 2000).

In the past decades, a growing number of universities in Europe are collaborating with local community partners beyond business. Based on a teaching format originally developed in the US, civic/public engagement is an integral part of curricula. *Community Service Learning* and its didactic and strategic approach has led to (mostly temporal, sometimes permanent) *Campus-Community Partnerships* which have become more relevant for higher education institutions who want to focus on a "social responsibility mission" beyond teaching and research. They aim not only at initiating social change and innovation within their local communities based on their academic resources, but simultaneously enhance individual values for social responsibility for their students and staff (Altenschmidt et al., 2009; Hofer & Derkau, 2020). As a result, a variety of national/regional Higher Education Networks on "Community Service Learning" and "Education for Societal Responsibility" have been growing since 2009.[3] The German University Network for Societal Responsibility[4] by now is the largest non-partisan university/college network in Germany. The European Association for Service Learning in Higher Education (EASLHE – https://www.easlhe.eu/) has been established as an international resource to expand the idea of community service learning for students, teachers, researchers and national/regional networks on a European scale.

Civic Engagement, Community Service Learning and Campus-Community Partnerships are closely interconnected. Community Service Learning is a pedagogical method which integrates Civic Engagement into academic teaching by addressing real-world problems of the community within the framework of student projects (Berger Kaye, 2010; Rosenkranz et al., 2019; Seifert et al., 2019). In Community Service Learning, practical Project-Based Teaching connects academic fields and disciplines with needs of real-life communities and challenges (Altenschmidt et al., 2009). Thus, society will benefit from Campus-Community Partnerships, while students can address significant actual issues in self-organized and responsible ways. Community Service Learning produces action- and experience-oriented learning environments that encourage strategies beyond linear problem-solving routines, substantive and continuous reflection, and the experience of practical problem-solving (Sliwka, 2007). New formats of Problem-

---

[3] Please find more information on Service Learning in Europe at https://www.easlhe.eu/

[4] More information at https://netzwerk-bdv.de/en/home/#about

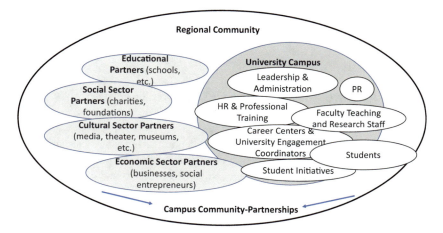

Fig. 7.1 Actors Represented in Community Service Learning. (Adapted from Ruda et al., 2015)

Based Learning combined with digitalized learning have been developed into a concept of "deeper learning" (Sliwka & Klopsch, 2021).

Community Service Learning can show positive impacts on the personal and social development of students and future leaders: they can gain a clearer sense of their identity, self-worth, and belonging, and develop fundamental key competences and social responsibility. Community Service Learning, on the one hand, can make education more meaningful and relevant. On the other hand, Campus-Community Partnerships have the potential to close the gap between educational institutions and their communities (Eyler & Giles, 1999).

Many actors may contribute to the field of Community Service Learning: the picture above (Fig. 7.1) shows which actors are represented or are likely to play a role in Community Service Learning and Campus-Community Partnerships.

Community Service Learning as a teaching approach is linking universities and civil society and is well known in some places on the globe (North and South America, Asia).[5] Elsewhere, Community Service Learning is still a relatively new

---

[5] International university networks on service learning, see https://talloiresnetwork.tufts.edu; https://www.researchslce.org

approach to teaching in Higher Education. In Europe, Ireland and Germany have been on the forefront to adopt this innovative teaching approach since around 2005.

7.4 An Innovative Approach Towards Teaching and Learning

Community Service Learning facilitates academic teaching and learning in collaboration with civil society: teaching is student-driven and practically oriented, linked to research, connected to real societal challenges, and aims to develop innovative solutions.

Project-Based Community Service Learning related to real-world challenges teaches students how to take responsibility for their own actions and for social concerns: *Programming a handicapped-accessible website, designing and implementing a sensory garden for dementia patients, developing PR or quality concepts for social institutions,* or *inventing new fundraising ideas*—depending on the field of study, many areas of application are conceivable. Off-campus involvement is embedded in the course of study. Many CSL projects are interdisciplinary: technical and methodological knowledge will be mutually shared and implemented in real-world settings.

Acting practically on the basis of theoretical knowledge promotes methodological and both social and personality-building skills in students. Depending on the learning setting, students test and expand their analytical, planning, and creative problem-solving strategies. They develop competencies for working in a team and dealing with conflicts, and demonstrate their communicative skills when working with "real" customers. Last but not least, the students experience how to make a difference and be significant, a decisive factor from a psychological point of view. Self-efficacy, the daily dose of "I am needed", is crucial for mental health and success. In this sense, Future Skills for Higher Education will be transformative and transdisciplinary, and may establish what Otto Scharmer calls "Vertical Literacy" (Scharmer, 2019; Stark, 2022).

One aspect that is very specific to Community Service Learning, and new to university teaching, is that CSL promotes the students' sense of social and democratic responsibility. An essential moment can be found here, which especially favors the development of social and personal competencies. The students perform a community service, move out of their "comfort zone" and view their social environment from different perspectives.

7.5 Universities and Students Co-Creating and Re-Designing Civil Society

The concept of Community Service Learning therefore opens up a multidimensional "added value" with regard to personality development of students, the networking of universities and the civil society environment, and the concrete benefit for public organizations and society in general.

"Universitas" emerges—in a novel sense—when scholars cross disciplinary and academic boundaries into practice, and help practitioners generate and bring new realities into the world. For research, another move may be equally important: practitioners cross the boundary into reflection and theoretical concepts inherent in their practice and outcomes will become accessible and fruitful to research discourses. A vibrant transformation of the university and higher education requires opening up to practice and its inherent potential for the future; to the practice of organizations, to the practice of individuals, to societal practice.

Learning within civil society projects generates a different depth of processing than is the case with lectures or even seminars. Experiential learning in the sense of John Dewey (1963) plays an important role here. According to his assumption, learning appears to be successful when it is oriented towards solving practical problems of action. If, in addition to imparting specialized knowledge, education also is important for promoting the potential of individuals and groups to proactively and collaboratively shape our democratic society (Scharmer, 2019), the actors of the universities, and especially the students, need to play an active part in these community-oriented efforts.

In this respect, universities need to develop their social and civic responsibility. They need to go beyond sustainability in the ecological sense, but also promote concrete civic engagement for democratic education (Baltes et al., 2007; Sliwka, 2007) and, through concepts such as service learning, enable a learning community of civil society and academic institutions for mutual benefit.

Promoting a sense of social responsibility in community-oriented projects (Community Service Learning) among students additionally raises the potential for engagement and innovation among students and faculty as a potential of universities; both of which are resources of civic development that have been underutilized in Germany to date. According to destatis,[6] approximately 2.9 million

---

[6] https://www.destatis.de/DE/Presse/Pressemitteilungen/2022/11/PD22_503_21.html

students at universities and colleges in Germany hold an invaluable potential for public engagement on federal, regional or community levels. If academic learning and civic engagement can be combined, not only the gap between democratic education and engagement in schools and later professional activity will be closed, but countless examples and role models for an active civil society will be developed.

7.6 Future Universities: Activating Resonance Spaces for Societal Innovation

Higher Education Institutions—being one of the core institutional system actors in our societies—are highly relevant for academic teaching and research but will play another crucial role for future societies. Future Universities also may develop as *Activating Resonance Spaces* for our society (Rosa & Endres, 2016; Stark, 2022). To establish universities as resonance spaces, and to exchange and share implicit and explicit knowledge (Stark et al., 2018), skills, and wisdom, we will need to establish an expanded and transparent "communication and reference framework" for societal innovation (Sailer et al., 2019). We will need to go beyond a mutual understanding of those acting within the academic system.

A mutual and collaborative eco-system within the scientific community will still be central, but not sufficient. Rather, through its various formats (teaching, research, transfer) and institutions, universities need to recognize, understand, and respond to the demands and challenges of society—in other words, "relate" and "resonate". At the same time, universities as "resonance spaces" need to be heard and echoed in society, as an active member of a societal discourse on science-based discoveries, insights, and innovations.

Therefore, the idea of university becomes—in the sense of Carayannis and Campbell's (2012) quintuple helix (Goldsmith, 2018)—an active (and vibrating) part of society (Fig. 7.2).

Following Carayannis and Campbell (2012), the idea of Future Universities can be sketched as a university "in Modus 3" (Roessler, 2016).[7] It is characterized not only by well-developed Campus-Community Partnerships (Stark et al., 2014), but based on a fully developed transformational literacy (Scharmer, 2019) and

---

[7] According to Roessler (2016), Modus 1 universities focus on traditional academic research and teaching, Modus 2 Universities focus on transferring academic knowledge for societal challenges, and Modus 3 features a reflective and transformative learning experience for all partners.

7 Future Universities as Activating Resonance Spaces …

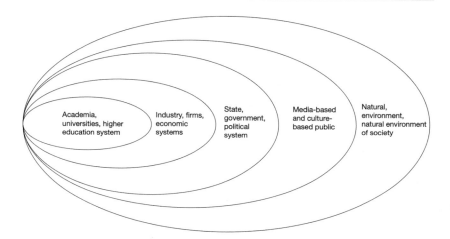

Fig. 7.2 Quintuple Helix Innovation. (Adapted from Carayannis & Campbell, 2012)

transdisciplinary, transformational research with a strong focus on societal (not only technical) application (Schneidewind & Singer-Brodowski, 2013), which is linked to research-based teaching and community-based research (Altenschmidt & Stark, 2016; Hacker, 2013). Transformational research and education as well as the strong link to civic society can also provide an important 'missing link' between applied research and basic research at different types of universities (Schneidewind, 2019).

Similar to "Industry 4.0", which is replacing the original idea of mass industrial production by individualized products and services, the learning, research and development in *"Universities as Activating Resonance Spaces of/for society"* will become more individualized. Lifelong learning, research, new forms of production (Ming et al., 2022), and new work will constantly intertwine. The different actors of society (students, teachers, or partners from companies, civil society organizations, entrepreneurs, creative people, artists, politicians…) will interact actively and contextually.

Teaching and learning in this context will go beyond a one-dimensional transfer of knowledge (from teacher to student; from university to society). It will be a continuous, mutual reflective experience. Learning will take place in coordinated and negotiated ways; in a continuous exchange of different actors in physical as well as virtual spaces. A multidimensional and resonating space, which will enable, create, and maintain its references for research and learning will not simply fade away after finishing projects or degrees. Mutual knowledge and skills from academia, arts, and experience will resonate to current challenges and enable an urgently needed re-reflection for responsible innovation. In short: "Activating Resonance Spaces" are needed as innovative enablers for communication between all social actors. Future Universities (like Modus 3-Universities) should act as, and provide, resonance spaces for the future of our societies and planet.

7.7   Shapes of Future Universities

Specific shapes of Future Universities as described below may act as a common framework for transformative learning, teaching, and research.

1. *Future Universities will act as an initiator, co-designer, enabler, and one of the active players in a societal resonance and learning space.* Actors will establish a concept of theory as "practice understood" (Dewey, 1963). Experiential knowing does not end at lecture hall doors (Killius et al., 2003). Learning is not restricted to a short time in life (at schools and universities), it develops as learning in the time of life ("lifelong learning"), applying even more to working life and social practice as an Open Loop University.[8] Relations between university, working life, and social practice therefore must be reorganized online and offline.

2. *The architecture (the buildings) of the Future Universities as Resonance Spaces* therefore will meet requirements needed in the interaction of its technology, building style, and design. *Resonating Spaces need to be enabling spaces* to allow various forms of active learning (skills for Co-Creation, Future Skills for innovative communities and transformational learning). These requirements will need to go beyond traditional "classroom-office" structures still dominating many of our universities today and towards Open Spaces like "Learning Hubs", "Co-Working Spaces", and "Experimental Floors" in which students, teaching and university staff, and civil society will be supported by digitalized features to learn mutually how to transform our future.[9]

---

[8] http://www.stanford2025.com/open-loop-university, extending the study experience towards "a lifetime of learning opportunities" by integrating practical professional experience into the learning process. "Open Loop" means that you bring back your professional experience to your university and link universities with your learning at the workplace.

[9] It is striking, that the "Futurium" in Berlin acts like an open and participative museum (https://futurium.de/en) and is not an active part of the university-eco-system. What we learn: There are open spaces in many cities which need to be re-discovered by the universities.

3. *Regionally-based international networking as part of Future Universities:* "Think global, act local" narrows this down. Many medium-sized companies embedded in their regional environment often and successfully act as global players. The resonance space takes this anchoring in the region into account, but also creates international networking beyond digitalization. Future Universities will highlight the poles global vs/and local to provide a complementary frame of reference in the resonance space.

4. *Resonance Spaces may act as a framework curating its own physical-virtual structural potential.* From the point of view of intellectual capital (human, structural, relational potential), the resonance space will enable smart links between micro-, meso- and macro-levels of a "Knowledge Society". Resonance Spaces will help to transparently classify insights generated on a macro- or meso-level and co-creatively inspire transdisciplinary research. They also will initiate practical-research applications and exchange with experiential knowledge in (regional) micro-levels.

5. *Resonance Spaces may act as "scaling spaces" for individual and societal impact.* They will open opportunities to share, evaluate, and reflect insights, innovations, and open questions with the community. They will enable actors previously unknown to meet and collaborate with new questions and projects. Both academic and practical routines may become re-vitalized by involving external actors; mutually best practices will be shared and resonated with.

6. *Future Universities as Resonance Spaces will expand previous approaches to a university of the future,* which have been addressing "educational processes" from a university perspective only. If members of the university dip into working and community life and community members will be part of the academic life in return, universities finally will become and serve as a resonance space for a responsible knowledge society (Open Loop University). Alumni will become populi. Universities as a Resonance Space will be identified as a citizen university: master classes will mutually use and reflect experiences that have not been made in university life and by non-university members. This will require a participatory intellectual constitution to support a citizen- and society-driven research life, enhanced within the resonance space.

7. *Resonance Spaces will re-invent traditional universities* in structural and hierarchical terms: Transformational learning and teaching implies that planning and administrative processes (enrollment, curricula, exams, formatting study programs) gradually will develop into a joint process between teaching and research staff, students and civil society. The practice of learning and teaching, as well as respective results, will be a joint responsibility. The best way to link learning and leadership is to teach what you learn, and to experience research.

7.8 Transformative Literacy Links Learning and Leadership

In essence, Future Universities will integrate not only different scientific-academic levels but also the experiential level (learning by doing). They will create transformative eco-systems in the sense of "systems thinking" and individual change. "From Ego to Eco" will broaden and deepen a perspective of transformative learning, building on, but even going beyond, what we believe to be core elements (properties) of a "university of the future".[10] Scharmer (2019) argues that in our Higher Education Institutions (HEIs) there still is a growing "blind spot" when it comes to transformational learning and collaborative and co-creating ecosystems (see Fig. 7.3).

A quest for transformative literacy is particularly of concern in transitional and uncertain situations: not only "in year 2 of a global pandemic", but even more

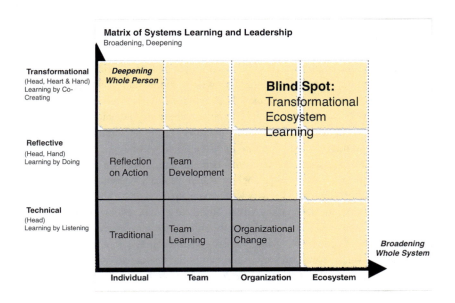

Fig. 7.3 Matrix of Systems Learning and Leadership. (Adapted from Scharmer, 2019)

---

[10] See Sickinger & Baumgartner, 2015, and https://medium.com/presencing-institute-blog/vertical-literacy-12-principles-for-reinventing-the-21st-century-university-39c2948192ee

in times of war and a highly threatened international security. In which stage of a global transition process are we actually? How can we, as universities, react to turmoil and uncertainty for students, teachers, researchers, and citizens? Are we walking together or are we (institutionally, but also individually) in different stages that will make "walking together" difficult? What is the role of higher education institutions in designing transformative learning spaces and formats in times of uncertainty? How can we support each other—and especially students, teachers, researchers and citizens, who have lost their home and safe places?

Based on the results of an iconic workshop conference at the Tutzing Academy in 2021 which brought together students, presidents, staff, researchers, and teachers from universities in Germany, Austria, and Switzerland (Fig. 7.4), major challenges for Future Universities may be developed around reflective questions instead of answers:

- *How can we learn to work and collaborate together?* Shaping our future together with different perspectives is already a challenge for disciplines and stakeholders within universities. Co-creation between civil society and

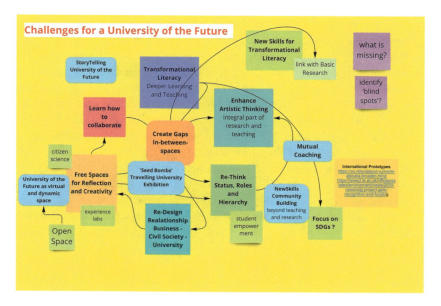

Fig. 7.4 Results from "Universities of the Future"—Wolfgang Stark, 2022

academia[11] additionally requires an exchange between different forms of how experiences and insights are processed.

- *Can spaces for reflection, creativity, and freedom be developed at universities and in civil society for new forms of collaborative learning?* Not only digitalization processes will require to re-purpose and re-design traditional spaces (classrooms, offices) in universities. The collaboration of science, civil society, and companies to transform our society also needs new (both virtual and analog) creative, free, reflective, and open spaces inside and outside universities.
- *How do we reshape the triangle of civil society—universities—business?* Relationship dynamics between civil society, universities, politics, and economic stakeholders are changing. In the context of global societal change, universities can, and need, to play an active and important role as a "resonance chamber of our society" in reshaping cooperation.[12]
- *In what ways can we rethink and test our respective roles?* If new forms of collaboration and co-creation also produce spaces for reflection and freedom within/between universities and civil society, the roles of stakeholders will also be re-negotiated. Students as (co-)designers of study programs, or as co-teachers, will change traditional hierarchies in higher education. Civil society as "agenda setters" and co-producers for research and teaching will enable new forms of knowledge and methods in the academic world.
- *How can we connect creative-artistic thinking with research and teaching?* Artistic thinking (Bertram, 2018; Kagan, 2011; Stein Greenberg & Kelley, 2021) is emerging and will take over a new significant role in the academic, societal, and business world. Artistic thinking and artistic research and reflection will shape knowledge processes and change more dynamically than the rational world of science. If both art and science and art and social change will develop into the "Art of Transformation" (Kagan, 2011; Schneidewind, 2019), new possibilities and potentials we have not been aware of before will arise.
- *In what ways do we develop competencies necessary for transformation?* The necessary competencies we need to transform our society often only become visible in the spaces between disciplines, between science and civil society, and between institutions.

---

[11] Witnessing a cruel war of Putin in the Ukraine at the time of writing this paper, "The Art of Co-Creating" (Walmsley, 2019a) may be of high significance for the future of our planet.

[12] https://futureuniversities.com presents a business-oriented version of universities as a resonance space to society.

The core of a new university therefore should rather promote transdisciplinary *thinking out-of-the-box*, systematically encourage *learning by mistakes and experimentation*, and use this experience to foster *a culture of critical and productive questioning*, promote the *development of a learning culture in and between social organizations*, and, last but not least, *build the personalities and identities of future generations and leaders* by strengthening social and societal responsibility and a sense of community.

Initial steps and open questions toward transformational teaching and research in Universities of the Future has started in many places.[13] Beyond national and international "flagships", there is an abundance of small "pockets" of innovative and transformational teaching and research in the universities of the world. Yet, at the same time, the vast majority of teaching still is based on the traditional one-way-street. Small innovative "pockets" rarely are connected, so innovation—in a more traditional way—has to be re-invented over and over again.

To break the wave, an interactive, dynamic, and adaptive market and information place—which should consist of an interactive online platform as well as offline elements—can serve. This marketplace makes it possible to match and further develop the different actors with their ideas, competencies, questions, searches, and resources as well as existing projects and results in a dynamic process.

7.9   Systematic Self-Reflection on "Transformation"

Talking about transformation can create the feeling of talking about the same thing but meaning very different goals (Göpel, 2016).[14] One way to start a target debate on "transformational literacy" is to share beliefs, concerns, and innovative ideas between students, teachers, and civil society as an integral part of each university program.

This is also where Maja Göpel's (2016) "tractions of transformation" come into play:

- Back to economic growth—at the expense of…?
- Inventing a new, sustainable, and safe world, do we, like always, start from a northern/western hemisphere perspective, or which one?

---

[13] Inspiring examples can be found for the US at http://www.stanford2025.com; for Germany at https://www.leuphana.de/en/university/history.html

[14] http://greatmindshift.org/key-concepts/

- What is the future "eco-system" of universities? What role do they play in it?
- Who are the real "transformers" (students, teachers, university administrators, politicians, companies…)?

The last question may be an important one for future scenarios. It is clear that universities and civil society are (supposed to be) connected. Will it be also clear that the students' point of view takes a more prominent place?[15] Actually, who belongs to civil society—who do we need to perceive?

Future Universities will need to add social responsibility and experiential wisdom to academic knowledge in order to increase their practical and societal relevance. Therefore, Future Universities will be competitive, but also emerge into collaborative universities in terms of civic relevance and excellence. That is how Future Universities will contribute to mastering the major future challenges of our society.

References

Altenschmidt, K., Miller, J., & Stark, W. (Eds.). (2009). *Raus aus dem Elfenbeinturm?: Entwicklungen in Service Learning und bürgerschaftlichem Engagement an deutschen Hochschulen*. Beltz.

Altenschmidt, K., & Stark, W. (Eds.). (2016). *Forschen und Lehren mit der Gesellschaft: Community Based Research und Service Learning an Hochschulen*. Springer.

Aramburuzabala Higuera, P., McIlrath, L., & Opazo, H. (Eds.). (2019). *Embedding service learning in European higher education: Developing a culture of civic engagement*. Routledge.

Baltes, A., Hofer, M., & Sliwka, A. (Eds.). (2007). *Studierende übernehmen Verantwortung: Service Learning an deutschen Universitäten*. Beltz.

Berger Kaye, C. (2010). Service learning: Engagement, action, results! *Colleagues, 5*(1), 4–7.

Bertram, U. (2018). *Artistic transfer: Efficiency through unruly thinking* (1st ed.). transcript.

Carayannis, E. G., & Campbell, D. F. (2012). *Mode 3 knowledge production in quadruple helix innovation systems: 21st-century democracy, innovation, and entrepreneurship for development*. Springer.

Dewey, J. (1963). *Experience and education*. Collier Books.

Eyler, J., & Giles, D. E. (1999). *Where's the learning in service-learning?* (1st ed.). Jossey-Bass.

---

[15] See inspiring ideas about future universities from a student's view at http://move.ariane-hagl.de/

7 Future Universities as Activating Resonance Spaces … 157

Goldsmith, P. (2018). The quadruple helix: Tackling the issues of the left behind (Radix Paper 10). https://radixuk.org/wp-content/uploads/2019/08/Quadruple-Helix-E-Final.pdf.

Göpel, M. (2016). *The great mindshift: How a new economic paradigm and sustainability transformations go hand in hand.* Springer Nature.

Hacker, K. (2013). *Community-based participatory research.* Sage.

Håkansson, A. (2005). The impact factor -a dubious measure of scientific quality. *Scandinavian Journal of Primary Health Care, 23*(4), 193–194. https://doi.org/10.1080/02813430500287232

Heidbrink, L., & Hirsch, A. (Eds.). (2006). *Verantwortung in der Zivilgesellschaft: Zur Konjunktur eines widersprüchlichen Prinzips.* Campus.

Hofer, M., & Derkau, J. (Eds.). (2020). *Campus und Gesellschaft: Service Learning an deutschen Hochschulen: Positionen und Perspektiven* (1st ed.). Beltz Juventa.

Kagan, S. (2011). *Art and sustainability: Connecting patterns for a culture of complexity* (2nd ed.). transcript.

Killius, N., Kluge, J., & Reisch, L. (Eds.). (2003). *Die Bildung der Zukunft* (1st ed.). Suhrkamp.

Latour, B. (2005). *Reassembling the social: An introduction to actor-network-theory.* Oxford University Press.

Latour, B. (2021). *After lockdown: A metamorphosis.* Polity.

Ming, Z., Nellippallil, A. B., Wang, R., Allen, J. K., Wang, G., Yan, Y., et al. (2022). *Architecting a knowledge-based platform for design engineering 4.0* (1st ed.). Springer International Publishing; Imprint: Springer.

Mittelstraß, J. (2003). Universität als Lebensform. In N. Killius, J. Kluge, & L. Reisch (Eds.), *Die Bildung der Zukunft* (1st ed., pp. 256–260). Suhrkamp.

Ramaley, J. (2000). Embracing civic responsibility. *Higher Education* (Paper 123).

Reimers, F. M. (2021). *Implementing deeper learning and 21st century education reforms: Building an education renaissance after a global pandemic* (1st ed.). Springer International Publishing; Imprint: Springer.

Robinson, K., & Robinson, K. (2022). *Imagine if: Creating a future for us all.* Penguin.

Roessler, I. (2016). Haben Hochschulen für angewandte Wissenschaften das Potential, Mode 3-Universitäten zu werden?: Dissertation zur Erlangung des akademischen Grades Doktor der Philosophie (Dr. phil.). Technische Universität Dortmund. https://www.che.de/wp-content/uploads/upload/Dissertation_Roessler_2016_06_22.pdf.

Rosa, H. (2018). *Resonanz: Eine Soziologie der Weltbeziehung.* Suhrkamp.

Rosa, H., & Endres, W. (2016). *Resonanzpädagogik: Wenn es im Klassenzimmer knistert* (2nd ed.). Beltz.

Rosenkranz, D., Roderus, S., & Oberbeck, N. (Eds.). (2019). *Service Learning an Hochschulen: Konzeptionelle Überlegungen und innovative Beispiele.* Beltz Juventa.

Ruda, N., Miller, J., Stark, W., & Meyer, P. (2015). Service learning in higher education: A pattern language. In R. Sickinger & P. Baumgartner (Eds.), *PURPLSOC: Pursuit of pattern languages for societal change: The workshop 2014* (pp. 348–365). Danube University Krems.

Sailer, K., Stark, W., & Szogs, G. (2019). Hochschule als ResonanzRaum der Gesellschaft Ausgangspunkte gesellschaftlicher Entwicklungen: Working Paper. Tutzing. https://www.researchgate.net/publication/333149490_Hochschule_als_ResonanzRaum_der_Gesellschaft_Ausgangspunkte_gesellschaftlicher_Entwicklungen.

Scharmer, O. (16. April 2019). Vertical literacy: Reimagining the 21st-century University. *Medium: Field of the Future Blog*. https://medium.com/presencing-institute-blog/vertical-literacy-12-principles-for-reinventing-the-21st-century-university-39c2948192ee.

Schneidewind, U. (2019). *Die große Transformation: Eine Einführung in die Kunst gesellschaftlichen Wandels* (3rd ed.). Fischer.

Schneidewind, U., & Singer-Brodowski, M. (2013). *Transformative Wissenschaft: Klimawandel im deutschen Wissenschafts- und Hochschulsystem*. Metropolis Verlag.

Seifert, A., Zentner, S., & Nagy, F. (2019). *Praxisbuch Service-Learning: "Lernen durch Engagement" an Schulen* (2nd ed.). Beltz.

Sickinger, R., & Baumgartner, P. (Eds.). (2015). *PURPLSOC: Pursuit of pattern languages for societal change: The workshop 2014*. Danube University Krems.

Sliwka, A. (2007). Giving back to the community. Service learning as university pedagogy for social problem solving. In A. Baltes, M. Hofer, & A. Sliwka (Eds.), *Studierende übernehmen Verantwortung: Service Learning an deutschen Universitäten* (pp. 29–34). Beltz

Sliwka, A., & Klopsch, B. (2021). *Deeper Learning in der Schule: Pädagogik des digitalen Zeitalters*. Beltz.

Smith, R. (2001). Measuring the social impact of research—Difficult but necessary. *BMJ Clinical Research, 323*(7312), 528. https://doi.org/10.1136/bmj.323.7312.528

Stark, W., Miller, J., Ruda, N., Altenschmidt, K., & Stieger, A. (2018). *Service learning in higher education: A pattern language for successful service learning*. Pattern Publishing.

Stark, W. (2022). Universities as a resonance space for future societies: Accepted paper to the 3rd world higher education conference organized by UNESCO in Barcelona. In *UNESCO World Higher Education Conference 2022*.

Stark, W., Miller, J., & Altenschmidt, K. (2014). *Zusammenarbeiten – Zusammen gewinnen: Was Kooperationen zwischen Hochschulen und Gemeinwesen bewirken können und was dafür nötig ist: Potenzialanalyse Campus-Community-Partnerships*. Organisation Development Lab Publications, University of Essen

Stark, W., Vossebrecher, D., Dell, C., & Schmidhuber, H. (Eds.). (2017). *Improvisation und Organisation: Muster zur Innovation sozialer Systeme* (1st ed.). Transcript Publishers, Bielefeld

Stein Greenberg, S., & Kelley, D. (2021). *Creative acts for curious people: How to think, create and lead in unconventional ways*. Penguin Business.

Walmsley, B. (Ed.). (2019a). *Audience engagement in the performing arts: New directions in cultural policy research*. Palgrave Macmillan.

Walmsley, B. (2019b). Co-creating art, meaning, and value. In B. Walmsley (Ed.), *Audience engagement in the performing arts: New directions in cultural policy research* (pp. 165–198). Palgrave Macmillan. https://doi.org/10.1007/978-3-030-26653-0_7.

Weber, C., Kröger, A., & Demirtas, C. (2015). Scaling social impact in Europe: Quantitative analysis of national and transnational scaling strategies of 358 social enterprises. Gütersloh. https://www.bertelsmann-stiftung.de/fileadmin/files/user_upload/BST_ScalingSocialImpactInEurope_final.pdf. Accessed 26 Febr 2023.

Wolfgang Stark, Dr. phil., Professor em. for Organizational and Community Psychology, has been founder and director of the Organizational Development Laboratory (www.orglab.org) and Center for Societal Learning and Social Responsibility (www.uniaktiv.org), both based at the University of Duisburg-Essen in Germany. His research specializes in community empowerment processes in organizations and society, and in organizational/societal learning and organizational culture. In linking the arts and community/organizational science, he is keen to establish a transdisciplinary knowledge base for societal innovation. Since 2010, Wolfgang Stark is director and CEO of Steinbeis Center for Innovation and Sustainable Leadership. He is also founding member and president of the European Community Psychology Association (ECPA), founder and president of the German Service Learning Network, and co-founder of the European Association for Service Learning in Higher Education. Since 2015, he is guest researcher at Strascheg Center for Entrepreneurship in Munich, Germany. In 2021/2022, he has been Visting Fellow at VU Amsterdam, NL (Free University Amsterdam, Netherlands).

Open Access This chapter is licensed under the terms of the Creative Commons Attribution 4.0 International License (http://creativecommons.org/licenses/by/4.0/), which permits use, sharing, adaptation, distribution and reproduction in any medium or format, as long as you give appropriate credit to the original author(s) and the source, provide a link to the Creative Commons license and indicate if changes were made.

The images or other third party material in this chapter are included in the chapter's Creative Commons license, unless indicated otherwise in a credit line to the material. If material is not included in the chapter's Creative Commons license and your intended use is not permitted by statutory regulation or exceeds the permitted use, you will need to obtain permission directly from the copyright holder.

Building a Creative Ecosystem of Intentional Serendipity

8

A Future Skills conversation with Tom Wambeke

Ulf-Daniel Ehlers and Laura Eigbrecht

> **Abstract**
>
> Tom Wambeke (Fig. 8.1) is a United Nations Senior Executive with a focus on learning innovation and digital transformation, working with cross-functional teams on innovation projects across more than 50 countries. Wambeke has been the Chief of Learning Innovation of the Training Centre of the International Labour Organization (ILO) since 2015, specializing in providing sustainable learning solutions with the objective to generate impact and organizational change. Change and transformation are also at the core of this conversation—discussing how we can learn from, for and in uncertain times.

Ehlers: In recent years, Tom, you were really trying to grasp the future of education. As I understand it, you see ITCILO, the International Training Centre of the ILO, as an engine and a nucleus to develop impulses needed to invent and reinvent education. Can you tell us more about this organization that you're working at?

U.-D. Ehlers
Professor for Educational Management and Lifelong Learning, Business Faculty,
DHBW Karlsruhe, Karlsruhe, Germany
e-mail: ulf-daniel.ehlers@dhbw-karlsruhe.de

L. Eigbrecht (✉)
Educational Management and Lifelong Learning, Business Faculty, DHBW Karlsruhe,
Karlsruhe, Germany
e-mail: laura.eigbrecht@dhbw-karlsruhe.de

© The Author(s) 2024
U.-D. Ehlers and L. Eigbrecht (eds.), *Creating the University of the Future*, Zukunft der Hochschulbildung - Future Higher Education,
https://doi.org/10.1007/978-3-658-42948-5_8

Fig. 8.1 Tom Wambeke

Wambeke: The ILO, the International Labour Organization, is a specialized tripartite UN agency with a focus on promoting decent work and advancing the global social justice agenda. The ITCILO, its training center, is a kind of experimental innovation hub where we focus on sustainable learning solutions, reaching out to 80,000 people on an annual basis in 42 different areas of expertise which relate to the recent work agenda in function of social justice.

My role as Chief of Learning Innovation is one that we have created; I didn't apply for that specific job. I started it at a time when innovation was about how we can infuse technology during the early days of technology-enhanced learning and e-learning. My first assessment of the training center was that we basically try to transform a training center beyond training. In other words, that we need to make sure that the world of learning doesn't become an eternal workshop factory, where we just replicate the same thing that we have always done. Technology was initially an excuse to change things.

We also realized that it's not only about learning technology, but about learning methodology, about digital media design. How can we innovate across the entire spectrum that will influence learning? And this is how this department actually was born, because the 42 areas of expertise replicate exactly what the ILO

8 Building a Creative Ecosystem of Intentional Serendipity

is doing, from international labor standards to social dialogue, social protection, just transition, gender mainstreaming et cetera. There are about 42 areas of expertise, but what they do not have is expertise in innovation in the field of learning, and this is where we are providing an answer. After many years, it has become a cross-cutting strategic driver of the overall strategy of the center—and I have the privilege to lead this program with my team.

Ehlers: I think it's quite impressive what you and your team achieved to become for your entire organization. It is a big achievement to make innovation and learning such an important issue in your organization. For you, what are the three words which are describing the future of education?

Wambeke: The future of education in three words—it's a creative ecosystem of intentional serendipity.

Ehlers: So, improvisation is probably one thing which you really like, right?

Wambeke: Yes, but not in the way that educational scientists use it sometimes—rather in the way that jazz musicians use it. Their high mastery of skills to become a top-notch jazz musician took them years to acquire, but it's only that kind of mastery of skills which gives you the freedom to improvise. Any jazz musician will tell you that you can only improvise when you're fully prepared. It's just not like the kind of improvisation where you experiment a little bit in a classroom.

Ehlers: We want to talk about Future Skills today. Is there any Future Skills moment or any anecdote that you remember from your life where you think that this was a moment where Future Skills really mattered, and you really learnt something?

Wambeke: Future Skills, in the sense of what I understand, with all the disruption ahead of us, are basically about the question of how I can I survive in the twenty-first century. I have a background in educational sciences and also in philosophy. I was suddenly wondering: what do I want to do in life? I was very much into the cultural scene in Belgium, so I decided to follow a master in cultural management.

At that time, we were setting up festivals—it was the age of what we would call the experience economy. Festivals were becoming an experience and I learned many skillsets in that kind of area that, later in my life, have come back to me. Because coincidence brought me to become, again, a learning professional. If I see how I positioned learning in my own professional context, I would see it as a kind of a learning festival where learning becomes an experience. If I talk about Future Skills, it's about the capacity to transfer from one discipline to another, to come up with innovative and creative ideas.

For me, this is a recurrent pattern in my life and in my professional life. Most of my ideas, I don't get from educational experts anymore because I became one myself, thinking with the same glasses. But if I talk to someone specialized in beer or wine, in completely different fields, I can try to translate that into my field. That's where my personal Future Skills have been quite successful—in the field of innovation science.

I've seen some interesting examples that reconfirmed that. One of the American e-learning gurus, Elliott Masie, asked to his ten thousand followers: what's the difference between learning and cooking? And from the thousands of answers he received, he produced his first book "What's the difference between learning and cooking?". It's an interesting experiment, asking two different disciplines and finding out what can they learn from each other. Maybe that's also a lesson for the Future Skills discussion. If you look at all the problems that we are facing, for example, in the world of work, labor migration or informal economy, there is no topic anymore where there is a unidisciplinary reaction on how to we have to address it. These problems are all fundamentally interdisciplinary and extremely complex. For promoting Future Skills, we will have to recreate our profiles of the way we think about problems. And that is going to be a high urgency point in how we shape the future of education and learning in general.

Ehlers: What we always say is that problems do not think about disciplines—so they are always interdisciplinary. A lot of teachers and professors we talk to tend to say: we are already very good at teaching our curriculum—but what we are looking for more and more are possibilities for students to develop life skills and interdisciplinary skills. Or in other words: how can we create intentional serendipity, where you see beyond what is obvious in front of you to discover new things? In our research on this important concept of Future Skills, we discussed with partners from industry and people in the labor market in interviews and Delphi studies and so on, and our partners in the economy and people who are already in the labor market. We asked them what they think are the most important things they would like universities to focus on and to help students develop. They were naming all kinds of things, but they did not really focus on knowledge, but a lot on skills. So, while we are mostly focusing on knowledge transmission in universities, they think the most relevant issues they experience in their work-

8 Building a Creative Ecosystem of Intentional Serendipity

ing and private lives are actually how to deal with unexpected experiences, how to communicate, how to collaborate across borders. This is why we started to further develop this concept of Future Skills into a framework to make people understand them.

"But as the problems we are facing are becoming more and more complex, with an extremely high level of urgency, we need to become something that I would call human chameleons, having to change colors many times."

Wambeke: I think it's extremely important to have a new narrative. We didn't invent the need for interdisciplinary thinking, it has kind of become common sense. As long as knowledge has existed, there probably has always been an interdisciplinary element. But there is one thing we need to make sure, looking at all these different skills frameworks, mostly listing cognitive flexibility, innovation, creativity as top skills—we need to use new images and create narratives that also inspire people. Future Skills is a good one already. But as the problems we are facing are becoming more and more complex, with an extremely high level of urgency, we need to become something that I would call human chameleons, having to change colors many times. What I like about this animal are its independently mobile eyes, allowing for a 360 degree view—I wish we had a similar vision to this as humans.

However, there is an element of substance related to these, let's say, soft skills—communication, collaboration and so on. Talking about creativity, for example: there is a whole discipline in creativity, almost like an engineering discipline. We thus also need to generate substantial knowledge on these disciplines that will help us become more interdisciplinary, to co-create, collaborate and communicate. And this is definitely more complex than soft versus hard.

Ehlers: I would agree to that. We see it like a compound in which knowledge, or the crystallized result of science, always needs some context in which your values are addressed so that you can start to act. In this view, values are the underlying mechanisms which are guiding your actions. But there is also a third element of what you're trained to do: your abilities and experiences—and all these three things have to come together. Knowledge alone is not enabling you to act—it is knowledge plus that we need, value-infused and contextual.

Moreover, our understanding is that Future Skills always have to do with a vision of the future, a narrative. In your job, you probably have a lot to do with convincing people that learning innovation is an important issue. How do you so successfully build this narrative around learning innovation?

Wambeke: One of the first things I learnt was to never use the word innovation or related words such as systems thinking or interdisciplinarity—because this is the specialist language and might be alienating to others, considering this as a specialist conversation which is not for them. For creating a narrative, I will come up with a story—for example about the human chameleon, which is very adaptive to the changing environment, able to survive the COVID crisis. Because that could have been the death of our training center, at that time mostly based on face-to-face training. What you then need is a narrative that focuses on what we want to achieve, and that is reach more people for making the world a better place, with innovation tools and mechanisms as something that might be a way to get there. For me, communication and the art of persuasive storytelling have become as important as the strategic plan behind it—because you need to move people. They need to be part of that story, and that's not the story written by a few experts. It's a human kind of collaboration act, and only when they are convinced, they will come along.

However, as you said, context is extremely important. I work in a global center—facing the entire world. So, if context is king, then I definitely say that value is queen, and maybe even more important than king. Different global systems have different values, with interculturality as only one very specific dimension. We need to reorganize our diversity wheels in a much more complex and nuanced way in order to go beyond standard parameters reduced to single categories such as language, culture, ethnicity. It is so much richer and complex than that!

And if you have the navigational capacity to work with all these different parameters on your dashboard, you will also be able to drive a culture of innovation ahead. And that is not an easy thing to do, because the narrative will also evolve over time. While we often think of innovation as a kind of almost technological solution, it has actually been more like muddling through, step by step. But if you do that consequently, you will move forward. Maybe this kind of long-term thinking has been partly lost in our plans and strategies that barely go beyond five years.

What is your plan for the next 20 years? That would be an interesting question but is rarely asked or answered. That's why I was surprised about the Agenda 2063: The Africa We Want by the African Union, going even beyond 2060. This is because the entire long-term thinking skill which we could call foresight or even strategic foresight is a muscle that needs to be trained and would be one of my most important Future Skills.

8 Building a Creative Ecosystem of Intentional Serendipity

Eigbrecht: Some things you said really resonated with me—I think because you create a lot of images: festival of learning, navigation tools, a compass, a chameleon. Sometimes we are facing all these challenges and not knowing where to go, so it's nice to have some images, maybe even utopian, of where to go and how to describe what is happening.

However, it's also important to have some concrete examples of how Future Skills can actually look like in successful practice. Do you have a story to share on that?

Wambeke: There's one website that I would like to share and which I use in making it very concrete—it is called hubot.org and created by a Dutch foresight agency. Basically, you take a job test and apply for a job in the future, such as Artificial Womb Nutritionist or the Organ Designer or Walker Inspector.

To make it very concrete: I live in North Italy, renowned for their mastery of high-quality products such as fashion or shoes. In the region where I live at, I still see some people with this kind of artisanal skillsets which are on the brink of basically disappearing but reflecting generations of knowledge into the quality of a product.

So, I ask: how could we start to combine these more future-oriented skills related to technology or ecological thinking and combine it with these old mastery skills of artisanal crafts? So, what if we combine two different skills into something new? Could that create a new future where we will be more innovative, more creative, rather than have these things disappear? If we have this kind of combinational skill set, we might revive and retrieve some of these things from the past to come up with more efficient and eco-friendly technologies, new value chains that create circular sustainable economies instead of thinking about utopian or rather dystopian science fiction scenarios where the machine will replace us. This might also influence how we organize the global economy. Recently, production lines have been moved back from China to Germany by Adidas, where factories will be locally producing shoes with robots instead of humans based on the final market needs. Let's not make this a utopian technological story, but let's see what other values emerge and how we can combine this with skill sets that are already here. Let's again make it a multidimensional question which is much more interesting than separating all the different elements.

Eigbrecht: I also wonder, when we talk about Future Skills, we often talk about individuals. But, as we see, all the challenges that we need Future Skills for are collective, basically shared by everybody on this planet. So how can we make

Future Skills learning not a pressure on individuals, but a shared social experience?

Wambeke: It's for an important reason that collaboration or co-creation is also seen as one of these future trends out there, at any level. For example, at work—looking at the team I am leading right now, I don't see any project managers—they're all working in mixed teams on different projects that change all the time. The challenges they face are not only technical problems, but also how we collaborate in teams towards a shared goal which requires different skill sets.

We shouldn't wait for people to learn this at work. Project-based learning, for example, is already conceptualized accordingly as an educational experience in which you will only find a solution if you undergo a group working process with assessment through systems of peer feedback within your own group. There are many other approaches, but they are still seen as the innovative way of learning while the majority of universities still lag behind, broadcasting knowledge. We need to make these approaches more common, starting from kindergarten towards university so that it becomes normal that a solution is not provided by an expert, but we are confronted with a challenge we cannot handle on our own—we will then tap into collective intelligence.

It's more of a mindset that we need to cultivate across the entire generation, a way of thinking—and this aspect will be important in organizing learning in the future. This is not something new but a recurring pattern, but if we don't keep on emphasizing it, we might lose it again—such as with the risk to go back to exactly how things were pre-COVID. So, after being exposed to many different experiences, also failures, it is important to ask: what is the next step? Where can we learn more?

Ehlers: One issue which we always come across in these conversations is that of putting it into practice. You already mentioned that you think that the education process needs chunks of knowledge, wisdom and values, but also peer feedback and Problem-Based Learning environments. You're constantly designing and thinking about training opportunities. How do you proceed?

"What I say is: it's not really about the headsets, it's more about the mindsets."

Wambeke: In university, I was still shaped in a more linear vision, not of how I see the world, but of how we do things, taking different steps, one after the other. Applying this to the field of educational science would be an instructional cycle from analysis towards evaluation. Today, I would probably get stuck in the first

8 Building a Creative Ecosystem of Intentional Serendipity 169

phase, in a kind of analysis paralysis. We probably need to have a more non-linear look at things, starting much faster, including feedback loops and reiterations, until things become clearer. We also need to have the courage to take a step back to do some piloting and reorganizing. However, this is often difficult to do in an organizational context asking for clear results and steps. So, what we are talking about is a kind of navigational capacity: how can I bring in some more complexity-oriented tools and approaches on my path towards success? It is a big challenge, and this is why I said my innovation journey was basically muddling through, but always towards a larger goal. I haven't gotten lost on my way muddling through. However, tools, approaches and mindsets need to be adapted in the whole educational sector. What I say is: it's not really about the headsets, it's more about the mindsets.

Ehlers: The way we would like to see our education processes in a seminar with our students or a lecture or a project is a very sophisticated and avant-garde vision very close to yours, bringing in complexity and making people understand that mindset matters. They need to develop questions and inspirations and creative solutions. But this is kind of a cultural break, because students are socialized in a totally different way, being agents in the process of answering safe questions. Now we come in, with our ambition to create complex learning scenarios in which we only want to deal with problems and questions which do not have any answers but plausibility, feedback, debates. So, there is a clash of learning philosophies, cultures and socializations—what is your approach of how to deal with this?

Wambeke: Of course, there are different takes, and maybe I will be answering a different question now. I started to be somewhat afraid of a challenge that I would call info-tension. Looking at mass information overloads and what I would call weapons of mass distraction, meaning social media, it's like our focus has been stolen. And the educational learning market has almost become a fast-food circus where bite-sized learning is served just in time. This sounds sexy and understandable and a perfect solution when I don't have a lot of time and I'm overwhelmed with everything—but let's step back.

And here again, my local environment comes in—I live in a slow-food region. And what if we applied the slow-food movement to other contexts? There's already travel, but what about slow-learning? What if we start to focus again? You can find this kind of Manifesto for Slow Thinking online—I think it says let's focus on questions rather than on answers, let's move into observation rather than immediate evaluation or judgment, let's focus on change of perspective instead of your point of view. It actually is a nice narrative that fits extremely well with the methodologies that I would like to use.

My approach is part of a larger vision on how I see change and behavioral change and learning, but I need to tell people about the bigger picture behind it—and this is what we are often lacking, focusing on short-term solutions. Once you have a vision, you have an overall purpose—but how do you translate that vision into practical instruments, making people go with the flow?

This is one of the problems that I see with some of the tools that are hyped now, including Design Thinking: you need extremely talented, skilled facilitators that really understand the entire process of conducting such an exercise. If this person does not have the skill set to pave the way ahead for students, they're going to get stuck, bored and confused very fast. We saw this happen when one university introduced systems thinking as a topic, but in the wrong way, with students complaining that they felt completely lost. And this was because there was not a sound methodological process with tools, approaches and well-trained people. This of course changes your role: you're not the sage on stage anymore, but the guide at the side, and this requires a different kind of expertise. However, you cannot just learn that in a workshop, but it's a process of experience, retesting and learning from it.

"You're not the sage on stage anymore, but the guide at the side, and this requires a different kind of expertise."

Eigbrecht: You supposedly just gave the answer to my next question. In the beginning you said that your future vision of education was an ecosystem of intentional serendipity. If we want to create deep learning opportunities for students and also more moments of unintentional learning opportunities—how can we do that?

Wambeke: Ultimately, it's making people aware that every second is a potential learning opportunity, even if they are not aware of it—having this conversation is already a learning opportunity. I always thought one of Einstein's quotes was quite interesting: I have no special talent. I am only passionately curious. For me, this would be the only kind of attitude that I would like to ask of anyone who's with me on a learning journey which is not locked up into a classroom. Because talking about informal learning or serendipity, it's always the stereotyped conversation at the coffee table that we go back to. In Italy, we drink a lot of coffee—a

8 Building a Creative Ecosystem of Intentional Serendipity 171

lot of potential serendipity out there. But how can we make sure that our entire environment, including the coffee bar, becomes a space and time where we learn from the dialogue and become conscious of it? We probably need to transform and translate a lot of different elements from it, and this might be the only possibility to give a new shape to the definition of lifelong learning: almost every single second until you die could be a potential learning opportunity. This should also be translated for different targets audiences, so that being confronted with a YouTube instructional video could make you see to something new through a new kind of glasses. This for me would be a way to create intentional serendipity, but again—not in a linear fashion, because then we would make the same mistakes again. Before, you need to create an open space for these kinds of ideas to come up and not lock them up in specific fields such as technology or governance.

Maybe we could learn from new technologies here. Currently, the debates on new technology are completely dominated by artificial intelligence, blockchain, et cetera, but why don't we dive deeper again? What if you look at the underlying structure of a phenomenon of blockchain? It is the first decentralized network that could create a completely new model of how we currently learn. I would like to see these kinds of narratives and not just the technological engineering discussions around them. And this might create a fascinating future where educational institutions might not be institutions anymore, but networks of learning with space for slow thinking and slow learning.

"Almost every single second until you die could be a potential learning opportunity."

Ehlers: So, you have guided us to the future of learning. I always like to think ten years back, where I was and how things were then, and ten years ahead as a thought experiment. So, if you think ten years ahead—will we still be discussing the future of learning in the same way, or will the future of learning need a different discussion?

Wambeke: This is a very difficult question, and sometimes I see people try to answer it with easy answers, such as that the future of learning is going to be the metaverse. With this kind of attitude, I think it will almost become the metaperverse, in one way or another. However, the underlying discussion here is on how we can make learning more immersive and get an experience that was not possible ten years ago. You can get a first glimpse of that when diving into my VR experiments, but it needs to go one step further and really make people have a completely different discussion about it. And that's where we are going to be confronted with our limitations. Today, we are certainly confronted with technological limitations, but there are still a lot of other limitations, such as the lack of connection with neuroscience specifically in the field of learning. I find that somewhat hilarious—that's the instrument that we basically use to learn, but the knowledge on it is in these extremely specialized fields and not a lot of people have the capacity to translate it into how to make it work in order to change the future of learning. For me, this would be a take on how to give a different twist to how we think about the future of learning. Secondly, as the world is becoming more diverse, we should also think about how to make future learning as inclusive as possible, with a lot of people now feeling a little bit left behind, either because of speed or access. Here again, the discussion needs to be radically different, with everything reduced to an accessibility discussion, whether it's infrastructure, technology, literacy. We need to have the courage to connect inclusion to innovation in order to come up with radically different solutions. Again, it will be less about headsets and more about mindsets.

And last but not least—I think this should not be only the discussion of educational specialists and stakeholders. It should become a societal type of discussion with a co-creation approach—such as with the UN Sustainable Development Goals. There is a difference here to the Millennium Development Goals where the discussion was rather expert-driven. The Sustainable Development Goals had a different approach, asking: what is the world we want? Having an entire population or at least an important part of that population think about the same question—that would be the greatest way to think about the future of education. We would probably see different narratives, because we as education specialists are also locked up in our own narratives—and I would also like to see different questions being addressed.

"We need to have the courage to connect inclusion to innovation in order to come up with radically different solutions."

Prof. Dr. phil. habil. Ulf-Daniel Ehlers is an internationally renowned Professor for Educational Management and Lifelong Learning at the Baden-Wuerttemberg Cooperative State University (DHBW) Karlsruhe which he headed as Vice-President between 2011 and 2017.

Laura Eigbrecht is principle investigator, teacher and doctoral student at the Baden-Wuerttemberg Cooperative State University (DHBW) Karlsruhe and holds degrees in European Media and Culture and Media Pedagogy.

Open Access This chapter is licensed under the terms of the Creative Commons Attribution 4.0 International License (http://creativecommons.org/licenses/by/4.0/), which permits use, sharing, adaptation, distribution and reproduction in any medium or format, as long as you give appropriate credit to the original author(s) and the source, provide a link to the Creative Commons license and indicate if changes were made.

The images or other third party material in this chapter are included in the chapter's Creative Commons license, unless indicated otherwise in a credit line to the material. If material is not included in the chapter's Creative Commons license and your intended use is not permitted by statutory regulation or exceeds the permitted use, you will need to obtain permission directly from the copyright holder.

Beyond Future Skills in Higher Education: A New Theory of Change

9

Eglis Chacón⊕, Emma Harden-Wolfson⊕, Luz Gamarra Caballero⊕, Bosen Lily Liu⊕ and Dana Abdrasheva⊕

Abstract

The role of higher education in equipping students for future paths that are being shaped by major global challenges and yet which remain unpredictable is an area of ongoing concern. This chapter proposes a new theory of change that supports efforts to identify the skills needed by future generations that higher education can provide. It extends the conceptualization to focus on how, through higher education, these skills could shape and refine people and societies. The theory of change is based on the findings of a survey conducted by the

---

E. Chacón (✉)
Boston College, Chestnut Hill, USA
e-mail: chaconce@bc.edu

E. Harden-Wolfson
McGill University, Montreal, Canada
e-mail: emma.harden-wolfson@mcgill.ca

L. G. Caballero
Newcastle University, Newcastle, Australia
e-mail: luz.gamarracaballero@uon.edu.au

B. L. Liu
UNESCO International Institute for Higher Education in Latin America and the Caribbean, Caracas, Venezuela
e-mail: b.liu@unesco.org

D. Abdrasheva
Korkyt Ata Kyzylorda University, Kyzylorda, Kazakhstan
e-mail: Dana.abdrasheva@alumni.nu.edu.kz

© The Author(s) 2024
U.-D. Ehlers and L. Eigbrecht (eds.), *Creating the University of the Future*, Zukunft der Hochschulbildung - Future Higher Education,
https://doi.org/10.1007/978-3-658-42948-5_9

UNESCO International Institute for Higher Education in Latin America and the Caribbean (UNESCO IESALC) during 2021, which was completed by almost 1,200 respondents in nearly 100 countries. This theory of change identifies the main skills that will be needed in the future, the accelerators that will facilitate the adoption of these skills, and the ways in which these skills and accelerators might lead to transformation at individual, institutional, and societal levels.

9.1 Introduction

Higher education has a critical role in equipping students for future paths. However, these paths are simultaneously being shaped by major global challenges and are unpredictable, causing ongoing concern. Calls to transform and reimagine all levels of education have only increased as the urgency around the impending environmental catastrophe collides with the persisting inequalities being put under the spotlight by new global crises (UNESCO, 2021). In this context, higher education institutions 'must impart knowledge, competencies and skills which will enable their graduates to function effectively in our rapidly changing society and world' (Jelinek & Fomerand, 2013).

Thinking about the future enables the generation of policies, strategies, and plans for the current time that can also lead to creating better and plausible future scenarios (Dator, 2009; Inayatullah, 2008, 2022). This offers the opportunity to individuals to be able to decide on possible future paths (Facer & Sandford, 2010). Yet, the realm of education, which has as a main objective to better prepare individuals for the future, is sometimes far from considering how these desirable futures could be achieved. This problem is often exacerbated by visions generated from other parts of the world, making it important to review future higher education scenarios that can create the conditions for paradigm shifts towards new, more desirable, and more locally relevant futures (Makoe, 2022).

This chapter proposes a new theory of change that supports efforts to identify the skills needed by future generations of students in higher education. It extends the conceptualization to focus on how, through higher education, these skills could shape and refine people and societies, facilitating the identification of solutions to address obstacles to progress and guiding the selection of the optimal strategy to reach the desired change (UNDAF, 2017). The theory of change was developed from the findings of a global public consultation on the futures of higher education organized by the UNESCO International Institute for Higher

Education in Latin America and the Caribbean (UNESCO IESALC) during 2021. Using an inductive approach, data from almost 1,200 respondents in nearly 100 countries was analyzed to generate a theory of change that identifies the main skills that will be needed in the future, the accelerators (outputs) that will facilitate or increase the adoption of these skills, and the goals (outcomes) for which these skills and accelerators might lead to transformation at individual, institutional, and societal levels.

Before introducing the theory of change, the chapter provides background on UNESCO's major initiative on the futures of education within which UNESCO IESALC conducted its work on the futures of higher education. The visions of higher education to a 2050 horizon emerging from the public consultation are presented and then connected methodologically to the identification of the future skills, accelerators and goals that inform the theory of change.

9.2 The Futures of Education

UNESCO's major global initiative on the futures of education aimed to 'reimagine how knowledge and learning can shape the future of humanity and the planet' (UNESCO IESALC, 2021a, p. 5).[1] Begun in 2019, the initiative engaged around one million people around the world in looking ahead to a 2050 horizon, recognizing that there should not be a single vision of the future (hence the use of 'futures' in the plural). The project centered on the transformative power of education to support better futures for all, building on UNESCO's track record of rethinking the role of education in periods of societal change (Delors, 1996; UNESCO, 1972, 2021).

As the only specialized institute of the United Nations system with a mission to contribute to the improvement of higher education, UNESCO IESALC initiated a project on the futures of higher education within the framework of this UNESCO global initiative. The project had three phases enabling rigorous engagement with a range of different stakeholders in the context of higher education. Overall, the project ran from November 2020 to May 2022.

In Phase I, an expert consultation, 25 global higher education experts were selected from all world regions. The selection of experts was based on their experience in teaching, research, and/or enacting higher education, with considerations of regional and gender balance taken into account. Experts representing a

---

[1] https://en.unesco.org/futuresofeducation/

range of knowledge traditions were invited to join the process.[2] Through this process, the experts shared their understanding of the concept, goals, and functions of higher education to propose opportunities and challenges that higher education can resolve looking into 2050. This phase culminated in the report *Thinking Higher and Beyond: Perspectives on the futures of higher education to 2050* (UNESCO IESALC, 2021b), which was published in May 2021.

During Phase II, a public consultation, almost 1,200 responses from nearly 100 countries were collected through an online survey tool. The survey was open to everyone and disseminated across all world regions.[3] Participants ranged in age from under 15 to over 60 with 57% identifying as female, 42% as male and 1% as nonbinary. Just over half of the respondents (55%) reported their location as being in Latin America and the Caribbean, 26% were in Asia and the Pacific, 13% in Europe and North America, 4% in Africa and 1% in the Arab states (based on UNESCO world regions). While the survey was open to all members of the public, 84% of respondents had some connection to the higher education sector, whether as teachers, students, or staff. The survey was available in English, French, Portuguese, and Spanish; respondents were also able to submit their responses in Chinese. The public consultation demonstrated a wide range of views and ideas on the role of higher education and the role of higher education in societal development. This phase led to the report *Pathways to 2050: Findings from a public consultation on the futures of higher education* (UNESCO IESALC, 2021a), which was published in November 2021.

Phase III of the project was a youth consultation. The aim of this phase was to raise the voices from the generations who will be the future beneficiaries and shapers of higher education. The consultation took place in two parts, the first being an online Global Youth Forum hosted in December 2021 and the second being in-person Regional Youth Workshops held in China and Venezuela in April and May 2022. Participants in the Global Youth Forum were selected through national networks convened by UNESCO's Associated Schools Network; the youth participants in China and Venezuela are students in local high schools in Shenzhen and Caracas, cities where UNESCO offices are based.

---

[2] A list of experts and further details about the expert consultation can be found at https://www.iesalc.unesco.org/en/futures-of-higher-education/expert-consultation/.

[3] Additional information about the methodology can be found in UNESCO IESALC (2021b).

9 Beyond Future Skills in Higher Education: A New Theory of Change

This chapter draws from data from phase II, the public consultation. The findings presented in this chapter focus on the public's responses to the higher education-specific questions in the consultation, highlighted in bold:

1. When you think about 2050, what are you most hopeful about?
2. When you think about 2050, what are you most concerned about?
3. **How would you like higher education to be in 2050?**
4. **How could higher education contribute to better futures for all in 2050?**

The logic of the consultation questions was to support respondents to reflect on the futures of higher education through linking higher education to broader societal shifts, challenges, and opportunities. These two questions encouraged people to extend their thinking on the role of higher education in reaching or addressing their hopes and concerns.

9.3 Higher Education in 2050 and Beyond

UNESCO IESALC's public consultation on the futures of higher education led to the development of a holistic conception of pathways to 2050 and beyond (see Fig. 9.1). From the general hopes and concerns for the futures as well as the futures of higher education specifically, four interconnected pathways were identified. These form the foundation for our futures, each pathway representing a root from which we can grow. In **quality of life** (pathway one) there are healthy humans living well and, due to **social change** (pathway two), we live in a socially just society. Through **care of the environment** (pathway three), we inhabit a flourishing planet that is better cared for; the advanced **development of technology** (pathway four) supports these harmonious relations with the self, others, and nature.

Nourished by these roots, higher education in the future has a number of branches. Opening access to higher education and striving for greater equity were key messages from respondents and discussed under the theme of **higher education for all**. Respondents' suggestions focused on **student-centered** future learning processes, emphasizing quality, student choice, skills, and values. The **organization of knowledge** for teacher development, what is taught, and the place for research and innovation were also reflected in respondents' ideas. Respondents also envisioned higher education in 2050 as being much more integrated than today and **connected at multiple levels** with society, with the planet, within and across borders.

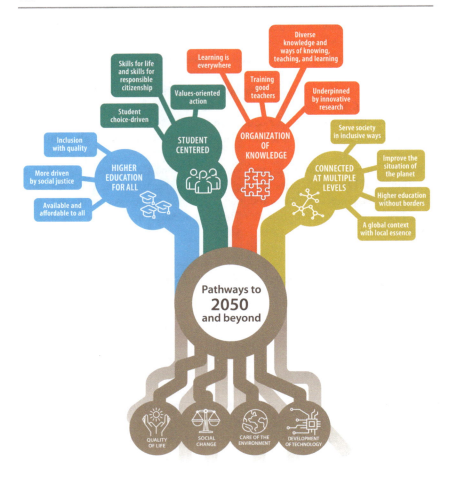

Fig. 9.1 Pathways to 2050 and beyond (UNESCO IESALC, 2021a, p. 39)

9.4 Connecting Higher Education in 2050 to Future Skills

The findings of the phase II public consultation and the phase I expert consultation were brought together in a joint vision for the futures of higher education (Fig. 9.2). This shows that higher education should be accessible to all, with

Fig. 9.2 Vision of the futures of higher education based on the expert and public consultations (UNESCO IESALC)

students at the very heart of everything higher education does and is for. This student-centeredness is surrounded by well-trained teachers and researchers, and flexible teaching and learning modalities. It is nurtured by intercultural and epistemic diversity, takes active and innovative responsibility for our common humanity, promotes wellbeing and sustainability, and is connected at multiple levels. This common humanity recognizes that existence and wellbeing are collective, and therefore that our destiny as humans is shared.

Given the importance of student-centered focus in the consultations, and taking into consideration one of higher education's main goals in training/forming students, this became the starting point for the inductive analysis of skills conducted for this chapter. In total, the public consultation received valid responses from 1,199 participants, each of whom provided free text input for the consultation's four questions:

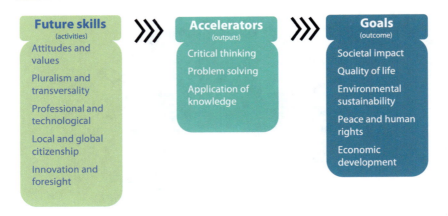

Fig. 9.3 Future skills and beyond: Theory of change (UNESCO IESALC)

1. When you think about 2050, what are you most hopeful about?
2. When you think about 2050, what are you most concerned about?
3. **How would you like higher education to be in 2050?**
4. **How could higher education contribute to better futures for all in 2050?**

Before reaching these questions, the following explanation was provided to respondents:

Higher education will shape the future of humanity and the planet. Regardless of where you live and work, or whether you have experienced higher education, you have the right to voice your opinion on the futures of higher education.

By higher education, we mean all types of study programs and courses of study at post-secondary level. Higher education can take place in universities, colleges, academies, conservatories, and specialized institutes. We invite everyone to join UNESCO IESALC in exploring the futures of higher education.

This public consultation is linked to UNESCO's Futures of Education, a global initiative to reimagine how knowledge and learning can shape the future of humanity and the planet.

From the total number of responses, 1,025 entries had a link to the student-centered pathway, meaning that participants referred to the importance of student-centered higher education in their answer. These entries were extracted from the dataset,[4] with a total of 445 entries identified in response to question 3 (as listed above) and 580 in response to question 4. The entries were manually coded by two people working independently, with the project coordinator reviewing the entire coding operation. This improved reliability and reduced duplication/repetition of codes.

The coding process was conducted in two parts. The first was descriptive and focused on identifying what respondents stated about the skills needed for the future, i.e., the specific skills or competencies that were mentioned. The second part was interpretive and examined the implied impact/significance of these responses, i.e., for what purpose these skills could be used/deployed to contribute to better futures for all. In total, 2,327 codes were generated. These were subsequently grouped according to commonalities as indicated by the participants and based on previous definitional work by UNESCO IBE (2013) and UNICEF (2022). From the descriptive codes, a total of 31 skill categories were identified and classified according to their frequency of occurrence (see Fig. 9.4 in next section). These were then grouped according to the major categories of skills and accelerators identified for the analysis.

The interpretive codes were also grouped to form the goals categories. The following section presents the findings in the form of a theory of change.

9.5 Future Skills and Beyond: A New Theory of Change

The UNESCO IESALC public consultation had a forward-thinking character that emphasized positive change. As a result, participants referred to promising and bright futures based on their view of the futures of higher education. It was in this context that respondents mentioned various skills, competencies, capabilities, and qualities that would be necessary to improve performance: in everyday life, at work, to impact society positively, to combat climate change, and for human or economic development.

A theory of change is an approach that explains how a given intervention or series of interventions is/are expected to result in a specified change in development. It frequently uses a causal analysis based on available evidence (UNDAF,

---

[4]The full dataset from the public consultation is available open access at https://www.iesalc.unesco.org/en/futures-of-higher-education/public-consultation/.

2017). The application of this framework facilitates the identification of obstacles to progress. It guides the selection of an optimal strategy to offer solutions to address the problem effectively. It can also identify the risks that could prohibit the achievement of the desired change.

The theory of change (Fig. 9.3) derived from this analysis connects these groups of skills to a smaller number of accelerators, and from there to a series of goals. From the public consultation, **future skills** can be defined as groups of attributes and/or abilities that can support students towards better futures and which can be developed while participating in higher education. Future skills include attitudes and values, pluralism and transversality, professional and technological, local and global citizenship, and innovation and foresight. In this idea of obtaining attributes and/or abilities for those futures, participants stressed the role of higher education in developing, enhancing, promoting, strengthening, and sharpening the ability to think critically, solve problems, and apply knowledge.

These three areas of skills – critical thinking, problem solving, and application of knowledge – are presented as **accelerators** in the theory of change, meaning that they are tangible outputs, or results. They are produced from the participation of the higher education experience and play a fundamental role in enabling the movement from delivering the skills to achieving outcomes. The addition of the accelerators as a mediator between skills and goals highlights the unique roles that higher education can play in enabling people to achieve positive personal and societal objectives (outcomes). While the future skills could be developed in other sectors beyond education, and the goals could similarly be achieved in other ways, the unique factor connecting them together is higher education. More specifically, the accelerators are areas that students should *expect* to develop and/or master as a result of participating in higher education.

Coupling together the skills and accelerators leads to the different **goals** that could be achieved through higher education and beyond. The goals expressed by survey respondents are: societal impact, quality of life, environmental sustainability, peace and human rights, and economic development. They are a good reflection of the ways that people tend to think about the future(s). People may not know precisely what they are aiming for or how they might achieve it, but they have certain desires or ambitions which are typically stated in broad and/or high-level terms.

Although the theory of change puts forward all factors as equally important, some were selected by respondents more often than others (see Fig. 9.4). This visualization helps to understand the relative prioritization of the elements within the theory of change when examining the responses as a whole. The order in

9 Beyond Future Skills in Higher Education: A New Theory of Change

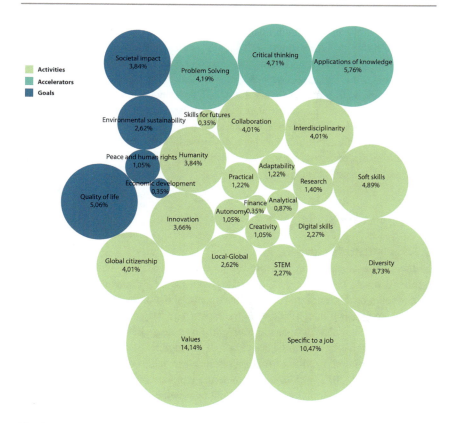

Fig. 9.4 Frequency of elements in the theory of change (UNESCO IESALC)

which the categorized factors appear in the theory of change also reflects this prioritization, with the categories that were mentioned most higher in the list.

Figure 9.4 shows graphically how the theory of change is adjusted according to the relevance (number of mentions) that participants gave in their answers when referring to the competencies they felt are needed in the different pathways towards 2050. Values, job-specific skills, the ability to think diversely or pluralistically, and soft skills are among the **future skills** most mentioned by respondents, among others that together account for 72% of the mentions when participants refer to the skills of the future. The skills that are developed and/or mastered as a result of participation in higher education (the **accelerators**) account for 15% of total mentions. Finally, looking ahead, participants gave relevance to future purposes (the **goals**) such as quality of life, societal impact, environmental sustainability, and others that together total 13% of the mentions.

The following sub-sections walk through each of the three parts of the theory of change, providing further detail about each area and showcasing through direct quotes from respondents (translated by the research team into English as applicable) the ways in which these categories were derived. In this way, the evidence for the theory of change that has been developed derives both from the quantitative data on frequency of elements as well as qualitative data from the free text responses of survey participants.

9.5.1 Future Skills

9.5.1.1 Attitudes and Values

In the public consultation, the futures look inclusive, more equitable, and culturally diverse. In this regard, a striking finding was the emphasis placed by respondents on attitudes and values, the sets of skills and attributes that are less tangible and measurable. These were the most frequently mentioned of all the different types of skills (28% of the total). In this category are future-oriented soft skills, with soft skills defined as a 'set of intangible personal qualities, traits, attributes, habits and attitudes that can be used in many different types of jobs' (UNESCO IBE, 2013, p. 53). In respondents' words, this included attributes such as communication, empathy, flexibility, and teamwork.

> *"Investigating problems in depth with a realistic and ethical sense and preparing students for their reflective possibilities, for the exercise of solidarity and respect as citizens, and for the possibility of generating multi-diverse and solid education." (age >60, female, Argentina)*

Respondents emphasized personal qualities such as self-management, ability to communicate assertively, to work in a team, authenticity, and sharing beliefs. Attributes included future vision, curiosity, solidarity, listening to multiple knowledge and people, ancestral wisdom for the regional and global development of the community, non-discrimination, learning to understand the diversity of the world and appreciate diversity, design strategies for the future; and habits such as respect for human rights, commitment to nature, plural thinking, tolerance, capacity for nondiscrimination, environmental and social awareness, understanding how to live with others and with nature, learn how to care.

Values, which in the theory of change are attributes that fit within future skills, are 'culturally defined principles and core beliefs shared by individuals and groups that guide and motivate attitudes, choices and behavior, and serve as broad guidelines for social life' (UNESCO IBE, 2013, p. 60). In the consultation, respondents discussed ethics, honesty, integrity, justice, sensitivity to the needs of others and so on, and the importance of these in improving relationships with people and human living conditions.

> "Education based on values should be weighed more than education based on skills or knowledge. Let humans be humans, not just tools." (age 31–45, male, China)

9.5.1.2 Pluralism and Transversality

The second most frequent category of skills are those relating to pluralism and transversality (19% of the total mentions). Three main skillsets inform this category: diversity, interdisciplinarity, and creativity.

As a skill, participants discussed respect for diversity as an interpersonal skill that 'goes beyond tolerance and understanding to actively acknowledge and promote the equal worth of peoples without condescension' (UNICEF, 2022). Respondents mentioned the need to be more compassionate, tolerant, supportive, committed to others, to the community, to humanity and the environment and to reduce extremism and violence, while others highlighted the importance of values to democratize knowledge for the common good.

When respondents think about futures, they emphasized skills that generate an understanding of themes and ideas that cut across disciplines and the connections with different disciplines and their relationship to the world. These were termed by participants as interdisciplinarity, multidisciplinary, transdisciplinary, transversal, diversified or integral skills.

> "Working together on multidisciplinary solutions to global challenges" (age 40–60, female, Vietnam)
> "Embracing inter-and transdisciplinarity from the undergraduate level to address the complex challenges of our realities and maximizing diversity among its students and academics" (age 31–45, female, Chile)

Creativity is seen by respondents as an essential future skill to respond adaptively to the needs for new approaches and new products using imagination and vision, and thinking every day about how to act collaboratively with a social focus across different fields and with diverse applications.

> "Help students increase their creativity and develop new technologies" (age 16–30, male, China)

9.5.1.3 Professional and Technological Skills

Most of the responses in this skill group (17% of total responses) referred to skills that are typically connected to professions and jobs. Those who related their response to the importance of skills training for entering the labor market stated the importance of higher education in generating the capacity to meet industry and market needs.

> *"The university must be the real vector of access to employment for graduates" (age 46–60, male, Angola)*

Skills in science, technology, engineering and math (STEM) are another group of skills that respondents associated with basic sciences, science understanding, and the technological know-how required for the future.

> *"To develop technical and technological capabilities of individuals" (age 31–45, male, Ecuador)*

Respondents defined digital skills as a range of abilities for e-learning, the use of digital devices, communication applications and social networks, in general with the purpose of greater access to digital information.

> *[Higher education contributes to better futures for all] "By developing digital skills and knowledge" (age 46–60, male, Senegal)*
> *"Equal education opportunities, as well as adaptive learning and technology use, and digital literacy improvement" (age 46–60, male, China)*

As well as digital literacy, participants also mentioned the importance of financial literacy and how the business world works. Respondents emphasized the importance of skills not only from a labor perspective (productivity-related) but also as instruments that enables people to progress (in the various ways that 'progress' can be defined) in employment. In addition to developing skills for work, participants also highlighted the importance of this for resolving everyday problems related to the common good and humanity.

> *"Educating people who can then start a career in a related research field and develop the necessary tools we need for our future as humanity" (age 31–45, female, Switzerland).*

9.5.1.4 Local and Global Citizenship

Participants referred to a range of skills that could help generate strong links with society, support global citizenship, and increase collaboration (16% of total mentions). Many respondents took an outlook that combined both the local and global, skills to support people to be more conscious about local places or communities while maintaining a global vision and looking for synergies among them. This included the capacity to learn from the knowledge of the people around you, the ability to understand multiple contexts and realities by addressing the local context, without missing regional and global contexts and the ability to generating synergies among them.

> *"Forming citizens able to take responsibility locally, nationally, regionally and globally with deep spiritual commitment and strong moral values" (age >60, female, Canada).*

Respondents also mentioned global citizenship as a skill integrated into the futures, referring to the importance of being a world citizen with civic values and developing international, intercultural, and global competencies for sustainable futures.

> *"By developing skills for life (not just professional ones) and skills for responsible citizenship (including fighting against climate change)" (age 34–45, female, Romania)*

In the futures, the ability to collaborate and be more inclusive was also mentioned, as was the possibility of appreciating the cultural characteristics of each individual. Understanding how to reduce bias towards gender and race were noted as relevant for the common good.

> *"Educating learners to become leaders of change, educating them on colonial pasts, giving them the skills required to tackle issues, such as climate change, and to become inclusive and respectful of others, no matter their background/origin/etc." (age 16–30, female, France)*

9.5.1.5 Innovation and Foresight

The final group of skills covers research, innovation, practical, analytical, adaptive, and foresight skills (15% of total mentions). Respondents mentioned that research and innovation skills can contribute to the overall capability of achieving general job tasks. Research skills were also related to producing new knowledge, transfer knowledge, or research thinking and innovation skills connected to the ability to turn knowledge into creating new things, with an entrepreneurial mindset and social impact.

Participants in the public consultation refer to practical skills. This group of skills relate to the ability to apply knowledge that has been acquired, not only for employment goals but also for life. This element differentiates practical skills from other types of skills. Respondents also emphasize the importance of acquiring these skills and developing the capacity to transmit and impart knowledge.

> *"Continue to provide for the needs to individuals and the economy through an accessible system and teaching relevant skills" (age 31–45, male, Singapore)*

Analytical skills mentioned by respondents referred to cognitive development and applying knowledge by contributing to scientific, social, economic, and cultural development, without forgetting the ethical component.

> *"Developing cognitive skills with an ethical backbone" (age 46–60, male, United States of America)*

Autonomy is also one of the skills mentioned by respondents, referred to as the ability to manage, regulate, and apply one's learning. Autonomy empowers students to take ownership of their own knowledge and make decisions based on values, respect, humility, and enrichment.

> *"Human skills development approach and self-management skills" (age 46–60, female, Colombia)*

The ability to adapt to change was also mentioned to integrate a society that benefits itself as changes occur and the capacity to use acquired knowledge to develop different connections at various levels in such a way that we can anticipate changes for the future.

> *"Emphasis more on cultivating ability or skills needed in future rather than the form of thesis" (age 16–30, female, China)*

9.5.2 Accelerators

The three areas of skills categorized as accelerators are, in order of their prioritization by respondents, critical thinking, problem solving, and the application of knowledge. While some participants referred to this specific group as skills for the future, others emphasized the importance of higher education in accelerating these skills during the higher education experience.

> *"I would like higher education to remain a place of emancipation, of critical debate, of academic freedom" (age 31–45, female, France)*
> *"Tailored to develop critical and innovative thinking" (age 31–45, male, Spain)*

For critical thinking, respondents highlighted the importance of thinking for themselves critically without yielding to peer pressure or believing what others say, holding their reflection for a common future.

> *"Better understanding of our world, be more critical citizens and be willing to challenge the status quo in a meaningful way" (age 40–60, prefer not to mention gender, Canada)*
> *"A well-educated population makes better decisions and votes with critical thinking for the long term." (age 16–30, male, Spain)*

According to respondents, problem solving is another relevant skill required to tackle issues and orient people to act on global problems with commitment; being resourceful to solve global issues to offer solutions for society and humanity with the knowledge gained.

> *"It [problem solving] can increase the knowledge and skills of young people and make them instrumental in resolving issues of climate change, poverty and unemployment" (age 40–60, female, Pakistan)*
> *"[Higher education should] have close connections with industry and motivate students to engage in real-life problem solving" (age 34–45, male, China)*

For respondents, the application of knowledge refers to the ability to provide diverse knowledge, academic or technological, in any field for the common good to improve the quality of life. This also includes competence, defined as 'the ability to apply learning outcomes adequately in a defined context' (UNESCO IBE, 2013, p. 12). These are not limited to the use of theory/concepts and can also include technical skills, interpersonal attributes, and ethical values.

> *"I would like to change the vertical model, where the teacher is the source of knowledge and cedes it to the student and adopt a model where the student explores and empowers his or her capacity to acquire, produce and apply knowledge" (age 31–45, male, Argentina)*

> *"Higher education must above all train students to think for themselves, to be aware of diversity, to be able and willing to engage in dialogue across cultures and identities, and to be able to apply their knowledge/learning (in whatever field) for the common good"* (Prefer not to mention age/gender, Canada)

9.5.3 Goals

The nature of research on the futures of education of UNESCO lies in how 'knowledge and learning can shape the future of humanity and the planet' (UNESCO, 2021, p. 2). From this forward-looking perspective, respondents comment on their contribution on how the skills and accelerators mentioned can shape the future to impact society. The skills, capabilities, and attributes will help to, in order of relevance: improve quality of life, improve environmental sustainability, preserve peace, and ensure human rights and economic development.

9.5.3.1 Societal Impact

Participants recognize that the purpose of higher education extends beyond national borders and serves both global and local societies. Through ideas and knowledge born in classrooms, students are expected to positively impact their surroundings. This impact is realized by putting into action students' technological skills, their consciousness, and abilities to incorporate values in their system of viewing the world, and awareness of environmental threats. Particularly, further advancements in knowledge can contribute to human's everyday life.

> *"Through the sophistication of knowledge and the inclusion of subjects that encourage and generate greater social and environmental awareness across all degree courses. Changing the purpose of studying from monetarist to social, community and environmental"* (age 31–45, male, Spain)

Higher education is expected to nurture and help students grow into mindful, confident, and holistic individuals. In this sense, students strengthen their agency while obtaining their higher education qualification. Higher education institutions contribute to the shaping of the citizen of the future by helping them understand and know themselves better. In this sense, skills, as highlighted by the respondents contribute to responsible citizenship.

> *"I hope the higher education can be a real garden of spirits, enhancing people's comprehensive abilities and letting them know themselves better"* (age 31–45, female, China)

9 Beyond Future Skills in Higher Education: A New Theory of Change

Understanding the human dimension in its broadest sense is an important element of a better life. Higher education can play a critical role in preparing students for life.

"Improve the living conditions of human beings, based on the values and the thought of living better, in a place that we care for, protect and give us what we need to live" (age 46–60, male, Mexico)

9.5.3.2 Environmental Sustainability

In 2050, participants hope to live in more harmony with nature. Conscious citizens with skills such as values, empathy, and a sense of justice will be capable of pursuing this goal within local and global settings. Awareness of worsening environmental situations will alert future students to seek solutions to tackle and prevent further damage to the planet.

"By helping all people to understand that human beings are part of nature and therefore must learn to live in and with nature" (age >60, male, Brazil)

9.5.3.3 Peace and Human Rights

Participants highlighted the importance of developing skills for peacebuilding. Citizens of the world with talents such as a holistic sense of humanity will contribute to building brighter futures for all.

"In my view, higher education won't be restricted to limited individuals or society in 2050. I think higher education will create more empathy among the people and broaden the vision of human society for the prosperity of people, the planet and global peace" (age 31–45, male, Thailand)

By placing an emphasis on human development, respondents demonstrated their concern with the ongoing state of human rights around the world. In their understanding, higher education has the potential to expose students to become advocates for human rights. It is through this learning that a student obtains an understanding and awareness of the potential violations of human rights.

Maintain a balance between technical and technological training and humanistic and ethical training; it will not be possible to change the world if we train good technicians and bad people (age 46–60, female, Colombia)

9.5.3.4 Economic Development

Economic development was the least emphasized purpose in the consultation. Where mentioned, participants believe that economic development cannot occur without human development. Higher education helps learners to become leaders of change to help the world and the economy, both should be viewed holistically.

> *"Students study not just for personal living, but with a commitment to build a better world by helping the economies of developing countries" (age >60, nonbinary, China)*

9.6 Conclusion

This chapter presented a new theory of change that moves the conversations about future skills to the next level by contextualizing skills with three core accelerators that together lead to a series of goals. As the UNESCO Futures of Education initiative makes clear, the paths ahead vary, reflecting different realities and contexts around the world. Nevertheless, this theory of change captures an approach towards those multiple avenues that could lead to our plural futures. In the shared vision, higher education offers a concrete set of skills that are accelerated by critical thinking, problem solving, and the application of knowledge, and then transformed into the possibility to reach the goals. In this theory of change, higher education institutions act as catalysts of change because it is through higher education that the accelerators can be developed in students. In this lies the unique role of higher education because it is higher education that provides the accelerators that connect future skills to goals.

The theory of change devised from the results of the public consultation conducted by UNESCO IESALC on the futures of higher education can be taken up and implemented at both a theoretical and a practical level. While the public consultation was wide-ranging, it was far from being universal. Its coverage could have been diversified both in terms of regional coverage and by incorporating the views and ideas of stakeholders without existing connections to (and therefore 'insider' knowledge of) higher education. As such, the first recommendation for developing the theory of change is to see whether the future skills → accelerators → goals links continue to hold true after sampling different population segments.

Finally, it is important to note that while this theory of change offers a unique and novel way of deepening the future skills debates, it is equally important, if not more so, to acknowledge diversity among different contexts. Such contexts can be regions, countries, institutions, and even individuals. Each context has its own opportunities and challenges that demand specific skills that may not be as relevant in other contexts. Contextualization in the discussion of skills is essential in providing the optimal outcomes of skill trainings. At the same time, while one of the missions of higher education is to provide training—whether knowledge-based or skill-based—it is a constant reminder for all stakeholders that higher education offers more than this single mission. Higher education's practices should always remain human-focused to serve the realization of the common good for all.

> **Future Skills in Practice: Our Recommendations**
>
> On a more hands-on level, there are a wide range of possibilities for putting the theory of change into practice. Here we delineate how key stakeholders could promote the future skills, accelerators and goals put forward in the theory of change through higher education:
>
> - **Future students:** When choosing a course of study in higher education, look beyond the subject matter to consider what skills can be obtained during the study period. Select a higher education institution because it can provide you with skills and accelerators to meet your personal and societal goals as well as opportunities to practice these outside the classroom.
> - **Current students:** Through governance structures (student unions, representation on committees, etc.), advocate for greater inclusion of future skills and accelerators in all courses. Seek out students based in other departments and faculties through cross-institutional opportunities to learn from each other and share skills and knowledge. This inclusive process accelerates the possibility of promoting the skills mentioned in the theory of change, such as diverse and pluralistic thinking and interdisciplinarity.
> - **Higher education teachers:** Redesign courses to emphasize future skills but particularly to promote the accelerators. For example, where assignments/evaluations are required, evaluate students' progress in developing the accelerators and not only subject expertise. Work with colleagues in other departments to create transdisciplinary courses. Build up links with relevant societal sectors to support students to build up relevant skills.

- **Higher education researchers:** Engage students in transdisciplinary research, both blue skies and applied, either as part of their courses or as extracurricular provision. Provide training to students to enhance their abilities when it comes to the accelerators.
- **Student support teams:** Work with students to outline their own theory of change, identify those skills that have yet to be developed, or even the inclusion of those that they did not expect to develop but which as a result of their participation in the higher education experience, they have managed to acquire or master. Also, complementing the theory of change, engage with students to brainstorm the new skills that could emerge in the future.
- **Institutional leaders:** Conduct whole-of-institution reviews using the theory of change to support future planning. Integrate the Sustainable Development Goals into the institution's strategic plans as a way of promoting the connections between future skills, accelerators and goals.
- **National policymakers:** Review course evaluation/quality assurance requirements for higher education institutions to integrate future skills and accelerators. Where national development plans for higher education exist, use the goals in the theory of change to update the mission/objectives section, suitably adjusted to the local context.

References

Dator, J. (2009). Alternative futures at the manoa school. *Journal of Futures Studies, 14*(2), 1–18.

Delors, J. (1996). *Learning: The treasure within: Report to UNESCO of the international commission on education for the twenty-first century.* Unesco Publishing.

Facer, K., & Sandford, R. (2010). The next 25 years?: future scenarios and future directions for education and technology. *Journal of Computer Assisted Learning, 26*(1), 74–93. https://doi.org/10.1111/j.1365-2729.2009.00337.x.

Faure, E., Herrera, F., Kaddoura, A.-R., Lopes, H., Petrovski, A. V., Rahnema, M., et al. (1972). *Learning to be: The world of education today and tomorrow: Report of the international commission on the development of education.* Unesco Publishing.

Inayatullah, S. (2008). Six pillars: futures thinking for transforming. *Foresight, 10*(1), 4–21. https://doi.org/10.1108/14636680810855991.

Inayatullah, S. (2022). *Anticipation to emancipation: Toward a stage theory of the uses of the future.*

Jelinek, V., & Fomerand, J. (19 December 2013). Higher learning institutions and global citizen education. *United Nations Chronicle*. https://www.un.org/en/chronicle/article/higher-learning-institutions-and-global-citizen-education.

Makoe, M. (2022). *The futures of higher education. Reimagining the futures of higher education: Insights from a scenario development process towards 2050. Paper commissioned for the World Higher Education Conference 18–20 May 2022.*

UNDAF. (2017). Theory of change: UNDAF Companion Guidance. https://unsdg.un.org/sites/default/files/UNDG-UNDAF-Companion-Pieces-7-Theory-of-Change.pdf.

UNESCO. (2021). *Reimagining our futures together: a new social contract for education: Report from the international commission on the futures of education.* Unesco Publishing.

UNESCO IBE. (2013). IBE glossary of curriculum terminology. http://www.ibe.unesco.org/fileadmin/user_upload/Publications/IBE_GlossaryCurriculumTerminology2013_eng.pdf.

UNESCO IESALC. (2021). Pathways to 2050 and beyond: Findings from a public consultation on the futures of higher education. https://unesdoc.unesco.org/ark:/48223/pf0000379985/.

UNESCO IESALC. (2021). Thinking higher and beyond: Perspectives on the futures of higher education to 2050. https://unesdoc.unesco.org/ark:/48223/pf0000377530.

UNICEF. (2022). Mission #9 – Respect for diversity. https://www.unicef.org/lac/en/mission-9-respect-diversity.

Eglis Chacón, MSc, is a PhD student and a research assistant at the Center for International Higher Education at Boston College (USA). Her research interests include forcibly displaced people and refugees in higher education, international higher education, student mobility, and international aid in higher education. She worked as a policy analyst at the UNESCO International Institute for Higher Education in Latin America and the Caribbean (UNESCO IESALC) and as a consultant for the Interamerican Development Bank. ORCID ID: 0000-0003-2432-7748

Emma Harden-Wolfson, PhD, is an Assistant Professor at McGill University (Canada). She is a comparative and international higher education specialist with two decades of international expertise in research, teaching, policy analysis, consultancy, and practice. Previously Head of Research and Foresight at UNESCO IESALC, she led flagship projects including the futures of higher education, digital transformation and artificial intelligence, and the right to higher education. Website: https://emmahardenwolfson.com/; ORCID ID: 0000-0001-7849-6411

Luz Gamarra Caballero, MPSP, is a PhD student in Sociology and Anthropology with a scholarship from the UNESCO Chair in Equity, Social Justice and Higher Education at the University of Newcastle (Australia) where her thesis topic is identifying the factors in Indigenous women's success in higher education in Australia and Peru. She was previously a Policy Analyst at UNESCO IESALC. Twitter: @lgamarrac. ORCID ID: 0000-0003-2390-8364

Bosen Lily Liu, MSc, is the Head of Partnership and UN Liaison Unit at UNESCO IESALC where she leads agenda-setting and consensus-making on higher education globally. She was previously a Policy Analyst at UNESCO IESALC where she participated in a range of projects. She has been an educational development researcher and practitioner for 12 years with diverse regional experiences. ORCID ID: 0000-0002-2763-5394

Dana Abdrasheva, PhD, works at Korkyt Ata Kyzylorda University (Kazakhstan) and is a higher education reform expert. Formerly a Policy Analyst at UNESCO IESALC, her research interests are internationalization (including study abroad and international partnerships between universities), governance, and digitalization of higher education. Twitter: @DanaAbdrasheva. ORCID ID: 0000-0001-9881-945X

Open Access This chapter is licensed under the terms of the Creative Commons Attribution 4.0 International License (http://creativecommons.org/licenses/by/4.0/), which permits use, sharing, adaptation, distribution and reproduction in any medium or format, as long as you give appropriate credit to the original author(s) and the source, provide a link to the Creative Commons license and indicate if changes were made.

The images or other third party material in this chapter are included in the chapter's Creative Commons license, unless indicated otherwise in a credit line to the material. If material is not included in the chapter's Creative Commons license and your intended use is not permitted by statutory regulation or exceeds the permitted use, you will need to obtain permission directly from the copyright holder.

Part III
Future Skills in Practice – Teaching and Learning

Part III provides a deep dive into higher education practices in different countries and institutions through insight into teaching and learning Future Skills. A Future Skills expert-talk with Angela Duckworth (Character Lab) will lead the way, followed by selected examples of Future Skills-ready higher and tertiary education on a larger scale such as 42 Coding Schools or Team Academy.

Future Skills in Practice - Teaching and Learning

"If You Really Want to Change the World, the Smartest Way to do so is Through Education"

10

A Future Skills conversation with Angela Duckworth

Ulf-Daniel Ehlers and Laura Eigbrecht

> **Abstract**
>
> Angela Duckworth (Fig. 10.1) is the Rosa Lee and Egbert Chang Professor of Psychology at the University of Pennsylvania and the founder of Character Lab, a nonprofit that advances scientific insights to help kids thrive. Before her research career, Angela Duckworth was a math and science teacher at public schools, founding her passion for education. With one of the most-viewed TED talks of all time and the bestselling book Grit: The Power of Passion and Perseverance as well as as a podcast host, Angela Duckworth shares her research to a broader audience. In this conversation, we discuss the concepts of Future Skills and character strengths and what they can contribute to shape the future of education.

Eigbrecht: When you think of the future of higher education or the future of education, what are the three first words that come up to your mind?

U.-D. Ehlers
Professor for Educational Management and Lifelong Learning, Business Faculty,
DHBW Karlsruhe, Karlsruhe, Germany
e-mail: ulf-daniel.ehlers@dhbw-karlsruhe.de

L. Eigbrecht (✉)
Educational Management and Lifelong Learning, Business Faculty, DHBW Karlsruhe,
Karlsruhe, Germany
e-mail: laura.eigbrecht@dhbw-karlsruhe.de

© The Author(s) 2024
U.-D. Ehlers and L. Eigbrecht (eds.), *Creating the University of the Future*, Zukunft der Hochschulbildung - Future Higher Education,
https://doi.org/10.1007/978-3-658-42948-5_10

Fig. 10.1 Angela Duckworth

Duckworth: Curiosity, independence and connection.

Eigbrecht: Tell us about your personal "Future Skill moment", where you learnt something for the future.

Duckworth: Well, I was very lucky to have the same teacher for writing twice when I was a high school student and his name was Mr. Carr. I was very lucky because he was so wonderful. And to have him twice, I think I had a double dose of a teacher who really helped me discover my curiosity again.

We know today from research: many of the students are, by the time they get to high school, really tuned out, there's nothing in the hours of the school day that peaks their curiosity. But with Mr. Carr, every day was an adventure. He would come in with stories, and in one class we stood on the desks just to see what it would be like to have a different perspective. He brought his own personal stories.

There were countless moments where I felt vividly alive again as a student. And I believe today that, to the extent that I'm a writer, it is because I had Mr. Carr as my writing teacher during those two years.

So, for me, the lesson of Mr. Carr is that education and teachers make enormous differences in the lives of young people.

Ehlers: Angela—I am still thinking about the three words you chose before: curiosity, independence and connection. How do independence and connection go together?

Duckworth: Those three words represent three dimensions of human functioning that all young people, especially in the twenty-first century, but frankly for all of the centuries of humanity, need in order to thrive, to lead a good life for themselves and for others. We already talked about curiosity, which is a strength of mind. When I talk about independence, I think of it as a strength of will. And when I talk about connection, I think of it as a strength of heart. Consider what you want for a young person in life: I am a mother of two daughters, as well as a scientist and an educator. And what would be my fondest hopes for my daughters to live good lives for themselves and for others is to develop these strengths of heart, mind, and will.

So, I have my stories of Mr. Carr, but there's a lot of new science on how important curiosity is in the most fundamental ways for learning. And when I mentioned independence, I related to the fact that in the twenty-first century, no matter what you end up doing, there's going to be increasingly a need for you to manage yourself. In other words, rather than other people managing you through contracts, through power, I think increasingly it is our responsibility to manage our own time, our own attention. There are infinite distractions and competing things that we could be doing and now more than ever again, no matter what you do for a living. You have to learn how to set goals, make plans, carry through, be clear about what you want, make sure that what you're doing is aligned with your values and so forth.

And then when you think about strengths of heart, I think about the need for people to relate to other people. So, when I talk about connection, I mean empathy and compassion, social and emotional intelligence. So very briefly, that is why I said curiosity, a strength of mind, independence, a strength of will and connection, a strength of heart.

We already talked about curiosity, which is a strength of mind. When I talk about independence, I think of it as a strength of will. And when I talk about connection, I think of it as a strength of heart.

Ehlers: I would like to directly hook into that: we developed a Future Skills model which is centering around the concepts of learning, creativity, and co-creating. The first relates to the personal development of an individual, the second—creativity—is a dimension which refers to creating solutions for subject matter problems, and the third is referring to one's ability to relate to the (social) world—which we call co-creation. All three are similar to curiosity, independence, and connection.

Eigbrecht: Angela, please tell us a bit about how you came to work with what you're working with now and your pathway to this.

Duckworth: As I mentioned, I was very lucky to have not one, but a few teachers who really changed my life. Then when I went to college, I was not thinking about education in particular. I was thinking I was going to be a doctor, which is what my father absolutely wanted me to be—in fact, he had very specific plans. I was supposed to get an MD and a PhD and then become a medical school professor, like many people in my family.

I started out and studied Neurobiology, and that sounded like the plan was going exactly as he wanted. At that time though in college, I started working with children as a volunteer, tutoring them after school. I then became what we call a Big Sister[1], which is a mentor who meets with a young person every week, and I was a big sister for five years to a little girl named Maria. And the more time I spent in schools, the more I realized that not all students had the same experiences that I had. And I glimpsed, I think for the first time, the equity gap between the haves and the have-nots. To see it so young in life, to see a five-year-old on the other side of an advantage, it was to me not only heartbreaking, but I thought to myself: if you *really* want to change the world, the smartest way to do so is through education—to begin at the beginning.

And if you want to solve any problem, climate change, how to help people live longer lives, everything starts with young people and education. So, I shifted—and I told my father that I was not going to go to medical school. Instead I was

---

[1] Big Brothers Big Sisters is a mentoring network for children and youth. For more information see https://www.bbbs.org/.

going to do something in education. He literally stopped speaking to me for six months, he wouldn't even answer the phone. He was very disappointed, because for him coming from his background—he immigrated to the United States from China—it was a lower status job than to be a medical school professor. So, he thought I was in a way sort of throwing away all of the opportunities he had worked so hard for.

So, I became a teacher. I created and I ran a summer program for low-income children. I worked in non-profit education policy, and now I'm a psychologist who studies the development of young people in order to help them develop the skill sets and mindsets that enable them to thrive.

You know, my father has now passed away, but I will say that before he died, I think we reconciled in one very important way. He came to understand that education was my passion. You're right: I am burning for it. And I haven't changed my mind at all about the importance of education as the lever to change the world—and I think he came to respect that. I'm very grateful to have had the personal experiences that led me to this lifelong interest in education.

To see it so young in life, to see a five-year-old on the other side of an advantage, it was to me not only heartbreaking, but I thought to myself: if you really want to change the world, the smartest way to do so is through education—to begin at the beginning.

Eigbrecht: You are a podcast host and host the podcast show "No Stupid Questions". Can you tell us a little bit about how this contributes to what you aim at with your work?

Duckworth: I have a podcast with Stephen Dubner, who is a journalist. It's called No Stupid Questions and part of the Freakonomics podcast family. The idea behind Freakonomics is that you can actually take any question that you would want to, like a question about public policy or social welfare or air pollution or dogs, apply a social science lens and ask yourself what's really going on here. The reason why I think this is so relevant to our conversation about education and young people is that when you think about our grandparents, our great-grandparents and maybe even our own parents, they were raised by adults who just used their own intuition and their own experience in this—but now we have science. I think intuition and our own personal experience are important. But if a teacher is trying to help young people develop a growth mindset about their abilities or trying to help a young person overcome frustration or learn how to get along better and make friends, there's now science on literally everything that

I mentioned—and more. For me, the podcast No Stupid Questions is part of a much larger movement to introduce science into the mainstream. If you asked me what's my magic wand vision, it's that every child in the world will grow up with a psychologically wise adult in their lives. By that, I mean somebody who is saying and doing things that in the wisest way possible enables that young person to grow up well. And again, intuition is great, personal experience is great, but why not harness modern twenty-first century science just like medicine and just like the most vibrant areas of the economy?

If you asked me what's my magic wand vision, it's that every child in the world will grow up with a psychologically wise adult in their lives. By that, I mean somebody who is saying and doing things that in the wisest way possible enables that young person to grow up well.

Ehlers: When I read about you and your work, the concept of character and character strengths comes out strongly. How would you describe that and why is it so important for you? Why did you focus on this particular concept?

Duckworth: Character is a word that some people love and other people hate—I love it. Let me tell you how I define character and why it's important to me: to me, character is what Aristotle said was important for a life well lived. A more modern definition with a little more specificity is: character is how we think, act, and feel in ways that are good for us and good for others. I think this is what Aristotle meant by character—and that the relevance to young people is obvious then. That's also why we use a phrase like character development. Some people would say they prefer other terms like social, emotional learning, or twenty-first century skills. Economists often talk about non-cognitive skills, or soft skills. I personally am almost agnostic about these alternative terms—I think there are good reasons for each of these terms, but they can be used almost synonymously.

So, character to me goes all the way back to Aristotle, and, more recently, Martin Luther King, the civic activist. When he was only 18 years old, he wrote an essay for his college newspaper—he went to Morehouse College. Martin Luther King, in so many words, had been reflecting on what education is for. And he said: character and intelligence, that is the true purpose of education. And by that he meant: it's not only that we learn math, it's not only that we learn to write well and express ourselves. It's not only that we learn knowledge. When we grow up in schools, we also must learn character. We also must learn all the ways to think, act and feel that are good for us and good for others. So, by character, I mean gratitude, compassion, curiosity, creativity, humility, grit, a growth mindset, optimism, productivity—I mean, everything that I want for my own daughters and for myself.

Ehlers: Angela—when I talk about Future Skills in my community, there is usually an initial fascination and then people start to think about it more deeply. They start to question the normative framework our development is based on and want to discuss the fundamentals. So, let me ask you the same question about your research subject: what is a good character? What is a wise person? What is "developing well" in life and society, and to which degree can we as educators create this idea of wellbeing and impart it on the pupil or the learner? Actually: to which degree are we allowed to do that? Because education is, is in a way, looking from a different perspective. It is also about this small line of educating somebody for freedom and autonomy so that they develop their own ideas. What is your reaction towards that dilemma? Character, in my community here, would be understood as a very normative concept. To have a good character means: you don't steal, you don't drink, you don't lie and so on, this has this biblical, Christian heritage to it. How do you deal with that as a psychologist? Also, when you go into a school that you tell the teachers that we are going to develop character strengths now, how do you bring the message across without going into this danger of being seen as somebody with just another list of important things?

Duckworth: I think it's an excellent question. There is a normative connotation to character, maybe it's even built into the definition. When you talk about character, we mean good character, not bad character. And then the question is: is that okay? Is there a place for that in schools? And how much agreement is there about what is normative? If you asked parents and teachers to make a list of the things that they would put on the good side and then a list of things they would put on the bad side, how much disagreement would there be? If there's a lot of disagreement, then maybe you would say that it should absolutely not be in schools. For example, there's a lot of agreement that young people should be numerate and they should be literate—so we have math and writing, and there are not a lot of parents or educators who would disagree that numeracy and literacy are important goals for all young people to achieve at least at some level.

So, I think for me, the question is, well, how much agreement is there first? And then we can kind of cross the bridge of how much of a role should schools really have in it. I think that most parents actually agree and most educators agree that it's better for a child to be grateful than ungrateful. A child who says 'thank you' sincerely is a child who's learning something which is good for themselves and good for others unambiguously at really no cost to themselves. I think likewise, the same for curiosity or empathy. What about honesty? When's the last time I met a teacher who said: 'No, I actually like my students to be dishonest'? Of course, everyone agrees that that's a good thing. What about believing that you can make a difference in the world, a kind of optimism that I think in a way is so important now more than ever in the twenty-first century? What about hard work? When's the last time I met a teacher who said: 'Oh, I believe all children are born knowing how to work hard'?

Teachers know that children need to learn how to work hard and how to work smart. I think there is enormous consensus about the list of things that would go on the good side, and then the contrary side of bad. I think the question then is: is there a place in schools for character to enter? Because even if you agree on that list, maybe you say that really happens in the home, that's the job of the parents. For me, like Aristotle and like Martin Luther King, and like Maria Montessori, and I think John Dewey and other great thinkers in education, I think there is absolutely a role.

Children spend more waking hours in school and doing school-related activities than pretty much anything outside of the home. And in some cases, it actually is literally more hours than hours spent under their own roof and all that time where they are with other young people watching adult role models who are their teachers, they're learning lessons about how to live life, how to act, think, and feel in ways that are good for themselves and good for others. So, to me to say no, we don't do character development in schools, we don't care about helping children learn how to be grateful, how to be honest, how to be hardworking, how to discover their curiosity, that to me, first of all, is naïve, second of all, that's never been the way that education has been. Simply by not talking about it just means that you're being unintentional, but children are still going to learn. And because there is new scientific research, new understanding about how the brain develops, about healthy child development, to me, it would be almost immoral not to allow educators to make use of these new insights.

Ehlers: Super interesting, thank you. I was once visiting Bogotá in Columbia. I was invited by the Ministry of Education to work with some school teachers in 2004. They had just won the election and they were thinking: How can we create better schools for our country? And what they did is that they were making a big television campaign, newspaper campaign, and social media campaign and asked people to call on hotlines and internet portals and tell their story about what they believed should be taught in schools. They had 47,000 inputs coming in within three months. Amongst the top five were learning how to live in, keep, and develop peace, and the second one was learning to deal with technology, and there was learning to live together as well. These are normative objectives as well—I think it's just important to be explicit about the normative basis.

But there is another concept you work on which is grit. As a scientist, I had the pleasure to work with John Erpenbeck in Germany, who is one of the big researchers in competencies and skills. I remember a phone conversation with him after I had done a lot of work on frameworks and questionnaires. What he told me is that after all the years of research on competencies and how they should be developed—subject-matter competencies, personal and social competencies and so on—one thing always came up as very important in his research and that is what he called "activity competence", or "action competence". And he said that it seemed that apart from all other competencies, this kind of competence that somebody takes the initiative, that somebody is curious, that somebody wants to go forward, wants to learn more, wants to go beyond, is a driver which makes people successful. Everything else doesn't matter *as* much as this particular issue. Is that what you would call grit?

Duckworth: I would need to learn more about action competence or activity competence—you've really aroused my curiosity and I would like to learn more. In general, I think there must be some overlap, because grit is about effort. Grit is something that, when I first started my training as a PhD student in Psychology, I began to want to understand. It was a term, a name, a label that I gave to a specific combination that I found in my research.

From the very beginning, when I looked at super achievers, people who are in the Olympics, for example, or win the Nobel prize, they have this combination of two things: they have perseverance over very long periods, which is kind of obvious, because the things they do are very hard and require long hours. They require resilience in the face of many setbacks and failures, because how else are you going to get to the Olympics or become a Nobel prize scientist? But they also had passion for the same long-term goals. In other words, when you come back to somebody who's really gritty five years from now, 10 years from now, if we have an interview a decade or two decades from now, and you say: 'Wonder what Angela Duckworth is thinking about. Maybe she's moved on to something else. Maybe now she wants to be a chef. You know, maybe she's retired early and maybe she doesn't care so much about children and psychology and education.' But I will guarantee you that if I am alive in 20 years, I will be interested in exactly these topics. I will be like: 'Oh, remember we had that conversation about activity competence'. Like I've been thinking about it for 20 years. And that's what I find about Olympic athletes, about Nobel prize winners, about people who are really at the top echelons of any field. They have perseverance over extremely long periods of time.

It's really more about stamina than it is about intensity. And then they have this kind of abiding devotion. It's like they are voluntarily obsessed with something, but not just for a day or two. So that's what I mean by grit—and when I say that this plays into what I think must be overlapping with activity or action competence, and that is effort, I mean that in the following way: there is the rate at which young people or you or I learn, and that's what is usually called talent—so if I'm very talented, I learn so fast. I was a math teacher, and some children, I could show them once and they would get it—so they were talented. Other students were like, what? I don't get it. But they would try it another time and then eventually get it. What I actually want to say is: the rate at which a young person or an older person learns is talent, but that is separate from how much effort they put in.

Take that very bright student: I teach them once and they understand it. Well, are they going to go home and try to think about their math? Are they going to do their homework? Are they going to study? To me, these are two very different categories of things that actually we have to develop in young people. One is talent, the other is effort. And in the effort family lives grit, that's effort towards very long-term goals, but also delay of gratification and self-control. Can I do things that are good for me? That's proactivity and initiative. Do I start the effort without being pulled?

There are many things in the effort family, but when I look at education and I say, what's going to happen to young people? To me, people are not born understanding how to optimize their efforts. They're not born knowing how to avoid procrastination.

Think about phones and screens and games—young people need our help in developing strategies to not be on their phones all day so they're not completely distracted. They need our help to learn how to set goals, how to make plans, how to learn when our plans don't work, how to take initiative.

I think taking initiative is a skill—it's not something you're born knowing how to do. So, to me, whether we call it activity competence, action competence, grit, delay of gratification, self-control—when I said that when I think of three words that leap to mind for my hopes for twenty-first century education, when I said independence, many philosophers and every religious tradition have said that true freedom is to be able to rule yourself, your own conflicting desires. That independence, self-rule, self-management, self-reliance to me is going to be more important, not less, with the technology and changes that are coming in the twenty-first century and that are already here.

10 If You Really Want to Change the World, the Smartest ...

I think taking initiative is a skill—it's not something you're born knowing how to do. So, to me, whether we call it activity competence, action competence, grit, delay of gratification, self-control—when I said that when I think of three words that leap to mind for my hopes for twenty-first century education, when I said independence, many philosophers and every religious tradition have said that true freedom is to be able to rule yourself, your own conflicting desires.

Eigbrecht: That's an interesting aspect, the time perspective. Thinking about character strengths, would you say they're timeless or are they more important now than ever—and why is that?

Duckworth: You can call them character skills—just as some economists like James Heckman, the Nobel prize-winning economist from the University of Chicago, in order to emphasize that they can be learned. I would say that they are timeless and they are timely—timeless in the sense that since the dawn of humanity, there has been a need to develop curiosity, kindness, gratitude and all the things that we're talking about. In every religious and philosophical tradition, going back to its very earliest writings or even its oral tradition, you can see evidence that people were talking about these exact themes. It's not only Western traditions, it's also Eastern traditions, every tradition. But another question is: how are they timely? What is happening in the future of work? I have new research that I haven't even published yet, where we are analyzing data from millions of workers in the United States, partly from the bureau of labor statistics kept by the U.S. government. We're looking at wages and job growth, and at the characteristics of jobs over more than a decade of recent history, asking what the trends are.

To me, that's a much more scientifically evidence-based way of thinking about the future of work. And I will tell you that the clearest trend that we see is a trend where the jobs requiring a, what we're calling, "intellectual tenacity" are not only growing, but most importantly, the wages are increasing, in a kind of monotonic, steady way.

So, what do I mean by this? These are the jobs that require a kind of curiosity and lifelong learning. Every day I'm solving a new problem. I'm learning something new and I have to take some initiative, I have to keep going because these problems don't solve themselves. Some might have predicted that with artificial intelligence and with automation, maybe people would not need to have intellectual tenacity because computers and machines and the internet do all of our thinking, our problem-solving for us. But I think digital technology is making it more important, not less important, for people of all ages to be lifelong learners, and to have that strength of will, the sort of effort to rule themselves and say:

'Okay, I could give up on this puzzle that I can't figure out or I could keep going'. That, to me, is some suggestion that there is a timeless, but also a timely need for strengths of mind and strengths of will. I want to add one other piece of evidence because it's important research from David Deming who was an economist at Harvard, and his research suggests that in addition to these strengths of mind and will, or intellectual tenacity, there is increasingly a premium on social skills, these strengths of heart, being able to relate to other people, knowing how to work with each other, how to read others' emotions, finding out how people are feeling. This to me says strengths of heart, mind, and will are timeless and are timely and there is an important role for education, from an equity perspective, to enable all young people to develop these capabilities.

Eigbrecht: In your book on grit, you had an example of Teach for America, and I've been a fellow in Germany myself for a year doing that program. It was really nice to see in practice how it can work, promoting a growth mindset with students that maybe normally in our school system, in Germany with being graded all the time, is kind of hard to promote—to see that it's possible to help people along the way to get that idea. How would you describe the changes that have happened in the last years for promoting character strengths, Future Skills, et cetera, and what still needs more change?

Duckworth: When Jim Heckman won the Nobel prize in 2000 for his contributions to econometrics, things really changed for him as an economist. He started to look at what he began to call the non-cognitive and, eventually, the character elements of human capital. As a labor economist, he began to see that there was an enormous, unexamined aspect of human capacity that was not being picked up by standardized tests, that was not exactly the same thing as knowing how to do math or how to write or read well. These dimensions are what we've been talking about—character. In in those 20 plus years that have passed since Jim won the Nobel prize, shifting 100% of his scientific research towards illuminating these other aspects of human capital that one could call character, there has been a groundswell of research interests across all sciences, neuroscience, economics, sociology, psychology, to try to better understand how these capabilities develop.

And I think that is the thing that needs to be done. I think we have an enormously deeper appreciation that when young people grow up, when we think if education has been successful, it can't just be if they can do math problems. Can they read and write well? It also has to be: can they relate to other people? Can they regulate their own effort? Can they maintain curiosity and honesty? What needs to be done is to now move beyond an appreciation of these capabilities being important and getting more into how—how do we support that?

And if you ask me like, you've been thinking about it for 20 years, you must have a curriculum. You must have maybe a five-page memo that you could simply hand out to school leaders and say, okay, this is a recipe, just do that. But I'm nowhere close to that, and I don't think anybody is—we're at the beginning of the beginning.

I think this to me is the important work—and this is why I'm so excited about this project that you have underway, understanding how to teach these things. Maybe it's not even the right word, teach, it's got to be some combination probably of modeling these things, embedding the programs within the school day, but maybe even if it's in sports and in music, things that extend beyond the classroom that support growth mindset, collaboration, et cetera. So, we're at the beginning of the beginning and I don't want to rush into a simplistic solution. I have no curriculum to sell.

I do think, though, that it's important to say one thing as we move into this exciting new chapter: as a psychologist who studies the data on this, one thing to assure those policymakers who are worried that this is going to crowd out traditional academics, saying oh, no, we can't focus on these things, it's very important that our children are able to read and to write and to do math. Well, I have two daughters and, also, I have a lot of data and I will tell you that both my personal experience and also the scientific research suggests that these are complementary. Young people cannot succeed academically without these strengths of character. And when you have both, you're enormously more effective, not only as a student, but as a person.

Ehlers: That was really fascinating—thank you!

Duckworth: And there's nothing more important than what we're all working on together. So, I'm happy to be, in some ways, I say on the same team.

Prof. Dr. phil. habil. Ulf-Daniel Ehlers is an internationally renowned Professor for Educational Management and Lifelong Learning at the Baden-Wuerttemberg Cooperative State University (DHBW) Karlsruhe which he headed as Vice-President between 2011 and 2017.

Laura Eigbrecht is principle investigator, teacher and doctoral student at the Baden-Wuerttemberg Cooperative State University (DHBW) Karlsruhe and holds degrees in European Media and Culture and Media Pedagogy.

Open Access This chapter is licensed under the terms of the Creative Commons Attribution 4.0 International License (http://creativecommons.org/licenses/by/4.0/), which permits use, sharing, adaptation, distribution and reproduction in any medium or format, as long as you give appropriate credit to the original author(s) and the source, provide a link to the Creative Commons license and indicate if changes were made.

The images or other third party material in this chapter are included in the chapter's Creative Commons license, unless indicated otherwise in a credit line to the material. If material is not included in the chapter's Creative Commons license and your intended use is not permitted by statutory regulation or exceeds the permitted use, you will need to obtain permission directly from the copyright holder.

Team Academy: Future Skills and the Future of Learning 11

Michael P. Vogel

Abstract

This chapter reviews and refines the concept of Future Skills before introducing and discussing a radically innovative higher education model for Future Skills development called Team Academy. The chapter argues that Future Skills are acquired best not through teaching but learners' self-directed action and reflection in authentic contexts. The Team Academy model of entrepreneurship education combines real-life action learning, team learning, and team coaching uniquely to create favorable conditions for, and actively foster, the acquisition of a range of Future Skills. Based on the example of Germany's first Team Academy in Bremerhaven, the chapter addresses some challenges of implementing the model in a public higher education context and offers first-hand learnings.

11.1 Introduction

Almost 30 years ago, Barr and Tagg (1995) contrasted two paradigms of higher education. The traditional, dominant Instruction Paradigm emphasizes the importance of teachers, their actions, and their expert inputs to the student learning process.

M. P. Vogel (✉)
Professor of Entrepreneurship Education; Founder and Director of Team Academy
Program, Bremerhaven University of Applied Sciences, Bremerhaven, Germany
e-mail: mvogel@hs-bremerhaven.de

© The Author(s) 2024
U.-D. Ehlers and L. Eigbrecht (eds.), *Creating the University of the Future*, Zukunft der Hochschulbildung - Future Higher Education,
https://doi.org/10.1007/978-3-658-42948-5_11

Institutional responsibility lies in quality teaching. On the other hand, the Learning Paradigm emphasizes the importance of students' experience, discovery, and active knowledge construction. Here, institutional responsibility is co-responsibility (with students) for learning outcomes.

Barr and Tagg (1995) criticized universities that consider teaching as their mission for confusing means and ends. Teaching, they argued, is only one possible means to achieve the actual end, which is student learning. In their view, the Learning Paradigm is superior because of its focus on results and its pragmatic stance on the choice of means. Its pragmatism is not arbitrary, though, but grounded in the psychology of learning. The Learning Paradigm shifts the focus from the 'what' to the 'how' of learning, from content to process and context:

> *"In the Learning Paradigm [...], a college's purpose is not to transfer knowledge but to create environments and experiences that bring students to discover and construct knowledge for themselves, to make students members of communities of learners that make discoveries and solve problems. The college aims, in fact, to create a series of ever more powerful learning environments."* (Barr & Tagg, 1995, p. 15)

The paradigm shift implies a fundamental shift also in roles. *"If the Instruction Paradigm faculty member is an actor—a sage on a stage—then the Learning Paradigm faculty member is an inter-actor—a coach interacting with a team."* (Barr & Tagg, 1995, p. 24)

Barr and Tagg could have made these two statements in direct reference to the Team Academy model presented in this chapter, so aptly did they describe some of its characteristics. The quotes also make clear how long the road to Future Skills readiness is for many universities (Ehlers, 2020, pp. 97–103). This is because Future Skills, at least as I understand, define, and discuss them below, cannot be taught in any traditional sense but require action and reflection by students in authentic contexts.

11.1.1 Team Academy

Team Academies may offer exactly this authentic context for learning through action and reflection. A Team Academy is a radical approach to entrepreneurship education from Finland. All students form teams of 12–18 who stay together for three years of study. Right from the start, each team builds a real company according to their ideas. These team companies serve as experiential learning spaces in which students test their business ideas, develop customer projects, pool

11 Team Academy: Future Skills and the Future of Learning

their resources and risks, acquire practical innovation and leadership skills, and have experiences of self-efficacy.

Challenges, problems, and the inevitable failures along the way are important learning opportunities. Reflection, dialogue, and extensive reading and writing complement the entrepreneurial action. The students assume leadership responsibilities at project, company, and Team Academy levels. Lecture inputs are limited to homoeopathic doses. Instead, teaching staff act as team coaches and focus on team dynamics and process facilitation, providing methods and tools on demand, and on accompanying their teams through ups and downs.

The kind of self-directed, team-based, feedback-intensive action learning, which is characteristic of the Team Academy model, is probably unique in higher education. Whether it is superior to more traditional entrepreneurship education in supporting the students' competence development is unclear to date due to a lack of systematic research and comparable results. However, having taught for 15 years in conventional business studies and having been a team coach since 2018 in Germany's first Team Academy at the Bremerhaven University of Applied Sciences, I know both worlds quite well. And I am very impressed with the progress that many Team Academy students are making in developing their Future Skills.

In this chapter, I first take a critical look at different Future Skills concepts, before proposing a definition as a synthesis. In the second section, I introduce the competence model underlying Bremerhaven's Team Academy and discuss which competences might qualify as Future Skills according to my definition. The third section outlines the Team Academy model to give a better idea of the particular setting in which the students acquire and practice their Future Skills. In the two final sections, I address some challenges of the Team Academy model and offer first-hand learnings.

The Team Academy at the Bremerhaven University of Applied Sciences is a three-year Bachelor's program. Its official name is 'Gründung, Innovation, Führung' (GIF), which translates as 'Venture Creation, Innovation, Leadership'. For the remainder of this chapter, I will refer to it simply as GIF.

11.2 Future Skills Concept

Even though, as humans, we are undoubtedly at a critical juncture in our existence and will need different skills to meet the challenges ahead than we did to meet past challenges, I am somewhat reluctant to summarize them under the term Future Skills. The future can be anything between now and infinity. Every user of the term may have a specific time horizon in mind, and unless it is made explicit, chances are that people refer to different time horizons without realizing it. As Dede (2010) points out, "many educational reforms have failed because of a reverse Tower-of-Babel problem, in which people use the same words, but mean quite different things" (Chap. 3, page 51).

The term "skill" in (capitalized) Future Skills is also far less clear than it may seem at first. A skill is "an ability or proficiency acquired through training and practice" (American Psychological Association, 2022) or "an ability to do an activity or job well, especially because you have practiced it" (Cambridge Dictionary, 2014). Skills are a constituent of competences. The OECD (2019) Learning Compass 2030, for example, presents competences as the combination of knowledge, values, attitudes and skills required to act responsibly and effectively according to given standards of performance in a given situation. Similarly, for Mitchelmore and Rowley (2010), competences "can be described in terms of essential personality traits, skills, knowledge and motives" (p. 94) that lead to superior performance. And for Bird (2019), entrepreneurial competences are the "underlying characteristics such as generic and specific knowledge, motives, traits, self-images, social roles, and skills which result in venture birth, survival, and/or growth" (p. 115).

Future Skills, however, are no constituent but a particular category or subset of competences (Ehlers, 2020; González-Pérez & Ramírez-Montoya, 2022; Kotsiou et al., 2022; Spiegel et al., 2021; Stifterverband, 2022). Even self-efficacy, which is an empowering belief,[1] is considered a Future Skill (Ehlers, 2020; Ternès von Hattburg, 2021). So, skills and Future Skills are quite different concepts.

Ehlers (2020) defines Future Skills as "competences that allow individuals to solve complex problems in highly emergent contexts of action in a self-organized way and enable them to act (successfully). They are based on cognitive, motivational, volitional and social resources, are value-based and can be acquired in a learning process." (p. 53).

This definition is 'timeless' in the sense that the future is only implied by the reference to highly emergent contexts of action, which are assumed to be characteristic of the future. "Emergence thus defines the dividing line that separates previous or traditional work areas from future work areas" (Ehlers, 2020, p. 54). It is timeless also by not considering the possibility of technological obsolescence

---

[1] Self-efficacy, according to Bandura (1997), is "the belief in one's capabilities to organize and execute the courses of action required to produce given attainments" (p. 3).

of human competences. I doubt that a problem-solving competence would still be regarded as a Future Skill after smart machines have demonstrated their ability to solve the same class of problems automatically.

Ehlers's definition raises another question. (Why) does it exclude individuals' competences that may enable others to solve complex problems, e.g. by providing leadership or organizing a collective problem-solving process? Of course, one might argue that leadership is itself a complex problem, so leading a team successfully in highly emergent contexts of action meets the criteria of a Future Skill. But if every competence is potentially a form of problem-solving, the definition loses clarity.

Kirchherr et al. (2019) take a very different and rather pragmatic approach. For them, Future Skills are "skills that will become more important for professional work and/or participation in society in the next five years—across all industries and branches" (Kirchherr et al., 2019, p. 4). This definition is not timeless but covers a specific time horizon. Its only selection criterion is increasing future importance.

Both definitions have their merit. But for someone who is "preparing students for jobs that don't yet exist, using technologies that haven't been invented, to solve problems we don't even know are problems yet" (Beers, 2010, p. 347), a five-year time horizon is too short and the limitation of Future Skills to competences related to individuals' problem-solving is too constraining.

Therefore, as a synthesis of elements of both definitions and my critique of them, I propose the following new definition: *Future Skills are competences that*

(a) enable individuals to pursue demanding professional or societal goals particularly effectively and in a socially acceptable manner, across many industries or sectors of society, alone or with others, in a self-organized way and under VUCA conditions; and
(b) are unlikely to become obsolete due to technological change in the foreseeable future.

I agree with Ehlers that Future Skills draw on cognitive, motivational, volitional, and social resources, are value-based and can be learned, but I prefer not to include this part in the definition. What I do include, however, are criteria to filter out competences that are relevant only in a few specific contexts or that may soon be automated. For reasons of familiarity, I replace Ehlers's "highly emergent contexts of action" with the term VUCA (volatility, uncertainty, complexity, and ambiguity).

11.3 Future Skills Model

In this section, I introduce the competence model underlying the GIF program. The model came into existence only after GIF had already taken off. It is not a model with universal pretensions, like the European Commission's EntreComp Framework (European Commission, 2017) or the U.S. Department of Labor's Entrepreneurship Competency Model (Employment & Training Administration, 2021). Rather, it is a simplified, proprietary model intended to provide orientation for program development, program operation, and stakeholders.

The starting point for the model development was the mission statement from 2019:

> "GIF aims to prepare people to live and work self-determined, productive, and cooperative lives in a volatile, uncertain, complex, and ambiguous (VUCA) world. To this end, GIF promotes competences in three domains: entrepreneurship, team, and self."

Entrepreneurship may be defined as "[t]he process by which individuals [...] pursue opportunities without regard to the resources they currently control" (Stevenson & Jarillo, 1990, p. 23). Note that, according to the GIF mission statement, preparing for entrepreneurship is not the purpose of GIF, but a means. The purpose is to prepare the students for work and life under VUCA conditions. Since entrepreneurs operate under VUCA-like conditions, organizing GIF in parts like a business incubator and requiring the students with practically no initial preparation to start real companies with real customers and real money is a good way of familiarizing them with the volatilities and uncertainties of the VUCA world.

The other two domains of competence, team and self, serve the same purpose. A team is "a small group of people with complementary skills who are committed to a common purpose, performance goals and approach for which they are mutually accountable" (Katzenbach & Smith, 1993, p. 70). Teams can display extremely complex social dynamics, which may paralyze them with conflict, turn them dysfunctional or dramatically boost their performance. As the term Team Academy suggests, GIF is entirely team-based, giving the students full exposure to VUCA-ish team dynamics for three years.

This experience is amplified by the students' transformation. Typically, in the course of the GIF program, their self-concept and self-awareness, their professional and life objectives, their priorities, perception of others, reflexivity, self-leadership and perceived self-efficacy undergo profound change. GIF makes productive use of this 'inner VUCA' by providing settings, methods, and coaching support to address and reflect those changes and turn them into conscious learning processes and competences. Examples include dialogue sessions, the constant use of learning contracts, learning journals and reflective essays, as well as a vivid feedback and formative evaluation culture.

The GIF competence model is built around the above mission statement's 'holy trinity' of entrepreneurship, team, and self. It comes in two forms, as GIF Competence Diamond and as GIF Competence Matrix. In Fig. 11.1, the Diamond's four sides are meant to represent entrepreneurship, broken down into four areas of practice in which the students are expected to plan and carry out their activities: building new ventures, innovating to make things better, leading with head, hand, and heart, as well as learning through action, reflection and sharing.

In each field of entrepreneurial practice, the students acquire self-competences, team competences, and world-related competences involving interactions with customers, investors, suppliers, partners, competitors, and authorities.

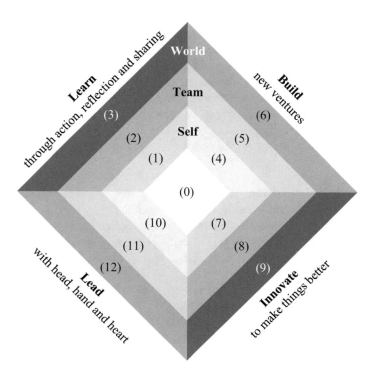

Fig. 11.1 GIF Competence Diamond. (Own representation)

Table 11.1 GIF Competence Matrix

	Self	Team	World
Basic	(0) Personal initiative, collaboration, digital literacy		
Learn	(1) Self-directed learning, digital learning, reflection	(2) Dialogue, feedback, generosity, diversity	(3) Learning community
Build	(4) Alertness, self-efficacy, ambiguity tolerance, perseverance, resilience	(5) Project management	(6) Business and marketing, financial literacy, resource mobilization
Innovate	(7) Critical thinking, creativity, research	(8) Innovation	(9) Networking
Lead	(10) Self-leadership	(11) Team leadership, coaching	(12) Lateral leadership, ethics

The numbers in the Diamond refer to competences, which the students' activities at the micro (self), meso (team) and macro (world) levels in each area of entrepreneurial practice are supposed to foster. The competences are listed in Table 11.1, with the words 'competence' and 'skill' omitted for ease of reading. The central rhombus is the only part of the Diamond which does not belong to any single practice area. It represents competences, denoted (0), that are foundational for all practice areas.

I will only provide short explanations for the less common competences in Table 11.1.

- Dialogue (2), literally the art of thinking together, is a form of communication central to team learning. There are four dialogue skills (Bohm, 1996; Isaacs, 1999): listening (and simultaneously perceiving our own reactions and resistances without reacting directly to them), respecting (i.e. recognizing the other's position, which we can never fully understand), suspending (our assumptions, certainties, emotions and judgments to explore the question behind the question) and voicing (what moves and engages us at the moment without holding back part of our own truth).
- Generosity (2) in this context means actively sharing our ideas, opportunities, skills, knowledge, experience, contacts, and other resources, as well as recognition, feedback, encouragement, and moral support with our team, trusting that this generosity will be reciprocated, strengthen our relationships, renew trust, benefit the team as a whole and enhance our collective performance.

- Learning communities (3) are characterized by "a culture of learning in which everyone interacts in a collective effort of understanding" (Overbaugh & Lin, 2006, p. 206). In addition to sharing and reciprocating, relevant skills include 'Working Out Loud' (Stepper, 2020), giving feedback, cross-pollinating between community groups, and other networking skills.
- Alertness (4) has been defined as "the ability to notice without search opportunities that have hitherto been overlooked" (Kirzner, 1979, p. 48) and is often considered a quintessential entrepreneurial competence (Chavoushi et al., 2021; Tang et al., 2012; Valliere, 2013).
- Resource mobilization (6) refers to the entrepreneurial skill of securing new and additional financial, human, and material resources to advance their mission (Clough et al., 2019; Kotha & George, 2012).
- Lateral leadership (12) means leading 'sideways', i.e., without hierarchical authority or formal power. It is a key skill in cross-functional projects, process chains without process owners, self-organized agile environments, and network structures (Kühl et al., 2005; Strathausen, 2015).

Which of the competences in Table 11.1 can count as Future Skills? Or, to use the words of my definition, which of these competences (a) enable individuals to pursue demanding professional or societal goals particularly effectively and in a socially acceptable manner, across many industries or sectors of society, alone or with others, in a self-organized way and under VUCA conditions; and (b) are unlikely to become obsolete due to technological change in the foreseeable future?

Ambiguity tolerance, perseverance, and resilience are particularly valuable in coping with VUCA-related adversities. I would therefore nominate them as Future Skills. The same holds for self-directed learning, self-efficacy, and self-leadership, which are important for the self-organized pursuit of goals. Social skills will continue to be indispensable in the future when it comes to achieving goals through collaboration. Therefore, the skills required to lead teams, coach others, lead laterally, give and accept feedback, and network are on my Future Skills list as well, especially since 'soft' leadership approaches suit the needs of highly qualified, self-organizing knowledge workers.

Also dialogue skills are social skills. However, although dialogue is highly effective in fostering team learning and resolving conflict, it leads a shadowy existence in our culture. Dialogue demands that, and only works if, all participants respect and adhere to its rules of interaction. If a skill becomes effective only when mastered by many (like a language), the barrier to it becoming a Future Skill is high.

Empirically, it is not clear whether ethical behavior favors or obstructs the pursuit of professional goals (Bazerman & Tenbrunsel, 2011; Boyer, 2002; Carucci, 2016). But since my definition of Future Skills emphasizes not only the effective, but also the socially acceptable pursuit of demanding goals, and unethical behavior is unlikely to be socially acceptable, I consider ethical competence (Kulju et al., 2016; Pohling et al., 2016) a Future Skill.

Projects have become ubiquitous in working, civic and private life. 'Projectification' (Jensen et al., 2016; Maylor & Turkulainen, 2019) is an answer to a volatile environment. Agile project management is a response to accelerating volatility or to VUCA conditions. I cannot imagine a plausible scenario in which this tendency would reverse. Therefore, the ability to manage projects successfully in a VUCA environment seems to be an obvious Future Skills candidate.

On the other hand, I do not include business and marketing skills, financial literacy, and the skills to participate in learning communities in my Future Skills candidate list. Their scope of application seems to be more limited than that of other competences in Table 11.1.

As to digital literacy and digital learning, I am undecided. Over the next decade or so, they will probably meet the criteria of my definition. But as digital devices become smarter, more intuitive, and better capable of processing natural language, the distinction between digital and non-digital skills will become increasingly blurred. The appropriate, discerning, and responsible use of digital technology will then no longer depend on digital skills, but on critical thinking, reflexivity, self-leadership, and other non-digital competences. For me, these are the real (and timeless) Future Skills.

11.4 Our Approach to Future Skills

Like the previous section, this one is not only about Future Skills but about all competences listed in Table 11.1. The GIF program I am about to present cannot be meaningfully deconstructed into parts with relevance for Future Skills and those without.

I begin by introducing the "flipped curriculum". This design principle applies the "flipped classroom" pedagogy[2] to an entire educational program. In Fig. 11.2,

---

[2] The flipped or inverted classroom is "a set of pedagogical approaches that (1) move most information-transmission teaching out of class; (2) use class time for learning activities that are active and social; and (3) require students to complete pre- and/or post-class activities to fully benefit from in-class work" (Abeysekera & Dawson, 2015, p. 3).

11 Team Academy: Future Skills and the Future of Learning

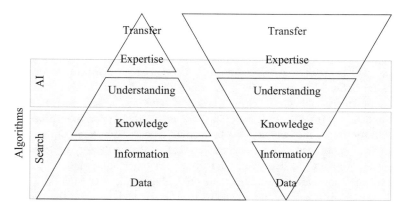

Fig. 11.2 Flipping the curriculum (Holmes et al., 2019, p. 28)

the triangle on the left represents, in simplified form, a conventionally designed curriculum. Students spend the vast majority of their time in lectures and learning-prescribed content. Only little time remains for building expertise in areas of their interest and transferring what they have learned to new contexts.

The triangle on the right of Fig. 11.2 reverses this relationship. Students gain access to relevant knowledge and acquire it independently outside of courses. This makes valuable time at the university and with fellow students available for practicing the higher-order cognitive activities of application, analysis, synthesis and evaluation (Gary, 2018), which promote competence development. In addition, this way the students spend relatively less time on acquiring new knowledge that tends to outdate increasingly quickly, and relatively more time on developing and practicing competences, some of which may be Future Skills that will not be rivalled by smart machines for the time being.

The GIF program looks almost as if it were designed with the idea of the flipped curriculum in mind. However, the Team Academy model, on which GIF is based, originated in Finland, where it was developed in the early 1990s. It promotes experience rather than theory as the starting point for learning and aims to empower the students to choose what, how, when, and with whom they learn. Rote learning of facts, stockpile learning, and cramming theory without personal relevance have no place here. Instead, the Team Academy's pedagogical cornerstones are action learning, team learning, self-directed reading, and team coaching.

11.4.1 Action Learning

Action learning is a method of experiential learning. It is learning to act effectively, which requires actual action, not theories about action or recommendations for action (Mumford, 1995). Learning is based on collective reflection on the experiences of action. Action learning always takes place in teams, which distinguishes it from learning by doing. The teams should consist of like-minded people for whom the challenge to be learned from is important and new: "It is recognized ignorance, not programed knowledge, that is the key to action learning: men [sic] start to learn with and from each other only when they discover that no one knows the answer but all are obliged to find it" (Revans, 1997, p. 6).

In the Team Academy, the students' team companies provide the framework for action. They continually produce situations and questions that are new to the students and to which they have to react. The collective reflection on their actions takes place in the special format of team learning.

11.4.2 Team Learning

Team learning is a process of thinking together through dialogue, in the course of which experiences, insights, knowledge, and perspectives are exchanged. Dialogue is neither a discussion about being right and getting one's way, nor does it aim at consensus (Bohm, 1996; Isaacs, 1999). I have already presented the principles of dialogue above, so I will not go into them further here. In the Team Academy, the members of each team company meet twice a week for three to four hours in a circle of chairs with their team coach for team learning sessions. According to Senge (1990), team learning is one of the five disciplines of learning organizations, which is what every Team Academy strives to be.

11.4.3 Self-Directed Reading

Students plan and decide for themselves what, when, and how they read. The use of books plays a very important role in the Team Academy, reflecting the strong Finnish reading culture. Books are preferred to shorter articles because they give ideas more room to unfold and provide more context. Students choose 5–7 books each semester that promise to help them solve problems or answer questions related to their customer projects, business ideas, team situations, or personal development. They formulate a guiding question for each book to direct and focus their attention. After reading, they produce and share an essay, podcast, video, or give a live presentation with a book review and a report on what they see as the most important insights from the book, how they used them to answer their guiding question and, if applicable, how the transfer of key insights to their own practice went.

11.4.4 Team Coaching

Team coaching is a process designed to develop groups of people into high-performing teams. In GIF, team coaches like myself take great care to create and sustain a friendly, welcoming, and open learning environment. We are constantly testing, evaluating, and learning how to do this better. Every rule, structure, and process introduced since the start of GIF in 2018 was co-designed by our students and us. Students and coaches collaborating at eye level is a key success factor for Team Academy programs. This is why we team coaches are on a first-name basis with the students, which is not at all common in German higher education.

Our other focus is on the teams we coach. Each team of students has its coach who accompanies them for a year, spends six hours a week with them in a chair circle for team learning sessions (see above), supports them for another five hours a week in their client projects and with their business ideas, works intensively with the team company's executive board, helps them through impasses, conflicts, and crises, and celebrates their successes and failures with them.

Team coaches do not usually impart their expert knowledge to students, solve their problems, or deliver solutions for them. This would be teaching or consulting. Coaching, as Team Academies understand it, is "the art of facilitating the performance, learning, and development of another" (Downey, 2003, p. 21). We want the students to shed their fear of not knowing something, overcome their initial helplessness when faced with new problems, strengthen their initiative, and cultivate their self-directed learning. We help them by asking good questions, not by giving the answers (Stanier, 2016).

Figure 11.3 summarizes the Team Academy's four pedagogical cornerstones just described and the relationships between them.

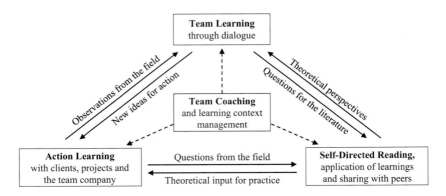

Fig. 11.3 Pedagogical cornerstones of the Team Academy. (Own representation)

11.4.5 Teams, Companies and Leadership

The Team Academy model is not oriented towards the ideal of the outstanding individual, the heroic entrepreneur (Boutillier & Uzunidis, 2014; Papi-Thornten, 2016; Pilotta, 2016), but towards the ideal of high-performing teams (Katzenbach & Smith, 1993) and entrepreneurship for everyone (Faltin, 2015). To prevent birds of a feather from flocking together, the team coaches put together the student teams of 12–18 students each, ensuring maximum heterogeneity and complementarity within each team. Factors we take into account include age, gender, work experience, region of origin, and the results of a Belbin team role test (Belbin, 2010).

Regardless of business ideas, each team sets up or takes over a real company (cooperative) early in the first semester. These team companies act as the students' learning environment, laboratory for experimentation, and formal bond with each other for the duration of their studies. In Germany, establishing a cooperative requires no specific initial capital. Liability risks are limited to the company's funds. Moreover, to limit risk, the team companies may not borrow money.

The teams move into a co-working space that is available to them around the clock. The students' spatial proximity to each other ensures lots of informal communication. Meeting rooms, an event area, a reference library, and a large kitchen are part of the infrastructure. Almost from day one, the students work in client relationships, which are initially helped by the team coaches. All students are expected to complete regular visits to actual or potential clients to learn from and with them, co-create business ideas and build productive, lasting relationships.

11 Team Academy: Future Skills and the Future of Learning

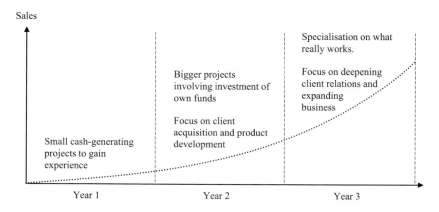

Fig. 11.4 Typical evolution of team companies. (Own representation)

The students generate their first sales with simple offers that are within their experience horizon and possibilities (e.g., hosting parties and organizing e-sports tournaments at corporate events; drop shipping; creation and search engine optimization of websites; setting up pop-up stores; mapping processes for service companies). With growing experience and increasing sales, they specialize in certain sectors, products, and processes. Figure 11.4 illustrates team companies evolve ideally.

Not all students in a team work for the same client, on the same product, or even in the same industry. Rather, each team company has a spectrum of projects at any given time, which take place independently of each other, involve different people, but are decided, financed, controlled, and evaluated jointly by all members. In this way, the students can pursue their different interests, try out a variety of business ideas and learn from one another.

The team companies do not form isolated learning units. On the contrary: The spatial, organizational and curricular conditions of the GIF program work to ensure that the teams network with each other, share ideas, knowledge, and competences across cohorts, share resources, coach each other, cooperate and create an open, dynamic, self-organizing ecosystem for entrepreneurial learning.

In GIF, with its 150 students, nine team companies, a plethora of projects and a large network of external stakeholders, leadership is needed everywhere all the time. Some students are elected CEO, CFO or to the supervisory board of their companies and assume legal responsibility. Others manage client projects, organize a Rocket Day (one-day learning and community building events for the whole

Team Academy) or a Learning Circus (a team trip lasting several days to several weeks, during which companies, conferences, and other Team Academies are visited), or act as Academic Leaders (ensuring their team's academic progress). All students take turns hosting team learning sessions. We team coaches interfere as little as possible.

11.4.6 Self-Leadership

The Team Academy is designed to give students plenty of freedom to pursue their personal learning and development goals and business ideas and to respond to the needs of their team companies and clients. However, freedom comes with responsibility and the expectation of serious commitment. This is a tough lesson to learn for many because parents, school, and work typically do not prepare them for freedom. In fact, for most students, the biggest leadership challenge is their self-leadership.

As a support measure, we require all of them before the beginning of each semester to draw up a personal learning contract for the next six months, in which they answer the following five questions (Cunningham, 1999):

1. Where do I come from?
2. Where am I now?
3. Where do I want to go?
4. How do I get there?
5. How do I know that I have arrived?

The students discuss their draft contracts with their team coaches, coordinate and agree on them with their team, and sign them. When taken seriously, learning contracts are an effective tool for the students to reflect on themselves and to practice goal orientation, focus, commitment, and evaluation of own progress. During the semester, learning contracts serve as a basis for conversations with the team coach. In addition, Academic Leaders use the learning contracts to keep track of their whole team's progress and to coordinate support within the team for students who are struggling.

An important role model for self-leadership is students' corporate clients. From them, they can (ideally) learn what professionalism, productivity, and reliability mean. The best clients are those who demand exactly this from the students.

11.5 Challenges for the Team Academy Model

There are many challenges to setting up and running a program like GIF in a bureaucratized, risk-averse public higher education institution. In this section, however, I will address three challenges we face in GIF concerning the development and assessment of the students' Future Skills.

11.5.1 The Challenge of Letting Go

In the introduction, I pointed out the importance of action, reflection, and an authentic learning context for the acquisition of entrepreneurial competences and related Future Skills. By an authentic learning context, I mean a learning environment in which it is natural for students to do the things that promote their competence development. Giving a talk in a seminar, having an appearance in front of the camera in a public speaking course, or discussing an ethical dilemma as part of a case study are not natural situations but artificial ones, producing artificial behavior, which may or may not be transferred to real-world situations outside the classroom.

The Team Academy works differently. Everything is real or as close to real as possible. If a client project is due to be completed, the students work very hard to meet the deadline, not because a team coach tells them so, but because it is their client, their project, and their ambition. If three students want to start a new project and need the financial support of their team, they pitch their project idea in front of their peers, respond to their questions and concerns, and show how everybody will benefit. They do this to gain support and not to practice their presentation skills that might be useful later in life. And eventually, when the students are fed up with their chaotic way of running projects, they begin to impose discipline on themselves for proper project management. They learn this lesson for life without any intervention by a team coach.

One rule of thumb for team coaches is therefore to "grant them their mess". Mess is part of the authentic learning environment in a Team Academy. It makes the students realize what they want to avoid in the future and start looking for improvements and solutions on their initiative. For us Team Coaches, however, watching students struggle with their mess or driving projects against the wall can be hard to bear, and I am often the first team coach who shows mercy. Not saying no, just letting go and trusting the process, is not for the faint at heart.

11.5.2 The Challenge of Unlearning

Learning from mistakes takes time. However, getting new students to just go ahead and try something that may fail, takes even more time. In their first months in the GIF program, many are hesitant to experiment because they expect to receive guidance, to need permission, or be discouraged from pursuing their ideas. The belief that they must learn something before being allowed to do it is as common as it is limiting. In addition, a deficit-oriented self-image gets in the way for some, leading them to focus on their weaknesses rather than their strengths.

Another big challenge for students, besides dealing productively with freedom, is unlearning. The socialization by parents and school may have prepared them for a well-defined job in a stable, hierarchical organization, but not for experiential, entrepreneurial, failure-prone learning in a self-organizing, frequently messy environment. They need to unlearn the way they used to learn at school. They need to unlearn the idea that every question has one correct answer, that there is a certain body of knowledge to be mastered, that learning is the mental stockpiling of knowledge and that everyone in GIF has to learn the same things. They have to unlearn the idea that they must be able to do everything themselves because that is exactly what does not apply in complementary teams. They have to unlearn that someone else is responsible for them, makes decisions for them, and tells them what to do. And they have to unlearn their fixation on grades, for otherwise they will never take risks, make courageous decisions, look for new ways and grow as entrepreneurs.

11.5.3 The Challenge of Balancing Assessment and Authenticity

Grades bring me to our third major challenge, namely the assessment of the students' competence levels and gains fairly and comparably. In GIF, the vast majority of assessments take the form of portfolio examinations.

During the semester, the students collect evidence for everything they do in the context of GIF. Evidence can be project or product plans, budgets, pitch decks, websites, web shops and apps created, results of own market research, prototypes, minutes of client talks and internal meetings, correspondence, offers sent out, order confirmations received, contracts, client feedback, team feedback, etc. At the end of the semester, the students decide which modules they want to complete

11 Team Academy: Future Skills and the Future of Learning 233

with the documentation of their activities. For each module, they compile the evidence required, explain each piece of evidence, and write a reflective piece on their learning journey in the course of the module.

So, in GIF, we wholeheartedly share Mintzberg's (2005) credo of "using work rather than making work" (p. 313) for assessment. The downside is, however, that while portfolios are a great way to make learning and demonstrated competences visible, no two portfolios look even remotely alike. This is because no two GIF students pass through our program in the same way. Some may work on the same projects for the same clients, but in different roles. Some look for business opportunities at their doorstep in Bremerhaven, while others seek opportunities abroad. And since team dynamics vary greatly among the teams, the CEOs of our nine team companies typically face very different leadership challenges, which are reflected by their equally different portfolios.

One consequence of this is that implementing fair assessment standards is extremely difficult. The students who are the most successful in identifying business opportunities, managing projects, or creating a positive team culture may not be the best with words. On the other hand, the most impressive portfolios by academic standards often come from students who would probably excel in more traditional, structured study programs and who know how to present their minor entrepreneurial activities in the best light. Moreover, if we team coaches evaluated portfolios purely based on the desired learning outcomes specified in the module handbook, we would have to disregard other valuable competences the students may have developed or applied successfully. The more we stick to the formalized intended learning outcomes, the more we reduce the perceived freedom to experiment and the authenticity of the GIF learning environment. We tend to deal with this trade-off by using 'soft' assessment standards; focusing on the strong points of each portfolio; and giving students extensive development-oriented written feedback.

11.6 Three Learnings

In this final section, I share three learnings from the design and implementation of GIF over four years, which may be valuable for those planning to develop or adopt a Future Skills oriented curriculum.

11.6.1 Higher Education is Changing

A frequently heard argument against originality in program design is that (not only) German higher education laws and accreditation regulations are too restrictive, hostile to innovation, and do not allow anything other than the established program formats. However, in view of something as radical and unorthodox as a Team Academy being a reality, this argument seems more like a protective assertion.

So, the first lesson is that public higher education in Germany is changing! Change may be painfully slow compared to the agile world around, but there are windows of opportunity for innovative, unconventional Future Skills oriented approaches to learning.

11.6.2 Start with Why

When I set out to convince management and committees at my university to establish Germany's first Team Academy as a degree program, I was confronted with the argument that coaching was not academic teaching and that GIF was too much about procedural knowledge (know-how) and too little about declarative knowledge (know-that) (Berge & van Hezewijk, 1999; Herz & Schultz Jr, 1999; Jiamu, 2001).

The same argument might be used against the introduction of practically any Future Skills-related curricular elements. Therefore, it is important to realize that the argument is flawed because it confuses the means and ends of education (see the introduction). The end is student learning. Teaching is a means, just like coaching. The choice of the means should be determined by effectiveness to achieve the given end, not by personal preference or historic conventions.

To counter the above argument, it is important to first focus on the purpose of the study program and get everybody to agree on it. In the case of GIF, I presented to my skeptical colleagues the draft of the program's mission statement (see the Future Skills Model section). It was well received, especially for its entrepreneurship aspect. Next, I explained the particular nature of entrepreneurship and how it differs from business studies or engineering. This made it much easier for management and committee members to agree that GIF needed a tailored pedagogical approach. People began to accept my point that coaching was the most authentic way and lectures were largely optional. Mentally, they had made the shift from the Instruction Paradigm to the Learning Paradigm (see the Introduction section).

11 Team Academy: Future Skills and the Future of Learning

So, when faced with resistance against the curricular integration of Future Skills, "Start with Why" (Sinek, 2019). Move on to How only after the purpose has been agreed upon explicitly by decision makers. Then derive How from Why with a watertight argument.

11.6.3 Let the Medium Be the Message

Learning Future Skills requires students to be active, to do something and preferably in a setting that does not feel artificial but authentic. As mentioned before, artificial situations generate artificial behavior. For this reason, special attention should be paid to the design of the setting or learning environment.

When McLuhan (1964) stated that "The medium is the message" (p. 7), his point was that the particular technology used to communicate a message will affect the content of that message. From a pedagogical perspective, the statement can be read as advice to align the medium of a study program, i.e., how its content is mediated, with that content, so that the medium supports the intended message, rather than contradicting or changing it (Yazon et al., 2002; Zvonimir, 2018). An example of how not to do it is a frontal lecture to prospective teachers on why frontal teaching in schools is a poor practice from a pedagogical perspective. Unfortunately, this example is not fictitious.

I think of the pedagogical medium broadly as a composite of the processes and methods of program delivery, physical spaces and objects, technology, formal and informal rules and roles, rituals, the use of language, and more. Ideally, all elements work together to ensure that students naturally engage with the intended message of their study program. Ask yourself what medium could trigger, guide, and sustain student learning without the need for any further message. How could you design the medium so that students acquire Future Skills all by themselves? Then, the medium becomes indeed the message, as McLuhan suggested.

> **Future Skills in Practice: My Recommendations**
> The decreasing half-life of knowledge and its ubiquitous availability will lead to a significant shift in the focus of (higher) education from knowledge to future-proof competences, especially future skills. Based on my experiences with the Team Academy approach in Germany, I have five recommendations to get the change process off the ground.

1. Let us not wait for political initiatives, new higher education laws, more money or anyone's approval to begin working on Future Skills oriented learning programmes. We can get far with what we have and control today, as the Team Academy example shows. The most limiting factor is the belief that the familiar is all that is possible.
2. We should be clear and stubborn about desired learning outcomes, but flexible about the methods to achieve them. Functionality and effectiveness need to take precedence over convention and habit.
3. The transition from the old to the new requires creativity, experimentation, courage and occasional non-conformity in the design of learning environments, curricula and interaction with students. We can invite them to be our 'beta testers' and co-developers.
4. Let us systematically prepare and empower students to take greater control of their learning. Self-directed learning is a Future Skill, and as this chapter has argued, learners acquire Future Skills best by acting and reflecting in authentic contexts.
5. Empowering students in this way will affect our role and professional identity as academic teachers. Actually, the term teacher with all the authority and power distance it implies will become increasingly inadequate to characterize what we do. Since language creates reality, we should identify or invent more suitable terms and use them on ourselves. This is why Team Academies have team coaches, not lecturers and professors.

References

Abeysekera, L., & Dawson, P. (2015). Motivation and cognitive load in the flipped classroom: Definition, rationale and a call for research. *Higher Education Research & Development, 34*(1), 1–14. https://doi.org/10.1080/07294360.2014.934336.

American Psychological Association. (2022). APA dictionary of psychology – Skill. https://dictionary.apa.org/skill.

Bandura, A. (1997). *Self-efficacy. The exercise of control*. Freeman.

Barr, R. B., & Tagg, J. (1995). From teaching to learning – A new paradigm for undergraduate education. *Change, 27*(6), 12–25.

Bazerman, M. H., & Tenbrunsel, A. E. (2011). *Blind spots: Why we fail to do what's right and what to do about it*. Princeton University Press.

Beers, K. (2010). The 2009 NCTE: Presidential address: Sailing over the edge: Navigating the uncharted waters of a world gone flat. *Research in the Teaching of English, 44*(3), 340–352.

Belbin, R. M. (2010). *Team roles at work* (2nd ed.). Butterworth-Heinemann.

Ten Berge, T., & van Hezewijk, R. (1999). Procedural and Declarative Knowledge: An Evolutionary Perspective. *Theory & Psychology, 9*(5), 605–624. https://doi.org/10.1177/0959354399095002.

Bird, B. (2019). Toward a theory of entrepreneurial competency. In J. A. Katz & A. C. Corbet (Eds.), *Seminal ideas for the next twenty-five years of advances* (pp. 115–131). Emerald Publishing Limited. https://doi.org/10.1108/S1074-754020190000021011.

Bohm, D. (1996). *On dialogue*. Routledge.

Boutillier, S., & Uzunidis, D. (2014). The theory of the entrepreneur: From heroic to socialised entrepreneurship. *Journal of Innovation Economics, 14*(2), 9–40. https://doi.org/10.3917/jie.014.0009.

Boyer, A. (2002). *L'impossible éthique des entreprises*. Edition d'Organisation.

Cambridge Dictionary. (2014). Skill. https://dictionary.cambridge.org/dictionary/english/skill.

Carucci, R. (2016). Why ethical people make unethical choices. https://hbr.org/2016/12/why-ethical-people-make-unethical-choices.

Chavoushi, Z. H., Zali, M. R., Valliere, D., Faghih, N., Hejazi, R., & Dehkordi, A. M. (2021). Entrepreneurial alertness: A systematic literature review. *Journal of Small Business & Entrepreneurship, 33*(2), 123–152. https://doi.org/10.1080/08276331.2020.1764736.

Clough, D. R., Fang, T. P., Vissa, B., & Wu, A. (2019). Turning lead into gold: How do entrepreneurs mobilize resources to exploit opportunities? *Academy of Management Annals, 13*(1), 240–271. https://doi.org/10.5465/annals.2016.0132.

Cunningham, I. (1999). *The wisdom of strategic learning* (2nd ed.). Routledge.

Dede, C. (2010). Comparing frameworks for 21st century skills. In J. Bellance & R. Brandt (Eds.), *21st century skills: Rethinking how students learn* (pp. 51–76). Solution Tree Press.

Downey, M. (2003). *Effective coaching. Lessons from the coaches' coach* (3rd ed.). Texere.

Ehlers, U.-D. (2020). *Future Skills – Lernen der Zukunft, Hochschule der Zukunft*. eBook ISBN: 978-3-658-29297-3, DOI: 10.1007/978-3-658-29297-3. https://nextskills.org/wp-content/uploads/2020/03/Future-Skills-The-Future-of-learning-and-higher-education.pdf.

Employment and Training Administration. (2021). Entrepreneurship competency model. https://www.careeronestop.org/competencymodel/competency-models/entrepreneurship.aspx.

European Commission (2017). *EntreComp: The entrepreneurship competence framework*. Luxembourg.

Faltin, G. (2015). *Wir sind das Kapital* (1st ed.). Murmann.

Gary, R. (2018). Bloom's Taxonomy. In B. B. Frey (Ed.), *The SAGE encyclopedia of educational research, measurement, and evaluation* (pp. 206–210). Sage.

González-Pérez, L. I., & Ramírez-Montoya, M. S. (2022). Components of education 4.0 in 21st century skills frameworks: Systematic review. *Sustainability, 14*(3). https://doi.org/10.3390/su14031493.

Herz, P. J., & Schultz, J. J., Jr. (1999). The role of procedural and declarative knowledge in performing accounting tasks. *Behavioral Research in Accounting, 11*(1), 1–26.

Holmes, W., Bialik, M., & Fadel, C. (2019). *Artificial intelligence in education.* The Center for Curriculum Redesign.

Isaacs, W. N. (1999). *Dialogue and the art of thinking together.* Doubleday.

Jensen, A., Thuesen, C., & Geraldi, J. (2016). The projectification of everything: Projects as a human condition. *Project Management Journal, 47*(3), 21–34. https://doi.org/10.1177/875697281604700303.

Jiamu, C. (2001). The great importance of the distinction between declarative and procedural knowledge. *Análise Psicológica, XIX*(4), 559–566.

Katzenbach, J. R., & Smith, D. K. (1993). *The wisdom of teams. Creating the high-performance organization.* Harvard Business School Press.

Kirchherr, J., Klier, J., Lehmann-Brauns, C., & Winde, M. (2019). Future skills: Which competences are lacking in Germany? https://www.stifterverband.org/medien/which-skills-are-lacking-in-germany.

Kirzner, I. M. (1979). *Perception, opportunity and profit.* University of Chicago Press.

Kotha, R., & George, G. (2012). Friends, family, or fools: Entrepreneur experience and its implications for equity distribution and resource mobilization. *Journal of Business Venturing, 27*(5), 525–543. https://doi.org/10.1016/j.jbusvent.2012.02.001.

Kotsiou, A., Fajardo-Tovar, D., Cowhitt, T., Major, L., & Wegerif, R. (2022). A scoping review of future skills frameworks. *Irish Educational Studies, 41*(1), 171–186. https://doi.org/10.1080/03323315.2021.2022522.

Kühl, S., Schnelle, T., & Tillmann, F. (2005). Lateral leadership: An organizational approach to change. *Journal of Change Management, 5*(2), 177–189. https://doi.org/10.1080/14697010500098205.

Kulju, K., Stolt, M., Suhonen, R., & Leino-Kilpi, H. (2016). Ethical competence: A concept analysis. *Nursing Ethics, 23*(4), 401–412. https://doi.org/10.1177/0969733014567025.

Maylor, H., & Turkulainen, V. (2019). The concept of organisational projectification: Past, present and beyond? *International Journal of Managing Projects in Business, 12*(3), 565–577. https://doi.org/10.1108/IJMPB-09-2018-0202.

McLuhan, M. (1964). *Understanding media: The extensions of man.* McGraw Hill.

Mintzberg, H. (2005). *Managers not MBAs: A hard look at the soft practice of managing and management development.* Berrett-Koehler Publishers.

Mitchelmore, S., & Rowley, J. (2010). Entrepreneurial competencies: A literature review and development agenda. *International Journal of Entrepreneurial Behaviour & Research, 16*(2), 92–111. https://doi.org/10.1108/13552551011026995.

Mumford, A. (1995). Learning in action. *Industrial and Commercial Training, 27*(8), 36–40.

OECD. (2019). Skills for 2030. Conceptual learning framework: OECD future of education and skills 2030 concept note. Paris. https://www.oecd.org/education/2030-project/teaching-and-learning/learning/skills/Skills_for_2030_concept_note.pdf.

11 Team Academy: Future Skills and the Future of Learning

Overbaugh, R. C., & Lin, S. (2006). Student characteristics, sense of community, and cognitive achievement in web-based and lab-based learning environments. *Journal of Research on Technology in Education, 39*(2), 205–223. https://doi.org/10.1080/153915 23.2006.10782480.

Papi-Thornten, D. (2016). Tackling heropreneurship. https://ssir.org/ticles/entry/tackling_heropreneurship.

Pilotta, J. J. (2016). The entrepreneur as hero? In V. Berdayes & J. W. Murphy (Eds.), *Neoliberalism, economic radicalism, and the normalization of violence* (pp. 37–52). Springer International Publishing. https://doi.org/10.1007/978-3-319-25169-1_4.

Pohling, R., Bzdok, D., Eigenstetter, M., Stumpf, S., & Strobel, A. (2016). What is ethical competence? The role of empathy, personal values, and the five-factor model of personality in ethical decision-making. *Journal of Business Ethics, 137*(3), 449–474. https://doi.org/10.1007/s10551-015-2569-5.

Revans, R. (1997). Action learning: Its origins and nature. In M. Pedler (Ed.), *Action learning in practice* (3rd ed., pp. 3–13). Gower Publishing.

Senge, P. (1990). *The fifth discipline: The art and practice of the learning organization.* Doubleday/Currency.

Sinek, S. (2019). *Start with why.* Penguin Business.

Spiegel, P., Pechstein, A., Ternès von, A., & Grüneberg, A. (Eds.). (2021). *Future Skills. 30 zukunftsentscheidende Kompetenzen und wie wir sie lernen können.* Vahlen.

Stanier, M. B. (2016). *Coaching habit: Say less, ask more & Change the way your lead forever.* Box of Crayons Press.

Stepper, J. (2020). *Working out loud.* Page Two Books.

Stevenson, H. H., & Jarillo, J. C. (1990). A paradigm of entrepreneurship: Entrepreneurial management. *Strategic Management Journal, 11*, 17–27.

Stifterverband. (2022). Future skills. https://www.future-skills.net/.

Strathausen, R. (2015). Lateral leadership. In R. Strathausen (Ed.), *Leading when you're not the boss: How to get things done in complex corporate cultures* (pp. 85–91). Apress. https://doi.org/10.1007/978-1-4842-1748-1_7.

Tang, J., Kacmar, K. M., & Busenitz, L. (2012). Entrepreneurial alertness in the pursuit of new opportunities. *Journal of Business Venturing, 27*(1), 77–94. https://doi.org/10.1016/j.jbusvent.2010.07.001.

Ternès von Hattburg, A. (2021). Selbstwirksamkeit. In P. Spiegel, A. Pechstein, A. Ternès von Hattburg, & A. Grüneberg (Eds.), *Future Skills. 30 zukunftsentscheidende Kompetenzen und wie wir sie lernen können* (pp. 250–257). Vahlen.

Valliere, D. (2013). Entrepreneurial alertness and paying attention. *Journal of Enterprising Culture, 21*(01), 1–17. https://doi.org/10.1142/S0218495813500015.

Yazon, J. M. O., Mayer-Smith, J. A., & Redfield, R. J. (2002). Does the medium change the message? The impact of a web-based genetics course on university students' perspectives on learning and teaching. *Computers & Education, 38*(1), 267–285. https://doi.org/10.1016/S0360-1315(01)00081-1.

Zvonimir, K. (2018). Pedagogical theory of medium. *Sodobna Pedagogika/journal of Contemporary Educational Studies, 69*(4), 290–304.

Michael P. Vogel is Professor of Entrepreneurship Education at the Bremerhaven University of Applied Sciences and the founder and director of Germany's first Team Academy program. Previously, he was Professor of Tourism Management, a tourism manager with TUI, and a management consultant. He holds doctorates in Economics and Education. In 2009, Michael founded a social business for homeless people and served as its director until 2019, for which he was awarded the German Order of Merit.

Open Access This chapter is licensed under the terms of the Creative Commons Attribution 4.0 International License (http://creativecommons.org/licenses/by/4.0/), which permits use, sharing, adaptation, distribution and reproduction in any medium or format, as long as you give appropriate credit to the original author(s) and the source, provide a link to the Creative Commons license and indicate if changes were made.

The images or other third party material in this chapter are included in the chapter's Creative Commons license, unless indicated otherwise in a credit line to the material. If material is not included in the chapter's Creative Commons license and your intended use is not permitted by statutory regulation or exceeds the permitted use, you will need to obtain permission directly from the copyright holder.

Education for Future Skills Development: Cognitive, Collaborative and Ethical Skills

12

Carmen Păunescu and Mary McDonnell-Naughton

Abstract

This chapter focuses on the cognitive, collaborative, and ethical skills that the future higher education student will need to acquire to meet the skills wanted for the future. It explores learning methods that may be of interest in this field. The encouragement of reflective practice will encompass the competencies that will help to make sense of new concepts and policies underpinning good critical thinking. This will lend itself to the student gaining a competency level to drive efficient and effective decision making, thus ultimately contributing to society. The students themselves, through a thirst for knowledge and skills, will become self-directed learners, and learn how to work collaboratively with colleagues, all of which is essential for the Future Skills society. Based on two case studies, the chapter illustrates how the students develop their Future Skills and connect their learning experiences to explore various opportunities, whilst thinking and working in an ethical manner, adhering to a code of practice.

C. Păunescu (✉)
Professor, Bucharest University of Economic Studies, Bucharest, Romania
e-mail: carmen.paunescu@ase.ro

M. McDonnell-Naughton
Senior Lecturer, Technological University of the Shannon, Athlone, Ireland
e-mail: Mary.McDonnell@tus.ie

© The Author(s) 2024
U.-D. Ehlers and L. Eigbrecht (eds.), *Creating the University of the Future*, Zukunft der Hochschulbildung - Future Higher Education,
https://doi.org/10.1007/978-3-658-42948-5_12

12.1 Introduction

As the future needs of the global economy change it is imperative that education-alists must also adapt and identify what has to be achieved to equip students with Future Skills and attributes that are fit for purpose. It is important to develop critical thinking, problem solving, ethical skills and competencies that they will need to lead and manage the innovations of the future.

Critical thinking, for instance, calls for a persistent effort to analyse and evaluate any form of knowledge, belief or experience that leads to reasoning and decision-making (Ehlers, 2020). Reasoning, sensemaking and, further, problem-solving draw on individuals' existing understandings, worldviews, and collaborative interactions (Muñiz, 2020), with the purpose to create new meanings that ultimately lead to innovation. The development of these cognitive skills will be on a continuous growth curve as the student moves through higher education.

This chapter explores the cognitive, collaborative and ethical skills that the future higher education student will need to develop. It illustrates some learning methods that may be critical to developing Future Skills. The study adopts a qualitative research approach: (1) a case study at a public university business school in Romania with participation of students in a master course of Entrepreneurship and Sustainable Business Development, and (2) a discourse on the importance of ensuring that nursing students gain ethical knowing whilst completing a BSc in Nursing, in Ireland. The chapter introduces good practice examples of alternative teaching and learning methods that support the development of student Future Skills, through discussions, reflections, cooperative efforts, and collaborative practical work. Awareness is also placed on how students encourage the making of associations between problem, place, entrepreneurship, and ethical knowledge. The knowledge presented in this paper has been gleaned from a case study based on practice and a reflection on gaining competent knowledge within an ethical framework. The expansion of both of those areas is an example of development and knowledge-building in specific areas of expertise. However, upon reflection, lessons can be learned that can be replicated in other areas of education.

The chapter is structured as follows: the coming section introduces an operational definition of the term 'Future Skills' and its structural components. Sects. 12.3 and 12.4 illustrate how development of cognitive and ethical skills is sustained in two different situations, one practical and the other reflective. Practical implications and further recommendations regarding implementation of Future Skills in practice follow.

12.2 Future Skills Meaning and Understanding

Promoting and acknowledging the importance of cognitive, socio-emotional and ethical skills to student success is paramount to higher education governing policies, educational leaders and legislators (Portela-Pino et al., 2021; Radwan et al., 2021; Torrence et al., 2017). These are evolutionary components of the Future Skills framework for future higher education created by Ehlers (2020), which beg the question as to how educators, students or researchers examine and make sense of new concepts, new phenomena, or new policies.

As the future needs of society change, it is imperative that higher education institutions must prop students to become self-directed learners, engage in knowledge exchange and work collaboratively in an ethical manner. The knowledge gained through self-learning, exchange and collective work will assist the student with clearer thinking and logical reasoning, including self-reflection and an opportunity to practice those skills within the confines of an academic institution. These practices can encompass real-life problem-solving, role-play and various case scenarios, under the watchful eye of accredited educators. Therefore, gaining cognitive independence becomes critical to skill development success (Espinoza Freire, 2021). Rouleau and Balogun (2011) claimed that critical thinking and sensemaking skills for middle managers underpin discursive competence and lie in an intimate knowledge of the setting and a good understanding of multiple interactions. As such, relational context and collaborative mindsets are very important (Hendarwati et al., 2021).

Moreover, ethical competence has an emerging requisite to be embedded in all higher education programmes in the twenty-first century. It begs the question as to what we understand by being ethically competent. Underpinning this concept is the "human quest for knowledge and action that defines right and wrong behaviour" (Menzel, 2016, p. 4). Ethical competence is an attractive, powerful, and promising concept, with several advantages for research and practice (Schrijver & Maesschalk, 2013 in Cooper & Menzel, 2013) and is also a fundamental but complex concept for learning (Dierckx de Casterlé et al., 2008). Most ethical competencies have arisen mainly from healthcare ethics (Koskenvuori et al., 2019). These comprise character strength, ethical awareness, moral judgement skills and the willingness to do good (Kulju et al., 2016).

Following the preceding conceptions and ideas, the current chapter describes Future Skills as a term that encompasses three types of skills: (1) cognitive independence (such as critical thinking, logical reasoning, sensemaking, decision-making, problem-solving skills), (2) collaborative (relational) and (3) ethical

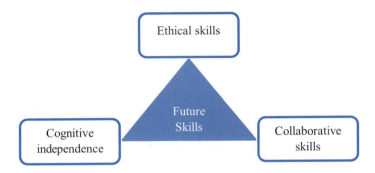

Fig. 12.1 Future Skills conceptualization

skills (Fig. 12.1). Accordingly, Future Skills integrate those competencies that enable individuals to independently and flexibly use their knowledge to meet complex demands and handle compound situations, whilst thinking and working in an ethical manner, adhering to a code of practice. These Future Skills are aimed to increase employees' prospects for success, being more adaptable to increasing complexity of their work.

12.3 Blending Problem-Based Learning with Place-Based Education to Develop Cognitive Independence

12.3.1 Developing Cognitive and Collaborative Skills in Entrepreneurship Education

Entrepreneurship education has rapidly emerged as a topic of high importance in multiple domains of knowledge in higher education institutions and continues to have a significant role for promoting job creation, innovation and the growth of national economies (Mohamed & Sheikh Ali, 2021). Higher education institutions are striving to equip their graduates with entrepreneurial skills that will elevate their capacity to pursue a self-employment career (Rasiah et al., 2019), whilst also developing students' capabilities to become future generators of sustainable value for business and society at large (Igwe et al., 2021). Developing entrepreneurship and other future work-ready skills, for enhancing entrepreneurial intentions of students to start successful businesses, raises continuous challenges. As such, the physical closure of higher education institutions due to

COVID-19 shed a brighter light on the need to implement alternative teaching pedagogies (Morgado et al., 2021) that allow the Future Skills development in an online or a blended learning context. An earlier work of Sánchez Contreras and Murga Menoyo (2019) stressed the importance of adopting adequate learning methods that support the students' acquisition of meaningful abilities and skills, but also values and characteristics of a citizenship consciously and actively committed to the great challenges posed by the existing socio-ecological crises. A hybrid system that combines online Problem-Based Learning (PBL) and onsite Place-Based Entrepreneurial Learning (PBEL) can be considered a viable setting for developing Future Skills when utilized within the specific context of entrepreneurship education. A recent work published by Wong and Kan (2022) stressed that PBL is an effective teaching pedagogy for knowledge acquisition and cognitive skill development (such as problem-solving, critical thinking, and logical reasoning), encouraging students to become self-directed learners, exchange knowledge and work collaboratively. Also, Takano's (2022) study outlined the importance of gaining learning and developing sensemaking skills through participation in meaning-making processes and by being exposed to real-life contexts, as this proved to have an impactful result in practice later.

Real-life problem-solving and collaborative skills are essential and valuable in entrepreneurship education. Problem-Based Learning is a broadly used pedagogical method to encourage interactivity, stimulate learning, construct reasoning, improve the learning outcomes and enhance the overall student's experience (Espinoza Freire, 2021; Wang et al., 2021). The collaborative, sensemaking, and problem-solving skills are very important Future Skills for students, necessary to organize the division of tasks in solving entrepreneurial problems, and work on solutions jointly and innovatively (Hendarwati et al., 2021).

The switch to online or blended learning due to the coronavirus pandemic stressed the need for inventing new combinations of alternative teaching pedagogies that enhance lifelong learning. One solution is online PBL. Recent research (Wong & Kan, 2022) found that online PBL stimulates self-directed and collaborative learning and knowledge-sharing behaviour of students that consequently lead to enhanced problem-solving skills. Yet, current studies uncovered that the students' engagement in offline and online PBL did not show significant difference (Kristianto & Gandajaya, 2022). This is possible when using the PBL approach, as it requires the students to be actively engaged in gaining and exchanging knowledge to advance meanings, while collaboratively working in teams and interacting with their peers and educators.

The concept of Place-Based Entrepreneurial Education was established only recently, the intention being to develop entrepreneurship education that takes the environmental, cultural, socio-economic, and political challenges of a place into account (Sesigür & Edeer, 2020; Wright et al., 2021). It blends Place-Based Learning and Problem-Based Learning within the entrepreneurship educational settings and context of university to develop student skills that matter. Yet, the importance of place for entrepreneurship education has received little attention by higher education institutions (Larty, 2021). There is still a lot of work to do in connecting students to places and engaging them in understanding the relationship between entrepreneurship, local communities, and their challenges within the entrepreneurship curriculum. Recent research by LaDuca et al. (2020) exemplifies how universities use place-based community engagement in developing student reasoning and sensemaking skills, by extending partnerships with communities that create meanings and make sense to address critical twenty-first-century challenges. They showed that applied creativity and transdisciplinarity acted as valuable ingredients in fostering reciprocal partnerships, aimed at creating value, benefits and a long-term impact for all involved. Cincera et al.'s (2019) study stressed that Placed-Based Education in programmes for sustainable development increased the teachers' self-effectiveness, developed the students' socioemotional competence, and improved the atmosphere at the schools involved. Also, research by Thomas (2020) showed that place-based inquiry situated in the students' outdoor surroundings can provide high relevance in classrooms for critical skill development, by connecting the curriculum content that can be highly standardized with the systemic dilemmas that challenge communities.

The coming section of the paper illustrates how the theoretical approaches underpinning the PBL and PBEL methods sustain the development of cognitive and collaborative skills as Future Skills required in entrepreneurship education. These are valuable Future Skills in other areas of education alike.

12.3.2 Reshaping Learning Methods in Entrepreneurship Education

To foster innovation and allow future skill development, higher education institutions need to internalize new forms of education. These can extend from blended learning, online work, practices with enterprises, volunteering to experiential learning trips among other, as formal practices that engage students in organizations. Students are expected to work closely with the local actors, either public, private sector or civil society, to develop their skills and increase their awareness and understanding of the local place (Sánchez Contreras & Murga Menoyo,

2019). The collaborative work with local actors enables students to develop and practice their entrepreneurial skills in a safe environment and contribute to complex problem solving. In this way, higher education institutions help them secure future entrepreneurial skills and potentially become tomorrow's entrepreneurs.

An example of a course that offers students opportunities for developing and practicing their cognitive and socio-emotional skills is "Entrepreneurship and Sustainable Business Development (ESBD)", taught at a public university business school in Romania. The course aims at producing work-ready graduates with entrepreneurial skills. Following a classroom action research approach, ESBD was developed as an intensive five-week graduate course (with four teaching and learning hours per day) aimed at a cohort of business students in the first year of study of their master programme. The course is run in collaboration with partner-companies, communities, or other organizations from the local environment in which the university is embedded. As part of their course assignments, students are demanded to examine, evaluate, and solve a real-life business dilemma defined by the partner-organizations, by employing a Design Thinking methodology (Teodoro, 2021). The learning process considers integration of the interests of all actors involved, use of technology, and the requirement for business success, and uses systemic reasoning, sensemaking and intuition to explore the most desirable alternative solution to the problem.

The ESBD course combines two teaching methods: Place-Based Entrepreneurship Education and (online) Problem-Based Learning. This combination of teaching methods increases the motivation of students, inviting them to become more actively involved in the problem-solving process. Also, it allows them to approach the given situation rigorously and professionally. Additionally, the methodology allows the educators to improve the relevance of teaching by integrating specifics of the place in the learning process. For instance, Wang et al. (2021) found that PBL significantly improved students' self-learning abilities in the theoretical framework of the course. At the same time, employing PBEL as a teaching method helps the students diagnose the real problem, generate alternative timely solutions and develop concrete action plans that consider the local context.

Working in groups of four to five members, by using their cumulative knowledge and applying the Design Thinking tools, the students can provide creative business solutions to the problem identified. Initially, the students describe the core problem and subsequent relevant issues taking into consideration the existing challenges of the local place. The solutions they come up with latter are framed in a hybrid learning environment that combines online learning for problem explanation and onsite learning for problem exploration and resolution. The collaborative work that the students undertake include successively clarifying priorities, doing required field work, acquiring and exchanging new knowledge, designing creative solutions and developing concrete action plans embedded into the local context (Fig. 12.2).

Educators play a facilitating role aimed at supporting and guiding students with their learning, more deeply and effectively, through their individual study and peer-to-peer interaction in a group. Partner organizations support the field research with real-time feedback, data collection, interviews, and validation of the intermediary and final results. Five to six different real-life scenarios are developed each academic year and the students, as teams, traverse the real factory virtually and/or onsite to assess the situation. The live online classes are carried out both via the PBL approach and via teacher-based methods by using the Zoom application. Group work for problem definition and solution generation is organized using breakout rooms.

The employment of online PBL combined with onsite PBEL demonstrated the improvement of students' self-directed learning, for which they were willing to take full responsibility, which led to improved critical thinking, logical reasoning and decision-making skills. These are skills that characterize cognitive independence (Espinoza Freire, 2021). Moreover, the students' problem-solving abilities improved through the well-planned intervention of both educators and local partners, containing clear guidelines for student learning and their involvement during the process, and through regular group discussions held via various channels (Wong & Kan, 2022). Students generally reported positively on the use of

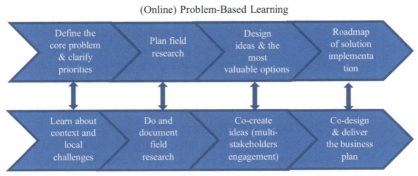

Fig. 12.2 Learning Method Design

a blended learning environment. Also, students found that while teachers were indispensable to implementation of the PBL process, the local partners played a key role in helping students understand the PBEL context.

There were some tension points reported in the integration of the learning principles of PBL along the different phases of PBL, given the variety of students' individual preferences, learning priorities, or understandings of the topic. These were mainly reported during the group formation and distribution of tasks, problem definition and analysis, and alternative solution prioritization. Other research also reported similar obstacles (Hermann et al., 2022). Additional tensions were registered during the validation of the learning insights gained as a result of the PBEL exploration process. To tackle these tensions, the teachers suggested early integration of formative feedback in every step of the learning process and progressive problem analysis and resolution. All the above highlights the importance of learning principles in relation to PBL. However, it is also imperative that those principles are grounded in ethical knowledge which lends itself to ethical knowing.

12.4   Developing Ethical Competence

12.4.1 Conceptual Understanding in Nursing Ethics Education

Ethics education reflects on ethical decision-making, professional and research practices (Torrence et al., 2017). Ethics as a discipline addresses moral issues at the junctures of health care delivery, medical, nursing and health research, technological advancement, and environmental studies, to name a few. Access to ethics training is important for all future and practicing professionals. Nurses, for instance, should be well versed in the ethical implications of their actions as clinicians (Purtilo & Doherty, 2011). Nursing is a practice-based discipline and clinical placement is a vital part of nursing education in Bachelor programmes (Plathe et al., 2021). Advances in health science and technology have led to profound changes in nursing practice and nursing education (Park, 2012). Nurses, in delivering care for patients, resort to their ethical knowing. It is well recognised in educating nurses that they must be also prepared to be ethically competent in their practice and decisions making (Park et al., 2009; Ujvarine, 2008). A nurse develops over time in their role as a responsible health care professional (Fowler & Tschudin, 2006). At times there may be a lack of critical reflection amongst students. At all times, critical reflection must be nurtured and encouraged.

The prerequisites for ethical competence such as professional virtues and ethical knowledge (Robichaux, 2016) is inherent in the skills deemed necessary to be taught to higher education students. Knowledge regarding ethical concepts and ethical knowing has enormous benefits for instructional effectiveness (Watts et al., 2017). An example of such a programme will focus on theoretical concepts such as ethical reflection and ethical decision-making (Lechasseur et al., 2018) amongst other skills such as analysis and judgement (Paganini & Yoshikawa Egry, 2011). The work will have a Future Skills profile as ethical leadership is needed to be at the forefront for an ever-changing future society. It is essential that the graduate of the future has the critical skills and knowledge to make decisions based on ethical reasoning. It is envisaged that a specific purpose module in ethical competences will ensure that the participants of an educational programme will acquire the essential components of ethical competence and awareness whilst ensuring that they safeguard the vulnerable in society. This is already embodied within the discipline of nursing and could also be replicated by other disciplines within higher level education.

Education in ethics (reasoning) and values (ideals) is important in every phase of life (Nirupama & D'Souza, 2021; Singh & Stückelberger, 2017). The development of ethical reasoning in an individual is essential to the development of society (Simkins & Steinkuehler, 2008). More importantly, ethics underpins how we live and treat each other. All educational institutions have the responsibility to educate their students in an ethical way. Socrates placed emphasis on ethics as a branch of philosophy that dealt with morality and stressed that it was more important than a religious, moral, or legal concept (Wilberding, 2014).

The idea of ethical competency development also involves acknowledging multiple perspectives, whilst allowing for deeper reflection upon an individual's ethical values (Ward, 2020). In teaching ethics, it is important to reflect on different backgrounds and be respectful of different cultures. Cultural competence is important in relation to ethics. Deardorff (2006) defined intercultural competence as "the ability to communicate effectively and appropriately in intercultural situations based on one's intercultural knowledge, skills, and attitudes" (pp. 247–248). He also reflected on the personality component in the definition with emphasis placed on openness to and respect for other cultures. This is essential in the ethical component of educational programmes.

The importance of research ethics training has led academic institutions to require that students obtain such training at various stages of their careers (Ahmed & Nebeker, 2021). This also extends to other ways of knowing regarding ethics and ensuring that there is an increased awareness around the value of ethics education. Resilience and mindfulness were positively correlated with moral competence and work engagement with reference to the use of experiential discovery learning practices and high-fidelity simulation (Rushton et al., 2021). This assists in empowering individuals and building their confidence to assist them in making sound ethical decisions.

12.4.2 Teaching and Learning Approach in Nursing Education to Support Ethical Skills Development

Theoretical concepts underpinning key ethical theories with specific reference to various disciplines ought to be embedded in all undergraduate programmes. Critical reflection and the utilisation of ethical knowledge is evident and documented in various tertiary modules that will equip the student with the appropriate skills for the future in dealing with complex issues. An example of the format for teaching ethics is undergraduate nurses completing a BSc in Nursing in Ireland. It is taught in year one where the student works on specific ethical concepts, year two on their application, with years three and four critically reviewing, analysing and synthesizing the concepts and merging the theory into practice. The students are supported by having the concepts explored in a simulation laboratory. It can also be brought into the concept of Problem-Based Learning such as devising a simulation within a lab scenario and giving challenges for the student to solve. This is then reviewed, so that the students demonstrate the necessary knowledge, skills and ethical competences in the area. This in line with the Quality and Qualifications Ireland accreditation (QQI, 2022).

There are opportunities to practice ethical competence with other disciplines. Another practical example may be through the development of e-health. According to the eHealth Action Plan 2012–2020 of the European Commission (2012), "eHealth can benefit citizens, patients, health and care professionals but also health organisations and public authorities. eHealth—when applied effectively—delivers more personalised 'citizen-centric' healthcare, which is more targeted, effective and efficient and helps reduce errors, as well as the length of hospitalisation. It facilitates socio-economic inclusion and equality, quality of life and patient empowerment through greater transparency, access to services and information and the use of social media for health". The Faculties of Engineering (Designing the Technology), Science (Exact recordings to be taken), Business (Budgets and costings) and Healthcare (Interpretation of results) can be all involved in reviewing the ethical issues underpinning these concepts. This, too, can be taught in a simulation lab and reviewed by a panel of experts as part of an overall assessment.

It is not unusual to witness a lack of critical reflection amongst students (Benner, 2012). This must also be taught with an ethical component. Strengthening cognitive skills and reflection strategies within a programme can be effective and a robust approach to learning (Ravik, 2020). It also lends itself to teaching ethics. The concept of scaffolding plays a crucial role in shaping the quality of classroom learning with the utilisation of a classroom discourse analysis approach as shown by Li and Zhang (2022) with a different topic.

Enriching skills with reference to ethics and ethical conflict also needs to focus on enabling inclusiveness and empower individuals with the right ability so that they can make decisions based on evidence. Ethical conflict such as moral uncertainty, moral dilemma, moral distress and moral outrage (Falcó-Pegueroles et al., 2015) must be discussed and developed within a case scenario. An ethical conflict is defined as a problem that arises when one senses that the idea of "good," "right" or "doing the right thing" with reference to other people's best interests are being compromised (Falcó-Pegueroles et al., 2016). Influences such as e-health and digitalisation have an impact on education in relation to ethics. Scenarios inclusive of these topics need to be developed and embedded in third-level education. Codes of ethics and malpractice law must also review computer software recognising that professional ethics of software developers are scrutinized within the classification of computing as a profession under U.S. tort law (Choi, 2021). In principle, a module is developed throughout each year of an undergraduate programme. As the student progresses through the programme, their knowledge is built upon in line with the National Qualifications Framework which allows for levels of education from level 6 to level 10 (see www.qqi.ie).

Ethical challenges in practice affect frontline nurses, which can undermine safety, quality, and compassionate care (Rushton et al., 2021). For instance, the key elements that underpin professional conduct and ethics for Registered Nurses and Registered Midwives in Ireland are respect for the dignity of the person, professional responsibility and accountability, quality of practice, trust and confidentiality and collaboration with others (NMBI, 2021). These principles are taught in each year of the undergraduate nursing programme and built upon inclusive of various legislative frameworks in line with the European Convention on Human Rights.

Educators, in imparting ethical knowing, may use a framework to teach and assess the range of critical knowledge and skills for ethical decision-making. Ethics education in nursing should promote the development of moral sensitivity amongst reasoning skills based on codes of ethics, ethical principles, and professional responsibilities (Gastmans, 2002; Jaeger, 2001; NMBI, 2021). The Ethical Competence Framework (Berghofer & Schwartz, 2011) is also a tool that may assist educators, and the use of experiential discovery and simulation scenarios can be effective in addressing moral adversity (Rushton & Sharma, 2018). It may also provide a rigorous assessment tool that can improve the understanding for what is required to achieve and gain ethical competence. Findings from research by Koskenvuori et al. (2019) revealed that healthcare professionals' ethical competence is a limited research area in relation to assessing conceptualization, measuring, and realization of the ethical competence. An example of instruments to measure ethical competence in terms of moral competence is offered by Asahara et al. (2015). Reflection on and in practice is very important to ensure that competent caring practitioners work in a professional manner. Therefore, allocating time during a working schedule on reflection is vital.

12.5 Challenges and Practical Implications

The COVID-19 pandemic has demanded changes to students' learning experiences and Future Skills development across all domains of knowledge. The jobs and companies of the future might not have yet been created, but there is a need to understand what will be necessary for a graduate to be considered qualified in the future. Higher education is very beneficial to any country's economic and societal development, accompanied with a demand for financial and productivity accountability (Waller et al., 2019). Higher education students are expecting to be engaged in learning environments that better acquaint them not only with discipline-specific concepts and principles, but more importantly, with relevant practices and competencies regarded essential for their future (Kruskopf et al., 2021).

Our synopsis informs higher education institution leaders and, particularly, entrepreneurship education faculty about how to explore their own curricula, educational settings, and institution's context. Also, it encourages educators to explore how Placed-Based Education can combine with Problem-Based Learning to create opportunities to teach students about innovation and develop Future Skills. Although PBL and PBEL have different focuses, their combination can enhance teaching effectiveness in various domains of knowledge and practice. Our methodology was effective in terms of enhancing students' interest in entrepreneurship and resulted in improved learning, but also in better preparation for the job market. The scenario presented contributes to the debate on Future Skills development within the entrepreneurship education literature. The scenario can also serve as an inspiration for entrepreneurship course designers in higher education, but also for other knowledge areas alike.

From ethical knowledge perspective, the work that the students engage in mirrors what takes place in clinical practice and in real acute hospital and community-based healthcare scenarios. They can utilise an ethical decision-making framework and explore and address relevant ethical issues. The element of reflection and reflective practice can also be utilised to encourage ongoing learning in this field. It is in the interest of everyone to develop an ethical code of professional conduct. It is also vital that empirical evidence is collected regarding ethics education, and that there is a sharing of professionals' experiences of teaching ethics. Pedagogical research relevant to diverse healthcare professionals will provide essential evidence as to how to teach this so that future generations are grounded in ethical knowing. It is vital that retaining the brightest nurses in the profession is an ethical mandate (Rushton et al., 2021). This is becoming more difficult in an era where nurses are leaving the profession due to the stress of the service demands.

The implications are that unfortunately different countries have different codes of ethics and practices. Implementing one programme across Europe may not suffice but it is important that ethical education respects the rights and dignity of all human beings. Ethics education inherent to upholding research integrity is different to ethical knowing essential for various professional disciplines. It is essential for society that it is taught properly and respectfully in all higher education institutions.

It is extremely important to ensure that the future graduates are competent practitioners, who work in a professional and ethical manner. This can be achieved through participation of the students in meaning-making learning processes and by exposing them to real-life contexts. Moreover, allocating time for reflection during a training course schedule is vital. This time may be challenging to attain in different environments, but students who are afforded this opportunity will perform better. Within a classroom environment, time needs to be allocated to sense-making and reflection. In educational programmes that have a professional qualification along with an academic award, it is imperative that reflection is part of the programme and time is allocated to it in practice.

Future Skills in Practice: Our Recommendations
- Regardless of the areas of knowledge in higher education, Future Skills should encompass cognitive independence (such as critical thinking, logical reasoning, sensemaking, decision-making, problem-solving skills), collaborative (relational) skills and ethical (character strength, ethical awareness, moral sensitivity, willingness to do good) skills.

- It is essential that the graduate of the future has the critical skills and knowledge to make decisions based on ethical reasoning.
- Adopting adequate learning methods (e.g., blended learning, online learning complemented by onsite work), relevant to different areas of education, is crucial to support the students' acquisition of meaningful abilities and skills.
- Higher education institutions must encourage students to become self-directed learners, actively engaging in gaining and exchanging knowledge to advance meanings, while collaboratively and flexibly working in teams and interacting with their peers and educators.
- Higher education institutions must develop students' Future Skills through their participation in meaning-making processes and by being exposed to real-life contexts.
- In educational programmes that have a professional qualification along with an academic award, it is imperative that reflection is part of the programme.

References

Ahmed, W. S., & Nebeker, C. (2021). Assessment of research ethics education offerings of pharmacy master programs in an Arab nation relative to top programs worldwide: A qualitative content analysis. *PLoS ONE, 16*(2), e0238755. https://doi.org/10.1371/journal.pone.0238755

Asahara, K., Kobayashi, M., & Ono, W. (2015). Moral competence questionnaire for public health nurses in Japan: Scale development and psychometric validation. *Japan Journal of Nursing Science, 12*(1), 18–26. https://doi.org/10.1111/jjns.12044

Benner, P. (2012). Educating nurses: A call for radical transformation —How far have we come? *Journal of Nursing Education, 51*(4), 183–184. https://doi.org/10.3928/01484834-20120402-01

Berghofer, D., & Schwartz, G. (2011). Ethical leadership: Right relationships and the emotional bottom line: The gold standard for success. http://www.ethicalleadership.com/BusinessArticle.htm. Accessed 9 Febr 9 2023.

Choi, B. H. (2021). Software professionals, malpractice law, and codes of ethics. *Communications of the ACM, 64*(5), 22–24. https://doi.org/10.1145/3457193

Cincera, J., Valesova, B., Krepelkova, S., Simonova, P., & Kroufek, R. (2019). Place-based education from three perspectives. *Environmental Education Research, 25*(10), 1510–1523. https://doi.org/10.1080/13504622.2019.1651826

Cooper, T. L., & Menzel, D. C. (Eds.). (2013). *Achieving ethical competence for public service leadership*. Sharpe.

Deardorff, D. K. (2006). Identification and assessment of intercultural competence as a student outcome of internationalization. *Journal of Studies in International Education, 10*(3), 241–266. https://doi.org/10.1177/1028315306287002

Dierckx de Casterlé, B., Izumi, S., Godfrey, N. S., & Denhaerynck, K. (2008). Nurses' responses to ethical dilemmas in nursing practice: Meta-analysis. *Journal of Advanced Nursing, 63*(6), 540–549. https://doi.org/10.1111/j.1365-2648.2008.04702.x

Ehlers, U.-D. (2020). *Future skills.* Springer Fachmedien Wiesbaden.

Espinoza Freire, E. E. (2021). Problem-based learning, a challenge to higher education. *Revista Conrado, 17*(80), 295–303.

European Commission (2012). *EHealth action plan 2012–2020 – Innovative healthcare for the 21st century.* Publications Office of the European Union.

Falcó-Pegueroles, A., Lluch-Canut, M. T., Martínez-Estalella, G., Zabalegui-Yarnoz, A., Delgado-Hito, P., Via-Clavero, G., et al. (2016). Levels of exposure to ethical conflict in the ICU: Correlation between sociodemographic variables and the clinical environment. *Intensive and Critical Care Nursing, 33*, 12–20. https://doi.org/10.1016/j.iccn.2015.10.004

Falcó-Pegueroles, A., Lluch-Canut, T., Roldan-Merino, J., Goberna-Tricas, J., & Guàrdia-Olmos, J. (2015). Ethical conflict in critical care nursing: Correlation between exposure and types. *Nursing Ethics, 22*(5), 594–607. https://doi.org/10.1177/0969733014549883

Fowler, M. D., & Tschudin, V. (2006). Ethics in nursing: A historical perspective. In A. J. Davis, L. de Raeve, & V. Tschudin (Eds.), *Essentials of teaching and learning in nursing ethics: Perspectives and methods* (pp. 13–26). Churchill Livingstone.

Gastmans, C. (2002). A fundamental ethical approach to nursing: Some proposals for ethics education. *Nursing Ethics, 9*(5), 494–507. https://doi.org/10.1191/0969733002ne539oa

Hendarwati, E., Nurlaela, L., Bachri, B. S., & Sa'ida, N. (2021). Collaborative problem based learning integrated with online learning. *International Journal of Emerging Technologies in Learning, 16*(13), 29–39. https://doi.org/10.3991/ijet.v16i13.24159

Hermann, R. R., Bossle, M. B., & Amaral, M. (2022). Lenses on the post-oil economy: Integrating entrepreneurship into sustainability education through problem-based learning. *Educational Action Research, 30*(3), 480–506. https://doi.org/10.1080/09650792.2020.1823239

Igwe, P. A., Okolie, U. C., & Nwokoro, C. V. (2021). Towards a responsible entrepreneurship education and the future of the workforce. *The International Journal of Management Education, 19*(1), 100300. https://doi.org/10.1016/j.ijme.2019.05.001

Jaeger, S. M. (2001). Teaching health care ethics: The importance of moral sensitivity for moral reasoning. *Nursing Philosophy, 2*(2), 131–142. https://doi.org/10.1046/j.1466-769X.2001.00045.x

Koskenvuori, J., Stolt, M., Suhonen, R., & Leino-Kilpi, H. (2019). Healthcare professionals' ethical competence: A scoping review. *Nursing Open, 6*(1), 5–17. https://doi.org/10.1002/nop2.173

Kristianto, H., & Gandajaya, L. (2022). Offline vs online problem-based learning: A case study of student engagement and learning outcomes. *Interactive Technology and Smart Education, 20*(1), 106–121. https://doi.org/10.1108/ITSE-09-2021-0166

Kruskopf, M., Ketonen, E. E., & Mattlin, M. (2021). Playing out diplomacy: Gamified realization of future skills and discipline-specific theory. *European Political Science, 20*(4), 698–722. https://doi.org/10.1057/s41304-020-00305-7

Kulju, K., Stolt, M., Suhonen, R., & Leino-Kilpi, H. (2016). Ethical competence: A concept analysis. *Nursing Ethics, 23*(4), 401–412. https://doi.org/10.1177/0969733014567025

LaDuca, B., Carroll, C., Ausdenmoore, A., & Keen, J. (2020). Pursuing social justice through place-based community engagement: Cultivating applied creativity, transdisciplinarity, and reciprocity in catholic higher education. *Christian Higher Education, 19*(1–2), 60–77. https://doi.org/10.1080/15363759.2019.1689204

Larty, J. (2021). Towards a framework for integrating place-based approaches in entrepreneurship education. *Industry and Higher Education, 35*(4), 312–324.

Lechasseur, K., Caux, C., Dollé, S., & Legault, A. (2018). Ethical competence: An integrative review. *Nursing Ethics, 25*(6), 694–706. https://doi.org/10.1177/0969733016667773

Li, D., & Zhang, L. (2022). Exploring teacher scaffolding in a CLIL-framed EFL intensive reading class: A classroom discourse analysis approach. *Language Teaching Research, 26*(3), 333–360. https://doi.org/10.1177/1362168820903340

Menzel, D. C. (2016). Ethical competence. In A. Farazmand (Ed.), *Global encyclopedia of public administration, public policy, and governance* (pp. 1–4). Springer International Publishing. https://doi.org/10.1007/978-3-319-31816-5_2458-1.

Mohamed, N. A., & Sheikh Ali, A. Y. (2021). Entrepreneurship education: Systematic literature review and future research directions. *World Journal of Entrepreneurship, Management and Sustainable Development, 17*(4), 644–661. https://doi.org/10.1108/WJEMSD-07-2020-0084

Morgado, M., Mendes, J. J., & Proença, L. (2021). Online problem-based learning in clinical dental education: Students' self-perception and motivation. *Healthcare, 9*(4), 420. https://doi.org/10.3390/healthcare9040420

Muñiz, R. (2020). Muddy sensemaking: Making sense of socio-emotional skills amidst a vague policy context. *Education Policy Analysis Archives, 28,* 114. https://doi.org/10.14507/epaa.28.5235.

Nirupama, M., & D'Souza, D. J. (2021). Values and ethics in education. *International Research Journal of Modernization in Engineering Technology and Science, 3*(2), 732–741.

NMBI. (2021). Code of professional conduct and ethics for registered nurses and registered midwives. https://www.nmbi.ie/NMBI/media/NMBI/Code-of-Professional-Conduct-and-Ethics.pdf?ext=.pdf. Accessed 9 Febr 2023.

Paganini, M. C., & Yoshikawa Egry, E. (2011). The ethical component of professional competence in nursing: an analysis. *Nursing Ethics, 18*(4), 571–582. https://doi.org/10.1177/0969733011408041

Park, E.-J. (2012). An integrated ethical decision-making model for nurses. *Nursing Ethics, 19*(1), 139–159. https://doi.org/10.1177/0969733011413491

Park, J., Kim, W. O., & kim, Y. (2009). The present status and future directions of nursing ethics education. *Korean Journal of Medical Ethics, 12*(3), 251–260. https://doi.org/10.35301/ksme.2009.12.3.251.

Plathe, H., Solheim, E., & Eide, H. (2021). Nursing students' and preceptors' experiences with using an assessment tool for feedback and reflection in supervision of clinical skills: A qualitative pilot study. *Nursing Research and Practice*, 1–9. https://doi.org/10.1155/2021/5551662.

Portela-Pino, I., Alvariñas-Villaverde, M., & Pino-Juste, M. (2021). Socio-Emotional skills as predictors of performance of students: Differences by gender. *Sustainability, 13*(9), 4807. https://doi.org/10.3390/su13094807

Purtilo, R. B., & Doherty, R. R. (2011). *Ethical dimensions in the health professions*. Elsevier Saunders.

QQI. (2022). Statement of strategy 2022–24. https://www.qqi.ie/sites/default/files/2022-02/statement-of-strategy-2022-24.pdf.

Radwan, O., Ghavifekr, S., & Abdul Razak, A. Z. (2021). Can academic leadership competencies have effect on students' cognitive, skill and affective learning outcomes? Higher education perspective. *Journal of Applied Research in Higher Education, 13*(2), 430–445. https://doi.org/10.1108/JARHE-05-2020-0144

Rasiah, R., Somasundram, S., & Tee, K. (2019). Entrepreneurship in education: Innovations in higher education to promote experiential learning and develop future ready entrepreneurial graduates. *Journal of Engineering Science and Technology, 14*(SI), 99–110.

Ravik, M. (2020). Improving simulation-based learning of a practical skill in nursing education. *The Journal of Practice Teaching and Learning, 17*(1), 36–50. https://doi.org/10.1921/jpts.v17i1.1315

Robichaux, C. (2016). *Ethical competence in nursing practice: Competencies, skills, decision-making*. Springer Publishing Company.

Rouleau, L., & Balogun, J. (2011). Middle managers, strategic sensemaking, and discursive competence. *Journal of Management Studies, 48*(5), 953–983. https://doi.org/10.1111/j.1467-6486.2010.00941.x

Rushton, C. H., & Sharma, M. (2018). Creating a culture of moral resilience and ethical practice. In C. H. Rushton (Ed.), *Moral resilience: Transforming moral suffering in healthcare* (pp. 243–280). Oxford University Press.

Rushton, C. H., Swoboda, S. M., Reller, N., Skarupski, K. A., Prizzi, M., Young, P. D., et al. (2021). Mindful ethical practice and resilience academy: Equipping nurses to address ethical challenges. *American Journal of Critical Care, 30*(1), e1–e11. https://doi.org/10.4037/ajcc2021359

Sánchez Contreras, M. F., & Murga Menoyo, M. Á. (2019). Place-based education: An approach for a sustainable curriculum in higher education. *Bordón Revista de Pedagogía, 71*(2), 155–174. https://doi.org/10.13042/Bordon.2019.68295.

de Schrijver, A. & Maesschalk, J. (2013). A new definition and conceptualization of ethical competence. In T. L. Cooper & D. C. Menzel (Eds.), *Achieving ethical competence for public service leadership* (pp. 29–51). Sharpe.

Sesigür, A., & Edeer, Ş. (2020). Place-based critical art education: An action research. *International Journal of Education and the Arts, 21*(25), 1–24. https://doi.org/10.26209/ijea21n25.

Simkins, D. W., & Steinkuehler, C. (2008). Critical ethical reasoning and role-play. *Games and Culture, 3*(3–4), 333–355. https://doi.org/10.1177/1555412008317313

Singh, D., & Stückelberger, C. (Eds.). (2017). *Ethics in higher education: Values-driven leaders for the future*. Globethics.net.

Takano, T. (2022). How experiences transform over time: A retrospective study on place-based education in Micronesia and the Philippines. *Journal of Adventure Education and Outdoor Learning, 22*(1), 12–23. https://doi.org/10.1080/14729679.2020.1854098

Teodoro, J. (2021). Design Thinking for Competency-Based Entrepreneurship Education: The ToolBoard Methodology. In F. Matos, M. de Fátima Ferreiro, A. Rosa, & I. Salavisa (Eds.), *Proceedings of the 16th European Conference on Innovation and Entrepreneurship* (Vol 2, pp. 1027–1035). UK: Academic Conferences International Limited Reading.

Thomas, T. G. (2020). Place-based inquiry in a university course abroad: Lessons about education for sustainability in the urban outdoors. *International Journal of Sustainability in Higher Education, 21*(5), 895–910. https://doi.org/10.1108/IJSHE-07-2019-0220

Torrence, B. S., Watts, L. L., Mulhearn, T. J., Turner, M. R., Todd, E. M., Mumford, M. D., et al. (2017). Curricular approaches in research ethics education: Reflecting on more and less effective practices in instructional content. *Accountability in Research, 24*(5), 269–296. https://doi.org/10.1080/08989621.2016.1276452

Ujvarine, A. S. (2008). Ethics in Hungarian nursing education programs. *Nursing Ethics, 15*(5), 696–697. https://doi.org/10.1177/0969733008092877

Waller, R. E., Lemoine, P. A., Mense, E. G., Garretson, C. J., & Richardson, M. D. (2019). Global higher education in a VUCA world: Concerns and projections. *Journal of Education and Development, 3*(2), 73. https://doi.org/10.20849/jed.v3i2.613.

Wang, H., Xuan, J., Liu, L., Shen, X., & Xiong, Y. (2021). Problem-based learning and case-based learning in dental education. *Annals of Translational Medicine, 9*(14), 1137. https://doi.org/10.21037/atm-21-165.

Ward, S. (2020). Reconceptualizing the teaching of ethics in a global classroom. *International Journal of Ethics Education, 5*(1), 39–50. https://doi.org/10.1007/s40889-020-00087-y

Watts, L. L., Medeiros, K. E., Mulhearn, T. J., Steele, L. M., Connelly, S., & Mumford, M. D. (2017). Are ethics training programs improving? A meta-analytic review of past and present ethics instruction in the sciences. *Ethics & Behavior, 27*(5), 351–384. https://doi.org/10.1080/10508422.2016.1182025

Wilberding, E. (2014). *Teach like socrates: Guiding socratic dialogues and discussions in the classroom*. Routledge.

Wong, F. M. F., & Kan, C. W. Y. (2022). Online problem-based learning intervention on self-directed learning and problem-solving through group work: A waitlist controlled trial. *International Journal of Environmental Research and Public Health, 19*(2), 720. https://doi.org/10.3390/ijerph19020720

Wright, D. S., Crooks, K. R., Hunter, D. O., Krumm, C. E., & Balgopal, M. M. (2021). Middle school science teachers' agency to implement place-based education curricula about local wildlife. *Environmental Education Research, 27*(10), 1519–1537. https://doi.org/10.1080/13504622.2021.1960955

Carmen Păunescu, PhD, is a Professor of Entrepreneurship in the UNESCO Department for Business Administration at the Bucharest University of Economic Studies, Romania. Her research interests lie in the areas of social entrepreneurship, innovation and impact engagement, sustainable entrepreneurship, and higher education. Carmen has been engaged as expert and local coordinator in various Erasmus+ projects focused on community learning, such as "CLLC—Community Learning for Local Change" and "VISEnet—Village social enterprise: learning material, guidance, and networking". Currently, she supervises PhD students on research topics that concern development of social entrepreneurship and creation of impact innovations across sectors and disciplines. Carmen co-edited the Springer book "Social Innovation in Higher Education: Landscape, practices, and opportunities" issued in 2022.

Mary McDonnell-Naughton, PhD, is a Registered Nurse, Midwife, and Registered Nurse Tutor, and is currently a Senior Lecturer at the Technological University of the Shannon, Athlone Campus and Chairperson of the College's Research Ethics Committee. She holds a PhD from the College of Medicine – University College Dublin, Ireland, has extensive research experience with members of the interdisciplinary team, and has been involved in collaborating international research across disciplines. Mary has supervised students and engaged in various areas of research from Child Health, Smoking, Alcohol and Learning Disability to various aspects associated with the Older Person, especially the Centenarian. Along with an interest in Ethics, Mary has an interest in Innovation, Social, and Community Engagement work, and has engaged in various community research projects.

Open Access This chapter is licensed under the terms of the Creative Commons Attribution 4.0 International License (http://creativecommons.org/licenses/by/4.0/), which permits use, sharing, adaptation, distribution and reproduction in any medium or format, as long as you give appropriate credit to the original author(s) and the source, provide a link to the Creative Commons license and indicate if changes were made.

The images or other third party material in this chapter are included in the chapter's Creative Commons license, unless indicated otherwise in a credit line to the material. If material is not included in the chapter's Creative Commons license and your intended use is not permitted by statutory regulation or exceeds the permitted use, you will need to obtain permission directly from the copyright holder.

The World Citizen School Model. Learning Philosophy and Learning System for Global, Socially Innovative and Value-Based Future Learning

13

Michael Wihlenda

Abstract

This chapter presents the learning philosophy and learning system of the World Citizen School. The project started in 2013 at the Weltethos Institute of the University of Tübingen (The Global Ethic Project goes back to Küng (1997). 'Weltethos' is the German name for Global Ethic after which the Weltethos Institute and the Weltethos Foundation, which Küng co-founded, are named). Early in the development process, the founder and author of this paper was particularly influenced by the concept of the so-called "twenty-first Century Skills", the 4C skill set of collaboration, critical thinking, communication, and creativity. Against this background, the ability to think and act procedurally (following the inquiry-based learning approach) receives special attention as an action-guiding process logic. This is practiced in particular with the didactic method which can be described as "dialogue around a common vision, mission, goals, and values, based on the concept of the 'learning organization'". With the latter, the primary focus of the learning philosophy moves to ethical competence development, for which the Weltethos Project and the Capability Approach serve as a reflective framework.

M. Wihlenda (✉)
Founder, World Citizen School, Tübingen, Germany
e-mail: wihlenda@worldcitizen.de

© The Author(s) 2024
U.-D. Ehlers and L. Eigbrecht (eds.), *Creating the University of the Future*, Zukunft der Hochschulbildung - Future Higher Education,
https://doi.org/10.1007/978-3-658-42948-5_13

13.1 Introduction

The following article represents an updated and revised adaptation of the text published in German under the title "Das World Citizen School-Modell" (Wihlenda et al., 2020).

The model was developed at the Weltethos Institute of the University of Tübingen. Over the years, the learning model has developed from a purely extracurricular network for civically engaged student initiatives into a holistic learning system with its own learning philosophy and various co-curricular learning opportunities. The model, presented in detail in the following chapter, can serve as a blueprint for student engagement centers, hubs, labs, start-up schools, departments and chairs as well as program leaders and lecturers for their own work. The model follows a social innovation school of thought, which promotes changemakers and change agents, initiatives and social start-ups (Alden-Rivers et al., 2015; Rüede & Lurtz, 2012). The free learning space promotes voluntary student engagement, as well as self-determined and value-oriented learning. More than 350 committed students, from over 40 community and sustainability-oriented initiatives and social start-ups, learn from and with each other, enter into cooperation, and jointly launch new projects, programs or organizations (see Fig. 13.1). The unifying normative goal of all participants is the creation of "social added value" and the promotion of a strong global civil society. All initiatives and start-ups typically, explicitly or implicitly, pursue one or more goals of the United Nations Sustainable Development Goals (Borges et al., 2017; Surie & Ashley, 2008; United Nations, 2019). The model was developed as a project of the Weltethos Institute at the University of Tübingen and is still part of the Institute today. The Weltethos Project (also called Global Ethic Project) goes back to the theologian Hans Küng; the Global Ethic values describe the commonalities of all religions and cultures worldwide. The project was launched against the background of the economic ethics and globalization ethics focus of the Institute, and the associated criticism of the neoclassical doctrine of economics (Dierksmeier, 2019).

The World Citizen School is, at a glance, a(n):

- umbrella organization for student initiatives and start-ups (community)
- voice amplifier for student engagement (advocacy)
- free learning space for global, socially-innovative and value-based learning
- incubator for socially innovative projects and social start-ups
- supporter of cosmopolitan identity
- shaper of a global civil society
- transformer of individualistic learning scenarios into new dialogue-based social learning cultures

13 The World Citizen School Model. Learning Philosophy ...

Fig. 13.1 Member initiatives of the World Citizen School—Status 12/2022

The World Citizen School sees itself as an alternative business school, in the sense of a "School for Organizing" (Parker, 2016) and a "School for Democracy" (Dodge & Ospina, 2016). The school was established at the Weltethos Institute in the context of complementary business courses on business ethics, globalization ethics and humanistic management (Gohl, 2018; Rendtorff, 2015), closely linked to the work of the Institute is the criticism of business and management schools, as formulated by Nobel Prize winner Amartya Sen (Sen, 1999), among others.

Students can participate in the World Citizen School in a variety of ways. For example, they are regularly invited to networking events and topic-specific, engagement-supporting workshops, which are offered partly as co-curricular or extracurricular activities. In order to help organize the networking events and workshops themselves and to promote student engagement, students can participate in "team study," a co-curricular learning program. The teams support student engagement through communication work (reporting), using project methods (project coaching), facilitating events (hosting) or impact measurement and evaluation of engagement (research) (see Sect. 13.4 on the learning system for more details).

Against this background, the School was developed as a laboratory that supports value-oriented social learning, and the (self-)education of responsible leaders and change agents, to promote the common good (Cauthen, 2016; Gentile, 2013; Gohl, 2018; Maak & Pless, 2009). In the development process, the so-called twenty-first Century Skills served as a foundation for Future Skills.

In the following chapter, the reference to the *Future Skills* discourse is outlined (Sect. 13.2), followed by a presentation of the central learning approach of the World Citizen School, and the emergence of the model as a *story of change* (Sect. 13.3). This starts with a critique of neoliberal *individualistic learning*, which is then contrasted with *social learning* in communities and teams, to derive and present the holistic learning system that exists today with its different levels. In Sect. 13.4, the *learning philosophy* underlying the model is presented. Section 13.5 describes the *learning system* and its various components in detail. Section 13.6 highlights possibilities for (higher education) teachers and program developers to participate in the further development of the model, to test individual components at their universities and institutions, and to become part of the collegial university network for transformational teaching and learning in Germany. The article ends with a short outlook towards the future (Sect. 13.7).

The criticism is aimed primarily at the neoclassical paradigm of economics that prevails worldwide, the associated dominant theory of *homo oeconomicus*, and the limited scope for theoretical and methodological diversity (Dierksmeier, 2016). This critique also includes a purely positivist understanding of science that leaves little room for normative questions (Decker et al., 2019).

13.2 Future Skills

Early in the development process of today's World Citizen School learning system, the so-called 4C skills—*creativity, communication, critical thinking*, and *collaboration*—often referred to as "twenty-first Century Skills"—served as a reflexive frame of reference (Ananiadoui & Claro, 2009; Widiawati et al., 2018). Twenty-first Century Skills generally refer to core competencies of digital learning, critical thinking, and problem-solving in the real world (Singh, 2021). These skills are developed to support students in keeping up with the evolving pace of the modern world. These skills can be applied in any field of study and professions of teaching, as a civic environment in the life of the students (ibid.). To compete in a global society, students must be able to communicate, create, think critically, and collaborate. With this in mind, educators are urged to supplement all subjects with the fostering of these skills to prepare young people for citizenship and the global workforce (Erdoğan, 2019).

In the daily work of the past years of the World Citizen School, these four skills (4C) have already been reflected upon informally and pragmatically. However, assessments have not yet been systematically developed (with the exception of the use of a learning diary aligned with these skills). This section therefore serves to frame current thinking in the discourse around Future Skills (Ehlers & Kellermann, 2019).

The World Citizen school model that has emerged does not represent ordinary and formal learning settings; the model focuses on self-organized social learning in teams and initiatives. *Collaboration* within these (learning) communities, as well as between student initiatives, characterizes the learning spaces presented in the following sections. *Creativity* is supported in particular by, among other things, the voluntary engagement of student initiatives as well as the provision of creative ideation methods. *Communication* skills are practiced on an organizational level, in the sense of corporate communication, as well as on an interpersonal level within the initiatives and the network of all initiatives. *Critical thinking* is practiced in the groups, either voluntarily and self-organized or supported by the organizers through workshops on systemic problem solving, with the help of the specially developed Social Innovation Education Toolbox (see Sect. 13.4).

In the course of the development process, it became clear that two more important skills should be defined to better describe and promote the learning space that was created and its effectiveness, thus creating a 6C skill set. First, *Civic literacy*, which expresses the ability to self-organize and civically engage on one or more socially relevant issues (Gut, 2011). This is linked to the ability to acquire content-related knowledge. Further, it became clear that for the self-understanding of learning organizations and teams, the ability to self-reflect on learning and project goals both at the individual and organizational level and their interaction is an important skill (Gut, 2011; Nissilä, 2005). The sixth C chosen was *Character and Collective Reflection* (Collin & Karsenti, 2011). The chosen term "Character" refers in particular to personal ethical value reflection, which is also related to a global ethical framework, not least through the Global Ethic Values. In the ability to think critically, to reflect retrospectively, presently and in the future, procedural thinking in the sense of Research-Based Learning gets special attention (Dimova & Kamarska, 2015).

At this point, the discourse on Future Skills will not be further deepened. The subject of future development work of the model will be to compare the outlined 6C skill set with the Future Skill Set according to Ehlers (2020). The three dimensions proposed by Ehlers (subject and individual development, object-related skills, and social world/organization-related skills) will be compared with the previous considerations in order to enable an appropriate self-assessment of the committed students (Ehlers & Kellermann, 2019).

13.3 Learning Approach: Story of Change

The entire learning philosophy of the World Citizen School is based on the idea of accompanying young people on the path of their personal competence development in the specific context of group-specific and organizational change activities.

Based on the concept of "Theory of Change" (Connell & Kubisch, 1998), the learning approach of World Citizen School was formulated as a "Story of Change" inspired by the ideals of critical pedagogy. Such pedagogy accentuates the criticism of individualistic learning settings. At the same time, this accentuation aims to make clear the potential of social learning settings for humanistic learning, as it is successfully implemented in numerous project seminars, service-learning seminars or diverse experience-based learning settings at schools and universities. The *Story of Change* highlights the core of the learning philosophy, and at the same time articulates the wish that there may, or should be, more of such learning opportunities at universities.

13.3.1 Moving Away from Individualistic Learning

The school's learning approach starts from the individual and his or her dignity and uniqueness, and consistently places the individual at the center of social entities, in which human uniqueness unfolds and the need for reciprocity and belonging finds its support (Küng, 2012). Within the framework of the model, the individual is never seen in isolation from the necessary process of dialogue with the other(s). The learning process is seen as an open, pluralistic identity learning, which finds its expression in the social learning of engagement (Geboers et al., 2014; Geijsel & Meijers, 2005).

13.3.2 Moving Towards Social Learning in Teams

Collectivism is often mentioned as the dialectical counterpart of individualism. It is typically attributed to a system of values and norms that gives the highest priority to the well-being of the collective. In collectivist systems, the individual should subordinate his or her interests to those of the group.

In view of the apparent contrast between individualism and collectivism, self-determined and social learning in community appears to be mediating in a special way in the context of student initiatives and social start-ups. Social and emotional competences develop, above all, in group and team structures, and form the foundation for a fulfilled life in an open society. Social learning supports a culture of relationships and participation, and promotes a balanced relationship between the students' self-, social and professional competences (Bartsch & Grottker, 2018; Pless et al., 2011; Reed et al., 2010).

Member initiatives and social start-ups are seen as communities of practice and learning. In communities of practice, students who have a concern or a passion for something they do, have the opportunity to learn how to do it better by regularly exchanging ideas (Wenger, 2015). In mostly interdisciplinary teams, exchange occurs across disciplinary boundaries. The students receive feedback and recognition from the people who are affected by their activities and services, or within the groups in which they organize them. Beyond abstract grading, in the reality of engagement, success criteria regarding the actual or desired impact are negotiated and evaluated in dialogue at eye level.

13.3.3 Moving Towards a Learning System for Socially Innovative Learning Communities[1]

The student teams and initiatives form the starting point, the place of learning, and thus the heart of the learning philosophy. Together, they form a social learning system (Wenger, 2010). The World Citizen School moderates a network characterized by a plurality of topics and diverse social and organizational challenges, and provides a support system in which projects, cooperations and organizations can develop further, or new ones can emerge. Students are enabled or empowered to take on social responsibility and to further their education according to their

---

[1] It is called "socially innovative learning communities" based on our recent study on entrepreneurial competencies, which surveyed more than 1000 engaged students from different initiatives and non-engaged students. The results show clear differences in social-entrepreneurial and social-innovative competencies between students engaged in initiatives like the World Citizen School and other engaged and non-engaged students (Wihlenda et al., 2023).

own interests. The self-organized educational activities are integrated into the teaching and research activities of the university from the bottom up—through the initiative and intrinsic motivation of those involved. The topics about which the school informs the public, and at the same time strengthens the commitment of its member initiatives, have also grown from the bottom up from the participating student communities and initiatives. Topics include human rights, democracy, sustainable development, fair opportunities, development cooperation, business ethics and intercultural learning. The central goal in community facilitation is *empowering each other*, understood as mutual support in the pursuit and realization of one's own ideas, interests and desires for a good life (Ehrlich, 2000; Nussbaum & Sen, 1993). The individual initiatives and teams are themselves social learning systems: they have a structure, consist of complex relationships, and are characterized by self-organization and the constant negotiation of identity and cultural meaning of joint activities. These learning systems, in turn, belong to broader social systems and are, like the school as a whole, part of further communities themselves. These include the university community, the student body in particular, but also the urban society and the idea of a global civil society.

13.4 Learning Philosophy: "Empowering Each Other"

The learning philosophy of World Citizen School is based on the roots of humanistic pedagogy. Our pedagogical approach is fundamentally characterized by the attitude and practice of paying particular attention to aspects of freedom, appreciation, dignity, maturity, emancipation, self-determination, and integrity of persons as emphasized in various pedagogies (Buddrus et al., 1995).

World Citizen School Education (Fig. 13.2) is an educational approach that combines aspects of the existing learning approaches of Global Citizenship Education (Global Responsibility) (Suša, 2019), and Social Innovation Education (Social Problem-Based Learning) (Wihlenda et al., 2020), with value-based learning (world ethos as a learning program), and thus didactically unfolds the dialogue around shared values, goals and visions (Haan, 2008; Küng, 1997; Senge, 2014). In the dialogical empowerment process of the learning system, students are to form their personal identity in the ideal of an open-minded, critical, and ethical power of judgment and power of creation. Figuratively speaking, the individual goes through a lifelong spiral process of experiential learning in plural communities (Pedaste et al., 2015), in which he or she recognizes and develops him- or herself (see Fig. 13.3). The cosmopolitan identity is of particular importance. It is assumed that this is realized particularly well in mutual support in

13 The World Citizen School Model. Learning Philosophy …

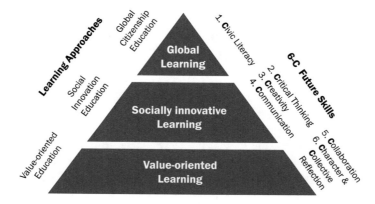

Fig. 13.2 World Citizen School Education

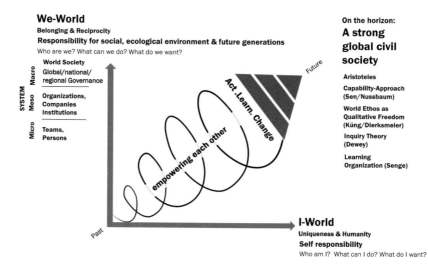

Fig. 13.3 Learning spiral: "Learning journey of the individual (I) in social contexts (We)"

open, plural communities, as well as in the joint search for and creation of solutions to the problems of our world. A "world citizen" is convinced that one's identity transcends geographical and political borders, and that his or her responsibilities and rights arise from belonging to a global community. Social and economic justice, equality of genders, ethnicities and nations, and religious peace, are the roots of world citizenship as understood in the model. The pragmatist ethics of discovering the world, shaping the world and developing a world-ethical attitude in the form of research-, problem- and project-based learning, forms the didactic guide (Wihlenda & Brahm, 2020).

The Global Ethic core values of humanity and reciprocity, and the values of justice, honesty, peacefulness, partnership and sustainability serve pragmatically in the educational process as a confidence-building conversation starter for ongoing dialogue at personal, team, organizational and global-societal levels, in the sense of a learning program for global society (Hemel, 2019). The ethical coordinate system of Global Ethic values ideally promotes trust between the *I-world* of the individual and the *We-world* of the community(ies) in which the self-organized learning communities are the places of learning.

A strong global civil society, guided by Global Ethic as an idea of qualitative freedom for the development of a good life for the benefit of all, forms the target horizon (Dierksmeier, 2019). Students learn to take responsibility for themselves and other people, teams and organizations—starting from their individual *I-world* through co-determination and co-design of the social entities of the *We-world*. Conversely, the learning system ideally promotes the development of such a *We-world*, which in turn does justice to the responsibility for human development of each individual world citizen. Both worlds, the *I-world* and the *We-world* together, and in the ideal, mutually reinforce each other for the realization of the well-being of all, in the sense of the global ethic as qualitative freedom.

13.5   Learning System

The World Citizen School is envisaged as a learning organization (Senge, 2014), pursuing the vision that all people learn together in dialogue, to use their abilities for a more peaceful, just and sustainable world. The learning system opens up a free learning space for committed students to learn how to learn from and with each other, in a self-responsible and value-oriented way.

One of the greatest challenges for student initiatives is the high member and knowledge turnover, as well as efficient organizational development. The institutional anchoring of volunteering in the school, and the knowledge network and institutional memory, counteract these challenges and promote the transfer of knowledge between the volunteers, the student generations, university staff, and practice partners.

13 The World Citizen School Model. Learning Philosophy ...

For the purpose of efficient organizational development, the school teaches initiatives and start-ups professional methods and makes them available, for example, in the form of the *Social Innovation Education Toolbox* (Wihlenda, 2020b). A special feature of the didactics is that the methods taught are applied in the self-organization of the school. From a pedagogical point of view, this is a central prerequisite for strengthening the learning success of the entire learning system in non-formal learning settings, in the sense of authentic leadership (Mazutis & Slawinski, 2008). These individual components form the learning system and will be described in the following section (see Fig. 13.4):

- Self-Education: Activities and offers of initiatives & start-ups
- Community: Moderated network of initiatives & startups
- Social Innovation Program: Team study, Learning Camp, toolbox
- Student Governance: Students participating in team studies
- Learning support: Master coaches

Fig. 13.4 Learning system based on the impact logic of the Learning Orchestra Canvas

13.5.1 Self-Education: Activities and Offerings of Initiatives and Start-Ups

Student initiatives and start-ups are serious educational spaces and educational providers in the university context (Wihlenda 2020a). The active citizens, change-makers, or responsible leaders involved in these initiatives develop their ethical leadership and design competences. They typically develop a wide range of activities and offerings. These include both products and services in the form of projects, events, political campaigns, as well as team building, self-organization, leadership and management activities. Numerous examples of these activities from our network can be found on our website, for example, in the engagement calendar (www.worldcitizen.school) and in various publications in the download section.

In the context of social innovation education, social entrepreneurial competence development in volunteering is particularly relevant, which mostly takes place in non-formal learning settings of the student groups. In our recent study, in which we surveyed over 1000 engaged and non-engaged students at different universities, we were able to show significant differences between engaged and non-engaged students with regard to their (social) entrepreneurial competences. In addition, sustainability- and public welfare-oriented volunteers have significantly higher social entrepreneurial attitudes than all others (Wihlenda et al., 2023).

Many student initiatives are also providers of formal educational offers such as seminars, workshops, reading groups, lecture series or conferences. In these contexts, the focus is on content-related learning.

13.5.2 Community: Moderated Network

In the Moderated Community, the members' needs and interests as well as collegial consultation, cooperation, and partnership networking play an important role.

In a narrow sense, the community consists of the member initiatives, the start-ups and local university partners, and in a broader sense also of partners from urban society, business, and politics. In addition, a university network for transformative teaching has emerged in recent years across institutions.

On the organizational side, an elaborate online moderation structure, with the help of project management tools, as well as the offline moderation structure through moderated social marketplaces, and two-hour learning sessions by and for committed people, play a supporting role. These ensure efficient networking for the purpose of knowledge transfer for, and between, the initiatives, as well as with and between the university partners. The latter includes, in particular, networking with the Career Service (which enables the recognition of volunteering activities through credit points), with university didactics, the Centre for Technology Transfer, the Foreign Language Centre, the Centre for Sustainable Development and/or the Centre for International and European Studies.

Numerous cooperations between the initiatives and other external partners are taking place in the organized community. Prominent examples include various small collaborative projects and joint workshops. It is common for member initiatives to exploit synergies and cooperate in workshops, or invite students from other initiatives, for example, for short presentations on their own initiative. One example of the more visible collaborative projects is the so-called "Education Weeks", in which different initiatives come together and offer various workshops and activities during the week, sometimes in cooperation. The "Human Rights Week" and a "World Climate Week" followed the first "Week of Links—Week for Sustainable Development" in 2014.[2]

13.5.3 Social Innovation Program: Team Study, Camp, Toolbox

The Social Innovation Program serves to professionalize initiatives and start-ups. All formats of the program are based on an emancipatory educational approach that encourages initiative, entrepreneurship, and participation. The program strengthens leadership, design, and self-organization skills.

All formats and methods support those involved in developing their social entrepreneurial competences in order to professionalize their own projects, or to start new projects, initiatives, or social enterprises. Through the orientation towards the 6Cs (Civic literacy, Creativity, Collaboration, Communication, Critical Thinking, Collective Reflection), the program promotes co-determination and co-design competences for future activities in business, politics, science or society (Ananiadoui & Claro, 2009; Collin & Karsenti, 2011; Passila et al., 2013).

Formats include:

- The Agile Team Study for Learning Initiatives & Start-ups
- The Social Innovation Camp
- Demand-based (spontaneous) workshops
- Personal group coaching

---

[2] For details, see https://mrw-tuebingen.de/ and https://nez-tuebingen.org.

An important tool for teaching social-innovative methodological skills is the Social Innovation Education Toolbox (SIE-T). The SIE-T is a systemic toolbox developed over the years, consisting of numerous visual templates (so-called canvases) for the development of learning, value-oriented projects, organizations, and companies. With the SIE-T students are able to simplify complex organizational functions, levels, and work processes. The SIE-T functions didactically as the center piece of all organizational and educational processes of the learning system. It is equally applicable on different levels for (informal) working groups, project teams, non-profit organizations or enterprises, irrespective of the stage of development. The core of the SIE-T is the "Learning Orchestra Canvas" (LOC, see Fig. 13.5; see also Fig. 13.4) in its function as a systemic meta-template into which all other canvases can be integrated.

Organizing and managing projects and organizations often quickly becomes a confusing and complex endeavor. The LOC helps to systemically align and combine different levels, departments, processes and activities. The remedy is visual modeling through the LOC—an image that can give orientation and identity to those involved. In this sense, the canvas contains, in a systemic way, all the topics of organizational development, which can be dealt with by further canvases of the toolbox.

13.5.4 Student Governance: Internal Team Study

For the overall management of the learning system, in addition to the general knowledge domain of world citizenship, four aspects (arts) for a strong civil society were identified, which are highly relevant for all initiatives and start-ups as well as for the own organization: A) the art of communicating, B) the art of organizing, C) the art of hosting, and D) the art of researching and reflecting on one's own effectiveness.

Accordingly, the management team, in its role as master coaches, is currently focusing on training three teams who, with their respective work focus, act as multipliers and knowledge carriers in the community.

1. In the *Social Reporting Team*, members learn the art of communication. The main task is to communicate for and about the community, to present good examples of self-organized learning, and the effectiveness of individual initiatives or the community as a whole to the public (e.g., via newsletter, social media, website, video, and personal presentations).

13 The World Citizen School Model. Learning Philosophy … 275

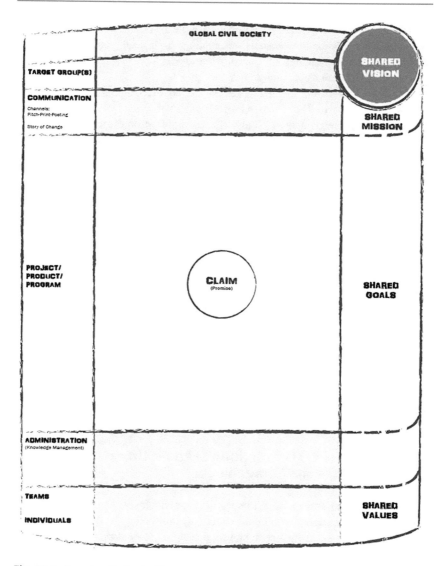

Fig. 13.5 Learning Orchestra Canvas

2. In the *Social Research Team*, students learn the art of research, primarily using qualitative and quantitative social research methods. The focus is on questions about learning in engagement, evaluation research on learning programs, and the social effects of the community.
3. The *Social Coaching Team* focuses on the art of coaching, organizing, and learning support. The focus is on learning of organizational-pedagogical basics, questioning methods, and the actual application of agile learning. The coaches support those involved, jointly identify knowledge needs, give tips on knowledge sources, or create knowledge maps for their clients.

All teams also learn the art of hosting and moderating, with the purpose of fostering good relationships within their teams as well as collaborations in the community and between all stakeholders. Different formats such as workshops, marketplaces, conferences, world cafés, exhibition stands, workshops, and so forth, serve this purpose.

13.5.5 Learning Support: Master Coaches

The basis for the implementation of the entire learning system is the management team, which consists of two employees who assume the role of learning coaches as well as managers. The team is responsible for the orchestration of the entire learning system. They act also as master coaches for the student teams, and coordinate student assistants (trainees), who also act as the main coordinators of the student teams (reporting, coaching, research).

13.6 Transfer for Universities, Schools, Urban Societies and Companies

In summary, it can be stated that this learning system enables an efficient circulation of knowledge for the promotion of student civil society. At the same time, the learning model is a sensitive social entity that needs to be carefully nurtured and developed.

In order to establish the learning model at one's own university, it requires, above all, trained management staff who have relevant experience in the areas of organizational development, (social) entrepreneurship, and systemic coaching. They should also be familiar with the methods of agile learning, working, and leadership. The greatest challenge at the University of Tübingen was, and is, to establish such a management team with this professional profile—despite the uncertainties of the founding process—and to stabilize the staff positions. If the knowledge in these central positions is sustainably secured, the model promises to raise further potential for the promotion of innovative and transformative teaching and learning, not least due to the integrated junior staff work. Here, transformative learning is understood equally as a change of the self and the world (Singer-Brodowski, 2018).

The World Citizen School Association was founded for the further development of the model and the individual programs, as well as for the purpose of collegial knowledge transfer between educational institutions. The association, based at the Weltethos Institute, promotes the collegial transfer of knowledge between university lecturers, engagement promoters, and program managers, and offers train-the-trainer formats in the form of workshops and collegial conferences, as well as educational counselling services.

This includes organizing the *"Colloquium for Transformative Learning and Teaching"* and the *"World Citizen Train-the-Trainer"* program launched in 2022, which consists of five-day workshops, an online learning platform, and coaching services offered on a biannual basis.

13.7 Outlook

The World Citizen School model complements the discourse around Future Skills, which has so far focused heavily on individual skills, by consistently incorporating collective and group-based learning environments.

We hope that the model can serve as a stimulus for teachers to design their own context-specific learning spaces, because group work, learning in projects, and teams, can be established in many different ways at universities. Student (voluntary) engagement in initiatives and teams is generally a widely underestimated learning space in which Future Skills are trained in a special way. For the further development of the model, a (self-)assessment tool for the various student initiatives and teams involved is to be developed. In particular, the three dimensions proposed by Ehlers and Kellermann (2019) (subject and individual development, object-related competencies, and social world/order competence) will be compared with the previous considerations as a starting point, and a competence framework tailored to the World Citizen School will be developed. At this point, I would like to express my sincere gratitude to the editors as well as the many contributing authors in this volume, whose contributions I and my team are very much looking forward to.

Here you can find further information about our work:

- www.worldcitizen.de
- www.worldcitizen.school
- www.entrepreneurship.tools
- www.socialinnovation.education

Future Skills in Practice: Our Recommendations
For Student Engagement Centers

- Look at student initiatives and startup teams as serious learning spaces in the sense of the core task "teaching" of universities.
- Establish engagement centers as holistic learning systems with the integration of student self-governance as well as through (co-)curricular connection of engagement-promoting workshops and the inclusion of external public and private partner organizations.

For Startup Schools (Entrepreneurship Centers)

- Understand student initiatives and organizations as serious (social) entrepreneurial learning spaces.
- Involving agile student teams in the entrepreneurial self-governance of the center.

For Departments and Chairs
- Develop an "on-the-job" learning program for co-organizing student teams in faculty or departmental self-governance (e.g., a team for coaching of student projects, a research team, an event organization and facilitation team, or an editorial communications team, etc.).

For Program Leaders and Lecturers
- Recognize the opportunities of project and Problem-Based Learning in groups as well as participatory teaching for a wide variety of learning scenarios (lectures, seminars, workshops, etc.)

References

Alden-Rivers, B., Armellini, A., Maxwell, R., Allen, S., & Durkin, C. (2015). Social innovation education: Towards a framework for learning design. *Higher Education, Skills and Work-Based Learning, 5*(4), 383–400.

Ananiadoui, K., & Claro, M. (2009). *21st century skills and competences for new millennium learners in OECD countries* (OECD Education Working Papers 41).

Bartsch, G., & Grottker, L. (2018). Do it! Handlungsleitfaden: Das Programm für gesellschaftliches Engagement von Hochschulen. https://www.agentur-mehrwert.de/wp-content/uploads/2018/05/Praxisleitfaden.pdf.

Borges, J. C., Cezarino, L. O., Ferreira, T. C., Sala, O. T. M., Unglaub, D. L., & Caldana, A. C. F. (2017). Student organizations and communities of practice: Actions for the 2030 Agenda for sustainable development. *The International Journal of Management Education, 15*(2), 172–182.

Buddrus, V., Pallasch, W., Sielert, U., & Winschermann, M. (1995). *Humanistische Pädagogik: Eine Einführung in Ansätze integrativen und personenzentrierten Lehrens und Lernens.* Klinkhardt.

Cauthen, T. W. (2016). Developing socially responsible leaders in academic settings. *New Directions for Higher Education* , June 2016 (174), 69–78.

Collin, S., & Karsenti, T. (2011). The collective dimension of reflective practice: the how and why. *Reflective Practice, 12*(4), 569–581. https://doi.org/10.1080/14623943.2011.590346.

Connell, J. P., & Kubisch, A. C. (1998). Applying a theory of change approach to the evaluation of comprehensive community initiatives: Progress, prospects, and problems. *New Approaches to Evaluating Community Initiatives, 2*(15–44), 1–16.

Decker, S., Elsner, W., & Flechtner, S. (2019). *Principles and pluralist approaches in teaching economics: Towards a transformative science.* Routledge.

Dierksmeier, C. (2016). Reframing economic ethics: The philosophical foundations of humanistic management. Springer/Palgrave Macmillan.

Dierksmeier, C. (2019). *Qualitative freedom – Autonomy in cosmopolitan responsibility.* Springer Berlin Heidelberg

Dimova, Y., & Kamarska, K. (2015). Rediscovering John Dewey's model of learning through reflective inquiry. *Problems of Education in the 21st Century, 63*(1), 29–39. https://doi.org/10.33225/pec/15.63.29.

Dodge, J., & Ospina, S. M. (2016). Nonprofits as "Schools of Democracy." *Nonprofit and Voluntary Sector Quarterly, 45*(3), 478–499. https://doi.org/10.1177/0899764015584063.

Ehlers, U.-D., & Kellermann, S. A. (2019). *Future skills – The future of learning and higher education: Results of the international future skills delphi survey.* Karlsruhe. https://nextskills.org/?smd_process_download=1&download_id=4281.

Ehlers, U.-D. (2020). Studium der Zukunft – Absolvent(inn)en der Zukunft. *Future Skills zwischen Theorie und Praxis.* Springer VS. http://link.springer.com/10.1007/978-3-658-29427-4.

Ehrlich, T. (Ed.). (2000). *Civic responsibility and higher education.* Oryx Press.

Erdoğan, V. (2019). Integrating 4C skills of 21st century into 4 language skills in EFL classes. *International Journal of Education and Research, 7*(11), 113–124.

Geboers, E., Geijsel, F., Admiraal, W., & ten Dam, G. (2014). Typology of student citizenship. *European Journal of Education, 49*(4), 514–528.

Geijsel, F., & Meijers, F. (2005). Identity learning: The core process of educational change. *Educational Studies, 31*(4), 419–430.

Gentile, M. C. (2013). *Educating for values-driven leadership: Giving voice to values across the curriculum.* Business Expert Press.

Gohl, C. (2018). Weltethos for business: Building shared ground for a better world. *Humanistic Management Journal, 3*(2), 161–186.

Gut, D. M. (2011). Integrating 21st century skills into the curriculum. In G. Wan & D. M. Gut (Eds.), *Bringing schools into the 21st century* (pp. 137–157). Springer.

de Haan, G. (2008). Gestaltungskompetenz als Kompetenzkonzept der Bildung für nachhaltige Entwicklung. In I. Bormann (Ed.), *Kompetenzen der Bildung für nachhaltige Entwicklung: Operationalisierung, Messung, Rahmenbedingungen, Befunde* (1st ed., pp. 23–43). VS Verlag. https://doi.org/10.1007/978-3-531-90832-8_4.

Hemel, U. (Ed.). (2019). *Weltethos für das 21. Jahrhundert.* Herder.

Küng, H. (1997). *Weltethos für Weltpolitik und Weltwirtschaft.* Piper.

Küng, H. (2012). *Handbuch Weltethos: Eine Vision und ihre Umsetzung.* Piper.

Maak, T., & Pless, N. M. (2009). Business leaders as citizens of the world. Advancing humanism on a global scale. *Journal of Business Ethics, 88*(3), 537–550.

Mazutis, D., & Slawinski, N. (2008). Leading organizational learning through authentic dialogue. *Management Learning, 39*(4), 437–456.

Nissilä, S. P. (2005). Individual and collective reflection: How to meet the needs of development in teaching. *European Journal of Teacher Education, 28*(2), 209–219. https://doi.org/10.1080/02619760500093354.

Nussbaum, M. C., & Sen, A. (Eds.). (1993). *The quality of life: A study prepared for the World Institute for Development Economics Research (WIDER) of the United Nations University.* Clarendon.

Parker, M. (2016). Towards an alternative business school: A school of organizing. In B. Czarniawska (Ed.), *A research agenda for management and organization studies* (pp. 147–154). Elgar. https://doi.org/10.4337/9781784717025.00020.

Passila, A. H., Oikarinen, T., & Harmaakorpi, V. (2013). Collective voicing as a reflexive practice. *Management Learning, 46*(1), 67–86.

Pedaste, M., Mäeots, M., Siiman, L. A., de Jong, T., van Riesen, S. A. N., Kamp, E. T., et al. (2015). Phases of inquiry-based learning: Definitions and the inquiry cycle. *Educational Research Review, 14*, 47–61.

Pless, N. M., Maak, T., & Stahl, G. K. (2011). Developing responsible global leaders through international service-learning programs: The Ulysses experience. *Academy of Management Learning & Education, 10*(2), 237–260.

Reed, M. S., Evely, A. C., Cundill, G., Fazey, I., Glass, J., Laing, A., et al. (2010). What is social learning? *Ecology and Society, 15*(4), 1–10.

Rendtorff, J. D. (2015). Theories of business ethics in a cosmopolitan perspective. In *Business and Society. General Track.01. Uncertainty is a Great Opportunity. EURAM 2015. 17–20 June. Kozminski University, Warsaw.* EURAM.

Rüede, D., & Lurtz, K. (2012). Mapping the various meanings of social innovation: Towards a differentiated understanding of an emerging concept. *EBS Business School Research Paper Series* (12–03).

Sen, A. (1999). *Development as freedom.* Oxford University Press.

Senge, P. M. (2014). *The fifth discipline fieldbook: Strategies and tools for building a learning organization.* Currency.

Singer-Brodowski, M. (2018). Über die Transformation von Selbst- und Weltverhältnissen hin zu einer Weltbeziehungsbildung. In VENRO (Ed.), *Globales Lernen: Wie transformativ ist es?: Impulse, Reflexionen, Beispiele* (pp. 27–33). Venro.

Singh, M. (2021). Acquisition of 21st century skills through STEAM education. *Academia Letters*, April 2021, 0–7.

Surie, G., & Ashley, A. (2008). Integrating pragmatism and ethics in entrepreneurial leadership for sustainable value creation. *Journal of Business Ethics, 81*(1), 235–246.

Suša, R. (2019). *Global Citizenship Education (GCE) for unknown futures: Mapping past and current experiments and debates.* Helsinki. https://www.bridge47.org/sites/default/files/2019-07/bridge47_gce_for_unknown_futures_report-compressed_0.pdf.

United Nations. (2019). *The sustainable development goals report.* United Nations.

Wenger, E. (2010). Communities of practice and social learning systems: The career of a concept. *Social Learning Systems and Communities of Practice,* 179–198. https://doi.org/10.1007/978-1-84996-133-2_11.

Wenger, E. (2015). Communities of practice: A brief introduction. http://hdl.handle.net/1794/11736.

Widiawati, L., Joyoatmojo, S., & Sudiyanto, S. (2018). Higher order thinking skills as effect of problem based learning in the 21st century learning. *International Journal of Multicultural and Multireligious Understanding, 5*(3), 96–105.

Wihlenda, M. (2020a). Das World Citizen School-Modell. In M. Wihlenda, T. Brahm, & L. Greger (Eds.), *Social Innovation Education. Transformierende Lernprogramme für Hochschulen* (pp. 121–142). Tübingen Library Publishing. https://doi.org/10.15496/publikation-50433.

Wihlenda, M. (2020b). Social innovation education – Toolbox (SIE-T). In M. Wihlenda, T. Brahm, & L. Greger (Eds.), *Social Innovation Education. Transformierende Lernprogramme für Hochschulen* (pp. 179–186). Tübingen Library Publishing. https://doi.org/10.15496/publikation-50433.

Wihlenda, M., & Brahm, T. (2020). Social Innovation Education. Transformierende Lernprogramme für Hochschulen. *Journal of Social Entrepreneurship.* Universität Tübingen.

Wihlenda, M., Brahm, T., & Greger, L. (Eds.). (2020). *Social Innovation Education. Transformierende Lernprogramme für Hochschulen.* Tübingen Library Publishing.

Wihlenda, M., Brahm, T., & Habisch, A. (2023). Responsible management education: Social entrepreneurialcompetences of civically-engaged students. *The International Journal of Management Education, 21*(1), 100756.

Dr. Michael Wihlenda is the founder of the World Citizen School, managing director of the association of the same name, and did his doctorate at the Weltethos Institute of the University of Tübingen on the topic of 'Social Innovation Education'. Since 2013, he has been conducting research on topics of global citizenship education and entrepreneurship education. At the Catholic University of Ingolstadt-Eichstätt, he has been developing train-the-trainer programs for transformative teaching since 2022. Before founding the World

Citizen School, he was involved as a project manager in the development of the Master program in Responsible Management at Steinbeis University Berlin. From these experiences, as well as from his own student volunteering during his studies, he developed the learning philosophy of the World Citizen School.

Open Access This chapter is licensed under the terms of the Creative Commons Attribution 4.0 International License (http://creativecommons.org/licenses/by/4.0/), which permits use, sharing, adaptation, distribution and reproduction in any medium or format, as long as you give appropriate credit to the original author(s) and the source, provide a link to the Creative Commons license and indicate if changes were made.

The images or other third party material in this chapter are included in the chapter's Creative Commons license, unless indicated otherwise in a credit line to the material. If material is not included in the chapter's Creative Commons license and your intended use is not permitted by statutory regulation or exceeds the permitted use, you will need to obtain permission directly from the copyright holder.

Learning Design for Future Skills Development in Small State Contexts

14

Sandhya Gunness, Karen Ferreira-Meyers and Thanasis Daradoumis

Abstract

The small Southern African states of Mauritius and Eswatini, with respect to their high levels of digital literacy and telecommunications infrastructure, have great potential for meeting future challenges as regards capacity building and developing a globalized workforce. However, the weaknesses of a decoupled University-Industry R&D collaboration, low-level business sophistication, a lack of appropriate knowledge workers, and manifest skills mismatches could create a difficult future for university graduates in these two countries. Within an African context, and with heavy reliance on imported and globalized products and resources, there is a common need for building resilience, self-efficacy, intra- and entrepreneurial skills, emotional intelligence, and growth mindsets as essential competencies for our future "peopleware", as opposed to

---

S. Gunness (✉)
Senior Lecturer at the Centre for Innovative and Lifelong Learning,
University of Mauritius, Ebène, Mauritius
e-mail: s.gunness@uom.ac.mu

K. Ferreira-Meyers
Associate Professor and Coordinator of Linguistics and Modern Languages at the
Institute of Distance Education, University of Eswatini, Kwaluseni, Eswatini

T. Daradoumis
Professor in the Department of Computer Science, Multimedia and
Telecommunications, Open University of Catalonia, Barcelona, Spain
Professor in the Department of Cultural Technology
and Communication, University of Aegean, Mytilini, Greece
e-mail: adaradoumis@uoc.edu

© The Author(s) 2024
U.-D. Ehlers and L. Eigbrecht (eds.), *Creating the University of the Future*, Zukunft der Hochschulbildung - Future Higher Education,
https://doi.org/10.1007/978-3-658-42948-5_14

hardware and software. This concept, made popular by Lister and DeMarco, in the context of increasing digitization, brings back the softer and more discerning human elements in times where algorithms are increasingly making decisions and influencing our behavior. This chapter presents an attempt to equip recently graduated young citizens with a set of transdisciplinary skills and competencies which can build the above-mentioned important attributes and values along with the depth of academic knowledge gained at the university. As small state developing countries with colonial backgrounds, our strong sense of community, togetherness, resilience, faith, and tolerance should permeate within our intellectual siege.

14.1 Introduction

The small Southern African states of Mauritius and Eswatini, with respect to their high levels of digital literacy and telecommunications infrastructure, have great potential for meeting future challenges as regards capacity building and developing a globalized workforce. However, the weaknesses of a decoupled University-Industry R&D collaboration, low-level business sophistication, a lack of appropriate knowledge workers, and manifest skills mismatches could create a difficult future for university graduates in these two countries. Within an African context, and with heavy reliance on imported and globalized products and resources, there is a common need for building resilience, self-efficacy, intra- and entrepreneurial skills, emotional intelligence, and growth mindsets as essential competencies for our future "peopleware", as opposed to hardware and software. This concept, made popular by Lister and DeMarco (1999), in the context of increasing digitization, brings back the softer and more discerning human elements in times where algorithms are increasingly making decisions and influencing our behavior. This chapter presents an attempt to equip recently graduated young citizens with a set of transdisciplinary skills and competencies which can build the above-mentioned important attributes and values along with the depth of academic knowledge gained at the university. As small state developing countries with colonial backgrounds, our strong sense of community, togetherness, resilience, faith, and tolerance should permeate within our intellectual siege. The chapter starts from a general overview of the contexts of both studied countries, and details the concept of Future Skills, before describing the study undertaken.

This action research study proposes an innovative approach to embedding Future Skills within university graduates in a developing country context. Our research focuses on how developing-state universities can breed more innovative and resilient workforces for a thriving and balanced work-life. What types of teaching and learning relationships and actionable strategies should we invest in for developing Future Skills for our graduates? We start with providing a background of the innovative stances of our two countries, and the disparities in terms of skills mismatch and areas where we should focus our policies and higher-education teaching and learning strategies. In the next section, we talk of the Future Skills requirements for a just, resilient, and eco-aware workforce, with increasing demands for better work-life balances as a result of the Covid-19 pandemic where our life priorities drastically changed. The third section then brings in the concept of transdisciplinarity, whereby in order to thrive in the future world, we need to be breaking down the silos created in higher education and get our graduates to cross-fertilize ideas, cultures and innovative creations. The fourth section proposes a pedagogical framework as well as learning design approaches to embed transdisciplinary skills and competencies within a university co-created module. In the fifth section, we describe the methodology for gathering information from students who had experienced the module as well as having a discussion with the academics to engage with them on the transdisciplinary competencies acquired by the students during the learning activities. The sixth section presents the findings from the focus group discussions and interviews with students. We conclude this book chapter with challenges and future research for developing transdisciplinary skills and competencies in the small country contexts. With a lack of critical mass and opportunities for wide scale research, we should be able to learn from collaborating with each other to find common areas for developing our graduates with Future Skills.

14.2 Small States Contexts—Potentials and Pitfalls

Mauritius is a rapidly developing Small Island State with a stable population of around 1.4 million inhabitants, banking on its natural beauty, stable political environment, and resourceful human resources for emerging into a high-income nation. The people of Mauritius value education highly and are fortunate to have free state-supported education from pre-primary up to university level. Higher education (HE) and even transportation to educational institutions are free for full-time students, and one of the political manifestos for the elections was to have "one graduate per household". Out of 132 countries, Mauritius is ranked

INNOVATION STRENGTHS AND WEAKNESSES

The table below gives an overview of the strengths and weaknesses of Mauritius in the GII 2021.

Strengths and weaknesses for Mauritius

Strengths			Weaknesses		
Code	Indicator name	Rank	Code	Indicator name	Rank
1.1.1	Political and operational stability	6	2.3.3	Global corporate R&D investors, top 3, mn US$	41
1.2.3	Cost of redudancy dismissal	23	2.3.4	QS university ranking, top 3	74
1.3	Business environment	21	4.3.3	Domestic market scale, bn PPP$	125
1.3.1	Ease of starting a business	19	5.1	Knowledge workers	110
2.1.2	Government funding/pupil, secondary, % GDP/cap	6	5.1.3	GERD performed by business, % GDP	81
3.3.1	GDP/unit of energy use	8	5.1.4	GERD financed by business, %	85
4.2	Investment	14	5.2.1	University-industry R&D collaboration	109
4.2.1	Ease of protecting minority investors	18	5.2.3	GERD financed by abroad, % GDP	86
4.2.3	Venture capital investors, deals/bn PPP$ GDP	1	5.3.5	Research talent, % in businesses	72
4.3.1	Applied tariff rate, weighted avg., %	13	6.1.1	Patents by origin/bn PPP$ GDP	108
6.2.2	New businesses/th pop. 15–64	18	6.1.5	Citable documents H-index	118
7.1	Intangible assets	14	6.2.1	Labor productivity growth, %	99
7.1.1	Trademarks by origin/bn PPP$ GDP	17	6.2.5	High-tech manufacturing, %	106

Fig. 14.1 Global Innovation Index showing strengths and weaknesses for Mauritius (Dutta et al., 2021)

52nd within high income groups on the Global Innovation Index (GII 2021) in the following categories: Institutions (Rank 21), Infrastructure (Rank 65) and Creative outputs (Rank 31) (Dutta et al., 2021). Figure 14.1 depicts that Mauritius is thus at par with high-income economies in these three categories, but shows weaknesses in knowledge production, namely for higher education-related indices and development of relevant knowledge workers. Another study reports that the main cause of skills mismatch put forward by stakeholders in Mauritius is "a misalignment between university/educational institution curricula and industry requirements that is a disconnect between the education system of the country and the needs of the economy" (Tandrayen-Ragoobur, 2020, p. 95). Her findings correspond with the World Intellectual Property Organization (Dutta et al., 2021) reports of low ranking for Mauritius in knowledge-specific indicators: Knowledge workers (GII Rank 110); University-Industry R&D collaboration (GII rank 109); Business sophistication (GII rank 111). This shows weaknesses in the transitions from secondary/tertiary education to the world of work and lack of coherent guidance and policies for career mapping, succession planning and sustainable development.

Another Small State in the SADC (Southern African Development Community) region is the Kingdom of Eswatini. It is not an island in the geographical sense of the word, but it remains fairly isolated, especially as it is located between South Africa and Mozambique. Eswatini's population stood at 1,148,130 in 2019. It has a primary net enrolment rate of 82.5% in 2017 and a secondary school completion rate of 41.7% in 2015 (Commonwealth of Learning, 2021). Like Mauritius, Eswatini is part of the Commonwealth of Learning's VUSSC (Virtual University for Small States of the Commonwealth) program. Primary school children benefit from free education, but secondary and tertiary education come at a cost to parents or education-seeking individuals themselves. Internet connectivity is available to 30% in 2017 of the population, and mobile-cellular subscriptions are at 94 per 100 people. Infrastructure is available for distance and technology-enabled learning and for expanding access to education and training in Eswatini. The Ministry of Education and Training's National Education and Training Sector Improvement Programme 2018/19—2020/21 intends to place a greater emphasis on teaching ICT as a subject and using ICT in education (Ministry of Education & Training, 2018).

For the sake of comparison, Mauritius and Eswatini are interesting cases as both have good technology infrastructure, having a positive impact on the ability to familiarize with the internet and digital devices as important indicators and enablers of digital literacy as per Fig. 14.2. Both Mauritius and Eswatini are open to collaboration and, in August 2018, the World Bank Board of Directors took note of the good progress made of The Country Partnership Strategy 2015–2018 for Eswatini and thus extended the ongoing projects and advisory service for another two years, until 2020, focusing on two program pillars: (i) promoting growth and productivity, and (ii) strengthening state capabilities. However, the rate of development for both countries is not the same. The unemployment rate for Mauritius in 2020 was 7.11% and that of Eswatini was 23.4% for respective working-age populations of 607,122 (18–64-year olds) to 482,400 for Eswatini. Also, for the year 2021, Eswatini does not appear on the Global Innovation Index. This comparative study thus helps to determine areas for collaboration and knowledge-sharing to mutually mitigate the weaknesses for both the countries

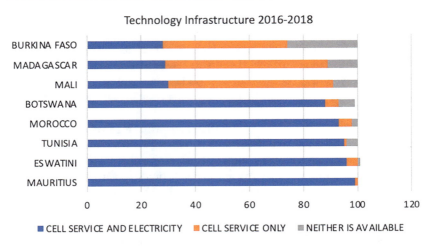

Fig. 14.2 Technology Infrastructure 2016–2018. (Modified from Krönke, 2020)

and provide **custom-designed graduate development training** that is tailored to individual needs.

This study responds to the following research questions:

1. How can developing-state universities breed more innovative and resilient workforces for a thriving and balanced work-life?
2. What types of teaching and learning relationships and actionable strategies should we invest in for developing Future Skills for our graduates?

Fig. 14.2 shows the level of technology infrastructure and indicates the technological proximity of Mauritius and Eswatini for development prior to Covid 19. While Mauritius has a vibrant and fast-developing infrastructure, especially relating to modern transportation and commercial buildings and centers, Eswatini faces more challenges owing to its low employment to population ranking—145th of the 150 country listings—and negative international student mobility at -34.4 (UNDP).

We thus find that both Mauritius and Eswatini have adequate infrastructure but lack the developing professional competencies for their future workforce. However, they understand the importance of focusing on a globally connected and needs-based human development for a more sustainable and resilient future (Ferreira-Meyers et al., 2022; Krönke, 2020). In the next section, we focus on the literature and recommendations for the future workforce for both Mauritius and Eswatini. We propose a framework for the development of transdisciplinary competencies based on innovative approaches for co-creation and student ownership.

14.3 Future Skills for a Resilient Workforce

Studies with respect to Future Skills required regularly conducted in Mauritius (Armoogum et al., 2016; Dubois & Juwaheer, 2012; Hardin-Ramanan et al., 2019) and the Human Resources Development Council (HRDC, 2021) revealed that students were less interested in Science, Technology, Engineering and Mathematics (STEM) subjects. These studies predict a mismatch in what would be required for the future workforce in Mauritius—namely higher-order thinking skills, problem solving and creativity amongst others. van Velsor and Wright (2012) had already identified specific transferable skills such as problem-solving, leadership, teamwork, empathy, and social/emotional intelligence, which were still being left out of the curricula of most higher education institutions (HEI), thus contributing to the widening of the skills gap. The Deloitte report on The Future of the Workforce—Critical drivers and challenges (Schwartz et al., 2016) reveals the pitfalls of focusing extensively on STEM. In the UK and Australia, this has resulted in higher unemployment rates compared to non-STEM graduates. Also, this extensive STEM focus might obliterate the more important perspective of **quality education**. Schwartz et al. believe that the STEM hype should be reassessed and improving technological infrastructure and connectivity, teacher quality, and digital literacy should be re-centered as key success factors for the future workforce. It should be noted, therefore, that focusing on STEM is a narrow viewpoint, since, arguably, "It is about balance: technical skills are not sufficient by themselves" (p. 9). Research shows that, increasingly, the focus on Science, Technology, Engineering, Arts, Mathematics (STEAM) or Science, Technology, Relationships, Engineering, Arts, Mathematics (STREAM) and other STEM variants are now shifting the paradigm to include more relationship-building or the arts and social science disciplines.

Kelly et al. (2022) pragmatically respond to the Covid-19 pandemic and propose that universities should consider how the pandemic has altered the world of work and that students should be assessed for more authentic, collaborative, and real-life case studies that offer opportunities to build professional resilience in the face of future uncertainty. Linking this to sustainability, the International Labour Organisation (ILO) published a report on the importance of Green Skills as essential for the diversification of the Mauritian economy (ILO, 2018) with main growth sectors identified as agriculture, manufacturing, tourism and energy. A green economy is one that results in improved human well-being and social equity, while significantly reducing environmental risks and ecological scarcities (UNEP, 2011). Green jobs are defined by the ILO as any decent job that contributes to preserving or restoring the quality of the environment, leading to environmentally, economically, and socially sustainable enterprises and economies.

The emphasis on greening the economy and its intricate link to sustainable development is a major priority for our developing Small States. The ILO report also encourages Mauritius to engage in "smart cities and ocean economy as two emerging sectors together with climate change adaptation projects that cut across several economic sectors" (p. 18) within the greening and sustainable development programs of the government. However, in these specific sectors, it has to be noted that probably owing to high specialization and lack of critical mass, skills related to sea-bed exploration for hydrocarbons, deep ocean water applications, marine renewable energies, for instance, are still in a state of uncertainty and there is at present no major move to offer a wide range of training in ocean-based teaching and learning activities, or Smart City planning and development, other than conventional and existing types of skills development. It would be more reasonable therefore to follow Schwartz et al.'s (2016) argument for a dynamic workforce that can constantly upskill and reskill, and enable innovation and workforce inclusiveness.

As noted in the Commonwealth of Learning (Commonwealth of Learning, 2021) country report, the Kingdom of Eswatini is a Small State with a primary school net enrolment rate of 82.5% (2017) and a secondary school completion rate of more than 40%. The University of Eswatini (UNESWA) offers degrees in agriculture, commerce, education, health sciences, humanities, sciences and social sciences and incorporates the Institute of Distance Education (IDE). The institute's mission is to increase access to tertiary education by providing demand-driven educational and training opportunities to individuals, offering quality courses using the distance education delivery mode.

Some research has been done on the concept of Future Skills in Eswatini and its possible impact on the educational sector. Gama and Edoun (2020) sought the relationship between Graduate Trainee Programs (GTP) and Talent Management (TM) in corporate organizations in Eswatini and posit that more research and focus is required since the resource-intensive administration of both these programs lack coherence and integration with each other. Another gap in skills development was revealed by Brixiová and Kangoye (2018) suggesting that entrepreneurial training programs in Eswatini and elsewhere could be more effective if they were better targeted to women's needs and in particular encompass soft skills such as confidence-building to address social-cultural barriers. Peppler (2013) links STEAM to cross-disciplinary education for a program in e-textiles and posits that "the creative problem solving, flexible thinking, and risk taking integral to e-textile design are ideal by-products of a STEAM-powered approach to education, which aims to balance technical expertise with artistic vision" (p. 39). By appealing especially to young girls and women, e-textiles offer a compelling medium to broaden participation in computing. Another area where coaching and life skills' development in Eswatini are discussed is that of sports (Huysmans et al., 2022). Also, Dulvy (2020) affirms that Technical and Vocational Education and Training (TVET), and post-primary skills training more broadly, is a largely unregulated sector which lacks sufficient coordination in Eswatini. The skills training sector is not sufficiently guided by labor market needs, and there are no system-level institutions to encourage linkages between training providers and employers. In the World Bank development project on "Strengthening Education and Skills Training Systems to Support Human Capital Development in Eswatini", Dulvy proposes that the project should support a selected number of training institutions, in collaboration with the private sector, to review and update existing programs or develop new ones to impart to trainees the competencies (which would include digital skills, green skills and other non-cognitive skills) identified within the occupational standards.

To summarize, we find that, for both Eswatini and Mauritius, there is a need to rethink our program offerings in HEIs to include graduate skills for more equal, equitable, ecological, and economical sustainability. In particular, we think that the Future Skills required for our graduates should be in line with the current government strategies, with a strong emphasis on the Sustainable Development Goals. For Mauritius and Eswatini, both hard and soft skills will be required. However, while the universities are innovating with more technology-based degree courses at post-graduate level, we need to also provide our undergraduate students with more transdisciplinary skills where they can collaborate, co-create and contribute with more dynamism, resilience and inclusiveness (empathy). We thus see the co-creation process as imperative to both develop and define the more important Future Skills for our developing countries. Our definition of Future Skills would thus be characteristic of our people, especially as our environments and technology are rapidly changing. We need, therefore, to give more importance in the curriculum to Digital Literacies, Green Skills, and how to forge ethical relationships within the world of work and Higher Education. It is also difficult to pin down an actual definition of Future Skills, given the fast pace at which our environments are changing, but we can work towards building the right mindsets so that our graduates can thrive in a very uncertain future. For the purpose of this chapter, we would want to define Future Skills as to include not only knowledge and competencies, but also thought processes, values, attitudes and empathy so that we can nurture well-rounded fully-fledged citizens who can collaboratively and confidently address future challenges.

14.4 Countering Vulnerability with Transdisciplinarity, Visibility and Resilience

The future is transdisciplinary. Future Skills should thus comprise competencies, values and thought processes which enable graduates to be at least aware, if not totally cognizant, of impacts of other disciplines on their own. The world is increasingly complex, interdependent, and interconnected—with "wicked" problems that need concerted efforts and skills to be resolved (Kłeczek et al., 2020). The more we delve into real-world problems and challenges, the more we realize that working in silos, continuously engaging with people from our own disciplines, and not connecting our students with students from other departments is a grave lacuna in our higher education system. Indeed, the transdisciplinary approach is important to address the challenges in society; the industry also requires graduates to become transdisciplinary specialists (Walther et al., 2017).

It would seem that it was Jean Piaget who coined "transdisciplinarity" so as to transcend the established framework of traditional academic disciplines and encourage freedom of thinking (Nicolescu, 2005). Piaget (1972) advocated for the unity of knowledge beyond disciplines, and his approach implies full interaction *between, among, and beyond* disciplines from a real-life problem-based perspective. The definition of the term transdisciplinary, however, is still in a constant state of flux (Mokiy, 2019). Nevertheless, we understand the term to refer to 'trans-sector solution finding' that focuses on the study of mega- and complex problems drawing on the mix of expertise and experiences from different disciplines and sectors of society, companies and stakeholders (Repko, 2012).

The diagram proposed by Jahn and his colleagues (2012), and reproduced below (Fig. 14.3), is useful as it shows the link between societal and scientific praxis that happens through transdisciplinary integration. A feedback mechanism allows for interdisciplinary knowledge sharing, which combines and integrates knowledge from both social and natural sciences, to influence social and scientific discourses. This knowledge will in turn consider both societal and scientific problems to define a common research object. This nexus approach is also based on the premises that both scientific and practical knowledge are equally valid.

14 Learning Design for Future Skills Development in Small State …   293

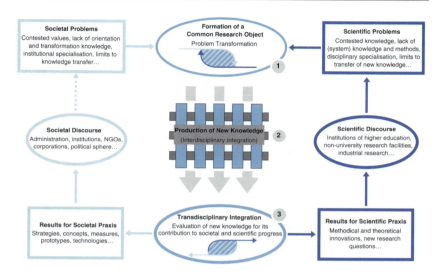

Fig. 14.3 The integration of societal and scientific praxis in transdisciplinary research. Reprinted with permission from Jahn et al., (2012, p. 8)

Correspondingly, as we move from STEM to STEAM (Science, Technology, Engineering, Arts, Mathematics), and ultimately STREAM (Science, Technology, **Relationships**, Engineering, Arts & Mathematics), thus adding the Creative and Humanities aspects with more empathy, this chapter proposes a transdisciplinary approach for developing Future Skills for our undergraduate students. As Haugen (2020) argues, we need to bring learners to explore relationships that we have with our peers and our environment, which is why there's a need to involve children as early as possible in STREAM and to make a profound impact by grounding our teaching and support for children in the context of really seeing children, getting curious with them, and valuing their ideas. The impetus for developing such a transdisciplinary course stems from the multiple reports from Industry-Academia instances elaborating on the need for developing "softer" skills for our graduates. As a universal feature, while university graduates have "savoir-faire", they lack "faire-savoir"—roughly translated as the ability to let others know, be more visible about their knowledge, their core competencies and their personal strengths, thus needing to develop stronger relationships with their stakeholders.

As the future cannot be tackled from a mono-disciplinary point of view, having a transdisciplinary perspective is of utmost importance for sustainable and inclusive development (Di Giulio & Defila, 2017). It makes much more sense, as Galafassi et al. (2018) have found, to have "open and engaging transdisciplinary processes with large and diverse populations aimed at sharing experiences, co-creating knowledge and reimagining public goals" (p. 73). McGregor (2017) proposes nine possible transdisciplinary higher education pedagogies that have the potential to enable graduates to become more skilled at reflecting on data, concepts, and real-world items, as well as the activities of the problem-solving system/community and their modes of participation and inquiry. McGregor further suggests embedding the curriculum with the following teaching and learning approaches:

1. Double loop learning,
2. Deep education/learning,
3. Integrative curriculum,
4. Inquiry-based learning,
5. Value analysis,
6. Transformative learning,
7. Authentic curriculum,
8. Paradigm shifts,
9. Learning communities.

Considering that there are as many frameworks that have been developed for key competencies and Future Skills (Davies et al., 2011; Ehlers, 2020; OECD, 2018; UNESCO, 2018; World Economic Forum, 2020; Young & Chapman, 2010) as disciplines, there are obvious areas of commonality, overlaps, and variations of similar competencies that we would like our graduates to develop, and it would be impossible to come to a final, definite list. We contemplated transdisciplinary skills and competencies that would provide the students a strong basis to explore further, with better awareness and honing of their personal strengths, choices, and affinities. This made even more sense in the spirit of co-creation that we had adopted for developing this module while at the same time avoiding the one-size-fits-all approach.

With the above learning design approaches in mind, the module that was proposed in Mauritius to 1st-year undergraduate students was designed to enhance or develop autonomy in choices of learning resources and educational technologies through four main blocks of learning which included the following transdisciplinary competencies:

1. Collaborative networking—Cultural awareness, Personal branding, Team playing, Networking and Trust building.
2. Communication—Emotional intelligence, Technology-enhanced communication, Verbal and non-verbal communication and Conflict management.
3. Growth mindsets—Solution-orientedness, Grit and perseverance, Opportunity-seeking, Design thinking, Critical and creative thinking.
4. Professional and ethical practices—Social responsibility, Sustainable competencies, Ethical dilemma management, Model Ethical situational leadership, Best practice application.

This module was actually designed and developed as an Open Educational Resource (OER) for the purpose of the Open Educational for a Better World (OE4BW) project and is available at: https://oe4bw.org/project/transdisciplinary-teaching-and-learning/.

The design of the Transdisciplinary Skills and Competencies project was inspired by the Delors Report which was prepared for UNESCO in 1996—"Learning: The treasure within". The report provided an insight into the still relevant societal challenges of globalization, knowledge societies, inclusion, social cohesion, and democratic participation (Tawil & Cougoureux, 2013). The four pillars of learning (Learning to be, Learning to do, Learning to know, and Learning to live together) underpinned the development of learning activities for the module on Transdisciplinary Skills and Competencies (Table 14.1).

Because of COVID-19, our 1st-year students were not able to get placements in industry which was a requirement of the BSc (Hons) Web and Multimedia development program. We thus proposed the module to the students so that they would be introduced to notions of work-place skills and competencies. The module would account for the required number of credits that the students would have otherwise lost and thus was a very timely opportunity to engage the students, and, eventually, get some university academics on board for feedback and enhancing the module, aiming to be as transdisciplinary as possible (Fig. 14.4).

The various learning activities were presented to both academics and students from different departments at the university. Based on sound socio-constructivist pedagogical approaches, the learning activities comprised metacognitive processes, peer interactions, portfolios, and tangible outcomes of cooperative or sole projects (Felix, 2003, p. 159). The module rationale and learning outcomes as well as the assessment criteria used to appraise the student learning are presented in Table 14.2.

As can be observed, the list of competencies is non-exhaustive and interconnected, with obvious overlaps throughout the different learning activities. It is

Table 14.1 Mapping the Delors Report (1996) to Future Graduate Skills

Learning: The treasure within	Transdisciplinary skills and competencies
Learning to be	Self and Cultural Awareness Personal branding Acknowledging, and appreciating differences Transformative leadership
Learning to know	Creative and critical thinking Design Thinking, Social and Emotional Intelligence Personal Branding Cognitive Bias Analysis
Learning to do	Social responsibility Sustainable development Managing ethical dilemmas Problem solving
Learning to Live together	Collaborative Networking Innovation Competence Design thinking Conflict management and resolution Negotiation Skills Creativity and Visual literacies

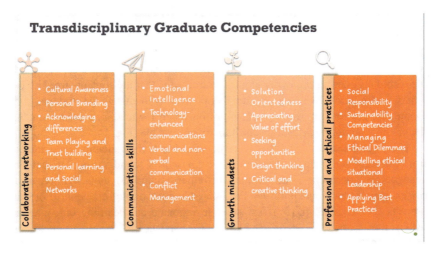

Fig. 14.4 Main competencies to be developed during the Transdisciplinary Skills and Competencies Module for 1st-year students

14 Learning Design for Future Skills Development in Small State ... 297

Table 14.2 Table of Learning activities for the Transdisciplinary Skills and Competencies Module

Learning Outcomes - At the end of the module learners are expected to:	And will be assessed through the:	Transdisciplinary skills and competencies
• Identify their own personal competencies and strengths in a digital world • Display Self-efficacy, resourcefulness, and Ethical Leadership qualities	• Creation of an Ikigai[1] model for self-assessment of personal strengths and development areas	Self and Cultural Awareness, Personal branding, Acknowledging, and appreciating differences
	• Role Play in class/online on Future job preparation—Jobs can be in any field • Storyboarding and Video recording of discussions around Emotional Intelligence, Cultural Sensitivity and Ethical practices during the role play	Technology-enhanced Communications, Transformative leadership
• Discuss about deep learning and authentic learning events • Reflect upon cognitive processes and how these can be optimized for assessment • Develop alternative solutions through deep and complex thinking	• Annotating the Curriculum—Taking ownership of your learning • Design and development of a Digital portfolio using digital tools and techniques for note taking, screen casting, and Social Reading and share its contents with peers • Create an influence diagram related to what should be displayed on a Social Network Site and what influences these decisions	Creative and critical thinking, Design Thinking, Social and Emotional Intelligence, Personal Branding Cognitive Bias Analysis

(continued)

---

[1] Ikigai is a Japanese concept that refers to a person's sense of purpose and meaning in life. It is often described as the intersection of four elements: what you love, what you are good at, what the world needs, and what you can be paid for.

Table 14.2 (continued)

Learning Outcomes - At the end of the module learners are expected to:	And will be assessed through the:	Transdisciplinary skills and competencies
• Build an online collaborative empathy map using Design thinking • Resolve an issue pertaining to problems from a different faculty	• Drawing a Future Spokes and Wheels diagram related to the first, second and third order consequences pertaining to a given Signal or trend (For example Design Future Thinking approaches for Small State Workforce) • Infographic pertaining to the faculty problem and its resolution (With statistical references and concept analysis)	Social responsibility, Sustainable development, Managing ethical dilemmas Problem solving
• Planning, Organising and Presenting a University Wide Workshop	• Compile a Who's Who for a particular Field • Designing and Developing Digital Poster – SDG Theme-based • Designing Promotional and registration packaging • Compiling Sponsorship lists and costing sheets • Delegating team responsibilities and task	Collaborative Networking Innovation Competence Design thinking Conflict management and resolution Negotiation Skills Creativity and Visual literacies Budgeting skills

expected that the redundancies would only reinforce the different competencies required from these students, allow for a fail-fast method to develop resilience, and enable learners to value the opportunities for a second chance. The first-year students would need to document their individual learning paths and provide evidence of having achieved the various competencies through artefacts, videos or audio-recordings. If competencies were not reached, the students would need to indicate self-help resources (books, online videos, learning circles, and social networks, etc.) which would help them reach their personal levels of competencies. Both formative and summative assessments were carried out to enable the students to develop and nurture the different skills and competencies required. Since these were mostly qualitative, the learning and collaborative interactions were made "visible" through transcripts (of discussions for doing the activity) and reflections on competencies acquired.

14.5 Study Methodology

The present small-scale study sought to get feedback on a number of questions related to the concept of Future Skills. This was done through an online questionnaire (Annex 1a) sent to purposely sampled interviewees who had followed the Transdisciplinary Skills and Competencies module. The criteria used for determining the sample of students was to ensure a fair balance of gender-responses and that they were in different years of study (not only freshers or final year students).

The interview protocol (Annex 1b) sent to academics in both countries included open-ended questions. These were meant as an indication of the focus areas for the actual interview so that the academics could think and prepare prior to the focus group meetings.

A focus group discussion (FGD) was organized with 9 academics and 6 students to present the Transdisciplinary Skills and Competencies Module. Participation was purely voluntary, followed research ethics protocol, and the respondents gave their informed consent. The profiles of the academics can be viewed in Annex 2.

The 6 students who participated in the group discussion were mostly from the first year of Web and Multimedia development undergraduate program and had followed the module during the lock-down period. The majority of them were female and only one male student had responded positively to the call for participation.

Their views were recorded, transcribed, and analyzed using thematic analysis. Most of the lecturers (7) had over 20 years' experience in higher education, while the remaining 2 academics had between 10- and 20-years' experience. In our judgement, the length of experience is a good indicator of their opinion and experience with skills' development in students and how best to undertake this in future.

14.6 Academics' View of Future Skills

The main aim of the discussions was to gain consensus around the module outcomes and activities set and whether there should be any modifications or improvements that needed to be made.

From the focus group discussions with the academics, Future Skills is equivalent to new pedagogical developments (beyond online teaching and learning), indispensable skills in the future, skills leading to a sustainable society, skills required to respond, adapt, enhance learning to our ever-changing world, and skills which increase graduate employability. The academics noted the mismatch between what is done in universities and what is needed "on the ground", in society. They highlighted the scarcity of IT and technological skills in particular.

Five out of nine respondents feel it is the university's responsibility to develop graduates' Future Skills. Nevertheless, they also thought some Future Skills needed to be acquired by the students in an autonomous manner. For the participating academics, the skills that students should develop individually are those related to communication (language, data manipulation, and visualization), entrepreneurship, and analysis.

The impact of the Covid-19 pandemic will be long-felt and thus better preparing the students to position themselves in the world of work is an important role of the higher education institutions (Kelly et al., 2022). Unsurprisingly, the academics focused their answers on the need for enhanced communication skills, as well as collaboration skills. Nevertheless, the same respondents indicated that lack of time, lack of appropriate training, lack of departmental/institutional support towards online tools and technology, as well as inability to identify Future Skills' needs in the job market were all challenges educational systems face when trying to incorporate what they perceived as the more commonly referred-to twenty-first Century Skills (such as critical thinking, communication, social responsibility, creativity, etc.) in their daily teaching approaches. While these are important challenges shared by many countries world-wide, some factors related to the "smallness" or lack of critical mass of Mauritius and Eswatini can be mitigated through the use of case studies from other countries/regions and follow-up discussions when teaching learners about Future Skills.

Regarding the methodology or pedagogical approach to use when teaching Future Skills, the respondents were unanimous in preferring the integration of Future Skills in the existing curricula (modules). This could mean that irrelevant course content is struck off so that space and time is available to the embedding of Future Skills. In addition, Future Skills could be developed through the implementation of more work-based, project-based, experiential learning opportunities and through the use of oral student presentations and team-based work on case studies.

As a follow-up activity, a second cohort of Web and Multimedia students who are currently following the LLC 1080 module and who were assigned the Event Management learning activity were given the opportunity to voice out on which areas they would like to be assessed. The instructions were purposely left unstructured to allow for the students to make decisions pertaining to themes, duration, costs, roles, and responsibilities. The steps for the activity are as below:

Organizing a University-Wide Online Workshop on the Future of the University

1. Organize yourselves into 6 teams and, using any collaborative organizational tool of your choice (Slack, Google Docs, Discord, etc.), start brainstorming about: **How to organize a university-wide workshop/conference/seminar on a collegially chosen Theme.**
2. List the tasks and assign responsibilities to people in your team.
3. Define the themes and objectives of this online event along with who you would like to invite to (1) participate and (2) facilitate the event.
4. Make a list of possible speakers and prepare the promotional material required to disseminate the information to both your Workshop presenters and attendees.
5. Use Canva to create posters and share these with your networks.
6. Take minutes of your organizing committee meetings and have regular debriefing sessions which are also minuted after each task is completed.
7. Reflect on the organizational process—What were the challenges you faced? What were the most important decisions you had to take? How were conflicts managed, if any? What would be the next steps required to make this event happen? Post all your communication material on a shared drive and link this back to this module.

The assumptions for designing this activity were that Web and Multimedia students should be able to fit into as many disciplines as possible. Developing a professional mindset, they should be able to engage into sense-making discussions with their "clients". In order to allow them to take ownership of the activity, they were allowed to define their own assessment criteria.

A word cloud was generated showing the main skills on which fifty (50) 1st-year students would want to be assessed. They were given the opportunity to define areas where they felt they needed to get additional skills before getting onto the job market.

The word cloud shows that students are majorly concerned with attributes pertaining to professionalism and communication skills, which appeared 49 and 30 times respectively in the discussion forum that was set up for this learning activity. What is more interesting are the finer details at the periphery of the world cloud: concepts such as "Educated Judgement Calls" or "Sense of Self" show that some students have a more sophisticated understanding of graduate attributes than others. We see this as a positive step towards self-determined areas of improvement, but at the same time observe the students' lack of investigation into more contemporary needs of Future Skills; for example, green skills or sustainable development-related skills and competencies. Some of the verbatim comments from the students show that they had really put in a lot of effort and thinking into defining their own yardsticks for assessing their competencies. One student mentioned: "The most crucial life skill is the ability to communicate effectively. It is what allows us to communicate with others and comprehend what is communicated to us. To appreciate how basic the need to communicate is, just watch a newborn listening carefully to its mother and attempting to imitate the noises she makes."

This highly emotional reference to communication and linking it to the affective relationship between mother and child shows the level of empathy that some students had engaged with for this activity. They deeply appreciated the ability to have a say in the assessment process: "Usually, as students we are assigned tasks or even assignments by lecturers. Grades are allocated in the light of how much we succeeded. However, having the opportunity to choose on which graduate attributes I want to be assessed on is a blessing."

As they neared the end of the Module, the students could identify areas where they felt they had been able to perform the best and in which they would prefer to be assessed for the skills and competencies required. Assessments were based on well-defined rubrics linked to levels of skills demonstrated. For instance, for communication skills, we asked them to provide transcripts of their team organization using WhatsApp or Zoom. This enabled a transparent view of who was leading the discussion or who was free riding, who had more creative ideas, etc.). Students would then be assessed on their communication types: idea generator, supportive arguments, devil's advocate (critical thinking).

14.7 Challenges and Further Research

As barriers to this study, we find that academics are quite hesitant to work with students as co-creators. This could possibly be owing to an already heavy workload, and the responsibility of supervising students on key projects will prove to be time-consuming. Also, some academics feel that because of lack of exposure, or possibly apathy to real world problems that reveals itself in the responses from the students, they would need to make an extra effort to on-board these students and convince them of the importance of this work-based learning opportunity. Additionally, an insular mentality prevents students from looking at bigger-picture world problems. More internationalization of the university (Kletz & Almog-Bareket, 2017) with more creative pedagogies, higher level of research in collaboration with industry, and engagement into international networks would help these graduates to have deeper learning opportunities. Already by reaching out to different faculties, the students have been able to experience the importance of creating personal networks and becoming more visible, and therefore present their capabilities to the academic and student community. Future research in this area will need to include other students and academics from different faculties, so that the interaction between the students can lead to identifying common areas of interest which might in turn lead to synergies for developing sustainable solutions to these.

14.7.1 Learnings and Recommendations

Whilst we have not yet worked with students in Eswatini, the feedback and learning experiences from the first two batches at the University of Mauritius (one cohort is ongoing) has supported reflection on practice (Schön, 1987) and provided the opportunity for continuously improving on this mutual learning experience. Some suggestions for improvement were made by the students as follows:

1. Assign a problem/project that highlights the content you want students to learn in your program *(It can be related to the program course)*.
2. Feature a guest speaker in the field of study to celebrate a "day in the life of". *(The guest can be an ex-student of the same course or those who have been on internship)*.
3. Encourage students to work alone and in groups, knowing that they need to communicate, share ideas, and participate in class discussions. (*Choosing*

groups for teamwork would help students feel comfortable with people other than their friends).

4. Nominate an "employee of the week/student of the week" each week based on the best assignments. *(To motivate and to encourage participation in the program).*
5. Include embedded videos with local cases of workplace conflicts and learning experiences that could be discussed by students who had gone for short work placements.
6. Ensure that students create healthy working relationships and that toxic events are openly discussed so that consensus for mutual benefits can be agreed upon.
7. Make students realize that their behavior will impact on future cohorts through story-telling activities from previous cohorts sharing their experiences.

While some students felt that they could do with more instructions and guidance, in general students found that the module had helped them build confidence and that they had discovered sides of their personality that they had not thought of:

> "There were some concepts which were a bit difficult. For example, I had difficulties understanding the future wheel but I also got some feedback from my friends who said the content was not related to web multimedia. I think that they did not understand the concept of the module, it was more about preparing us for the world of work. For me, it was okay."
>
> "I'm much more confident because once we looked up T-graduates and that really helped me get into the mind of an employer and what he's looking for, that really helped me. And then with the Viva Sessions, we were given some prompts as to what we have to talk about."
>
> "I think after the Ikigai one, it really got me thinking and re-evaluating all of my dreams because there are some aspects that we miss that we forget, like how it will contribute to the world and everything. And when you put all that together, that's when you realise that we did not think about it thoroughly. So we really need a reality check, maybe a one to one session to make us realise sometimes we don't even realise what we need and what we lack until we get the opportunity to. So that would be good."

Eventually, the co-creation of a module on Future Skills and competencies is one that students are very keen to participate in and would provide academics with greater variety of learning experiences and cases for their students to learn from. Of course, this requires some organization to bring the academics and students together to work towards breaking down existing silos. Also, it would be important to include more learning activities related to sustainable development, frugal innovation, and green skills. Having a consortium or special interest group approach could provide the necessary structure and is worth investigating further.

14.8 Conclusion

This chapter started off with a general look at Future Skills and transdisciplinary approaches to teaching and learning. A two-fold method—a questionnaire sent to academics in two Southern African Small States (Mauritius and Eswatini) followed by interviews and discussions with Mauritian 1st-year university students having taken a module on Transdisciplinary Skills and Competencies allowed us to identify some of the Future Skills both Small States perceive as most important, and also to list some of the possible teaching and learning approaches to incubate these.

The current education system in Mauritius and Eswatini, like in many developing countries, is based on traditional teacher-centered approaches where students are not provided with adequate opportunities to develop transdisciplinary skills and competencies. The discussions from both the students and academics suggest that self-efficacy and self-directed learning are not being promoted sufficiently. Students expect that their lecturers will determine "the knowledge that needs to be transferred, design and conduct training and monitor and evaluate the outcomes" (Santos Rocha & van Berg, 2017). For self-directed learning (Knowles, 1975), learners should take control—make decisions, and take responsibility for their learning process. Clearly, the first-year students were still requiring the scaffolding that they were used to, and as this module was asking them to co-construct their own knowledge and various competencies not only individually, but also collaboratively with more knowledgeable others (Vygotsky, 1978), it was important to enhance the module to clearly enunciate the more self-reliant competence that was required from the students.

This chapter has its obvious limits. It is exploratory in nature, and thus the results are inconclusive; owing to the small sample population. However, we attempted to provide authentic information based on teaching and learning experiences. The chapter gives a clear indication of the Future Skills' gaps, how these might be filled and what additional research would assist the communities of both Small States to build resilience, in particular after two years of the Covid-19 pandemic.

> **Future Skills in Practice: Our Recommendations**
> - Upgrade the education system from teacher-centered to more learner-centered approaches; providing students with more ownership, empowerment, and discernment for their learning capabilities to transform these into core competencies.
> - Enhance co-creation across disciplines for more authentic skill building.
> - Build upon existing frameworks for Education with strong moral compasses—For instance the Delors report which emphasizes the four pillars of learning (Learning to know, Learning to do, Learning to live together, and Learning to be) and taking into consideration the challenges and opportunities of globalization, knowledge societies, inclusion, social cohesion, and democratic participation.
> - Humbly accept that for sustainable development, we need to be more frugal in our approach to innovation, and that Small States are a great lesson to the world in terms of providing its people with skills for Resourcefulness, Resilience, Relationships and Reliability for Sustainable Development.

Annex 1a) Interview Protocol for Students

The survey questions asked to students were as follows:

1. For you, what does the concept of Future Skills refer to?
2. In which of the courses you took did you encounter references to Future Skills?
3. Was this your first time to learn about some of these skills?
4. Which [future] skills do you value the most for your own personal development?
5. Which [future] skills do you value the most for your own professional development?
6. What did your work placement/internship teach you about Future Skills?
7. What competencies have you developed during the work placement and would recommend to your juniors?
8. What competencies and skills have you realised were important from the LLC1080 Module?

9. How prepared are you to develop these skills after work placement?
10. Which Future Skills did you expect to gain from your studies?
11. Which Future Skills did you expect to gain from your work placement/internship?
12. Which Future Skills did you expect to have to develop individually/autonomously?
13. In which of the courses you took did you encounter references to Future Skills?
14. Was this your first time to learn about some of these skills?

Annex 1b) Interview Protocol for Academics

1. For you, what does the concept of Future Skills refer to?
2. Which Future Skills did you expect your students to have to develop individually/autonomously?
3. What is specific to Mauritius/Eswatini in terms of skills development? Have we got the right mix of talents/workforce?
4. How do we mitigate the effects of smallness and "lack of critical mass?"
5. To what extent is it the responsibility of the university to develop graduates' Future Skills?
6. How do you embed these skills without overloading the existing curriculum?
7. Your Existing Module/Course Catalogue Structure—Can it be improved to embed Future Skills within the assessments?
8. Can you please provide three or more practical recommendations for others when implementing Future Skills into higher education?

Annex 2

The academics had the following profiles:

- Faculty of Social Sciences and Humanities: F—Lecturer in Psychology—8 years' experience
- Faculty of Law and Management: M—Senior Lecturer in HRM—25 years' experience
- Faculty of Agriculture: M—Associate Professor Biometry—28 years' experience

- Faculty of Agriculture: M—Senior Lecturer in Agricultural Sciences—26 years' experience
- Faculty of Engineering: F—Senior Lecturer in Town and Country Planning—20 years' Experience
- Faculty of Medicine and Health Sciences: F—Associate Professor in Medicine—26 years' experience
- Faculty of Information Communication and Digital Technologies: F—Senior Lecturer Software and Information Systems—15 years' experience
- Faculty of Science: M—Associate Professor in Mathematical Modelling—20 years' Experience
- Centre for Innovative and Lifelong Learning: F—Senior Lecturer Graphic Design—22 years' experience

References

Armoogum, N. Y., Ramasawmy, B., & Driver, B. M. F. (2016). The need to enhance the employability competences (knowledge, skills, autonomy, and attitudes) of undergraduates in Agriculture. Evidence from students' perceptions and employers' expectations. *Tuning Journal for Higher Education, 4*(1), 169. https://doi.org/10.18543/tjhe-4(1)-2016pp169-219.

Brixiová, Z., & Kangoye, T. (2018). *Skills as a barrier to women's start ups: A model with evidence from Eswatini* (ERSA working paper 768).

Commonwealth of Learning. (2021). Eswatini 2015-2021: Country Report. http://hdl.handle.net/11599/3814.

Davies, A., Fidler, D., & Gorbis, M. (2011). Future work skills 2020. Palo Alto. https://www.voced.edu.au/content/ngv%3A49812.

Delors, J. (1996). *Learning: The treasure within: Report to unesco of the international commission on education for the twenty-first century*. Unesco.

Di Giulio, A., & Defila, R. (2017). Enabling university educators to equip students with inter- and transdisciplinary competencies. *International Journal of Sustainability in Higher Education, 18*(5). https://doi.org/10.1108/IJSHE-02-2016-0030.

Dubois, R., & Juwaheer, Y. (2012). *Skills for green jobs in Mauritius: Unedited background country study*. ILO.

Dulvy, E. N. (2020). *Concept Project Information Document (PID) – Strengthening education and skills training sytems to support human capital development in ESwatini – P173151*. United States of America.

Dutta, S., Lanvin, B., Rivera León, L., & Wunsch-Vincent, S. (2021). Global innovation index 2021: Tracking innovation through the COVID-19 crisis. https://www.wipo.int/edocs/pubdocs/en/wipo_pub_gii_2021.pdf.

Ehlers U-D (2020) *Future Skills*. Springer, Germany. https://doi.org/10.1007/978-3-658-29297-3.

Felix, U. (2003). Pedagogy on the line: Identifying and closing the missing links. In U. Felix (Ed.), *Language learning online: Towards best practice* (1st ed., pp. 147–170). Swets & Zeitlinger.

Ferreira-Meyers, K., Barkhuizen, A., & Schmid, K. (2022). Educating french teachers in the digital era. In J. Olivier, A. Oojorah, & W. Udhin (Eds.), *Perspectives on teacher education in the digital age* (pp. 205–222). Springer Nature Singapore. https://doi.org/10.1007/978-981-19-4226-6_12.

Galafassi, D., Kagan, S., Milkoreit, M., Heras, M., Bilodeau, C., Bourke, S. J., et al. (2018). 'Raising the temperature': The arts in a warming planet. *Current Opinion in Environmental Sustainability, 31*, 71–79. https://doi.org/10.1016/j.cosust.2017.12.010.

Gama, L. Z., & Edoun, E. I. (2020). The relationship between the graduate trainee programme and talent management in corporate organisations in Eswatini. *SA Journal of Human Resource Management, 18*. https://doi.org/10.4102/sajhrm.v18i0.1249.

Hardin-Ramanan, S., Ballasoupramanien, L., Gopee, S., Rowtho, V., & Charoux, O. (2019). Graduate work-readiness challenges in mauritius. In S. Dhakal, V. Prikshat, A. Nankervis, & J. Burgess (Eds.), *The transition from graduation to work* (pp. 143–160). Springer Singapore. https://doi.org/10.1007/978-981-13-0974-8_9.

Haugen, K. (2020). From STEM to STEAM to STREAM. *Exchange* (235), 40–43.

HRDC. (2021). An assessment of secondary school students' interest in STEM subjects. https://www.hrdc.mu/index.php/projects/349-an-assessment-of-secondary-school-students-interest-in-stem-subjects. Accessed 4 March 2023.

Huysmans, Z., Whitley, M. A., Clement, D., Gonzalez, M., & Sheehy, T. L. (2022). "The relationship was a big success–the bond": Exploring coaching strategies to foster life skills development in Eswatini. *Journal of Applied Sport Psychology, 34*(4), 751–779.

ILO. (2018). Skills for green jobs in Mauritius. https://www.ilo.org/skills/projects/WCMS_706879/lang--en/index.htm.

Jahn, T., Bergmann, M., & Keil, F. (2012). Transdisciplinarity: Between mainstreaming and marginalization. *Ecological Economics, 79*, 1–10.

Kelly, A., Moore, C., & Lyons, E. (2022). Traditional exams, 21st-century employability skills and COVID-19: Disruptive opportunities for rethinking assessment design in higher education. In R. Ammigan, R. Y. Chan, & K. Bista (Eds.), *COVID-19 and higher education in the global context: Exploring contemporary issues and challenges* (pp. 67–79). STAR Scholars.

Kłeczek, R., Hajdas, M., & Wrona, S. (2020). Wicked problems and project-based learning: Value-in-use approach. *The International Journal of Management Education, 18*(1), 100324.

Kletz, P., & Almog-Bareket, G. (2017). Higher education in management: The case of Israel. In S. Dameron, & T. Durand (Eds.), *The future of management education: Volume 1: Challenges facing business schools around the World* (pp. 181–203). Palgrave Macmillan.

Knowles, M. S. (1975). *Self-directed learning: A guide for learners and teachers.* Association Press.

Krönke, M. (2020). *Africa's digital divide and the promise of e-learning* (Afrobarometer Policy Paper 66).

Lister, T., & DeMarco, T. (1999). *Peopleware: Productive projects and teams: Second edition featuring eight all-new chapters.* Dorset House.

McGregor, S. L. (2017). Transdisciplinary pedagogy in higher education: Transdisciplinary learning, learning cycles and habits of minds. In P. Gibbs (Ed.), *Transdisciplinary higher education: A theoretical basis revealed in practice* (pp. 3–16). Springer International Publishing. https://doi.org/10.1007/978-3-319-56185-1_1.

Ministry of Education and Training. (2018). The national education and training improvement programme 2018/19–2020/2021. Eswatini. https://planipolis.iiep.unesco.org/sites/default/files/ressources/eswatini_netip.pdf.

Mokiy, V. S. (2019). International standard of transdisciplinary education and transdisciplinary competence. *Informing Science, 22*, 73.

Nicolescu, B. (2005). Towards transdisciplinary education and learning. *Science and Religion: Global Perspectives, 1–12*.

OECD. (2018). The future of education and skills: Education 2030. https://www.oecd.org/education/2030/E2030%20Position%20Paper%20(05.04.2018).pdf.

Peppler, K. (2013). STEAM-powered computing education: Using e-textiles to integrate the arts and STEM. *Computer, 46*(09), 38–43.

Piaget, J. (1972). The epistemology of interdisciplinary relationships. *Interdisciplinarity: Problems of teaching and research in universities, 127–139*.

Repko, A. F. (2012). *Interdisciplinary research: Process and theory* (2nd ed.). Sage.

Santos Rocha, J., & van Berg, M. M. den. (2017). *Agricultural extension, technology adoption and household food security: Evidence from DRC*. Wageningen University.

Schön, D. A. (1987). *Educating the reflective practitioner: Toward a new design for teaching and learning in the professions*. Jossey-Bass.

Schwartz, J., Bersin, J., Bourke, J., Danna, R., Jarrett, M., Knowles-Cutler, A., et al. (2016). The future of the workforce: Critical drivers and challenges. https://www2.deloitte.com/content/dam/Deloitte/au/Documents/human-capital/deloitte-au-hc-future-of-workforce-critical-drivers-challenges-220916.pdf.

Tandrayen-Ragoobur, V. (2020). Addressing the education and skills mismatch in the mauritian economy. https://www.researchgate.net/project/Addressing-the-Education-and-Skills-Mismatch-in-the-Mauritian-Economy.

Tawil, S., & Cougoureux, M. (2013). *Revisiting learning: The treasure within: Assessing the influence of the 1996 Delors report* (Occasional Papers). Paris.

UNDP. Country Insights. United Nations. https://hdr.undp.org/data-center/country-insights#/ranks.

UNEP. (2011). Towards a green economy: y pathways to sustainable development and poverty eradication. A synthesis for policy makers. https://sustainabledevelopment.un.org/content/documents/126GER_synthesis_en.pdf.

UNESCO. (2018). UNESCO ICT Competency Framework for Teachers: Version 3. Paris. https://unesdoc.unesco.org/ark:/48223/pf0000265721.

van Velsor, E., & Wright, J. (2012). Expanding the leadership equation: Developing next-generation leaders (White Paper).

Vygotsky, L. S. (1978). *Mind in society: Development of higher psychological processes*. Harvard University Press.

Walther, J., Miller, S. E., & Sochacka, N. W. (2017). A Model of empathy in engineering as a core skill, practice orientation, and professional way of being. *Journal of Engineering Education, 106*(1), 123–148. https://doi.org/10.1002/jee.20159.

World Economic Forum. (2020). The future of jobs report 2020. http://www3.weforum.org/docs/WEF_Future_of_Jobs_2020.pdf.

Young, J., & Chapman, E. (2010). Generic competency frameworks: A brief historical overview. *Education Research and Perspectives, 37*(1), 1–24.

Sandhya Gunness is a senior lecturer at the Centre for Innovative and Lifelong Learning—University of Mauritius. She is the online tutor and content developer for the BSc and MSc Educational Technology Programs, especially related to Open Educational Resources. She is also coordinating the MA Educational Leadership program in collaboration with the University of Seychelles and has reviewed and adapted the COL OER content for the SIDS contexts. She has conducted many workshops with COL, UNESCO, COMESA and the SADC on numerous e-learning and digital literacy projects and is currently pursuing her PhD studies in the field of Horizontal Collaborative Networks and development of T-Shaped graduates.

Prof. Ferreira-Meyers is an Associate Professor and Coordinator of Linguistics and Modern Languages at the Institute of Distance Education, University of Eswatini (Eswatini). Her research interests vary, from Open Education to distance and e-learning, from the teaching and learning of languages to online assessment and facilitation, from autofiction and autobiography to crime and detective fiction, from women's writing to African literatures. She publishes regularly and is a keen translator and interpreter.

Thanasis Daradoumis holds a PhD in Computer Science from the Polytechnic University of Catalonia. He combines his role as a Joint Professor between the Computer Science, Multimedia and Telecommunication Department at the Universitat Oberta de Catalunya and the Department of Cultural Technology and Communication at the University of the Aegean. His research interests are: Emotional Intelligence, Alternative (Holistic) Education, Learning Analytics, E-learning, Collaborative, Affective and Adaptive Systems, and CSCL.

Open Access This chapter is licensed under the terms of the Creative Commons Attribution 4.0 International License (http://creativecommons.org/licenses/by/4.0/), which permits use, sharing, adaptation, distribution and reproduction in any medium or format, as long as you give appropriate credit to the original author(s) and the source, provide a link to the Creative Commons license and indicate if changes were made.

The images or other third party material in this chapter are included in the chapter's Creative Commons license, unless indicated otherwise in a credit line to the material. If material is not included in the chapter's Creative Commons license and your intended use is not permitted by statutory regulation or exceeds the permitted use, you will need to obtain permission directly from the copyright holder.

Boosting Future Skills in Higher Education. Lessons Learned from Funding Programs, Networking, Establishing Standards & Curricular Integration

15

Felix Suessenbach, Judith Koeritz, Andreas Wormland and Henning Koch

Abstract

Facing challenges at an individual, professional, and global level, individuals need a new set of competencies: Future Skills. Higher education plays a central role in teaching these, but their curricular integration can be challenging. The Stifterverband organization has contributed to Future Skills education in higher educations by providing two Future Skills frameworks and funding programs such as "Entrepreneurial Skills", "Data Literacy Education", and "Curriculum 4.0.nrw". Here we share our experiences from these programs to aid decision makers in higher education when implementing Future Skills education. Working with several institutions tackling a variety of challenges

---

F. Suessenbach (✉)
Researcher, Stifterverband, Berlin, Germany
e-mail: felix.suessenbach@stifterverband.de

J. Koeritz · H. Koch
Program Manager, Stifterverband, Berlin, Germany
e-mail: judith.koeritz@stifterverband.de

H. Koch
e-mail: henning.koch@stifterverband.de

A. Wormland
Program Manager, Stifterverband, Essen, Germany
e-mail: andreas.wormland@stifterverband.de

© The Author(s) 2024
U.-D. Ehlers and L. Eigbrecht (eds.), *Creating the University of the Future*, Zukunft der Hochschulbildung - Future Higher Education,
https://doi.org/10.1007/978-3-658-42948-5_15

when implementing entrepreneurial education allowed us to distill several guidelines for sustainable entrepreneurship education. Including a wide range of experts in our Data Literacy networks, we developed a mutual understanding of and commitment to Data Literacy education—the Data Literacy Charter—and gained valuable experiences working in these networks. Funded with 7.5 mio. €, the large-scale "Curriculum 4.0.nrw" program has been supporting the curricular integration of a range of Future Skills related to digitization. Here we collected the most common obstacles as well as supporting factors when integrating Future Skills into existing curricula as well as suggested solutions to these obstacles.

15.1 Introduction

The many accomplishments of our modern society such as an interconnectedness of the world both digitally and physically, the increase in wealth and health and the ability to produce and consume in large quantities have introduced a range of new and pressing societal challenges such as climate change, resource shortage, pandemics, or ageing of society. As these great and complex problems permeate all domains of our life, it seems clear that economy, politics, science, and civil society must work together to overcome these challenges and perform the much-needed transformation of our world (e.g., Domanski & Kaletka, 2017; Suessenbach et al., 2021; United Nations, 2023). To do so requires a range of distinct skills, tools, and mindset, subsumed under the umbrella term Future Skills (e.g., OECD, 2023; Suessenbach et al., 2021).

These Future Skills include competencies which allow individuals to partake in a digitized world, enable awareness and understanding of transformative challenges, foster innovative thinking, planning, development of products to implement transformation, promoting and utilizing open science and open innovation. A sharp increase in publications on Future Skills in the past decade reflects the rising efforts in Future Skills education—especially in higher education (Ehlers, 2020). The Stifterverband organization has contributed to this effort with several programs funding Future Skills education, creating networks between various stakeholders in- and outside academia as well as a multitude of analyses and other publications. The Stifterverband is well suited for this endeavor as it is the only organization in Germany advising, funding, and connecting stakeholders in a wholistic approach at the intersection of education, science, and innovation.

Based on our Future Skills work, this chapter will provide insights, learnings, and examples relevant to institutional policy makers in higher education to help them implement Future Skills education. First, we will introduce the Stifterverband's two Future Skills frameworks which underpin our programmatic work. Second, we will introduce the Stifterverband's Entrepreneurial Skills program for sustainable entrepreneurship education. Here we present the Entrepreneurial Skills Charter including eleven theses on how higher education institutions can successfully teach entrepreneurial thinking and action. Third, we present the Data Literacy Education program which—with its Data Literacy Charter—laid the groundwork to develop the first uniform data literacy framework. Here, learnings from working in data literacy networks are discussed. Fourth, we will provide insights on our large-scale project Curriculum 4.0.nrw supporting a range of Future Skills relevant to digitization. Here we provide an overview of obstacles as well as supporting factors when integrating these skills into existing study programs. Finally, we leave the reader with some concluding remarks and three practical recommendations from our programs to support Future Skills development in higher education.

15.2 Future Skills Frameworks by Stifterverband and Partners

The Stifterverband's Future Skills work is based on two Future Skills frameworks—Future Skills 2021 (Suessenbach et al., 2021) and Future Skills for Openness (Hoffmann et al., 2021) —which have been developed with partners McKinsey & Company and the innOsci forum, respectively. In this section, we will present the frameworks' key definitions, briefly outline how each of these frameworks was developed, as well as provide an overview of the two frameworks showcasing a range of selected Future Skills central to the funding programs in the following sections.

Future Skills are broadly defined as a set of competencies that will gain importance within the next five years across all industries and disciplines. Added to this general aspect, each framework targets the specific needs in a certain field: Future Skills 2021 is aimed at the labor market and the competencies employees and (self-)employers need now and even more so in the future. Future Skills for Openness is aimed at academics in science and business and their competencies needed for open science and open innovation. The timeframe of five years was selected to anticipate future demands but at the same time provide reasonably robust predictions given rapid technological advances and other unforeseen global developments (e.g., a pandemic). Our understanding of competencies is based on Boyatzis' definition as an effective mix of motives, traits, skills, aspects of one's self-image or social role, and of body of knowledge used by an individual (Boyatzis, 1982; Weinert, 2001a). It also comprises Erpenbeck and Heyse's (1999) understanding of competencies as self-organization dispositions. Thus, Future Skills go beyond passive knowledge and abilities but empower and encourage individuals to act (cf. Seidl et al., 2018). In short, Future Skills in our frameworks are conceptualized as action-oriented competencies based on an interplay of knowledge, skills/aptitude, and attitude (Hoffmann et al., 2021; Suessenbach et al., 2021).

15.2.1 Future Skills 2021

The Future Skills 2021 framework is an update to the Stifterverband and McKinsey's first Future Skills framework from 2018 (Kirchherr et al., 2018). The latter is a result of a workshop with a wide range of stakeholders in business, education, and politics, expert interviews with human resource officers, as well as focus groups of experts in business and education from Stifterverband and McKinsey (more details in Kirchherr et al., 2018). The updated framework includes feedback from stakeholders in business and education having put the first framework to the test as well as from many exchanges with experts in both fields. Again, focus groups from Stifterverband and McKinsey analyzed the current needs of the labor market but also distilled and added on relevant bits from other Future Skills frameworks, for example, by the United Nations (2015), OECD (2023), World Economic Forum (2021, more details in Suessenbach et al., 2021). The 2018 and the 2021 framework were each validated in representative surveys of CEOs and human resource officers in 607 and 500, respectively, businesses and public administration institutes across Germany. These surveys included questions about the importance of each Future Skill for the development of the respective organization now and in five years, how many employees currently have these skills and how many will be needed.

The Future Skills 2021 framework consists of 21 Future Skills in 4 skills dimensions: classic, transformative, digital, and technological (see Fig. 15.1). Classic skills refer to competencies which have been important in the past but increasingly so in the future across all domains of professional life such as creativity or Entrepreneurial Skills. Transformative skills refer to competencies needed to comprehend transformative challenges such as climate or demographic change, find innovative solutions and be able to convey them. Digital skills refer

15 Boosting Future Skills in Higher Education. Lessons Learned …

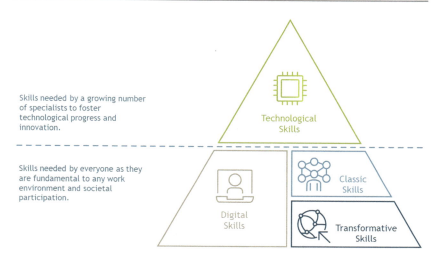

Skills needed by a growing number of specialists to foster technological progress and innovation.

Skills needed by everyone as they are fundamental to any work environment and societal participation.

Fig. 15.1 Illustration of the Future Skills 2021 framework containing 21 competencies across 4 skill dimensions: classic, transformative, digital, and technological

to the basic and more advanced digital competencies required at almost any workplace and key to participate in the digital world. Technological skills refer to specialist IT competencies such as data analytics & artificial intelligence needed for technological progress and innovations (see Table 15.1 for a selection of Future Skills 2021 relevant to the following funding programs).

15.2.2 Future Skills for Openness

The development of the Future Skills for Openness framework was based on the question, "which competencies do academics in science and business need to be able to operate successfully in a working world, characterized by open science and open innovation?". At the beginning, data answering this question were collected in structured discussions of a network of 11 academic experts in these fields from both scientific and commercial institutions. This was supplemented by a literature review of 26 key publications on Openness, open science, and open innovation. This data was then clustered in focus groups consisting of the Stifterverband and said experts, upon which several Future Skills were identified and compiled into a framework (see Hoffmann et al., 2021 for more details).

Table 15.1 Selection of Future Skills from the Future Skills 2021 framework relevant to the Stifterverband's programs: Entrepreneurial Skills (ES), Data Literacy Education (DLE) and Curriculum 4.0.nrw (C4)

Name	Description	Dimension	Program
Creativity	Developing of original ideas to improve processes such as in professional, communication or innovation contexts	Classic	ES
Entrepreneurial Skills	Self-initiated working and acting; high self-efficacy. Taking responsibility for outcomes and processes (ownership)	Classic	ES
Dialogue and Conflict Management	Overcoming disciplinary and functional silos; balancing tensions and solving dilemmas; acknowledging contradictory perspectives and dealing with ambiguities; engaging in open discussions and sharing one's opinion	Transformative	ES
Change Competencies	Developing and implementing strategies to obtain change. Understanding of dynamics between different groups, institutions, networks and systems. Acceptance for sustainable and cultural changes	Transformative	ES
Innovation Competencies	Generating innovation (products, services, processes, activities) in professional and private contexts which contribute to solving societal challenges and ensure independence (e.g., prevent cyber-attacks or changes to critical supply chains etc.). Challenging the status quo and implementing new ideas	Transformative	C4
Judgement Abilities	Reflecting on societal challenges (ecologic, social, economic goals, UN Sustainable Development Goals, circular economy, energy literacy); evaluating scientific findings and media reports	Transformative	DLE
Digital Learning	Evaluating digital information from various sources; accumulating knowledge for specific topics; use of educational software	Digital	C4
Digital Collaboration	Use of online channels to efficiently interact, collaborate and communicate with others independent of physical distance; appropriate etiquette in digital communication	Digital	C4

(continued)

Table 15.1 (continued)

Name	Description	Dimension	Program
Data Analytics & AI	Analysis and interpretation of large amounts of data (cf. Big Data) to make evidence-based decisions. This includes using Artificial Intelligence and Machine Learning	Technological	DLE

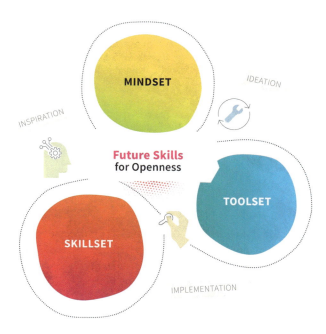

Fig. 15.2 Illustration of the Future Skills for Openness framework containing 20 competencies across 3 dimensions: tool set, skill set, and mindset

The Future Skills for Openness consist of 20 competencies in three dimensions: tool set, skill set, and mindset (see Fig. 15.2). Competencies in the tool set relate to open practice methods as well as (legal) knowledge needed for open science and open innovation, such as open-mass collaboration, open-technology in- and outsourcing, or the knowledge of collaboration tools and platforms. The skill set dimension consists of psycho-social and social-communicative competencies enabling the use of the above methods, such as the ability to communicate, con-

Table 15.2 Selection of Future Skills from Future Skills for Openness frameworks relevant to the Stifterverband's programs: Entrepreneurial Skills (ES), Data Literacy Education (DLE) and Curriculum 4.0.nrw (C4)

Name	Description	Dimension	Program
Data Literacy	Ability to critically collect, manage, evaluate, and use data based on a range of competencies from fields such as mathematics, statistics, or programming	Tool set	DLE
Openness to experience	Personality trait related to seeking new experiences, intellectual curiosity, and creativity	Mindset	ES
Social problem-solving skills & Resilience	Ability to initiate and moderate group processes leading to a clear cooperative advantage over individual performance. Ability to overcome unforeseen stressors (e.g., in heterogeneous interdisciplinary teams), and misfortunes flexibly and faster	Skill set	C4

flict-resolution skills and integration skills. Mindset competencies lay the foundation to establishing a culture of openness in which the above skills and tools can thrive; these include empathy, openness as a personality dimension, and tolerance for ambiguity (see Table 15.2 for a selection of Future Skills for Openness relevant to the following funding programs).

15.3 Entrepreneurial Skills

The first program to foster the development of Future Skills in higher education we would like to introduce here is called Entrepreneurial Skills. Entrepreneurship describes the ability to seize opportunities, develop ideas and turn them into added value for others. This added value can be financial, cultural, or social (European Union, 2018). Entrepreneurship Education encompasses a variety of Future Skills that promote entrepreneurial thinking and action such as Creativity, Entrepreneurial Skills, Dialogue and Conflict Management, Change Competencies and Openness to experience (Suessenbach et al., 2021).

15.3.1 Entrepreneurship as Action-Oriented Future Skills

Entrepreneurial Skills are cross-sectional and include the ability to perceive opportunities, creativity, visionary thinking, sustainability skills, the ability to mobilize resources, to motivate oneself and others, and economic competencies. In addition, Entrepreneurial Skills include leadership, judgment, problem-solving, and reflection skills, as well as the willingness to take risks, seek collaborations, and work in interdisciplinary teams and take entrepreneurial responsibility (Suessenbach et al., 2021). Entrepreneurial Skills are thus action-oriented and promote a hands-on mentality, self-initiative and experiencing self-efficacy. These are key competencies for solving current and future challenges and actively shaping a sustainable future under the influence of volatility, uncertainty, complexity, and ambiguity (VUCA). The development of Entrepreneurial Skills promotes an understanding of the future working and social environment and empowers people to recognize, develop and implement entrepreneurial opportunities offered in daily life, society, and the workplace (Mccallum et al., 2018).

15.3.2 The Entrepreneurial Skills Program

The "Entrepreneurial Skills" funding program is a collaboration program between Stifterverband, Dieter Schwarz Foundation, Campus Founders and Allianz SE. The aim is to anchor Entrepreneurial Skills as key Future Skills in the curricula of higher education institutions and offer students from all faculties and disciplines the opportunity to acquire key skills in the field of entrepreneurship during their studies. All 423 German public and private higher education institutions were invited to apply for the Entrepreneurial Skills program with a specific challenge they faced when implementing Entrepreneurial Skills teaching and learning concepts. Based on the challenges submitted by 69 higher education institutions, the 16 most interesting challenges were selected by a jury of experts and brought together in a network for the first funding phase. The call for proposals was deliberately kept open, on the one hand to provide a broad overview of the challenges faced by the higher education institutions, and on the other hand to allow the participating higher education institutions to formulate their challenges as individually as necessary. That's why this network was characterized by a broad range of challenges. During the first funding period, the 16 selected higher education institutions worked collaboratively for several months on their self-defined challenges and were supported through so-called curriculum workshops. The content of these curriculum workshops was prepared and conducted together with entrepreneurship experts. As a result, the higher education institutions developed peer-reviewed solutions. This collaboration has proven to be very productive and beneficial, as many higher education institutions face similar challenges. During the workshops, all 16 higher education institutions refined, revised, or developed their concepts and applied for the second funding phase, for which five received financial funding to implement their concepts.

15.3.3 The Entrepreneurial Skills Charter

Starting from the challenges identified by the more than 50 participants of the Entrepreneurial Skills program, and the solutions and approaches they developed on how Entrepreneurial Skills can be structurally integrated into universities as cross-sectional or Future Skills, the Stifterverband and Campus Founders initiated the Entrepreneurial Skills Charter.[1] With the support of numerous higher education institutions representatives from the Entrepreneurial Skills funding network and an additional co-creative process with a diverse group of other entrepreneurship education experts, eleven theses for the development of successful, sustainable entrepreneurship education were developed. They serve as a guideline to support teachers and administrations of higher education institutions in designing their entrepreneurship education formats and was published July 4th 2022. The Charter aims to contribute to making the relevance of Entrepreneurial Skills visible. In this way, the role of Entrepreneurial Skills can be strengthened in the higher education policy debate and at the same time, the Charter can provide orientation for higher education institutions to further develop their own entrepreneurship education programs.

In these eleven theses, the Entrepreneurial Skills Charter formulates how higher education institutions can successfully teach entrepreneurial thinking and action:

---

[1] The full charter can be accessed here: https://www.stifterverband.org/entrepreneurial-skills-charta.

1. Entrepreneurship Education encompasses a variety of competences relevant to the future
2. Entrepreneurship Education needs an impact-oriented and data-based scientific monitoring
3. Entrepreneurship Education is practical, evidence-based and uses holistic methods
4. Entrepreneurship Education is oriented towards the needs of the target group
5. Entrepreneurship Education must be further developed in a subject-specific manner
6. Entrepreneurship Education must be comprehensively anchored in the organizational structure
7. Entrepreneurship Education must be developed as an intersectional topic in relation to transfer, research, start-up services and the economy
8. Entrepreneurship Education needs a cultural change at higher education institutions
9. Entrepreneurship Education must be structurally anchored in the curriculum
10. Entrepreneurship Education is interdisciplinary and cooperative
11. Entrepreneurship Education signifies education for social responsibility, sustainability, and future viability

By the time of publication in January 2023, 62 higher education institutions have committed themselves as signatories to implementing the Charter and strengthening Entrepreneurship Education at their institutions. Other interested higher education institutions and organizations can decide to sign at any time and be added to the list of signatories. These theses can also give orientation for further developing educational profiles in higher education aimed at promoting Future Skills.

The signatory higher education institutions and organizations of the Entrepreneurial Skills Charter for successful Entrepreneurship Education will take measures to disseminate this understanding of entrepreneurship education and to integrate the associated competences structurally and in curricula. They call on other actors to do the same in their sphere of influence.

The next program we would like to present—Data Literacy Education—is in many ways similar to Entrepreneurial Skills in that it also concerns a narrow set of Future Skills and in that our work culminated in a Charter setting educational standards.

15.4 Data Literacy Education

"Data is the new oil!" This phrase—which exists in many different variations[2]—was perhaps the first global metaphor for the digital age (Spitz, 2017). Although the metaphor has since been criticized as data, unlike oil, can be used multiple times to extract valuable information (better: Data is the new soil; Voß, 2020), the metaphor still captures the increased relevance of data in a global society and the importance of enabling students to use data responsibly as a *"raw material of the twenty-first century"* (Merkel, 2018). Being able to evaluate and manage data critically—which can be subsumed under the Future Skill Data Literacy (see Table 15.2)—also acts as a catalyst to other Future Skills concerning the competencies to evaluate transformative challenges or to analyze complex data (see the skills Judgement Abilities and Data Analytics & AI in Table 15.1). Hence, Data Literacy ranks very high among the Future Skills.

Data Literacy is the ability to collect, manage, evaluate, and apply data in a critical manner (Ridsdale et al., 2015). It comprises the data competencies that are important for all people in a world shaped by digitalization (Schüller et al., 2021a, b). But Data Literacy "is often misunderstood as a set of technical skills, limited to data management and analysis and to the development and application of algorithms. However, data and AI literacy as a Future Skill of the twenty-first century serves to promote autonomy in a modern world shaped by data and its application as well as new technologies like AI and is therefore important for all people—not only for specialists" (Schüller et al., 2021b). In this sense, Data Literacy provides a fundamental understanding of the world of data which is essential to everyone to get along in our future world (Morrow, 2021).

Critically, Germany and most other countries have not yet established a comprehensive, uniform and framework-based data culture which recognizes the value of data and fully guarantees the security of data and data providers (Ebeling et al., 2021). Hence, the need for Data Literacy education permeates all sectors of society—private, public, political, social, and economic. Thus, Data Literacy plays a particularly prominent role in the Stifterverband's Future Skills Initiative addressing a multitude of stakeholders. One of the program's initiatives has been the Data Literacy Education network which—with the publication of a Data Lit-

---

[2] E.g.: "Data is the new oil. It's valuable entity, but if unrefined it cannot really be used" (Palmer, 2006); "Just like oil was a natural resource powering the last industrial revolution, data is going to be the natural resource of this industrial revolution" (Mugge et al., 2021); "The world's most valuable resource is no longer oil, but data" (The Economist, 2017).

eracy Charter—laid the groundwork to develop an initial uniform data literacy framework.

15.4.1 The Data Literacy Education Network

The Stifterverband's "Data Literacy Education" funding program wants to ensure that students across all universities and subjects acquire data literacy. As a first step, a data literacy education network was established. All members of the network worked on the question of how to integrate data literacy education into university teaching across all disciplines. In this network, representatives and experts from more than 25 German universities were working on the question of how data literacy can be integrated into the curriculum and how it can be implemented as broadly as possible in different learning settings. For this purpose, existing study programs were being revised and new learning opportunities created. Higher education institutions have been supporting each other in this network and benefitted from mutual exchanges.

Beyond tackling the curricular integration of Data Literacy, network members discussed other topics and challenges relevant to Future Skills education on a broader scale such as digital teaching methods, lecturer qualifications or data ethics. With the digital transformation of our world, new opportunities and requirements have emerged which pose new challenges such as the systematic reflection and negotiation of the values associated with data-related processes, technologies, and practices. A cross-university example of the network's work is the Data Literacy Charter.

15.4.2 The Data Literacy Charter

Developed in cooperation with numerous partners, the Stifterverband's Data Literacy Charter seeks to draw social and political attention to the topic of data literacy (Schüller et al., 2021b). The full charter can be accessed here: https://www.stifterverband.org/data-literacy-charter. Since its publication in January 2021, signatories of the charter have expressed their common understanding of data literacy in the sense of comprehensive data literacy and its overall importance in educational processes.

To gather support from as many institutions and people as possible, the charter needed to include as many different perspectives on this common theme as possible. This prerequisite for any charter was necessary to make sure future action and work would be based on a common understanding. Five guiding principles of Data Literacy Education emerged from this work which characterize the importance and role of data literacy as a key Future Skill. They create a common basic understanding and serve as a stimulus to jointly shape educational processes in a future-oriented way:

1. Data literacy must be accessible to all people.
2. Data literacy must be taught throughout life in all areas of education.
3. Data literacy must be taught as a transdisciplinary competence across all subjects from three perspectives (application-oriented, method-oriented, socio-culturally-oriented).
4. Data literacy must systematically cover the entire process of insight and decision-making with data.
5. Data literacy must include knowledge, skills, and values for a conscious and ethically sound handling of data.

Following the Data Literacy Charter, the Stifterverband is now committed to the development of an international "Standard for Data and Artificial Intelligence (AI) Literacy, Skills, and Readiness". Under the institutional umbrella of the IEEE Standards Association,[3] both international data literacy experts and German experts from the Stifterverband's data literacy network will take part in this work. The development of the Data Literacy Charter has provided many valuable lessons which may help others to implement and further data literacy education.

15.4.3 Lessons from Working in Data Literacy Networks

Decision-makers, particularly at universities, may not be aware of the importance of Future Skills like Data Literacy. This is because Future Skills address prospective needs some may struggle to grasp in the present. This work inevitably moves in a field that remains unpredictable despite all the forecasts on which there can be different justified opinions. Particularly when it comes to institutionally integrating Future Skills into higher education or including them in the curriculum, it is of great importance to have a convinced representative in the institution.

---

[3] The Institute of Electrical and Electronics Engineers Standards Association is an operating unit within the Institute of Electrical and Electronics Engineers (IEEE) that develops global standards in a broad range of industries.

Achieving this is by no means self-evident or trivial. Especially in higher education institutions, various topics compete for special consideration of the university management at the same time. A charter that articulates the will of education policy is highly promising for this purpose, especially if it has already been signed by many other universities and institutions and thus signals that a topic is currently of great importance for society and other universities.

Setting up Data Literacy education in an institution or organization can be supported through external incentives and networking. People interested in fostering Data Literacy may benefit from applying for external resources through funding programs such as the Stifterverband's Data Literacy Education to offset initiation costs. With the growing importance of data education, in general more funding opportunities will arise. In addition to financial support for individual projects, networking is equally important. The exchange of ideas leads to synergy effects that make the integration of Future Skills such as Data Literacy much more effective.

To support the cultural change towards a greater focus on data education in general and Data Literacy education in particular, proponents of Data Literacy must not only work on theoretical issues but also contribute to Data Literacy promotion in practice. This includes conferences, publications, and online communication, for example, via social media. These aim to create a social and political awareness for Future Skills and Data Literacy and set a nourishing and enabling environment for Future Skills education.

Somewhat different to Entrepreneurial Skills and Data Literacy Education, the next program we would like to introduce concerned a wider range of Future Skills and their integration on a larger scale.

15.5 The Curriculum 4.0.nrw Program: Learnings from Large-Scale Integration of (Digital) Future Skills into Curricula

The increasing digitisation of industries and work environments has led to a shift in the skill set higher education graduates need to acquire. These skills include highly specialised technical skills such as *Data Analytics and AI* or quantum technology but also a broad range of digital skills such as *Digital Literacy*, *Digital Learning* or *Digital Collaboration* that empower students to work in digital environments. Especially new forms of collaboration and individual responsibilities that evolve from working in interdisciplinary teams require an emphasis on skills such as *Social Problem Solving & Resiliency*. However, study programs are only rarely structured to teach these skills systematically. Hence, in its Curriculum 4.0.nrw Program, the Stifterverband in cooperation with the German state government of North Rhine-Westphalia supported universities in adjusting their curricula to the students' need for competencies in a digitized world.

For this, 39 projects have been funded with up to 300.000 € over up to three years during which people involved in the projects were also part of a supporting peer network. Projects involved reforming modules and study programs within existing frameworks to avoid potentially restrictive and time-consuming accreditation processes. Most of the projects focused on a first introduction of Digital Literacy, Digital Learning and Digital Collaboration into the curriculum which in most cases was combined with repositioning Classic skills as defined in the Future Skills 2021 framework (see Suessenbach et al., 2021). Generally, projects in the network covered a diverse range of subjects such as computer science, mathematics, sport science, material science, architecture, medicine, child pedagogy, teaching and many more. Structurally, the program was equally diverse as 22 projects reformed single modules within a study program and 16 projects addressed the whole degree. Twelve projects have been developed at universities of applied sciences and 27 at universities. However, despite these differences, the projects faced similar obstacles and supporting factors.

15.5.1 Eleven Clusters of Obstacles and Supporting Factors When Integrating Future Skills into Curricula

These obstacles and supporting factors were discussed during a poster session in September 2021, which was open to all project participants and anyone else who was interested. Thirty-seven of 39 programs contributed posters; 11 clusters were identified (see Table 15.3). Interestingly, the three largest clusters consisted of obstacles as well as supporting factors showing both their importance during the curricular development process as well as how certain aspects such as communication can be both strength and weakness depending on their functionality. This presents the opportunity to not only overcome obstacles, but to transform them into supporting factors. The following section will describe these three largest clusters in more detail and outline our learnings from them as well as provide brief insights into the other clusters.

The cluster *Communicate and Coordinate* reflected the interdisciplinary nature of many of the projects that sought to integrate Future Skills into their curricula. Consequently, academic personnel from two or more institutes or even faculties

15 Boosting Future Skills in Higher Education. Lessons Learned ...

Table 15.3 Number of obstacles and supporting factors in eleven clusters during the process of including Future Skills into the curricula in the Curriculum 4.0.nrw program

Cluster	Obstacles	Supporting factors
Communicate and Coordinate	21	13
Participation	7	9
Covid-19	11	4
Assessing and Accrediting	6	
Redesigning	8	
Heterogeneity	6	
Legal Aspects	6	
Structural Support		9
Cultural Support		8
Conceptual Clarity		6
Procedural Approach		4

needed to be coordinated. This posed an organisational challenge on the one hand while also implying the need to establish new networks of collaboration and even bridging professional cultures. However, as stated on the supporting side, interdisciplinary exchange, once facilitated, was an important success factor. To turn this obstacle into a supporting factor, including structural elements to facilitate interdisciplinary exchange such as working groups and project teams as well as enabling room for exchanges via teaching compensations was important. As coordination may not only be necessary internally but also with external partners such as schools or businesses, a variety of arrangements needed to be considered.

Closely linked to the above was the cluster *Participation* which was seen as an important supporting factor as the reforms seemed to depend on co-creation and individual commitment by lecturers. This, in turn, was seen to increase acceptance of the reforms and allow both, lecturers and students, to design the courses according to their specific interests and needs. However, facilitating participation could be challenging. Possible solutions involved addressing students' needs by offering a variety of open teaching formats, such as inverted classrooms, self-checks, and personally selected micro-modules, most of which may be offered online.

The effects of the *Covid-19* pandemic as a (hopefully) exceptional event shall be discussed only briefly. The pandemic delayed planning and developing in several instances and rendered some on-site teaching formats impossible. On the other hand, reforms that were geared toward digitising teaching benefited from the steep learning curve and increased acceptance of online formats.

The six obstacles in the cluster *Assessing and Accrediting* were mainly related to the development of suitable credit point assignment methods and the assessment of Future Skills such as Creativity. The two major obstacles in the *Redesigning* cluster were the difficulty in restructuring a study program and the negotiation process of what to keep and what to kick involved when only partially redesigning. *Heterogeneity* in students' and lecturers' knowledge of the subject matter was a challenge in interdisciplinary projects, especially in computer science and programming. *Legal aspects*, especially licensing and copyright, and data privacy concerns were obstacles in projects related to Open Educational Resources. *Structural support*, *Cultural support*, and *Conceptual Clarity* were all crucial in supporting curricular reforms, while continuous evaluation and an agile development approach was a key factor in the success of the Procedural Approach.

Work in the Curriculum 4.0.nrw program has shown many successful projects to integrate Future Skills into existing or new curricula. As we hope this integration will happen more and more often, these 11 clusters of obstacles and supporting factors should contribute to aid curricular developers by including Future Skills more easily in the future.

15.6 Concluding Remarks and Practical Recommendations

The demand for Future Skills increases in all domains of our lives. They are not only essential to ensure social participation and future employability but also to tackle transformative challenges and turn them into societal progress. Higher education institutions play a central role in teaching these skills. By sharing the rich experiences from funding programs and initiatives, Entrepreneurial Skills, Data Literacy Education, and Curriculum 4.0.nrw to foster Future Skills education, the Stifterverband hopes to aid others in their implementation of Future Skills education. We leave the reader with three practical recommendations from these programs.

Future Skills in Practice: Our Recommendations
Besides motivated individuals, successfully reforming study programs to incorporate Future Skills relies heavily on a rich and functioning ecosys-

tem within the organization. While this is true for most curricular reforms, due to increased agility and uncertainty inherent in Future Skills education, these supporting structures are even more important. Providing this may be easier for larger institutions. However, if considered in the early stages, members of smaller organizations may be able to outsource some support or calculate additional personnel.

To effectively impart Future Skills to all researchers, students and young academics, higher education institutions must structurally anchor and integrate Entrepreneurship Education as a cross-cutting topic in the curriculum. Thus, entrepreneurial thinking and action is not only relevant for founders, but is also needed by employees to successfully meet the present challenges of the economy and society.

In addition to the technical integration of Future Skills into the curricula, a cultural change is needed—a cultural change across higher education institutions making clear that: there are Future Skills relevant to students of all subjects! Therefore, we must take care of these Future Skills together as an institution. Thus, we recommend to actively promote this cultural change. Our Data Literacy Charter and the framework conditions outlined in this chapter have paved the way for this.

References

Boyatzis, R. E. (1982). *The competent manager: A model for effective performance.* J. Wiley.

Domanski, D., & Kaletka, C. (2017). *Exploring the research landscape of social innovation: A deliverable of the project social innovation community (SIC).* Dortmund.

Ebeling, J., Koch, H., & Roth-Grigori, A. (2021). *Kompetenzerwerb im kritischen Umgang mit Daten.*

Ehlers, U.-D. (2020). *Future skills: The future of learning and higher education..*

Erpenbeck, J., & Heyse, V. (1999). *Die Kompetenzbiographie: Strategien der Kompetenzentwicklung durch selbstorganisiertes Lernen und multimediale Kommunikation.* Waxmann.

European Union (2018). *The Entrepreneurship Competence Framework.* Luxembourg. https://ec.europa.eu/social/main.jsp?catId=738&langId=en&pubId=8201&furtherPubs=yes.

Hoffmann, W., Grill, C., Remmert-Rieper, M., Bänfer, A., Mohr, V., & Höring, F. (2021). *Future Skills for Openness: Ein Framework zur Förderung von Offenheit in Wissenschaft und Wirtschaft.* https://innosci.de/wp-content/uploads/innOsci_Studie_Framework.pdf.

Kirchherr, J., Klier, J., Lehmann-Brauns, C., & Winde, M. (2018). *Future Skills: Welche Kompetenzen in Deutschland fehlen* (Future Skills—Diskussionspapier 1). https://www.future-skills.net/download/file/fid/118.

Mccallum, E., Weicht, R., Mcmullan, L., & Price, A. (2018). *EntreComp into action: get inspired, make it happen: A user guide to the European Entrepreneurship Competence Framework*. Luxembourg.

Merkel, A. (2018). *Speech by Federal Chancellor Angela Merkel at the World Economic Forum Annual Meeting in Davos on 24 January 2018*, 2018.

Morrow, J. (2021). *Be data literate: The data literacy skills everyone needs to succeed*. Kogan Page.

Mugge, P. C., Abbu, H., Gudergan, G., & Kane, G. C. (2021). *TRUST: The winning formula for digital leaders: A practical guide for companies engaged in digital transformation*. Patterns of Digitization Lab.

OECD (2023). *OECD Future of Education and Skills 2030*. https://www.oecd.org/education/2030-project/. Accessed 4. March 2023.

Palmer, M. (2006). *Data is the New Oil*. https://ana.blogs.com/maestros/2006/11/data_is_the_new.html. Accessed 4. March 2023.

Ridsdale, C., Rothwell, J., Smit, M., Bliemel, M., Irvine, D., Kelley, D., et al. (2015). *Strategies and Best Practices for Data Literacy Education: Knowledge Synthesis Report*.

Schüller, K., Deiner, H., & Koch, H. (2021). *Project Authorization Request for a IEEE Standard for Data and Artificial Intelligence (AI) Literacy, Skills, and Readiness*.

Schüller, K., Koch, H., & Rampelt, F. (2021). *Data Literacy Charter*. https://www.stifterverband.org/data-literacy-charter.

Seidl, T., Baumgartner, P., Brei, C., Lohse, A., Kuhn, S., Michel, A., et al. (2018). *(Wert-)Haltung als wichtiger Bestandteil der Entwicklung von 21st Century Skills an Hochschulen (AG Curriculum 4.0)* (Diskussionspapier 3). https://hochschulforum-digitalisierung.de/de/diskussionspapier-3-wert-haltung-als-wichtiger-bestandteil-der-entwicklung-von-21st-century-skills.

Spitz, M. (2017). *Daten* (1st ed.). Hoffmann und Campe.

Suessenbach, F., Winde, M., Klier, J., & Kirchherr, J. (2021). *Future Skills 2021: 21 Kompetenzen für eine Welt im Wandel* (Future Skills—Diskussionspapier 3). https://www.stifterverband.org/medien/future-skills-2021.

The Economist. (2017). *The world's most valuable resource is no longer oil, but data*. https://www.economist.com/leaders/2017/05/06/the-worlds-most-valuable-resource-is-no-longer-oil-but-data. Accessed 4. March 2023.

United Nations. (2015). *Resolution adopted by the General Assembly on 25 September 2015. Transforming our world: the 2030 Agenda for Sustainable Development*.

United Nations. (2023). *Multi-stakeholder partnerships and voluntary commitments*. https://sdgs.un.org/topics/multi-stakeholder-partnerships-and-voluntary-commitments. Accessed 4. March 2023.

Voß, O. (2020, November 3). Berliner KI-Forscher Markl: „Daten sind nicht das neue Öl". *Der Tagesspiegel*. https://www.tagesspiegel.de/wirtschaft/daten-sind-nicht-das-neue-ol-5380717.html.

Weinert, F. E. (2001a). Leistungsmessungen in Schulen. In F. E. Weinert (Ed.), *Leistungsmessungen in Schulen* (pp. 17–31). Beltz.

World Economic Forum. (2021). *Building a Common Language for Skills at Work: A Global Taxonomy*. https://www3.weforum.org/docs/WEF_Skills_Taxonomy_2021.pdf.

Dr. Felix Suessenbach graduated from the University of Edinburgh, UK, in 2017 with a PhD in Psychology. After this he was employed as a post-doc at the University of Munich, Germany, at the chair of Personality & Educational Psychology conducting research in personality and motivational psychology. Since 2021, he has been working as a researcher at Stifterverband—a nonprofit organization seeking to further science, education, and innovation in Germany—with a focus on Future Skills, Computer Science in schools, and equity in education. ORCID ID: 0000-0002-5479-6898

Judith Koeritz graduated with a Master of Arts in Political Economy of European Integration from the Berlin School of Economics and Law in 2021. She has been working at the Stifterverband since 2020. She began as a working student and has been the program manager of the programs Entrepreneurial Skills and Learning Architectures since November 2021.

Andreas Wormland studied History, English, and Social Sciences at Ruhr University Bochum. Since 2019, he has been working at Stifterverband focusing on the implementation of Future Skills in university curricula. Lately, he has been putting emphasis on exploring new ways to integrate quantum technologies into teacher education. He was also responsible for several communication activities directed at raising the reputation of education engagement.

Dr. Henning Koch graduated from the University of Bremen with a PhD in Educational Sciences. Before joining the Stifterverband, he gained work experience in the field of university didactics and as a personal advisor to a university president for studies and teaching. At the Stifterverband, he is working on Future Skills and their integration into different educational processes. An important focus of his work is data literacy and the question of how to establish data literacy education for students of all subjects.

Open Access This chapter is licensed under the terms of the Creative Commons Attribution 4.0 International License (http://creativecommons.org/licenses/by/4.0/), which permits use, sharing, adaptation, distribution and reproduction in any medium or format, as long as you give appropriate credit to the original author(s) and the source, provide a link to the Creative Commons license and indicate if changes were made.

The images or other third party material in this chapter are included in the chapter's Creative Commons license, unless indicated otherwise in a credit line to the material. If material is not included in the chapter's Creative Commons license and your intended use is not permitted by statutory regulation or exceeds the permitted use, you will need to obtain permission directly from the copyright holder.

May the Code Be with You: The 42 Learning Model in Germany

16

A Future Skills Conversation with Max Senges

Ulf-Daniel Ehlers and Laura Eigbrecht

> **Abstract**
>
> 42 is a series of software engineering schools in Wolfsburg, Heilbronn, and Berlin that offer humanistic and tech education for 1,800 students. Here, they learn Future Skills for a self-determined life in the digital age—without professors, schedules or grades. For the Global Future Skills initiative, we were able to talk to Dr. Max Senges (Fig. 16.1), director of 42 Wolfsburg/Berlin, about their pedagogy and approach to Future Skills.

Ulf-Daniel Ehlers: 42 proposes an exciting take on peer-learning for software engineering. Could you shortly summarize your future learning approach?

Max Senges: The 42 learning environments are composed of peer learning, gamification, and project-based software development challenges. Also, we want to go beyond coding: we offer an egalitarian form of Future Skills acquisition, aimed at enabling students to master fundamental digital and critical social competencies. 42 is a progressive educational approach that promotes collaborative learning, ini-

---

U.-D. Ehlers
Professor for Educational Management and Lifelong Learning, Business Faculty,
DHBW Karlsruhe, Karlsruhe, Germany
e-mail: ulf-daniel.ehlers@dhbw-karlsruhe.de

L. Eigbrecht (✉)
Educational Management and Lifelong Learning, Business Faculty, DHBW Karlsruhe,
Karlsruhe, Germany
e-mail: laura.eigbrecht@dhbw-karlsruhe.de

© The Author(s) 2024
U.-D. Ehlers and L. Eigbrecht (eds.), *Creating the University of the Future*, Zukunft der Hochschulbildung - Future Higher Education,
https://doi.org/10.1007/978-3-658-42948-5_16

Fig. 16.1 Max Senges

tiates critical-creative thinking, and relies on playful elements. We think that it is an approach which can be useful beyond software engineering education.

Today, 42 forms the largest network of software engineering schools in the world, with more than 40 coding schools of this kind in 25 countries worldwide and more than 13,000 students. In Germany alone, more than ten thousand applicants have registered on the school platform since 2021. Three cities offer the 42 coding school model in Germany: Wolfsburg, Heilbronn and Berlin, each one with a capacity of 600 students thus fueling a talent pipeline of about 1,800 software engineers per year.

Ehlers: This is pretty impressive indeed. Why the need to rethink coding education in this very different way?

Senges: Our different model allows us to support students whose learning needs don't fit in traditional academia. But it's not a primary objective, we are not—only—a second chance school. We are a school with a different approach that allows students who are different to find an interesting learning context—but more "regular" students can definitely come and succeed. And being unsuccessful

16 May the Code Be with You: The 42 Learning Model in Germany

in more 'classic' education does not mean being successful in 42. That means a new approach to access—but, maybe even more important, to learning.

It all started in France, in 2013. Then, the founder of the first 42 coding school, the French entrepreneur Xavier Niel, wanted to establish a new form of IT education, independent of universities and their interests. He was interested in a democratic form of education, accessible for everyone—including those who cannot afford expensive French private schools and those who cannot cope with the classic educational paths. It is following his vision that 42 coding schools with their unique pedagogy and curriculum have emerged.

Laura Eigbrecht: So why is coding the field that 42 schools have focused on?

Senges: The original trigger was the increasing shortage of skilled labor in this field in Europe. Across the continent, there is a shortage of engineers, software developers and IT experts. In Germany alone, at least 96,000 IT experts are needed, and significantly more in the coming years. In times of digital transformation, the shortage of IT specialists is becoming a real locational disadvantage. According to a study by industry association BITKOM, two out of three companies surveyed expect the staff shortage to worsen in the coming years.

There are different approaches to how this gap can be closed. Immigration is seen by many as an opportunity. In Germany, the current government is working on a new migration policy. One way to allow highly skilled workers from non-EU countries to live and work in the EU is the "Blue Card". This new admission system, which also facilitates family reunification, is intended to attract skilled workers. German Federal Minister for Economic Affairs and Climate Action Robert Habeck (Die Grünen/Green Party) wants to, as he puts it, "ease immigration requirements" so that qualified IT specialists can come to Germany.

In addition to immigration, however, there is an opportunity to break down educational barriers, and enable people to get technical training more quickly than via the pathway of traditional academia. 42 can give access to coding skills to people who otherwise would not be able to qualify for advanced studies in a university.

Eigbrecht: You say that learning how to code is one focus in 42 schools, Future Skills are another one. Can you elaborate on how this is actually done?

Senges: Future Skills are something we would like all our students to be equipped with. We think that these will help them professionally and personally to shape their life trajectory as well as our digital future, and we would like to highlight three dimensions that are particularly expressed at 42 in Germany here. Of course, literacy in coding and IT sets the foundation to ensure 42 learners feel empowered by technology rather than overwhelmed by it. Secondly, in their celebration of diversity and English as lingua franca, the schools promote planetary thinking—the realization that we all share a responsibility for our planetary spaceship and the need to collaborate across cultures, disciplines and beliefs. Lastly, a third Future Skill dimension facilitated at 42 in Germany is life entrepreneurship. Independent of students' professional interests and passions, the affordances of the 42 learning ecosystem require learners to identify, assess and pursue learning opportunities that are in line with their lives' ventures.

Very importantly, we don't scan diplomas or CVs at 42. We do not think in terms of deficits, we don't want to look at what our students are *not* capable of—we think in terms of opportunities, and we encourage our students to do so. From this point of view, educational institutions should be a place of opportunities, a place of inspiration, of creativity—and a place where people realize what they are capable of. And we think that this learning model at 42 really supports our students' Future Skills learning.

Ehlers: IT and coding literacy, planetary thinking and life entrepreneurship—these are very interesting and promising Future Skills you propose here. Can you elaborate how you use gamification, which you mentioned before, for promoting them?

Senges: It plays a very important role. Altogether, our learning model is software-based, project-focused and features peer-to-peer learning. For the whole experience, students are provided with a learning environment which looks a little bit like a mix between an online banking account and a fitness app. Students can see their active and future projects, get an overview of their time investments, of campus events and deadlines. They use this software to organize their project work. When they select a project, they receive a project description which outlines the goals, requirements and sometimes constraints of the project. Students then independently solve coding problems that are part of the projects, seek help from search engines or their peers.

Concerning problems, we follow a certain rule set: if you are stuck with a problem, ask Google. If you are still stuck, ask a fellow student. Throughout their studies, students determine their own learning paths and specializations. There are no teachers, schedules or books. At the end of each project, students submit the result of their work: functioning code. If they succeed, they advance to a new level, and new projects are proposed—or 'unlocked', in gamification jargon.

Ehlers: And why is gamification such a promising approach for Future Skills learning?

Senges: We observed that at regular universities, professors spend a significant amount of time to motivate their students, correct exams, and deliver the same lectures over and over again in the Prussian tradition of frontal teaching. Formalized, top-down bureaucracy leaves little time for real educational work, little time to help people learn better. What we try at 42 is to provide playful, self-organized, cooperative learning spaces where studying happens in a community and also in self-selected teams, virtually or face-to-face. At the German offshoots of 42, we select students who have the intrinsic motivation they need to become competent and skilled programmers. With this energy, students are able to build their own learning networks and have an experience that is rare in other schools: solving problems together in a group by sharing skills and perspectives. Here, it's always about project-based, hands-on problem solving. You can test yourself, challenge yourself, push yourself—and do it when you want to, not when a professor wants you to. In many cases, students learn only what they need to get through the current project. If they are particularly interested in a topic or an application area, they end up specializing with appropriate depth. We call it the "go as deep as you want" approach.

This is where gamification comes in: Gerald Hüther says, "The brain is not optimized for memorizing facts, but for solving problems". A gamified, self-determined educational setting takes away the learners' fear. Gamification in education means not only transparency, clear and fair rules and quantification, but above all motivation by visualizing learning progress by game elements such as "challenges" and "levels". "Rankings" as measures of success can provide additional motivation for learners, and cooperative games increase the collaboration effect by making participants experience how to play and learn better and more efficiently in a peer community.

Eigbrecht: So this peer-learning aspect seems to be central in your learning model. We often tend to conceptualize skills acquisition in a kind of individualistic perspective. What are the benefits of focusing on peer support and peer learning instead?

Senges: We use elements of peer learning in various programmatic components of the 42 learning ecosystem. For example, when a project is completed, the student submits it and can then spend evaluation points to receive an assessment as well as constructive feedback. To earn points, the student will offer to evaluate others. Also, some of the projects in the curriculum can only be solved as a team.

Peer learning means to be able to meet with others—in order to tackle coding challenges, to take a walk, to hang out, or to brainstorm. How and when students do that is up to them. The schools in Wolfsburg, Heilbronn and Berlin are open 24/7—and students who get stuck with a problem can turn to other students for help. There are no professors or teachers at the schools, but there is a dynamic local and world-wide knowledge network as a precious resource. So, peer learning is more than an element of our learning model—it is really central for our student selection process and our 42 culture. Students also offer talks and knowledge sharing sessions to pass on and consolidate their newly acquired competences and their knowledge.

In the course of studying at 42, students have to solve increasingly bigger and more complex coding projects. These are designed for learning flow and continuously optimized by using learner data. When a project is finished, it is submitted to two fellow students who review the coding solution and provide feedback. Only if students can explain their coding solutions to others, they truly understand what they have done—you have really learnt something if you can pass it on to others.

In order to validate the knowledge and skills acquired, students take exams at certain milestones in the course of their studies where they have to solve programming challenges in the areas of their recent study focus without internet or peer support.

Two sum up, the whole model is student-centered—both in terms of content and equipment. To support this, all schools have state-of-the-art digital work stations and equipment such as whiteboards, micro-kitchens or gaming areas which promote collaborative learning, informal knowledge-sharing as well as identity- and community-building.

But all this doesn't just run by itself—in order for peer learning to really work in a complex subject matter such as software engineering, you need a critical mass of students. We have observed that it takes approximately 150 students for peer-learning to really work; so that you can always find someone who knows or who is lucky enough to find a clue through trial and error.

Ehlers: It is really fascinating to have peer learning and collaboration as a foundation of an organizational learning culture. So, as I understand it, you really have to have students who are committed to this approach. So how do you find these students who are also willing to contribute to their fellow students' personal development?

Senges: Yes, it really is a central and important aspect here at 42—starting with the admission process which I would like to describe. Our coding schools are meritocratic in their selection of students: everyone over 18 can take the admission test. For this direct access to become an IT professional, students do not need high school diplomas or any other school certificates, and they neither need any prior coding experience. Applications from all nationalities are accepted and the program is offered entirely in English.

Students are selected after completing a four-week bootcamp called "Piscine"—which is French for swimming pool—during which the learners "dive" into the world of programming, and explore if software engineering and peer-learning are suitable for them. As said, the Piscine requires no prior knowledge, no degrees, no programming experience, but it comes with an intense workload in which all applicants experience the limits of their learning capacities—participants usually report that the Piscine has been a very profound learning experience for them. On average, 150 "Pisciners" start a bootcamp, from which about 50 students are selected to start in a cohort.

Eigbrecht: It really sounds like an immersive and intense experience. How do you ensure to also connect learning to the real or more professional world?

Senges: Well, that's where our focus on Future Skills comes in. For example, the social skills to give and receive feedback, to know when to ask, and to assess one's strengths and shortcomings all help to work in a professional setting. After 12 to 18 months at 42, depending on the individual pace of the student, the program requires learners to engage in 4 to 6 months of practical experience, either in an internship or in a startup-like project. Two-thirds of 42's graduates receive a job offer after their first internship. In addition, a number of exceptional entrepreneurs can be found among the thousands of graduates of 42 schools.

In Wolfsburg, students also have the opportunity to work in a so-called FabLab on questions and challenges relating to self-fabricated hardware and to mobility. The school is also developing a one-and-a-half-year specialization in Software Engineering Automotive & Mobility Ecosystem called SEA:ME. This program is developed in collaboration with around forty fellows—experts from academia and industry—as an Open Educational Resource. Once tested and successfully rolled out in Wolfsburg and Berlin, it will be offered as an addition to the existing curriculum after the undergraduate studies. At SEA:ME, students will learn about software development for the automotive and mobility sectors through hands-on projects divided into three modules. In the first module, challenges around sensors and actuators in embedded systems are covered by programming a model digital electric vehicle, a PiRacer. In the second module, participants learn to set up and administer machine learning systems for autonomous driving. In the last module, participants solve ecosystem projects that deal with interoperability and coordination between vehicles as well as with traffic signals and other roadside units like charging stations.

Ehlers: It seems like this is the kind of out-of-the-box thinking that promotes reflection and thus Future Skills learning. I would like to learn more about where your learning approach is rooted, theory-wise. What are your assumptions about how students learn that you build your didactic model on?

Senges: That's a very important question. This is how we think about learning: we come into the world as learners. We want to try things out, we want to develop our talents, we want to offer value to society. Learning is deeply rooted in every complex living organism. Monkeys, for example, learn in groups. Monkeys are copycats. Behavioral researchers such as Frans de Waal (2016) have been able to prove that apes always pass on what they have learned to their descendants and thus develop their own traditions in their respective groups. In an experiment that De Waal conducted, chimpanzees observed how to open a box, which contained fruit. Later, they showed it to others, who acquired the same ability. He proved that monkeys can acquire skills which they did not develop themselves. In another experiment, De Waal showed how monkeys also understand whether other monkeys are motivated by egoistic or altruistic behavior. When it comes to sharing, monkeys seem to have a clear sense for what is fair and what is not. And we think that peer learning works on a similar principle: here, the person who is able to pass on knowledge empowers others to make progress. At 42, this communal learning spirit replaces professors, books and schedules.

> At 42, this communal learning spirit replaces professors, books and schedules.

And we also consider learning a superpower. We learn to walk, we learn to speak, we learn to read and write. Others help us, but there are different views about what this help should look like. One of our role models here is Maria Montessori, the Italian reform pedagogue who developed her method at the beginning of the twentieth century to support children and young people in their learning journey. Montessori believed that everyone has their own rhythm, that everyone should be encouraged to be curious and independent. "Help me do it myself" is still the motto of Montessori education today. The pedagogy trusts in the strength and the cognitive abilities of each learner, it takes learners seriously and trusts them. The teachers are supportive in this concept and encourage the child, not entirely without rules, but without a restrictive teaching corset. In Montessori's eyes, the child is its own master. It is crucial that the students are able to participate in work that "moves" them, in which they are asked to be creators and not just reproducers. At 42 in Germany, we are guided by the Montessori philosophy and support our students in diving deeper into the parts of the curriculum that are interesting to them.

16 May the Code Be with You: The 42 Learning Model in Germany 343

Ehlers: Very interesting! To me, it seems like we rarely hear of Montessori and higher education pedagogy thought together, but it results in some very interesting questions and ideas. Is there any other inspiration for your teaching and learning model?

Senges: Another pedagogical role model is Mitch Resnick, currently professor of educational research at the MIT Media Lab in Boston. For decades, Mitch has been addressing the question of what learning needs to look like in the twenty-first century—and he cites four key points: Passion, Play, Peers and Projects. It is in free play that we discover the world—and that is why, for Resnick, it is and remains the strongest form of learning (Resnick & Robinson, 2017). Play helps us explore, understand and reimagine the world, in other words, to be creative. So we shouldn't stop playing, because it's in play that people grasp their possibilities, recognize their abilities, to know themselves. And education should always be about discovering one's horizons and thus options and possibilities.

Mitch says that it's depressing how many millions of young learners are still pigeonholed as "non-creative" at a ridiculously early age—but creative thinking is elemental to technological change. According to Resnick, creativity is a social process in which people cooperate, share, and build their work on the work of others. Accordingly, creativity is often the result of interaction with peers. Play and playful experimentation encourage people to take risks, to try things out. However, we feel that in conventional education, the message is: "Stop playing." We and the whole community of serious game designers disagree: we need more playrooms than classrooms. In play, people build their own understanding of the world because it excites them. And for that, they need spaces, real and imagined.

Eigbrecht: I do like this approach to creativity very much as it is a very different perspective than the one often advocated where you are born creative or not. This perspective empowers learners: looking at today's and tomorrow's challenges, we kind of need everyone to be creative!

Senges: Exactly—this is also why we promote it at our schools. At first glance, 42 is about learning programming skills, about coding, but it's about more than that. The development of character or, in contemporary English, mindset, is just as crucial for each individual as it is for their employers. And to have people have a digital-literate mindset is fundamental to successful digitization and competitiveness.

Allow us to elaborate: 42 in Germany is designed as a humanistic educational institution. In our view, education also means character building, embracing a canon of values like sustainability or an egalitarian view of humanity. At our coding schools the motto is: show us your dedication to learn and your willingness to openly share and learn with your peers. Your previous certificates, your diplomas, your career path are not relevant as they do not provide information about your current motivation and ability to learn—we give you a chance.

More explicitly, the 42 Network has set the goal to have 30% students who would otherwise not fulfill the requirements to access higher education.

Eigbrecht: It seems like we often disconnect this more humanistic vision from technology which we might perceive as cold, inhumane even. How can we think about humans and technology together?

Senges: Well, let's think about the internet: it has been a paradigm-shifting innovation for society and education. We believe that we are still in the beginning of embracing this new technology, and that the net will make new forms of learning common place—indeed it is the origin, incubator, and platform of planetary peer learning. It is humanity's biggest knowledge resource and the dynamics of virtual, location-independent co-creation and collaboration are still unfolding. In the best scenario, the internet is the homestead of a cosmopolitan open society, of meritocracy, a place where everybody can share and access all information at one's fingertips (Rheingold, 2012).

In Germany, "education for all" has been a guiding principle of education policy for many decades. It dates back to a time when social advancement was established to be dependent on education—but today, education can no longer guarantee socio-economic advancement, and many professions and traditional vocational education preparing for them are becoming quickly outdated. It thus becomes even more important to awaken the desire—the intrinsic motivation—to learn and to continue learning.

Ehlers: So why is it coding that your students should focus on learning?

Senges: At 42, we sometimes say that the programming language "C" is the Latin of digitization—coding C is as useful for a contemporary cosmopolitan life now as speaking Latin has been for centuries. C is a low-level, imperative programming language. It is closer to machine processes than object-oriented programming like Python or Java, and hence allows a deeper understanding of how computers work and organize their work stacks.

Building coding skills from the ground up helps to comprehend the algorithmic foundations of our digital life and our daily interactions with machines.

16 May the Code Be with You: The 42 Learning Model in Germany

Above all, programming stands for trying out ideas, which is the foundation of the scientific method as well as for creative thinking. Building repeatable processes through code is also closely related to an entrepreneurial mindset, and to pursuing innovative ventures. We truly believe that today, by solving big problems with software, coders can change the world.

> "We truly believe that today, by solving big problems with software, coders can change the world."

Ehlers: You, as educational institutions, thus provide a certain framework for students to learn to, as you just put it, change the world, and to learn Future Skills. Would you say that this should be the responsibility of all educational institutions?

Senges: I would say that the fundamental task of educational institutions today is to enable their students to learn to learn. The quest of education from kindergarten to higher education is to allow students to acquire and use knowledge, and to pursue self-formulated learning goals. Consider the cognitive learning goal taxonomy of the US-American psychologist Benjamin Bloom (see Fig. 16.2) as an orientation framework here—the more advanced and self-reflected learners are about their understanding and competence in a given field, the better our pedagogical approach at 42 Germany works for them. At the higher education level, the goals also include interdisciplinary competencies or Future Skills such as critical thinking, ethical behavior, or the ability to work in a team. Education for

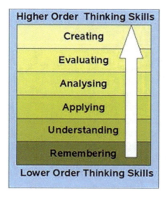

Fig. 16.2 Bloom's taxonomy (Xristina Ia, 2012)

"Weltanschauung" or "Bildung"[1] have always been more comprehensive than just subject-specific vocational training, and we at 42 in Germany embrace that challenge with our pedagogy.

To sum up, firstly, education should always offer a way to develop one's personality and character. Another important task for today's education is learning how to work together with other people, including an increased need to collaborate with diverse backgrounds and identities. We welcome a generation that is more aware of discrimination and unconscious biases. In the case of 42 in Germany, highly diverse communities that consist of different cultures and age groups learn together. For example, our communities span from 18-year-olds to professional veterans in their late fifties. This requires various strategies to promote effective and wide-spread inclusion. And last but not least, 42 Germany promotes the idea of planetary thinking. This concept entails a focus on sustainable living and development, as well as a new way to connect with other people—not through ways of binary thinking and stereotypes, but through sharing perspectives and offering allyship.

Eigbrecht: Your approach is indeed very student- and learning-centered. Could you shortly sum up the 42 learning model and your Future Skills approach?

Senges: In order to describe our overall approach to learning, let's have a look at today's and tomorrow's challenges. In today's globalized, multi-media, hypercomplex world, it is evident that no one's education is ever conclusive, and that there is no shortcut to learning through experience, as Confucius had already pointed out (see Fig. 16.3).

---

[1] "Weltanschauung" could be translated by *world view* or also *philosophy of life*. *Bildung* is a complex concept and has deep roots in European thinking and education. In the classical era, the Greek called it *Paideia*, and in the 1600s, protestant Pietists explored it as personal religious, spiritual and moral growth in the image (German: *Bild*) of Christ. From 1774 to around 1810, thinkers like Herder, Schiller, and von Humboldt explored *Bildung* as a secular phenomenon, relating it to emotional, moral, and intellectual development, to enculturation and education, and one's role as a citizen. An exemplary description could be: *Bildung* is the combination of the education and knowledge necessary to thrive in a society, and the moral and emotional maturity to live together in peace and gain personal autonomy. *Bildung* in a more structured view is the development of yourself, of the relation between yourself and an object (e.g. mathematics) and the relation between yourself and the world (Ehlers, 2020).

Tell Me and I Forget; Show Me and I May Remember; Involve Me and I Will Understand. - Confucius

Fig. 16.3 Confucius (work by Kanō Sansetsu, AMorozov, 2021)

Especially for Future Skills learning, it is important to offer a model to students that works in the long run—meaning throughout one's life. At 42 in Germany, students acquire skills not just to be prepared to solve big projects later in their career, but by learning meta-skills for problem-solving as such, and skills like goal-setting and planning. In a fast-paced socio-technological world where all knowledge is outdated within a few years, they are able to adapt and grow—and to empower their peers and problem-solve as a community.

Ehlers: And would it be possible to adapt this learning approach to other subject areas than coding?

Senges: Yes, we think that it is totally possible that peer learning environments and curricula can be developed for other Future Skills-relevant areas, such as design, business and entrepreneurship. In order to do this, we need to promote students to develop their own learning strategies, and build peer-learning capacity through exchange and cooperation with others. Then the educators' job is to "only" provide suitable thematic project work and learning environments that allow students to discover and develop their own talents and interests.

We also need to understand that the learning engine of any school are the students—and this goes hand in hand with a paradigm shift from teaching to learning. At 42, we hope to impact Future Skills learning far beyond our software engineering schools and promote open peer learning spaces with educators, experts and learners from everywhere.

References

AMorozov. (2021). Great Confucian Figures – Painting of Kongzi by Kanō Sansetsu. Wikimedia. https://commons.wikimedia.org/wiki/File:Great_Confucian_Figures_-_Painting_of_Kongzi_by_Kan%C5%8D_Sansetsu.jpg.

Resnick, M., & Robinson, K. (2017). *Lifelong Kindergarten: Cultivating creativity through projects, passion, peers, and play*. The MIT Press.

Rheingold, H. (2012). *Net smart: How to thrive online* (1st ed.). MIT Press; IEEE Xplore.

Waal, F. de. (2016). *Are We Smart Enough to Know How Smart Animals Are?*. W. W. Norton & Company.

Xristina Ia. (2012). Bloom's Taxonomy. Wikimedia. https://commons.wikimedia.org/wiki/File:Bloom%27s_Taxonomy.png.

Prof. Dr. phil. habil. Ulf-Daniel Ehlers is an internationally renowned Professor for Educational Management and Lifelong Learning at the Baden-Wuerttemberg Cooperative State University (DHBW) Karlsruhe which he headed as Vice-President between 2011 and 2017.

Laura Eigbrecht is principle investigator, teacher and doctoral student at the Baden-Wuerttemberg Cooperative State University (DHBW) Karlsruhe and holds degrees in European Media and Culture and Media Pedagogy.

Open Access This chapter is licensed under the terms of the Creative Commons Attribution 4.0 International License (http://creativecommons.org/licenses/by/4.0/), which permits use, sharing, adaptation, distribution and reproduction in any medium or format, as long as you give appropriate credit to the original author(s) and the source, provide a link to the Creative Commons license and indicate if changes were made.

The images or other third party material in this chapter are included in the chapter's Creative Commons license, unless indicated otherwise in a credit line to the material. If material is not included in the chapter's Creative Commons license and your intended use is not permitted by statutory regulation or exceeds the permitted use, you will need to obtain permission directly from the copyright holder.

Interdisciplinary Project to Build Teaching Skills: A Pedagogical Approach

17

Mônica Cristina Garbin and Edison Trombeta de Oliveira

Abstract

The concept of "competence" includes the knowledge to be acquired, skills and attitudes. It is not enough for the professional to have a lot of knowledge, but it is necessary that he knows how to mobilize his knowledge in solving problems or in creating something innovative. The Interdisciplinary Project (IP) developed by higher education students at Virtual University of São Paulo State—Univesp (Brazil) is guided by Project-Based Learning (PBL) and Human-Centered Design (HCD), in which the pedagogical action is based on the principle of the inseparability of the relationship between theory and practice. In this scenario, students develop at least six essential skills such as: Investigation; Problem Solving; Collaboration; Communication; Professional; and Technological Practice. The aim of this chapter is to correlate the skills proposed in the teacher's education at Univesp with the Future Skills proposed by Ehlers (2020). As a result, we assess that Univesp is a leader in this area and can train teachers with skills for a better education in the future.

M. C. Garbin (✉)
Professor in the area Methodology and Distance Education, Virtual University of the State of São Paulo, São Paulo, Brazil
e-mail: monica.garbin@gmail.com

E. T. de Oliveira
Adjunct Professor I, University of Sorocaba, Sorocaba, Brazil

© The Author(s) 2024
U.-D. Ehlers and L. Eigbrecht (eds.), *Creating the University of the Future*, Zukunft der Hochschulbildung - Future Higher Education,
https://doi.org/10.1007/978-3-658-42948-5_17

17.1 Introduction

The concept of "competence" is broader and includes the knowledge to be acquired, but it also includes skills and attitudes. It is not enough for a professional to have a lot of knowledge. It is necessary to know how to mobilize the knowledge in solving problems or in creating something innovative. It is the ability to mobilize knowledge, values, and decisions to act relevant in a given situation.

The UNESCO Delors Report—also known as "The Four Pillars of twenty-first Century Education"—is a cornerstone when we think about learning and skills needed in the contemporary world. It is the end product of the work of the International Commission on Education for the twenty-first Century, whose work was coordinated by Jacques Delors (1996). The report was published in book format in 1999, entitled "Learning: the treasure within". It also proposed an education aimed at the four skills that are expected to be necessary for a citizen of the twenty-first century: learn to know, learn to do, learn to live with others, and learn to be. According to Perrenoud (2000), the meaning of competence is endowed with multiple meanings, but he defines it as an ability to act effectively in a given type of situation, supported by knowledge, but without limit. His research demonstrates that a situation can be faced in the best possible way when we synergize various cognitive resources complementarily. Almost every action triggers the mobilization of some knowledge, sometimes sparse and elementary, and sometimes complex and networked. These actions manifest competences that are not only knowledge, but mobilize it. The construction of skills, therefore, is inseparable from the formation of knowledge mobilization schemes with discernment, in real time, at the service of effective action (Perrenoud, 2000).

Perrenoud (2000) also presents the school in a more utilitarian view, being a place where students learn to read, write, count, but also to reason, explain, summarize, observe, compare, draw and dozens of other general capabilities. Knowledge is organized into subjects and, therefore, into acquired knowledge, but the school is not concerned with linking these resources to life situations.

The author relates this issue to the process of training teachers, and it is up to the teacher to have developed skills to: design and manage problem situations adjusted to the level and students' possibilities; acquire a longitudinal view of the teaching objectives; establish links with the theories underlying the learning activities; observe and evaluate students in learning situations, according to a formative approach; make periodic assessments of skills and make decisions about progression (Perrenoud, 1999, 2000).

17 Interdisciplinary Project to Build Teaching Skills ... 353

In this context, he defends the need to develop ten essential skills: organize and direct learning situations; manage the progression of learning; design and evolve the differentiation devices; involve students in their learning and work; work in a team; participate in the administration of the school; inform and involve parents; use new technologies; face the duties and ethical dilemmas of the profession; as well as manage your own continuing education.

17.2 Skills for Now and Then

Many of these skills listed are related to the concept of Future Skills that this chapter is based on. Future Skills, in the context of teachers' training, allow individuals to solve complex problems in a professional and rapidly-changing context with an organized and successful action. The actions indicated require the development of communication, cooperation, reflection, decision-making capacity, pro-activity, ethics, innovation, and learning literacy skills.

It is recognized, therefore, the need to rethink education and pedagogical action to improve the quality of learning. However, little has been discussed about how to intentionally and explicitly develop twenty-first Century Skills, or Future Skills (Scott, 2015). Notice that, in the context of this chapter, it is more important to think about the skills needed to educate better teachers than a specific definition. We use several sources in order to build this foundation, as can be seen.

In this sense, Saavedra and Opfer (2012) recommend nine premises for teaching twenty-first Century Skills: (1) make learning relevant to the 'big picture'; (2) teach through the disciplines; (3) develop lower and higher order thinking skills to encourage understanding in different contexts; (4) encourage transfer of learning; (5) teach how to 'learn to learn' or metacognition; (6) address misunderstandings directly; (7) promote teamwork; (8) exploit technology to support learning; and (9) foster students' creativity.

Scott (2015) concluded that:

> Above all, studies have found that learners are more successful at acquiring new competencies when they build strong metacognitive abilities, reflect objectively on new concepts learned, and integrate that information with their existing knowledge and skills. The process of adapting new knowledge for their own use and incorporating it into their existing conceptual frameworks will support further learning. Once new learning is integrated into existing 'ways of knowing', this in turn nurtures creativity and originality and establishes new cognitive habits. Critical thinking skills are also enhanced. (Scott, 2015, p. 3)

From this, the author researched several methodologies or pedagogical aspects that allow the teacher to help in the development of the skills of the future. They are: focus on quality; foster participation; personalize and customize learning; emphasize project and Problem-Based Learning; encourage collaboration and communication; engage and motivate learners; cultivate creativity and innovation; and employ appropriate learning tools.

Many of these pedagogical aspects can be seen in the Interdisciplinary Project (IP) at Virtual University of São Paulo State—Univesp (Brazil). The IP is guided by Project-Based Learning—PBL (Araujo & Sastre, 2009) and Human-Centered Design—HCD (Brown, 2010; Plattner et al., 2011). Pedagogical action in the IP is based on the principle of the inseparability of the relationship between theory and practice. In this direction, in methodological terms, the projects are planned by the students to be carried out in teams, a fundamental condition for developing Future Skills, focusing on problem solving and the formation of collaborative knowledge networks.

The main aim of this chapter is to present the concept of the IP at Univesp and correlate the skills proposed in the teachers' education at Univesp with Future Skills. According to Ehlers (2020), Future Skills are related "to dealing with the social, organizational and institutional environment. This includes skills such as creating meaning and value, the ability to shape the future, to cooperate with others and to be able to communicate, criticize and reach a consensus, also in intercultural contexts" (p. 82). As a hypothesis, we assess that Univesp is a leader in this area, especially in Brazil, and can train teachers with skills for a better education in the future.

17.3 The Interdisciplinary Project Model

Created in 2012, Univesp is the fourth university in the state of São Paulo, Brazil, that offers education in the distance learning model. Currently, there are nine undergraduate programs on offer, totaling around 55,000 students. For face-to-face support for these programs, 330 learning centers are distributed in 290 cities, which allows the university to reach more than 44% of the territory of the state.

The university's pedagogical model consists of five fundamental axes, which connect and complement each other: expansion of access to higher education; focus on student; interaction; digital inclusion; training for professional practice (Garbin & Oliveira, 2019). This model gains an interface in a Virtual Learning Environment (VLE), the way in which the university makes available to its students the training paths of each program.

Univesp, which is a public institution, has a curriculum for teachers' education based on active methodologies, the Interdisciplinary Project (IP) and pedagogical use of technologies. Since its creation, its mission has been based on promoting knowledge as a public good, universalizing access to formal education and education for citizenship, applying innovative methodologies and intensive use of information and communication technologies applied to education.

The institution offers graduation in the distance modality, so it seeks to use the most effective and current technologies to support the entire learning process. Thus, the courses are offered through a Virtual Learning Environment, where all the contents are made available. In addition, all communication and learning are carried out with the support of digital technologies. Thus, teachers prepare a learning roadmap for students with materials and study guidelines. In addition, they have the support of tutors, who guide the development of activities, as a pedagogical facilitator.

In addition to the regular disciplines and internships, the university has what is called the Interdisciplinary Project (IP). The IP is guided by the concept of active learning methodologies such as Project-Based Learning (PBL) (Araujo & Sastre, 2009) and Human-Centered Design (HCD) (Brown, 2010; Plattner et al., 2011), that puts students in the center of the learning process. In PBL, students are invited to carry out actions in a collaborative way, based on curiosities, doubts and problematizations, giving rise to processes that will be researched in order to seek possible solutions. To arrive at solutions, students use the principles of HCD, which integrate multidisciplinary and interactive collaboration with the creation of innovative solutions, with an emphasis on the user. One of the foundations of this model is the construction of prototypes to solve the problem, which are continuously tested, until a model capable of being implemented is reached. Through problem solving and collaborative learning, students will be exposed to activities that aim to relate curriculum content to pedagogical foundations, to master not only the specific content, but also the pedagogical practices necessary to teach them.

This approach is supported by three phases for the development of these prototypes or solutions: hear, create, and implement, which are carried out continuously, as illustrated in Fig. 17.1.

In the "hearing" step, dialogue between the project team and the educational community for which the solution is being developed is required. Thus, it is from the data collected in the initial phase of "listening" that solutions are designed. During the "creation" phase, students use digital tools for collective work that helps in the search for solutions that really impact the solution. The last step

Fig. 17.1 The phases of the Interdisciplinary Project

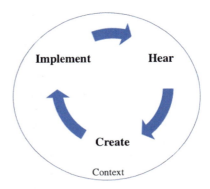

refers to the "implementation" of the solution, whose purpose is to verify whether the needs identified during the other processes with the community were met.

The focus on the subjects, which arises from curiosities, doubts, individual and collective problematizations, gives rise to themes that will be investigated by students in order to seek elements that help to respond to the problem that generated it.

The Interdisciplinary Project starts in the second semester and will be developed in each semester, totaling 6 projects over 480 h at the end of the program. Working in small groups and guided by a tutor, who works as a pedagogical facilitator, students must research and solve problem situations related to the reality and daily life of the program's knowledge area, so that they complete the following steps throughout the semester:

1. Define the work team (maximum 7 students per group).
2. Conduct theoretical research or research on practices that have already been developed on the topic.
3. Choose a partner school for the development of the project.
4. Research with the school the viable possibilities for the development of the project and the proposal.
5. Propose and apply the proposal at school, identifying the steps to be taken.
6. Deliver the partially fulfilled IP for the professor's assessment.
7. Finalize and deliver the activity, considering the professor's suggestions.

All teams have a tutor specifically chosen to accompany the pedagogical actions of the collaborative work and who holds fortnightly meetings with the teams.

Currently, the tutors are professionals from different areas, who are taking their master's or PhD at universities in the state of São Paulo (Brazil) and participate in a training program at the institution in question.

Throughout the semester, as an evaluation process, students deliver: action plan, partial report, final report and project presentation by a video, as well as performing a collaborative evaluation. Each of these activities is evaluated by the mentor, who provides constructive feedback to the teams.

When developing the IP, students come into contact with professionals in the area of their program and, in this way, experience aspects of their future professional practice. From this methodological context, the teams analyze the professional context in which they are inserted as student-researchers, to identify problem situations that constitute the observed practices and propose solutions to them that must, in turn, be implemented and tested in a cycle of carrying out the project.

To support the performance of collaborative work by IP teams, especially in the face-to-face modality, the centers are configured as strategic spaces for teams to carry out meetings and research, in addition to offering technological infrastructure that helps communication and interaction. It is also at the hubs that teams have the opportunity to meet face-to-face with their IP mentors.

The IP was created to provide students contact with the professional world, in this case, the schools and classrooms. However, it also aims at the development of different skills throughout their own development, which allows the teacher in training to develop skills that will be important to them in their daily work. Thus, teacher education at the university seeks to train professionals beyond that utilitarian view of knowledge, as seen in Perrenoud (1999, 2000).

Future Skills can be found in the development of the IP actions. Through problem solving and collaborative learning, students will be exposed to activities that aim to relate curricular contents to pedagogical foundations, in order to master not only the specific contents, but also the pedagogical practices necessary to teach them. The Basic Education teacher's competence is not restricted only to the specific knowledge of Pedagogy, but also to the relationship between this knowledge and "teaching–learning", as well as the ways of being a teacher and teaching. It is necessary that the future teacher in training be exposed to reflections on content to be taught in Kindergarten and Elementary School I; know the school reality and its context; be in contact with research in the area of Education that addresses difficulties identified in learning basic content; analyze content and new approaches to school programs; and discuss the potential of technological tools for learning Pedagogy and developing teaching activities in these different environments. To program and execute new teaching experiences, both from the point of view of basic education and from the methodological point of view, is to experience a teaching practice in the classroom.

Future Skills enable individuals to efficiently solve complex problems in any given context. The IP allows undergraduate students to experience their work context and to understand the school context in depth. In this way, it allows a professional experience for undergraduates, which will impact the way they conceive of their profession, as will be discussed in sequence.

17.4 The Interdisciplinary Project: Developing Skills for the Future of Learning

Zabala (1998), whose work as an advisor to the Spanish Ministry of Education revolutionized teaching in the country, states about competence in the professional field that the school system must train people for innovation. They should become capable of evolving, of adapting to a changing world, but without losing sight of the individual committed to the social and economic transformation and with a society that guarantees the right to work. For him, in order to teach skills, the starting point must be work centered on the context of real problem situations, with a global approach.

In addition, Paulo Freire (1996) qualifies the activity of teaching as a human specificity that requires competence, professional skill, methodical rigor, affection among those involved in the teaching–learning process.

For Tardif et al. (1991), teaching knowledge represents a set of knowledge from different sources, among them: textbooks, school programs, contents, as well as the experience acquired in the profession. In this way, they present four distinct categories of knowledge:

- *Professional*, which was built throughout the teacher's training, based on the science of education, therefore, related to pedagogy, techniques and teaching methods.
- *Disciplinary,* related to the different areas of knowledge offered in professional training institutions, for example, chemistry, physics, biology and mathematics.
- *Curricula* is specific to the organization of educational institutions, and related to the objectives, contents and methods present in the specific teaching programs of each organization.
- *Experiential* arises from the teaching action during the development of the profession, that is, from the pedagogical action.

Such knowledge is plural and heterogeneous, as the teacher, in his teaching practice, articulates it in different ways over time and in everyday situations. In contrast to this definition, Tardif (2008) points out that the practice of teacher training programs occurs in an applicational way, that is, future teachers consume theories in class formats and then apply their knowledge at the moment of practice, in the internship: "in a discipline, learning is knowing. But, in practice, learning is doing and knowing by doing" (Tardif, 2008, p. 271).

Therefore, teacher education acquires particular relevance in today's complex, unstable and globalized world and should encourage reflection so that teachers are able to analyze teaching situations, institutional and social contexts based on their experience (Oliveira, 2019). Thus, the logic of skills presupposes the integration between training and teaching work, valuing personal skills, know-how, know-how-to-talk, know-how-to-undertake, know-how-to-use different technologies. In this sense, there can only be a significant teaching action from the construction of knowledge aimed at Future Skills.

Given this context, it is important to think of a teacher training curriculum that seeks to articulate theory and practice, so that future teachers can develop new knowledge, such as new experiences, as indicated by Tardif (2008), or even articulate professional skills from an early moment as Zabala (1998) points out. In the curriculum developed at Univesp, moments of practice occur throughout the training program, precisely to provide new experiences to trainees and to be able to articulate and to build different skills.

The IP, as mentioned earlier, is an application of professional practice articulated with the contents of each of the training programs. In it, students, through the resolution of a problem, articulate and develop at least six important skills for the contemporary global world. The skills can be seen in Table 17.1.

Such skills are related to the concept initially defined in this work, which is Future Skills. The IP promotes an interaction between subjects, emphasizing the need for interpersonal communication, which generates negotiations of meanings for the establishment of a common aim and cooperation. In addition, it takes place in a school, a place of cultural plurality, where the teacher in training is placed in a situation that generates knowledge about their professional, intercultural and organizational context. According to Ehlers (2020, p. 278): "higher education would mainly be organized around one key objective: to enable the development of graduates' Future Skills, i.e. complex problem solving, dealing with uncertainty or developing a sense of responsibility".

The first skill is the **Investigative** in which it is expected that students are able to use academic knowledge already built and relate it to the problem under study. To this end, they carry out actions such as: Search the scientific knowl-

Table 17.1 Interdisciplinary Project Skills

Investigative	Problem Solving	Collaborative	Communication	Professional	Technological
Skills to use academic knowledge already built and relate it to the problem under study	Skills to understand and solve a problem scenario related to professional practice	Joint-building skills in which a group of people have a common goal to be achieved	Skills to communicate using different languages	Skills to relate the knowledge developed in the course with the professional field	Skills to use technological tools to solve a given problem
Search the scientific knowledge related to the program; Use scientific knowledge to solve the problem under study; Develop scientific knowledge related to the program area; Relate the scientific knowledge developed in the program with professional practice	*Understand PBL and HCD; Identify problem scenarios facing a subject; Define a problem scenario for project development; Define an action plan; Develop actions that lead to the solution of the problem (data collection, field visits, reflection on the problem); Implementation*	*Understand your role in the context of collaborative work; Understand the importance of establishing common goals; Interact with the team; Negotiate agreements and directions with group members*	*Make plans to systematize communication; Writing; Systematize and synthesize; Take ownership of collaborative writing; Academic writing*	*Make schemes, systematize and synthesize Search, Selection, Application of information in IP; Autonomy*	*Make schemes, systematize and synthesize Appropriation of digital tools*

edge related to the program; Use scientific knowledge to solve the problem under study; Develop scientific knowledge related to the program area; Relate the scientific knowledge developed in the program with professional practice.

The second listed skill is **Problem Solving** in which it is expected that students are able to understand and solve a problem scenario related to professional practice. To this end, they carry out actions such as: Understand PBL and HCD; Identify problem scenarios facing a subject; Define a problem scenario for project development; Define an action plan; Develop actions that lead to the solution of the problem (data collection, field visits, reflection on the problem); Implementation.

The third skill is the **Collaborative** one, in which it is expected that students are able to jointly build skills in a group of people that have a common goal to be achieved. To this end, they carry out actions such as: Understand your role in the context of collaborative work; Understand the importance of establishing common goals; Interact with the team; Negotiate agreements and directions with group members.

The next skill is related to **Communication**, in which it is expected that students develop the ability to communicate using different languages and channels. To this end, they carry out actions such as: Make schemes to systematize communication; Writing; Spiking; Systematize and synthesize; Take ownership of collaborative writing; Academic writing.

The fifth is related to **Professional** skills, in which it is expected that students develop the ability to relate the knowledge developed in the program with the professional field. To this end, they carry out actions such as: Make schemes, systematize and synthesize; Application of information in IP; Actions to exercise autonomy.

The last one is related to **Technological** skills, in which it is expected that students develop the ability to use technological tools to solve a given problem. To this end, they carry out actions such as: Make schemes, systematize and synthesize; Appropriation of digital tools.

Thus, in the development of the Interdisciplinary Project, students are expected to develop at least these skills, which connect with the skill profiles as indicated by Ehlers (2020). We can observe organization-related skills such as Communication and Cooperation Competence; object-related ones such as Digital Literacy, Design-Thinking Competence, Innovation Competence; subject development-related ones such as Self-Efficacy, Reflective Competence, Decision and Ethical Competence, as we can see in the publications referred to in the next passage.

In this proposed model, it is important to mention that Univesp is a very new university, and the IP model has been developed by people linked to the institution since its beginning. The proposed model starts with the offer of continuing education courses for teachers and is adapted until reaching the current model. The trajectory and some results of this process has been previously published (see Garbin et al., 2017, 2020a, 2020b, 2021; Garbin & Favaro, 2021). The creation of IP in particular is described in Araujo, Fruchter et al. (2014) and Garbin et al. (2017). However, it was during the years 2020 and 2021 that a group of people from the university began to identify what are the expected skills developed with the IP. Table 17.1, therefore, summarizes the work developed.

The work to identify skills has gone through the following phases: 1) identify the main points for the training of professionals in university programs that have the IP in their curriculum; 2) Review the didactic material of all IPs offered; 3) Identify the actions carried out by students within the HCD and PBL process (listening, creating and implementing); 4) Categorize actions into main categories; and finally, 5) Create a list of skills to be developed by students over 4 years.

In this sense, it is important to emphasize that the student is not expected to develop all the skills in a single IP. As mentioned, a total of six IPs is developed throughout the programs and in each of them, students advance in the construction of skills. In this process, the idea that students learn at different paces and in different styles is also valued.

Therefore, the process is open, although there is a suggested agenda for students, and they must deliver the assessment activities. Throughout the semester, as an evaluation process, students deliver: action plan, partial report, final report, and project presentation video, as well as performing a collaborative evaluation. Each of these activities is evaluated by the mentor, who provides constructive feedback with the teams.

Each of these activities presupposes assistance in the development of a skill. In the reports, students need to demonstrate through theoretical foundations how the knowledge developed in the other subjects studied helped in solving the problem, in addition to graphically demonstrating the evolution of the solution conceived by their group. They also need to describe the location or community for whom they are developing their solution, thus relating to their professional field.

In the action plan, students are expected to plan the actions that will be developed throughout the semester. In the video, students need to demonstrate what the problem under study was and how they managed to solve it, with the participation of the community.

Finally, they take stock of the team's participation, scoring how each member helped in the process and how they could improve their participation in future IPs. All activities are developed and delivered collectively.

The IP content is developed biweekly, precisely so that adaptations to the initial agenda provided by the university are possible. For the development of the PBL and HCD steps, the agenda initially indicates to students:

1. First fortnight—Definition of the group, approach to the topic, choice of location and on-site observation;
2. Second fortnight—Definition and study of the problem;

3. Third fortnight—Field visit and solution definition;
4. Fourth fortnight—Definition of the solution;
5. Fifth fortnight—Collection of suggestions with the external community;
6. Sixth fortnight—Rethinking the solution;
7. Seventh fortnight—Finalizing the solution;
8. Eighth fortnight—Delivery of the final solution and evaluation.

In this way, students and future teachers, through actions planned for the development of the IP, develop skills and abilities that will be useful to them in the future.

As mentioned by Perrenoud (2000) and Tardif (2008), teacher education needs to encompass practice together with content, so that students and teachers in training do not conceive theory as something disconnected from practice. And the interdisciplinary project at Univesp is the way the institution managed to transcend this relationship.

So, IP aims to provide students the skills that allow the formation of these teachers' skills. In order to educate individuals who will be able to solve complex problems in many emergent contexts in a self-organized way, this is how Univesp applies Future Skills:

- All the IP actions make the students develop and use their **communication** and **cooperation** skills, by working in groups, doing activities together and taking decisions collectively;
- Once they need to take decisions about how to approach the theme and how to solve the problem, the students are willing to develop **learning literacy, self-efficacy, self-determination** and **self-competence**;
- At the same time, since the educational process is virtual and directed by **Design Thinking**, the students need to be open to new technologies and methodologies for **innovation, systems, and digital competences**.

The rest of the Future Skills, obviously, are also developed by the IP actions. It is a complex set of educational issues that, in theory, can help to educate better professionals and better citizens.

17.5 Conclusion

The aim of this chapter is to correlate the skills proposed in the teacher's education at Univesp with the Future Skills as proposed by the NextSkills Study (Ehlers, 2020). The Interdisciplinary Project (IP) developed by higher education students at Univesp (Brazil) is guided by Project-Based Learning (PBL) and Human-Centered Design (HCD), in which the pedagogical action is based on the principle of inseparability of the relationship between theory and practice. In this scenario, students develop at least six essential skills, such as: Investigative; Problem Solving; Collaboration; Communication; Professional; and Technological.

It was possible to perceive that the skills expected in the Univesp IP relate to the skills indicated by Ehlers (2020) such as communication, cooperation, Digital Literacy, Design-Thinking, Innovation, self-efficacy, reflective, decision and ethical, among others.

The work of including these skills in the students' learning process is long and has been improved over the years. Although from the beginning, in 2014, the objectives of including the Interdisciplinary Project in the curriculum were clear, it was only in 2021 that it was possible to clearly identify which were the competencies involved in the pedagogical process. We believe that now new work must be tackled, which is to identify, in the students' learning process, evidence of the development of these skills and how the activities carried out by them throughout the semester can actually support this process.

One of the challenges found at the institution was precisely to think of an interdisciplinary project that could be developed by different people in different contexts and regions, since the university in question is present in a diversity of cities in Brazil. In order to solve that, it was important to initially think about the audience for whom to design the project and how this design can help in their professional growth. In addition, it is significant to have a multidisciplinary team that can assist in raising different issues.

In teacher education, as mentioned earlier, it is essential to break the dichotomy between theory and practice, providing students with a differentiated experience during their undergraduate course. The Interdisciplinary Project was the way Univesp managed to put this need into operation. Teaching about the importance of respecting ideas, new perspectives, values, and how to deal with difficulties is something to be considered in contemporary society.

We hope that the example set at Univesp can inspire other institutions to consider the inclusion of work with competences in their curricula, especially in teaching education, as it provides a consolidated training for the professionals of the future.

> **Future Skills in Practice: Our Recommendations**
> - Future teachers cannot be educated in the same way teachers were educated some years ago. We need to make them experience new teaching practices, like active methodologies and problem solving, in order to develop Future Skills.
> - In the same way, it is mandatory to include critical thinking about technology in teacher's education. This can be done by distance education, e-learning and massive online open courses (MOOCs).
> - Promoting the future teachers' skills such as collaboration, problem solving, and critical thinking can be a start of a new standard to the whole educational system.

References

Araujo, U. F., Fruchter, R., Garbin, M. C., Pascoalino, L. N., & Arantes, V. A. (2014). The reorganization of time, space, and relationships in school with the use of active learning methodologies and collaborative tools. *ETD – Educação Temática Digital, 16*(1), 84. https://doi.org/10.20396/etd.v16i1.1331.

Araujo, U. F., & Sastre, G. (2009). *Aprendizagem baseada em problemas no ensino superior*. Summus.

Brown, T. (2010). *Design thinking: Uma metodologia poderosa para decretar o fim das velhas ideias*. Elsevier.

Delors, J. (1996). *Learning: The treasure within: Report to unesco of the international commission on education for the twenty-first century*. Unesco.

Ehlers, U.-D. (2020). *Future skills: The future of learning and higher education*. Springer. Wiesbaden. ISBN: 9783750494268. Online Access https://nextskills.org/wp-content/uploads/2020/03/Future-Skills-The-Future-of-learning-and-higher-education.pdf

Freire, P. (1996). *Pedagogia da autonomia: Saberes Necessários à prática educativa*. Paz e Terra.

Garbin, M. C., Trombeta de Oliveira, E., Pirillo, N. R., & Telles, S. (2020a). Pedagogical practices based on areas of knowledge: Reflections on the technology use. *New Trends and Issues Proceedings on Humanities and Social Sciences, 7*(1), 134–141. https://doi.org/10.18844/prosoc.v7i1.4877.

Garbin, M., Oliveira, E. T., Rubio Pirillo, N., & Santos Azevedo, A. (2020b). Práticas pedagógicas inovadoras para a formação de professores. *Revista Brasileira de Aprendizagem Aberta e a Distância, 19*(1). https://doi.org/10.17143/rbaad.v19i1.388.

Garbin, M. C., Cavalcanti, C. C., & Araujo, U. F. (2017). Metodologias ativas de aprendizagem na formação semipresencial de professores: articulando teoria e prática. *International Studies on Law and Education*, 27, 13–28.

Garbin, M. C., & Favaro, R. F. (2021). O ensino superior a distância: o projeto integrador em momento de ensino remoto emergencial. *Revista Brasileira de Aprendizagem Aberta e a Distância, 20*(1). https://doi.org/10.17143/rbaad.v20i1.602.

Garbin, M. C., Oliveira, E. T. de, & Telles, S. (2021). Active methodologies supported by interaction and communication technologies in higher education. *Global Journal of Information Technology: Emerging Technologies, 11*(2), 47–54. https://doi.org/10.18844/gjit.v11i2.6117.

Garbin, M. C., & Oliveira, É. T. (2019). Práticas docentes na Educação a Distância: Um olhar sobre as áreas do conhecimento. *Revista Diálogo Educacional, 19*(60). https://doi.org/10.7213/1981-416X.19.060.DS02.

Oliveira, E. T. de (2019). *Distance education and virtual learning environments: Orienting dimensions for selection of media.* Thesis (Doctorate in Education)—Faculty of Education, University of São Paulo.

Perrenoud, P. (1999). *Construir as competências desde a escola.* Artmed.

Perrenoud, P. (2000). *Dez novas competências para ensinar.* Artmed.

Plattner, H., Meinel, C., & Leifer, L. (2011). *Design thinking research – Studying co-creation in practice.* Springer.

Saavedra, A. R., & Opfer, V. D. (2012). Learning 21st century skills requires 21st-century teaching. *Phi Delta Kappan, 94*(2), 8–13. https://doi.org/10.1177/003172171209400203.

Scott, C. L. (2015). *The futures of learning 3: what kind of pedagogies for the 21st century?* (Education Research and Foresight Working Papers 15).

Tardif, M. (2008). *Saberes docentes e formação profissional.* Vozes.

Tardif, M., Lessard, C., & Lahaye, L. (1991). Os professores face ao saber – Esboço de uma problemática do saber docente. *Teoria e Educação, 4*, 215–233.

Zabala, A. (1998). *A prática educativa: como ensinar.* Artmed.

Mônica Cristina Garbin is a graduate in Pedagogy and holds a PhD in Education from the State University of Campinas (UNICAMP). She is a professor at the Virtual University of São Paulo State in the area of Methodology and Distance Education and is a collaborating professor in the postgraduate programs in Education at the State University of Campinas (UNICAMP) and the University of São Paulo (USP). Dr. Garbin conducts research in the area of Education, working mainly on the following topics: Didactics, Educational Technologies, Teacher Training and Teaching Methodologies. ORCID ID: 0000-0002-4598-6032

Edison Trombeta de Oliveira is a Doctor in Education from the São Paulo University (USP). Currently he is Adjunct Professor I at the Postgraduate Program in Education (PPGE) at the University of Sorocaba (Uniso) and professor of higher education at the Faculty of Technology of São Paulo (Fatec). He was instructional designer at Virtual University of São Paulo State between 2014 and 2022. His main interest areas of research in Education are: Educational Technologies, Teacher Training, and Teaching Methodologies. ORCID ID: 0000-0001-9935-4260

Open Access This chapter is licensed under the terms of the Creative Commons Attribution 4.0 International License (http://creativecommons.org/licenses/by/4.0/), which permits use, sharing, adaptation, distribution and reproduction in any medium or format, as long as you give appropriate credit to the original author(s) and the source, provide a link to the Creative Commons license and indicate if changes were made.

The images or other third party material in this chapter are included in the chapter's Creative Commons license, unless indicated otherwise in a credit line to the material. If material is not included in the chapter's Creative Commons license and your intended use is not permitted by statutory regulation or exceeds the permitted use, you will need to obtain permission directly from the copyright holder.

Changemaking on Campus

18

Judit Costa

The world is changing: We live in a fluid and fast-paced world. Societies that were once oceans apart are now completely interconnected; jobs are being created and eliminated at record rates; technical innovation is accompanying our daily lives, as well as an ever faster environmental degradation. In such a world, fundamental questions arise: What does it mean to thrive in this society? What are the skills necessary to gain meaningful employment? How does one make an impact on society for the good of all?

Ashoka builds and cultivates a community of changemakers, comprised of social entrepreneurs, young changemakers and institutions. Together we mobilize a movement to create an "everyone a changemaker" world. We work towards a world in which everyone, including teachers, students, and university employees, feels capable and invited to drive change.

Regarding higher education, social innovation offers a twin benefit. Firstly, as an educational framework, social innovation has the power to develop relevant twenty-first-century skills in students. Secondly, as an approach to institutional change, it can also rewire the institutional ecosystem to become more innovative, resilient, relationship-oriented, and responsive to the needs of its core constituents and the community within which it is embedded.

Higher education is uniquely equipped to prepare learners of all generations with the hard and soft skills required to lead and to drive long-term change, such as empathy, creativity, collaboration, and systems thinking. We envision a sector

---

J. Costa (✉)
Partner, Ashoka Deutschland gGmbH, Berlin, Germany
e-mail: jcosta@ashoka.org

© The Author(s) 2024
U.-D. Ehlers and L. Eigbrecht (eds.), *Creating the University of the Future*, Zukunft der Hochschulbildung - Future Higher Education,
https://doi.org/10.1007/978-3-658-42948-5_18

characterized by interdisciplinarity, new models of hands-on education, active engagement with on- and off-campus stakeholders, and leadership and innovation opportunities infused across the organization.

Ashoka envisions a higher education sector where colleges and universities feel a responsibility to create positive social impact as part of and beyond core institutional operations. They cultivate students as changemakers with broad-based changemaking skills (empathy, creativity, collaboration, and systems thinking). Changemaker Campuses are adaptive, resilient, innovative, and collaborative organizations, increasingly breaking down traditional silos and hierarchies. They invest in new structures and norms that increase multidisciplinary, cross-campus collaboration, blending of theory and practice, and integration with local communities.

Since its launch in 2008, Ashoka has selected 51 Changemaker Campuses globally, engaged 600 colleges and universities in Ashoka U programs, and supported more than 4000 educators and senior administrators as they designed and taught courses, produced research, and created and implemented strategy. We also catalyzed over 2 million students to gain education and skill-building in changemaking and social innovation. In 2021, Ashoka U and the Changemaker Campus network started transitioning from a centralized, fully staffed, programmatic model to a decentralized model in which Changemaker Campuses collaborate on regional initiatives via Ashoka country offices and programs.

Ashoka's experience supports the idea that higher education should seek to align with the world at large: learning and social impact belong together. Responding to the challenges and needs of our society can only be learned by putting in place actions that generate a real transformation in context. This is why students recognize this purposeful approach and feel inspired when universities deliver on their promises and practice what they preach. Therefore, Ashoka believes that all colleges and universities can and should embrace social innovation, both as an educational framework and as a strategy for institutional change.

Judit Costa is a partner at Ashoka and based in Berlin. In order to create an everyone a changemaker world, she keeps on unlocking the potential of individuals and institutions. Further information on Ashoka can be found here: www.ashoka.org

18 Changemaking on Campus

Practical Advice, Frameworks and Supporting Material Can Be Found Here:

- Becoming a Changemaker Institution (2020): https://ashokau.org/publications/
- Evaluating Changemaker Education: A Practitioner's Guide (2019): https://ashokau.org/publications/
- Preparing Students for a Rapidly Changing World (2019): https://ashokau.org/publications/
- Practice Example Expert in Transformational Education, Universidad Camilo José Cela, Spain (2023): https://www.ucjc.edu/estudio/experto-educacion-transformadora/#Section6

Judit Costa

is a partner at Ashoka in Germany, focussing on what young people need to grow up as changemakers. She has extensive expertise in human rights, having worked at the United Nations and several non-governmental organisations, including Human Rights Watch. Judit holds an M.A. in modern history from the University of Zurich and a second M.A. in social management from Alice Salomon Hochschule in Berlin.

Open Access This chapter is licensed under the terms of the Creative Commons Attribution 4.0 International License (http://creativecommons.org/licenses/by/4.0/), which permits use, sharing, adaptation, distribution and reproduction in any medium or format, as long as you give appropriate credit to the original author(s) and the source, provide a link to the Creative Commons license and indicate if changes were made.

The images or other third party material in this chapter are included in the chapter's Creative Commons license, unless indicated otherwise in a credit line to the material. If material is not included in the chapter's Creative Commons license and your intended use is not permitted by statutory regulation or exceeds the permitted use, you will need to obtain permission directly from the copyright holder.

The "University of the Future" of the Philippines: The Case of University of the Philippines Open University's Master of Public Management Program

19

Juvy Lizette M. Gervacio

Abstract

One of the issues in the education sector is how to future-ready degrees and develop students' Future Skills essential in an agile environment. This will facilitate students not only to become lifelong learners but also enable them to adapt to various career tracks in the fast-paced world. The University of the Philippines Open University (UPOU) is envisioned to help equip Filipinos with the knowledge and skills they need for life and work in the twenty-first century. As the "University of the Future," UPOU, through the Open Distance Learning Law, is mandated to assist agencies, higher education institutions (HEIs), and technical and vocational institutions in developing distance education programs through training, research, and other academic programs. This paper discusses the following questions: (a) What is the concept of the University of the Future for UPOU?; (b) How is Open and Distance E-learning (ODeL) articulated towards future-ready degrees?; (c) What are the initiatives from the Master of Public Management (MPM) Program to develop the Future

---

J. L. M. Gervacio (✉)
Assistant Professor, Master of Public Management Program, University of the Philippines Open University, Quezon City, Philippines
e-mail: juvylizette.gervacio@upou.edu.ph

© The Author(s) 2024
U.-D. Ehlers and L. Eigbrecht (eds.), *Creating the University of the Future*, Zukunft der Hochschulbildung - Future Higher Education,
https://doi.org/10.1007/978-3-658-42948-5_19

Skills of public servants?; (d) Are the learning activities aptly designed to develop Future Skills of public servants?; and (e) How can online assignments be redesigned to incorporate development of Future Skills?

19.1 Introduction

Rapid technological advancements coupled with social, economic, and environmental problems pose the need to prepare students for the opportunities and circumstances of the future. Megatrends influence the skills needed to face uncertainties and challenges, as well as to navigate a more complex world. The Organization for Economic Cooperation and Development (OECD) identified megatrends as migration, climate change, and COVID-19 (not a megatrend but a significant shock event). It pointed out that these megatrends make lifelong learning imperative and that it is essential for all citizens to become full and active participants in the economy and society (OECD, 2021). In the post-pandemic world, it is also recognized that workers may not be able to return to their previous roles and must retrain and upskill to find a new job with new skill requirements. As tasks are automated in the future, today's worker skills will become redundant (OECD, 2021).

According to the World Economic Forum, 50 percent of employees need to reskill to respond to the pandemic's economic impact and the automation of jobs (Whiting, 2020). They estimated that in 2025, 85 million jobs may be displaced due to the division of labor among humans and machines. Despite this, 95 million jobs may emerge that are more adapted to this new division.

The OECD (2018) argued that the development of Future Skills for learners lies in the hands of the education sector. Aside from merely providing academic courses, Higher Education Institutions (HEIs) must also enrich the values and skills that will help learners become responsible citizens and enable them to actively participate in building a better and sustainable society.

In general, future-ready learners must possess the sense of agency in dealing with their own learning and other situations they will encounter in their lifetime (OECD, 2018). The Economist Intelligence Unit reported in 2015 that education systems were not providing enough skills needed by the students and in the workplace. As a result, the students are making up for these deficiencies. Agency implies an individual's duty to engage with people and events and make decisions for the better. One of the ways in which agency can be developed is through education. Educators must simultaneously acknowledge the individuality of learners and their relationships with people who influence their learning. This is the so-called "co-agency" or supportive relationships that help learners achieve their goals. The OECD (2018) identified two factors that contribute to inculcating agency in learners: (1) personalized learning environments and (2) building a solid foundation of literacy and numeracy. A personalized learning environment enables learners to pursue their passions and gain knowledge and experience from various learning methods.

In the Philippines, the concept of Future Skills can be gleaned through the University of the Philippines Open University (UPOU) as it adapts the concept of the "University of the Future." Since it is the premier University of online education in the country, it has articulated the use of digital technology as a tool to future-proof degrees as well as to upskill and reskill learners.

This chapter discusses the concept of Future Skills, particularly in the context of Higher Education. It also highlights the case of the Philippines' "University of the Future" and how assessment is redesigned to develop Future Skills of public servants.

19.2 The Concept of Future Skills

To provide a better understanding of Future Skills, it is important to define this concept and identify the role of HEIs and digital learning in the development of Future Skills.

19.2.1 Defining Future Skills

In 2020, the World Economic Forum observed that the future work had arrived for a large majority of online white-collar workforce, with employers rapidly digitalizing the working processes. This can be attributed to the remote work arrangement that has been adopted during the height of the COVID-19 pandemic. There is a need to incorporate knowledge and ideas that will enable workers to become competent with their actual jobs and to other work that will be available for them.

Ehlers and Kellermann (2019) define Future Skills as an individual's capability to successfully respond to and act on future changes and intricate problems in a self-organized way. In simpler words, these are the skills that will be instrumental to people's success in the future (Fidler, 2016).

Ehlers and Kellermann (2019) identified three dimensions of Future Skills. The first Future Skills dimension is the subjective dimension, which refers to the individual's personal capability to acquire and develop skills that will enable them to actively participate in the future workforce. This dimension contains seven skills: (1) ability to make a decision on their own and act suitably (autonomy); (2) ability to take on tasks without being asked to (self-initiative); (3) ability to effectively control their behavior and decisions (self-management); (4) desire to attain accomplishments and mastery (need/motivation for achievement); (5) receptivity to changes and various situations (personal agility); (6) ability to take charge of their own learning (autonomous learning competence); and (7) belief in their capabilities to succeed in tasks (self-efficacy).

The second Future Skills dimension is the object dimension, referring to an individual's capability with regard to objects, tasks, and issues (Ehlers & Kellermann, 2019). This dimension contains five skills: (1) ability to adapt to dynamic objects and contexts (agility); (2) ability to come up with new and unpredicted solutions to a certain task (creativity); (3) openness to uncertainty while performing different roles (tolerance for ambiguity); (4) ability to use digital technology in accomplishing tasks and goals (digital literacy); and (5) ability to examine one's experiences and learn from them (ability to reflect).

The third Future Skills dimension is the social dimension, which pertains to an individual's capability to act with regard to their social environment (Ehlers & Kellermann, 2019). This dimension contains four skills: (1) ability to understand the essence of given tasks or instructions (Davies et al., 2011) (sense-making); (2) ability to think ahead and motivation to pursue lifelong learning (future mindset); (3) ability to effectively work in teams and in culturally diverse working environments (cooperation skills); and (4) ability to facilitate dialogue and criticize when needed (communication competence).

To enable learners to keep pace with evolving jobs, the responsibility to transform current practices and approaches in education and work is shouldered by all stakeholders concerned, including policymakers, business leaders, sector specialists, and the civil society.

The Asian Development Bank (2021) outlined the following skills categories that had been brought upon by the task shifts in the 4th Industrial Revolution (4IR): (1) critical thinking and adaptive learning (2) written and verbal communication (3) numeracy (4) complex problem-solving (5) management (6) social (7) evaluation, judgment, and decision-making (8) technical (9) computer literacy (10) digital/ICT. The ADB added that 4IR technologies make it simpler to monitor workers, thus making management skills less important.

On the other hand, the International Labor Organization (2021) also declared its Global Framework on Core Skills for Life and Work in the twenty-first Century. The framework provides the foundation for lifelong employability, decent work, and well-being of all. It also suggests a robust, concise taxonomy and definition of core skills for policymakers, teachers, trainers and assessors. Lastly, it underpins and promotes the development of curricula in a variety of educational settings. The ILO Framework identifies 19 Core Skills needed to adapt to the future of work grouped into four categories:

(1) **Social and emotional skills** (Communication, Collaboration and Teamwork, Conflict Resolution and Negotiation, Emotional Intelligence)
(2) **Cognitive and metacognitive skills** (Foundational Literacies, Analytical and Critical Thinking, Creative and Innovative Thinking, Strategic Thinking, Problem-solving and decision-making, self-reflection and learning to learn; collect, organize, and analyse information; planning and organizing, career management)
(3) **Basic digital skills** (use basic software, use basic hardware, operate safely in an online environment)
(4) **Basic skills for green jobs** (Environmental awareness, waste reduction and waste management, energy and water efficiency).

At the regional level, the Association of Southeast Asian Nations (2021) listed the Future Skills which are incorporated, albeit partly, in the curriculum and assessment in general education, technical-vocational education, and higher education: (1) cognitive skills (numeracy and literacy; low-order cognitive skills on the level of understanding and applying; high-order cognitive skills on the level of analyzing, evaluating, critical thinking, creating, innovating) (2) ICT skills or digital literacy (3) STEM skills (4) learnability (5) social skills (6) character qualities (7) problem-solving in complex, technology-rich environments, and (8) "Green Skills" and environment awareness. Although Future Skills are part of curricula, assessments and teaching and learning materials and implementation are still in progress.

With all these discussions, it is evident that there is a recognition of the Future Skills needed to address current and future challenges. These various skills are identified in order to be able to craft the relevant policies, plans, programs and strategies that could develop them.

19.2.2 The Role of Higher Education Institutions (HEIs) in the Development of Future Skills

According to Ehlers and Kellermann (2019), the learning experience provided by higher education institutions (HEIs) will also undergo significant changes. They discussed the four drivers or pillars of change in higher education, which are categorized into content and curriculum-related drivers and organization-structure-related drivers. Under the content and curriculum-related drivers are (1) Future Skills focus and (2) multi-institutional study pathways. As opposed to the current learning system where the mere focus is to acquire knowledge and skills in preparation for a professional career, HEIs in the future will also emphasize development of Future Skills. Networked universities will also emerge, where multiple HEIs will collaborate to offer certain programs to learners. Under the organization-structure-related drivers are (1) personalization of academic learning and (2) the lifelong learning university. Learners will be granted more freedom in forming their own curricula depending on their personal preferences. This will lead to a more flexible learning environment where learners can also collaborate with educators in building the curriculum. Lastly, higher education will be supplemented by lifelong learning. HEIs will start offering lifelong learning programs such as those for learners who are seeking to develop skills and competence they need in the workplace.

Ehlers et al. (2022) also noted that Future Skills must be genuinely integrated in the curricula and not only through detached workshops and extracurricular training. This entails self-assessment with formative feedback processes to support the students' Future Skills development.

In the Philippines, the role of Higher Education Institutions (HEIs) is crucial in incorporating Future Skills. The country has a very young population. The Philippine Statistics Authority (PSA) estimated the Philippines population to be 110 million in 2020 with the percentage of youth representing 28.69% or about 31.9 million with ages 15 to 30. Moreover, the country is also ranked as one of the most vulnerable to climate change and is hit frequently with typhoons, floodings, earthquakes, among others.

However, even with about 2000 HEIs in the Philippines, it is the UPOU that has been actively promoting its concept of the University of the future, including reskilling and upskilling, through the development and implementation of microlearning courses. This is because of its nature as an institution that utilizes ICT in the delivery of education.

19.2.3 Digital Learning and Its Prospects in Developing Future Skills

A study by Sariyatun et al. (2021) showed that digital learning has potential in developing and improving social skills of learners. Through digital education, learners take part in intensive interaction and communication with each other and with educators, contributing to a collaborative learning environment. The authors noted that according to Schrage (1990), working with other learners on group tasks enhances learners' decision-making and task and time management skills (Sariyatun et al., 2021, p. 420). Using digital learning materials also prompts learners to explore other sources of information outside the classroom. There is also opportunity for learners to expand their technological knowledge and expertise. Despite the benefits of digital learning in honing the social skills of students, it is important to note that there are still values that can only be learned through physical interaction; hence, it will be more effective to utilize both digital learning and traditional learning in shaping social skills of learners.

Dede and McGivney (2021) also discussed the different digital technologies that can be used for lifelong learning. One of which is virtual reality, which can be useful for training learners in a simulated environment. Despite not being in the actual work environment, learners can still experience, develop, and put into practice the needed knowledge and skills through simulation. This digital technology can also help in developing learners' self-efficacy to accept new roles, which is one of the Future Skills identified by Ehlers and Kellermann (2019). Artificial intelligence can also be utilized for personalized tutoring systems, where learners are granted the freedom to choose what, when, and how they learn.

However, a study by Zwart et al. (2020) found that the confidence of nursing students decreased with the use of digital learning materials. For digital learning to be more efficient, and to encourage the learners to engage actively, the authors recommended the following points: (1) the learners should be able to conduct their own online assessment; (2) there should be set quality criteria for tasks; and (3) there should be rules regarding online collaboration and interaction. They also noted that the educators should also support learners in developing their self-efficacy, which can be strengthened through a more virtual-based learning environment.

Grand-Clement (2017) also expounded on the importance of integration of digital skills in formal education. The use of technology has led to the remodeling of learning into a lifelong process since learners have to be constantly up-to-date with new developments and skills in the digital world. These digital skills, such as the ability to use digital technologies and digital navigation skills, serve as a tool to help learners with their daily lives and future professions.

Governments are also given the significant responsibility of ensuring that workers possess the skills and knowledge to effectively adapt to the dynamic and high technology work environments of the future (OECD, 2017). This can be achieved through improving the quality of education and training, incentives to encourage individuals to invest in developing in-demand skills, high-quality assessment systems, and efficient information and guidance systems.

It is also important to note that there is still few existing literature on the direct relationship between digital education and Future Skills. Based on the reviewed literature regarding the future of higher education and due to the increased use and integration of digital technologies in education, workplace, and our daily lives, it is important to conduct further studies regarding the significant role digital education will play in the development of Future Skills. The lack of Future Skills literature in the Asian contexts, specifically in the Southeast Asian region, also opens up an opportunity to do research on this topic. Thus, this paper will attempt to contribute not only to the concept of Future Skills but also to the use of digital technology in higher education.

19.3 Research Design

This paper discusses the case of the Philippines in terms of skills education for the future, particularly in Higher Education Institutions (HEIs). The country is the fourth largest country in Southeast Asia and has the 13th largest population in the world, seventh in Asia. It is an archipelago consisting of more than 7000 islands with a large and young population. However, there are many challenges when it comes to higher education that are related to quality and accessibility which became more apparent during the COVID-19 pandemic. As the country bounces back, it should be important for the education sector to build forward better.

The study discusses the following questions: (a) What is the concept of the University of the Future for UPOU?; (b) How is Open and Distance E-learning (ODeL) articulated towards future-ready degrees?; (c) What are the initiatives for the Master of the Public Management (MPM) Program to develop the Future Skills of public servants?; (d) Are the learning activities aptly designed to develop Future Skills of public servants?; and (e) How can online assignments be redesigned to incorporate development of Future Skills?

The research is a descriptive study that utilized primary and secondary data. It reviewed and analyzed documents, reports, online articles related to the subject. Since the concept of Future Skills is in the process of being articulated in the

Philippines, the researcher relied on the recorded messages from conferences and webinars. For the primary data, an online survey was designed and conducted to determine their perceptions regarding the redesigned assignment as well as Future Skills.

The study focused on the case of the University of the Philippines Open University (UPOU) as it is the premier University that offers online education in the country. Moreover, it also pursues the concept of "University of the Future" as it envisions to escalate online learning to develop microlearning courses and immersive technologies; future-proof degrees including the development of Future Skills of students.

The Master of Public Management (MPM) Program was selected since the researcher also served as its Program Chair. The majority of the students under this program are public servants working in different aspects of government, civil society and the private sector. There were three courses that were selected since they were also handled by the Researcher.

In these three courses, collaborative assignments were designed to enable learners to collaborate and communicate with each other. Since it was the first time using the redesigned assignment, it was important to get feedback from the learners on how they perceived the group task and determine if it can be a mechanism to develop Future Skills of students. Thus, the skills that were utilized are the 17 competencies based on the research by Ehlers and Kellermann (2019) which are also discussed in the previous chapter. They include organizational, subject development-related, and object-related skills. Each of the indicators include a short description. This is also a way for the students to learn more about the importance of Future Skills. A Likert scale was utilized to determine the strength of their perceptions.

The online survey was deployed through Google Forms after the semester ended. It was sent to all the students of the three courses selected for the study. The survey contained questions regarding the basic profile of the student; their assessment on the different Future Skills based on their experience on the assessment and their comments regarding said activity. It lasted for two weeks from 14 to 27 February 2022 and the information was processed through the Statistical Package for Social Sciences (SPSS). The qualitative information was also categorized and analyzed according to recurring themes to provide further explanation of their scores.

19.4 Results and Discussion

19.4.1 The University of the Philippines Open University: The Philippines' "University of the Future"

It was in 1995 when the UPOU became the fifth autonomous campus of the UP System with the mission to provide Filipinos everywhere access to quality higher education through innovative methods of teaching and learning that are designed to be responsive to national development priorities.

The articulation of the University of the Future concept started in 2019 as it recognizes that it should contribute to shape the direction of future revolutions and developments, which can only be achieved by revisiting the essence of universities with regard to core functions in producing graduates who are competent, capable, and skilled enough to face the challenges and opportunities of the future (Bandalaria, 2021).

In a speech by Chancellor Melinda Dela Peña Bandelaria in November 2019, she defined significant thrusts of UPOU in propelling the "University of the Future." Such terminology pushes relevant concepts of future-ready degrees and future-ready leaders with ethical and open science perspectives. She has also delineated future-ready degrees, as they refer to the basic qualifications of training that would allow individuals and learners to undergo career shifts throughout their lifetime, which would eventually serve as pillars for their lifelong learning (Bandalaria, 2021).

The UPOU's Master of Public Management Program is one of the first programs offered in 1997 via distance learning to assist in democratizing education in the country. It is designed for policymakers, administrators, and managers of public, private, and non-governmental organizations; practitioners in local government and administration; and other individuals interested in good governance, public policy and administration. Thus, it is important to introduce innovations to continuously develop the skills of the learners.

19.4.2 The Reimagined Assessment Plan

Designing activities and assessment plans is quite challenging in an online set-up with learners not being able to see each other. Hence, the most convenient would be to deploy individual assignments for them to work on it at their own pace and time. However, one of the challenges that was noticeable during the COVID-19 pandemic was the lack of communication and collaboration among public servants. Although the government has called for a "whole of government" approach for various government agencies to address the situation, there have been some hits and misses. Thus, the researcher designed an activity/assessment that enabled learners to work as a team.

Three courses under the MPM Program were selected as part of the study, namely: Theory and Practice of Public Administration (PM201), Public Policy and Program Administration (PM241) and Local Government and Regional Administration (PM251) for the 1st Semester, Academic Year 2021–2022.

The group tasks entailed online collaboration in analyzing public administration issues in the Philippines within the context of national development. The tasks were designed since they are part of the course content which students need to understand.

The mechanics of the assignment were prepared and sent to the students. They were grouped into five to eight participants. Each group chose a coordinator who took care of the communication within and outside the group. Groups also assigned an editor who collected all outputs and integrated them in a cohesive manner. The rest of the group served as researchers.

They were given four weeks to do the task and there was a prescribed weekly activity for them to ensure that the groups will be able to finish on time and upload the output in the forum. All students were encouraged to go over the different outputs and give their comments and feedback to the other groups. They also had the opportunity to complete a peer rating form. The final activity was a 15-minute oral presentation for each team. The entire activity is equivalent to 30% of their total grade wherein 20% comes from the faculty and 10% of the grade is based on peer rating.

In terms of marking the group's output, the following are the criteria: Content (50%); Organization of thoughts (15%); Writing style (10%); Format (10%); Proper citation (10%) and On-time submission (5%). For the peer rating, the following criteria were followed: Quality of contribution to the process and final output (40%); Willingness to cooperate and communicate to the group (30%); Overall completeness of the tasks performed for the group (30%). Table 19.1 presents the description of the reimagined assessment.

19.4.3 Profile of the Research Participants

Table 19.2 presents the profile of the respondents. There were 50 students who participated in the survey out of 79 students for PM201, 50 students for PM241, and 27 students for PM251. Most of those who are in PM201 are likely to be

Table 19.1 Description of the Reimagined Assessment. *Source*: Gervacio (2022)

	PM201	PM241	PM251
Objectives	To be able to coherently document facts (i.e. details, photos) and analyses (i.e. ideas, assessments, insights) a Sustainable Development Goal (SDG) and how it is being implemented in work or locality	To assess a particular government policy or a program carried out by any implementing entity (i.e., government, NGO, private institution) that addresses a specific public issue in the Philippines	To document experiences with the issues and challenges confronted by local government units and provide recommendations or proposed amendments to the Local Government Code of 1992
Output	Journal/documentation/videos based on the chosen SDG an an oral presentation	Written assessment of a certain public policy and an oral presentation	Written amendments to the Law and an oral presentation
Ethical considerations	All outputs should be signed by the students that the output is their original work	All outputs should be signed by the students that the output is their original work	All outputs should be signed by the students that the output is their original work

enrolled in either PM241 or PM251 as well. Since the survey was conducted one month after the semester had ended, not everyone was able to participate. Out of the 50 students who participated, there were 42 respondents who were in the PM201, 27 students in PM241 and 14 students for PM251.

The basic profile of the students was also gathered to know more about the student body. About 74% were female compared to only 26% male. The age of the respondents ranged from 22 to 55 years old and the mean age is 33. About 24% of them are in the age group 30–39 years.

Almost half (46%) of the participants are occupying administrative/clerical positions. This is followed by the technical personnel with 20%. There were also 18% occupying managerial/supervisory positions. Others are either in academia or self-employed.

As regards the category of their offices, more than half (54%) work for the national government. This is followed by those who work at local government units with 16% and those working with private industries with 14%. In terms of the geographical location, 40% of the respondents work in Metro Manila, which

19 The "University of the Future" of the Philippines …

Table 19.2 Profile of the Research Participants

Profile	Number (Total: 50)	Percentage
PM201: Sustainable Development Goals (SDGs) PM241: Analyze a public policy and assess/evaluate based on a certain framework PM251: Recommendation of how the Local Government Code should be amended	42 27 14	84 54 28
Gender Male Female	13 37	26 74
Age Group 20–29 30–39 40–49 50–59 Mean Age of respondents Age Range of respondents	18 24 6 2 33 years old 22 to 55 years old	36 48 12 4
Current Position in Office Managerial Technical Frontliners Administrative/Clerical Others (Academe, self-employed, public affairs)	9 10 4 23 4	18 20 8 46 8
Agency/Office National Government Local Government Unit Government Owned and Controlled Corporations (e.g. HIGC, GSIS, NAPOCOR) Non-Government Organizations (NGOs) Private/Business Others (Constitutional Govt, overseas)	27 8 3 3 7 2	54 16 6 6 14 4
Geographical Location of Office Luzon Visayas Mindanao Metro Manila Others (Asia, Africa, Europe, US, Middle East, etc.)	18 5 5 20 2	36 10 10 40 4

is where the capital city is located. This is followed by Luzon which is the largest among the three major islands in the Philippines with 36%. There were four students who are based in other countries. The huge number of students from the urban areas can be attributed to availability of ICT infrastructure. This is one of the reasons why digital learning really depends on the ICT infrastructure of the country.

19.4.4 Assessment of Future Skills

The research participants were asked to give their perceptions regarding the 17 Future Skills profiles as proposed by Ehlers and Kellermann (2019), keeping in mind the group tasks that were given to them. The rating ranged from 1 (strongly disagree) to 5 (strongly agree) that the competency is being met through the assignment. Based on their answers, they all "strongly agreed" that the tasks have enhanced their competencies with "Digital Literacy" given a score of 4.74. This can be attributed to the nature of the task wherein they need to work collaboratively using digital communication.

This is followed by "initiative and performance competence" with 4.70. The task required commitment from each member to accomplish the goal. Hence, there was an effort not to wait but to initiate communication to get the task finished. "Cooperation Competence" was also given a score of 4.68 which is the ability to cooperate and collaborate. The lowest rating is "Future Design Competence" and "Ambiguity competence" with 4.40 each (See Fig. 19.1).

Based on the answers, it can be gleaned that the research participants agreed that the collaborative assignment helped develop various Future Skills. It can also be noted that the top three competencies represented the three categories of "object-related," "subject development-related," and "organization related."

19.4.5 Comments of the Respondents on the Group Task and Future Skills

The survey also included open-ended questions to enable the research participants to share their comments regarding the group task; their experiences and their perceptions about the competencies based on the Future Skills. The following is a summary of the student feedback.

The group task can be a strategy to develop Future Skills. This is the general observation of the students regarding the group task. Some noted that they tried various collaboration strategies and brainstorming that helped them come up with the best strategy on how to do the assignment given the deadlines. Another suggested to include more collaborative tasks in the future since they are effective in

19 The "University of the Future" of the Philippines ...

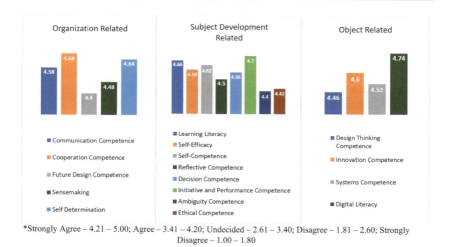

*Strongly Agree – 4.21 – 5.00; Agree – 3.41 – 4.20; Undecided – 2.61 – 3.40; Disagree – 1.81 – 2.60; Strongly Disagree – 1.00 – 1.80

Fig. 19.1 Perceptions of Students on the 17 Competencies Based on Future Skills

enhancing collaborative skills, which, in the actual practice is imperative in working with different agencies/organization towards a common purpose.

One also claimed that the task helped "not to immensely broaden the knowledge but to showcase the individual skills possessed by the students and to discover other skills of which can be applied in the future." Some noted that the activities have enhanced their analytical skills, improved digital literacy, and increased awareness on the stages of policies specially on the implementation and development.

Some also noted that these competencies (Future Skills) were being enhanced throughout the process of the activity. For example, they had to make sure that their data and information are accurate. Digital skills were also demonstrated through communication and creating the desired output and presentation. One respondent said that "the activities helped me a lot in terms of my writing and research skills." Some also noted that the group activity was a great tool in practicing camaraderie, interaction, coordination, as well as integration of all learnings since they have no opportunity for face-to-face interaction. Students still somehow get help from each other and refer to each other in terms of output and deadline, among other things through online platforms like Viber. This is also related to the idea of peer learning wherein interaction with other students with their preferred platform can also be beneficial for them.

Based on the feedback and comments from the students, it can be said that collaborative assignments can be an effective way to develop competencies for the future. Moreover, since the assignment entail the use of digital tools, this implies that digital learning also contributed to the success of this activity. The ability to decide on the accuracy of the data was also cited. Time management is also one of the skills which they have developed.

There is a need to increase awareness on futures skills or competences. Based on the comments of the students, they perceived that all these skills are important to face the VUCA (volatile, uncertain, complex and ambiguous) world which is also one of the topics discussed in one of their courses. It seems that the survey has also increased their awareness of the competencies that they need not only in their current job but could also prepare them to the demands of their work in the future. The comment that assignments can develop their competences also reveals that this is one aspect that should be explored by educators. Moreover, the Future Skills will enable an individual to become a more productive member of his/her organization and the country.

Collaborative assignments can be designed appropriately to develop competences. Based on the comments from students, it seems that collaborative assignments could be more challenging for online students since there is a higher possibility of non-participation. However, they also find it very important since most tasks nowadays require teamwork and collaboration. It is suggested that roles can be assigned to the students to facilitate the discussion. Moreover, it was also recommended to sustain the peer rating to make sure that only those who participated can have a grade for this activity.

19.5 Conclusions and Recommendations

The COVID-19 pandemic has affected all sectors of the society and served as a catalyst or game-changer particularly for the government and the education sector. As part of its plan to transition into the new normal, the Philippines has recognized that it will use its experiences in online learning and combine it with face-to-face learning or flexible learning. Moreover, it is also important to highlight the importance of HEIs and their administration in ensuring that reforms will be instituted.

The UPOU as a pioneer in open and distance e-learning (ODeL) is mandated to assist other HEIs on how to use ICT in education. Moreover, it has also acknowledged that the institution must adapt to the fast-changing world as it envisions the concept of the University of the Future.

As such, it has started the articulation of the concept to future-proof its degrees and skills to make learners be able to cope with the future challenges. A corollary to this is the challenge on how to design activities to develop Future Skills of learners. Hence, the MPM Program of the UPOU has redesigned and reimagined its assessment to determine if the Future Skills are being developed.

The study concludes that HEIs play an important role in the development of Future Skills. In the case of the UPOU, it has already articulated the use of digital technology including immersive technologies for skilling and upskilling and at the same time future-readying the degrees. It envisions itself as a lifelong university with the offering of micro-credential courses. In the case of the MPM Programs, it plans to develop its microlearning courses for public servants to be able to improve the delivery of public services and prepare them as well in the challenges that are brought in by the megatrends and the VUCA world.

The study also highlights that assignments can be a strategy to develop Future Skills of students, particularly group assignments. Group assignments enhance learners' decision-making and task and time management skills. It also allows learners to discern information provided online as well as develop digital skills. As mentioned by Zwart et al. (2020), it is necessary to set the criteria for the task and the rules regarding the online collaboration. This can be evident by the redesigned assignment wherein the criteria for grading were set including the mechanics on how to do the task to develop self-efficacy.

Moreover, digital learning is also an effective tool for learners to interact and communicate with each other that encourages collaborative learning. It also helps in developing learners' self-efficacy to accept new roles. This is one of the Future Skills identified by Ehlers and Kellermann (2019). Digital learning is also an effective tool for learners to interact and communicate with each other that encourages collaborative learning. It also helps in developing learners' self-efficacy to accept new roles as showed in the assignment wherein students take roles in the achievement of their assignment.

The study also contributes to the literature on Future Skills of public servants. So far, there has been very little information about the Future Skills of public servants and how to incorporate them in the curricula. Developing their skills is a big step since they are directly implementing policies, programs and projects towards development. They are also aware of the challenges brought about by the VUCA world and this could be addressed better if they are equipped with the competencies required for any disruption in the future.

Finally, this study contributes to the literature that establishes the relationship between digital learning and Future Skills, specifically for the public servants in the context of Southeast Asian region. It is also important to document other experiences in the future to enable Future Skills to be incorporated in the curricula of HEIs.

> **Future Skills in Practice: Our Recommendations**
> - Assignments can be a strategy to develop Future Skills of students, particularly group assignments. Group assignments enhance learners' decision-making and task and time management skills.
> - Digital learning is an effective tool for learners to interact and communicate with each other that encourages collaborative learning. It also helps in developing learners' self-efficacy to accept new roles.
> - There is a need to increase awareness on Future Skills, especially for HEIS.
> - There should be studies related to Future Skills specifically for the public servants in the context of Southeast Asian region. It is also important to document other experiences in the future to enable Future Skills to be incorporated in the curricula of HEIs.

References

Asian Development Bank. (2021). Reaping the benefits of industry 4.0 through skills development in high-growth industries in Southeast Asia: Insights from Cambodia, Indonesia, the Philippines, and Viet Nam. https://www.adb.org/sites/default/files/publication/671711/industry-skills-development-southeast-asia.pdf.

Association of Southeast Asian Nations. (2021). Human resources Development readiness in ASEAN: Regional report. https://sea-vet.net/images/seb/e-library/doc_file/892/asean-regional-hrd-reporten.pdf.

Bandalaria, M. d. P. (2021). *Unpacking the university of the future,* 2021. https://www.upou.edu.ph/uncategorized/unpacking-the-university-of-the-future/

Davies, A., Fidler, D., & Gorbis, M. (2011). Future work skills 2020. Palo Alto. https://www.voced.edu.au/content/ngv%3A49812.

Dede, C., & McGivney, E. (2021). Lifelong learning for careers that don't yet exist. In S. Jagannathan (Ed.), *Reimagining digital learning for sustainable development: How upskilling, data analytics, and educational technologies close the skills gap.* Routledge.

Ehlers, U.-D., & Kellermann, S. A. (2019). Future skills: The future of learning and higher education. Karlsruhe. https://www.learntechlib.org/p/208249.

Ehlers, U.-D., Geier, N., & Eigbrecht, L. (2022). Changing futures in higher education: Assessment of future skills learning. https://next-education.org/wp-content/uploads/2022/06/2022-06-07-Report-Self-Assessment-Version17-final.pdf.

Fidler, D. (2016). Future skills update and literature review. https://legacy.iftf.org/fileadmin/user_upload/downloads/wfi/ACTF_IFTF_FutureSkills-report.pdf.

Gervacio, J. L. (2022). Digital Education and future skills of public servants. *Embedded Selforganising Systems, 9*(4), 15–18. https://doi.org/10.14464/ess.v9i4.568.

Grand-Clement, S. (2017). Digital learning: Education and skills in the digital age. Santa Monica. www.rand.org/content/dam/rand/pubs/conf_proceedings/CF300/CF369/RAND_CF369.pdf.

International Labour Organization. (2021). Global framework on core skills for life and work in the 21st century (Report). https://iloskillskspstorage.blob.core.windows.net/development/resources/4944/wcms_813222.pdf.

OECD. (2017). Future of work and skills: Paper presented at the 2nd meeting of the g20 employment working group. https://www.oecd.org/els/emp/wcms_556984.pdf.

OECD. (2018). The future of education and skills: Education 2030. https://www.oecd.org/education/2030/E2030%20Position%20Paper%20(05.04.2018).pdf.

OECD. (2021). *OECD skills studies towards a skills strategy for Southeast Asia: Skills for post-COVID recovery and growth.* Paris.

Sariyatun, S., Suryani, N., Sutimin, L. A., Abidin, N. F., & Akmal, A. (2021). The effect of digital learning material on students' social skills in social studies learning. *International Journal of Instruction, 14*(3), 417–432. https://doi.org/10.29333/iji.2021.14324a.

Whiting, K. (2020). These are the top 10 job skills of tomorrow – And how long it takes to learn them. https://www.weforum.org/agenda/2020/10/top-10-work-skills-of-tomorrow-how-long-it-takes-to-learn-them/. Accessed 9 Febr 2023.

Zwart, D. P., Noroozi, O., van Luit, J. E., Goei, S. L., & Nieuwenhuis, A. (2020). Effects of digital learning materials on nursing students' mathematics learning, self-efficacy, and task value in vocational education. *Nurse Education in Practice, 44*, 102755. https://doi.org/10.1016/j.nepr.2020.102755.

Juvy Lizette M. Gervacio is an Assistant Professor and former Program Chair of the Master of Public Management of the University of the Philippines Open University. She has written several research papers and published articles on online education, capacity development of public servants, and public sector reforms. She obtained her PhD in E-learning at the Universitat Oberta de Catalunya (UOC), Barcelona, Spain. She finished her Master of Public Management from the University of Potsdam, Germany, and her Master of Arts in Demography at the University of the Philippines. ORCID ID: 0000-0001-6074-3496

Open Access This chapter is licensed under the terms of the Creative Commons Attribution 4.0 International License (http://creativecommons.org/licenses/by/4.0/), which permits use, sharing, adaptation, distribution and reproduction in any medium or format, as long as you give appropriate credit to the original author(s) and the source, provide a link to the Creative Commons license and indicate if changes were made.

The images or other third party material in this chapter are included in the chapter's Creative Commons license, unless indicated otherwise in a credit line to the material. If material is not included in the chapter's Creative Commons license and your intended use is not permitted by statutory regulation or exceeds the permitted use, you will need to obtain permission directly from the copyright holder.

Using Real-World Problems and Project-Based Learning for Future Skill Development: An Approach to Connect Higher Education Students and Society Through User-Centered Design

20

André Luiz Maciel Santana and Roseli de Deus Lopes

Abstract

Although technologies are increasingly present in people's pockets through powerful smartphones, the development of solutions centered on the user does not always follow this movement, creating a gap, mainly in hardware solutions. At the same time, the role of the modern engineer is rethought as the demands of the industry and the way the population consumes technology are also changing. Furthermore, Future Skills, such as Design Thinking, Real-World Problems Solving, User-Centered Design, and Digital Literacy, are increasingly necessary to connect higher education students with complex social problems and their contexts. This paper analyses and compiles the results of an engineering program to operationalize real-world problem solutions in higher education by a User-Centered Design that aims to approach Future Skills in a Computer Engineering Course. It promotes discussion on a case study with 49 students from a Microcontroller and Internet of Things

---

A. L. M. Santana (✉)
Professor, Insper Institute of Education and Research, São Paulo, Brazil
e-mail: andrelms4@insper.edu.br

R. de Deus Lopes
Associate Professor, Universidade de São Paulo (USP), São Paulo, Brazil
e-mail: roseli.lopes@usp.br

© The Author(s) 2024
U.-D. Ehlers and L. Eigbrecht (eds.), *Creating the University of the Future*, Zukunft der Hochschulbildung - Future Higher Education,
https://doi.org/10.1007/978-3-658-42948-5_20

class, from a Brazilian university, in the year 2020 and during the pandemic period. It was possible to conclude that the program stimulates the development of modern skills and encourages students to design solutions based on people's real needs. The results also indicate the enhancement of competencies such as Design Thinking, developing in teams, Digital Literacy, design with and for the user, solving complex problems by interacting with real-world issues, and communication skills.

20.1 Introduction

When facing complex problems, it is natural to involve people with different approaches and previous knowledge to find solutions that may be suitable for solving as many challenges as possible. Interacting with real users in each project step allows us to design a viable, feasible, and desirable solution (Dennehy et al., 2019). The role of engineers, designers, and scientists has undergone significant changes in the face of social and market demands. According to Goldberg and Somerville (2014) and Santana and Lopes (2020), educational institutions play a crucial role in this transformation. Studies such as Graham (2018) indicate the trend towards defining the user as a central part of a design process. Also, in Graham's review (2018), the author highlights those best practices in engineering education which include: (i) User-Centered Design, (ii) hands-on experiential learning and (iii) opportunities for entrepreneurial development within and beyond the curriculum.

From the design point of view, Coyne (2005) revisits the concept of Tame and Wicked Problems, describing Tame Problems as well-defined problems with a single goal and a set of well-defined rules. That kind of problem is part of many subjects in engineering courses, from solving mathematical problems to understanding and reproducing a phenomenon with solid restrictions. Students have a clear goal and can measure if they have completed the task or not. An example of that could be a challenge to connect two different devices that need to send a message between a predefined network system by the HTTP request. This challenge represents an excellent opportunity to practice different skills, such as *Programming a computer, specifying and understanding a network architecture, physical programming, teamwork and time management, and maybe defining a microcontroller or an embedded system and communicating* the solution. However, this approach does not represent real-world problems because the cases have solid frontiers: no user is required, and the problem is free of context. Also, students do not have to discuss with the user or revisit the problem definition because it is well-formulated and has a well-defined answer.

Rittel and Webber (1973), confirmed by Coyne (2005) and Skaburskis (2008), define problems of importance as Wicked Problems. Those problems, in contrast to Tame Problems, do not have a single solution; they usually need to be investigated and reformulated and depend on the viewpoint of those presenting them. Furthermore, those problems have a strong connection with the social context. By not having a well-defined structure or a unique strategy, we cannot specify a definitive solution. Thus, it is essential to choose one candidate solution that must be connected with a hypothesis based on user needs and incorporates the assumptions and restrictions designed by a team.

Following the same example of the Tame Problem, we can set a context: message exchange between an instructor and a student in a public school in the North Region (Brazil). Setting user/persona in an equation will make measuring and producing a more challenging, viable, feasible, and desirable solution than a solution designed for a sandbox classroom.

Consequently, students are faced with some questions: *what kind of message will the user send? Do users have connection issues? Do you have stable connectivity? Do you have full-time access to the internet? What is the primary goal of the solution? And if it rains, will the connection remain reliable?* That is an excellent opportunity to connect students with Real-World Problems Solving because, at this point, it is mandatory to go beyond the institution walls to answer those questions.

Sarathy (2018) describes that Real-World Problems are different from regular classroom problems because these problems are dynamic, not linear, with many reconnections, refactored scenarios, and subproblems. Fortus et al. (2005) define Real-World Problems as not well-defined state problems that start with identifying a context, followed by background research, and prioritize collecting feedback from the people impacted by the solution.

In this same scenario, it is essential to highlight that we live in the fourth industrial revolution, characterized by communication and information technology, prioritizing the capability to solve complex problems based on social, economic, and political changes. That also involves developing in short periods, prioritizing custom product development, and applying flexibility and a decentralization approach (Lasi et al., 2014).

This chapter presents a case study of a program for Real-World Problems Solving by Project-Based Learning with a User-Centered Design approach. This program was an adaption of approaches of the *Startup Garage Innovation Process* and *Design Thinking*, including materials and methods to operationalize the design of solutions for complex problems in engineering higher education in six (6) courses. The main results of a case study in Computer Engineering classrooms in 2020 are presented.

At the end of this chapter, the following questions are answered:

- What material and methods are necessary to introduce Real-World Problems Solving by Project-Based Learning into Higher Education?
- What Future Skills are developed with Real-World Problems Solving?
- How can we assess projects developed using this methodology?

This chapter will be divided into five sections. Section 20.1 is a short introduction to Real-World Problems and methods that could help engineering students work in teams to solve complex problems. Section 20.2 discusses Future Skills and how some of these can be applied by engineers to solve wicked problems in a real-world approach. Section 20.3 then introduces User-Centered Design and Real-World Problem Solving as necessary engineering skills for problem solving. Section 20.4 will then present the case study in which a method to develop Future Global Skills through Real-World Problems Solving is proposed. To finish the chapter, Sects. 20.5 and 20.6 will summarize and discuss the results of the case study, respectively.

20.2 Defining Future Skills

Santana and Lopes (2020) present a systematic review of the literature about expected skills for engineers in Industry 4.0 and Active Learning Methodologies. They conceptualize three different profiles of classroom engineering projects that involve Real-World Problems Solving:

1. Real-World Problems Solving by Project-Based Learning approach and without scope limitation by instructors/researchers. Additionally, the design process could be split into two directions: (i) one that starts by developing a prototype with an evaluation at the end of the process and (ii) one that has a minimum viable product with user evaluation in each step.

2. Real-World Problems Solving by Project-Based Learning with limited scope by instructors/researchers in the problem definition step of the design. Usually, the design process starts with a case study or has solid frontiers.
3. Project-Based Learning and well-defined problems with a well-defined scope, but with a focus on the main course themes to promote the development of pre-defined skills, tools, technologies, or theories/concepts.

Dos Reis et al. (2019) describe the main results of an innovation course at the University of São Paulo involving an innovative and entrepreneurial approach to connect students with user-centered learning. Several studies highlight the role of the university that needs to incorporate active-learning methodologies and changes in engineering and scientist profiles (see Fortus et al., 2005; Freeman et al., 2014; Goldberg & Somerville, 2014; Santana & Deus Lopes, 2020; Zappe et al., 2009). Those studies indicate that the curriculum needs to be more strongly connected to Real-World Problems and that active learning methods based on projects must include both soft and hard skills development.

Kamaruzaman et al. (2019) and Santana and Lopes (2020) emphasize which soft skills are expected by engineering professionals in the era of Industry 4.0. In Table 20.1, the left side highlights the skills expected in the labor market as described by Kamaruzaman et al. (2019). The author emphasizes non-technical skills that must be mastered by engineering graduates from three different points of view: (i) that follow the most cited skills from 18 of twenty countries that signed the Washington Accord in the report compiled by the World Economic Forum (2016); (ii) from the skills required for the Industry 4.0 era; and (iii) from skill demands expected by employers in Industry 4.0.

In the right side of Table 20.1, Santana and Lopes (2020) highlight a set of skills presented by studies in higher education for the era of Industry 4.0. The authors particularly emphasize the skills mentioned in papers about Project-Based Learning in engineering curriculums.

Let us compare the left and right tables. Some skills present in both studies can be checked: (i) Active Learning and Learning Autonomy, (ii) Creativity, Originality, and Initiative, (iii) Critical Thinking and Analysis, (iv) Leadership, Social Influence, and Teamwork, and (v) Problem Solving. Skills such as innovation, leadership, and initiative are indirectly connected with communication, creativity, and problem solving. However, from an employer's point of view, solving complex problems is more frequent in the real world of work than solving well-defined problems.

Given this context, it is possible to verify changes in the profile of engineers of the twenty-first century influenced by labor market expectations and social needs.

Table 20.1 Skills expected in Industry 4.0—employer's point of view (left) and academic papers point of view (right)

Kamaruzaman et al. (2019)	Santana and Lopes (2020)
Analytical Thinking and Innovation	Learning Autonomy
Active Learning and Learning Strategies	Collaboration
Creativity, Originality and Initiative	Communication—Writing/ Speaking
Technology Design and Programming	Creativity
Critical Thinking and Analysis	Time Management
Complex Problem Solving	Leadership
Leadership and Social Influence	Personal Organization
Emotional Intelligence	Critical Thinking
Reasoning, Problem Solving and Ideation	Problem Solving
System Analysis and Evaluation	Teamwork

There is also a change in the international posture concerning the expectations about the background and role of an engineer and how an engineer can collaborate to change the stance about the production of new products, services, and disruptive technologies. This type of change also affects competitiveness on a global scale, which requires developing skills related to solving increasingly complex problems in the classroom.

In terms of soft skills, engineering graduates' skills for the future are related to (i) **Design Thinking and user experience**; (ii) **Real-World Problems Solving** and how to design solutions for complex problems; (iii) Teamwork and mastering tools for collaborative design; (iv) **User-Centered Design** and the ability to create with and for the user; (v) **Analytical Thinking** and evidence-based decision-making; and (vi) **Self-knowledge-learning** management. From a technical point of view, skills for the future include (i) **Digital Literacy** and the ability to create technology rather than just consuming technology; (ii) **Computer programming**, in order to improve and operationalize solutions; (iii) **Co-design** tools and frameworks to design *with* and *for* the user; and (iv) **modeling tools** to elaborate Digital and Tangible Minimum Viable Products (MVP). In this way, the resolution of real problems primarily involves the participation of real users, which implies the need to develop non-technical social skills to approach problems, and technical skills to facilitate the gathering of requirements and the validation of results with key stakeholders. Additionally, those approaches improve access to the development of Future Global Skills, such as Design Thinking and user experience, Real-World Problems Solving, User-Centered Design, and the capability to design based on Analytical Thinking, *with* and *for* the user.

20.3   User-Centered Design and Real-World Problems Solving

Problem solving with an engineering method usually starts with a problem. However, engineering students often have difficulty in building a good definition of the problems to solve or even in adequately defining the scope of their projects. Usually, students anticipate a solution or technology that will be the subject of the project instead of understanding the problem itself. Other times, they choose a strategy in which they assume that they must control both the process of building a solution and the process of scaling it. Therefore, a problem-definition protocol was developed (see Sect. 20.4) that allows students to scale a problem. Those tools embody the main foundations of Design Thinking by Tim Brown (2008) and were designed based on principles highlighted by Schallmo et al. (2018), Dos Reis et al. (2019), and Leal et al. (2020).

The double-Diamond Design Process was developed by the British Design Council in 2005 and analyzed by Gustafsson (2019) to identify suitable methods for designing a solution based on design principles. In this study, this process was adapted to be applied to the engineering classroom, proposing to help students define a Point of View about a problem (see Fig. 20.1). Sometimes, students do not have an authentic experience with a situation. For example, if the point of view is "Visually Impaired People *need* a solution to walk on Sao Paulo streets **because** they feel as if they almost always need help from others, and this makes them feel dependent", frequently, students do not have experience or do not meet people that live with this problem. So it is essential to know the reality of those who experience this problem, reducing the number of doubts and uncertainties and designing solutions that are desirable by the user.

Wright et al. (2017), Dos Reis et al. (2019), and Leal et al. (2020) describe the Startup Garage Innovation Process as an entrepreneurship course that aims to develop an innovative and sustainable business model as fast as possible (based on agile methodology) besides collecting pieces of evidence with the user. Stanford Graduate School of Business (2020) defines Startup Garage as an "intensive, hands-on and project-based course, in which students design and test new business concepts that address real-world needs".

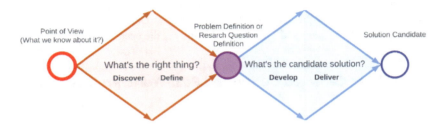

Fig. 20.1 Double-Diamond Process and Point of View Definition

Chanin et al. (2018) did a systematic mapping study to analyze and evaluate studies on software innovation in education. After reviewing 31 papers, the authors summarize the contributions, listing a couple of methodologies that contribute to (i) identifying the business model with Business Model Canvas, (ii) validating business hypotheses with the customer, (iii) developing User-Centered Design Thinking, and (iv) working with the Agile Software Development Method. Chanin et al. (2018) describe that the most challenging part of this methodology is identifying real-world problems and properly characterizing them. They highlight that the best methodological practices involve (i) *evaluating the process*, (ii) *working on real projects*, (iii) *providing opportunities for multidisciplinarity*, (iv) *creating opportunities for external validations and creating an appropriate environment for it, and* (v) *engaging in the next step* (what's the next level for the project?).

Agile Software Development Methods focus on simplicity and speed in the development flow. The Manifesto for Agile Software Development, proposed by Beck et al. (2001), focuses on the user and suggests that the development process is about individuals and interaction, working product, customer collaboration, and the capability to respond to change. This paper thus works on the hypothesis that bringing Agile Software Development in conjunction with Design Thinking and supported by Startup Garage Innovation Process is a significant first step to operationalizing Projects in Higher Education focusing on Real-World Problems.

Section 20.4 presents the methodology proposed in this study to operationalize Real-World Problems Solving Based-Learning in higher education. In the scope of this paper, students will develop a product with a business model, which may or may not accompany a service, and which necessarily involves physical programming with an ATMega328 microcontroller. To this end, an 18-week higher education program was designed based on the methods in this section to promote Future Skills development and allow students to scale solutions to real problems and test their creations with real users.

20.4 Case Study

The results in Sect. 20.5 were part of a Microcontroller and Internet of Things Program of a Brazilian University with students in the second year of Computer Engineering. The program lasted **18 weeks**, with classes of **3 h each**, and was a case study for this paper. Note that this is not a linear process. It is possible to advance and roll back in each stage until the student communicates the results in the presentation. The **class** was **split** into **two** parts: (i) the first one dealing with the design process, including entrepreneurship skills, and (ii) the second one dealing with the main themes of the Microcontroller and IoT course, with **1.5 h** each, followed by homework tasks.

20.4.1 Materials and Methods

During the development of solutions for Real-World Problems, one of the most important steps is to identify the problem and follow the best candidate solution to create a **viable, feasible,** and **desirable** solution. Figure 20.2 illustrates an adaption of the Startup Garage Innovation that includes protocols and frameworks for each step and a hypothesis-building stage before the Point of View (PoV) definition.

Initially, students are invited to think about different research areas, choosing between one of the five main areas shown in Fig. 20.3. After that, without any systematic process and individually, the students start to think about problems related to the theme they chose for a team discussion in class 2.

In this course, three restrictions were pre-defined: (i) students must develop projects related to one of the themes, (ii) the developed project must generate a solution capable of solving a problem for a group of people, and (iii) the project must contemplate a solution that involves physical programming, and possibly internet of things. The topics internet of things and "physical programming" were chosen because the course was written to develop technical skills in those fields and because these are critical themes in Industry 4.0. **Student groups** must have between **three** and **six members**.

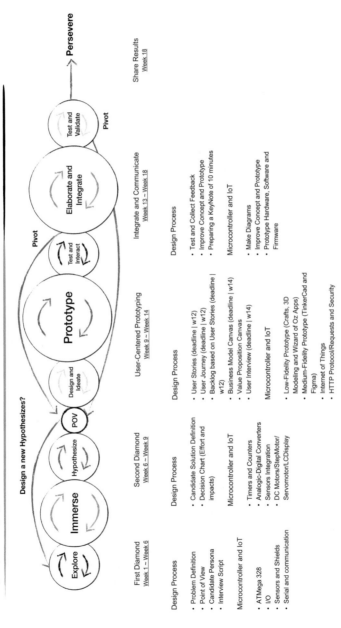

Fig. 20.2 Real-World Problems Solving Program, an Adaptation of Startup Garage Innovation

Accessibility and Assistive Technologies Energy and Sustainability

Food and Public Health Education and Access to Information

Environment and Circular Economy

Fig. 20.3 General topics suggested by the instructor

20.4.2 Program Block 1: First Diamond and Problem Definition

Firstly, in the **Explore Step**, students try to find a problem and work with non-guided brainstorming on topics suggested by the instructor (Fig. 20.3). After that, students are invited to think about **four** different dimensions of a problem, as represented in Table 20.2.

Still in the exploration stage, students write a point of view as follows:
[WHO?] needs [WHAT?] because [HOW DOES THAT IMPACT THE WHO?] or [TO SOLVE WHICH PROBLEM?]

After having drawn a Candidate's Point of View and a Candidate User Persona, students can start on the **Formulation Step** and begin to draw a proto persona, including:

- **A profile image** of a non-public figure, using an open-licensed image
- **A set of demographic data**, such as name, age, gender, salary range, and region where someone lives
- **Technological fluency**, evaluating experience with digital and analog technologies, but mainly focusing on applications for mobile devices, social networks, and intelligent solutions that use sensors
- **Needs and goals** related to the Point of View designed by the students in the previous stage.
- **A small biography**, including important information about the needs and objectives

Following this, the **Hypothesis Step** is started, in which students make significant doubts and assumptions about the problem and possible users in team. The results of this step are used to create an interview script for the **Immersion Step**, in which students are expected to interview at least three people who fit some of the characteristics of the proto persona they created.

Table 20.2 Problem Definition Protocol: four dimensions of a problem

Dimensions	Description	Protocol
Pillars of the Project	Secondary research to register primary references and how they contribute to understanding a problem, and different approaches used by other designers and researchers	**[THE REFERENCE]** is an inspiration for this project because it allows us to understand better **[HOW? or WHAT?]**
Design Constraints	Important conditions for the project to be coherent, viable, and feasible. In this block, students list which elements impose limits on the project and help define scope and alignment strategies	Given that **[WHAT/WHO]** constrains this project **[IN WHAT WAY?]**, so **[WHAT ARE YOU INTENDED TO DO?]**
Impacting the Persona	A mapping connects users who experience the proposed problem (structure as a user profile) with life changes that illustrate a genuine contribution to facing the proposed problem	By solving this problem, the **[TARGET AUDIENCE]** will be impacted **[IN WHAT WAY?]**
Gaps and Advantages	A mapping of genuine issues or opportunities that justify "why solving this problem?". Sometimes students target to develop a new product or process and ignore already tested solutions or do not recognize characteristics of the context that could generate a more well-defined problem. Here students are invited to think about differences that could be characterized as a contribution	This issue needs to be resolved, as the existing solutions were not built considering **[WHAT?]** This problem needs to be solved because it considers **[WHAT GAP?]**

In this process, it is crucial to understand that only a real user can describe a real problem. Therefore, students are invited to elaborate on their **interview script** to collect more information about user issues and refine their Point-of-View. It is suggested to structure the interview into four sections:

- **Sect. 1**: Present the project to the participants, highlighting the conversation objectives, and clarify the data usage and acquisition process.
- **Sect. 2**: Includes questions about demographics and trying to establish a relationship with the interviewee.
- **Sect. 3**: Discuss the problem, with questions such as "How does the user deal with the problem? How does the user search for solutions to this problem? What does he or she already know about solutions to this problem? What makes finding a solution to this problem difficult?".
- **Sect. 4**: Specific questions, including branch questions. For example: "if the user answers that, I will ask about ...".

Throughout the process, students are challenged not to ask the user's opinion about their solution but to understand what he/she feels about the problem. Also, questions that stimulate the "why?" and "how?" are better than multiple-choice or yes-or-no questions because, with more open questions, they can achieve more with real stories rather than pre-formatted answers. After that, they analyze the results, revisiting the Point of View and proto persona to consolidate it. This step usually occurs in class when students write Post-it notes with doubts and assumptions.

In parallel to these steps, students study themes and exercises related to (i) the elements and components of a project that involves embedded systems; (ii) the life cycle of an application that uses the ATMega 328p microcontroller; (iii) I/O in ATMega 328p; (iv) sensors and shields for Arduino[1]; and (v) serial and communication protocols.

At this moment of the course, students have spent *six weeks* structuring the first phase of the double diamond, as suggested in Fig. 20.1. As a result of this stage, students have a clear idea of who their target audience is, for whom they are developing, and with whom they should talk to gather knowledge. Also, they have the basics of microelectronics to start phase 2 of the course, which focuses on structuring models, prototypes, and the validation strategy.

---

[1] Open-source electronic prototyping platform enabling users to create interactive electronic objects.

20.4.3 Program Block 2: Second Diamond and Candidate Solution Selection

Before starting the prototyping step, students should decide on the best Candidate Solution that matches the problem defined in the **PoV Step**. For this, students should do a new brainstorming (following the second diamond suggested in Fig. 20.1), and each one needs to elaborate on at least one Candidate Solution. Each student needs to illustrate a Candidate Solution considering that their proposal for the other team members should highlight answers to the following questions: (i) How does the solution solve the problem and mainly, solve the problem of our persona? (ii) What resources are needed to prototype this solution? (iii) How does the solution relate to the program objectives? (iv) Our team can develop this solution because our team has *[STUDENT NAME]*, who is capable of *[WHAT;]* (v) Does our solution involve a product? A service? Both? Finally, it is also suggested that the students make a free sketch on paper to illustrate this. After that, students should vote on the Candidate Solutions using a Decision Chart, as represented in Fig. 20.4.

For the next step, students should receive a pair of cards with numbers 1, 2, 3, 5, 8, and 13 (Fibonacci Series), as shown in Fig. 20.5. This series was chosen because the weight of numbers in the lower or upper limit significantly impacts student choices. This process is like the Planning Poker used in software development with Agile Methods. However, students can establish criteria that are more aligned with the course theme or team characteristics (repertoire, technical skills, training, among others).

Students individually start to vote on Candidate Solutions; each student receives six yellow and six green cards containing the numbers identified in Fig. 20.5. After that, they distribute the team effort points and impact points (without sharing with teammates) for each Candidate Solution. For the yellow cards, 1 represents a solution quickly reachable and 13 represents a solution that is hard to reach. For the green cards, 1 has little impact on the user and 13 has a high impact on the user.

As a product of those steps, students finally complete the second diamond and need to start to prototype their solution. They need to select some tools that could contribute to that. As described in Fig. 20.2, students will do low-cost and low-fidelity prototypes to validate with the user as fast as possible. Furthermore, they need to draw a schedule with a 15–30 day sprint to generate the most value potential in their prototypes before creating the most elaborate prototype. For such a program, a two-week sprint is recommended.

20 Using Real-World Problems and Project-Based Learning …

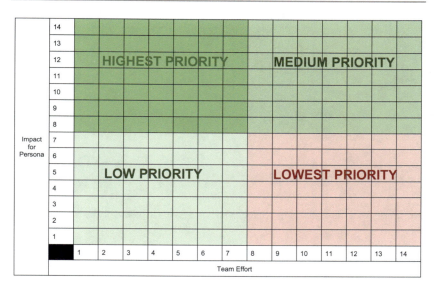

Fig. 20.4 Decision Chart

Fig. 20.5 Effort and Impact Points

At the end of this stage, students will be in **week 9**, that is, halfway through the course. During the classes, they will also have practiced traditional technical skills related to Microcontrollers and Internet of Things topics.

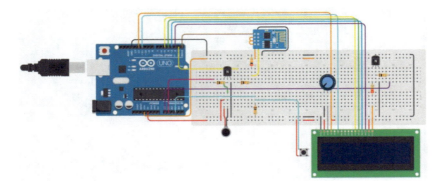

Fig. 20.6 A wearable that helps seniors with Alzheimer's in their daily tasks

20.4.4 Program Block 3: Prototyping and Validating with the User

In this step, students are invited to plan a backlog with the essential tasks that are of value for the user. The protocols designed in this step follow the principles of *Design Thinking* and *Agile Software Development Methodologies*.

They start the **Design and Ideate Step** and elaborate a low-cost prototype. If they develop software or an embedded system, the first version of the prototype will be made with paper, a pencil, and a ruler; after that, they will take pictures using the *POP Application* with their smartphones to simulate a flow. Alternatively, students can prototype an embedded system using a simulator such as TinkerCad (see Fig. 20.6) before starting to develop in real hardware. However, if they deliver a physical prototype, the prototype first version is drawn in a flat superior view, using a flip chart OR modeling clay (see Fig. 20.7).

After that, they need to interact with at least three users to show their solutions and collect feedback. They thus start to elaborate on a **User Journey** and **User Stories** to help define a backlog of development. For a **User Journey**, students draw a process that starts with the user's perception of having a problem that needs to be solved and ends with the user interacting with the proposed solution, using it, and providing feedback about the experience. Students must register user feelings and try to sketch "small sentences" that could illustrate the user's emotion during the process.

User Stories (see Fig. 20.8) are small clippings that contemplate the moments that make up the user's journey. For this, students must structure a story focused

Fig. 20.7 Motorcycle Support for a mechanic shop with constrained space

Fig. 20.8 User Story template—prioritizing team effort and story value (user point of view)

on the user and actions simply enough so that they can be prioritized and implemented according to the need and the value that these stories must compose a solution.

This stage has two breakpoints; the first in **week 12** (backlog list with user's story) and the second in **week 14** (user interview and measurement of features acceptance). At the end of this stage, students also advance with technical concepts related to the *Internet of Things*, *HTTP protocol*, *requests*, *encryption*, and *data security*. Furthermore, students work on **a business plan** and set the value of the task for the user, rethinking the Point of View with tools such as **Business Model Canvas** and **Value Proposition Canvas**.

20.4.5 Program Block 4: Integrating and Communicating

The last few weeks (between week 13 and week 18) will be studio classes (classes with developing project emphasis). In this sense, students reinforce the necessary technical concepts in the laboratory with the instructor, and in week 15, they perform an intermediate presentation to review and mature the projects.

The students demonstrate the results by preparing a presentation that should not exceed 10 min. This presentation must contain (i) information related to the problem and the primary references used to understand the problem; (ii) the results of the prototype development, highlighting each of the versions; (iii) the technical diagrams, which involve Physical Programming and Web Applications (if applicable); (iv) the results of the user interviews; (v) the business model; and (vi) the future steps, followed by the main conclusions. Students also need to elaborate a commercial pitch, between 1 and 3 min, to summarize the project from a business point of view.

20.4.6 Project Assessment

The grades are composed of the products generated in the Design Process and the incorporation of technical knowledge (Microcontroller and Internet of Things). Design process assessments involve the deliverables: (i) problem definition, (ii) persona definition, (iii) interviews, (iv) problem and persona review, (v) user journey, (vi) user stories and backlog, (vii) feature review, (viii) two interviews for prototype validation, preparing a benchmark to show the main differences (one in **week 12** and another until **week 17**). So, those deliverables are assessed by a formative assessment.

Design steps tend to encourage the development of **Future Skills** such as **Real-World Problems Solving** by connecting students with real users and their needs. In order to promote **Design Thinking,** the product is based on user-centered design, **Teamwork,** because in each step, students need to evidence the main contributions and how they can improve the contribution of each member, **Analytical Thinking** by an elaborate hypothesis based on evidence and defining paths by Primary and Secondary Research. **Self-learning management** is when students find new technical components or technologies to include in the MVP or a new tool to interact with the users to map their needs.

In parallel, this course targets traditional **technical skills** related to Microcontrollers and Internet of Things. By incorporating technical skills to operationalize the expected results from the design process, students develop Future Skills such as **Digital Literacy** when:

- Developing an MVP using a **programming language**.
- Scheduling meetings, defining goals, and planning together using **collaborative design tools**.
- Seeking computational resources to **optimize project** planning and **interact with the user**.
- Incorporating strategies to **develop digital prototypes**.

Also, students work in solutions that include three pillars of Industry 4.0, such as **rapid prototyping**, when students create models to prototype with a 3D printer, **computer simulation** to test solutions, and **cloud computing** and **the internet of things** to develop prototypes.

The final presentation involves a panel of external professors who appraise the projects and assess the students through rubrics.

The following section consolidates the main results of the research, mainly involving (i) the assessment of non-technical skills developed by students, (ii) the average score obtained at the end of the course, and (iii) some projects developed by students throughout the study.

20.5 Results

In addition to these assessments, students answered a self-assessment questionnaire, which included questions about technical and non-technical skills expected by the program and related to the *Future Skills* listed in the previous section. All in all, 49 students from the Computer Engineering program experienced the course and answered both the pre-test and the post-test anonymously (each student used a unique identifier to fill out the form). In general, students showed good progress in all the skills assessed throughout the program.

Whereas topics related to the business model and the value proposition concerning the technical knowledge of the Design process had a more significant increase in the score, topics related to hardware development with Arduino had the highest score increase in technical knowledge.

When dealing with non-technical skills, the score with the most significant increase was noticed to be related to the student's perception of solving problems using hardware; this is positive since the core of the discipline focuses on physical programming. However, the non-technical skills related to leadership and planning, respectively identified in the attributes (i) organizing goals for your team and (ii) creating a schedule and distributing tasks, did not validate the alternative hypothesis and indicated that there was no significant change after the practical experience in the program.

This may have occurred because: (i) a specific strategy was not implemented to define a leader; (ii) the project took the form of self-management on the part of the students, who, despite having decentralized the actions, did not identify leaders for each of the project's areas; and (iii) due to the maturity of the students, who, for the most part, had their first project experience in higher education and, for the first time, in designing with and for the user.

In addition to answering about skills development, the student also answered questions about the individual perception of the program. This course, in general, represented the students' first experience with the development of an unguided project without a pre-defined scope by the instructor (concerning the problem). The students' statements also highlight the importance of the students being monitored by the instructor in each stage and how other skills, not necessarily belonging to the course, are fundamental in the students' view for structuring the students' mindset. Furthermore, students' comments indicate that this approach supports the development of Global Future Skills such as Design Thinking and entrepreneurship, Real-World Problems Solving, Learning Literacy, Communication, and User-Centered Design.

20.5.1 Outstanding Projects

Twenty-Four projects were developed during the program by 24 different teams. The projects listed in Table 20.3 were the ones that stood out regarding the development of the solution at the hardware and software levels. They additionally structured a good business model with User-Centered Design.

Each project developed a physical prototype, accompanied by an article presenting the main results. The 4D1 team project involved only physical programming, while the 10D1 and 13D3 teams also involved the internet of things. All the projects experienced the entire cycle of the discipline, designed a set of personas, and validated their solutions with the user, collecting evidence of the use of the solution. The 13D3 team, for example, validated their solution with 54 people, of

20 Using Real-World Problems and Project-Based Learning ...

Table 20.3 Outstanding Projects in 2020

Team 4D1: **People who frequent small shops in São Paulo** need a *system of hand hygiene and access control to establishments*, as it is necessary to *reduce the proliferation of the new coronavirus and control the number of people in each place to avoid agglomeration*

Team 10D1: **Residents of the city of São Paulo** need a *more efficient electric cost control energy system* because, with the pandemic, it has become *necessary for better population autonomy regarding their expenses, or at least a double-check system for that*

Team 13D3: **Seniors who suffer from the condition degenerative Alzheimer's** need support *so that they do not get lost and carry out their daily tasks*, as *many lose their autonomy, get frustrated, and make their families worried because of the disease*

which 62% have a family member or know someone with Alzheimer's. The 4D1 and 10D1 teams performed the validations with at least five users.

All the teams indicated in their results that they generated changes in the project design due to interactions with the user. The 4D1 squad, for example, stated the need for changes to the user interface and concerns about fixing the equipment in public places. The 10D1 team, in turn, identified the need to improve the graphical interface and the usability of the Web system and incorporated the role of the person who performs measurements in homes (this action takes place manually in Brazil) into its business model. This was due to the frequent concern of the team, confirmed by the interviews, regarding the sustainability of the jobs. The 13D3 team was challenged to rethink the user interaction strategy and involve multidisciplinary health professionals as a central part of its user group.

In addition, all the teams performed a Pitch for the institution's technology incubator and received feedback regarding their business model (but did not incorporate this step in the discipline evaluation).

20.6 Discussion

This paper highlights the main results of a methodological process for Real-World Problems Solving in engineering courses based on innovation projects concerned with the sustainability of the solution and its impacts on a real user. In addition, the article also highlights a strategy for evaluating the project and the student's trajectory, considering that the discipline needs to incorporate technical subjects; in this context, related to Microcontrollers and the Internet of Things, in the engineering field.

The results indicated that the students improved the skillset designed for the discipline. These skills agree with what engineering professionals expect to fully exercise in their social and professional roles in the era of Industry 4.0.

Concerning the strategy and materials needed for this type of activity in the classroom, note that students must have access to computers, the internet, and materials that enable the construction of prototypes. However, for the context of the discipline, some simulators, such as TinkerCad and software for design, can favor the reduction of costs with physical products, considering that there are some losses regarding the tangibility of the built solutions and the validation process with users at more advanced stages.

Students understand that the process favored the development of Future Skills such as:

1. Learning autonomy.
2. The ability to solve real-world problems with different complexities and co-designing with real users.
3. Teamwork and negotiation to work with other people.
4. Thinking of different approaches to find more creative solutions, negotiation, and evidence-based judgment.

Wicked Problems and real-world problems, from an engineering point of view, are complex and are connected with the expectations of industry and society for the engineer of the XXI century profile. Thus, rethinking higher engineering education to promote, practice, and develop skills connected with the following social and environmental challenges, must be considered in constructing new engineering curricula. Furthermore, Global Future Skills are encouraged by this program when students start: (i) defining a real problem; (ii) improving the problem statement when interacting with real users; (iii) working within multidisciplinary teams; (iv) negotiating features and prioritizing tasks; (v) interacting with potential users; (vi) validating ideas or improving features; and (vii) when students work in an MVP approach, to evaluate how the solution could affect users' problems, by giving more value, and less risk.

Future Skills in Practice: Our Recommendations
Design Thinking, Real-World Problems Solving, Teamwork, User-Centered Design, Analytical Thinking, Self-Learning Management, Digital Literacy, and Programming Computers are important engineering

> **Future Skills.** It's important to make students conscious of these skills and integrate them into engineering curricula.
>
> Also, students strengthen the pillars of **Industry 4.0,** emphasizing the **internet** of **things, cloud computing, computer programming, computer simulation**, and **additive manufacturing**. This approach can be recommended for other contexts from other design disciplines.

References

Association for Computing Machinery. (Ed.). (2018). *Proceedings of the 22nd international conference on evaluation and assessment in software engineering.*

Beck, K., Beedle, M., Bennekum, A., Cockburn, A., Cunningham, W., Fowler, M., et al. (2001). Manifesto for agile software development. https://agilemanifesto.org/.

Brown, T. (2008). Design thinking. *Harvard Business Review, 86*(6), 84.

Chanin, R., Pompermaier, L., Sales, A., & Prikladnicki, R. (2018). A systematic mapping study on software startups education. In Association for Computing Machinery (Ed.), *Proceedings of the 22nd international conference on evaluation and assessment in software engineering* (pp. 163–168). https://doi.org/10.1145/3210459.3210478.

Coyne, R. (2005). Wicked problems revisited. *Design Studies, 26*(1), 5–17. https://doi.org/10.1016/j.destud.2004.06.005.

Dennehy, D., Kasraian, L., O'Raghallaigh, P., Conboy, K., Sammon, D., & Lynch, P. (2019). A Lean Start-up approach for developing minimum viable products in an established company. *Journal of Decision Systems, 28*(3), 224–232. https://doi.org/10.1080/12460125.2019.1642081.

Dos Reis, D. A., Fleury, A. L., Bento, T., Fabbri, K., Ortega, L. M., & Bagnato, V. (2019). Application of new agile approaches at University of São Paulo innovation agency's entrepreneurship and innovation course. *Gestao e Producao, 26*(4). https://doi.org/10.1590/0104-530X4122-19.

Fortus, D., Krajcik, J., Dershimer, R. C., Marx, R. W., & Mamlok-Naaman, R. (2005). Design-based science and real-world problem-solving. *International Journal of Science Education, 27*(7), 855–879. https://doi.org/10.1080/09500690500038165.

Freeman, S., Eddy, S. L., McDonough, M., Smith, M. K., Okoroafor, N., Jordt, H., et al. (2014). Active learning increases student performance in science, engineering, and mathematics. *Proceedings of the National Academy of Sciences, 111*(23), 8410–8415.

Goldberg, D. E., & Somerville, M. (2014). *A whole new engineer: The coming revolution in Engineering Education.* Threejoy.

Graham, R. (2018). *The global state of the art in engineering education.* Massachusetts Institute of Technology (MIT) Report.

Gustafsson, D. (2019). Analyzing the double diamond design process through research & implementation. Aalto University. https://core.ac.uk/download/pdf/224802861.pdf.

Kamaruzaman, M. F., Hamid, R., Mutalib, A. A., & Rasul, M. S. (2019). Comparison of engineering skills with IR 4.0 Skills. *International Journal of Online and Biomedical Engineering (iJOE), 15*(10), 15. https://doi.org/10.3991/ijoe.v15i10.10879.

Lasi, H., Fettke, P., Kemper, H. G., Feld, T., & Hoffmann, M. (2014). Industry 4.0. *Business and Information Systems Engineering, 6*(4), 239–242. https://doi.org/10.1007/s12599-014-0334-4.

Leal, L. F., Oliveira, M. S., Silveira, D. K. B., Santana, A. L. M., Junior, A. C. G., Reis, D. A., et al. (2020). Fábrica de ensino em indústria 4.0 proposição de modelo de negócios. *Revista de Ensino de Engenharia, 39*, 157–169.

Rittel, H. W., & Webber, M. M. (1973). Dilemmas in a general theory of planning. *Policy Sciences, 4*(2), 155–169.

Santana, A. L. M., & Deus Lopes, R. (2020). Active learning methodologies and industry 4.0 skills development – A systematic review of the literature. In IEEE (Ed.), *2020 XV Conferencia Latinoamericana de Tecnologias de Aprendizaje (LACLO)* (pp. 1–10). https://doi.org/10.1109/LACLO50806.2020.9381161.

Sarathy, V. (2018). Real world problem-solving. *Frontiers in Human Neuroscience, 12*. https://doi.org/10.3389/fnhum.2018.00261.

Schallmo, D., Williams, C. A., & Lang, K. (2018). An integrated design thinking approach – Literature review, basic principles and roadmap for design thinking. In ISPIM (Ed.), *ISPIM Innovation Symposium* (pp. 1–18). The International Society for Professional Innovation Management (ISPIM).

Skaburskis, A. (2008). The origin of "wicked problems." *Planning Theory & Practice, 9*(2), 277–280.

Stanford Graduate School of Business. (2020). Startup Garage. https://www.gsb.stanford.edu/experience/learning/entrepreneurship/courses/startup-garage.

World Economic Forum. (2016). *The future of jobs: Employment, skills and workforce strategy for the fourth industrial revolution.* Global Challenge Insight Report.

Wright, M., Siegel, D. S., & Mustar, P. (2017). An emerging ecosystem for student start-ups. *The Journal of Technology Transfer, 42*(4), 909–922.

Zappe, S., Leicht, R., Messner, J., Litzinger, T., & Lee, H. W. (2009). "Flipping" the classroom to explore active learning in a large undergraduate course. *American Society for Engineering Education.* 14.1385.1–14.1385.21. https://doi.org/10.18260/1-2--4545, https://peer.asee.org/4545.

André Luiz Maciel Santana is a Professor in the Computer Engineering Department at Insper in São Paulo and a Professor at Alura.Tech. He received his BSc. in Mechanical Engineering from the University of Vale do Itajaí in 2013 and his Master's degree in Applied Computer from the same university in 2015. Santana finished his PhD in Electrical Engineering at the Polytechnic School of the University of São Paulo and is a project leader and researcher at LSITec. His primary interest topics are STEAM, Computational Thinking, Rare Diseases, and Real-World Problems Solving Based-Learning. ORCID ID: 0000-0002-9807-3253

Roseli de Deus Lopes (Member, IEEE) received a bachelor's, master's and Ph.D in Electrical Engineering from the Universidade de São Paulo (USP), Brazil. She is an Associate Professor with the Escola Politécnica, Universidade de São Paulo (USP), São Paulo, Brazil. She is the Vice-Chair of the Interdisciplinary Center on Interactive Technologies and a Researcher with the Laboratory of Integrated Systems (LSI-USP), where she coordinates research projects in interactive electronic media, with emphasis on applications in education, inclusion, and health. She currently serves as a Deputy Director of the Institute of Advanced Studies, USP. ORCID ID: 0000-0001-8556-6473

Open Access This chapter is licensed under the terms of the Creative Commons Attribution 4.0 International License (http://creativecommons.org/licenses/by/4.0/), which permits use, sharing, adaptation, distribution and reproduction in any medium or format, as long as you give appropriate credit to the original author(s) and the source, provide a link to the Creative Commons license and indicate if changes were made.

The images or other third party material in this chapter are included in the chapter's Creative Commons license, unless indicated otherwise in a credit line to the material. If material is not included in the chapter's Creative Commons license and your intended use is not permitted by statutory regulation or exceeds the permitted use, you will need to obtain permission directly from the copyright holder.

Part IV
Future Skills in Practice – Assessment

Part IV focuses on questions of assessment of Future Skills in higher education. After an introduction to different Future Skills assessment models in higher education, authors present teaching, learning and assessment approaches and the role of concepts such as micro-credentials for Future Skills learning and assessment.

Part IV

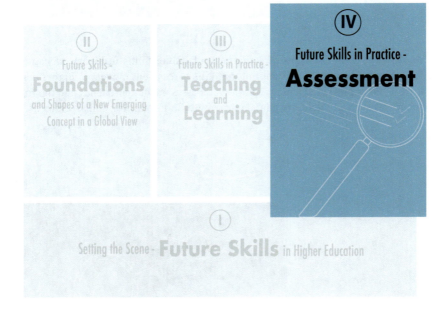

Assessment of Future Skills Learning: Changing Futures in Higher Education

21

Nicole Geier and Ulf-Daniel Ehlers

Abstract

Future Skills assessment is currently a hot debated issue. On the one hand it is the only way to move Future Skills into the center of learning in higher education, on the other hand it is difficult to achieve with the usual assessment practices in higher education institutions. In the project presented in this chapter we describe Future Skills modules in form of a concept that accompanies the whole student life-cycle of undergraduates and uses self-assessments and an e-portfolio tool to support students in their Future Skills development. The chapter presents a new vision of assessment based on the need to provide learners with what is called vertical transformation competence (Scharmer, 2018) and to make Future Skills development visible (Ehlers, 2013b, 2020d). Since student self-assessment has proven its potential in higher education, a model is presented that shows how student self-assessments can be integrated into learning and teaching practices at higher education institutions. Those recent concepts highlight the existing attempts to shift assessment culture in higher education from *assessment of learning* towards a new vision of *assess-*

N. Geier (✉)
Educational Management, Institute for Pedagogy, Carl von Ossietzky University Oldenburg, Oldenburg, Germany
e-mail: nicole.geier@uol.de

U.-D. Ehlers
Professor for Educational Management and Lifelong Learning, Business Faculty, DHBW Karlsruhe, Karlsruhe, Germany
e-mail: ulf-daniel.ehlers@dhbw-karlsruhe.de

© The Author(s) 2024
U.-D. Ehlers and L. Eigbrecht (eds.), *Creating the University of the Future*, Zukunft der Hochschulbildung - Future Higher Education,
https://doi.org/10.1007/978-3-658-42948-5_21

ment as learning. It represents a paradigm shift away from *what can be measured* to *what can we learn during and from the assessment* to create value for students' personal growth and professional development.

List of Abbreviations

AaL	Assesment as Learning
AfL	Assessment for Learning
AoL	Assessment of Learning
DHBW	Duale Hochschule Baden-Württemberg (Baden-Wuerttemberg Cooperative State University)
HEIs	Higher education institutions

21.1 Introduction

The concept of formative assessment has evolved in recent years to include the idea of *assessment as learning.* In higher education, this shift has implications for both students and instructors, as it views assessment not simply as a means of evaluating performance, but as a tool for promoting learning. In this chapter, we will explore the concept of assessment as learning and its application in higher education. We will examine the benefits of this approach, including improved student motivation, engagement, and deep learning. Additionally, we will discuss the ways in which technology and innovative assessment techniques can be used to support this approach and enhance the learning experience for students in higher education.[1]

Higher education institutions (HEIs) should take the responsibility to **empower students** to learn how to develop Future Skills independently in order to overcome future challenges on a personal, professional, and societal level (Ehlers, 2020). The question is: how to include them systematically into learning, teaching and assessment practices? Students need genuine opportunities to experience, reflect on and develop their Future Skills within higher educational

---

[1] This article is based on a report that was published within the *DIRK Dual* project in June 2022 (Ehlers et al., 2022). For more information on the project and the article (including a choice of good practices of e-portfolio cases at German universities), please refer to: https://www.dhbw.de/projekte/dirk-dual.

training. These opportunities need to be facilitated by educators and accompanied by means that make students' progress visible and creditable; the latter being a particular challenge, given that competencies cannot be measured like knowledge. Student self-assessments bear a great potential to realise this challenge by supporting **learner agency** (Schoon, 2018) and **self-directed development** of Future Skills (Ehlers, 2020). E-portfolios represent one the means to track the students' progress and support the shift from **assessments of learning (AoL) towards assessments as learning (AaL)** (Yan & Boud, 2022). This transformation of assessment practices at Higher Education Institutions (HEIs) is an essential step to empowering students for **lifelong learning**. This calls for the well-known, often discussed but still not completed shift from teaching to learning (Wildt, 2005) and for the autonomous, self-reflected learner and critical thinker. This poses a fundamental challenge to current practises in higher education, as most institutions and study regulations do not allow for the flexibility, nor are they equipped with suitable tools, concepts or staff resources for student self-assessments.

Following this introduction, the different assessment modes (assessment of, for, and as learning), the currently predominant practices at HEIs and the relevance of shifting towards assessment as learning are discussed (Sect. 21.2). This theoretical excurse is followed by a four-type model on how to integrate student self-assessment into teaching and assessment practices at HEIs (Sect. 21.3). Subsequently, we briefly introduce good practices for each of the four types (Sect. 21.4). We close with a conclusion on the current student self-assessment landscape in German HEIs and an outlook on how the project DIRK Dual at the DHBW Karlsruhe and Heilbronn can contribute to shaping the shift towards assessment as learning (Sect. 21.5).

21.2 From Assessment of Learning over Assessment for Learning towards Assessment as Learning

Three forms of assessments can be distinguished in relation to the role of learning: **assessment of learning (AoL), assessment for learning (AfL), and assessment as learning (AaL)** (see Fig. 21.1). The current call for a shift from AoL to AaL is in line with the demand to promote learner agency and empower students to manage their individual lifelong learning strategies (Ehlers, 2013). However, it requires fundamental changes in the assessment practices of higher education institutions towards a focus on students' long-term development processes rather than on snapshots of their knowledge-based performance.

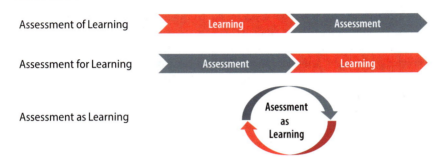

Fig. 21.1 Relationship of assessment and learning in the concepts assessment of learning, assessment for learning, and assessment as learning (in close accordance with Yan & Boud, 2022, p. 15)

The currently most popular form in higher education examination practice is **AoL** (Schindler et al., 2015), where students' knowledge is tested after the learning process, i.e. at the end of a course or module, using a summative instead of formative feedback after tests. It is usually knowledge-related. It therefore has a minimal impact on students' motivation and opportunities to improve their performance, and is considered unsuitable for equipping students with the future-relevant skill of lifelong learning (Boud & Falchikov, 2007; Ehlers, 2013).

The **AfL**-approach uses assessment as an integral part of the learning journey itself (Ehlers, 2013), with the aim of increasing students' motivation to learn and their overall performance and competence development, rather than simply monitoring it (Stiggins, 2008). However, following the current shift to self-organisation (Ehlers, 2020), there is also a need to move beyond AfL as a standard in higher education examination practice towards increasing the use of AaL. Primarily, and in contrast to AaL, AoL delivers a judgement showing students their learning achievements and how much more is needed to meet their goals. This usually refers to learning outcomes set by teachers or study programmes (learning what is asked in the exam) rather than personal development goals (Yan & Boud, 2022, p. 11).

In contrast, **AaL** requires students to learn new knowledge or develop their competences further while working on the assessment task (Yan & Boud, 2022, p. 16). Yan and Yang (2022) define AaL as a strategy rather than a pure assessment method. It *"requires students to learn from engagement with the assessment task itself as well as activities associated with it. An assessment-as-learning task has to generate learning opportunities for students beyond recalling and using their prior knowledge and foster the development of metacognition and self-regulation* *for students to monitor their performance and cater for their ongoing learning needs"* (Yan & Yang, 2022, pp. 1–2). Assessment as learning requires students to take active agency for their learning and supports them in developing self-regulatory abilities to facilitate their lifelong learning (Lee et al., 2019; Yan & Yang, 2022). Therefore, it can be seen as the basis for AoL and AfL, as it inspires students to learn and supports the learning process (Yan & Boud, 2022).

Feedback is one of the success factors which helps students to process the results of the AaL task (Yan & Boud, 2022) by helping students to answer the three questions: *"Where am I going? (What are the goals?), How am I going? (What progress is being made toward the goal?), and Where to next? (What activities need to be undertaken to make better progress?)"* (Hattie & Timperley, 2007, p. 86). Despite all the studies indicating the benefits of feedback, some argue that it can only be called feedback if the students are willing to receive and process it instead of solely restoring it (Yang, 2022). The process/criteria for giving and receiving feedback effectively (feedback literacy) should be carefully designed. There should be sufficient time for students and teachers to give and reflect on feedback. For more details on feedback use and accountability, see Yang (2022).

21.3 Assessment as Learning and Student Self-Assessment

Student self-assessment is one of the keys to operationalising effective AaL practices. They serve to shift more responsibility from teachers to learners and allow them to reflect and learn during the actual assessment. They integrate well with portfolio-based learning approaches when they are repeated, as they can show progress and setbacks in the learner's development process.

Before defining student self-assessment in particular, let us briefly consider the distinction between self-reflection, self-evaluation and self-assessment. So far, there is no consensus among researchers on the extent to which the three concepts can be distinguished from each other. What the three have in common is that they refer to the individual's feedback on his or her performance and learning progress, and that self-regulation and self-regulated learning serve as a framework for all three concepts. This is because monitoring one's own performance and learning and giving feedback to oneself leads to better development of self-regulation skills (Andrade, 2019).

Van Loon distinguishes self-reflection as monitoring learning attitudes and competence development qualitatively to identify learning opportunities from self-assessment, which is, in her opinion, a quantitative judgement of one's own performance (van Loon, 2018). Szűcs, with reference to Athanasaou, on the other hand, uses self-reflection and self-assessment interchangeably, both characterised by a cognitive and an affective domain, taking place during the learning process. Self-evaluation, in contrast, follows those two as the judgement of the achievements that have been made during the process (Szűcs, 2018). Boud (1994, 1995) and Ehlers (2013) reckon self-reflection as a broader, informal, and rather explorative concept, whereas self-evaluation and self-assessment follow a clear process and criteria. According to Boud (1991), self-assessment is characterised by the involvement of students in the process of defining standards and criteria against which they can later judge their achievements. Following the idea that the ability to reflect is a prerequisite for learning (Ehlers, 2013) and that self-assessment and self-evaluation are at least similar concepts, we will use the term **self-assessment as defined by Andrade and Du in the following elaborations:**

> "[Student self-assessment] is a process of formative assessment during which students reflect on and evaluate the quality of their work and their learning, judge the degree to which they reflect explicitly stated goals or criteria, identify strengths and weaknesses in their work, and revise accordingly. [...] Put simply, we see self-assessment as feedback for oneself from oneself." (Andrade & Du, 2007, p. 160)

Boud (1999) argued that student self-assessment is not an isolated or individualistic activity. On the contrary, students need to actively seek the feedback of peers, teachers, or other sources of information, and they should make student self-assessment a habit rather than a one-time activity. Student self-assessments omit self-grading, as self-grading focuses on collecting information about one's performance and how this matches a specific goal at the end of a learning process. Without having the opportunity for adjustment and improvement, as is the case with self-grading, student self-assessment is ineffective (Andrade, 2019). Also, self-grading distorts the genuine self-reflection, as students tend to award themselves higher grades when they know their academic grade is influenced by their self-assessment (Andrade, 2019; Yan & Boud, 2022).

According to this definition, student self-assessment qualifies as a form of AaL. Several studies line out beneficial effects of student self-assessment on students' learning, including:

- enhancing academic achievement (Guo et al., 2022; Ross, 2006; Yan, 2020)
- independent and self-regulated learning (Bakula, 2010; Panadero et al., 2017; Yan, 2020)
- critical and reflective thinking, and lifelong learning (Guo et al., 2022).

The focus of student self-assessments is not on gaining better grades but on learning about necessary skills to build the ability to actively participate in and design society (Future Skills, twenty-first Century Skills) (Wanner & Palmer, 2018). These aspects do not only correlate with the definition of AaL but also indicate that student self-assessments are suitable instruments to reflect on and develop Future Skills, as long as they fulfil three conditions: (1) The steps of the process should be clearly defined, (2) students must be well versed in self-assessment literacy, and (3) they must receive feedback from peers or teachers, respectively, have the opportunity to discuss the results with others. Ehlers (2013) and Yan & Brown (2017) defined similar processes, including four or three steps. First, students and teachers need to define the assessment criteria. Second, students carry out the assessment; this step is not explicitly mentioned in Yan and Brown's process but is logically necessary. Third, students seek feedback and process it. Fourth, students develop objectives, plans, and strategies for further learning. Yan and Brown call this step *self-reflection*. Various studies have adapted similar process steps (Guo et al., 2022; Nicol, 2020). Self-assessment literacy includes (1) comprehension: knowing what student self-assessment is and why one uses it, (2) application: knowing how to self-assess and being capable of setting criteria, seeking feedback, and reflecting on the outcomes, (3) interpretation: being able to process the results and derive a plan for improvement, and (4) critical engagement: being aware of the limitations of student self-assessment and possible errors during the process (Guo et al., 2022, p. 146). Feedback from others (e.g. peers and educators) increases the effectiveness of student self-assessment and the consistency and honesty of self-assessments (Andrade & Du, 2007, p. 161). However, the exact mechanisms and relations between formative feedback and learning effects are working (Andrade, 2019). Boud (1994) refers to feedback as a liberating factor in student self-assessment if carried out correctly.

As for the different types of student self-assessment, various attempts of typologies and taxonomies exist using different classification criteria. For instance, Panadero et al. (2016) summarise five different typologies. They demand a comprehensive typology including knowledge interest/purpose, involvement of teacher vs student on a continuum, power and transparency, presence and form of the assessment criteria, and student response format (Panadero et al., 2016). In contrast, Andrade focuses on the what (competence, process, or product), the why (formative or summative), and the how (methods, criteria, etc.) (Andrade, 2019). While a common taxonomy of student self-assessment types or formats would certainly help structure the variety and contribute to a commonly agreed definition, this paper aims not to find a generally applicable typology for all student self-assessment. Instead, the focus is on presenting examples/good practices that show how HEIs can operationalise Future Skills learning through student self-assessment in learning and teaching structures. This is why we present a classification model, which allocates different concepts of student self-assessment regarding its integration grade into the curricula of study programmes and/or strategies of HEI. When developing the model and selecting good practice examples, we focused on the fact that student self-assessments, as a form of AaL, help students reflect on their future skill development, as elaborated earlier, and therefore support the shift to self-organisation.

21.4 The Integration of Student Self-Assessments into Learning and Teaching Strategies at Higher Education Institutions—A Model

Following research on student self-assessment and e-portfolio use cases at German HEIs between October 2021 and February 2022, we discovered that the variety of these tools, instruments, and concepts can be categorised in four types referring to their strategic integration. What they all have in common is that the responsibility for reflecting on and dealing with the assessment of the subject matter is given to the learners themselves. The four types are: 1) individual/ stand-alone, 2) course-integrated, 3) programme-integrated, and 4) institution-integrated and beyond (Fig. 21.2). They vary in terms of their scope, the role of students and teachers, the way they are integrated into the curriculum (in terms of number of modules, voluntary or compulsory participation) and their usability beyond university purposes. The following guiding questions were used to categorise the examples and develop the four types:

- Is it a single instrument or rather a concept with various aspects?
- If it is a concept: Of what scope is it, i.e. how many different instruments/processes does it include? How many different (future) skills does it address?
- Is it voluntary or mandatory to participate for students?
- Is it anchored in the curriculum? If so, does it refer to one or more modules and do students receive credit points for it?
- Can the tool be used beyond the study, i.e. for lifelong learning processes?

The model is depicted as a house, with type one (individual) being the foundation of reflection and self-assessment. Type two concepts (course-integrated) act as pillars, and the more of them there are, the more stable the building is. Type three

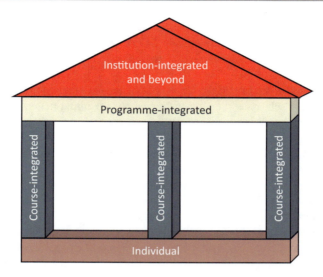

Fig. 21.2 Types of integration of portfolio and student self-assessment concepts in degree programmes

(programme-integrated) can be seen as the ceiling that connects the different pillars. Type four (institution-integrated and beyond) acts as the roof of the building, making it watertight and holding everything together.

Type one represents **stand-alone instruments** such as (online) questionnaires and personality tests. These are usually open access solutions developed by professionals, e.g. psychologists, universities or other institutions, and in most cases do not explicitly relate to higher education contexts, but are useful for all individuals. These tools can be integrated into study programmes in different ways. Usually, they are recommended or used by teachers in individual modules related to the development of key competences or similar, but they are neither embedded in the curriculum nor credited. Often, extra-curricular offerings work with this type one instruments by recommending them in learning management systems or on websites of university competence centres, without offering to discuss the results with students. Accordingly, these tools do not influence the learning and teaching strategies of higher education institutions. Concerning the success factors of student self-assessments, this type is unlikely to have a sustainable impact on students' competence development because of the lack of feedback and because teachers or institutions do not verify whether students are assessment literates or not. Examples are:

- **VIA inventory of strengths** by the University of Zurich: an online self-assessment for character strengths in 24 categories like creativity, judgement, social intelligence, leadership etc. (free online access) (Values in Action Institute, 2021)
- **KompetenzNavigator** by the University of Passau (eng. competence navigator): student self-assessment on the university's learning management system with 120 items. Students assess eleven competences in the three fields 1) personal competence, 2) social-communicative competence, and 3) methodological competence (Zentrum für Schlüsselkompetenzen, 2017).

Type two describes student self-assessment options that are guided by educators as learning facilitators. The process follows specific criteria set individually by educators and/or students or follows well-known reflection models such as Kolb's reflection cycle (Kolb, 2015; Kolb & Fry, 1977) and the four steps of self-evaluation (Ehlers, 2013, p. 189). These approaches are broader in scope. They consist of several building blocks rather than isolated tools. These can be, for example, certificates of competence, portfolios and cross-module assignments. It is characteristic that reflection is not a one-off exercise, but is applied repeatedly and linked to at least one course/module, i.e. initiated by teachers. In between, students should plan and implement development steps independently. The long-term impact of this type of student self-assessment is likely to be more sustainable as it involves cyclical repetition and guidance by teachers and feedback from various sources, e.g., peers. Depending on how the approaches are organised, there may also be a strategic impact. This is the case, for example, when interdisciplinary courses are offered or are compulsory for students in all programmes and university management is involved in the design, e.g. through the deans. One example is:

- **DigKom—Certificate of Digital Competences** by the TH Nuremberg: A networked and structured qualification programme for students from all degree programmes in which they can strengthen their self-learning and digital competences. Students learn about current digitalisation topics during the programme, work on their methodological skills for a digitalised world and are asked to process several self-reflection and self-assessment tasks. The programme is integrated into the university's strategy and involves bi-directional feedback of students and educators (Le Thi & Zinger, 2021)

Type three includes reflection and student self-assessment approaches which are compulsory for the duration of a whole programme, or at least for a significant part, and which carry ECTS points. At least in Germany this form is very popular in teacher training programmes. Successful implementation requires that student self-assessment is not simply added on top of the usual curricula, but is truly integrated into them. This means that students use the experience of their studies to reflect on and develop their student self-assessment. This reflection is in turn used to improve their personal and professional skills. The support of university management and programme directors is essential for mandatory integration into the curriculum. Otherwise, students and teachers may not value the use of such concepts. Type three approaches offer a high degree of strategic impact and sustainable growth in learning and teaching, but also require a high degree of coordination, communication between different stakeholders and consistent evaluation of the approach/process itself. Examples are:

- **p:ier e-portfolio** by the University of Bremen: Electronic portfolio tool for integrating theory and practice within teacher training along the whole student life-cycle (undergraduate, graduate and traineeship). The goal is to support students in developing a professional and reflective capacity to act and become *Reflective Practitioners*. In encompasses reflections of different practical phases in the training, but they do not necessarily built upon each other (Wulf, 2022).
- **Study Journal** by Cologne International School of Design: e-portfolio tool that encompasses the whole student life cycle and serves as a means for the documentation, reflection and dissemination of results/learning outcomes students achieve during their studies. The study journal is compulsory to pass courses and is justified by students having a high degree of autonomy in choosing their courses. It includes course reports, semester reports, a social learning environment and a mentoring concept (Großhans et al., 2019; Köln International School of Design, 2022).

Type four goes one step further. It describes concepts that are not only integrated into curricula and accompany students throughout their lifecycle, but can also be used after graduation. In terms of lifelong learning, both constant self-reflection and self-assessment are necessary for the continuous development of Future Skills (Ehlers, 2013; European Commission—Education and Training, 2019; OECD, 2021). These are development portfolios in terms of Baumgartner's typology (Baumgartner, 2012). Type four concepts encourage lifelong self-assessment, support the process with guidelines and criteria, and provide a platform for collecting artefacts and feedback among peers and/or coaches. In addition to their strategic relevance for improving the quality of learning and teaching, these approaches can have a lifelong impact on the development of Future Skills and therefore have societal implications. It goes beyond higher education and can be extended to professional and societal contexts.

- **Digitales Reflexionstool zur Kompetenzentwicklung im dualen Studium (DIRK Dual)** by DHBW[2]: the project's aim is to develop a concept for a module that integrates Future Skills learning systematically into the curricula of dual study programmes. It therefore combines face-to-face workshops, online self-learning modules on a set of 17 Future Skills reflection tasks and coaching sessions. The programme spans across the whole student life-cycle and is facilitated by an e-portfolio tool that can be used further on after graduating. The concept uses experiences of the practical phases and asks students to reflect on them in order to explore their Future Skills development. The concept, which is also scalable and adaptable for enterprises and organisations, is currently being tested and evaluated in various settings and faculties at DHBW (Geier et al., 2022).

21.5 Conclusion and Outlook

In the German higher education landscape, several lighthouse projects have included student self-assessment by means of e-portfolio concepts. Considering differences in scope, involvement of students and educators, integration into curricula, and usability beyond study programmes, four types can be distinguished: 1) individual/stand-alone, 2) course-integrated, 3) programme-integrated, and 4) institution-integrated and beyond (Fig. 21.2). Research revealed that most of the concepts are not systematically integrated into curricula and/or strategy. E-portfolios in teacher training represent an exception, as they have been included in study programmes in most universities some years ago. This becomes necessary to impact the 1) the shift from Assessment of Learning to Assessment as Learning, 2) the shift to self-organisation, and 3) the integration of Future Skills development strategies into curricula. To support these developments, pilot and practice projects need more attention and continuation. In particular, research should focus on:

---

[2] Students at DHBW study in turns of three months at the university (referred to as theoretical phase) and at a partner organisation/enterprise (referred to as practical phase).

- development of better definitions and more operational concepts for self-reflection, self-evaluation, and self-assessment, as the blurry lines between the definitions of those concepts complicate the differentiation of practice examples,
- a broader systematic benchmarking analysis of good practice examples in which criteria for selection and integration of good practices into higher education would be specified to give orientation to educators and leaders in higher education and provide a more transparent view on student self-assessment for learners,
- creation of an observatory to map the current situation at (German-speaking) higher education institutions and therefore foster peer exchange among the institutions leading to an accelerated progress.

What remains open is to gain a deeper understanding of the motivational, cognitive and attitudinal aspects which are addressed in and supported through student self-assessment. Andrade refers to it as *"the next black box: the cognitive and affective mechanisms of students who are engaged in assessment processes"* (Andrade, 2019, p. 10). In conclusion, student self-assessment practices are becoming more popular in higher education but are not yet considered a standard procedure or an integral part of assessments.

References

Andrade, H. (2019). A critical review of research on student self-assessment. *Frontiers in Education, 4*. https://doi.org/10.3389/feduc.2019.00087.

Andrade, H., & Du, Y. (2007). Student responses to criteria-referenced self-assessment. *Assessment & Evaluation in Higher Education, 32*(2), 159–181. https://doi.org/10.1080/02602930600801928.

Bakula, N. (2010). The benefits of formative assessments for teaching and learning. *Science Scope, 34*(1), 37–43.

Baumgartner, P. (2012). *Eine Taxonomie für E-Portfolios: – Teil II des BMWF-Abschlussberichts "E-Portfolio an Hochschulen": GZ 51.700/0064-VII/10/2006*. Krems.

Boud, D. (1991). *Implementing student self assessment*. HERDSA.

Boud, D. (1994). The move to self-assessment: Liberation or a new mechanism for oppression? In SCUTREA (Ed.), *SCUTREA 24th annual conference – Reflecting on changing practices, contexts and identities* (pp. 10–13). University of Leeds Department of Adult and Continuing Education.

Boud, D. (Ed.). (1995). *Enhancing learning through self-assessment*. RoutledgeFalmer.

Boud, D. (1999). Avoiding the traps: Seeking good practice in the use of self assessment and reflection in professional courses. *Social Work Education, 18*(2), 121–132. https://doi.org/10.1080/02615479911220131.

Boud, D., & Falchikov, N. (Eds.). (2007). *Rethinking assessment in higher education: Learning for the longer term*. Routledge.

Ehlers, U.-D. (2013). *Open learning cultures: A guide to quality, evaluation, and assessment for future learning*. Springer Berlin Heidelberg.

Ehlers, U.-D. (2020). *Future skills – Future learning and future higher education*. Springer VS.

Ehlers, U.-D., Geier, N., & Eigbrecht, L. (2022). Changing Futures in Higher Education: Assessment of Future Skills Learning: Report 2 for the project „DIRK Dual – Digitales Reflexionstool zur Kompetenzentwicklung im dualen Studium". https://www.dhbw.de/fileadmin/user_upload/Dokumente/Projekte/DIRK_Dual/2022-06-07-Report-Self-Assessment-Version17-final.pdf.

European Commission – Education and Training. (2019). Key competences for lifelong learning. Luxembourg. https://op.europa.eu/de/publication-detail/-/publication/297a33c8-a1f3-11e9-9d01-01aa75ed71a1. Accessed 30 Dec. 2021.

Geier, N., Eigbrecht, L., Ehlers, U.-D., & Winkler, K. (2022). Kompetenzlernen im Theorie-Praxis-Studium: Report 1 für das Projekt „DIRK Dual – Digitales Reflexionstool zur Kompetenzentwicklung im dualen Studium". https://www.dhbw.de/fileadmin/user_upload/Dokumente/Projekte/DIRK_Dual/2022-05-03-Report-Kompetenzlernen-Version11_final.pdf. Accessed 13 May 2022.

Großhans, J., Meinhardt, D., & Schuhwerk, V. (2019). Das Study Journal als kompetenzorientiertes Reflexions- und Beratungsinstrument (Zur praktischen Umsetzung der Kompetenzorientierung in Hochschulen). https://www.hrk-nexus.de/material/tagungsdokumentation/zur-praktischen-umsetzung-der-kompetenzorientierung-koeln/poster/poster-5/.

Guo, W., Huang, Y., & Yan, Z. (2022). The conceptualisation of student self-assessment literacy: A case study of Chinese undergraduates Wuyuan. In Z. Yan & L. Yang (Eds.), *Assessment as learning: Maximising opportunities for student learning and achievement* (pp. 143–157). Routledge Taylor & Francis Group.

Hattie, J., & Timperley, H. (2007). The power of feedback. *Review of Educational Research, 77*(1), 81–112. https://doi.org/10.3102/003465430298487.

Kolb, D. A. (2015). *Experiential learning: Experience as the source of learning and development*. Pearson Education Inc.

Kolb, D. A., & Fry, R. (1977). Towards an applied theory of experiential learning. In C. L. Cooper (Ed.), *Theories of group processes* (pp. 33–58). Wiley.

Köln International School of Design. (2022). Das Social Learning Environment Spaces. https://kisd.de/kisd/spaces/. Accessed 10 Febr 2022.

Le Thi, T. V., & Zinger, B. (2021). Förderung von digitalen Kompetenzen im Hochschulstudium. Ein Praxisbericht zum DigKom-Hochschulzertifikat für Digitale Kompetenzen der Technischen Hochschule Nürnberg. In L. Lehmann, D. Engelhardt, & W. Wilke (Eds.), *Kompetenzen für die digitale Transformation 2020. Digitalisierung der Arbeit – Kompetenzen – Nachhaltigkeit 1. Digitalkompetenz-Tagung* (pp. 229–244). Springer Vieweg.

Lee, I., Mak, P., & Yuan, R. E. (2019). Assessment as learning in primary writing classrooms: An exploratory study. *Studies in Educational Evaluation, 62*, 72–81. https://doi.org/10.1016/j.stueduc.2019.04.012.

van Loon, M. H. (2018). Self-assessment and self-reflection to measure and improve self-regulated learning in the workplace: Preprint version. https://www.researchgate.

net/publication/328215125_Self-Assessment_and_Self-Reflection_to_Measure_and_Improve_Self-Regulated_Learning_in_the_Workplace/citations. Accessed 30 Dec 2021.

Nicol, D. (2020). The power of internal feedback: Exploiting natural comparison processes. *Assessment & Evaluation in Higher Education, 46*(5), 756–778. https://doi.org/10.1080/02602938.2020.1823314.

OECD. (2021). OECD skills Outlook 2021. Paris. https://www.oecd.org/education/oecd-skills-outlook-e11c1c2d-en.htm. Accessed 29 Dec 2021.

Panadero, E., Brown, G. T. L., & Strijbos, J.-W. (2016). The future of student self-assessment: A review of known unknowns and potential directions. *Educational Psychology Review, 28*(4), 803–830. https://doi.org/10.1007/s10648-015-9350-2.

Panadero, E., Jönsson, A., Botella, J., & Jonsson, A. (2017). Effects of self-assessment on self-regulated learning and self-efficacy: Four meta-analyses. *Educational Research Review, 22*, 74–98. https://doi.org/10.1016/j.edurev.2017.08.004.

Ross, J. A. (2006). The reliability, validity, and utility of self-assessment. *Practical Assessment, Research, and Evaluation, 11*. https://doi.org/10.7275/9wph-vv65.

Scharmer, C. O. (2018). *The essentials of theory U: Core principles and applications.* BK, Berrett-Koehler Publishers, Incorporated, a BK Business Book.

Schindler, C., Bauer, J., Strasser, A., Schlomske-Bodenstein, N., Seidel, T., & Prenzel, M. (2015). Prüfungen als Indikatoren für Studienerfolg. In C. Berthold, B. Jorzik, & V. Meyer-Guckel (Eds.), *Handbuch Studienerfolg. Strategien und Maßnahmen: Wie Hochschulen Studierende erfolgreich zum Abschluss führen* (pp. 62–77). Edition Stifterverband.

Schoon, I. (2018). Conceptualising learner agency: A socio-ecological developmental approach (LLAKES Research Paper 64). https://www.llakes.ac.uk/wp-content/uploads/2021/03/LLAKES-Research-Paper-64-Schoon-I.pdf. Accessed 30 March 2022.

Stiggins, R. (2008). Assessment manifesto: A call for the development of balanced assessment systems. Portland. https://famemichigan.org/wp-content/uploads/2018/06/Stiggins-Assessment-Manifesto-A-Call-for-the-Development-of-Balanced-Assessment-Systems.pdf. Accessed 19 Nov 2021.

Szűcs, I. Z. (2018). Teacher trainers' self-reflection and self-evaluation. *Acta Educationis Generalis, 8*(2), 9–23. https://doi.org/10.2478/atd-2018-0008.

Values in Action Institute. (2021). VIA Inventar der Stärken: Fragebogen. https://charakterstaerken.org/questionnaire.php.

Wanner, T., & Palmer, E. (2018). Formative self-and peer assessment for improved student learning: the crucial factors of design, teacher participation and feedback. *Assessment & Evaluation in Higher Education, 43*(7), 1032–1047. https://doi.org/10.1080/02602938.2018.1427698.

Wildt, J. (2005). Vom Lehren zum Lernen. Perspektivenwechsel im Kontext hochschuldidaktischer Weiterbildung. In M. Kerres (Ed.), *Hochschulen im digitalen Zeitalter. Innovationspotenziale und Strukturwandel* (pp. 203–214). Waxmann.

Wulf, M. (2022). e-Portfolio (p:ier): Zentrale Ergebnisse der 1. Projektphase. https://www.uni-bremen.de/zflb/projekte-forschung/schnittstellen-gestalten-qualitaetsoffensive-lehrerbildung/teilprojekte/e-portfolio-pier. Accessed 11 Jan 2022.

Yan, Z. (2020). Self-assessment in the process of self-regulated learning and its relationship with academic achievement. *Assessment & Evaluation in Higher Education, 45*(2), 224–238. https://doi.org/10.1080/02602938.2019.1629390.

Yan, Z., & Boud, D. (2022). Conceptualising assessment-as-learning. In Z. Yan & L. Yang (Eds.), *Assessment as learning: Maximising opportunities for student learning and achievement* (pp. 11–24). Routledge Taylor & Francis Group.

Yan, Z., & Brown, G. T. (2017). A cyclical self-assessment process: Towards a model of how students engage in self-assessment. *Assessment & Evaluation in Higher Education, 42*(8), 1247–1262. https://doi.org/10.1080/02602938.2016.1260091.

Yan, Z., & Yang, L. (Eds.). (2022). *Assessment as learning: Maximising opportunities for student learning and achievement*. Routledge Taylor & Francis Group.

Yang, L. (2022). The role of feedback orientation in converting external feedback to learning opportunities for implementing assessment-as-learning in the context of feedback. In Z. Yan & L. Yang (Eds.), *Assessment as learning: Maximising opportunities for student learning and achievement* (pp. 53–76). Routledge Taylor & Francis Group.

Zentrum für Schlüsselkompetenzen. (2017). *Kompetenz-Navigator*. Universität Passau.

Nicole Geier has been working as a research assistant in the field of educational management at the University of Oldenburg since September 2023. Before, she was an academic assistant at the Baden-Wuerttemberg Cooperative State University Karlsruhe in the Department of Educational Management and Lifelong Learning from 2021 to 2023. Her main areas of research there included Future Skills, competence development in theory-practice study programs and digitally enhanced learning and teaching. She studied Leisure and Tourism Management (B.A.) and Human Resource Management (M.Sc.) at the universities of Stralsund (GER), Palma de Mallorca (ES) and Koblenz (GER).

Prof. Dr. phil. habil. Ulf-Daniel Ehlers is an internationally renowned Professor for Educational Management and Lifelong Learning at the Baden-Wuerttemberg Cooperative State University (DHBW) Karlsruhe which he headed as Vice-President between 2011 and 2017.

Open Access This chapter is licensed under the terms of the Creative Commons Attribution 4.0 International License (http://creativecommons.org/licenses/by/4.0/), which permits use, sharing, adaptation, distribution and reproduction in any medium or format, as long as you give appropriate credit to the original author(s) and the source, provide a link to the Creative Commons license and indicate if changes were made.

The images or other third party material in this chapter are included in the chapter's Creative Commons license, unless indicated otherwise in a credit line to the material. If material is not included in the chapter's Creative Commons license and your intended use is not permitted by statutory regulation or exceeds the permitted use, you will need to obtain permission directly from the copyright holder.

Active Learning and Integrated Assessment: Minerva's Approach to Teaching Future Skills

22

Megan K. Gahl, Abha Ahuja, Raquel H. Ribeiro, Maia Averett and James Genone

Abstract

The Minerva Project works with global higher education partners to build transformational education programs based on Future Skills. Within our learning taxonomy, we identified practical knowledge as distinct Learning Outcomes (LOs). What differentiates Minerva programs from other Future Skills-focused programs is: 1) active learning pedagogy, 2) direct feedback and assessment of Future Skills, and 3) systematic reinforcement throughout students' learning experience. The goal in our lessons is to practice skills and broad concepts, therefore we use flipped classrooms with active learning tech-

---

M. K. Gahl (✉)
Senior Director of Curriculum and Pedagogy at Minerva Project/Professor of Natural Sciences at Minerva University, Minerva Project/Minerva University, San Francisco, USA
e-mail: mgahl@minervaproject.com

A. Ahuja
Academic Director at Minerva Project/Associate Professor of Natural Sciences at Minerva University, Miverva Project/Minerva University, San Francisco, USA
e-mail: abha@minervaproject.com

R. H. Ribeiro
Senior Manager of Partner Programs at Minerva Project/Associate Professor of Computational Sciences at Minerva University, Minerva Project/Minerva University, San Francisco, USA
e-mail: ribeiro@minervaproject.com

© The Author(s) 2024
U.-D. Ehlers and L. Eigbrecht (eds.), *Creating the University of the Future*, Zukunft der Hochschulbildung - Future Higher Education,
https://doi.org/10.1007/978-3-658-42948-5_22

niques. To guide students' improvement of Future Skills in our programs, we directly assess LOs and provide feedback on specific LO applications in both synchronous (e.g., in-class polls) and asynchronous (e.g., assignments) aspects of each course. Learning Outcomes from the learning taxonomy may be introduced in one course but are assessable in any other course in the curriculum, ensuring that skills are reinforced throughout a student's learning experience. In this chapter, we outline principles that underlie the development of learning taxonomies and curricular approaches in Minerva programs. We employ the same principles to collaborate with partners and build custom learning taxonomies and curricula; throughout this chapter we illustrate partner adaptations using examples from our collaborations.

22.1 Introduction

The foundation of our learning approach at both Minerva Project and Minerva University is a learning taxonomy based on practical knowledge, rather than focusing on transmission of content as in many higher education systems. The practical knowledge in our learning taxonomy includes both skills and broad concepts that students need to adapt to a changing world. We use the same principles that underlie the development of our own learning taxonomy to collaboratively develop learning taxonomies with global partners based on their own program goals.

Minerva Project (Minerva) collaborates with a variety of higher education institutions to design and deliver comprehensive interdisciplinary educational programs focused on teaching critical skills for academic and professional success. Our programs integrate curriculum focused on practical knowledge, active

---

M. Averett
Senior Academic Program Manager at Minerva Project/Professor of Computational Sciences at Minerva University/Professor of Mathematics at Mills College, Miverva Project/Minerva University/Mills College, San Francisco, USA
e-mail: maverett@minervaproject.com

J. Genone
Managing Director of Higher Education Innovation at Minerva Project/
Professor of Social Sciences at Minerva University,
Minerva Project/Minerva University, San Francisco, USA
e-mail: jgenone@minervaproject.com

learning pedagogy based on learning science, outcomes-based assessment, and systematic reinforcement and scaffolding of Learning Outcomes (LOs) throughout the curriculum. We have worked closely to help design and implement Minerva University (MU) and have collaborated with higher education partners globally to introduce transformational learning to their students.

While other Future Skills projects have also identified core sets of skills that all students should learn, what differentiates our approach are our 1) pedagogical approach, 2) direct assessment of the skills in the learning taxonomy, and 3) systematic reinforcement of these skills and concepts (i.e., LOs) across courses and other aspects of the student learning experience.

In this chapter, we outline the principles that underlie the development of learning taxonomies in Minerva programs and illustrate their adaptation using examples from our collaborations. Throughout this chapter, we include salient examples from our experience with our flagship partner, MU, and our global higher education partnerships. Minerva University is illustrative of our approach as an integrated system. We highlight the varying degrees of programmatic change in partner collaborations to illustrate the different scales of programmatic and curriculum changes that can be made to move towards skills-based teaching and learning.

22.2 Principles of a Minerva-Designed Learning Taxonomy

Minerva's approach to practical knowledge is a learning taxonomy composed of four core competencies derived from empirical literature: thinking critically, thinking creatively, communicating effectively, and interacting effectively. Our core competencies were derived from literature research into the qualities of effective innovators and leaders and surveys and interviews with employers to identify qualities they value when hiring new employees (see Kosslyn, 2017). The four core competencies align with the 4 C's concept commonly described as an effective approach to twenty-first century education: critical thinking, creativity, communication, collaboration (Kivunja, 2014).

Within each of these core competencies, sub-competencies contain sets of fundamental skills and concepts focused on in the general education curriculum that provides a common foundation for students (Case Study 1, Kosslyn & Nelson, 2017). The practical knowledge that our education system is based on should be broadly useful and aid a student to be successful in a changing world. Because information is so readily available with the internet, instead of focusing on information transfer common in traditional education, we focus on application of the skills needed to think clearly about and access the information needed for a specific task (Kosslyn, 2017). This core learning taxonomy is used at MU (see "Case Study 1: Minerva University" below). Some Minerva partners use either a subset of this taxonomy or an expanded version, depending on how many Minerva courses they adopt (see "Case Study 2: Partially Minerva-Designed Program" below). Other Minerva partners do not use this learning taxonomy at all, but instead collaborate with us to develop a custom learning taxonomy using the principles below (see "Case Study 3: Custom Collaboratively Designed Program" below).

Under the umbrella of each competency and sub-competency, we have identified practical knowledge as distinct Learning Outcomes. Each learning outcome is one of two types of practical knowledge: a habit of mind or foundational concept. Habits of mind are cognitive skills that with practice can be applied automatically. Foundational concepts are broad concepts that can be applied in multiple disciplines (Kosslyn, 2017). The LOs identified for a specific program provide focus and clear goals for the rest of the curriculum within the program. Therefore, the LO identification and selection is a key step and undertaking in the program design process. Our principles for developing LOs in core learning taxonomies include that the prospective LO should:

1. Be derived from one of the four core competencies (noted above);
2. Lead students to master practical skills or knowledge;
3. Be broadly applicable (i.e., be applicable to more than one discipline);
4. Be justified either by empirical findings, proofs, or well-established best practices; and
5. Lead to specific behaviors that can be evaluated systematically and reliably with rubrics (Kosslyn, 2017).

For example, in a Minerva course, a student may be scored on any LO to which they were introduced in any other course within a Minerva-designed curriculum, even if those LOs are from different competencies and sub-competencies and introduced in different disciplines (Table 22.1).

LOs in Minerva programs and at MU are not static. As we teach with these LOs we often find the need to redefine the scope or focus of a skill. For example, we used to teach 4 different LOs that represent different types of biases: #attentionbias, #perceptionbias, #emotionalbias, #memorybias (Gahl & Chandler, 2017). But in practice we realized that the scope of these LOs was too narrow and caused students to focus on differentiating between the type of bias, when the focus of the skill was to identify that bias was occurring and when the bias required mitigation.

22 Active Learning and Integrated Assessment … 441

Table 22.1 Learning Outcome (LO) examples from four core competencies and example sub-competencies (Appendix A, Kosslyn & Nelson, 2017)

Competency	Sub-competency	LO
Thinking Critically	#reasoning	#fallacies: *Identify and correct logical fallacies*
Thinking Creatively	#ideation	#heuristics: *Identify when to use heuristics and when to avoid them*
Communicating Effectively	#communicationstrategy	#audience: *Tailor oral and written work by considering the situation and perspective of the people receiving it*
Interacting effectively	#systemsthinking	#networks: *Apply network analysis to explain outcomes that arise out the structure of connections*

These example LOs are from Minerva Project's learning taxonomy

These skills are now clarified as #biasidentification and #biasmitigation, focusing student attention on identifying any bias present and then determining whether mitigation is appropriate (see "Case Study 1: Minerva University" for more information). To adapt LOs we collect feedback from instructors at the end of each lesson and course. We also adapt LOs in the program design phase of a partnership, when we are designing a learning taxonomy with a partner.

With partners we use the same principles for development of learning taxonomies as we do for our Minerva learning taxonomy, whether they are adapting our taxonomy or developing their own. For example, a partner business school with a focus on entrepreneurship selected different core competencies oriented towards entrepreneurial skills: Future Business Orientation, Innovation & Thinking Critically, Effective Communication, and Freedom & Self.

22.3 Pedagogical Approach

Learning skills and broad concepts, as opposed to the disciplinary content in most traditional education systems, depends upon similar learning processes, but supporting these different types of knowledge requires different approaches. For example, to learn a vast amount of disciplinary content, a student would ideally engage with the content in multiple ways to reinforce the content over time (spaced practice, Brown et al., 2014; Cepeda et al., 2006), such as reading, attending a lecture, doing homework, taking a test, and then working on an assignment. Similarly, for a student to learn practical skills they need to engage with the skills in multiple ways with repeated practice applying the skill. But, for a student to improve their applications of the skill, the practice requires receiving actionable, formative, and constructive feedback from the instructor or peers. For example, if we want students to learn how to problem solve, we need to give them opportunities to apply problem solving skills so that they become habits. They cannot necessarily improve their problem solving skills by learning about problem solving in a lecture or reading, though those are assuredly supplemental. If we want students to learn how to identify biases and mitigate them, we need to give them opportunities to practice identifying bias in different mediums and then mitigating bias or clearly articulating how one might mitigate bias, not just learn what biases are in a lecture or reading (though again, these are supplemental). Therefore, our pedagogical approach to teach practical knowledge in Minerva-designed courses is fully active learning, so that students are engaged at least 75 percent of the time while in class and therefore collaborate in their own learning (Fost et al., 2017).

Active learning has been shown to improve learning and retention in many different types of classrooms (Freeman et al., 2014; Kilgo et al., 2015; Prince, 2004). In part, this is because students' focused attention span in lectures has been shown to be about 15 min (numerous studies cited in Hartley & Davies, 1978; Wankat, 2002), thus, engaging the students actively can improve retention (Prince, 2004). Improved retention from active learning is not limited to content, for example, Styers et al. (2018) demonstrated that students in flipped, active learning biology courses exhibited gains in critical thinking. The largest critical thinking gains in their study were in intermediate and upper-level courses (Styers et al., 2018), likely because of the increase in problem solving and more theoretical content of upper level science courses. Most importantly, for underrepresented students in math, technology, science and engineering, active learning has narrowed achievement gaps (Haak et al., 2011; Theobald et al., 2020).

Our pedagogical approach at Minerva is designed to nurture student's development of practical knowledge, through the LOs that make up the learning taxonomy. We do not employ lectures in class sessions; instead, students prepare using asynchronous learning materials before class and then in-class time is spent engaging in activities designed to provide deeper processing of the material and spaced practice with the Learning Outcomes. In flipped learning, passive learning such as lectures and reading happens outside of class and in class is reserved for homework, such as problem sets (Jenkins et al., 2017). Minerva's pedagogical approach is radically flipped, the learning outside of class includes both the reading/lectures and the homework, and in class time is reserved for active learning. We design highly structured, active learning-based lessons that allow students to apply LOs specified for the course by engaging in higher-order cognitive tasks such as problem solving, peer instruction, and analysis (Resnick, 1987; for examples of applications in an upper-level ecology class, see Gahl et al., 2021).

Using an active learning approach requires a modification of the traditional class roles of instructor, student, and classroom. The instructor in a Minerva active learning session is a facilitator and coach, guiding the group of participants through a series of activities structured for engagement. The instructor is rarely engaged in information transfer except where to provide feedback, clarify confusion, or re-focus the class. A key role of the instructor is to provide feedback to students, in real time and asynchronously, on their applications of LOs. This feedback is integral for coaching students to improve applications over time directly on the Future Skills targeted by the learning taxonomy.

In a radically flipped active learning class, the pedagogical structure of the sessions requires participation by the students. Therefore, the students must prepare for in-class sessions by completing pre-class reading and work before the session, which is typically a large departure from lecture-based classrooms, in which students can arrive to a class unprepared. In Minerva courses, we nudge students to fully prepare ahead by including preparatory assessment polls in each session and assessing students on in-class contributions. To ensure creative engagement of students throughout the lesson, course designers assess student engagement with each activity in a lesson plan by asking "what are the other students doing?". We attempt to create a culture that embraces and celebrates this more engaged vision of a student.

Although one could teach a Minerva-designed active learning session in person, Minerva partners typically use our active learning platform, Forum™, because it was designed for active learning and teaching. Some of the classroom features necessary for active learning include space for students to collaborate, with the ability to move around (i.e., breakouts), some way for students to provide long form answers in real time and receive feedback on those responses, and a way to be looking at the same prompt (e.g., slide, text, image, blackboard, etc.). In Forum, we can do all of these easily and create a similar experience for every student taking that course. The speed at which we can make classroom changes in Forum outpaces the physical classroom. Imagine the logistics involved in telling students in an in-person class to go into small groups with pre-defined group members and instructions. Consider the amount of time it takes for students to find their peers, pick up their things, move around, receive a document that explains what they will do, and settle back into learning. With set-up beforehand, this can be done in Forum with the click of a button; students arrive in a breakout room, with instructions in front of them, with little chance for distraction or loss of focus during the transition. The instructor, meanwhile, can listen in or visit any breakout group, watch their responses being typed in the breakout workbook in real time, move students to other breakouts as needed with drag and drop, monitor who is talking more or less, chat a specific group, respond to raised hands, follow the progress of all breakout groups at a glance, pin specific groups for later debrief, and modify the breakout time as needed based on their observations of the groups' progress.

22.4 Assessment in Minerva Programs

Each skill or concept that we include in our learning taxonomy is directly assessed, providing students with focused formative feedback directly on that skill or concept. Feedback is focused because each application of an LO is assessed, rather than one score on that LO for the entire work. Feedback from instructors is also formative in Minerva programs, with comments that clearly identify how the student could improve their application of a specific LO. LO statements and rubrics are clearly articulated and outline what students should know and be able to do as a result of applying a particular concept or skill. Instead of emphasizing high-stakes exams, our assessments are scaffolded, from contributions in classroom discussions to open-ended, inquiry-based projects and assignments. Instructors are trained to assign rubric scores and provide qualitative assessments to provide students targeted, actionable feedback on specific LOs. In addition, we evaluate students' ability to transfer that skill or concept to other content areas through assessment of those same LOs across courses.

LOs in the Minerva and MU learning taxonomies are each introduced in the relevant interdisciplinary general education course, for example in Minerva's general education Collegiate Foundations courses. Once introduced, LOs can be assessed in any other course in a student's program. Because LOs are assessed by faculty of different disciplines in multiple courses across the curriculum, we need to ensure consistency in the feedback that we provide to students on their applications. We approach this in two key ways: 1) high levels of collaboration among faculty and 2) clear rubrics with measurable outcomes. Faculty team teach many courses at MU and at Minerva partner institutions. In our context, team teaching is a scenario of multiple faculty teaching the same course to different groups of students, and meeting regularly to discuss lesson plan implementation and corroborate grading. Team teaching in Minerva programs allows for conversations about applications and potential scores to occur both synchronously in team meetings and asynchronously in discussion threads. Faculty provide feedback and advice for each other's assessments by both means. Rubrics are core aspects of the assessment process in Minerva-designed courses. Rubrics are developed along with the LO and reflect the aspects of LO applications that are being assessed (for example, consider the rubric for the LO #biasidentification in Table 22.2).

Rubrics are made visible to and used by both students and faculty. For students, rubrics provide clear instructions for strong applications and can help students self-reflect on their applications. For faculty, they are instrumental tools for assessing student applications, though faculty may assess applications made quickly in a class session (i.e., in class polls and verbal comments) with a bit more leeway than applications made with time to think and plan such as those in assignments.

Forum tools integrate the use of rubrics for assessment. Instructors can provide feedback on poll responses, student in-class verbal contributions, pre-class work, and assignments all within Forum. Rubrics are available within the Forum grading tools so that instructors have them at their fingertips while grading. In their Outcome Index in Forum, students can view each LO they have been introduced to, the LO rubrics and examples. Students can also see their average scores for each LO, how their scores for that LO have changed over time, and in which courses, sessions, and assignments the LO has been assessed (Fig. 22.1).

Table 22.2 Example rubrics for the Learning Outcome #biasidentification

#biasidentification: Identify and explain how biases result from psychological mechanisms or use of heuristics

Rubric Score	Rubric
1	Does not recall or recognize psychological biases when prompted; identifies the existence or type of psychological bias mostly or entirely inaccurately
2	Identifies the existence or type of psychological bias and its potential effects only somewhat accurately
3	Accurately identifies the existence and type of psychological bias and its potential effects
4	Accurately identifies the existence and type of bias and clearly explains the potential effects of a psychological bias; (when applicable) effectively analyzes the relationships among psychological biases and their impact

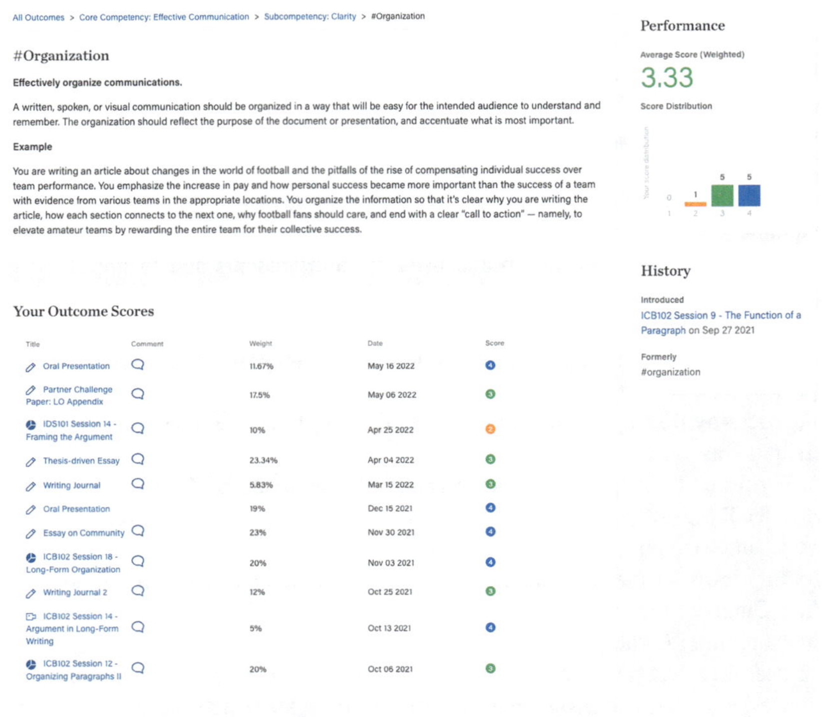

All Outcomes > Core Competency: Effective Communication > Subcompetency: Clarity > #Organization

#Organization

Effectively organize communications.

A written, spoken, or visual communication should be organized in a way that will be easy for the intended audience to understand and remember. The organization should reflect the purpose of the document or presentation, and accentuate what is most important.

Example

You are writing an article about changes in the world of football and the pitfalls of the rise of compensating individual success over team performance. You emphasize the increase in pay and how personal success became more important than the success of a team with evidence from various teams in the appropriate locations. You organize the information so that it's clear why you are writing the article, how each section connects to the next one, why football fans should care, and end with a clear "call to action" — namely, to elevate amateur teams by rewarding the entire team for their collective success.

Performance

Average Score (Weighted)

3.33

Score Distribution

Your Outcome Scores

Title	Comment	Weight	Date	Score
Oral Presentation	Q	11.67%	May 16 2022	4
Partner Challenge Paper: LO Appendix	Q	17.5%	May 06 2022	3
IDS101 Session 14 - Framing the Argument	Q	10%	Apr 25 2022	2
Thesis-driven Essay	Q	23.34%	Apr 04 2022	3
Writing Journal	Q	5.83%	Mar 15 2022	3
Oral Presentation		19%	Dec 15 2021	4
Essay on Community	Q	23%	Nov 30 2021	4
ICB102 Session 18 - Long-Form Organization	Q	20%	Nov 03 2021	4
Writing Journal 2	Q	12%	Oct 25 2021	3
ICB102 Session 14 - Argument in Long-Form Writing	Q	5%	Oct 13 2021	4
ICB102 Session 12 - Organizing Paragraphs II	Q	20%	Oct 06 2021	3

History

Introduced
ICB102 Session 9 - The Function of a Paragraph on Sep 27 2021

Formerly
#organization

Fig. 22.1 Example student view of a single Learning Outcome (LO) in the Outcome Index in Forum, Minerva Project's proprietary learning platform. A student can track all assessments of a single LO across courses in the Outcome Index, can view where the LO was introduced, and see an average across all scores

22.5 Systematic Reinforcement of Learning Outcomes

A key aspect of the Learning Outcomes in Minerva programs is their scaffolding throughout the curriculum, leading to their reinforcement across contexts and domains, providing students with opportunities to transfer their knowledge (Dunlosky & Rawson, 2015; Hopkins et al., 2015). We track the improvement of student's mastery of the LOs over time, as well as their facility in applying LOs under different conditions (such as different assignment types versus in class verbal comments and polls) and in different ways (such as applying a skill directly versus critique the application of a skill by someone else). LOs are integrated throughout a student's experience, including reinforcement in experiential learning and internship opportunities. Minerva University provides the most illustrative example of the systematic reinforcement of LOs throughout the program; other global partners may implement varying degrees of integration of LOs throughout a specific program depending on their own constraints.

LOs are typically introduced in a specific course, and then may be scored in other courses. Though many LOs are revisited in subsequent courses, in these instances, the reintroduction of the LO may focus on LO applications that are more complex or highlight a different aspect of the LO (Fig. 22.2). For example, #organization is introduced in a first-year communications course and practiced in many different kinds of courses including arts and literature courses, philosophy courses, natural sciences and computational sciences and its application varies depending on the domain. This LO is scored in the course it is introduced, but is also scored in other courses where organization of written and verbal material is important and applied by students.

Forum tracks all assessments that a student receives on any specific LO, and the student has visibility of each assessment in the Outcome Index (in Forum). For example, a student could view the LO #organization and see each instance of assessment they received on #organization and the context of the assessment (i.e., course, class session, assignment/poll/verbal response). This creates a cohesive view of the student's application of each LO across courses and allows students to track their improvement on LOs over time (Fig. 22.1).

One challenge with systematic reinforcement of LOs across courses and disciplines is that LOs are then assessed by varied faculty from different disciplines. Clear rubrics are key for ensuring consistency in scores across disciplines. We also encourage faculty collaboration about grading specific LOs, either through discussion boards and collaborative meetings.

22.6 Case Studies

22.6.1 CASE STUDY 1: Full Implementation at Minerva University

Minerva University (MU) is the flagship partner of Minerva Project (Minerva) and best illustrates the full application of Minerva principles. Minerva University embodies the active learning pedagogical approach, the direct assessment of prac-

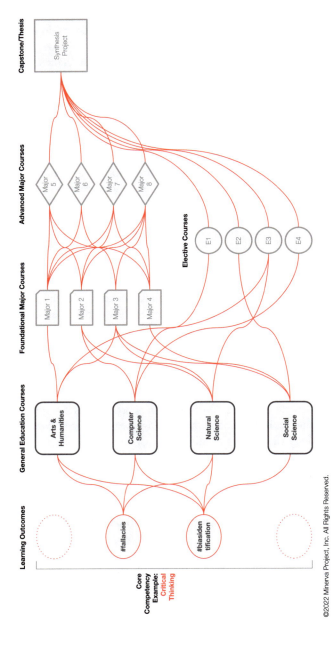

Fig. 22.2 Learning Outcomes (LOs) are scaffolded throughout the Minerva curriculum to promote knowledge transfer. Future Skills oriented LOs are typically introduced in the first-year courses. Students apply these LOs in upper year courses in the context of their chosen disciplines. At MU students apply these skills in fourth year capstone projects

tical knowledge, and the systematic reinforcement throughout the program (Kosslyn & Nelson, 2017).

Future Skills in MU's learning taxonomy are called Habits of Mind (H) and Foundational Concepts (C); HCs (Kosslyn, 2017). Minerva University uses a learning taxonomy of the full set of 78 HCs within the four core competencies: thinking critically, thinking creatively, communicating effectively, and interacting effectively. While the core learning taxonomy of MU and Minerva are similar, the key difference between HCs and LOs (in Minerva programs) is that LO scores are retained within the course where the LO was scored. In contrast, HC scores are always added to the first year Cornerstone course in which they were introduced, and not to the second-, third-, or fourth-year course in which they were scored (see discussion in Kosslyn & Nelson, 2017).

The pedagogy at MU reflects and implements the principles of active learning in every aspect of a student's education. MU's faculty design and teach structured active learning lesson plans in courses on Forum. Faculty use features of Forum in class to ensure that the class activities are engaging and equitable, including all students in the activity (e.g., TalkTime™ tool lets faculty see which students have talked less in the session and could be called on next). The strength of this pedagogy on MU students is best exemplified by two final year traditions of tutorials and Civitas at MU. Tutorials are fourth year courses that are guided by a faculty member, but are taught by students in a seminar format. At Civitas, soon to be graduates lead discussions with external experts on pressing global topics. MU students excel in leading these sessions because of their vast experience and practice with active learning over 4 years at MU.

Systematic reinforcement of Future Skills is best illustrated in MU's implementation. Students are assessed on HCs throughout their 4 years at MU in any course they take. Students are also assessed on HCs in civic projects (collaborative experiential projects with local partner organizations), internships (students provide a self-reflection of HC applications that is scored for credit), and capstone projects (a final year project for all MU students).

22.6.2 CASE STUDY 2: Partially Minerva-Designed Program

Minerva Project established a partnership with a university to adapt the Minerva foundational education courses as part of a new entrepreneurship program focused on leadership and social impact. The overall program is a three-year program, with an additional year reserved for a specialization track. Students are exposed to fundamental skill sets covering management, humanities, and technology to later apply in disruptive and innovative projects in the subsequent years. The overarching learning methodology is offered via three tracks, each of which exposes students to sets of cognitive and social skills that foster the ecosystem of innovation and entrepreneurship. Students take online and offline classes and embark on project-based scenarios that focus on prototyping and problem solving throughout the entire program.

Minerva Project's partnership is focused on the foundational education track, which offers twelve carefully curated Minerva-developed active learning structured courses and the subset of LOs that are introduced in those courses. In this partnership, the learning taxonomy is based on the Minerva/MU learning taxonomy, but customized to include the LOs that are specific to the courses to be taught by the partner. In this case, because the partner is teaching a 12-course foundation sequence, instead of MU's typical 8-course sequence, the learning taxonomy includes additional LOs not found in the MU taxonomy that are introduced in the additional four courses that are part of this track. Assessment for the LOs are done using Minerva rubrics and Forum tools. Systematic reinforcement of LOs is primarily done within the 12 Minerva-developed courses, and not throughout the rest of the program, unlike the MU implementation.

In light of the existing program at the university that focuses on leadership, innovation, and Socratic dialogue, Minerva courses have been customized for the partner by building activities in the classroom where students engage with concepts and techniques that help create synergy between the different components of the program. This tailoring process results from a deep collaboration between Minerva and university faculty, who meet regularly to discuss the previous lesson plans and how the new lesson plans address the program's focus, driving the choice of topics our curriculum offers.

The threading of Learning Outcomes throughout the curriculum is strategically designed to allow students to revisit priorly introduced skills and to have the opportunity to master those later. This is done by having one or even more LOs shared by different courses, which offer breadth and depth for their application scope. This repetition mechanism guarantees mastery of the skill set powered by the instructors' regular assessment and feedback of in-class contributions and assignment work.

Students' focus on skills in the Minerva-developed courses can then be applied to the other tracks in the program to build a solid foundation that fast-tracks students to innovate as they work on company business projects. For example, a student who has learned how to effectively communicate with an audience while using rhetorical appeals can directly apply these when prototyping a business

22 Active Learning and Integrated Assessment …

model. By supporting their foundation years with LOs, our curriculum enhances the interdisciplinary skill set that program students develop by the end of the program.

Through this collaboration, we have developed a partnership that thrives as a model of learning and practicing. Far from a plug-and-play method, the curriculum takes shape through our continuous collaboration between Minerva and university faculty. Further, using a single focused skill-based track in the foundation years can provide a thread that will weave through the entire student experience.

22.6.3 CASE STUDY 3: Custom Collaboratively Designed Program

A large private university engaged Minerva Project to design and develop an entirely custom new flagship program centered around innovation, entrepreneurship, and design, with the goal that this program would blossom into a hub for educational innovation across the university. This partner set their sights high, with a vision of what was possible with creative ideas and bold changes in how we understand the ways and modes in which students learn. Together we imagined a program for students who are unconventional, driven, and eager for challenging experiences. These students would seek to develop skills from engineering to business, coding to visual arts.

Minerva collaborated with the university to develop four core structural components of the program: the academic model, the learning taxonomy, the student experience, and the depth of the major. We co-designed a three-year undergraduate degree that eliminates the large breaks that delay student learning and growth and increases the ability of students to take advantage of experiential learning activities through employer and civic engagements during a summer term. Underlying the design was understanding that learning takes place in a myriad of ways and across a variety of scales, from small moments of insight in peer discussions during class to hands-on collaborative projects to engagement with relevant problems with real-world partners.

The program's custom learning taxonomy is focused on Future Skills for innovation and design and was collaboratively designed by Minerva and the university team. These skills are to be taught and assessed repeatedly, in diverse contexts, and on varied scales of complexity in order to enable ample opportunity for practice and to help students recognize opportunities for transfer. To achieve this solid foundation, the program requires all students to take a core set of foundational courses in their first year in which these skills are introduced. These courses are intentionally integrated and their Learning Outcomes persist over time and across program components, including design challenges. Students learn, broadly: to communicate in a compelling manner, to understand themselves, their society, and the similarities and differences among individuals and groups, to think critically and use computational methods, and to solve problems in a structured and creative manner.

The way in which these skills are woven into the fabric of the program is central to its ethos. The skills in the learning taxonomy do not simply make an appearance in a single course and then disappear. Rather, they are introduced in foundational courses, reinforced through experiential learning and design challenges, and revisited and reassessed in higher level courses. For example, the learning outcome *Maker Mindset* encourages students to have an approach to building and learning that embraces tinkering and learning from failure. It is organized in the taxonomy within the Adaptability and Growth sub-competency of the core competency of Self, Difference, and Power. This LO is introduced in a foundational course on designing for innovation and appears in the early design challenges. Later, it is foregrounded in a prototyping course and explicitly called out in a reflection students write as part of their final year capstone project. Importantly, *Maker Mindset* is always available as an outcome on which faculty can provide feedback, even if the specific activity did not explicitly call it out in its construction. This allows students to identify how the skills within the learning taxonomy appear in various intensities across contexts, and enables faculty ample opportunities to give formative feedback to encourage growth.

22.7 Challenges and Further Research

Each of the key aspects of the Minerva approach to learning presents challenges. We have worked with these challenges at MU and with our higher education partners to create some solutions, but there is still ample room for improvement as we continue to iterate on these programs.

Developing the learning taxonomy of practical knowledge is an ongoing process. As we teach, apply, and assess LOs, we continue to revise and hone their scope. Every academic year since MU's inception we have revised LOs to ensure that they are of a similar scale (i.e., are not too broad or too narrow) and are assessing the skill we are targeting. It can be challenging to then ensure clarity of the new or merged LO throughout the curriculum and for instructors who will assess this skill in practice.

As effective as active learning is for student retainment of skills and knowledge, student preparation and the amount of design work needed to create lesson plans are persistent challenges. Students who are conditioned to attend lectures without having to prepare ahead often struggle to do the pre-class work necessary for an effective active learning session. We have implemented preparatory polls to assess student preparation, score pre-class work deliverables, and underscore the need for preparation in class sessions. And yet, until there is a strong culture of preparation and buy-in for active learning, this change for some students can be challenging. Additionally, to design an effectively structured active learning session takes time and expertise, much more time than instructors typically have available for class preparation. For lesson plan design, we collaborate with partners to either 1) use Minerva-designed active learning courses or 2) collaboratively design courses as a team to spread the work. We have also worked on ways to speed design efforts, using templates and instructional designers, who may be savvy in designing active learning courses but not in a specific content area.

Lastly, although rubrics help guide assessment across disciplines and faculty, some skills are not readily applied and assessed in a typical academic classroom (e.g., #teamwork, #confidence). Project-based assignments and experiential learning along with self-reflection can help to fill this gap, but this remains an area of challenge. Rubrics also help to guide assessment towards consistency, but without collaboration and discussion among instructors, consistency may be difficult to achieve.

22.8 Learnings and Recommendations

From our work with multiple partners implementing practical knowledge focused programs, our key learnings and recommendations are centered on alignment in both curriculum and students throughout the institution. Alignment among LOs, class activities, assignments, and assessments is key to a successful program. Effectively applying LOs is the overall goal, therefore each aspect of the overall implementation should be built to drive towards that goal. The learning taxonomy provides the blueprint for the rest of the curriculum. To focus a program on Future Skills along with active learning pedagogy and direct assessment of LOs, rather than holistic scores, is an approach that is transformational and requires a cultural and mindset shift in a higher education system. Stakeholder buy-in is important from administration, faculty, and students. The culture can be built, but it takes focused effort. When the culture is achieved, we have found that the students themselves begin to speak up to reinforce that active learning with focus on LOs continues to be implemented in their classrooms.

Having a clear learning taxonomy based on skills can be a powerful tool. Within our own organization we apply LOs in our work, in meetings, and with feedback from peers. We have also integrated active learning into our internal processes, for example, large meetings are almost always engaging, active learning sessions with time for small group collaboration and opportunities for input from all involved. In addition, we intermittently facilitate internal trainings and workshops for non-academics at Minerva Project, to improve understanding of our learning taxonomy and pedagogy. Integrating these skills internally allows us to build an effective and focused team culture and to cultivate an education organization that tries to exemplify its own philosophy in practice.

> **Future Skills in Practice: Our Recommendations**
> - For successful whole program implementation, align Learning Outcomes with class activities, assignments, and assessments throughout a program.
> - Directly assess the skills that you would like students to learn, providing formative feedback at many stages throughout the program.
> - Stakeholder buy-in is important across all levels of a program from administration to teachers to students.

References

Brown, P. C., Roediger, H. L., & McDaniel, M. A. (2014). *Make it stick: The science of successful learning*. Harvard University Press.

Cepeda, N. J., Pashler, H., Vul, E., Wixted, J. T., & Rohrer, D. (2006). Distributed practice in verbal recall tasks: A review and quantitative synthesis. *Psychological Bulletin, 132*(3), 354–380. https://doi.org/10.1037/0033-2909.132.3.354.

Dunlosky, J., & Rawson, K. A. (2015). Practice tests, spaced practice, and successive relearning: Tips for classroom use and for guiding students' learning. *Scholarship of Teaching and Learning in Psychology, 1*(1), 72–78. https://doi.org/10.1037/stl0000024.

Fost, J., Levitt, R., & Kosslyn, S. M. (2017). Fully active learning. In S. M. Kosslyn & B. Nelson (Eds.), *Building the intentional university: Minerva and the future of higher education* (pp. 165–178). MIT Press.

Freeman, S., Eddy, S. L., McDonough, M., Smith, M. K., Okoroafor, N., Jordt, H., et al. (2014). Active learning increases student performance in science, engineering, and mathematics. *Proceedings of the National Academy of Sciences of the United States of America, 111*(23), 8410–8415. https://doi.org/10.1073/pnas.1319030111.

Gahl, M. K., & Chandler, V. (2017). Empirical analyses and creative thinking. In S. M. Kosslyn & B. Nelson (Eds.), *Building the intentional university: Minerva and the future of higher education* (pp. 97–108). MIT Press.

Gahl, M. K., Gale, A., Kaestner, A., Yoshina, A., Paglione, E., & Bergman, G. (2021). Perspectives on facilitating dynamic ecology courses online using active learning. *Ecology and Evolution, 11*(8), 3473–3480. https://doi.org/10.1002/ece3.6953.

Haak, D. C., HilleRisLambers, J., Pitre, E., & Freeman, S. (2011). Increased structure and active learning reduce the achievement gap in introductory biology. *Science, 332*(6034), 1213–1216. https://doi.org/10.1126/science.1204820.

Hartley, J., & Davies, I. K. (1978). Note-taking: A critical review. *Programmed Learning and Educational Technology, 15*(3), 207–224. https://doi.org/10.1080/0033039780150305.

Hopkins, R. F., Lyle, K. B., Hieb, J. L., & Ralston, P. A. S. (2015). Spaced retrieval practice increases college students' short- and long-term retention of mathematics knowledge. *Educational Psychology Review, 28*(4), 853–873.

Jenkins, M., Bokosmaty, R., Brown, M., Browne, C., Gao, Q., Hanson, J., et al. (2017). Enhancing the design and analysis of flipped learning strategies. *Teaching & learning Inquiry, 5*(1). https://doi.org/10.20343/teachlearninqu.5.1.7.

Kilgo, C. A., Ezell Sheets, J. K., & Pascarella, E. T. (2015). The link between high-impact practices and student learning: Some longitudinal evidence. *Higher Education, 69*(4), 509–525. https://doi.org/10.1007/s10734-014-9788-z.

Kivunja, C. (2014). Innovative pedagogies in higher education to become effective teachers of 21st century skills: Unpacking the learning and innovations skills domain of the new learning paradigm. *International Journal of Higher Education, 3*(4), 37–48. https://doi.org/10.5430/ijhe.v3n4p37.

Kosslyn, S. M. (2017). Practical knowledge. In S. M. Kosslyn & B. Nelson (Eds.), *Building the intentional university: Minerva and the future of higher education* (pp. 19–44). MIT Press. https://doi.org/10.7551/mitpress/11142.003.0005.

Kosslyn, S. M., & Nelson, B. (Eds.). (2017). *Building the intentional university: Minerva and the future of higher education*. MIT Press.

Prince, M. (2004). Does active learning work? A review of the research. *Journal of Engineering Education, 93*(3), 223–231. https://doi.org/10.1002/j.2168-9830.2004.tb00809.x.

Resnick, L. (1987). *Education and learning to think*. National Academy Press.

Styers, M. L., van Zandt, P. A., & Hayden, K. L. (2018). Active learning in flipped life science courses promotes development of critical thinking skills. *CBE—Life Sciences Education, 17*(3), ar39. https://doi.org/10.1187/cbe.16-11-0332.

Theobald, E. J., Hill, M. J., Tran, E., Agrawal, S., Arroyo, E. N., Behling, S., et al. (2020). Active learning narrows achievement gaps for underrepresented students in undergraduate science, technology, engineering, and math. *Proceedings of the National Academy of Sciences of the United States of America, 117*(12), 6476–6483. https://doi.org/10.1073/pnas.1916903117.

Wankat, P. C. (2002). *The effective, efficient professor: Teaching, scholarship and service*. Allyn and Bacon.

Megan K. Gahl is Senior Director of Curriculum and Pedagogy at Minerva Project and Professor of Natural Sciences at Minerva University. Megan has been with Minerva University since its inaugural class began its first year curriculum in 2015. Megan leads the curriculum team at Minerva Project in developing engaging, active learning curriculum for Minerva partners and oversees Minerva faculty training programs. ORCID ID: 0000-0001-9697-1925

Abha Ahuja is an Academic Director at Minerva Project and Associate Professor of Natural Sciences at Minerva University. Abha was one of the first faculty members at Minerva University and helped to shepherd through the inaugural class in their first year at MU. Abha oversees curriculum design and delivery with University Partners at Minerva Project. ORCID ID: 0000-0002-2496-669X

Raquel H. Ribeiro is a Senior Manager Partner Programs at Minerva Project and Professor of Computational Sciences at Minerva University. Raquel builds on a career in academia as a theoretical physicist and in the industry as a data scientist to guide a data-based approach to teaching since 2018. ORCID ID: 0000-0002-5434-252X

Maia Averett is a Senior Academic Program Manager at Minerva Project, Professor of Computational Sciences at Minerva University, and Professor of Mathematics at Mills College. ORCID: 0000-0002-0834-4356

James Genone is the Managing Director of Higher Education Innovation at Minerva Project and Professor of Social Sciences at Minerva University. James has been with Minerva University since its inaugural class began its first-year curriculum in 2015. ORCID: 0000-0002-4395-0730

Open Access This chapter is licensed under the terms of the Creative Commons Attribution 4.0 International License (http://creativecommons.org/licenses/by/4.0/), which permits use, sharing, adaptation, distribution and reproduction in any medium or format, as long as you give appropriate credit to the original author(s) and the source, provide a link to the Creative Commons license and indicate if changes were made.

The images or other third party material in this chapter are included in the chapter's Creative Commons license, unless indicated otherwise in a credit line to the material. If material is not included in the chapter's Creative Commons license and your intended use is not permitted by statutory regulation or exceeds the permitted use, you will need to obtain permission directly from the copyright holder.

Developing a More Granular and Equitable Approach to the Learner-Earner Journey. The Role of Badging, Micro-Credentials and Twenty-first Century Skills Within Higher Education to Enable Future Workforce Development

23

Grame Barty, Naomi Boyer, Alexandros Chrysikos, Margo Griffith, Kevin House, Tara Laughlin, Ebba Ossiannilsson, Rupert Ward and Holly Zanville

Abstract

This chapter introduces trends within the global skills economy and explores how our learner-earner journeys can best align to these trends. It starts with a discussion of future global workforce skills requirements from higher education courses and discusses emerging Future Skills. It then considers how

---

G. Barty
Co-Leader ICoBC Global Workforce Development Working Group/Head of Issuing Authorities, ICoBC/Credshare, Neutral Bay, Australia
e-mail: hello@credshare.com

N. Boyer
Executive Director, Education Design Lab, Washington, DC, USA
e-mail: nboyer@eddesignlab.org

A. Chrysikos
Senior Lecturer and Researcher in Computing Science (Cyber Security), London Metropolitan University, London, UK
e-mail: a.chrysikos@londonmet.ac.uk

© The Author(s) 2024
U.-D. Ehlers and L. Eigbrecht (eds.), *Creating the University of the Future*, Zukunft der Hochschulbildung - Future Higher Education,
https://doi.org/10.1007/978-3-658-42948-5_23

schools can align with higher education and workforce requirements through a skills-based approach to delivery and how higher education courses can better align to schools, workforce requirements and other potential outputs. The chapter then explores validation models, micro-credentials, and alternative credentials, considering alongside this the role of equity within skills-based education and hiring systems. Finally, it concludes with some key policy and process considerations.

23.1 Introduction

The global skills economy is increasingly reliant on an agile skilled workforce that can quickly adapt to changing consumer behavior and labor market demands. This agility has already seen profound changes to the careers and opportunities of learner-earners around the world. Workforce migration has increased signifi-

---

M. Griffith
Edalex Pty Ltd, Hobart, Australia
e-mail: info@edalex.com

K. House
Education Futures Architect, Education in Motion, Singapore, Singapore
e-mail: Kevin.House@eimglobal.com

T. Laughlin
Education Designer, Micro-Credentialing Project Manager, Education Design Lab,
Washington, DC, USA
e-mail: tlaughlin@eddesignlab.org

E. Ossiannilsson
Professor and Research Fellow, Victoria University of Wellington, Wellington,
New Zealand

R. Ward (✉)
Director of Strategic Partnerships & 21St Century Skills Working Group Co-Lead/
Professor of Learning Innovation and Associate Dean,
ICoBC/University of Huddersfield, Berlin, Germany
e-mail: rward@icobc.net

H. Zanville
Executive Committee of the ICoBC/Research Professor and Co-Director of the Program
Skills, Credentials & Workforce Policy (GWU), ICoBC/George Washington University,
Washington, DC, USA

cantly, job security has reduced, economies have transformed from local skill low income to high skill high income and vice versa through responding quickly to opportunity and through strategically planning skills development amongst their workforce, or by neglecting both of these. From the learner-earner perspective there are both opportunities and threats from this agile globalized economy. How can we best respond to this agility as learner-earners? What socio-technical solutions can assist us in managing this agility? What do we need to consider when looking to change careers, job roles or when trying to plan our learner-earner journey?

This chapter considers these questions from a social constructivist perspective, outlining some current trends which will be part of answering these questions. It considers, for example, how learner-earners will need to consider how they carry evidence of their skills around with them within digital wallets rather than as a traditional resume/CV, how they will be able to communicate to themselves and others what skills they have and how reskilling and adapting to new roles may become much more agile with specific skills being upskilled rather than the traditional requirement to completely retrain or undertake a full qualification. These changes introduce a new, more granular, and more lifelong learner-earner journey, based on badges, micro-credentials, and skills, which enable us all to better communicate our capabilities and competencies, and in so doing provide opportunities to address long standing structural inequalities by providing more equitable education and employment mechanisms.

Within this chapter, the term Future Skills relates to the NextSkills definition i.e. *competencies that allow individuals to solve complex problems in highly emergent contexts of action in a self-organized way and enable them to act (successfully). They are based on cognitive, motivational, volitional and social resources, are value-based and can be acquired in a learning process* (Ehlers, 2020; NextEducation, 2023). They are also contextualized in respect to subjects, objects (e.g. systems) and organizations. In comparison, the term twenty-first Century Skills remains contested. For example, Partnership for twenty-first Century Learning provides a Framework for twenty-first Century Learning based on key subjects and twenty-first Century Themes (P21 – Partnership for twenty-first Century Learning, 2019), whilst Assessment and Teaching of twenty-first Century Skills (ATC21S) provided a framework based on tools for working, ways of thinking, and living in the world (ATS2020 Project, 2023). Twenty-first Century Skills also tend to be contextualized with respect to different perspectives which further adds to the lack of clarity when using the term.

In this chapter, twenty-first Century Skills are viewed from a personalized learning perspective (Ward, 2020); i.e., where Future Skills focus on the competencies that permit learner agency, twenty-first Century Skills focus on how the learner can develop agency through competencies; i.e., how learners develops themselves. In this chapter we therefore define twenty-first Century Skills as *competencies gained by a learner that enable them to self-reflect, self-regulate, and self-optimize their capabilities within highly emergent contexts*. This is a very subtle difference and for the most part this means both terms can be seen as almost interchangeable throughout these discussions. The twenty-first Century Skills definition provided here lists many areas that can be seen as Future Skills. It is in their application to, or by, the learner therefore that there is this subtle difference.

23.2 Future Skills and the Global Workforce: The Challenge for Higher Education

What global workforce employers require, in terms of Future Skills from Higher Education, at its simplest is for new employees to be able to engage in productive work immediately upon appointment. We agree with the analysis that students want to undertake Higher Education training that is flexible, affordable, and with the high potential to lead them to the job or career they seek (Pichette et al., 2021). However, a number of factors are conspiring to force educators, employers and students to better understand the 'future' skills required for the global workforce. For example, one factor is that access to digital technology and platforms is increasingly ubiquitous. Satellite broadband, 5G Mobile Networks, and Artificial Intelligence are providing levels of broadband access and capability for the first time in the world's largest markets such as Greater China, South Asia, the countries of Africa and Latin America.

Low-cost smart devices available today can now also provide a high-performance computing capability to individuals in these markets to access new global digital services—including education and training. Given these technological developments, twenty-first Century Skills capabilities have become increasingly critical, not just desirable, for individuals to participate in the global workforce. For Future Skills, we also need to understand where the future source of global talent resides. Global demographics show us very large populations in emerging markets are proportionally younger and will require an unprecedented level of jobs, and require twenty-first Century Skills to match (Adekeye, 2019). In addition, in any future global workforce, the importance of skills that can be transferred between different jobs is critical. Young people entering the workforce today may have many employers and different careers over their working lives (Foundation for Young Australians, 2017).

Another once in a generation change in new skills needed for workers has been brought on by the COVID-19 pandemic. What does that mean for employees' skills going forward? Growth in global sourcing and recruitment for nearly any job role is now more possible, even more attractive, because of the positive COVID remote working productivity experience of most of the world's businesses. However, this places a new emphasis on both worker and manager skills to maintain an esprit de corps, corporate culture and worker and business technical performance without the benefit of in-person communication. At the same time, we are moving to a more automated and global workforce. Alongside many jobs disappearing, as they become automated, the digitization of roles increasingly means global workforce fluidity in both how we can work and how we can be employed (Foundation for Young Australians, 2017).

The key element of this changing environment for Higher Education is that, over a career, lifetime tertiary knowledge expires (sometimes referred to as a 'half-life' of higher education) whilst skills and reskilling requirements are ongoing. Future Skills will need to be delivered differently, be affordable and flexible, and be able to relate 'exactly' to the employer's requirements as it's employers needs that are being met. Furthermore, significant employers, such as IBM, can no longer wait three or four years for students to graduate (Leaser, 2020). Short courses with the right skills for the role are now equally valuable. There are numerous interpretations of what Future Skills are. A recent International Council of Badges and Credentials (ICoBC) twenty-first Century Skills Report identified the categories of 'future' skills (ICoBC, 2021). These included **Learning/Cognitive/Thinking Skills** such as analysis, creativity, innovation, problem solving, researching, reasoning, synthesis; **Life Skills** such as adaptability, communication, initiative, planning, resilience, self-regulation; **Career/Working Skills** such as collaboration, entrepreneurship, leadership, management; **Digital Literacy/ Tools for Working Skills** such as data analysis, presentation, reporting; and **Citizenship/Ways of Living in the World Skills** such as economics, ethics, health, professionalism, socio-cultural awareness, sustainability.

Interestingly, much of the discussion regarding future workforce skills refers not to technical competence, but rather to 'human capability'. That is, an individual's character, disposition, and mindset. In one workforce example, The Institute for Working Futures (IWF) has developed 'A Future Capability Reference Model on Human Capability Standards' which is available to educators and policy makers to improve graduate employability, and to accelerate the development of a future-ready workforce (The Institute for Working Futures, 2020). IWF claims these are the non-technical worker and leadership capabilities that will form over 62% of all future job profiles.

Cheryl Oldham, Senior Vice President of Education and Workforce, U.S. Chamber of Commerce Foundation refers to these as 'durable skills' as a combination of how you use what you know, skills like critical thinking, communication, collaboration, and creativity, as well as character skills like fortitude, growth mindset and leadership (America Succeeds, 2021).

Durability, by definition, infers "enduring capabilities" which in turn delivers what America Succeeds describes as "Future Ready Capabilities". The challenge for higher education institutions in preparing students for the global workforce is to understand not only what it can provide in terms of historical, unique teaching methods, but how they can integrate internationally acceptable human capability and durable skills as an essential component of any course curriculum. Getting this right will provide institutions with a competitive ability to both source and attract the right students for the training for which they are best suited, as well as provide them with the level of immediate work skills employers require (The Institute for Working Futures, 2020).

23.3 Teaching and Learning in Schools: An Opportunity for Higher Education

23.3.1 Connecting High School with Higher Education

For an increasing number, one of the important transition points in lifelong learning is that between school and university. However, much of the contemporary literature examining Future Skills largely overlooks a learner's credential journey from compulsory to tertiary education. Therefore, this next section raises issues with this transition before going on to offer two examples of how there might be a better knowledge and skills alignment between the two education systems. Over the last 30 years, we have seen a continuation of the twentieth-century tradition of recognizing only a narrow range of 'academic' knowledge and skills as the core requirements for pre-tertiary student graduation. This means the final two to four years of the student learning experience in compulsory schooling prioritize a well-established, and largely siloed, set of disciplinary subjects, which then benchmark end point evidence of student knowledge using high stakes summative examinations that have remained unchanged since the eighteenth-century (Shackleton, 2014).

In the context of the twenty-first century future of work agenda, this means that most compulsory schooling provides little opportunity to nurture, practice or recognize the development of durable, soft skills amongst school leavers. The aim of this section of the chapter is to first provide a summary of the common current forms of school graduation recognition (credentialing), and their skills gaps, before moving to explore scenarios of how the final years of schooling might look in a future that better anticipates both tertiary and workplace learning and skills development.

23.3.2 The School Graduate Picture Today: A Tale of Two Worlds

Global school graduate credentialing is dominated by two systems, both of which historically evolved in Western education systems on both sides of the Atlantic Ocean. From North America we find various iterations of the Carnegie high school transcript model. This delivers a cumulative student transcript built over four years and based on credits that are directly related to what is known as 'seat time.' This term refers to the hours of instruction provided to cover the pre-established content of a specific disciplinary subject. A student's accumulation of knowledge and skills in these disciplinary areas is then evidenced by an assessment process that uses end-point examinations. The scores drawn from these examinations then lead to pass or fail judgements that directly relate to the credit entered on the four-year high school student transcript. On successful completion, this transcript leads to the award of diploma or diploma with honors. Today, in many contexts, advanced subject specialism is recognized by leveraging externally benchmarked examinations such as College Board's Advanced Placement or individual subject certificates drawn from the International Baccalaureate's Diploma Program. These specialist advanced qualifications often lead to students having recognized undergraduate credit with selected North American universities.

However, much of the rest of the world defaults to a qualification rather than transcript-based pre-tertiary approach. The reason for this, we would suggest, is largely to do with the level of centralization at the ministry of education level. The transcript model evolved because of a largely devolved approach to, and little centralized management of, education. Qualifications, on the other hand, grew out of more central government management of educational provision and its credentialing.

Qualification approaches come in many guises and are either awarded by a nation state's ministry of education or by a government-regulated awarding body that is external to the school system. However, qualifications rely on hours of instruction of a predetermined curriculum scope and sequence over a set period, which is not dissimilar to the transcript notion of seat time. Examples of centralized, ministry-awarded qualifications would be the French Baccalaureate and the German Abitur. Examples of regulated, externally-awarded credentials would include the English GCSE and A Levels and the International Baccalaureate's Diploma Program.

By and large, transcripts nor qualifications identify, evaluate, or award credentials for what are now referred to as twenty-first Century Skills. However, whilst not prioritized, there are many instances where the learning experiences do incorporate the development of these skills as a by-product of the school experience in traditional academic knowledge and skills curricula. However, they are to date doing nothing to recognize such skills development using credential systems, and this creates distinct problems related directly to any Diversity, Equity, Inclusion and Justice (DEIJ) agenda and impacts future citizens globally (Zhong & Shetty, 2021).

23.3.3 The Gaps

There are simple changes to high schooling that could both empower the Diversity, Equity, Inclusion and Justice agenda and better meet the needs apparent in the well-documented 'future of work' crisis. The current narrowness of knowledge and skills delivered through compulsory education limits the credentialing and recognition of a more diverse range of skills, knowledge, and dispositions. This is largely driven by well-established qualifications such as A Levels (United Kingdom), Advanced Placement (United States), and the International Baccalaureate's Diploma Program. Their global dominance is maintained by a university system that continues to view them as 'gold standard' qualifications, which dominate entry to undergraduate degrees. Consequently, this has led to vocational qualifications being regarded as second-class qualifications even though many deliver on Future Skills better than traditional academic qualifications. The institutional privileging of these qualifications, even when they have equivalency in nation qualification frameworks, creates a social hierarchy that leads to inequity in skills recognition, and ultimately limits access to lifelong learning, whereas better tertiary recognition of a wider range of knowledge, skills and dispositional traits would lead to a more inclusive education environment. Building wide-ranging micro-credentials could break the current qualifications hierarchy by evidencing a wider knowledge and skills matrix, and this would enable better recognition of all learners' social capital and make the institutional practices of education and employers more just (Young & Hordern, 2022).

23.3.4 The Future

Few would deny that more equity is not desirable in future education and employment, but the question remains as to how we redesign compulsory schooling so that it better connects with higher education and workforce needs. To explore this further, below is a summary of two approaches currently being developed in high school contexts.

Here, we present two current high school models that each seek to build non-traditional learning experiences alongside recognition of longstanding and traditional knowledge and skills. The first example is built around a deep commitment to nurture dispositions, skills, and knowledge that will provide young people with a clear sense of their role in harnessing understanding to create a more sustainable relationship between human beings and the planet. Green School International[1] is a group of schools that have built a high school program that balances traditional academics with Project-Based Learning experiences to provide students with multiple opportunities to both apply learned skills and identify pathways for new learning. The second example is the School of Humanity,[2] which is an online first and hybrid high school model. Beyond traditional academics, School of Humanity again uses a PBL backbone to fully equip young learners with the digital fluency to navigate a world in which technology has become ubiquitous. However, this high school program is also founded on somatic and intellectual skills that aim to accelerate student awareness of human flourishing as a core educational principle in compulsory schooling.

Both models use the Mastery Transcript Consortium (MTC)[3] (see Fig. 23.1) online platform to build a competency-based credits system that captures durable, soft skills development as well as academic knowledge. This is done by mapping specific learning outcomes to a high school credit matrix, which students accu-

---

[1] https://www.greenschool.org/

[2] https://sofhumanity.com/

[3] https://mastery.org/

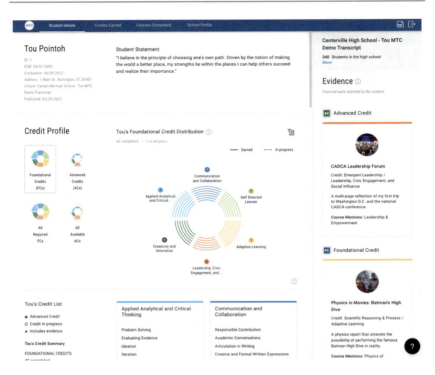

Fig. 23.1 Mastery Transcript Representation by MTC (2023)[4]

mulate over the four years of the program. It ensures that a predetermined range of core credits are accumulated whilst also allowing for high levels of personalization through self-identified areas of knowledge and skills specialism. The MTC platform also gives students the opportunity to curate a digital portfolio of extended knowledge artefacts, which provide evidence to their credited knowledge and skills being used.

Alongside this transcript approach, each school is designing a digital wallet that houses the entire digital record of a student's learning during the four years. This entails, for example, peer and faculty awarded Non-Fungible Tokens (NFTs) for soft skills displayed in collaborative activities, or badges recognizing participation in learning events such as workshops or short-term externships. These wal-

---

[4] See https://mastery.org/what-we-do/mastery-transcript/.

23 Developing a More Granular and Equitable Approach …

Fig. 23.2 Credential Ecosystem (own representation by Kevin House)

lets also house both verified micro-credentials issued by the school and certified ones issued by embedded industry and tertiary partners (Fig. 23.2).

In summary, the digital wallet becomes the repository for all learning and speaks to a learner's future learning pathways and future work trajectory. Fundamentally, the MTC transcript represents the pragmatic need to curate and represent granular components from the digital wallet in a form that speaks to the reality of today's tertiary admission industry processes. However, both these school models anticipate a time when the transcript concept falls to the wayside as it is replaced by the digital wallet. As societies move toward digital forms of identity across a wide range of areas such as taxation, health care, insurance, formal, non-formal, and informal credentialing will also follow suit. When digital credentialing is fully embedded there will be no need to rely on narrow academic qualifications or seat time-based transcripts because micro-credential wallets will reflect learners' full skill sets, bringing about more equity and a frictionless integration into higher education and continued lifelong learning.

This section has argued there is a problematic relationship between compulsory schooling and tertiary education, one that requires the development of digital wallets at school level, which contain a range of micro-credentials that can be added to during university and beyond. Therefore, it is now important to consider how such micro-credentials have been evolving in the tertiary system.

23.4 Future Skills and Teaching and Learning Within Higher Education: Contextualizing Micro-Credentials

Crawford (2021), president of Miami University, claims:

> "Degree programs are no longer sufficient in supporting student success and meeting industry needs. Micro-credentials can do both, affordably and conveniently. As

> *higher education aims to meet the needs of a rapidly changing post-COVID world and workplace, micro-credentials are emerging as a quick, compact, targeted way to instill and certify the particular skills that add value to a résumé and empower individuals to move toward their goals. These tools vastly expand the traditional education options that stretch from the two-year associate degree to the four-year bachelor's, additional-years master's and multi-year doctorate. They can be earned fast, and they provide employers with specific information about the person's qualification. A micro-credential can stand alone, become part of a curriculum or stack with other micro-credentials to demonstrate increasing knowledge".*

Micro-credentials are growing rapidly in the higher education world (Ossiannilsson & Kaur, 2021). Their growth is especially notable in colleges and universities committed to workforce development and alternative credentialing; in academic programs aligned with employers who require micro-credentials for entry (whether combined with academic degrees or not); and in regional, national, and international initiatives that focus on providing micro-credentials sought by individuals and employers for skilling and reskilling of workers.

While there is no common definition of micro-credentials, they can be defined as "proof of learning outcomes that a learner has acquired following a short learning experience" (European Commission, 2020, p. 10). These may be focused on a discrete set of competencies or a particular area of expertise, for example. They tend to be flexible in delivery and require demonstration of mastery. The term badges, which is often used synonymously with micro-credentials, is often used to represent the digital iconography associated with the micro-credential, that when clicked on provides information called metadata about the specifics of the earned digital credential, though it can also refer to the learning achievement itself.

According to OECD (2021a) "[t]he association of micro-credentials with a specific organized learning distinguishes them from badges" (p. 2–3); i.e., badges can represent a very broad range of learning achievements, whereas micro-credentials represent specific learning achievements aligned to organized learning, or indeed to a component of a credential, hence the term micro-credential. Where specific learning achievements are aligned to organized non-degree learning, and especially when these relate to workforce requirements, the term alternative credential is often used (Fong et al., 2016).

Micro-credentials are often designed as micro-learning modules (skills, knowledge, and attributes); and are often related to other credentials, stacked together, and portable (see Table 23.1).

Digital Credentials, or the digital representation of previously paper-based academic credentials such as degrees, diplomas, certificates, and certifications,

23 Developing a More Granular and Equitable Approach …

Table 23.1 Examples of Definitions of Micro-credentials

European Commission (2021, p. 1): "A micro-credential is the record of the learning outcomes that a learner has acquired following a small volume of learning. These learning outcomes have been assessed against transparent and clearly defined standards. Courses leading to micro-credentials are designed to provide the learner with specific knowledge, skills and competences that respond to societal, personal, cultural or labour market needs. Micro-credentials are owned by the learner, can be shared and are portable. They may be standalone or combined into larger credentials. They are underpinned by quality assurance following agreed standards in the relevant sector or area of activity."

National Education Association (2020): Micro-credentials are a digital form of certification indicating demonstrated competency/mastery in a specific skill or set of skill

UNESCO (2022, p. 20): "[…] typically focused on a specific set of learning outcomes in a narrow field of learning and achieved over a shorter period of time. Micro-credentials are offered by commercial entities, private providers and professional bodies, traditional education and training providers, community organisations and other types of organisations. While many micro-credentials represent the outcomes of more traditional learning experiences, others verify demonstration of achievements acquired elsewhere, such as in the workplace, through volunteering, or through personal interest learning. Micro-credentials are often promoted as an efficient way to upskill workers across the lifespan. A micro-credential: Is a record of focused learning achievement verifying what the learner knows, understands or can do. Includes assessment based on clearly defined standards and is awarded by a trusted provider. Has stand-alone value and may also contribute to or complement other micro-credentials or macro-credentials, including through recognition of prior learning. Meets the standards required by relevant quality assurance."

Wikipedia (04/2023): In higher education, a micro-degree and also micro-credentials and micro-masters is a qualification focused upon a specified professional or career discipline and typically comprises one or more sources of accelerated educational experiences

provide a means for electronically documenting, awarding, and sharing information about learning achievements and skills. While digital credentials is a term encompassing a broad swath of academic achievements, there is great variety in the deployment of these credentials for various purposes. For example, in terms of stackability, there are various models of accommodating micro-credentials within degrees, such as Reece's model for UK degrees (The Quality Assurance Agency for Higher Education/QAA, 2021) and the growth of micro-credentials has taken off particularly where there are policy directives from a governmental entity like a state higher education agency or national qualifications framework. In such instances, policy describes what micro-credentials are and how they fit among the array of approved credentials in an academic system.

Micro-credentials, digital badges, and industry-recognized certificates have expanded their scope considerably in recent years, driven by increasing demand for upskilling, retraining, and lifelong learning, as well as the sharp reduction in unit costs made possible by digitization. In the United States, the State University of New York (SUNY) policy sets standards guiding principles for development and support for a broad range of micro-credential types. A SUNY micro-credential is (1) competency-based, (2) endorsed by the issuing campus, (3) developed through faculty governance, and (4) meaningful and of high quality. Six guiding principles have been established: (a) academic quality is paramount, (b) faculty governance engagement is required, (c) aligned with campus mission and strategic goals, (d) aligned with industry-sector standards, (e) portable and stackable, and (f) online or in class, non-credit to credit, credit (State University of New York, 2023a, 2023b). SUNY further plans to launch a searchable database of micro-credentials, streamlined application processes, a data tracking and reporting system, and identify gaps in areas of focus and academic disciplines to ensure there are pathways from the undergraduate to graduate levels in high-demand fields (Proctor, 2021).

In Canada, there has been an explosion of micro-credentialing initiatives over recent years. Ontario's government-backed digital learning organization, E-Campus Ontario (2020), has been established alongside strategic micro-credential development at the University of New Brunswick, Dalhousie University, and the University of British Columbia (Macdonald, 2022).

In Europe, small learning experiences, such as short courses leading to micro-certificates, enable targeted acquisition of skills and competencies adapted to a rapidly changing society and labor market, without replacing traditional qualifications. Their aim is to be complementary. The European approach to micro-credits aims to provide a clear definition and European standards so that the learning outcomes of these small experiences can be easily recognized and understood by employers, learners and education and training institutions, and to develop guiding principles to be considered when designing or issuing high-quality micro-credits. Common approaches to the development and use of micro-credentials at European Union level can support and enhance national efforts to ensure their quality, transparency, cross-border comparability, recognition, and transferability. They can also help build confidence in micro-credentials for the benefit of learners, employers, and education and training institutions (European Commission, 2023a).

Continuing Education Units are particularly well positioned to facilitate the adoption of micro-credentials. "Continuing Education teams rely upon their understanding of student demand, employer demand and regional economic development to ensure their viability. Continuing Education teams have the ability to share our market identification, program design and operational skills that support short-cycle learning as a partner to academic faculties that are ready to venture into the micro-credential space" (LeBlanc, 2021).

There is growing recognition that infrastructure capacity must be bolstered to accelerate micro-credentialing. Key to infrastructure capacity are government policy and funding incentives. The latter will be particularly needed to assist (1) micro-credential providers to develop micro-credentials; (2) learners to participate in micro-credentials through loans/grants; (3) employers to offer work-integrated learning experiences and provide learners the opportunity for skilling and upskilling; and (4) development of interoperable data systems to track the acquiring of micro-credentials needed to determine the return on investments of these credentials in the workforce. Better data on the value and utility of micro-credentials will encourage postsecondary education institutions to create more micro-credentials, whilst governments, employers and publicly funded postsecondary institutions must work together to accelerate this work in response to policy and resource requirements.

The OECD (2021a) has issued several recent reports on micro-credentialing and is continuing to work in this area, especially in partnership with the European Commission (EC). The EC has undertaken an extensive consultation to help underpin a European approach to micro-credentials. Based on extensive consultation and evidence gathering, the Commission adopted a proposal for a Council Recommendation on a European approach to micro-credits for lifelong learning and employability in December 2021 (European Commission, 2023a). The proposal aims to:

- Enable individuals to acquire the knowledge, skills, and competencies to succeed in a changing labor market and society, and to benefit fully from a socially just recovery and an equitable transition to a green and digital economy.
- Support the readiness of micro-credit providers to improve the flexibility and transparency of their learning offerings to enable individuals to design personalized learning and career pathways.
- Promote inclusion and equity as a contribution to achieving resilience, social justice, and prosperity for all, in the context of demographic change and across business cycles.

To achieve these goals, the proposal outlines a European approach that recommends member states to apply a common EU definition, standards, and basic principles for the design and issuance of a micro-credit, including its portability;

develop an ecosystem for micro-credentials; and exploit the potential of micro-credentials to support lifelong learning and employability. As a result, micro-credentials can be developed, used, and benchmarked in a coherent manner by member states, stakeholders, and various providers (from education and training institutions to private companies) across different sectors, domains, and borders. The European approach aims to support ongoing work on micro-credits by Member States, stakeholders, and diverse groups of providers across the EU. The proposal was subsequently adopted together with a proposal for a Council Recommendation on Individual Learning Accounts, which can support the development, use, and uptake of micro-credentials.

The OECD (2021a, 2021b) has identified three key drivers of micro-credentials in many countries: (1) incredibly rapid innovation on the part of the higher education institutions; (2) surge in learning platforms and training programs providing micro-credentials; and (3) a struggle on the part of governments to understand what's happening and to make use of micro-credentials as a way of improving their education and training offerings. Also, across the span of OECD member countries, there are three emergent and distinct purposes to micro-credentials: employment and wage advancement; educational advancement; and enjoyment and personal growth.

The micro-credential and alternative credential offerors include those outside higher education — business firms, professional bodies, training firms, and vocational education institutions. These developments have and will continue to occur in competition with higher education institutions or in collaboration with higher education institutions. In the latter case, micro-credentials are often embedded in the higher education curriculum (Kato et al., 2020). One recent development, for example, is linking micro-credentials from organizations such as LinkedIn Learning, to recognition of academic credit (University of Huddersfield, 2023).

The ICoBC has developed a taxonomy and quality grid for micro-credentials (Ossiannilsson & Kaur, 2021). This taxonomy, quality criteria, and quality grid are based on current research and discourse in this field, and are intended to be universal and interoperable for use and implementation. The target groups for these guidelines include learners, employees, employers, program coordinators, and organizations of all sizes.

Based on the characteristics of the MicroHE[5] (2020) and the EC-suggested quality indicators (relevance, valid assessments, flexible learning pathways, recog-

---

[5] Support Future Learning Excellence through Micro-Credentialing in Higher Education, see https://microhe.microcredentials.eu/ for more information.

nition, portability, learner-centered, authentic, stackability, validation, and information and guidelines), the ICoBC have also proposed the following as overarching quality criteria: (i) accessible; (ii) authentic; (iii) digital; (iv) and universal. These four quality criteria are the suggested minimum requirements to guarantee the success of micro-certificates, their validity and reliability, their ability to sustain learners, and their overall value to all stakeholders. These four criteria can be subdivided into sub-criteria that provide more clarity by defining the measurement parameters when assessing the quality of micro-certificates (Ossiannilsson & Kaur, 2021).

ICoBC research conducted for the proposed ICoBC taxonomy, quality criteria, and quality grid show that all major organizations and stakeholders in education worldwide (for example, UNESCO, OECD, COL, MQA, EC, ICDE, and others) are currently strongly emphasizing the paradigm shift for education and labor markets, as well as the movement toward lifelong learning and everything related to it—not least the movement toward badges and micro-credentials. Thus, the development of digital credentials is urgently needed. This will require the use of best practices for badges and credentials on a regional and global scale, such as the design of badges and credentials (curriculum, testing, verification); use (internal marketing, practices); and taxonomies and alignment with official certification systems.

For micro-credentials to take their place among the array of valuable and trusted credentials (e.g., degrees, certificates, certifications, and licenses), governments, credential providers (colleges, universities, and third-party providers), employers, and other key stakeholders in the learn-and-work ecosystem will face many challenges ahead. Four will be key:

1. *Governments* will have the key role in setting policy to guide and incentivize through resources the development of micro-credentials. There will particularly be a two-fold challenge to governments: how can micro-credentials meet both labor market demand and the learning needs of students? Policy must incentivize pathways to study that are more open and more flexible than what students have today, allowing individuals to pause in their work journeys to return to resume education and training and update their education credentials. Policy will also need to support employer labor market needs by, for example, incentivizing employment-focused skill building and recognition. Governments will have to devise new funding models for micro-credentials, including funding for these credentials along with other types of credentials such as degrees. This will include funding formulas by federal and state governments, and revisions to traditional student aid systems.

2. *Data systems* must be in place to assess micro-credentials with an explicit vocational orientation, monitoring of occupational and earnings outcomes. The challenge is including micro-credentials in current education records systems since they are not generally included now. Until data systems are updated, education data cannot be linked to employment information systems that allow the type of assessment and monitoring of outcomes that will be needed.
3. *Quality assurance systems.* Countries will need appropriate systems to assure the quality of the micro-credential providers and the programs they offer. The current processes for higher education quality assurance are generally not fit for this now. Micro-credentialing will require revised or entirely new procedures for accreditors, standards bodies, and others concerned about the value and quality of micro-credentials.
4. *Trust and value.* The related issues of building trust and understanding among educators about micro-credentials, especially to achieve recognition and portability, will be a major challenge for all the stakeholders in the learn-and-work ecosystem.

23.5 Beyond Higher Education: Connect Learning to Opportunities Through twenty-first Century Skills

As the global skills economy develops, we are increasingly suffering the effects of what Ward et al. (2021) refer to as the ***Capability-Competency Chasm***. Capability (learning a skill along with any knowledge required to perform the skill) is different from competency (application of a skill with proficiency within a particular context). To be competent we need to know not just what (knowledge) and how (skills), but also why (dispositions) (CC, 2020, 2020), this is done through application.

Within schools and higher education, the traditional pedagogical model is one based on knowledge imparting and the development of capabilities within learners, the educational analogy of teaching a driver to pass their driving test. However, in the global skills economy they need to be able to drive in different road conditions, different weather conditions and with different amounts of traffic, i.e., they need to be a competent driver rather than simply a capable one. The skills economy therefore requires learners to experience different contexts, to apply their learning within these and through this to develop competence. Traditionally, this has been achieved to some extent at least within schools and higher education through work experience, work-based learning, internships/placements and live projects, but these tend to represent non-compulsory or insubstantial elements of the overall learning experience and therefore when looking from an employment perspective it is little wonder that employers continue to complain that graduates lack the skills that are needed for employment.

The Capability-Competency Chasm, however, is as much a communication chasm as it is an educational one. The fundamental problem is really with how learning, and earning, are expressed rather than the learning and earning activities themselves. A chasm persists because of the language that is used to define learning and earning. On the capability side of the chasm, learning is defined and measured as learning outcomes, i.e., has this learning been gained? Or, perhaps more usefully in this discussion, has this capability been achieved? On the competency side of the chasm, earning is defined and measured as competencies expressed within competency frameworks and job roles, i.e., can this learner-earner demonstrate that they can apply their learning to a particular earning context?

A further difficulty when considering this chasm is the ability to communicate across subjects, organizations, and countries. On the capability side of the chasm, there exist national and international educational standards where comparability and value can be easily understood and exchanged. For example, in Europe, the European Qualifications Framework (CEDEFOP, 2023) provides an eight-level structure defining qualifications in terms of learning outcomes and enabling individual national qualifications frameworks to interconnect. It has also been piloted in Australia, New Zealand, and Hong Kong and UNESCO is seeking to agree on comparability for qualifications around the world through its Global Convention on the Recognition of Qualifications concerning Higher Education. On the competency side of the chasm, however, things quickly get more complex and fragmented. Considering the equivalent system within Europe, for example, the European Skills, Competences and Occupations (ESCO) classification (ESCO, 2023) provides a reference language for education and employment, and attempts to align non-formal and informal learning through open badges and digital credentialing, with qualifications, skills, micro-credentialing frameworks and employment. However, this is a very large undertaking. ESCO describes 13,485 skills and 2942 occupations. ESCO needs to connect with the Europass framework (Europass, 2023) in order to provide transparency and understanding of formal, non-formal, and informal qualifications and skills and how they are recorded and represented. The EU's Digital Education Action Plan (2023b) then intends to incorporate micro-credentials within all educational levels by aligning micro-credentials with the existing qualification framework structures. This alignment and interconnectivity is to be applauded, however there are still significant gaps when making these connections, not least of which is the lack of clearly defined international agreement on standardized competency frameworks. Whilst there are international standards on competency frameworks, such as those developed through the IEEE (2023), they only standardize what competency frameworks should do and do not define what they are; i.e., a common competency framework standard. The challenge then is two-fold, how to better define competency standards, and how to better connect capability and competency.

The solution to these challenges is through the development of an intermediary that bridges the Capability-Competency Chasm. This solution (Ward et al., 2021) involves the use of a set of twenty-first Century Skills descriptors that enable skills profiles to be developed for both learners and earners. By translating learning outcomes into skills gained, and by breaking down job roles and competency frameworks into the skills required, educationalists, employers and learner-earners themselves can better understand what they have and what they need to have to proceed through their lifelong learner-earner journey. The choice of twenty-first Century Skills and the agreement on a universal taxonomy are perhaps still some time away, but there are clear benefits that can already be seen from adopting a twenty-first Century Skills approach to link Future Skills with education and employment.

For example, in the United States, Education Design Lab (hereby, Lab), a non-profit organization located in Washington D.C., uses human-centered design thinking to respond to complex issues that inhibit equity and quality of the learn to work talent pipeline. Two early design challenges that the Lab tackled were: 1) How might we capture and credential learning outside the classroom in ways that will be meaningful to employers? and 2) How might we demonstrate in different job markets that twenty-first century skill credentials have hiring value? As a result of this foundational work over the last eight years, the Lab co-designed, prototyped, tested, and scaled, a twenty-first Century Skills Framework with employers, higher education partners, and learners, which includes nine in-demand competencies: critical thinking, collaboration, creative problem solving, oral communication, resilience, intercultural fluency, empathy, initiative, and self-directed learning (Boyer & Payne, 2022). These high level, durable, cross-domain competencies are built upon four measurable sub-competencies creating a taxonomy over overlapping, complementary skills. Figure 23.3 below provides a visual representation of the framework, with the concentric hubs depicting the intersections between the 27 competencies.

The Lab's open framework has been adopted in a variety of secondary schools, higher education and career and technical institutions, alternative edu-

23 Developing a More Granular and Equitable Approach … 477

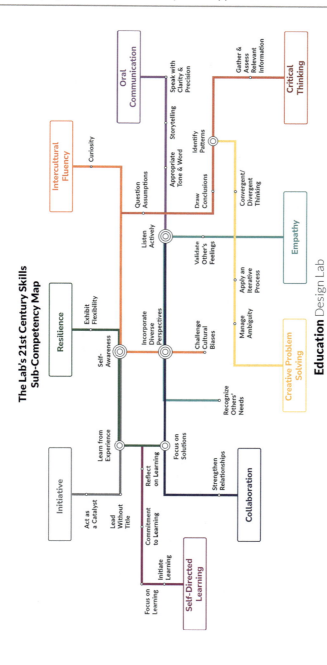

Fig. 23.3 Education Design Lab twenty-first Century Skills Framework Representing Nine Digital Micro-credentials and 27 Sub-Competencies (Education Design Lab, 2023)

cation providers and employers in the United States, South Africa, Australia, Pakistan, and Canada. Despite the global interest in the structure and specifications of the twenty-first Century Skills, the implementation strategy, and technical processes of deployment present challenges to scalability and the tracking of learner-earner progress. To support this work, the Lab constructed "Rich Skill Descriptor" collection(s) that provide data schema for capturing the metadata, specific information about the individual sub-competencies, and can empower organizations and technology vendors when aligning curriculum, assessments, and earner achievements (Open Skills Network, 2023).

The twenty-first Century Skills have been emerging in importance over a number of decades. However, more recently the demand for these skills has escalated due to technological advancements, virtual work, and the lack of social development due to COVID isolation. The implementation of programs and structures to explicitly address the twenty-first Century Skills in practice through the award of digital micro-credentials involves a targeted learning pedagogy and a plan for delivery. The integration of digital micro-credentials provides the opportunity for higher education institutions to alter traditional learning practices to optimize: learner personalization; engaging learning methodologies; communication of competencies to be mastered; and critical reflection throughout the learning experience. Optimizing learner personalization, for example, supports twenty-first Century Skills development as competencies are gained by the learner that enable them to perform best in highly emergent contexts, and thus allow them to act successfully, with their Future Skills competencies communicated as they are mastered. Assessment of the twenty-first Century Skills is therefore both a critical component of the micro-credential delivery and award process, and a way of demonstrating Future Skills acquisition.

The Lab has two types of assessment available to validate mastery of the sub-competencies within the framework. First, activities called *proving grounds*, which incorporate performance-based, employer-informed scenarios that result in a variety of evidential artefacts that are assessed by facilitators against a binary rubric. The criteria in this rubric also underscores the second form of assessments that have been developed utilizing two next generation technologies, text-based simulations and extended reality immersive experiences, to create innovative auto-graded assessments. Quality, rigor, and consistency is maintained across the assessments through the common criteria, as any award of the Lab's twenty-first Century Skills digital micro-credentials is validated against the same standard.

Higher education institutions have implemented the Lab's twenty-first Century Skills framework in a variety of models. The base information and content of the twenty-first Century Skills credentials can be accessed through openly available resources in a resource Toolkit, such as https://eddesignlab.org/. Institutions are able to craft their own learning experiences from the provided information. In addition, organizations, for non-commercial use, can "map" their curriculum to the criteria in the rubric, capitalizing on existing content and courses being delivered in the curriculum across disciplines and programs. Finally, the most seamless and supported mode is the availability of online content modules that can be applied within a variety of academic delivery models. Organizations have deployed the twenty-first Century Skills in a plethora of ways from credit, non-credit, and extracurricular to workforce focused and humanities infused.

Implementation models of twenty-first Century Skills digital micro-credentials in higher education institutions include **credit-based approaches** such as modules integrated into existing traditional academic coursework, alignment of the twenty-first Century Skills framework and assessment criteria to course and program learning outcomes, optional opportunities for learners in required or elective coursework (e.g., University of Dayton, Fisher, 2021), stand-alone courses representing twenty-first Century Skills (with each digital micro-credential representing about 15 h of coursework), clustering of credentials into certificates in elective courses and upper secondary education ($11^{th}+12^{th}$ grade in the United States) and integrated into existing curriculum (e.g., Propel Polk Initiative). **Non-credit-based approaches** include continuing education for non-admitted learner enrolment, designed and deployed directly for business partners (e.g., San Antonio Goodwill, UpSkill San Antonio), open enrolment in response to local workforce needs and in partnership with community agencies (workforce boards, youth groups, advocacy groups) to elevate a local citizenry. **Extracurricular approaches** include infused in workplace learning experiences (i.e., internships, co-ops, apprenticeships, and clinicals, etc.), as part of clubs and student groups (student government and affinity groups such as sports and academic achievement), open enrolment as an optional value added for learners to connect the higher education experience to specific job requirements, as part of an extracurricular STEM program, coupling content, support services, and twenty-first century digital micro-credentials in an extended industry support program such as Unity in Africa (https://www.uina.co.za/) and aligned to student affairs required compliance training to communicate job value of skills such as financial management and diversity, equity, and inclusion. **Liberal Arts and Sciences examples** include integrated and aligned across general education requirements and assessments utilized as accreditation documentation of mastery of required standards. **Workforce examples** include credentials coupled with industry certifications to form micro-pathways in either credit or non-credit learning options and direct response to economic development and talent pipeline needs identified by local or prospective employers.

23.6 Challenges and Further Research

There is a clear set of next steps required in research, policy, and processes in order to better connect higher education with schools, with employment, and with Future Skills. Firstly, it is critically important that global approaches to granularizing learning through badges, micro-credentials and alternative credentials are better understood, collated and communicated to a broader audience that for the most part are aware of, but not fully understanding of, how these approaches work and can provide significant benefit to society. ICoBC, for example, is developing an approach to recognizing organizations who work in this sector, enabling best practice to be shared and fostering growth in the skills ecosystem. Secondly, mechanisms for representing badges, micro-credentials, and alternative credentials need to work better with one another. Recognition will help with this, but a further key step is to identify skills framework structures, such as the twenty-first Century Skills approach highlighted above, that can work with badges, micro-credentials, and alternative credentials to support the transfer of value within the skills economy, i.e., by being able to break down qualifications and work experience into component skills which can be understood and recognized individually. This has enormous benefits for learners, earners, and employers as it will mean that less retraining is required and that the workforce can be more adaptable and responsive to skills economy needs. Thirdly, this greater interconnectedness can foster a more granularized and bespoke approach to education and employment. This has two key benefits that will benefit from further research. The first of these is the opportunity to reduce and remove many existing impediments to optimal learner-earner progress based on structural and societal barriers. This area of research is commonly referred to in the United States skills-based hiring and represents a broader focus on more equitable and fairer education and employment practices. The second of these is a more expansive version of the first. As well as the potential to reduce barriers to learner-earner journeys based on existing modes of education and employment, there is also the potential to optimize learner-earner journeys, i.e., to personalize learning and earning such that each learner-earner can take on a journey that optimizes their productivity within the skills economy but also optimizes their happiness, fulfilment and purpose within life. This has clear benefits not only within the skills economy but also in the better functioning of society as a whole.

The challenges to enacting this are both structural and socio-cultural. Structurally existing standards and frameworks need to be leveraged or new structures developed that enable friction-free interoperability amongst education and employment and between them. This chapter discusses some mechanisms to do this. Socio-culturally, trust in the currency of badging and micro-credentialing needs to increase. The currency value can be pegged to known value such as micro-credentials linked to existing formal qualifications, but challenges remain in particular in employment and in how we recognize non-formal and informal learning in commonly understood ways. Without this understanding within key stakeholder groups, such as employers, parents, teachers and learners, the use of and exchange through badges and micro-credentials will be limited. However as greater use is made of these mechanisms, familiarity, uses, and trust will all increase and therefore the main challenge is in widespread use of standards, frameworks, and ecosystem processes that facilitate interoperability and interconnectedness of badging, micro-credentialing, and skills-based hiring to enable a friction-free learner-earner journey.

23.7 Learnings and Recommendations

This chapter has sought to provide an overview of the current challenges facing higher education in connecting better with schools, employment, and indeed the learner-earner themselves. In terms of practical recommendations, the key focus within higher education should be on how granularizing learning can benefit all of these stakeholders. Badges, micro-credentials, and alternative credentials present an opportunity to review why and how learning is delivered within higher education (Ward et al., 2022). Higher education institutions should look on this as a critically important moment for them. The world, in the form of the global skills economy, is changing at an ever-faster pace. Education can and should respond to this by reflecting on what it delivers and how this best meets the needs of those it seeks to serve. Learning outcomes have long been the currency of education, and can easily be traded amongst many parts of the global education system, but they do not exchange well with the world of work and as we seek a more fluid lifelong learner-earner journey there are some key steps that higher education needs to take to minimize barriers and maximize opportunities for learner-earners. We propose a four-step plan for higher education to meeting Future Skills requirements:

1) Map existing provision to skills through the approach outlined by Ward et al., (2021, 2022).
2) Introduce opportunities to badge and micro-credential content using the approaches outlined by Ossiannilsson and Kaur (2021).

3) Review the skills developed within higher education courses against those sought by the global skills economy through working with existing labor market information data and organizations.
4) Develop a more personalized learner-earner journey through higher education by working better with schools to ensure better onboarding and recognition of existing capabilities, and with employers to ensure better transitioning and development of competencies for the global skills economy.

By taking these steps we can address many of our current global skills economy challenges and meet Future Skills demands, and in so doing, we can develop more effective, and indeed more fulfilled, lifelong learner-earners.

Future Skills in Practice: Our Recommendations
- Granularizing learning, through the increased use of badging and micro-credentialing, benefits all
- Badges, micro-credentials, and alternative credentials support restructuring of higher education
- Badges, micro-credentials, and alternative credentials support greater labor marker alignment
- Personalizing the learner-earner journey through twenty-first Century Skills can address Future Skills gaps
- Granular learning-earning routes optimize our lifelong adaptability in highly emergent contexts

References

Adekeye, O. (2019). These are the 5 skills African employers are looking for. https://www.weforum.org/agenda/2019/09/skills-african-employers-are-looking-for/. Accessed 8 Feb 2023.

America Succeeds. (2021). The high demand for durable skills. https://americasucceeds.org/portfolio/the-high-demand-for-durable-skills-october-2021. Accessed 8 Feb 2023.

ATS2020 Project. (2023). Assessment of transversal skills resource portal. https://resources.ats2020.eu/resource-details/LITR/ATC21s. Accessed 8 Feb 2023.

Boyer, N. R., & Payne, S. S. (2022). Leveraging self-directed learning in the skills-based economy. In J. Keengwe, P. Hughes, & J. Yarbrough (Eds.), *Self-Directed learning and the academic evolution from pedagogy to andragogy* (pp. 78–96). IGI Global. https://doi.org/10.4018/978-1-7998-7661-8.ch005.

CC2020. (2020). *Computing curricula 2020: Paradigms for future computing curricula* (Computing Curricula Report).

CEDEFOP. (2023). European qualifications framework (EQF). https://www.cedefop.europa.eu/en/projects/european-qualifications-framework-eqf. Accessed 8 Feb 2023.

Crawford, G. (30 November 2021). Microcredentials empower change and growth. *The Evolllution.* https://evolllution.com/programming/credentials/microcredentials-empower-change-and-growth-2/.

E-Campus Ontario. (2020). Micro-credential principles and framework. https://micro.ecampusontario.ca/wp-content/uploads/2020/12/Micro-credentials-en_v2.pdf.

Education Design Lab (2023). The Lab's 21st Century Skills Micro-credentials: Pedagogy. Available at: https://eddesignlab.org/microcredentialing/microcredentials/pedagogy/.

Ehlers, U.-D. (2020). *Future skills: The future of learning and higher education.* BoD–Books on Demand.

ESCO. (2023). ESCO. https://esco.ec.europa.eu/en. Accessed 8 Feb 2023.

Europass. (2023). What are digital credentials. https://europa.eu/europass/en/what-are-digital-credentials. Accessed 8 Feb 2023.

European Commission. (2020). A European approach to micro-credentials: Output of the micro-credentials higher education consultation group. https://education.ec.europa.eu/sites/default/files/document-library-docs/european-approach-micro-credentials-higher-education-consultation-group-output-final-report.pdf.

European Commission. (2021). A European approach to micro-credentials. https://education.ec.europa.eu/sites/default/files/2022-01/micro-credentials%20brochure%20updated.pdf. Accessed 4 Apr 2023.

European Commission. (2023a). A European approach to micro-credentials. https://education.ec.europa.eu/education-levels/higher-education/micro-credentials. Accessed 8 Feb 2023.

European Commission. (2023b). Digital education action plan (2021–2027). https://education.ec.europa.eu/focus-topics/digital-education/action-plan. Accessed 8 Feb 2023.

Fisher, J. (21 September 2021). Closing the skills gap: Why UD teamed up with a national nonprofit. *Dayton Business Journal.* https://www.bizjournals.com/dayton/news/2021/09/21/ud-micro-credentials.html.

Fong, J., Janzow, P., & Peck, K. (2016). Demographic shifts in educational demand and the rise of alternative credentials. https://upcea.edu/wp-content/uploads/2017/05/Demographic-Shifts-in-Educational-Demand-and-the-Rise-of-Alternative-Credentials.pdf.

Foundation for Young Australians. (2017). The new work order: Ensuring young Australians have skills and experience for the jobs of the future, not the past. https://www.fya.org.au/app/uploads/2021/09/new-work-order-2015.pdf.

ICoBC. (2021). The role for 21st century skills in badging, micro-credentialing and skills-based hiring. https://icobc.net/wp-content/uploads/2022/07/20211028_ICoBC_21st_Century_Skills_Environmental_Scan.pdf.

IEEE. (2023). P1484.20.2 – Defining competencies working group. https://sagroups.ieee.org/1484-20-2/. Accessed 8 Feb 2023.

Kato, S., Galán-Muros, V., & Weko, T. (2020). *The emergence of alternative credentials* (OECD Education Working Papers 216). Paris.

Leaser, D. (2020). New volume: How IBM used badges to connect on-the-job learning to academic credit. https://www.ibm.com/blogs/ibm-training/new-volume-how-ibm-used-badges-to-connect-on-the-job-learning-to-academic-credit/. Accessed 8 Feb 2023.

LeBlanc, S. (23 December 2021). How continuing education can facilitate the adoption of microcredentials. *The Evolllution.* https://evolllution.com/programming/credentials/how-continuing-education-can-facilitate-the-adoption-of-microcredentials-2/.

Macdonald, M. (2022). Are microcredentials the future of higher ed? https://www.universityaffairs.ca/features/feature-article/are-microcredentials-the-future-of-higher-ed/. Accessed 8 Feb 2023.

NEA. (2020). Microcredentials. http://web.archive.org/web/20200531060136/http://www.nea.org//home/microcredentials.html. Accessed 25 June 2023.

NextEducation. (2023). Future skills. https://nextskills.org/future-skills-overview/future-skills/#:~:text=Future%20Skills%20are%20competences%20that,acquired%20in%20a%20learning%20process. Accessed 8 Feb 2023.

OECD (2021a). *Micro-credential innovations in higher education: Who, what and why?* (OECD Education Policy Perspectives 39).

OECD. (2021b). *OECD skills Outlook 2021: Learning for life.* OECD Publishing.

Open Skills Network. (2023). Rich skill descriptors. https://www.openskillsnetwork.org/rsd. Accessed 8 Feb 2023.

Ossiannilsson, E., & Kaur, A. (2021). *ICoBC taxonomy, quality criteria, and quality grid.* Lund.

P21 – Partnership for 21st Century Learning. (2019). Framework for 21st century learning. BoD–Books on Demand.

Pichette, J., Brumwell, S., Rizk, J., & Han, S. (2021). Making sense of microcredentials. Toronto. https://heqco.ca/pub/making-sense-of-microcredentials/.

Proctor, C. P. (28 December 2021). Defining a role for high-quality microcredentials in higher education. *The Evolllution.* https://evolllution.com/programming/credentials/defining-a-role-for-high-quality-microcredentials-in-higher-education-2/.

QAA. (2021). Quality compass: Which way of micro-credentials? https://www.qaa.ac.uk/docs/qaa/news/quality-compass-which-way-for-micro-credentials.pdf?sfvrsn=25c6d481_8.

Shackleton, J. R. (2014). The history of qualifications and the role of competition. In G. Heller Sahlgren (Ed.), *Tests worth teaching to*: *Incentivising quality in qualifications and accountability* (pp. 6–27). The Centre for Market Reform of Education.

State University of New York. (2023a). Microcredentials – SUNY. https://www.suny.edu/microcredentials/. Accessed 8 Feb 2023.

State University of New York. (2023b). SUNY launches new micro-credential policy. https://system.suny.edu/academic-affairs/microcredentials/suny-launches-new-micro-credential-policy/. Accessed 8 Feb 2023.

The Institute for Working Futures. (2020). Human capability standards: Reference model. https://www.workingfutures.com.au/wp-content/uploads/2020/06/HumanCapabilityStandards_7Level_FULLSUMMARY_290420.pdf.

UNESCO. (2022). Towards a common definition of micro-credentials. Paris. https://unesdoc.unesco.org/ark:/48223/pf0000381668.

University of Huddersfield. (2023). LinkedIn learning pathways. https://www.hud.ac.uk/postgraduate/linkedin-learning-pathways/. Accessed 8 Feb 2023.

Ward, R. (2020). *Personalised learning for the learning person.* Emerald Publishing Limited.

Ward, R., Phillips, O., Bowers, D., Crick, T., Davenport, J. H., Hanna, P., et al. (2021). Towards a 21st century personalised learning skills taxonomy. In IEEE (Ed.), *2021*

IEEE Global Engineering Education Conference (EDUCON) (pp. 344–354). IEEE. https://doi.org/10.1109/EDUCON46332.2021.9453883.

Ward, R., Shamim, T., Hull, B., Hayes, A., Davenport, J., Lengyel, D., et al. (2022). QAA collaborative enhancement project report on badging and micro-credentialing within UK higher education through the use of skills profiles. https://www.qaa.ac.uk/docs/qaa/members/report-on-badging-and-micro-credentialing-within-uk-he-through-the-use-of-skills-profiles.pdf?sfvrsn=f710a481_18.

Wikipedia. (2022). Microdegree. https://en.wikipedia.org/w/index.php?title=Microdegree&oldid=1107268820. Accessed 8 Feb 2023.

Wikipedia (04/2023). Microdegree. Available at: https://en.wikipedia.org/wiki/Microdegree.

Young, M., & Hordern, J. (2022). Does the vocational curriculum have a future? *Journal of Vocational Education & Training, 74*(1), 68–88. https://doi.org/10.1080/13636820.2020.1833078.

Zhong, M., & Shetty, T. (2021). Diversity, equity and inclusion in responsive career pathways. https://fsc-ccf.ca/wp-content/uploads/2021/11/FSC-RCP-DEI-EN.pdf.

Grame Barty is an entrepreneur, education technology, and global innovation commercialization specialist currently working with Credential Exchange provider CredShare. He is a member of the ICoBC Future Skills Working Group and co-leads the ICoBC Global Workforce Development Working Group.

Dr. Naomi Boyer is an educational strategist and innovative leader at Education Design Lab with over 20 years of education experience. Currently serving as the Executive Director, Digital Transformation, she focuses on the future of work catalysts of 21st Century Skills, digital micro-credentials, the learner-earner data ecosystem, and competency/skill frameworks. Dr. Boyer has expertise on competency-based education, leads many non-profit Boards, and maintains scholarship on self-directed learning.

Dr. Alexandros Chrysikos received a BSc (Hons) in Computing Science at the Computing department of the University of Huddersfield in June 2010. In October 2011, in the same institution, he completed a MSc degree in Information Systems Management and in June 2016, he completed his PhD Thesis. Currently, he works at the London Metropolitan University as a Senior Lecturer and Researcher in Computing Science & Cyber Security. ORCID ID: 0000-0003-0550-3128

Margo Griffith is a recognised leader in educational technologies as they relate to open and digital recognition. She has decades of experience working nationally and internationally for corporate organisations involved in education sectors and currently serves as the head of growth for Edalex. Her work focuses on technology enablement of the emerging skills ecosystem by providing equitable opportunity through skills visibility. She is a consultant on digital recognition technologies and represents Edalex as a member of the Open Skills Network and Skills Validation Network. In Australia Margo chairs several working parties on microcredentials and skills based learning.

Dr. Kevin House is International Curriculum Director for Dulwich College International and most recently led quality assurance processes for the International Baccalaureate Organization as the Head of IB World Schools. Previously, he was Head of High School at the German European School of Singapore, Director of Curriculum at Suzhou Singapore International School, and Head of English at the International School of Valencia. Kevin recently completed his doctoral thesis in International Education at the University of Bath and has been working to align program standards across awarding bodies such as CIS, WASC and IB. Kevin is also a qualified trainer for global safeguarding practices and protocols.

Dr. Tara Laughlin is an Education Designer focused on Micro-Credentialing, who facilitates the design of next-generation skills assessments and contributes to Education Design Lab's 21st Century Skills Micro-credentials in the vsbl platform. Tara previously spent four years as Director of Curriculum and Training for edtech startup PAIRIN, leading the development of a comprehensive competency-based curriculum focused on soft/social-emotional skills. Tara has also spent over a decade as an educator, teacher leader, and district administrator for school districts in Colorado and South Carolina. Tara holds an EdD in Curriculum and Innovation, for which she developed a framework for the systematic integration of soft skills into the K12 classroom.

Professor Ebba Ossiannilsson, Sweden, is an independent researcher, expert, consultant, quality reviewer, and opinion leader in the areas of open, flexible, online and distance education related to SDG4 and the future of education, with a focus on quality, innovation, leadership, and personalized learning. She is a member of the ICDE Board of Directors and chairs the ICDE OER Advocacy Committee. Ossiannilsson is a visiting professor at several international universities and was recently appointed professor and research fellow at Victoria University of Wellington, New Zealand. She is a member of the Digital Skills and Jobs Coalition Sweden and vice president of the Swedish Association for Distance Education. ORCID ID: 0000-0002-8488-5787

Rupert Ward is a former Special Adviser and Project Lead for iDEA, one of the world's most successful digital badging platforms. He is Director of Strategic Partnerships for the International Council on Badges and Credentials (ICoBC), a National Teaching Fellow and Principal Fellow of the Higher Education Academy. His technology acceptance model, GETAMEL, is one of the most highly cited technology acceptance models globally since publication. He has authored two books on Personalized Learning and is Professor of Learning Innovation and Associate Dean (International) within the School of Computing and Engineering at the University of Huddersfield. ORCID ID: 0000-0003-1514-5870

Dr. Holly Zanville is a Research Professor and Co-Director of the Program on Skills, Credentials & Workforce Policy at George Washington University, Washington, DC. Previously, she served as a strategy director at Lumina Foundation, overseeing portfolios on adult learners, student success, future of learning and workforce, and research. She has held leadership positions at state higher education systems/boards in Oregon and Washington, and the Western Interstate Commission for Higher Education (WICHE); and held academic positions at community college and non-traditional university programs in multiple states. She serves on the Executive Committee of the International Council on Badges and Credentials (ICoBC).

Open Access This chapter is licensed under the terms of the Creative Commons Attribution 4.0 International License (http://creativecommons.org/licenses/by/4.0/), which permits use, sharing, adaptation, distribution and reproduction in any medium or format, as long as you give appropriate credit to the original author(s) and the source, provide a link to the Creative Commons license and indicate if changes were made.

The images or other third party material in this chapter are included in the chapter's Creative Commons license, unless indicated otherwise in a credit line to the material. If material is not included in the chapter's Creative Commons license and your intended use is not permitted by statutory regulation or exceeds the permitted use, you will need to obtain permission directly from the copyright holder.

Formative Assessment of 21st Century Skills

24

Tobias Seidl

> **Abstract**
>
> Since 2016, the Faculty of Information and Communication at Stuttgart Media University has integrated comprehensive key competence modules in all its BA study programs. The aim is to prepare students for a demanding study program as well as an uncertain and therefore challenging future. Part of the modules is a sophisticated formative assessment approach, which supports the individual learning journey of the students. This chapter describes the design of the modules, as well as the assessment setting, in detail. The good practice example encourages reflection on one's own approaches and perspective to teaching and assessing 21st Century Skills.

24.1 Towards a New Model of Teaching and Learning

In 2016, the Faculty of Information and Communication at Stuttgart Media University made fundamental changes to the curricula of its bachelor programs. The starting point of the change process was the shared insight that current curricula did not prepare students well enough for a dynamic future. Faculty and external stakeholders identified two central questions:

T. Seidl (✉)
Professor for Academic Key Competences at the Faculty of Information and Communication, Stuttgart Media University, Stuttgart, Germany
e-mail: seidl@hdm-stuttgart.de

© The Author(s) 2024
U.-D. Ehlers and L. Eigbrecht (eds.), *Creating the University of the Future*, Zukunft der Hochschulbildung - Future Higher Education,
https://doi.org/10.1007/978-3-658-42948-5_24

- What do students need in order to be well prepared for a dynamic present and future?
- How should teaching & learning at university level look like in the twenty-first century?

Three fundamental challenges for the higher education sector were addressed in the change process:

- Study skills: What competences do students need to successfully complete their studies and master complex learning arrangements throughout the course of their studies (cf. eg., van den Berk et al., 2016)?
- 21st Century Skills: Which competences are gaining importance in an economy and society shaped by digitization and other future trends? How can these competences be appropriately addressed in higher education (cf. eg., AG Curriculum 4.0, 2018)?
- Didactic issues: Which teaching and learning scenarios are suitable for supporting students' competency development in the mentioned areas (cf. e.g., the EDUCAUSE Horizon Reports)?

The result of the change process was a new standardized study model/curriculum for all bachelor's degree programs within the department (cf. also Burmeister & Seidl, 2020; Mildenberger & Vonhof, 2020). One aspect of the new model was the implementation of three mandatory 21st Century Skills modules (5 ECTS[1] each) for all BA students. The modules focus on the development and improvement of metacognitive strategies (especially reflective skills) and the acquisition of important 21st Century Skills. About 450 students attend the modules each semester which are taught by one quarter of the departmental staff.

The term 21st Century Skills indicates that the skills "are more related to the needs of the emerging models of economic and social development than with those of the past century, which were suited to an industrial mode of production" (Ananiadoui & Claro, 2009, p. 5). In 2014–16, when our change process took place, the term 21st Century Skills was much more prominent in the political and scientific debate than the term Future Skills. Therefore, the term continues to be used in in the presented good practice example.

---

[1] 1 ECTS = 30 learning hours.

24 Formative Assessment of 21st Century 491

An operationalization of the term 21st Century Skills—using the KSAVE[2] framework (Binkley et al., 2012)—is presented in Sect. 24.2. Section 24.3 explains how teaching and learning of (some) of these skills is organized at Stuttgart Media University. In this context, the main focus is on the assessment of 21st Century Skills. The paper concludes with learnings and recommendations.[3]

24.2 How to Identify the Relevant Competences

However, the decision to introduce the new 21st Century Skills modules was only the first step. It then became necessary to determine which learning objectives should be achieved in the modules. According to Schaper (2012), two different approaches in academic program development can be distinguished. On the one hand, needs- or standard-oriented approaches, which are primarily oriented toward professional contexts and students' later labor market. On the other hand, perspective- or progression-oriented approaches, which focus on the competence requirements during study (cf. Schaper, 2012, p. 54). Key competences are highly relevant in both variants of academic program development. Therefore, both approaches were combined and translated into three guiding perspectives and related questions (Seidl, 2017):

1. Today: what key competences do students need to succeed in their studies?
2. Tomorrow: what key competences do students need to succeed in the current society and world of work?
3. In the future: what key competences do students need to succeed in a future society and world of work?

The relevant competences from perspective 1 and 2 were identified through surveys of stakeholders (such as students, university teachers, employers and graduates). In addition, job-related qualification frameworks were evaluated. Such frameworks are developed jointly by universities, industries and professional associations. They describe competence profiles for graduates, which can serve as orientation for academic program development. Suitable frameworks are also available for the third perspective. There are different '21st Century Skills' frame-

---

[2] K = Knowledge, S = Skills, AVE = Attitudes, Values & Ethics.
[3] Central ideas of this paper were first published in Seidl (2017) and Seidl (2021b).

works, which can be used as important orientation points in academic program development.

Since the 1970s, there has been intensive discussion within German universities about the integration of generic competences into the curriculum. Initially under the label of 'key competencies,' for the past five years the term '21st Century Skills' or 'Future Skills' have been increasingly used. Pioneering work in this area has been done by the Curriculum 4.0 working group of the Hochschulforum Digitalisierung[4] (Hochschulforum Digitalisierung, 2022). Nevertheless, no uniform definition nor prioritization has yet been established in the German higher education sector. For this reason, each university must find its own way of defining and prioritizing these skills.

In the example presented in this paper, the KSAVE (Knowledge, Skills, Attitudes, Values and Ethics—see Binkley et al., 2012) model was utilized in the academic program development process. The KSAVE model is a meta-model, which consolidates the contents of various other 21st Century Skills frameworks. In total, twelve frameworks from organizations and institutions, such as the EU, the OECD, the partnership for twenty-first century learning, and the Center for Research and Educational Testing Japan, were integrated into the model (for a complete list, see Binkley et al., 2012, p. 35). The resulting meta-model consists of ten skills that are organized into four groupings:

Ways of Thinking

1. Creativity and innovation.
2. Critical thinking, problem solving, decision making.
3. Learning to learn, metacognition.

Ways of Working

4. Communication.
5. Collaboration (teamwork).

Tools for Working

6. Information literacy.
7. ICT literacy.

---

[4] Hochschulforum Digitalisierung (HFD) is a German-wide think tank which connects people engaged in digitalization in university teaching: https://hochschulforumdigitalisierung. de/en.

Living in the World

8. Citizenship—local and global.
9. Life and career.
10. Personal and social responsibility—including cultural awareness and competence.

Each skill is described in three categories:

- Knowledge (K): "This category includes all references to specific knowledge or understanding requirements for each of the ten skills" (Binkley et al., 2012, p. 37).
- Skills (S): "This category includes the abilities, skills, and processes that curriculum frameworks are designed to develop in students and which are a focus for learning" (Binkley et al., 2012, p. 37).
- Attitudes (A), Values (V) and Ethics (E): "This category refers to the behaviors and aptitudes that students [need to] exhibit in relation to each of the ten skills" (Binkley et al., 2012, p. 37).

The framework has not been updated since 2012. In 2014–16, when our change process took place, it represented the best-backed model available. Nevertheless, the empirical basis of 21st Century Skills/Future Skills frameworks was and is rather weak so far.

The KSAVE model has two advantages for program development and instructional planning:

- On the one hand, the framework can be used as a valid source for deriving necessary future competences for work and everyday life;
- On the other hand, the competences in the model are operationalized and formulated to such an extent that they can be easily transferred into learning objectives.

To illustrate this, Table 24.1 shows the operational definitions of creativity and innovation in the KSAVE model.

In addition, the model is highly compatible with the traditional understanding of key competences at German universities. In terms of integration into study programs and the organization, there is an important continuity between key competencies and 21st Century Skills at German universities (cf. Seidl, 2021b). If we consider Orth's definition (which is often referred to in this context) according to

Table 24.1 Operational definitions of creativity and innovation in the KSAVE model (Binkley et al., 2012, p. 38)

Knowledge	Skills	Attitudes/values/ethics
Think and work creatively and with others –Know a wide range of idea creation techniques (such as brainstorming) –Be aware of invention, creativity, and innovation from the past, within and across national boundaries and cultures –Know the real-world limits to adopting new ideas and how to present them in more acceptable forms –Know how to recognize failures and differentiate between terminal failure and difficulties to overcome *Implement innovations* –Be aware of and understand where and how innovation will impact the field in which the innovation will occur –Be aware of the historical and cultural barriers to innovation and creativity	*Think creatively* –Create new and worthwhile ideas (both incremental and radical concepts) –Be able to elaborate, refine, analyze, and evaluate one's own ideas in order to improve and maximize creative efforts *Work creatively with others* –Develop, implement and communicate new ideas to others effectively –Be sensitive to the historical and cultural barriers to innovation and creativity *Implement innovations* –Develop innovative and creative ideas into forms that have impact and can be adopted	*Think creatively* –Be open to new and worthwhile ideas (both incremental and radical) *Work creatively with others* –Be open and responsive to new and diverse perspectives; incorporate group input and feedback into the work –View failure as an opportunity to learn; understand that creativity and innovation is a long-term, cyclical process of small successes and frequent mistakes *Implement innovations* –Show persistence in presenting and promoting new ideas

which key competences are to be understood as "skills, attitudes and knowledge elements" (Orth, 1999, p. 107), the similarities to the KSAVE model become apparent. Due to its structure, its level of detail and its broad content focus, the KSAVE model is very well suited as a starting point and source for academic program development.

24 Formative Assessment of 21st Century

Table 24.2 Layout of the key competence modules

Module	Tools for working	Ways of working	Working in a media world
Compulsory course	Project Management	Intercultural Skills and Communication	Media Law
Elective courses	Project Management Deepening	Communication	Ethics and Responsibility
	Creativity	Leadership & Teamwork	Data protection and data security: Customer data processing in the company
	Self-Management	Moderation	Data privacy and data security: Data privacy and the Internet
Colloquium	Colloquium tools for working	Colloquium ways of working	Colloquium working in a media world

24.3 Teaching and Learning 21st Century Skills

The three key competence modules are integrated in all four bachelor's degree programs within the information and communication department at Stuttgart media university (Information Design, Information Science, Online Media Management, Information Systems and Digital Media—duration of study, 7 semesters) in the second, third and fourth semesters. In each course, the students work in mixed groups in order to learn how to work with people from different professional backgrounds. Students equip themselves with important 21st Century Skills which help them both to master their study program as well as prepare for a dynamic future (Seidl, 2017). The three modules all follow the same structure:

- Compulsory course of the module (2 ECTS),
- Elective course within the competence area of the module (2 ECTS),

- ePortfolio[5] and key competence colloquium (1 ECTS). For more details on both teaching & learning settings see subsection 24.3.2 and 24.3.3.

Table 24.2 shows the layout of the modules.

The key competence modules focus on the development and improvement of metacognitive strategies.[6] In addition, students should acquire relevant skills, which could be used inside and outside of the university. To reach these learning goals, the teacher always links the content of the courses with current challenges in students' subject-specific courses (taking place at the same time) and their daily lives. This provides students with important chances for reflection and opens up opportunities to test new skills. The setting therefore enables situated and sustainable learning.[7]

With the key competence modules, the department implements the goal of personality development for university studies, as defined by the German Accreditation Council (Akkreditierungsrat, 2013, p. 2013). On the one hand, by creating opportunities for reflection and setting individual development goals by the students. On the other hand, by integrating electives within the compulsory modules in which students are given the opportunity to (at least partially) achieve these goals and consciously shape their own learning path in the key competence domain.

24.3.1 Assessment

The focus on the promotion of metacognitive strategies also made it necessary to think about adequate assessment formats. In summative assessment, the focus is

---

[5] "e-Portfolios are a form of authentic assessment with formative functions that include showcasing and sharing learning artifacts, documenting reflective learning processes, connecting learning across various stages and enabling frequent feedback for improvements" (Yang et al., 2016, p. 1276).

[6] Metacognition: "Metacognition is generally understood as the ability to contemplate one's own thinking, to observe oneself when processing cognitive tasks, and to organize the learning and thinking processes involved in these tasks" (Seel, 2012a, 2012b).

[7] Situated learning: "Learning does not take place in an individuals' mind, it is situated in a context in which participation of individuals to the communities of practice plays a vital role on situated learning process. [...] Situated learning take place when learning is specific to the situation in which it is learned" (Ataizi, 2012).

on assessing the learning outcome. Feedback is given as a differentiating grade. In formative assessment, the focus is on feedback on the learning process and progress. In this type of feedback, grades are not used. It is also referred to as assessment for learning. The quality levels presupposed for summative testing are generally not achieved in examination scenarios that focus on metacognitive strategies (Schaper & Hilkenmeier, 2013). The faculty also experienced that the use of formative assessment formats increased students' motivation to engage in new and uncertain courses of action and supported self-reflection processes. This perception is consistent with findings from research in higher education didactics. For example, Wildt and Wildt point out that a "continuous orientation towards (final) grades damages rather than promotes learning in the sense of self-controlled learning and intrinsic motivation to work on the subject matter" (2011, p. 30). Moreover, in a formative setting, the teacher can assume the role of a learning guide far more authentically, as there is greater role clarity for all stakeholders involved. For these reasons, a purely formative assessment approach was chosen for the key competence modules (for the relationship between summative and formative assessment approaches, see Gaus, 2018).

The exam for each of the key competence modules consists of three individual components, all of which must be successfully completed in order to pass the module:

- Transfer task in the compulsory course
- Transfer task in the elective course
- ePortfolio and colloquium (for specific tasks see Sects. 24.3.2 & 24.3.3)

The module is passed (ungraded) if all three examination parts (compulsory, elective course, portfolio/colloquium) have been worked out to a sufficient degree.

The transfer tasks support students in the development of practical skills and help them to be able to connect theory to practice. The tasks involve the transfer of theoretical aspects into one's own daily practice. For example, in the course 'Leadership & Teamwork', students must analyze a situation from their everyday lives using a theoretical model. Based on their analysis, they develop and test suitable intervention options. In the course, students get formative feedback on their transfer tasks.

The core element of the formative assessment in the key competence modules is the ePortfolio, which supports students to reflect on the learning process during their course of study. The ePortfolio is used across all courses of the three modules. The results of the reflection are presented in a small group at the end of the semester in the colloquium. In the colloquium, students also receive feedback on their learning process and their portfolio. The colloquium and ePortfolio support the learning of the students in different ways:

- It increases students' ability to reflect
- It helps students achieve a better understanding of their current skills and the skills they want to acquire
- It encourages students to be more intentional about their choice of academic courses
- It helps students to train in important media production skills (through the use of WordPress as the portfolio platform).

Study results show that the concept works. In the winter semester 2017/18, parts of the portfolio concept were comprehensively evaluated ($N = 226$, response rate $= 90.4\%$). A standardized questionnaire with predominantly closed questions was used for the evaluation. The constructs measured consisted of reflective and formative indicators. Over the period of portfolio use, students showed a significant increase in their writing competence, media competence and their reflective ability (Schütz-Pitan et al., 2019).

24.3.2 Design and Use of the ePortfolio

The ePortfolio is primarily used to document and reflect on the learning and competence acquisition process. Students work with the ePortfolio in every course of the three modules. Through this continuous use, students are able to recognize and establish content-related connections between individual courses and can document and review their own development.

There are three mandatory task blocks for each compulsory and elective course in the ePortfolio (of course, more intensive use by students is possible and is encouraged accordingly by the lecturers):

1. Reflection at the beginning of the semester. With regard to the competency goals (knowledge, skills, attitudes, values & ethics) of the course (as stated in the module description), students answer the following questions:
   a. What specifically do I already know? What am I already able to do? Which relevant skills did I acquire in the past?
   b. What in particular interests me in this area? What do I really want to learn or be able to do?

2. Learning artifacts to document the learning process. During the semester, students have to collect at least three artifacts to document their learning process and skill development in the portfolio. Artifacts can be a wide variety of things, such as quotes, assignments, exercises, etc. In addition, students reflect on the artifact and explain why they think the artifact is particularly important to their learning process and why they chose it for their portfolio.
3. End-of-semester reflection. With regard to the competency goals of the course, students answer the following questions:
   a. What did I learn in the course? What skills did I acquire? Which routines or perspectives have changed?
   b. In which contexts (study, work, private, etc.) have I used my new skills? In which contexts can I use or train them in the future?
   c. How can I prove that I have these skills?
   d. Where do I want to develop further in this domain? What else am I interested in in this domain?
   e. What influence does the course content have on my further study planning?
   f. What impact does the course content have on my job aspirations/career planning?

Technically the ePortfolio is a WordPress blog. Each student gets their own WordPress blog in the first semester. The students are able to and should design and organize their blogs according to their own preferences. WordPress is a free content management system that enjoys great popularity worldwide and is used in many industries. By working with WordPress on a regular basis, students thus acquire important digital skills 'along the way'. There is deliberately no introduction to WordPress, as there are sufficient freely accessible resources available online.

Reflective work with the ePortfolio is new and unfamiliar to most students. Therefore, it is important to give a comprehensive and profound introduction into the work with the ePortfolio. It has proven to be useful to explain goals, tasks and expectations with regard to ePortfolio and colloquium at the beginning of each course (regardless of the semester level). There is no general introduction course for the ePortfolio. In addition, the instructors regularly connect to the portfolio in the courses (keyword artifacts) and explain the aim of the ePortfolio (as an important instrument to support the learning and reflection processes). In the past, the four stages model of competence (Howell, 1982) has proven useful for clarifying and communicating the meaning and purpose of the portfolio to students. The idea is that the learning process consists of four stages:

1. Unconscious incompetence
2. Conscious incompetence
3. Conscious competence
4. Unconscious competence

To put it simply, learning processes start by getting a sense of what one already knows and is able to do on the one hand, and doesn't know / is not able to do on the other hand, with regard to a new field (cf. task block 1 of the ePortfolio). This step leads from unconscious incompetence to conscious incompetence: the knowledge of one's own learning needs. Within the course of the semester, the step from conscious incompetence to conscious competence can then usually be completed. This means new knowledge and skills are developed but not yet internalized nor transferred into ones' own routines. The learning artifacts and the reflection at the end of the semester in the ePortfolio help to make visible what has been achieved (cf. task block 2 and 3 of the ePortfolio). However, what is achieved at this point is often not yet a genuine competence since the new skills are neither internalized nor part of ones' routines. A genuine competence can only be achieved through further training and experience-based learning. The colloquium has an important linking function here. On the one hand, the students should become aware of in which domains and in which ways they want to continue working on their competences. On the other hand, the instructors provide assistance and feedback on the past and future learning processes at this point.

24.3.3 Implementation of the Colloquium

At the end of the semester, all students present their semester reflections of the key competence modules in a small group (3 students plus one instructor) in a colloquium. Each student has the opportunity to present their own ePortfolio and to discuss it with the other students and instructors. The colloquium is primarily about discussing one's competence-related development path in the group and next steps in the learning process. For this reason, the instructor who accompanies the colloquium does not take on a classic examiner's role (in which the students' statements are evaluated as correct or incorrect), but rather the role of a coach or feedback provider. Feedback is usually given on the following levels:

- Acknowledgment of the student's competence development and their further learning path. The aim is to foster the self-efficacy of the students.

24 Formative Assessment of 21st Century

Table 24.3 Levels of reflection according to Bräuer (2014, p. 17–71)

Level 1	Documenting individual activities
	Describing the overall action
Level 2	Analyzing one's own accomplishments
	Interpreting the quality of one's own accomplishments
Level 3	Comparing different options for action
	Evaluation based on recognized criteria

- Practical hints and advice for the further learning process (e.g. which elective courses are suitable, which further input would be interesting, etc.).
- Feedback on the quality of the reflection presented in the colloquium. This should help students to continually increase their depth of reflection as they continue their work with the ePortfolio in subsequent semesters.

It has proven useful to briefly explain the format, the role of the teacher as coach/feedback provider and the aim of the colloquium at the beginning of the colloquium.

Prior to the colloquium, students complete the following assignments:

1. Complete the reflection assignments and documentation of your competence development for the key competence courses in the ePortfolio.
2. Summarize your most important results/findings on an additional WordPress page. Use this page as a visualization for your presentation during the colloquium. You have complete liberty in designing the layout of the page. The following guiding questions will help you to create the content of the page:
   a. Which newly acquired competences/skills/knowledge from the key competence courses do you consider particularly important? Why?
   b. Which events/moments/elements (artifacts) were particularly important for your own learning? Why?
   c. To what extent were your learning expectations for the key competence courses met this semester?
   d. In which (sub-)areas of the courses do you want to develop your skills further? What else are you interested in? How have the events influenced your further study or career planning?

After the presentation, the instructor can use a variety of questions to provide students with assistance in self-reflection. For example, "If you imagine your learning journey as a mountain hike, what is the next section you need to tackle? If you had to give a fellow student exactly three tips that would be helpful for their personal development based on your experiences this semester, which tips would these be?" (Seidl, 2021a, pp. 11–12).

When providing feedback on the quality of students' self-reflections, the instructor can use the model of self-reflection levels developed by Bräuer (2014) as a guide. Bräuer distinguishes three levels of reflection (Table 24.3).

The instructor should address which level of self-reflection was accomplished by the student. If necessary, the instructor should also provide hints and advice on how to reach a higher level of self-reflection. In addition to feedback from the instructor, students in the colloquium should also support each other through peer feedback. To encourage this, there are guiding questions/observation assignments for the students in the colloquium, which can help them to structure their feedback. For example, "Which important resources and competences do you think the fellow student has acquired in the module? What priorities should the fellow student set for their further development? What key qualities do you see in the fellow student?" (Seidl, 2021a, p. 13). The observation assignments significantly increase the quality of peer feedback. It has proven useful to print out the questions before the colloquium begins and place them on the wall or table for all students to see. The students who are not presenting are asked to pick out one or two of the questions and give the fellow student specific and appreciative feedback on this topic/aspect after the presentation.

24.3.4 Further Developments and Challenges in Assessment

Assessments have the purpose of verifying the results of the students' learning process, but also support the learning process itself. It therefore makes sense to combine summative with formative assessment formats in the curriculum. At many universities, however, formative assessment formats are still sparsely developed and implemented. The assessment concept of the key competence modules has stimulated reflections on the examinations practice within the department. Two aspects in particular became apparent:

- Reflection of instructors on their own roles: a qualitative survey showed that the specific style of teaching and assessment in the key competence modules enables a higher quality of communication between instructors and students and stimulates instructors' reflections on their own roles and teaching habits

(Buhl et al., 2019). These reflection processes will probably also have a positive impact on teaching and assessment activities in other courses.

- Imitation and inspiration: due to the key competence modules, there is a functioning ePortfolio infrastructure within the department that is familiar to the students. In recent semesters, instructors have increasingly begun to integrate ePortfolios into other modules. For example, the documentation and reflection of the mandatory internship semester in the Information Science study program is also realized through the combination of ePortfolio and colloquium. As the example shows, good practice examples can therefore contribute to organizational development.

Assessment always takes place in a field of tension with (at least) three poles:

- Didactics: how can I optimally support the learning process or verify the level of competence of the students?
- Legal issues: which forms and modalities of assessment are compatible with legal frameworks and guidelines (e.g. accreditation and administrative law)? What legal risks am I/is the organization willing to take?
- Economics: which assessment settings can be implemented in view of the available resources (e.g., working hours of staff)? Are there possibilities for shifting resources (e.g., within curricula or modules) and setting new or other priorities?

Dealing responsibly with this tension and finding a good middle ground between these poles is one of the central challenges with regard to assessment at universities. For the department, the assessment model in the key competence modules is such a middle ground. Of course, more regular feedback on the contents of the portfolio would be useful and desirable from a didactical point of view (cf. eg., Hansen & Rachbauer, 2018), but unfortunately this cannot be realized with regard to the available resources of teachers.

24.4 Learnings and Recommendations

The integration of 21st Century Skills into the curriculum is a challenge on several levels. First, it must be discussed whether and to what extent 21st Century Skills should be part of the competence goals of a study program. In addition, the relevant competences must be identified and operationalized. Here, one can utilize models like the KSAVE model. Furthermore, the necessary resources and timeslots in the curriculum must be provided. The next step is to develop a suitable didactic design at both the micro and macro levels. This also includes assessment formats. This list shows that the integration of 21st Century Skills into the curriculum is a complex organizational development challenge.

The presented concept of the key competence modules at the Faculty of Information and Communication at Stuttgart Media University shows that this challenge can be mastered. The concept followed an iterative development approach from the beginning. Continuous innovation based on accumulated experience and empirical data has helped to successfully develop the concept and has proven to be a successful strategy for implementing such a teaching and learning innovation. In this sense, the good-practice example described here should not be seen as finished, but as a successful work in progress. This agile approach was very helpful for the project presented.

An important prerequisite for the success of the concept is and was the support within the faculty and department. One of the most important success factors in the change process was comprehensive and early integration of the stakeholders involved, as well as transparent communication. When new content is added to the curriculum, existing content must be deleted. In our experience, this is one of the most critical points. Here it is worthwhile to develop a common vision of higher education in the future and to openly address the concerns of individual stakeholders. This usually requires a comprehensive strategy process. Furthermore, the scaling of the colloquia (and the associated integration of more instructors) has shown that regular structured exchange (in the form of workshops or information material) is important to reduce fears and to develop new skills and perspectives among the instructors.

The structured and transparent derivation of learning objectives for the modules (utilizing the KSAVE model and other sources) has several positive effects:

- The courses and modules are well structured in terms of content and learning goals.
- The concept can be well communicated and explained (both internally and externally).
- Students recognize the relevance of the course content for their own lives and further development. This motivates them to engage in new ways of learning.

The fact that students do not receive grades does not have a negative impact on their engagement (this fear did exist beforehand). On the contrary, in the context of regularly used classroom assessment techniques and the colloquia, students stress that the grade-free environment makes it easier for them to engage in new, 'risky' ways of learning. Therefore, it is necessary to think about new examination formats when integrating 21st Century Skills in the curriculum.

Future Skills in Practice: Our Recommendations

Based on my experiences as a faculty developer, these five recommendations help you to get Future Skills into your curriculum successfully:

- Understand the integration of Future Skills into the curriculum as a holistic change process.
- Lobby for Future Skills and form a powerful coalition.
- Agree on a common understanding of Future Skills and operationalize them accordingly
- Take all aspects of constructive alignment into account (outcome, assessment, learning activities).
- The integration of Future Skills needs (usually) organizational changes and sufficient resources.

References

AG Curriculum 4.0. (2018). *Curriculumentwicklung und Kompetenzen für das digitale Zeitalter: Thesen und Empfehlungen der AG Curriculum 4.0 des Hochschulforum Digitalisierung* (Arbeitspapier 39).

Akkreditierungsrat. (2013). *Regeln für die Akkreditierung von Studiengängen und für die Systemakkreditierung: Beschluss des Akkreditierungsrates vom 08.12.2009, zuletzt geändert am 20.02.2013.* https://www.akkreditierungsrat.de/sites/default/files/downloads/2019/AR_Beschluss_Regeln_Studiengaenge_Systemakkreditierung_2013.02.20_Drs.20-2013.pdf.

Ananiadoui, K., & Claro, M. (2009). *21st century skills and competences for new millennium learners in OECD countries* (OECD Education Working Papers 41)

Ataizi, M. (2012). Situated learning. In N. M. Seel (Ed.), *Encyclopedia of the sciences of learning* (pp. 3084–3086). Springer US. https://doi.org/10.1007/978-1-4419-1428-6_878.

Binkley, M., Erstad, O., Herman, J., Raizen, S., Ripley, M., Miller-Ricci, M., et al. (2012). Defining twenty-first century skills. In P. E. Griffin, B. McGaw, & E. Care (Eds.), *Assessment and teaching of 21st century skills* (pp. 17–66). Springer Science+Business Media B.V. https://doi.org/10.1007/978-94-007-2324-5_2.

Bräuer, G. (2014). *Das Portfolio als Reflexionsmedium für Lehrende und Studierende* (1st ed.). UTB GmbH, Barbara Budrich.

Buhl, V., Seidl, T., & Zeiner, K. M. (2019). Einfluss eines ePortfolio-Einsatzes in der Lehre auf Selbstverständnis und Perspektiven der Lehrenden. *die hochschullehre, 5*, 249–264.

Burmeister, M., & Seidl, T. (2020). Lehr-Lernkontexte in einer transformativen Fakultät. In R. Stang & A. Becker (Eds.), *Zukunft Lernwelt Hochschule: Perspektiven und Optionen für eine Neuausrichtung* (pp. 86–95). De Gruyter Saur.

EDUCAUSE. (2023). *Horizon reports*. https://library.educause.edu/resources/2021/2/horizon-reports. Accessed 3 April 2023.

Gaus, D. (2018). *Kompetenzorientiertes Prüfen: Handreichung der Prüfungswerkstatt*. https://www.zq.uni-mainz.de/files/2018/08/2_Kompetenzorientiertes-Pruefen.pdf.

Hansen, C., & Rachbauer, T. (2018). *Reflektieren? Worauf und Wozu?: Arbeiten mit dem E-Portfolio – ein Reflexionsinstrument für die LehrerInnenbildung am Beispiel der Universität Passau*. https://www.e-teaching.org/etresources/pdf/erfahrungsbericht_2018_hansen_rachbauer_arbeiten_mit_dem_e_portfolio_reflexionsinstrument_fuer_die_lehrerbildung.pdf.

Hochschulforum Digitalisierung. (2022). *Curriculum 4.0*. https://hochschulforumdigitalisierung.de/de/themen/curriculum-40. Accessed 8 Febr. 2023.

Howell, W. S. (1982). *The empathic communicator*. Wadsworth Publishers.

Mildenberger, U., & Vonhof, C. (2020). Neues Studienmodell und organisatorische Herausforderungen: Wege zu einer transformativen Fakultät. In R. Stang & A. Becker (Eds.), *Zukunft Lernwelt Hochschule: Perspektiven und Optionen für eine Neuausrichtung* (pp. 26–34). De Gruyter Saur.

Orth, H. (1999). *Schlüsselqualifikationen an deutschen Hochschulen: Konzepte, Standpunkte und Perspektiven*. Luchterhand.

Schaper, N. (2012). *Fachgutachten zur Kompetenzorientierung in Studium und Lehre* (Projekt Nexus). Bonn. https://www.hrk-nexus.de/fileadmin/redaktion/hrk-nexus/07-Downloads/07-02-Publikationen/fachgutachten_kompetenzorientierung.pdf.

Schaper, N., & Hilkenmeier, F. (2013). *Umsetzungshilfen für kompetenzorientiertes Prüfen* (Projekt Nexus). https://www.hrk-nexus.de/fileadmin/redaktion/hrk-nexus/07-Downloads/07-03-Material/zusatzgutachten.pdf.

Schütz-Pitan, J., Seidl, T., & Hense, J. (2019). Wirksamkeit eines fächer- und modulübergreifenden ePortfolio-Einsatzes in der Hochschullehre. *die hochschullehre, 5*(41), 769–796

Seel, N. M. (Ed.). (2012a). *Encyclopedia of the sciences of learning*. Springer US.

Seel, N. M. (2012). Metacognition and learning. In N. M. Seel (Ed.), *Encyclopedia of the sciences of learning* (pp. 2228–2231). Springer US. https://doi.org/10.1007/978-1-4419-1428-6_108.

Seidl, T. (2017). Schlüsselkompetenzen als Zukunftskompetenzen: Die Bedeutung der „21st Century Skills" für die Studiengangsentwicklung. In B. Berendt, A. Fleischmann, N. Schaper, B. Szczyrba, M. Wiemer, & J. Wildt (Eds.), *Neues Handbuch Hochschullehre*. DUZ Verlags- und Medienhaus.

Seidl, T. (2021). ePortfolios und Kolloquien als formative Prüfungsinstrumente nutzen: Ein Beispiel aus der Schlüsselkompetenzausbildung. In B. Berendt, A. Fleischmann, N. Schaper, B. Szczyrba, M. Wiemer, & J. Wildt (Eds.), *Neues Handbuch Hochschullehre*. DUZ Verlags- und Medienhaus.

Seidl, T. (2021). Förderung von Schlüsselkompetenzen. In R. Kordts-Freudinger, N. Schaper, A. Scholkmann, & B. Szczyrba (Eds.), *Handbuch Hochschuldidaktik* (pp. 117–128). wbv.

van den Berk, I., Petersen, K., Schultes, K., & Stolz, K. (Eds.). (2016). *Studierfähigkeit: Theoretische Erkenntnisse, empirische Befunde und praktische Perspektiven*. Universität Hamburg, Universitätskolleg.

Wildt, J., & Wildt, B. (2011). Lernprozessorientiertes Prüfen in "Constructive Alignment": Ein Beitrag zur Förderung der Qualität von Hochschulbildung durch eine Weiterentwicklung des Prüfungssystems. In B. Berendt, A. Fleischmann, N. Schaper, B. Szczyrba, M. Wiemer, & J. Wildt (Eds.), *Neues Handbuch Hochschullehre*. DUZ Verlags- und Medienhaus.

Yang, M., Tai, M., & Lim, C. P. (2016). The role of e-portfolios in supporting productive learning. *British Journal of Educational Technology, 47*(6), 1276–1286. https://doi.org/10.1111/bjet.12316.

Prof. Dr. Tobias Seidl is Professor for Academic Key Competencies at the Faculty of Information and Communication at Stuttgart Media University. He teaches and researches in the field of key competencies/Future Skills, creativity, university development and innovative methods in teaching. In 2017, he was a member of the Curriculum 4.0 working group of the "Hochschulforum Digitalisierung". As a coach and expert, he supports universities, companies, and public institutions in generating and implementing new ideas.

Open Access This chapter is licensed under the terms of the Creative Commons Attribution 4.0 International License (http://creativecommons.org/licenses/by/4.0/), which permits use, sharing, adaptation, distribution and reproduction in any medium or format, as long as you give appropriate credit to the original author(s) and the source, provide a link to the Creative Commons license and indicate if changes were made.

The images or other third party material in this chapter are included in the chapter's Creative Commons license, unless indicated otherwise in a credit line to the material. If material is not included in the chapter's Creative Commons license and your intended use is not permitted by statutory regulation or exceeds the permitted use, you will need to obtain permission directly from the copyright holder.

The State of Skills: A Global View from Burning Glass Institute and Wiley

25

How Skills Are Disrupting Work: The Transformational Power of Fast-Growing, In-Demand Skills. A "State of Skills" Report from the Burning Glass Institute, the Business-Higher Education Forum, and Wiley

Ulf-Daniel Ehlers and Laura Eigbrecht

just limited to specialized programs. Educational institutions should ensure that learners are aware of the importance of these emerging skills to virtually all career paths. Schools should continuously assess and reassess the relative importance of key skills in the labor market and collaborate closely with local and regional businesses and other industries or sectors for which the new emerging skills may well prove qualifying. By doing so, higher education can play a critical role in preparing individuals for success in the workforce. Furthermore, businesses should adopt the expectation that the workforce will constantly acquire new skills and center learning in the entire enterprise. They should track pressing skill needs and relevant skill adjacencies and use this information to identify or build effective talent pipelines internally. Companies can also partner with higher education institutions

---

U.-D. Ehlers
Professor for Educational Management and Lifelong Learning, Business Faculty, DHBW Karlsruhe, Karlsruhe, Germany
e-mail: ulf-daniel.ehlers@dhbw-karlsruhe.de

L. Eigbrecht (✉)
Educational Management and Lifelong Learning, Business Faculty, DHBW Karlsruhe, Karlsruhe, Germany
e-mail: laura.eigbrecht@dhbw-karlsruhe.de

© The Author(s) 2024
U.-D. Ehlers and L. Eigbrecht (eds.), *Creating the University of the Future*, Zukunft der Hochschulbildung - Future Higher Education, https://doi.org/10.1007/978-3-658-42948-5_25

While Future Skills are widely discussed, there is also a profound debate on how to measure and assess skills in order to identify skills gaps and design measures to address them. Job markets are undergoing significant changes due to the constant demand for new skills in almost all industries. One in eight U.S. job postings in 2021 require skills in **Artificial Intelligence/Machine Learning, Cloud Computing, Social Media, and Product Management**, which are among the fastest-growing and most rapidly spreading skills. Workers have had to replace or upgrade over a third of their skills to keep up with their occupation's demands in the past five years. Skills disruption can have positive effects on innovation, productivity, and compensation, but it can also lead to job loss and make education and training systems obsolete. The Burning Glass Institute and the Business–Higher Education Forum have identified these four high-demand emerging skill sets as a laboratory for understanding how to prepare workers and students for skills disruption, with a focus on the U.S. The report includes profiles of recent innovations from the BHEF network to illustrate how programs can help learners acquire essential skills.

This report's methodology as well as the section "How Emerging Skills Are Spreading" (p. 25) are shortly described in this info box, showing how technology-related skills are becoming transversal skills across sectors.

Coming Soon to a Job Near You: How Emerging Skills Are Spreading Beyond the World of Tech

The section discusses how the four skill sets laid out (Artificial Intelligence/Machine Learning, Cloud Computing, Social Media, and Product Management) are spreading beyond the tech sector to other industries. This reflects a fundamental shift in adoption from niche technologies to broad acceptance across fields (Fig. 25.1). Additionally, the geographic concentration of people with these skills is decreasing, with significant declines in AI/ML and Cloud Computing skills. The trend of dispersion is consistent, and many more jobs for people with these skills are available across the country. This shift is driven by the explosion of demand and the deeper integration of these skills into the core of everyday work, and not just the post-pandemic shift toward remote work.

Beyond Tech: How (Higher) Education Institutions Should Address Emerging Skills

The chapter also discusses the implications of the spread of emerging skills for higher education and businesses. It is argued that emerging skills, such as AI/ML, should become staples in a wide array of courses and curricular areas, not

25 The State of Skills: A Global View from Burning Glass Institute ...

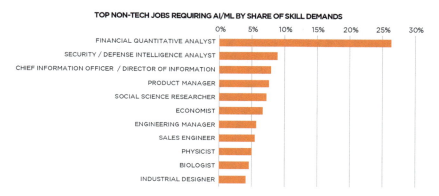

Fig. 25.1 Top non-tech jobs requiring AI/ML by share of skill demands (own representation by the Burning Glass Institute, the Business-Higher Education Forum, and Wiley)

and others to deliver high-quality, just-in-time learning for existing and entering employees, either inside their companies or in higher education or other settings.

Methodology

The Burning Glass Institute conducted a landscape analysis to identify areas of great transformation in emerging skills that change jobs, workplaces, and industries, and to inform leaders on how they can respond to this phenomenon. The study analyzed 228 million job postings from 2015 to the present and identified four clusters of skills that are experiencing rapid rates of growth, high demand, and are spreading across industries and regions. The study prioritized identifying new skills that have emerged over the past decade and do not require a university degree as a prerequisite. The paper examines the growth, demand, spread, and transition pathways of these skill clusters throughout firms, occupations, regions, and industries.

Further Information: https://www.burningglassinstitute.org/research/how-skills-are-disrupting-work

Prof. Dr. phil. habil. Ulf-Daniel Ehlers is an internationally renowned Professor for Educational Management and Lifelong Learning at the Baden-Wuerttemberg Cooperative State University (DHBW) Karlsruhe which he headed as Vice-President between 2011 and 2017.

Laura Eigbrecht is principle investigator, teacher and doctoral student at the Baden-Wuerttemberg Cooperative State University (DHBW) Karlsruhe and holds degrees in European Media and Culture and Media Pedagogy.

Open Access This chapter is licensed under the terms of the Creative Commons Attribution 4.0 International License (http://creativecommons.org/licenses/by/4.0/), which permits use, sharing, adaptation, distribution and reproduction in any medium or format, as long as you give appropriate credit to the original author(s) and the source, provide a link to the Creative Commons license and indicate if changes were made.

The images or other third party material in this chapter are included in the chapter's Creative Commons license, unless indicated otherwise in a credit line to the material. If material is not included in the chapter's Creative Commons license and your intended use is not permitted by statutory regulation or exceeds the permitted use, you will need to obtain permission directly from the copyright holder.

Part V
Future Skills in Higher Education – The Wider View

Part V widens the perspective and presents selected national and international Future Skills initiatives and approaches. All initiatives aim at making society and lifelong learning future-proof and are integrating educational policy and higher education practices. Singapore's Future Skills approach is described from two perspectives, followed by examples from the Japanese and European Union context and with an inspirational outlook from New Zealand on the concept of creating a Universal Learning Community for Future Skills.

Future Skills in Higher Education - The Wider View

(II) Future Skills - **Foundations** and Shapes of a New Emerging Concept in a Global View

(III) Future Skills in Practice - **Teaching** and **Learning**

(IV) Future Skills in Practice - **Assessment**

(I) Setting the Scene - **Future Skills** in Higher Education

Future-Skilling the Workforce: SkillsFuture Movement in Singapore

26

Soon-Joo Gog, Edwin Tan and Kelsie Tan

Abstract

Workforce development is an ongoing undertaking in Singapore. This includes both the pre-employment education of students in the education system, and the continuing education and learning of incumbent workers. The workforce development system in Singapore is anchored on the tradition that stakeholders within the skills ecosystem must collaborate and coordinate closely to anticipate skills needs, disseminate insights, and measure skills progression and training outcomes. This is achieved through the regular charting of industry transformation from the business and economic perspectives, and the parallel review of human capital and skills demands for the future economy. A skilled and competitive workforce is the foundation of an inclusive society where everyone benefits from economic growth.

S.-J. Gog (✉) · E. Tan · K. Tan
SkillsFuture Singapore, Singapore, Singapore
e-mail: GOG_Soon_Joo@ssg.gov.sg

E. Tan
e-mail: Edwin_TAN@ssg.gov.sg

K. Tan
e-mail: Kelsie_TAN@ssg.gov.sg

© The Author(s) 2024
U.-D. Ehlers and L. Eigbrecht (eds.), *Creating the University of the Future*, Zukunft der Hochschulbildung - Future Higher Education,
https://doi.org/10.1007/978-3-658-42948-5_26

26.1 Introduction

Human capital investment has always been a priority in Singapore; this includes both general to tertiary education, and lifelong learning (Koh, 2014). The lifelong learning policy in Singapore, also known as the education and training policy, serves both economic and social purposes. On one hand, as the economy transforms towards becoming more knowledge-based and digitalized, Singapore maintains her competitiveness by ensuring that the workforce is adequately skilled to meet emerging demands. On the other hand, the lifelong learning policy serves to facilitate the continual career mobility of all citizens, regardless of starting points, so that every citizen can realize their fullest potential (Shanmugaratnam, 2015). Lifelong learning is pertinent in ensuring individuals can take advantage of inevitable economic changes and can continue to benefit from economic development—regardless of the disruptions brought on by technological advancement and other exogenous forces.

The SkillsFuture Movement was launched in 2015 as a continuation of Singapore's human capital investment effort. It was born at a time when Singapore was experiencing demographic change, including an ageing workforce, a falling total fertility rate, and rapid changes due to globalization, technological advancement, and urgency in pushing for a digital economy and greening of the economy. The need to anticipate emerging skills and potential job content changes, and to embark on pre-emptive upskilling in tandem with industry transformation, laid the foundation of SkillsFuture Movement.

The lifelong learning policy manifests through SkillsFuture Movement. SkillsFuture Movement supports economic development through facilitating education, offering training options, and ensuring employer recognition—all of which are "focused on encouraging economic growth through skills development and labor force enhancement" (Woo, 2017). Notably, the Movement will also support Singaporeans to realize their fullest potential in achieving their career aspiration. This notion is supported by ongoing reskilling and skills-based career pathways across life stages, as part of the social movement to value skills mastery.

The Future Economy Council (FEC) drives the growth and transformation of Singapore's economy in anticipation of future growth. Chaired by Deputy Prime Minister and Coordinating Minister for Economic Policies, the Council comprises members from the government, industry, trade associations and chambers, unions, and educational and training institutions. FEC oversees the implementation of the Industry Transformation Map (ITM) and SkillsFuture initiatives (Ministry of Trade & Industry, 2023b). Specifically, each ITM consists of a growth and competitiveness plan, supported by four pillars: productivity, jobs and skills, innovation and trade, and internationalization. As observed by Fung et al. (2021) in *SkillsFuture: The Roles of Public and Private Sectors in Developing a Learning Society in Singapore*, "[the] public sector has the opportunity to rethink existing education and training structures" to enhance the growth of "learning societies adaptive to the increasing pace of change" (Fung et al., 2021). The SkillsFuture Movement serves to testify that policy-led initiatives can bring about effective and wide-scale change in Singapore's education system, and beyond.

This chapter will explain Singapore's future-skilling planning and implementation through a skills-based approach, for targeted stakeholders including individuals and enterprises. It will also discuss the transformation of Singapore's higher education sector to comprise Institutes of Continuous Learning (ICLs). The challenges involved and SkillsFuture Singapore Agency (SSG)'s adaptive innovation will be explored. The chapter will end with sharing the vision of a learning nation, where the skills ecosystem is progressive, responsive, and effective.

26.2 Future-Skilling

In Singapore, it is a national imperative to help citizens acquire and utilize skills, to enable them to take up quality jobs, and seize opportunities in the future economy (Ministry of Trade & Industry, 2023a). This is the foundation of an inclusive economy where citizens benefit from economic growth, enjoy high quality of living standard, and lead a fulfilling life.

As the national skills authority, SSG leads the collaboration in skills anticipation, skills identification, ensuring adequacy of training supply, removing barriers to skills acquisition (e.g., information asymmetry and affordability issues), and monitoring the outcome of the interventions. A high-level process flow is depicted in Fig. 26.1. On the skills radar, SSG leverages data science approaches and expert input to monitor in-demand skills, emerging skills, and future skills for the economy. In-demand skills are skills currently deemed as important by employers to keep their business going. Emerging skills are skills anticipated to be high-growth in sectors where such skills are highlighted as essential to support their industry transformation. Future skills are skills not currently demanded but are expected to be critical for the future economy, in accordance with industry strategies. The skills definitions serve to inform SSG on the speed to reskill and upskill the workforce.

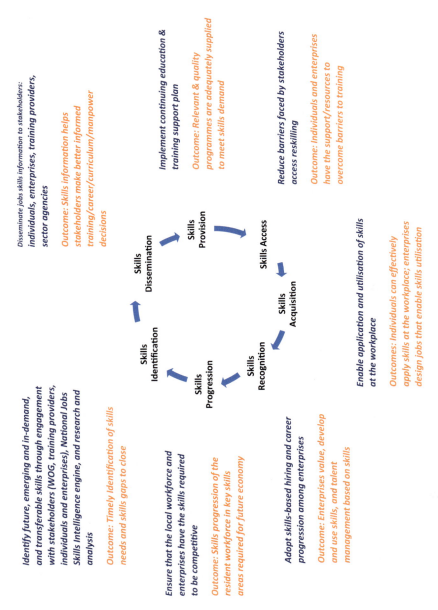

Fig. 26.1 Skills identification to skills progression cycle (own representation)

From 2015 to 2020, a massive sectoral engagement exercise as part of ITM development was carried out to identify the job roles and skills needs of the respective sectors. The approach was primarily via expert input, where employers and experienced professionals identified the skills requirement by job roles. This contributed to the establishment of the *Singapore Skills Frameworks*. Skills demand is categorized into immediate needs (in-demand skills), near-term needs (emerging skills) and intermediate term needs (future skills). This categorization allows stakeholders to prioritize training programs to support reskilling and upskilling capacity planning.

Since 2020, SSG has leveraged on data science approaches and available data sources to enhance Singapore's skills identification capability. These data sources include job posting data, curriculum vitae data, training participation data, wage data, and business performance data. The developed Jobs-Skills Insights (JSI) are validated with the industry and experts. This is further supplemented by the annual labor force survey and annual business survey, conducted at the national level. Results from ongoing monitoring and analyses are disseminated regularly to stakeholders within the skills ecosystem. The primary goals are to ensure that the workforce has the requisite skills to support businesses and the economy, and that reskilling efforts are carried out in a timely manner.

The skills development process from identification to progression (see Fig. 26.1) is done at three levels: economy, sector, and organization/individual. At the economy level, four future economies have been identified to power the nation ahead: the Green Economy, the Digital Economy, the Care Economy, and the Industry 4.0 Economy. Skills clusters commonly required by job roles within each economy, are determined via data science approaches supplemented by industry validation. These skills clusters are communicated to citizens to help them gain access to the future economies (SkillsFuture Singapore, 2021). At the sector level, Industry Transformation Maps have been developed and are refreshed regularly, to keep sectoral strategies updated. This is to meet accelerated changes arising from a dynamic operating environment, supported by good jobs and in-demand skills (Ministry of Trade & Industry, 2023a). At the organization/individual level, schemes and initiatives are put in place to help these entities acquire the skills they need, to advance their business/goals and to facilitate business transformation and career progression. Taken together, this forward planning presents a multi-level future-skilling approach, to pre-empt and position the nation for inclusive and sustainable growth based on skills as the common currency.

The outcomes of future skilling are monitored at multiple levels. At the course level, the *Training Quality and Outcomes Measurement (TRAQOM)* survey is administered at the end of the course and six months after course completion. Overall skills progression and skills gaps analysis are monitored at sectoral and national levels. This is complemented by the ongoing monitoring of labor market data, including employment participation rate, unemployment rate, medium wage of the workforce, average household income growth, productivity growth, and economic competitiveness.

26.3 Rolling Out Targeted Programs for Individuals and Enterprises

SkillsFuture Movement continues to support citizens in developing their fullest potential throughout life, regardless of their starting points. Citizens can confidently participate in career transition programs along their work journey, which may entail moving across to a new sector or job role, or moving up their career path. The Movement also supports reskilling for industry transformation. At present, the Next Bound of SkillsFuture is under way. This is the second five-year plan for SkillsFuture Movement. It will enable individuals to continue reskilling, enhance the role of enterprises in developing their workforce, and have a stronger focus on helping mid-career workers stay employable and move to new jobs or new roles (SkillsFuture Singapore, 2020).

26.3.1 Empowering Individuals

In 2015, SkillsFuture Credit was introduced to give all Singapore citizens aged 25 and above a training credit of S$500. The intent was and still is to put reskilling and upskilling decisions in the hands of citizens; individuals need to take ownership of their productive asset—skills, and not be solely dependent on their employers. In 2020, a time-limited further S$500 credit was provided to citizens, to nudge timely reskilling and upskilling to seize opportunities in the future economies. At the same time, an additional S$500 credit was provided to mid-career workers, to support their career transitions. These credits aim to defray out-of-pocket expenses, on top of the highly subsidized course fees that range from 50 to 90% subsidy. Courses are curated and pre-approved by SSG and sector agencies for quality and relevance. These courses are modular, bite-sized, and involve multiple learning modes (e.g. in-person, online, or hybrid). Some of the courses offered by local universities, polytechnics and Institutes of Technical Education are stackable towards full qualifications.

The MySkillsFuture portal is a one-stop digital platform for Singapore individuals' skills need. Individuals can use MySkillsFuture to access information on jobs-skills trends and developments, search for courses, apply for courses, download their training certificates, and assess their skills and career interests. Most recently, the portal is being enhanced to provide more customized recommendations to individuals on their training options.

Besides the online self-help functions, SSG also offers one-to-one skills and training advisory to citizens, through its network of Skills Ambassadors who are trained to provide career-learning advisory. SkillsFuture Work-Study Programs provide citizens with work-study pathways to obtain a Diploma, post-Diploma or Degree, that comes with job-matching and mentorship, as well as sign-on incentives and training sponsorships. By 2025, this pathway will be made mainstream, involving 12% of each yearly cohort of students (Chan, 2022a). To help mid-career workers stay employable and access good jobs, Train-and-Place programmes (TnP) and Place-and-Train programmes (PnT) have been progressively rolled out to provide skilling options for mid-career workers with different needs. The TnP and PnT programmes are two modes of career transition programmes. The former entails screen-and-train before the trained individual seeks employment, while the latter entails the individual's secured employment prior to embarking on the reskilling programme.

26.3.2 Engaging Employers

In 2020, SkillsFuture Enterprise Credit was introduced to encourage employers to invest in enterprise transformation and the capabilities of their employees. Eligible employers receive a one-off S$10,000 credit to cover up to 90% of out-of-pocket expenses, over and above existing programme subsidies. In 2022, the requirement of a minimum employer contribution to the Skills Development Levy was removed, to allow more enterprises to qualify for and benefit from the scheme.

SkillsFuture Queen Bees (SFQBs) are industry leaders who take on a leading role to champion skills development in organisations, particularly small and medium enterprises (SMEs). As SFQBs, these leaders provide skills advisory and support to guide organisations in identifying and acquiring skills needed for business transformation. Interested organisations join a SFQB network to benefit from an ecosystem support, which includes a skills manager who works with the organisation to curate training programmes and tap on government schemes.

The National Centre of Excellence for Workplace Learning (NACE) was established in 2018 as a collaboration with the Swiss Federal Institute of Vocational Education and Training, and the German Chamber of Industry & Commerce. NACE aims to help organisations build and develop their workplace learning capabilities, solutions and systems, through training and consultancy projects. The goal is to build up workplaces in Singapore, to be able to undertake workplace training and learning for their own employees, to support ongoing business transformation and growth. This involves, for instance, incorporating internships, work-study programmes, and upskilling employees as part of workplace practices.

26.4 Transforming Institutes of Higher Learning into Institutes of Continuous Learning

Singapore is working towards a higher education system with multiple upgrading pathways, so that citizens may choose the pathway that best fits their individual aspirations and needs. To support such a system, a citizen's relationship with Institutes of Higher Learning should last for a much longer time, than if education were to be frontloaded before an individual formally embarks on their career.

As such, Singapore is repositioning Institutes of Higher Learning (IHLs) as Institutes of Continuous Learning (ICLs). This is to signal that there is no limit to lifelong learning, and that there is no need to rush for the highest possible qualification before entering the workforce (Chan, 2022b). This approach is coherent with the strategy of helping mid-career workers to stay employable and access good jobs. Since 2018, all IHLs (post-secondary education and above) have set up their continuing education and training services, to be the major providers of continuing education and training. Singapore's twelve autonomous universities, polytechnics, and Institutes of Technical Education cater to the reskilling needs of the economy, alongside private training providers.

Besides supporting skills-based reskilling initiatives, ICLs have their core capability in research and development. The polytechnics are set up with their specialization as centers of innovation to support SMEs in adoption of advanced technological applications.

The revision of the mandate is not without its challenges. Firstly, reskilling of incumbents in the workforce requires a different pedagogical consideration and learning design as compared to educating students without work experience. To do this, the ICLs partner industry practitioners to design and deliver the continuing education and training programs as part of their capability development plan.

Secondly, with demand being from employers who sponsor their employees for skills acquisition, learning is expected to be applicable in nature and relevant for workplace. As such, more ICLs are partnering with enterprises to design part of the workplace learning curriculum. Thirdly, the demand for career facilitation by adult learners has led it to become an essential service. Adult learners who are keen on career transition expect ICLs to support their successful transition. This calls upon ICLs to ensure that the courses they offer lead to jobs in high demand areas, and that career-learning advisory to learners is part of the services rendered.

26.5 Further Steps to Enhance Lifelong Learning Participation and Design

By 2021, the SkillsFuture Movement was in its 6th year of implementation. The training participation rate of the resident labor force was 50% in 2021, as compared to 35% in 2015 (Ministry of Manpower, 2021). As of 31 December 2021, 27% of eligible Singaporeans have used their SkillsFuture Credit; and 24,000 enterprises and 660,000 individuals participated in SkillsFuture-supported reskilling programs, an increase of 22% and 71% respectively from 2020 (Ministry of Education, 2021).

Challenges remain in encouraging more individuals in the workforce to initiate their reskilling journey. Statistically, professionals, managers, executives, and technicians (PMETs) have the highest training participation rate (58.7%). Comparatively, clerical, sales and services workers, and production and related workers have lower training participation rates at 38.3% and 21.5% respectively (Ministry of Manpower, 2019).

With the speed of change increasing at the business front and the half-life of skills shortening, there is a need to sustain the validity and relevance of one's knowledge and skills (Chan, 2022c). On this front, SSG has been producing regular and up-to-date JSI through ongoing data analytics, to support individuals' skills development decision making. Starting from 2021, SSG has released and will be releasing annual Skills Demand for the Future Economy reports for Singapore citizens (SkillsFuture Singapore, 2021). SSG also partners with education and training partners to strengthen job placement services, to support vulnerable segments of the workforce in their career pivot journey. Depending on the needs of individual adult learners, career-learning advisory through jobs-skills adjacency analysis and training pathway advisory services are provided.

Skills needs and skills utilization are primarily determined by workplaces. As Singapore pushes forth for a digital and green economy, enterprises are expected to drive innovation and growth globally and locally. While the anticipation of future skills and identification of emerging skills involve enterprises large and small, SMEs continue to lag behind larger firms in skills development efforts (Institute for Adult Learning Singapore, 2018). This is particularly worrisome when SMEs employed 70% of the workforce in Singapore (Department of Statistics, 2023). To scale up engagement with Singapore's community of SMEs, SSG identifies Skills Development Partners (SDPs) to help SMEs aggregate their skills needs and source for reskilling supplies (Gan, 2022). SDPs will work on the ground to validate the skills needs of the professional community and curate reskilling pathways to support the skills needs of SMEs. This new initiative is currently in its pilot phase. The pilot will allow SSG and its partners to learn alongside the SMEs' journeys, and adjust their support to SMEs along the way.

Singapore recognizes the need to empower citizens in their extended working lives, and the need for the workforce to continuously learn and pivot their career throughout life-stages (National Research Foundation, 2021). To these imperatives, the Singapore government has been investing in research and development, to better design and deliver learning to the workforce. In 2019, SSG and the National Research Foundation convened a taskforce to establish The Future of Adult Learning Research Agenda (Institute for Adult Learning Singapore, 2020). The taskforce made four recommendations:

(1) Four highly complex priority research areas to advance adult learning research in Singapore in the next 5-10 years;
(2) Data infrastructure to support adult learning research, policy evaluation and data-driven practices;
(3) Research co-laboratories as new mechanisms to facilitate large-scale research-practice collaborations, driven by use-inspired transdisciplinary research;
(4) New flagship platforms to signal the building of a leading research-user learning community in Singapore.

The Agenda has guided research investment and capacity building in Singapore. The Workforce Development Applied Research Fund (WDARF) is established by SSG to encourage interdisciplinary research in the areas of workforce development and lifelong learning, administered by the IAL (Institute for Adult Learning Singapore, 2023). Besides leading adult learning research, IAL also leads the professional development of adult educators and drives learning innovation in continuing education and training in Singapore. The commitment to research, innovation, and adult educator development is pertinent to SkillsFuture Movement.

26.6   Conclusion

As the economy and businesses continue to evolve and restructure, continuous reskilling effort will be a policy priority worldwide. Especially in Singapore, the human capital investment strategy serves both economic and social purposes. SkillsFuture Movement will continue to adapt to the needs of the economy and the workforce. To support this ongoing adaptation, SSG has put in place monitoring and evaluation mechanisms to evaluate the effectiveness of SkillsFuture's schemes and programs. These measurements will allow SSG to enhance its programs and services. At the same time, SSG invests in research and development to develop future models of adult learning, career-facilitation, and skills anticipation capability. Only through continuous enhancement and adaptation can Singapore ensure a progressive, responsive, and effective skills ecosystem.

The Singapore experience suggests that skills development agenda is integral to economic transformation and inclusive growth. One form of institutional arrangement is for the government to play an active role as convenor: to coordinate the skills demand and skills supply of the economy through working with stakeholders in the skills ecosystem. Quality and responsiveness of training provision is critical to the success of the reskilling agenda and having a committed and responsive community of training providers requires the right incentive and nurturing. Being mindful of the barriers to reskilling and upskilling means there is a deliberate need to address affordability to access training, and to actively address information asymmetry. Hence, the timely and targeted signposting of jobs-skills information through channel partners (such as including Trade Associations and Chambers, Professional Bodies, Labor Unions and other non-governmental organizations) will strengthen the outreach to target segments of the workforce and enterprises. Only when the whole nation is involved and all hands are on deck, can we achieve the future skilling agenda.

> **Future Skills in Practice: Our Recommendations**
> - A skilled and competitive workforce is the foundation of an inclusive society where everyone benefits from economic growth;
> - SkillsFuture Movement supports economic development through skills development and labour force enhancement;
> - SkillsFuture Movement also supports Singaporeans to realise their fullest potential in achieving their career aspiration;
> - One form of institutional arrangement is for the government to play an active role as convenor: to coordinate the skills demand and skills supply of the economy through working with stakeholders in the skills ecosystem;
> - National skills agenda requires tight coordination among key stakeholders within the ecosystem;
> - Skills are used as the common currency for individuals' skills development journey, for employers' talent and workforce planning, and for education and training partners to ensure courses are meeting skills needs;
> - Quality and responsiveness of training provision is critical to the success of the reskilling agenda; and,
> - Being mindful of the barriers to reskilling and upskilling means there is a deliberate need to address affordability to access training, and to actively address information asymmetry.

References

Chan, C. S. (2022a). *Learn for life: Confidence for a new tomorrow: MOE FY2022 committee of supply debate response by minister for education Chan Chun Sing,* February, 7.

Chan, C. S. (2022b). *Speech by Minister Chan Chun Sing at the launch of Prof Arnoud De Meyer's Book, "Building excellence in higher education: Singapore's experience", at the Singapore Management University,* Singapore Management University, February, 21.

Chan, C. S. (2022c). *Speech by Minister Chan Chun Sing at republic polytechnic graduation ceremony on 4 May 2022 at the Republic Cultural Centre (TRCC),* May, 4.

Department of Statistics. (2023). *Topline estimates for all enterprises and SMEs.* https://tablebuilder.singstat.gov.sg/table/TS/M600981.Accessed 11 April 2023.

Fung, M., Taal, R., & Sim, W. (2021). SkillsFuture: The roles of public and private sectors in developing a learning society in Singapore. In S. Ra, S. Jagannathan, & R. Maclean (Eds.), *Powering a learning society during an age of disruption* (pp. 195–208). Springer Singapore Pte. Limited. https://doi.org/10.1007/978-981-16-0983-1_14.

Gan, S. H. (2022). *MOE FY2022 ccmmittee of supply debate response by Minister of State Gan Siow Huang,* March, 7.

Institute for Adult Learning Singapore. (2018). *Business performance and skills survey (BPSS): Final Report.* https://ial.edu.sg/getmedia/32eb68f2-0073-496b-af8c-772ebb4a14c6/BPSS_Final_Report_20171012_RID_FINAL1_1.pdf.

Institute for Adult Learning Singapore. (2020). *Future of adult learning research.* https://www.ial.edu.sg/access-research/future-of-adult-learning-research.html.

Institute for Adult Learning Singapore (2023). *Workforce development applied research fund.* https://www.ial.edu.sg/research/wdarf-grant-call/. Accessed 11 April 2023.

Koh, B. S. (2014). *Learning for life: Singapore's investment in lifelong learning since the 1950s.* Workforce Development Agency

Ministry of Education. (2021). *Utilisation of skillsfuture credit.*

Ministry of Manpower. (2019). *Training participation rate of economically active residents.* http://stats.mom.gov.sg/iMAS_Charts/Training%20Participation%20Rate%20of%20Economically%20Active%20Residents/TRNG_001_Training_Participation_Rate_Economically_Active_Residents.xls.

Ministry of Manpower. (2021). *Supplementary survey on adult training.*

Ministry of Trade and Industry. (2023). *Industry transformation map overview.* https://www.mti.gov.sg/ITMs/Overview. Accessed 11 April 2023.

Ministry of Trade and Industry. (2023). *The future economy council.* https://www.mti.gov.sg/FutureEconomy/TheFutureEconomyCouncil. Accessed 11 April 2023.

National Research Foundation (2021). *Human Health and Potential.* https://www.nrf.gov.sg/rie2025-plan/human-health-and-potential. Accessed 11 April 2023.

Shanmugaratnam, T. (2015). *Budget speech 2015—Section C: Developing our people,* February, 25.

SkillsFuture Singapore. (2020). *Next bound of skillsfuture.* https://www.skillsfuture.gov.sg/aboutskillsfuture/nextbound. Accessed 11 April 2023.

SkillsFuture Singapore. (2021). *Skills demand for the future economy.* https://www.skillsfuture.gov.sg/docs/default-source/initiatives/ssg-skills_demand_for_the_future_economy_2021.pdf.

Woo, J. J. (2017). Educating the developmental state: Policy integration and mechanism redesign in Singapore's SkillsFuture scheme. *Journal of Asian Public Policy, 11*(3), 267–284. https://doi.org/10.1080/17516234.2017.1368616.

Dr. Soon-Joo Gog is the Chief Skills Officer at the SkillsFuture Singapore Agency, a statutory board under the Ministry of Education. She oversees the skills development system in Singapore, through working with tripartite partners in the identification, dissemination and measurement of skills needs of Singapore's economy. She works with global partners, including researchers and technologists, in shaping the skills ecosystem. Soon-Joo is an alumnus of Nanyang Technological University in Singapore, University College London, and Oxford University in the UK, and George Washington University and Singularity University in the US, and HEC-Paris in France. ORCID ID: 0000-0002-3170-7725.

Edwin Tan is a Deputy Director with the SkillsFuture Singapore Agency, a statutory board under the Ministry of Education. He leads a team of Jobs-Skills Analysts and Solutionists in developing insights to enable individuals, enterprises, training providers, and government agencies to make informed decisions relating to jobs and skills. Previously with the Ministry of Education, he has experience in policy formulation, stakeholder engagement, project management and skills development. Edwin is an alumnus of Osaka University and Tohoku University in Japan. ORCID ID: 0000-0002-5330-9146.

Kelsie Tan is a Jobs-Skills Analyst (JSA) at SkillsFuture Singapore Agency, a statutory board under the Ministry of Education. She works in a team of JSAs who study local and global trends affecting jobs & skills, towards developing timely jobs-skills insights for stakeholders including policy makers and educational institutions. Kelsie is an alumnus of the School of Humanities at Nanyang Technological University, Singapore. ORCID ID: 0000-0003-0513-6495.

Open Access This chapter is licensed under the terms of the Creative Commons Attribution 4.0 International License (http://creativecommons.org/licenses/by/4.0/), which permits use, sharing, adaptation, distribution and reproduction in any medium or format, as long as you give appropriate credit to the original author(s) and the source, provide a link to the Creative Commons license and indicate if changes were made.

The images or other third party material in this chapter are included in the chapter's Creative Commons license, unless indicated otherwise in a credit line to the material. If material is not included in the chapter's Creative Commons license and your intended use is not permitted by statutory regulation or exceeds the permitted use, you will need to obtain permission directly from the copyright holder.

Anticipating the Future: Continuing Education at the National University of Singapore

27

Miriam J. Green, Christalle Tay and Ye-Her Wu

Abstract

The chapter describes how the National University of Singapore contributes to strengthening Singapore's workforce through its approach to Future Skills, as well as through collaboration with government and industry. The authors show how a refreshed approach to undergraduate education, coupled with the development of a broad array of graduate programs, support the goal to prepare students for the future. NUS's approach includes efforts to inculcate a culture of lifelong learning on campus, providing opportunities for acquiring in-demand skills, and building data literacy among students as well as university staff. This approach aims at ensuring both broad- and deep-skilling in undergraduate education for a volatile and uncertain future.

M. J. Green
Principal Policy Analyst in the Office of the Provost,
National University of Singapore, Singapore, Singapore
e-mail: pvomjg@nus.edu.sg

C. Tay (✉)
Equal Dreams, Singapore, Singapore
e-mail: christxy@gmail.com

Y.-H. Wu
Advisor at the Futures Office and Associate Dean of SCALE-Global,
National University of Singapore, Singapore, Singapore
e-mail: yeher.wu@nus.edu.sg

© The Author(s) 2024
U.-D. Ehlers and L. Eigbrecht (eds.), *Creating the University of the Future*, Zukunft der Hochschulbildung - Future Higher Education,
https://doi.org/10.1007/978-3-658-42948-5_27

529

27.1 The Little Red Dot

Singapore, affectionately referred to as "the little red dot", is a city-state with a population of around 6 million and one of the world's most open and market-driven economies (The Heritage Foundation, 2023). Singapore has one of the world's largest and busiest cargo ports; its economy is also driven by services, tourism, chemicals, electronics, and financial services. The World Bank classifies Singapore as "a high-income economy [which] provides one of the world's most business-friendly regulatory environments for local entrepreneurs and is ranked among the world's most competitive economies" (The World Bank, 2019, Summary). Except for a pandemic-related contraction in 2020, Singapore has enjoyed steady economic growth since independence in 1964 (The World Bank, 2021a, b).

The World Bank's Human Capital Index (0–1) index measures how much health and education feeds into the productivity of the next generation of workers. In 2020 (the most recent year for which there is data), Singapore scores 0.9 on the World Bank's Human Capital Index, the highest of any country in the world (The World Bank, 2020a, b). This is also true for 2017 and 2018, the only other years for which there are data.

In this chapter we describe how the National University of Singapore (NUS) contributes to strengthening Singapore's workforce through its approach to Future Skills, as well as through collaboration with government and industry. We show how a refreshed approach to undergraduate education, coupled with the development of a broad array of graduate (primarily Master's) programs, support our goal to prepare our students for the future. We relate our efforts to inculcate a culture of lifelong learning on our campus, and to provide opportunities for acquiring in-demand skills. Finally we describe how Future Skills includes building data literacy among students as well as university staff.

27.2 The National University of Singapore's Approach to Future Skills

At NUS, Future Skilling means ensuring that our undergraduates acquire critical thinking skills and breadth of knowledge. We also stress interdisciplinary approaches. These strategies are intended to prepare them intellectually for openness to learning throughout their careers and lives. At the same time, we are launching new postgraduate programs that teach technical or specific skills, with as much flexibility as possible. As the flagship university of Singapore, it is part of NUS's mission to keep the national workforce relevant. However, our mandate is not just to churn out well-trained workers for industry, but also to teach students how to be good humans and citizens, and to develop in them resilience to confront a volatile and unpredictable future.

Our approach therefore also includes teaching our students that learning does not stop after university, nor does it end at the confines of a particular discipline. We have invested significantly in lifelong learning, expanding opportunities for adult learning, and infusing younger students with the spirit of lifelong learning.

Our approach to Future Skilling does present challenges. We work hard to balance general knowledge and up-to-the-moment expertise and skills—especially relevant, given that knowledge and skills can (and do) expire. And change is hard. To illustrate, figuring out how to make postgraduate programs more flexible, for example by making courses stackable toward diplomas and degrees, has demanded careful thought and planning. We confront these challenges with purpose and open eyes, and with confidence in our mission.

27.2.1 A Tight Coupling Between Government and Higher Education

The Singapore government works hand-in-hand with Singaporean institutions of higher learning and with industry to invest in the future, to ensure that both businesses and people can thrive in an increasingly diversified economy and are prepared to deal with whatever changes lie ahead.

Singapore set up the Workforce Development Agency in 2003, under the Ministry of Manpower to "[t]o enhance the employability and competitiveness of Singapore's workforce" by increasing access to Continuing Education and Training (CET) and ensuring that training meets industry-approved standards (Singapore Workforce Development Agency, 2011, p. 3). The Agency was subsequently split into Workforce Singapore (still under the Ministry of Manpower) and SkillsFuture Singapore (SSG), which is under the Ministry of Education, looping Singapore's universities and polytechnics into the effort to ensure future-readiness. SSG partners with educational institutions across Singapore—including NUS— to ensure that younger people and working adults have access to "high quality, industry-relevant training throughout life" (SkillsFuture Singapore, 2020, paragraph 2).

Singapore's Ministry of Trade and Industry developed an Industry Transformation Program, to allow the government, firms, industries, trade associations and chambers to partner and address industry issues (Ministry of Trade & Industry, 2023). This program, launched progressively between 2016 and 2018, is used by Singapore's institutions of higher learning to ensure that the workforce has access to training in areas that are in high demand by employers. This means frequent review and updating of programs, curricula, and pedagogical tools, and working with national initiatives such as SkillsFuture Singapore, which provides educational and training opportunities to Singaporeans. There is demand for upskilling and reskilling: the number of adult learners enrolled in Singapore's higher education system has doubled, from around 165,000 in 2018 to 345,000 in 2020, and is expected to continue to increase, according to the Minister of Education (Ng, 2022).

27.2.2 Knowledge and Skills Are Quickly Obsolete

The World Economic Forum (WEF) reported in 2020 that employers believe 50% of their employees will need reskilling, and 94% expect employees to pick up new skills on the job, a sharp uptick from 65% in 2018. For workers who remain in their roles, about 40% of the skills a typical role requires will change in the next five years (World Economic Forum, 2020). A 2018 McKinsey report claims that between 2016 and 2030, the need for physical and manual skills is likely to fall by 14%, whereas social and emotional skills requirements will rise by 24%, and technological skills by 55% (Bughin et al., 2018).

As complex issues upend expectations of work and the workplace, job markets are becoming more unpredictable. For example, the Covid-19 pandemic caused some jobs to be designated as essential/non-essential and remote/non-remote. Many workers whose jobs could not be done remotely, or in industries hit by the pandemic, were displaced. The WEF reports that around 60% of workers in high-income countries (e.g. the United States and Switzerland) were unable to fully work from home (World Economic Forum, 2020). The figure is higher for countries with lower GDP per capita. It is vital that workers today have the agility to pivot their skills in an unstable world.

27.3 NUS—Educating the Workforce of the Future

The current leadership at NUS, sensitive to seismic changes in the labor market, has shifted the focus of undergraduate education. To help protect future Singaporean workers from becoming redundant, NUS is taking a two-pronged approach: interdisciplinarity and lifelong learning.

Path Options					Qualifications
Path 1[#]	Major	+	Contrasting Major		Double Degree
Path 2	Major	+	2nd Major		Degree
Path 3	Major	+	Minor		Degree
Path 4	Major	+	Minor	+ Minor	Degree
Path 5	Major				Degree

A Double Degree Programme (DDP) with the College of Design and Engineering (CDE) is a possible pathway for CHS students, where Common Curriculum modules read can be mapped between CDE and CHS

Fig. 27.1 Multiple pathways for undergraduates (NUS College of Humanities & Sciences, 2021)

27.3.1 Interdisciplinarity—Broadening Undergraduate Learning

To give students a broad foundation for lifelong learning, the university has begun a shift towards interdisciplinary learning. Through the merging of faculties, it recently created the College of Humanities and Science (CHS). CHS undergraduate students must complete a year and a half of general curriculum, then specialize for 18 months. In their final year, they either go deeper into their chosen area, or add another area of specialty. Figures 27.1 and 27.2 show the various paths CHS students may choose from, and the options for curriculum balance, depending on the level of focus or specialization preferred.

CHS students have the choice to pivot between disciplines or to learn about what lies in-between, as the problems of the future are unlikely to "fit nicely within one discipline". NUS president Tan Eng Chye, who propelled the merger, said: "Our challenge is this: if you are focused on one, what if this particular branch of knowledge becomes obsolete?" (Ellis, 2021, paragraph 10). The design and structure of CHS was led by a vision "to prepare students for the digital world and a future of change and complexity, while nurturing them to be adaptable, resilient and empathetic," said Professor Sun Yeneng, CHS Co-Dean and Dean of the Faculty of Science (National University of Singapore, 2020c, paragraph 13).

The general curriculum requirements for CHS students include the following courses:

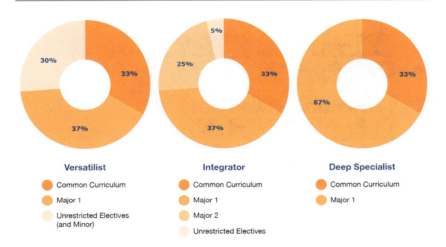

Fig. 27.2 Multiple pathways for undergraduates (NUS College of Humanities & Sciences, 2021)

i. *Artificial Intelligence* (uses, economics and ethics of AI),
ii. *Communities and Engagement* (for example, caring for the elderly, to encourage students to think beyond their immediate identities),
iii. *Digital Literacy* (tailored for whether the student intends to major in a science or in social science/humanities),
iv. *Design Thinking* (to develop potential for problem-solving) and *Data Literacy* (fundamentals of business analytics and data science), and
v. *Writing*

CHS's requirements aim to equip NUS undergraduates with the capacity to perceive and understand multiple perspectives, the skill to communicate effectively, an understanding of the value of contributing to their communities, and the ability to think beyond themselves.

Students also take a series of courses intended to promote independent learning, a rigorous approach to problem-solving, and an appreciation for tolerance and diversity. Finally, in their third and fourth year, CHS students take two interdisciplinary courses. This structure ensures that even a social science or humanities major will leave NUS with broad knowledge that includes data skills and, hopefully, an understanding of how a scientist thinks. And science students will know how a social scientist thinks.

An example of an interdisciplinary course is *Sporting Bodies*, offered jointly by the departments of Pharmacy, and Communications and New Media. *Sporting Bodies* covers issues like mental and physical health, gender and sexuality, and doping and substance abuse, through both cultural and scientific lenses (NUS College of Humanities & Sciences, 2023a). Another course, provided jointly by the departments of Economics and Chemistry, unites the physics and chemistry of technology with the environmental, economic, geopolitical and policy considerations of electric vehicles (NUS College of Humanities & Sciences, 2023b).

Like CHS, the College of Design and Engineering (CDE) was recently formed through the merging of faculties. The new College carves out a common curriculum (equivalent to 15 courses) and bumps up the number of electives students can take. CDE united the School of Design and Environment and the Faculty of Engineering, to "take advantage of the natural synergies and growing convergence between the fields of Engineering, Architecture, and Design" (NUS College of Design & Engineering, 2021, paragraph 1). Given the collaborative nature of so many professions, students need to know how to find integrated solutions for the real world by working across disciplines.

In addition to the interdisciplinary approaches of CHS and CDE, NUS offers a variety of programs and pedagogies that promote the kinds of skills and critical thinking we believe students will need throughout their careers.

27.3.2 Lifelong Learning at the School of Continuing and Lifelong Education

To build and support a culture of lifelong learning, NUS established a School of Continuing and Lifelong Education (SCALE) in 2016. SCALE unifies professional development and CET offerings at the university and supports the delivery of large-scale training. Its programs target the needs of working professionals and are therefore broad-based and multidisciplinary. To ensure its courses meet market demand, NUS works closely with industry associations, unions, and local and international employers.

In addition to programs open to any adult learner, SCALE services are available to corporations through "All-You-Can-Learn" (AYCL), a customizable training program to upskill and reskill employees. NUS currently has nine AYCL corporate clients.

27.3.2.1 Extended Enrollment Period, Stackable Courses, and New Master's Programs

To encourage alumni to return and to continue their learning journeys, enrollment at NUS is valid for 20 years from when students are first admitted as undergraduates. Alumni are eligible for continuing education courses curated from 17 NUS schools and faculties, with opportunities for an alumni discount of 5% as well as some government subsidies.

Where possible, programs are flexible, to accommodate the needs of working adults. This means not only short courses (which are compressed and typically last a few days) and evening/weekend offerings; some programs permit sequential credentialing. An expanding catalogue of courses and programs can be stacked into qualifications like graduate certificates, graduate diplomas, and Bachelor's or Master's degrees. For example, students in the Master of Social Sciences in Communication program receive a graduate certificate upon completion of 16 units, a graduate diploma with 24 units, and a Master's with 40 units (including a final project). This gives students the option to pause after completing the graduate certificate, and to return later to complete the Master's. Short courses can be taken all year round, whereas semester courses follow the academic calendar, with intakes in August and January.

In 2018, at the launch of the 20-year enrollment initiative, NUS Provost Ho Teck Hua observed:

> At NUS, we see lifelong learning as the key to ensuring that our students and alumni stay updated on the developments and disruptions that globalization and digital technologies are bringing to the workplace (...). It represents our strong commitment to our students and alumni, as well as our ambition to be their anchor for lifelong learning. (Teng, 2018, paragraph 7)

Some of NUS's new Master's programs offer specializations, and students can choose to get a graduate certification in that area, or to continue on for the full Master's. For example, our Master of Science in Industry 4.0 offers specializations such as Data Mining and Interpretation, Deep Learning for Industry, Digital Supply Chain, and Internet of Things. Some of these programs require students to complete a consulting project, working with a private, public, or non-profit organization, to invent an application, or solve an industry problem. They are mentored by a faculty advisor and a company representative, connections that may further tie the student to the industry.

A number of our new postgraduate programs (both Master's and Graduate Diplomas) are multidisciplinary, or interdisciplinary where relevant, and in some cases, allow prospective students with no prior domain knowledge to enroll in them. An example of a cross-disciplinary state-of-the-art CET course is the Lee Kuan Yew School of Public Policy's course, *3D Printing, Robots and Public Policy*. In this course, students explore the benefits and risks of 3D printing and robotics in a variety of industries, as well as the policy and regulatory implications in terms of growth, efficiency and equity, and competitiveness. This kind of course equips a future policymaker with the knowledge and skills to make informed decisions about how to maximize the benefits—and manage the risks—of 3D printing.

27.4 Building a Learning Culture

Lifelong learning needs to be more than just enabling working adults to take classes. Younger adults must be prepared—and desire—to learn, so they are driven to take up educational opportunities throughout their careers and lives. NUS has been working to increase the types of learning experiences we offer to our students, to excite and encourage them to take charge of their own learning.

27.4.1 Starting Them Young

In 2021, SCALE commissioned a survey to explore how polytechnic students and first-year undergraduates make decisions about their studies and future careers. Some 36% of survey respondents had not yet decided on a study or career path (many said they were too busy to even explore options). Another 43% had not made a study or career decision but were at least aware that they needed to do so. Only 21% of respondents had decided on a study and/or career path. While the university is committed to skilling its undergraduates for the future, students who do not seriously explore or understand their options are less likely to take maximum advantage of what we have to offer. From subsequent focus group discussions with selected respondents, teachers, and career counsellors, as well as representatives from youth organizations, SCALE found that the majority of youths today face challenges in:

1. Identifying their aspirations and career identity, including their skills and interests;
2. Understanding the impacts that issues of today and tomorrow will have on their future; and

3. envisioning how they can balance what they want in their future and what they value.

NUS, with funding from the Temasek Foundation, is developing short courses (typically three days) for pre-university students ages 15–19 to help them better appreciate the technological and cultural opportunities and challenges we/they will face in the future, e.g., sustainability, an ageing population, cyber security, and food security. These courses will urge them to start clarifying their interests and thinking about the future by considering where they want to make an impact, how will they make a living, and what careers are appealing. The courses will also familiarize them with NUS's approach to future skilling, by introducing critical thinking skills, interdisciplinary approaches, and openness to learning. Our hypothesis is that young people's ambitions and interests are only as diverse as those of the mentors and opportunities they have been exposed to; we aim to increase that diversity.

Through this project, we would like to help a young person better appreciate:

1. the linkages between topics learned in school and their applications in the real world;
2. the multi-disciplinary lenses and empathy that solving real-world problems requires; and
3. the drivers of change in Singapore, and the unique opportunities and challenges these pose, both for Singapore and for the young person.

Regardless of whether the young person chooses NUS, the intent is to encourage them to think rigorously about their higher education options, and to make decisions based on their own interests and abilities (rather than what their parents want them to do).

27.4.2 Design-Your-Own-Module (DYOM)[1]

DYOM was introduced in 2019, to encourage self-directed learning among undergraduates (Fig. 27.3). Students can take or design up to eight credits worth of electives (the equivalent of two courses). To push students to try new things,

---

[1] "Module" is the same thing as "course".

27 Anticipating the Future: Continuing ...

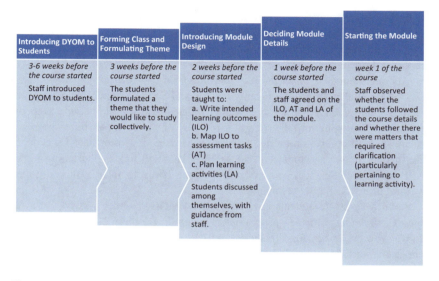

Fig. 27.3 Example of possible DYOM development timeline provided by Dr. Andi Sudjana Putra

DYOM courses are taken on a pass/fail basis. Students may choose from over 2,000 edX courses or an online course offered by AI Singapore (a program run by the Singapore government). Once completed, students receive NUS credit and are reimbursed for the cost of the course.

Alternatively, students may form groups based on their interests or social networks. The groups design their own course, with guidance from supervisors.

Students can create their own learning experiences, such as engaging guest speakers and conducting field trips and workshops (National University of Singapore, 2020b). In one DYOM course, students from diverse disciplines (engineering, arts and social sciences, and computing) worked together to create a rinser to prepare bottles and cans for recycling. In another course students learned to speak with their grandparents in the *Hokkien* dialect, which much of the younger generation has lost touch with.

Students may also choose to join recurring DYOMs. The Office of Student Affairs runs a course to train Peer Student Supporters. The curriculum includes mental health literacy, mental health issues and disorders, basic peer helping skills, and coping techniques. Peer Student Supporters provide a listening ear to fellow students, offer de-stressing activities like board games and craft work, and organize wellness projects. Social and emotional intelligence may go a long way in equipping students for the future (Bughin et al., 2018). There are currently about 40 Peer Student Supporters in training.

Another course, *Computational Reasoning in the Corporate World*, is a DYOM for students from the Faculty of Arts and Social Sciences who are interested in coding. Aimed at non-computing students who want to be able to incorporate simple coding into their work, this DYOM includes a part-time internship where students receive on-the-job training at participating companies. They learn the fundamentals of Python, how to analyze data, and link their training in the Arts and Social Sciences to problems they are likely to face in the corporate world: Future Skilling in action.

As of May 2022, students have taken 9,704 MOOCs under DYOM. An average of 248 students (or 13 groups) opted for group DYOMs. NUS's DYOM initiative won the award for "Teaching and Learning Strategy of the Year" at the Times Higher Education (THE) Awards Asia 2021 (National University of Singapore, 2021).

27.4.3 The Imaginarium

Learning can be intentional or incidental. The Imaginarium—a physical space housed in NUS's Central Library—is an example of a space that allows for incidental learning.

The Imaginarium offers an arsenal of technology, including a mixed reality room, a HoloLens, an Oculus, and 360 cameras that students can borrow. The Oculus has been used to test run a business idea, while 3D scanning and printing is used to print prototypes and other objects. The intention is for the space and tools to "future skill" our students by inspiring resourcefulness and creativity. For example, a designer might use Oculus to bring their designs to life; a media student might use a 3D printer to create props. The Imaginarium encourages students to think up applications for existing technologies and to look for new opportunities to apply their problem-solving skills. This allows them to transform future, unfamiliar challenges into opportunities.

Aside from providing a play space and tools, the Imaginarium supports experiential learning for specific courses. For example, the team developed apps for three Forensic Science courses that can be used with virtual reality and augmented reality technology, or on the web. In *Advanced Criminal Litigation—Forensics on Trial*, students inspect a crime scene through VR technology. They are able to view the evidence in detail, and to run tests. In *Forensic Toxicology and Poisons*, students can explore a crime scene in virtual reality, then use augmented reality to examine the evidence they find.

27.5 Emerging Area: Green Economy

In early 2021, the Singapore government unveiled *Green Plan 2030*, laying out sustainability and environmental goals for the next decade. Sustainability will be "a new engine for jobs and growth" (Ministry of Sustainability and the Environment, 2021, p. 5). The Green economy is also one of three high-growth areas identified by SkillsFuture (2021); the other two are the Digital and Care economies.

In a Hongkong and Shanghai Banking Corporation (HSBC) survey in 2021, 41% of institutional investors in Asia said that a lack of qualified candidates for hire has limited their ability to invest more heavily in Environmental, Social and Governance (ESG) (HSBC, 2021). An analysis of LinkedIn data by the Chartered Financial Analyst (CFA) Institute showed that while less than 1% of profiles listed sustainability-related skills, 6% of job postings sought them (Channel News Asia, 2021). There is a need to train the talent pool to meet the rising demand for Green Skills.

People are definitely interested in Green Jobs. According to a 2022 Accenture survey, 77% of Asia–Pacific respondents aged 15 to 39 said they want to work in the Green Economy within 10 years (Accenture, 2021). This means training for both young people and mid-career types. Rising participation in Green Skill training is part of a larger trend of increasing enrollment in CET, as adults want to add new skills and capabilities to their resumes or pivot to new industries and/or new job roles.

27.5.1 NUS: Matching Demand and Supply for Green Jobs

Using the labor research of SSG (2021), Green Skills were identified and clustered into groupings such as Environmental and Sustainability Management, Green Infrastructure, Resource Circularity and Decarbonization, etc. The skills groupings are used as a reference point for developing new (or reviewing existing) programs. After courses are developed, the learning outcomes are evaluated by selected stakeholders in government and corporates to ensure relevance.

Given the multidisciplinary nature of sustainability, NUS set up a CET Coordination Committee tasked with synchronizing efforts between Faculties/Schools that offer programs (everything from short courses to degrees) on sustainability and climate change. This is to minimize overlap in content and prevent internal cannibalization. It is also a forum to trade insights from the different experiences schools and faculties have from engaging their clients on sustainability.

27.6 Emerging Area: Data Everything

It is a data world. Much data is produced, and more organizations seek to leverage on the data collected. Naturally, they expect their employees to have data skills: how to get data, how to understand it, how to use it, how to protect it. McKinsey's survey of over 3,000 C-suite executives in seven countries, including the United States, Canada, and a few countries in Europe, showed that advanced IT and programming skills are seen as the most important expertise that will be needed in the next three years. The demand for basic cognitive skills, especially basic data input and processing skills, is expected to fall (Bughin et al., 2018).

Aside from relevant courses and programs, part of NUS's future skilling agenda is making sure that everyone—students, faculty, and staff—knows how to use data. Graduates will have to use data in their businesses and organizations: to increase efficiency, solve problems and try new ideas. NUS staff need data (and data skills) to figure out what new programs and courses the university should offer (and which should be retired), and to support policy changes in anything from HR to IT to infrastructure development. As a university, the community is the creator, author, and custodian of enormous amounts of data.

27.6.1 Data Literacy on Campus

In 2020, NUS introduced compulsory training in data literacy and basic artificial intelligence for all university staff. The two goals of this program were to foster data-driven decision-making on campus and develop staff capabilities. Using concepts and visualization skills taught in the course, students use data—often from campus sources—to address problems or inefficiencies, or to test new ideas. For example, a team from the Development Office found that there is a significant difference in how much NUS staff donated to the school, depending on their alumni status (National University of Singapore, 2020a). This information may be helpful in refining development strategies. This program has met some challenges in practice. Staff with some training and experience in data use did not find that the required introductory course challenged them or added to their knowledge base. Feedback is used to fine-tune each course run.

27.6.2 ALSET—Where Data is Pooled

The Institute for Applied Learning Sciences and Educational Technology (ALSET) maintains NUS's Data Lake, a living repository of educational data ready for research use by academics, policymakers, and innovators (Institute for Applied Learning & Educational Technology, 2022). The lake has data collected passively (such as LMS transaction logs, course bidding, and student housing), as well as those collected actively, through surveys and studies. NUS students and staff can access the data by submitting a request to the ALSET data governing bodies.

Dr. Robert Kamei, the founder of ALSET, formed an analytics team to pilot the use of educational data in his home school (Medicine). The team takes on research questions from management, faculty, or students. One project started with a student asking whether the order of clinical rotation affects student performance, and whether starting with a particular medical specialty is advantageous. The results showed only small differences, but these can probably be teased out as more data are accumulated.

The Data Lake is intended to be a resource to encourage inquiry and creative problem-solving. Access to the data is regulated (of course), but is available to staff or students who want, for example, to understand relevant behaviors (e.g., human traffic on campus) before they develop solutions for recycling. When curious-minded students or staff are empowered to question and develop answers to challenges, they are better prepared for the future.

27.7 Conclusion

As a major research institution enjoying a close relationship with the Singaporean government and with industry, we at NUS believe we are preparing our students for the future and for change. But the future remains difficult to predict. We recognize that the skills we teach today may become obsolete; there is of course no guarantee that our new programs provide "future-proofing". Predicting even five years into the future is difficult (otherwise we would have written this chapter five years ago!). Lifelong learning is a little like nuclear fusion: many people think it's a good idea, but perfection is always five or ten years in the future. And so, a degree of humility is warranted.

None of our challenges are unique to NUS. Universities, especially big research universities like NUS, can't change quickly or easily. Knowledge takes time to evolve, refine, and translate into classroom content. We can't lose sight of our primary mission as a research university—the production and dissemination of research. Nor should we forget the higher calling of a university: to help our students learn to be human. We cannot simply prepare students to be cogs in a machine, especially when the machine may change every few years. We must develop curiosity, creativity, and critical thinking. These are unlikely to *ever* become obsolete and may be what differentiates an exceptional worker from a good one.

By ensuring both broad- and deep-skilling in our undergraduate education, and with many new, more skill-specific and relevant master's programs, we look at a volatile and uncertain future with cautious optimism. We end our chapter with some recommendations.

Future Skills in Practice: Our Recommendations
- Allow and encourage undergraduates to explore a variety of approaches and perspectives, either through a set of broad requirements and/or by offering interdisciplinary approaches.
- Lifelong learning might not remain an optional education taken up by diligent and curious adults, but become a necessity for adults to stay relevant. Encouraging adult learners to return to school is not just the matter of opening courses, but understanding their needs and motivations. For example, where possible, offer flexibility and stackability in postgraduate studies.
- Not all learning must happen in the classroom, with a facilitator, and guided by a learning plan. Incidental, unstructured learning can happen within a university that provides the tools, space, and opportunities for students to stumble into. Without the pressure of grades, they learn to learn, and are empowered to find answers to challenges. These are skills that will last them beyond their undergraduate years.
- Build and maintain relationships with potential employers to ensure understanding of their needs and expectations in terms of competencies.

References

Accenture. (2021). *Youthquake meets green economy: Why businesses need to care*. https://www.accenture.com/ma-en/insights/strategy/youthquake-meets-green-economy.

Bughin, J., Hazan, E., Lund, S., Dahlström, P., Wiesinger, A., & Subramaniam, A. (2018). *Skill shift: Automation and the future of the workforce* (Discussion Paper). https://www.mckinsey.com/featured-insights/future-of-work/skill-shift-automation-and-the-future-of-the-workforce.

Channel News Asia. (27. December 2021). Green is the new gold: Focus on sustainability drives demand for ESG talent. *Channel News Asia*. https://www.channelnewsasia.com/business/money-mind-sustainability-demand-esg-talent-2402561.

Ellis, R. (7. December 2021). Talking leadership 5: Tan Eng Chye on fully embracing life-long learning. *Times Higher Education*. https://www.timeshighereducation.com/talking-leadership/talking-leadership-5-tan-eng-chye-fully-embracing-lifelong-learning.

HSBC. (2021). *Sustainable financing and investing survey—Asia report*. https://www.gbm.hsbc.com/en-gb/feed/sustainability/sfi-survey-asia-report.

Institute for Applied Learning and Educational Technology. (2022). *Data Lake*. https://nus.edu.sg/alset/data-lake/. Accessed 11 April 2023.

Ministry of Sustainability and the Environment. (2021). *Our key targets for the green plan*. https://www.greenplan.gov.sg/targets.

Ministry of Trade and Industry. (2023). *Industry transformation map overview*. https://www.mti.gov.sg/ITMs/Overview. Accessed 11 April 2023.

National University of Singapore. (2020a). *Enhancing capabilities with data literacy*. https://nus.edu.sg/inside-nus/stories/enhancing-capabilities-with-data-literacy. Accessed 11 April 2023.

National University of Singapore. (15. July 2020b). Hokkien, photography or food science? NUS students craft their own modules. *NUS News*. https://news.nus.edu.sg/hokkien-photography-or-food-science-nus-students-craft-their-own-modules/. Accessed 11 April 2023.

National University of Singapore. (8. December 2020c). New College of Humanities and Sciences by NUS delivers interdisciplinary learning at scale. *NUS News*. https://news.nus.edu.sg/new-college-of-humanities-and-sciences/.

National University of Singapore. (28. December 2021). Cultivating a generation of self-directed learners: NUS clinches Times Higher Education award for teaching strategy. *NUS News*. https://news.nus.edu.sg/cultivating-a-generation-of-self-directed-learners-nus-clinches-times-higher-education-award-for-teaching-strategy/.

Ng, W. K. (7. March 2022). Budget debate: More places for adult learners on the cards, new transition programme for mid-career workers. *The Straits Times*. https://www.straitstimes.com/singapore/politics/budget-debate-more-places-for-adult-learners-on-the-cards-new-transition-programme-for-mid-career-workers.

NUS College of Design and Engineering. (2021). *Introducing NUS college of design and engineering*. https://cde.nus.edu.sg/wp-content/uploads/2021/11/2021-1014-NUS-CDE-Brochure-Final-1.pdf.

NUS College of Humanities and Sciences. (2021). *Overview*. https://chs.nus.edu.sg/programmes/#prog-overview.

NUS College of Humanities and Sciences. (2023). *HS2903 sporting bodies: Interdisciplinary modules I & II*. https://chs.nus.edu.sg/programmes/common-curriculum/interdisciplinary-module-i-ii/.

NUS College of Humanities and Sciences. (2023). *HS2904 Driving Towards the Future: Battery Electric Vehicles: Interdisciplinary Modules I & II*. https://chs.nus.edu.sg/programmes/common-curriculum/interdisciplinary-module-i-ii/.

Singapore Workforce Development Agency. (2011). *Overview of Singapore workforce development agency: Workshop on structural reform Singapore 10–12 August 2011*. Asia-Pacific Economic Cooperation. http://mddb.apec.org/Documents/2011/SOM/WKSP/11_som_wksp_013.pdf.

SkillsFuture Singapore. (2020). *About us. SkillsFuture Singapore and workforce Singapore*. https://www.ssg-wsg.gov.sg/about.html.

SkillsFuture Singapore. (2021). *Skills demand for the future economy*. https://www.skillsfuture.gov.sg/docs/default-source/initiatives/ssg-skills_demand_for_the_future_economy_2021.pdf.

Teng, A. (6. March 2018). Lifelong learning scheme to be open to all NUS alumni. *The Straits Times.*. https://www.straitstimes.com/singapore/education/lifelong-learning-scheme-to-be-open-to-all-nus-alumni.

The Heritage Foundation. (2023). *Index of economic freedom—Singapore*. https://www.heritage.org/index/country/singapore.

The World Bank. (2019). *Overview*. https://www.worldbank.org/en/country/singapore/overview. Accessed 11 April 2023.

The World Bank. (2020). *Human capital index, Singapore, 2017–2020*. https://databank.worldbank.org/source/human-capital-index.

The World Bank. (2020). *The Human capital index 2020 Update: Human capital in the time of COVID-19*. https://openknowledge.worldbank.org/entities/publication/93f8fbc6-4513-58e7-82ec-af4636380319. Accessed 11 April 2023.

The World Bank. (2021). *World development indicators: GDP growth (annual %) of Singapore, United States, Europe & Central Asia, 2000–2021*. https://databank.worldbank.org/source/world-development-indicators.

The World Bank. (2021). *World development indicators: GDP per capita (current US$)—Singapore*.

World Economic Forum. (2020). *The future of jobs report 2020*. http://www3.weforum.org/docs/WEF_Future_of_Jobs_2020.pdf.

Miriam Green is a Principal Policy Analyst in the Office of the Senior Deputy President and Provost at the National University of Singapore. Miriam moved to Singapore in 2019 to join NUS, where her work focuses on lifelong learning. She has worked in higher education for many years, including at the University of California (Office of the President) and at the Central European University. Miriam holds a BA in German Language & Literature from the George Washington University, a Master of International Studies from the Claremont Graduate University, and an MBA from the University of Pittsburgh.

Christalle Tay was an analyst with the NUS Futures Office at the time of writing. The Futures Office is a unit within the President's Office that looks at the future of higher education, to provide alternative perspectives to the university leadership. She was trained in journalism, and obtained her BA in Communication and New Media from NUS. She now works for a social business that provides access services for people with disabilities.

Ye-Her Wu heads SCALE-Global, an incubator for lifelong learning models. She is also an advisor at the NUS Futures Office. Ye-Her works at the intersection of business and government. Previously, she oversaw executive education and alumni relations at the LKY School of Public Policy. Prior to NUS, she led public policy advocacy and business development at a social enterprise, served in strategy and policy appointments in government, and was a consultant at EY. Ye-Her has an MBA from MIT, which she attended under a Fulbright scholarship. She holds an MSc in Criminology from LSE, and a BSc in Sociology from University of Bristol.

Open Access This chapter is licensed under the terms of the Creative Commons Attribution 4.0 International License (http://creativecommons.org/licenses/by/4.0/), which permits use, sharing, adaptation, distribution and reproduction in any medium or format, as long as you give appropriate credit to the original author(s) and the source, provide a link to the Creative Commons license and indicate if changes were made.

The images or other third party material in this chapter are included in the chapter's Creative Commons license, unless indicated otherwise in a credit line to the material. If material is not included in the chapter's Creative Commons license and your intended use is not permitted by statutory regulation or exceeds the permitted use, you will need to obtain permission directly from the copyright holder.

Aiming to Build Future Skills for Society 5.0: Educational DX (Digital Transformation) of University Education in Japan

28

Keiko Ikeda

Abstract

This chapter focuses on the concept of Society 5.0, which emerged in response to the current trend of rapid internationalization and globalization in Japan. Society 5.0 aims to improve the quality of people's daily lives and make all diverse generations members of a "smart society" without leaving them behind. Higher education institutions (HEIs) will further promote close collaboration with industry and provide human resource development and education curricula that place the highest priority on the individual Future Skills needed by the rapidly changing society. In order to realize this new challenge, various urgent efforts are needed, including reform of university governance and introduction of curriculum design specialists into the institutional culture in Japan.

28.1 Introduction

There is a growing awareness in Japan of the critical need to promote the internationalization of universities (known as *Internationalization at Home*) with the purposeful integration of international and intercultural dimensions into the

---

K. Ikeda (✉)
Professor in the Division of International Affairs, Kansai University, Osaka, Japan
e-mail: keikoike@kansai-u.ac.jp

© The Author(s) 2024
U.-D. Ehlers and L. Eigbrecht (eds.), *Creating the University of the Future*, Zukunft der Hochschulbildung - Future Higher Education,
https://doi.org/10.1007/978-3-658-42948-5_28

549

formal and informal curriculum for all students within domestic learning environments. This internationalization is undertaken to ensure that a wider range of people can readily engage with more international educational experiences, including opportunities to have cross-cultural encounters and to afford for greater skill development of intercultural competencies to better become global citizens through their university studies. To make this opportunity inclusive, rather than relying solely on traditional student mobility exchanges, it is important to harness the use of digital technology. In this paper, I would like to focus on the fact that Japanese higher education institutions (hereafter 'HEIs') which have gained a great deal of experience and lessons learned from the COVID-19 pandemic, have finally upshifted their gears to actualize digital transformation (hereafter 'DX'). The prospective of Japan's transformation trend naturally foresees the 'next stage' of a post-pandemic future, with much advanced digitally enhanced infrastructure for every dimension of our lives.

One of the trends driving DX in Japanese university education is the promotion of building a next generation of society, namely "Society 5.0." In its argument to promote this concept, it is perceived that the society will transform through a new phase with much acceleration in the coming years. The phase perhaps better and more popularly known as "Industry 4.0" (the fourth industrial revolution) in the other parts of the world has started around 2011, with the digitalization of manufacturing and production. The social infrastructure represented by efforts to visualize information and link it to new business models has been established. With regards to the Society 5.0 conceptualization, following on from the several years since Industry 4.0 was proposed in Germany in 2016 (European Parliament, 2016), Japan has come up with 'Society 5.0.' Japan describes its initiative in these terms as making a purposeful effort to create a new social ecosystem and an economic model case by fully incorporating the technological innovations of the fourth industrial revolution.

This chapter will first introduce the basic concept of Society 5.0, describing what it captures as the design of the near-future society we are heading towards. It then ties the concept with the challenges and opportunities which Japan potentially holds to realize such a society. Finally, it revisits how higher education must be actively involved in producing the "agents" of Society 5.0 through their university curricula with an emphasis on the point that transformation of education, or paradigm shift in mindset in HEIs, is inevitable. This is precisely done in order to assure future ready skills that are seen as even more necessary graduate attributes of their students.

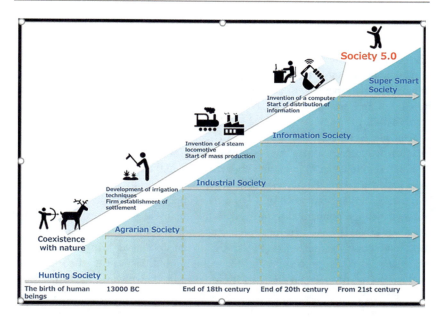

Fig. 28.1 Evolution of Societies up to Society 5.0 (Keidanren, 2016)

28.2 Emergence of the "Society 5.0" Concept

Society 5.0 was proposed in the 5th Science and Technology Basic Plan (Cabinet Office Japan, 2015) as representing a future society that Japan could and should aspire to. It follows from the development of the so-called hunting society (Society 1.0), agricultural society (Society 2.0), industrial society (Society 3.0), and information society (Society 4.0). Figure 28.1, adopted from the Keidanren (Japan Economic Organization) homepage, illustrates the increment of society in different stages thus far.

Digital transformation will dramatically change many aspects of society. It touches on private lives, public administration, industrial infrastructure, and education. Society 5.0 addresses several key pillars: infrastructure improvement, a rise of industries with tech-advanced system such as finance tech, agriculture tech, ed tech, healthcare, logistics, and widely used AI. AI exerts its capabilities not just in cyberspace, but in the physical world through robots. AI and robots will replace or support humans in carrying out routine tasks, for example with a transition in public transportation to the use of autonomous driving. We already have seen some realizations of these transformations in daily living, and it is likely such transformations will occur with greater frequency and across broader domains of activity. Distributed ledger technology in finance tech is worth remarking upon here, with such ledger technologies as blockchain representing possible improvements in transaction efficacy with a high level of transparency and reliability.

Finance technology, IoT (Internet of Things), AI, and robotics—the emergence of such technologies may fundamentally transform the way in which societies operate. As indicated in the figure above, Society 5.0 reflects on such emergence. It is called a *super* smart society, meaning that it not only uses information and communication technologies (ICT) to increase operational efficiency, share information with the public and improve both the quality of government services and citizen welfare, but also features higher degrees of integration, better collaboration, and value maximization. While digital transformation brings a new stage of society, it is also important that technologies and data are used so that people can pursue diverse and enriched lifestyles in their own ways. In realizing this increased diversity, the Basic Plan report states Society 5.0 requires rich imaginations to identify a variety of needs and challenges scattered throughout society, then come up with scenarios to solve the challenges creatively utilizing available digital technologies. Here, Society 5.0 is conceived as a product of the combination of DX with the imagination and creativity of diverse people (Keidanren, 2017).

Why is Society 5.0 important for a country like Japan? There are many reasons, but one significant example is that Japan is a rapidly aging country, and it needs innovative solutions to deal with rapidly occurring demographic changes. In 2050, an estimated 40 percent of the population will be 65 years and older, while the average life expectancy in Japan is now reaching 85 years. In such a "super-aging" society, challenges will not only be to have enough caretaking, but there needs to be ways to develop new pharmaceuticals or assist systems for the elderly to stay independent. With the lowering birthrate, the workforce population is declining. The rate of underpopulation is indeed hard to ignore. For example, the Japanese birthrate fell below 2 (births/woman) in 1975, hit a low of 1.3 in 2005, and has been as low as 1.4 from then until now (Cabinet Office Japan, 2019; Kato, 2018). One of the negative impacts of such demographic changes is increasing economic stagnation. The Japanese economy grew by less than 2% in 2017 for the sixth year in a row (UNESCO, 2019), due to ever-intensifying global competition, the changing structure of value creation in the new digital economy, shrinking population and ageing, and growing fiscal pressure from rising government expenditure on social security.

To compensate for these disadvantages, technology is seen as one way to remedy the challenge. Japan is already famous for its robot developments, and in Society 5.0 smart robotics are also seen as a key player to provide solutions. As assist systems could enable a prolonged independent life, robots can take over work in elderly care. And finally, AI can help to develop new pharmaceutical drugs as well as support elderly people in everyday life. While information society (in Society 4.0) enabled humans to access information from anywhere in the world, with AI innovation (in Society 5.0), people can gain ready access to a high level of abilities from anywhere (i.e., conceptualized as "distribution and commoditization of abilities") and this affordance will drastically enhance individual capabilities beyond what had been thought plausible. This means that digitalization and DX will not leave anyone behind with technological advancement facilitating and easing the use of technology by everyday citizens.

What does it look like in a more practical sense? A UNESCO online article (2019) illustrates some specific illustrations of how a life would look like in Society 5.0. In Society 5.0, autonomous vehicles and drones will bring goods and services to people in depopulated areas. A doctor will be able to consult her patients in the comfort of their own home via a special tablet, and medication will be delivered to them instantly. A robot may be vacuuming the carpet in a house. At the nursing home down the road, another robot may be helping to care for the aged ones. In the nursing home's kitchen, the refrigerator will be monitoring the condition of stocked foods to cut down on waste. The town will be powered by energy supplied in flexible and decentralized ways to meet the inhabitants' specific needs. On the outskirts, autonomous tractors will be toiling in the fields while in downtown, advanced cyber-physical systems will be maintaining vital infrastructure and standing by to replace retiring technicians and craftspeople, should there not be enough young people to fill the gap.

28.3 Aiming Global Employability for Society 5.0: New Pedagogy Through Education DX

While Society 5.0 sounds like a well-served philosophy, implementation of it as outcome (the goal) through actions will come with some challenges. There are some obstacles to realize this social transformation. Among various challenges, *Keidanren* points out lack of qualified personnel pools in order to bring out Society 5.0. This is a rather critical aspect to take up for educators at HEIs. What

Future Skills will the people in Society 5.0 need, particularly those who would become the main players to run the new ecosystem? In other words, we can elaborate to say that what is at stake here is to redefine (global) employability for Society 5.0; regardless of types of industry, an attractive future hire would require the ability to adapt to a rapidly changing world. They would also need to have a more complex level of understanding of information science so that they are able to stay productive and creative in their professions. What kind of education/training will be then expected at HEIs in Japan to meet these expectations? Are the Japanese HEIs ready to generate "future ready" graduates?

Smith et al. (2018) have defined that employability is not an outcome, but a process, and skills to facilitate the individual to employ their abilities in lifelong and life-wide contexts for private and public good are desired by future employers. Education must give students the skills to both cope with that changing society and, furthermore, for them to embrace and lead that change (Future Skills). One challenge will be to train enough IT engineers to drive Society 5.0. The Council for Science, Technology and Innovation (CSTI) estimates that by 2030, the IT industry will be short of 789,000 talents. This figure was released by the Ministry of Economy, Trade and Industry (Cabinet Office Japan, 2019).

Society 5.0 will demand multiple employability dimensions. Some of the illustrations can be shared here. In 2018, MEXT (Ministry of Education, Culture, Sports, Science and Technology) has issued a vision statement on human resources and forms of learning ("Building upon discussions in Minister's Meeting on Human Resource Development for Society 5.0"). In the document, the skills needed to discover and create leaps in knowledge towards technological innovation and to create new values were emphasized. To do so, they list the ability to accurately interpret and respond to writing and information, the ability to engage in and apply scientific thinking and inquiry, curiosity, and inquisitiveness to be of essential quality. All these represent important Future Skills in Society 5.0. Qasrawi and BeniAbdelrahman (2020) have proposed that Higher Order Thinking Skills (HOTS) should be a priority at HEIs to cultivate the skills requested. HOTS is an over-average cognitive thinking approach developed from cognitive concepts and methods. More precisely, HOTS comprises problem-solving, taxonomic flourishing and taxonomy learning.

In 2017, Society 5.0 took on a new significance by making a major contribution to the Sustainable Development Goals (SDGs). Keidanren even revised its Charter of Corporate Behavior in November 2017, calling for member corporations to proactively deliver on the SDGs through the realization of Society 5.0. Adopting goals that matter to all people in the world into the concept, Society 5.0's conceptualization further promotes global corporations to realize its targeted outcome. Naturally, those who become key players to make changes towards it must develop not just local employability but global employability. Candidates with soft skills and cross-cultural understanding and tolerance are qualities that are required for bridging the gap across cultural boundaries. Fostering learning attitudes which show a strong willingness to learn and constantly invest in new knowledge building is also highly valued (PwC, 2022). A powerful trend in Japanese HEIs in recent years has been the emphasis on global human resources, or in other words, people who have no difficulty in working transnationally. Traditionally, the Japanese have been conscious that international interaction is not their strength, largely due to their poor English (Sato & Arimoto, 2015). For quite some time, Japanese universities have been making it a priority to educate students in today's global context and to enroll international students. Due to the COVID-19 impact, and with a growing awareness of the importance of digital technology and online education modalities, I will highlight some of the efforts to nurture global employability at HEIs in aiming to meet the human resource demands for Society 5.0. Future Skills must thus relate to a global context and, in this approach, be reflective of the Sustainable Development Goals—and their promotion must be inclusive.

At Kansai University, a private comprehensive university with a student body of approximately 30,000 in the west of Japan (Osaka), an online symposium on Educational DX in Higher Education[1] was recently held dealing with the theme of what aims a university should focus on in any process of transformation. The keynote speaker, Dr. Toru Iiyoshi of Kyoto University, began by stating that it is important for education to be DX (as in "deluxe") (i.e., it should seek to spread and expand) through DX (as in "digital transformation"). The symposium considered that the significance of educational DX is *not* to simply use advanced digital technology, or opt for online education because of the pandemic impact, but to employ digital technology and online modalities to encourage socially engaged and innovative processes of learning and promote Future Skills. The pedagogy at HEIs will need an upgrade or even further, a paradigm shift from the conventional education.

What would happen if we shed the light of possibility of DX here? Not all problems will be solved, but issues of distance and traveling cost, as just one example, can be alleviated by enabling coordinated activities online. It would also be possible to use on-demand and social apps to enable high school students to learn and, if they wish, communicate with learning content provided by universi-

---

[1] March 2022, https://www.kansai-u.ac.jp/Kokusai/info/index.php?m=267.

Fig. 28.2 Global Smart Classroom (GSC) at Kansai University

ties, even when there are different times available for participation. Furthermore, with this concept, there is no need to keep the connectivity within the single country. It would also be possible to practice multiple university collaborations among global south-to-south countries, or global south-to-north regions, and so on. Equitable and inclusive international education has not been particularly successful until now, without having to travel abroad or have offshore campuses involved. Yet with DX, HEIs in isolated regions such as islands or rural areas of a country can now also be a part of active participation. The developmental realization of education beyond any conventional modality is the 'DX/deluxe of education', and DX (digital transformation) is what makes this possible.

As a case in point, Fig. 28.2 illustrates a global smart classroom at Kansai University, launched in March 2021. In this classroom, students can either be present on-site or participate online. There are sensitive ceiling microphone panels installed, so the students do not need to use individual microphones or speak loudly in order to hear and be heard well by the remote participants. A special application called CLASS is in use for the class conduct, in which multiple camera projections of image can be broadcast at the same time. The instructor, together with the students in the classroom, has access to a rich source of information to make themselves feel immersed in one shared space, no matter where they join from. The interactive support functions designed in the application facilitate further participation as well. In Society 5.0, no one should be left behind, and the sky should be the only limit to generate innovative and creative collaborative pedagogies with our technology. This environment was created to strengthen the student experience in a hyflex mode of classroom, connecting both those online and internationally participating, as well as those who are on campus. The impact by alternating to an online mode of international education has contributed to reducing inequality in internationalization by reaching out to more students from a wider range of regions, more global south allies than global north, through the use of virtual exchanges, collaborative online learning, and the explicit internationalization of the curriculum/at home.

When we bring an equity mindset to digitally transforming the education, those who gain more may be the ones who actually "give" and "share." Going into the 3rd year of the pandemic phase, many educators have had a recognition that teaching online does not mean simply recording a traditional lecture and posting it to the web or using a videoconference platform to deliver the same lecture online as the instructor would give on campus.

Effective online education requires teaching and learning methods that engage students dynamically in an enjoyable and stimulating education experience. Interaction and engagement are closely related and even used interchangeably. Student engagement is developed through interaction (Anderson, 2003), and fostering interaction is important in online learning. Engagement strategies must be embedded in online modes of pedagogy, to provide positive learner experiences including active learning opportunities, such as participating in collaborative group work, having students facilitate presentations and discussions, sharing resources actively, creating course assignments with hands- on components, and integrating case studies and reflections. For example, in a survey-based study, Martin and Bolliger (2018) found that icebreaker/introduction discussions and working collaboratively using online communication tools were rated the most beneficial engagement strategies in the learner-to-learner modes of learning activities. They also found that students mentioned working on real-world projects and having discussions with structured or guiding questions were the most beneficial. Utilizing education technology and digitally enhanced classrooms can bring out enriched social engagement in the learning process.

Digital transformation for education, as a part of the Society 5.0 picture, does not just stop at adopting simple e-learning modalities. Goger et al. (2022) consider how learning processes and modalities have evolved rapidly, possibly accelerated by the pandemic impact. The HEIs modes of teaching and learning now show Phase 2.0 mainly, meaning that for conceptual and foundational learning, online courses and remote instruction via video conferencing tools are the dominant cases. More recent technologies have come about, such as machine learning, learning platforms, virtual reality, and distributed ledger technologies including blockchain, and these have enabled many more fundamental shifts in how education functions. Technology advancement today is about to take us to a next phase, Education 3.0. The centralized, traditional education model today will be no longer sustainable in the near future. Learning happens increasingly *outside* the brick-and-mortar classrooms, but on online platforms, and people will start learning among the communities of the same needs, not necessarily those being one's school mates. Learning will be far more international than it used to be then. Students travel to different countries to improve their employability prospects by getting trained by various education providers. Given this projection in the future, we can clearly see that HEIs, in Japan and elsewhere, do not really have much affordance of time to resist the changes. This educational model thus engages students in an inclusive way to make Future Skills learning more accessible.

28.4 Challenges Ahead for Japan: Socio-Cultural Conservative Mindset as a "Pull" Factor

The pandemic undoubtedly led to a switch to online courses, but once things settled down the number of institutions switching to face-to-face courses increased across the board, and as of 2022 only a small percentage of institutions are maintaining and offering online courses. There are a variety of factors contributing to this face-to-face approach, but the most significant "pull" factor is the lack of trust in communication through digital communication technology. It is true that all the educational practices with digital technologies and internet connectivity should be further promoted in higher education today, yet at the same time all of them present challenges for those who are familiar with the conventional methods, which presumes education takes place in a brick-and-mortar classroom setting.

For instance, despite the renewed spread of the coronavirus, about 70% of the nation's 23 top universities have increased the ratio of face-to-face classes in the 2021 academic year compared to 2020 (Endo & Lee, 2021). The 23 institutions are former Japanese imperial universities such as the University of Tokyo and Kyoto University, and renowned private universities such as Waseda and Keio universities. According to the same survey report, at Waseda University, about 70% of students who responded to an interview survey requested face-to-face classes. "There is a clash between increasing students' opportunities to come to school and thoroughly preventing infection" (ibid.), a school representative said.

Similarly, many universities have switched to face-to-face classes even though there is no prospect of controlling the infection, they are concerned about students feeling isolated.

28.5 The "Push" Factors

There are some efforts to counteract the pulling factors at a national level. On January 7, 2022, the Japanese government released the "Roadmap for the Utilization of Educational Data", a 53-page document outlining an ambitious plan to harness information and communications technology to create "a society where anyone can learn in their own way, anytime, anywhere, with anyone" (Digital Agency Japan, 2022). They propose that they will realize the roadmap by 2030. The scope of this proposal is wide, extending to lifelong and recurrent education. The focus is on the creation of a school learning environment that makes optimal use of digital technology to shift from the teacher-centered, "chalk and talk" mode of instruction to a more personalized, interactive, and self-directed learning experience (Matsumoto, 2022).

At the higher educational level, a proposal to exceptionally relax credit limits for online classes at Japanese universities under certain conditions, currently set at 60 of the 124 credits required for graduation, was recently approved by a working team of the education minister's advisory body (Ministry of Education, Culture, Sports, Science and Technology, 2022). The reasons behind this push are diverse, but a few aspects worth remarking on here are prominent. The first is the significant paucity of incoming international students to educational institutions in the country. The more online classes are offered, the easier it will be for students in China, South Korea, and Southeast Asia, where the time difference with Japan is minimal, to "attend" classes at Japanese universities from their home countries. The cost required for their registration to a foreign institution will be reduced, thus it can provide a much wider population of students with opportunities to "study (virtually) abroad." Following the blended mobility framework that has been well adopted by European Commission's Erasmus+, Japan can also propose a combination of online and on-site learning at a university. Those who may not be able to afford the time and money for a full degree abroad can now consider undertaking a blended program provided the physical mobility component can be reduced in length.

Another reason is ease of management. For a large-scale university like Kansai University, maintenance of multiple large lecture halls (up to 1,000-person capacity) with air conditioning can use considerable electricity every day. By shifting the focus to online classes, large lecture halls may no longer be needed, leading to eased regulations on physical space such as site and building area. It also contributes towards SDGs by cutting down on energy consumption of large buildings on campus.

The third reason is most relevant to the discussion at stake in this paper; the need for digital literacy improvement is recognized now as an essential foundation for graduate attributes or Future Skills. Online class experience enables strengthening students' digital competence. Multi-lateralized learning, in which students can study specialized subjects in their pursuing discipline while simultaneously developing soft skills such as digital literacy will be actively encouraged in the future. The Japan Business Association (*Keidanren*) agrees, and they have called for the upper limit's removal in a January 2022 proposal so that students have access to flexible learning opportunities. The education ministry will continue discussing specific requirements for receiving the special exception and aims to revise the Standards for the Establishment of Universities by the end of academic year 2022. The transformation of work styles has already begun in Japan. The pandemic has certainly altered working sentiments. The country's willingness to change their ways is worth a remark to project a possible workplace dynamic of the future. According to a survey undertaken by Hays Japan, Asia prioritizes getting everyone on board the digitalization journey, to implement flexibility and encourage trust within employees who are working remotely. Additionally, the proliferation of remote working has exacerbated the need for remote orientation and remote leadership training (Hays, 2021, p. 46).

Commonly in Asia and elsewhere, e-learning represents a fast-growing space, with schools at various levels now looking at incorporating this into their curriculums. One of the most recent responses by HEIs in Japan has been the establishment of a cross-institutionally operated virtual learning platform called "Japan Virtual Campus (JV-Campus)". MEXT (Education ministry in Japan) has funded the platform and a total of 19 university projects are using it to offer their education programs to overseas as well as domestic student population cross-institutionally (Fig. 28.3).

Many of these programs are free of charge and available to anyone regardless of where they reside. Another feature about the education programs on the JV-Campus is that many of them are not given official credentials provided by a university. The length of learning planned for each program is relatively shorter than what is offered in a regular semester. This is intentional since the administration of JV-Campus is planning to implement a micro-credential system to advance the value of learning in the very near future, which will lead to upskilling and reskilling education for various targets, such as prospective university students (from

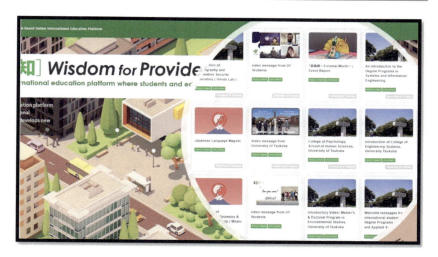

Fig. 28.3 Japan Virtual Campus (University of Tsukuba, 2023)

abroad or high schools within Japan), those who seek for new skill developments for career change, and/or those who wish to improve their skills needs to sustain their professions in business.

With a rapid shift in a workforce portfolio due to changing new business models and corporate strategies for Society 5.0, education and capacity building trainings for continuous learning regardless of their formal degree is high on demand in Japan, similarly to the rest of the world. In addition to macro-degrees, such as university degrees, micro-degrees obtained from micro-credentials and digital badge certificates will be given further acknowledgement to add value to one's employability.

28.6 Consequences of Skill Needs from the Reform Strategy

A report issued in 2020 by METI (Ministry of Economy, Trade and Industry) in Japan has clearly pointed out that companies need to modify their approaches to human capital management and their relationship with individuals according to changes in society and make a shift to an open and equal relationship with the aim of creating value, regardless of past successes (see Fig. 28.4).

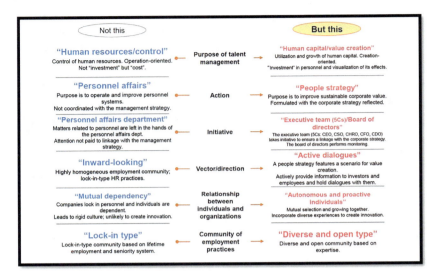

Fig. 28.4 Direction of Reformation for corporate strategy for human capital (adopted from METI, 2020)

The Report of the Study Group on Improvement of Sustainable Corporate Value and Human Capital (Ministry of Economy, Trade and Industry, 2020) as summarized in Fig. 28.4, emphasizes that the COVID-19 crisis is a good opportunity for questioning "common knowledge," resisting "inertial thinking" and initiating a movement for significant change. Corporate strength to transform will generate divides between companies who can make a creative and flexible transformation to make the maximum use of human capital and companies who cannot.

As shown in the above figure, people strategies of companies need to enable new business models and corporate strategies to be implemented, in order to lead to an improvement of sustainable corporate value—and the strategies can also promote Future Skills development of the employees. For this purpose, the report points out that the executive team of a company, in particular the CHRO (Chief Human Resource Officer), should take the initiative to formulate a people strategy, and core members (5Cs: CEO [Chief Executive Officer], CSO [Chief Strategy Officer], CHRO, CFO [Chief Financial Officer] and CDO [Chief Digital Officer]) of the executive team need to work together to implement the strategy. There are some specific contents of this people strategy worth remarking upon

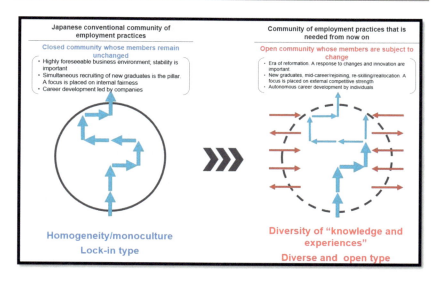

Fig. 28.5 Necessary change in a community of employment practices (Adopted by METI, 2020)

here. The report says a new workforce portfolio allows a diverse range of individuals to play an active role, and such a portfolio (named as "dynamic workforce portfolio") realizes diversity and inclusion of knowledge and experiences of individuals. The strategy promises re-skilling and continuous learning to fill a gap between skills for realizing the future vision and the current skills. With the diverse talents to be embraced, the factor of working without constraints in terms of time and place is given more importance as well, especially due to the impact of the COVID-19 pandemic.

Traditionally, Japanese companies have been operating in a closed community whose members remain unchanged, locked personnel. The belief behind this is that career development is supposed to be led by companies, but not by individuals. A closed network will end up in a rather homogeneous like-minded community. With the right transformation being pursued, individuals will become autonomous and proactive and have an equal relationship with companies, instead of locking-in individuals. For this to be realized, each company needs to promote a community of diverse and open employment practices based on mutual selection by companies and individuals (Fig. 28.5). A focus should be placed on external competitive strength (Future Skills) of the individual candidates, regardless of educational paths.

This personnel strategy reform certainly looks at Society 5.0 as providing the next context for the prospective human resources as projected in the report. To meet the industry expectations, Japan's educational models must seek a radical paradigm shift. Reflecting on this direction of transformation, the educational sector is also responsible to change its scheme of operation drastically. Competency-driven, inter-operable educational design with other education providers and institutions overseas should be the core curriculum at HEIs, instead of summative assessments to evaluate students on paper tests for a letter grade, which is only reputed by a specific university system. Flexible routes of education should be given more credit, allowing more student population to appreciate opportunities for higher learning and Future Skills development. Adopting new dynamics such as micro-credentialing is one of such efforts.

28.7 Conclusion

In this paper, I have explored various new trends for Japanese HEIs with regards to (i) internationalization, (ii) digitalization and digital transformation, and (iii) curriculum transformation to better meet the demands for the next phase "Society 5.0". The COVID-19 pandemic has certainly stimulated and convinced various stakeholders that this is an inevitable change. While there are many "pull" factors ahead, there are also "push" factors to strongly proceed with new ways. Perhaps the strongest push factor among many would be from pressure generated by private sectors. The industry sees the world demands with up-to-speed pacing, whereas the educational sectors tend to stay in their own bubbles (or "ivory towers") and miss out a chance to realize them. A Society 5.0 conceptualization assumes a backcasting approach, which is a planning that starts with defining a desirable future and works backwards to identify an (educational) program design to take place at present. In other words, it aims to generate a future ready skill set and mindset, i.e., Future Skills development. It is highly important and essential for the HEIs to attend to other sectors' actions sensitively and seek out to establish a multidimensional collaboration with them.

Future Skills in Practice: Our Recommendations

Suggestion 1. Build Multiple Communication Channels Across Different Sectors

Future Skills dynamics desired in different sectors may be different from each other. In order to have an accurate grasp of the needs, consistent communication among the sectors is essential.

Suggestion 2. Work with Professional Instructional Designers and Curriculum Advisors

For HEIs to design a successful and effective curriculum to build students' Future Skills, professional assistance is most desired. For many Japanese HEIs, typically, ID professionals are not on campus. Generating such a new role in a HEI is an urgent action on demand.

Suggestion 3. Work on the Governance and Institutional Culture to Dynamically Change Educational Curriculum According to the Needs of the Society

Perhaps the most challenging mission is to transform the HEI culture to become willing to stay flexible and ready to change its educational curriculum. The whole governance ecosystem may need to be addressed to enable the changes.

References

Anderson, T. (2003). Modes of interaction in distance education: Recent developments and research questions. In M. G. Moore & W. G. Anderson (Eds.), *Handbook of Distance Education* (pp. 129–144). Lawrence Erlbaum Associates.

Cabinet Office Japan. (2015). *Report on the 5th science and technology basic plan: Council for science, technology and innovation.* https://www8.cao.go.jp/cstp/kihonkeikaku/5basicplan_en.pdf.

Cabinet Office Japan. (2019). *Annual report on the declining birthrate 2019 (Summary).* https://www8.cao.go.jp/shoushi/shoushika/whitepaper/measures/english/w-2019/pdf/gaiyoh.pdf.

Digital Agency Japan. (2022). *Roadmap on the Utilization of Data in Education.* https://www.digital.go.jp/assets/contents/node/basic_page/field_ref_resources/0f321c23-517f-439e-9076-5804f0a24b59/20220307_en_education_outline_01.pdf.

Endo, H., & Lee, Y. (2021). *70% of 23 major Japanese universities to increase face-to-face classes: Mainichi survey.* https://mainichi.jp/english/articles/20210426/p2a/00m/0na/024000c. Accessed 9 Febr. 2023.

European Parliament. (2016). *Industry 4.0: Study for the ITRE committee*. https://op.europa.eu/en/publication-detail/-/publication/1b970736-9acb-11e6-868c-01aa75ed71a1.

Goger, A., Parco, A., & Vegas, E. (2022). *The promises and perils of new technologies to improve education and employment opportunities*. https://www.brookings.edu/wp-content/uploads/2022/03/Digital-innovations_FINAL.pdf.

Hays. (2021). *Uncovering the DNA of the future workplace in Asia*. https://www.hays.com.my/dna-of-the-future-workplace.

Kato, H. (2018). The analysis on disparities of fertility rate of Japanese municipalities. *Public Policy Review, 14*(1), 1–24.

Keidanren. (2016). *Toward realization of the new economy and society: Reform of the economy and society by the deepening of "society 5.0"*. http://www.keidanren.or.jp/en/policy/2016/029_outline.pdf

Keidanren. (2017). *Revitalizing Japan by realizing society 5.0: Action plan for creating the society of the future*. http://www.keidanren.or.jp/en/policy/2017/010_overview.pdf.

Martin, F., & Bolliger, D. U. (2018). Engagement matters: Student perceptions on the importance of engagement strategies in the online learning environment. *Online Learning, 22*(1), 205–222. https://doi.org/10.24059/olj.v22i1.1092.

Matsumoto, M. (2022). *Is the digital transformation of education a realistic, Sensible goal?*. https://www.tokyofoundation.org/research/detail.php?id=878.

Ministry of Economy, Trade and Industry. (2020). *Report of the study group on improvement of sustainable corporate value and human capital: Outline*. https://www.meti.go.jp/shingikai/economy/kigyo_kachi_kojo/pdf/20200930_2e.pdf.

Ministry of Education, Culture, Sports, Science and Technology. (2022). *Committee minutes on the 168th central education council meeting on university policies*. https://www.mext.go.jp/b_menu/shingi/chukyo/chukyo4/siryo/1422495_00022.html.

Moore, M. G., & Anderson, W. G. (Eds.). (2003). *Handbook of distance education*. Lawrence Erlbaum Associates.

PwC. (2022). *Reimagining the outcomes that matter: PwC's 25th annual global CEO survey*. https://www.pwc.com/gx/en/ceo-survey/2022/main/content/downloads/25th_CEO_Survey.pdf.

Qasrawi, R., & BeniAbdelrahman, A. (2020). The higher and lower-order thinking skills (HOTS and LOTS) in unlock english textbooks (1st and 2nd editions) based on bloom's taxonomy: An analysis study. *International Online Journal of Education and Teaching, 7*, 744–758.

Sato, Y., & Arimoto, T. (2015). Japan. In UNESCO (Ed.), *UNESCO science report: Towards 2030* (pp. 642–659). Paris

Smith, M., Bell, K., Bennett, D., & McAlpine, A. (2018). *Employability in a global context: Evolving policy and practice in employability, work integrated learning, and career development learning*. Wollongong.

UNESCO. (Ed.) (2015). *UNESCO science report: Towards 2030*. Paris.

UNESCO. (2019). *Japan pushing ahead with Society 5.0 to overcome chronic social challenges*. https://www.unesco.org/en/articles/japan-pushing-ahead-society-50-overcome-chronic-social-challenges. Accessed 13 April 2023.

University of Tsukuba. (2023). *Japan virtual campus*. https://www.jv-campus.org/. Accessed 9 Febr 2023.

Keiko Ikeda is a Professor in the Division of International Affairs, and KU-COIL Coordinator at Kansai University. Recently, she has taken the role as the principal project manager for an Inter-University Exchange Project funded by MEXT ("COIL Plus Program to Develop Global Career Mindset" 2018–2022, "Blended Mobility Project for Society 5.0 Human Resources" 2023–2028). Keiko is Vice-Director for the newly established organization at Kansai University, Institute for Innovative Global Education (IIGE). She has a PhD from the University of Hawai'i at Manoa, specializing in Japanese linguistics, foreign language education, and conversation analysis. Her interests in the international education field are internationalization at home, constructing active learning programs, and collaborating with universities overseas.

Open Access This chapter is licensed under the terms of the Creative Commons Attribution 4.0 International License (http://creativecommons.org/licenses/by/4.0/), which permits use, sharing, adaptation, distribution and reproduction in any medium or format, as long as you give appropriate credit to the original author(s) and the source, provide a link to the Creative Commons license and indicate if changes were made.

The images or other third party material in this chapter are included in the chapter's Creative Commons license, unless indicated otherwise in a credit line to the material. If material is not included in the chapter's Creative Commons license and your intended use is not permitted by statutory regulation or exceeds the permitted use, you will need to obtain permission directly from the copyright holder.

Future Skill Needs for IT Professionals— an Empirical Study

29

Marina Brunner and Ulf-Daniel Ehlers

Abstract

The currently EU-wide largest survey on the future of skills for professionals in the IT sector reveals a new configuration in skill demands. The skill study differentiated between three sets of skills: Business, Technical, and Future Skills and surveyed IT and HR professionals from more than 300 organizations in 27 European member states to assess the importance of skills today and within the next three to five years. It took place in the Blockchain sector, which stands exemplary for digital transformation of economies. It turns out that participants attribute high to very high importance to Future Skills over Technical and Business Skills. This brings up questions for new qualification pathways and strategies with a string focus on Future Skills. The study presented here provides an in-depth analysis of surveys and research skill demands for IT professionals and an analysis of skill supply, which has been investigated through a multi-method and multi-stakeholder research design.

M. Brunner (✉)
Chair of Innovation and Technology Management, Karlsruhe Institute of Technology, Karlsruhe, Germany
e-mail: marina.brunner@kit.edu

U.-D. Ehlers
Professor for Educational Management and Lifelong Learning, Business Faculty, DHBW Karlsruhe, Karlsruhe, Germany
e-mail: ehlers@dhbw-karlsruhe.de

© The Author(s) 2024
U.-D. Ehlers and L. Eigbrecht (eds.), *Creating the University of the Future*, Zukunft der Hochschulbildung - Future Higher Education, https://doi.org/10.1007/978-3-658-42948-5_29

29.1 Introduction

Skill development is high on the agenda of regional, national, and institutional decision makers in policy and institutions and counts for large parts of a regions' innovation capacity and an individual's resilience against biographical risks.[1] A growing number of studies is investigating the efficiency and effectiveness of such skill development of educational systems world-wide (Ehlers, 2022). For higher education, the investigations claim a mismatch between what graduates are able to do and what society and the labor market expects them to be able to do. The latter being the ability to deal with a volatile, uncertain, complex, and ambiguous environment ahead. The phenomenon has recently been termed as "skill gap" in a so-called Delta Study by McKinsey involving more than 18,000 participants (NSDC, 2020). The skill gap concept is also expressed in individuals' perceptions: As biographies become increasingly flexible, individuals have a growing responsibility to develop individual competence strategies for their biographies at large. In this context, the fit between educational opportunities and occupational requirements must increasingly be prioritized and translated into individual learning and action strategies, in which "Future Skills" play an essential role (Ehlers, 2020).

While the skill debate is led under various diverging flags and terminology, the Future Skills concept has now been precisely and operationally defined and conceptualized by Ehlers (2020, 2022) in the NextSkills Study resulting in 17 defined Future Skill profiles. The study is rooted in an analysis of the state of the art of research and is modelled on sociological theory, neo-institutionalism, and individualization approaches, involving educational theoretical approaches of action competences and new theories of organizational development (for a detailed account of research methodology and state of research on Future Skills see Ehlers, 2020). Section 29.3 describes the approach briefly.

The Future Skills model has been used as a basis for building a quantitative instrument to investigate IT professionals and human resource experts' opinions about the relevance of different skill sets in relation to Future Skills. The question being if what has been known as hard skills can be really understood as superior to so-called soft skills—or if on the contrary, the former soft skills are more relevant skills for the future. The quantitative study is part of a larger multi-part,

---

[1] The explicit focus of policy can be seen e.g. in the fact that 2023 has been declared the European Year of Skills (see European Commission, 2022).

multi-mix and multi-perspective study based on methods of the emerging field of labor market intelligence research (Brunner & Ehlers, 2021; Ehlers & Bonaudo, 2021). It has been conducted in 27 European member states and addressed to IT professionals and management staff in the IT sector. In addition to the analysis of skill demands, the study also investigates skill supply—looking at learning pathways for Future Skills in the IT sector through curricula analysis, expert interviews, as well as informal learning communities and fora.[2]

In Sect. 29.2 we will explain our Future Skill concept and describe two other different sets of skills which have been used to define skill demands in the IT sector. In Sect. 29.3 we will shortly describe the research methodology which has been followed to determine skill demands. We will also state the methodology used to analyze skill supply—although the results will not be part of this chapter. In Sect. 29.4 we summarize the results of the skills demand analysis.

Overall, the studies reveal a gain in importance for Future Skills against other skill sets.

Labor Market Intelligence Research

Skills intelligence relies on various qualitative and quantitative empirical research methods that collate existing and newly researched labor market information to analyze currently existing and projected future in-demand skills within a given labor market. It is building on demand and supply theory (typically attributed to Adam Smith), human capital theory (developed by economist Theodore Schultz in the 1960s), labor market segmentation theory (first proposed by economist Edna Ullmann-Margalit in the 1970s), and recently the so-called skill-biased technological change theory (suggested by economists David Autor and Lawrence Katz in the 1990s).

In theory, in such an ideal market environment, both individuals and organizations can take informed decisions efficiently, while education policy and practice can be further developed and grounded in (empirical) evidence that takes the future direction into account (International Labour Organization, 2017). Within the past five years notable works on labor market intel-

---

[2]The research has been conducted as part of the large-scale CHAISE Initiative together with 23 organizations from more than 16 European countries. CHAISE—in itself being an acronym—stands for "A Blueprint for Sectoral Cooperation on Blockchain Skill Development".

> ligence include: "OECD Skills Strategy 2019" and "OECD Skills Outlook 2021" by Organization for Economic Co-operation and Development (OECD, 2019, 2021), "The Future of Jobs and Skills in Africa" by the World Economic Forum (World Economic Forum, 2017) or "The Future of Jobs Report 2020" by the World Economic Forum (World Economic Forum, 2020).

29.2 Skill Sets for the IT Professional of the Future: Beyond Technical and Business Skills

For the study, three skill sets (see Fig. 29.1) have been selected in order to investigate their future relevance for professionals in the IT industry: a set of Technical Skills, a second set of Business and Managerial Skills and a third set of Future Skills resulting from a large-scale future skill study.[3]

1. Technical Skills (focus here on Blockchain) (Brunner & Ehlers, 2021): IT-specific skills relate to skills which are hard skills in the domain of digital technology and IT information technology development, informatics, programming, Distributed Ledger expertise, Blockchain security, Blockchain architecture, which in the core relate to domain-related knowledge, abilities, and attitudes of IT professionals.
   - Mathematics & Statistics.
   - Coding (C++, Python, Java).
   - Blockchain Solutions Design.
   - Protocol Engineering.
   - Cryptography Development.

---

[3] In a general understanding, we define "skills" as learnt or natural abilities of a person. Within the global debate on skills, talents, and competences, the discussion in literature is shifting to a more comprehensive concept of competences which includes skills and adds to it attitudes and knowledge (Erpenbeck et al., 2017). The European Skills, Competences, Qualifications, and Occupations (ESCO) initiative applies the same definition of "competence" as the European Qualification Framework (EQF). According to this framework, "competence means the proven ability to use knowledge, skills and personal, social and/ or methodological abilities, in work or study situations and in professional and personal development" (ESCO, 2022).

29 Future Skill Needs for IT Professionals ...

Fig. 29.1 List of skills for future IT professionals (Brunner & Ehlers, 2021)

- Distributed Network Engineering.
- Frontend & Backend Development.
- Data Analysis.
- Data/Network Security Design.
- Smart Contract Development.
- Dev. of decentralized Apps.
- Cloud & Infrastructure Design.
- UX Design.
- Scientific Computing.

2. Professional/Business Skills (Brunner & Ehlers, 2021): Domain-related skills are defined by skills which are related to the field of profession of IT development but are comprised of skills which can be described or called complementing skills, like project management knowledge for IT and Blockchain-specific projects, business analysis skills for IT and Blockchain projects and alike.
   - Business (Needs) Analysis.
   - Business Development.
   - (Blockchain) Use Case Development.
   - Product Development.
   - Product Management.

- Legal & Compliance.
- Marketing.
- Finance and Controlling.
- Human resource development.
- Customer Success Design.
- Affiliate Marketing.

3. Future Skills: Horizontal, transversal skills—often referred to as soft skills—are skills which enable professionals to act successfully in the changing and emergent environment of organizational future contexts. Research shows that these skills are of increasing importance (Ehlers, 2020) and the study is aimed to analyze the importance of these kind of skills for IT professionals in the Blockchain labor market development in Europe.

- Learning literacy & Metacognitive Skills.
- Self-efficacy & Self-confidence.
- Self-determination & Autonomy.
- Self-management/organization regulation & responsibility.
- Decision competence & Responsibility-taking.
- Initiative & performance competence.
- Ambiguity competence.
- Ethical & Environmental competence.
- Design-thinking competence.
- Innovation & Creativity Skills.
- Systems & Networked Thinking.
- Sensemaking.
- Future mindset & willingness to change.
- Cooperation competence.
- Communication competence.

Figure 29.2 shows a summary of the 17 Future Skills.[4]

On a more detailed level, Future Skills is a concept which is directly connected to the former debate on key competences or twenty-first century skills (OECD, 2018; World Economic Forum, 2020) and which is now gaining increasing importance as a concept in educational policy and individuals' lives (Dettmers & Jochmann, 2021; Samochowiec, 2020). The importance of Future Skills has been stated in many studies both for the field of university graduates (Ehlers,

---

[4]The 17 Future Skills identified in the NextSkills study by Ehlers (2020) were combined into 15 for the CHAISE study after consolidations with blockchain and IT experts.

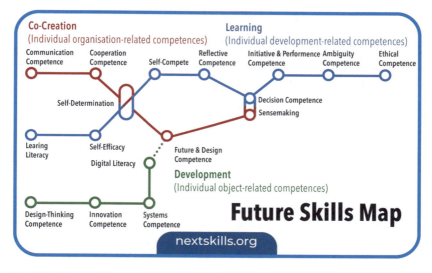

Fig. 29.2 Future skills profiles (Ehlers, 2022)[5]

2020; Huber, 2016, 2019; Schlaeger & Tenorth, 2020; Wild et al., 2018) as well as for professionals in their jobs (Agentur Q, 2021; Dettmers & Jochmann, 2021; Stifterverband & McKinsey, 2018), and also internationally (Ashoka Deutschland & McKinsey, 2018; Dondi et al., 2021; OECD, 2018; World Economic Forum, 2020). The body of studies indicates that research on Future Skills has established itself as a research field in its own right in recent years. Since 2016, 13 Future Skills studies are available within a Germany speaking context and at least 37 internationally. As a general trend, Future Skills concepts also include digital competencies, but place an emphasis on competencies of a transversal nature (e.g., ethical competence, dealing with ambiguity, etc.). In Chap. 2 in this book we have analyzed the digital dimension and importance within Future Skills studies.

This also finds expression in the currently growing international field of research on Future Skills. Since 2015, there have been more than 37 international studies on Future Skills, with more to be published soon. Amongst them, the Organization for Economic Co-operation and Development (OECD) Skill Com-

---

[5] An interactive Future Skills finder has been developed which can be accessed here: https://nextskills.org/future-skills-finder/.

pass and concepts from the World Economic Forum which indicate a skills shift, which demand moving away from a knowledge based understanding of (higher) education to a multidimensional concept, including knowledge, but going beyond it towards so-called "key competencies" or transversal "Future Skills" (Ehlers, 2020; OECD, 2018; World Economic Forum, 2020).

29.3 Methodological Design

A variety of methodological approaches from the social sciences have been used for the study on Future Skills for IT professionals, contrasting the demand for skills with the supply for skills (Table 29.1). A number of different studies has been conducted in order to gain information about the demand of skills in the IT sector, as well as the supply (see Ehlers & Bonaudo, 2021). Amongst them, qualitative interviews with IT experts and training and education providers, job-ad analyses, community and fora analyses, and a Europe-wide skills survey (Brunner & Ehlers, 2021).

For both perspectives—the skills demand as well as the skills supply—a number of data sources have been used.

Skills Demand
A detailed analysis of 314 job-ads collected from LinkedIn and further online job portals resulted in a description of preferred skills for job profiles. These data have been used to contextualize and define a Technical and a Business/Managerial skill set. Together with the previously collected set of Future Skills, both the Technical and the Business skill set built the basis for designing the quantitative research questionnaire. More than 300 IT experts across 27 European countries rated the importance of the individual skill sets for three selected roles: architect, developer, and manager for the application context of the Blockchain sector. In addition, data from interviews of 28 IT experts have been collected to complement the data from the standardized surveys.

Skills Supply
For the skills supply perspective, 120 online training offerings were simultaneously analyzed according to the predefined skill set. In addition, 17 IT communities and forums were analyzed according to skills and teaching methods. In order to get a more detailed insight into the training offered, 7 expert interviews were conducted with IT training providers, here with a focus on such forward-looking technologies like Blockchain.

29 Future Skill Needs for IT Professionals …

Table 29.1 Research Flow and Data Collection (Brunner & Ehlers, 2021)

Research methods	Research activities	Data collected & analyzed
Quantitative standardized online survey	European Survey on Skills for IT professionals	304 Survey participants
Qualitative guideline-based interviews	In-depth expert interviews	36 interviews conducted (29 skill demand perspective & 7 skill supply perspective)
Qualitative document analysis	Job Ad analysis	459 Job ads collected[6] 314 analyzed
Qualitative document analysis	Educational and training offerings with focus on Blockchain	133 Educational and training offerings collected[7] 120 analyzed
Qualitative document analysis	Analysis of online foras and communities	17 Communities and foras analyzed

29.4 Future Skills in the IT Profession

29.4.1 Overall Relevance of Future Skills

The quantitative data collected confirms that the Future Skills proposed in the NextSkills model are high on the agenda of IT professionals today and within the next three years. This holds true specifically if compared to skills sets on Technical Skills and Business Skills.

The companies' assessment of how important transversal skills will be today and in the next 3 years shows that more than 90% of the respondents describe Future Skills today as either "somewhat important" or "very important". For the importance of Future skills in the next three years the vast majority (93%) of firms responded with either "very important" or "somewhat important".

Figure 29.3 provides an overview of the percentage of participants who describe each skill as important.

---

[6] See registry of job ads: https://chaise-blockchainskills.eu/registry-of-blockchain-online-job-vacancies/

[7] See registry of educational and training offerings: https://chaise-blockchainskills.eu/registry-of-blockchain-educational-and-training-offerings/

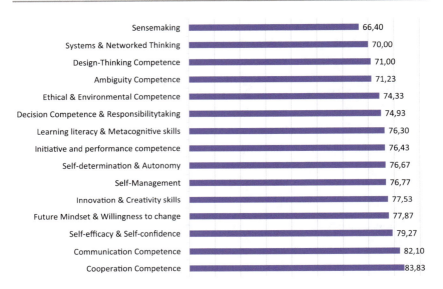

Fig. 29.3 Overview of the answers to the importance of the individual future skills[8] (Brunner & Ehlers, 2021)

As shown in Fig. 29.3 the most important Future Skills are cooperation competence (84%), communication competence (82,1%) and self-efficacy & self-confidence (79,3%). The following definitions and the definitions of the other skills can be found on nextskills.org:

- **Cooperation competence:** Cooperation competence as a Future Skill relates to the ability and disposition to cooperate and collaborate in (intercultural) teams either in face to-face or digitally supported interactions within or between organizations with the purpose of transforming differences into commonalities. Social intelligence, team-working competences, and consultation competence play a key role for this competence.

---

[8] In the EU Survey on Skills for IT professionals, 304 survey participants from IT industry have been asked for which of the three defined job profiles they consider the 15 Future Skills to be important (for more details on the survey see Brunner & Ehlers, 2021; Ehlers & Bonaudo, 2021). Figure 29.3 shows the average number of times participants rated the skills as important across all three roles.

- **Communication competence:** Communication competence as a Future Skill entails not only language skills, but also discourse, dialogue, and strategic communication aspects, which—taken together—serve the individual to communicate successfully and in accordance with the respective situation and context, in view and empathy of her/his own and other's needs.
- **Self-efficacy & Self-confidence:** Self-efficacy as a Future Skill Profile refers to the belief and one's (self-)confidence to be able to master the tasks at hand relying on one's own abilities and taking over responsibility for one's decisions (Ehlers, 2020).

The following skills were described as important by fewer participants in the survey: Sensemaking (66.4%), Systems & Network Thinking (70%) and Design Thinking Competence (71%). These differences can all be explained by strong variations in the ratings of importance for each role profile. We will discuss these differences and possible explanations further in sub-Sect. 29.4.3.

The interest in Future Skills for individual job profiles is also highlighted in comparison to the importance rating of other skill sets, as shown in Fig. 29.4.

As can be seen in Fig. 29.4, it is evident that Future Skills are regarded as very important skill sets across all job profiles. Even in a strongly IT-centric occupational field such as blockchain, they are rated more important than technical skill sets. This indicates a clear skill shift from technical knowledge to Future Skills.

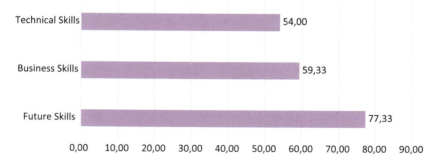

Fig. 29.4 Assessments of Importance of different Skill Sets (Brunner & Ehlers, 2021)

29.4.2 Comparing Importance of Different Skill Sets in IT Job Profiles

Skills are context-bound and—for professionals—a particular skill gains its value through enabling professional performance, understood as successful action. While the general context of the study was aiming at defining skills for IT professionals at a general level, an additional analysis step has been undertaken: An analysis of the perceived skills requirements for certain role-profiles within the sector of IT professionals. The participants of the study were therefore additionally asked to relate the importance of skills to three different job role-profiles: Architect, Developer and Manager – all related to the sector of Blockchain. In the study, the three role-profiles are clearly described. (1) The IT or Blockchain Architect designs the multileveled architecture of a large IT or Blockchain system and software landscape and ensures the coherence of all aspects of a project as an integrated system. (2) The Developer role-profile codes applications, in our case Blockchain applications, and takes care of problem solving at the micro level. (3) The Manager of Blockchain applications and systems is tasked to track implementation progress, maintain close cooperation with business managers, and monitor the process quality to ensure that products meet their technical and business objectives. In a role-profile-specific section of the study, participants have been asked to rate the important of the three different skills sets for the different role-profiles stated above.

304 participants from 13 countries took part in the survey, and rated different statements on a scale from very high to very low, depending on how important a skill is for the respective role. For the data evaluation, the highest two evaluation scores "very high" or "very important" and "somewhat high" or "somewhat important" were aggregated.

The data analysis shows that the skill set for Future Skills is the set rated with highest importance over all three role-profiles. Figure 29.5 gives an overview of the distribution of the importance of the different skills according to roles.

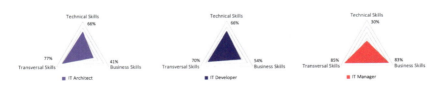

Fig. 29.5 Skill profiles per role for IT professionals (Brunner & Ehlers, 2021)

Secondly, the analysis shows that the three skill sets used have a distinct importance and can be distinguished from each other. Thirdly, the analysis shows that professional roles do not rely on one particular competence profile only, but that domain-specific skills and Future Skills complement each other in creating wholistic professional skill portfolios.

29.4.3 Future Skills in Comparison

In an additional step of analysis, the value and inner structure of the skill set of Future Skills has been questioned. The aim was to analyze which importance the participants attributed to each skill within the three given role-profiles and to extract the inner Future Skill characteristic for each role-profile. An overview is given in Fig. 29.6. While self-efficacy and self-determination are rated similarly important for all roles, there is a difference in skills such as creativity, system thinking, sensemaking, design thinking, future mindset, and ethical thinking. Here it can be seen that operational roles such as the Blockchain Developer are

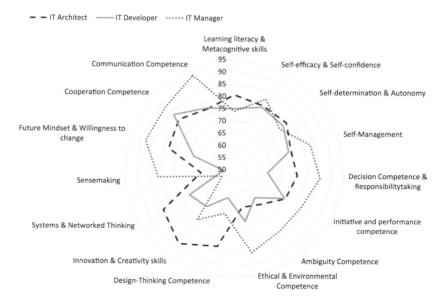

Fig. 29.6 Importance of transversal skills for different roles of IT professionals (Brunner & Ehlers, 2021)

assigned a lower importance for some skills than the strategic roles of the Blockchain Architect or the Blockchain Manager. The Blockchain Manager, in his connecting role between the teams, has a strong focus on organization-related skills (cooperation, communication, sensemaking, etc.), while the Blockchain Architect has a stronger focus on object-related skills (systems thinking, design thinking, innovation, etc.).

A clear skill shift from so-called hard skills to transversal Future Skills can be observed in this area. IT professionals predominantly require transversal skills, which is also related to the many changes and innovations in the IT working environment. It requires professionals who can continuously adapt to their fast-moving environment. Transversal Future Skills are indispensable in this context.

As far as formal education is concerned, the interviewed experts (n = 36) are divided. In many job-ads an academic education in the field of computer science or informatics is required, but some experts do not find traditional education particularly important and refer to short courses offered by numerous e-learning platforms such as Udemy and Coursera. On the other hand, these courses are also criticized for being too generic and superficial. In many cases they offer only a surface introduction to the topic. There is also a lack of face-to-face training sessions with supervision, which can be useful for practical training. To develop especially the missing Future Skills, it was clearly emphasized in the survey and in the interviews that training and education programs should be as interactive as possible. The focus should be on practical application, dealing with real world problems, and working on concrete projects. But also, entrepreneurial skills and working in interdisciplinary teams were highlighted as important for the learning process. Especially in solution and use case design, extensive industry knowledge is a basic requirement. This rising demand of real-world use cases and practical learning shows the need for work-based oriented learning modules. Specialized knowledge of the basics of IT technologies should be taught as well as project-related skills. The involvement of experts and needs from the public sector and the economy offers further added value. However, self-learning in forums and via videos should also be encouraged, as future professionals need to continuously develop themselves on the job and should internalize this ability to self-learn in their formal education.

29.5 Summary and Conclusion

The study shows that higher education will have to move quite a bit from its current position. The new paradigm of higher education will have to be geared towards supporting the development of new and emerging skill needs and focus on learner agency. Learner agency refers to the feeling of ownership and control that learners have over their own learning (Schoon, 2018). When students believe their actions can make a difference, they become more confident, engaged, and effective learners. Every student can develop their agency—but they must be supported by their teachers and learning community to do so.

The following conclusions can be drawn from the empirical research findings:

1. Skill profiles can be clearly defined: As shown in Sects. 29.4.2 & 29.4.3, the different job profiles have different skill needs according to industry experts. Even in the case of Future Skills, a distinction can be made depending on the role which skills are rated as important.
2. Sectorial needs can be clearly described: By means of a targeted approach, it is possible to identify a clear sector need. The blockchain sector that is the focus here is still growing and yet job profiles can be clearly defined and distinguished from each other, and the respective need determined.
3. Future Skills are on the rRise: Future Skills are not only described as increasingly important but exceed the importance of subject-specific skills for different role profiles (see Sect. 29.4.1)
4. The method for skill analysis employs expert-supported foresight procedures like Delphi studies and qualitative methods to avoid blind spot problems: In addition to the quantitative European-wide surveys and the analyses of job ads, forums and online courses, the expert interviews and focus groups provided important information on how the development of Future Skills can be promoted (see Sect. 29.4.3).
5. Future Skills are in general important, but some can be identified as more important for certain job profiles than others: Job profiles that are more generalist or have more interfaces in collaboration with other people or departments show a higher rated need for Future Skills than job profiles that have more isolated areas of responsibility (see Sect. 29.4.2).

The multi-method and multi-stakeholder approach in skill research in very dynamic fields of work, such as blockchain, provides a good information base for closing the skills gap. Especially between the advertisement in job ads, the discussion in online forums and the perspective assessment of blockchain experts, a lack of awareness for Future Skills in the high-tech community can be identified. Future Skills need to be codified in a way that is known to the general public in order to be properly used by recruiters in job ads and to find resonance in existing networks. The online communities are the first port of call for many blockchain enthusiasts, and this is where the topic of Future Skills should be addressed.

Through better anchoring in formal education especially in ICT programs, more attention can be created for Future Skills. Furthermore, human resource managers should be educated about the importance of Future Skills. Higher education institutions and industry players should join forces and facilitate practice-oriented training in this area. In addition, there should be a regular exchange to prepare students with real world use cases for the new dynamic challenges of the working world.

Future Skills in Practice: Our Recommendations

For Higher Education Institutions the following steps are important:

1. Include Future Skills elements systematically into the curriculum: Integrate forward-thinking topics like critical thinking, digital literacy, adaptability, and problem-solving across all grade levels and subject areas to equip students with essential skills for the ever-evolving job market.
2. Determine Future Skill foresight capacity: Establish a dedicated team or department within educational institutions to continuously monitor industry trends, emerging technologies, and labor market demands, ensuring that the curriculum remains relevant and responsive to Future Skill needs.
3. Support professional development for Future Skills teaching and assessment methodologies: Provide professional development opportunities for educators, empowering them with innovative teaching techniques and strategies that promote active learning, collaboration, creativity, and the integration of technology to effectively impart future-oriented skills to students.
4. Develop dedicated assessment methodologies for Future Skills in addition to existing assessment methods: Design new evaluation tools, such as performance-based tasks, projects, simulations, and portfolio assessments, that can accurately measure students' proficiency in future skills beyond traditional exams, fostering a comprehensive understanding of their capabilities.

References

Agentur, Q. (2021). *Future Skills: Welche Kompetenzen für den Standort Baden-Württemberg heute und in Zukunft erfolgskritisch sind.* https://www.bw.igm.de/news/meldung.html?id=101055. Accessed 1 Dec 2021.

Ashoka Deutschland, & McKinsey. (2018). *The skilling challenge: How to equip employees for the era of automation and digitization – and how models and mindsets of social entrepreneurs can guide us.* https://www.ashoka.org/de-de/files/2018theskillingchalleng eashokamckinseypdf.

Brunner, M., & Ehlers, U.-D. (2021). *Chaise – Blockchain skills for Europe: D2.5.1: Study on skills mismatches in the European Blockchain sector.* https://next-education.org/wp-content/uploads/2021/11/Chaise_WP2_D2.5.1_Study-on-Skill-Mismatch-in-the-blockchain-sector_v3.pdf. Accessed 27 Febr 2022.

Dettmers, S., & Jochmann, W. (2021). *Future skills – future learning.* https://media.kienbaum.com/wp-content/uploads/sites/13/2021/06/Kienbaum-StepStone-Studie_2021_WEB.pdf. Accessed 1 Dec 2021.

Dondi, M., Klier, J., Panier, F., & Schubert, J. (2021). *Defining the skills citizens will need in the future world of work.* https://www.mckinsey.com/industries/public-and-socialsector/our-insights/defining-the-skills-citizens-will-need-in-the-future-world-of-work.

Ehlers, U.-D. (2020). *Future Skills: Lernen der Zukunft – Hochschule der Zukunft.* Springer Fachmedien Wiesbaden.

Ehlers, U.-D. (2022). *Future skills compared: On the construction of a general framework model for future competencies in academic education.* https://nextskills.org/wp-content/uploads/2022/07/2022-06-15-Future-Skills-Bildungsforschung_final_Vs_2ENG.pdf.

Ehlers, U.-D., & Bonaudo, P. (2021). *Research methodology to gather labour market intelligence and identify skills mismatches.* https://next-education.org/wp-content/uploads/2023/01/CHAISE-WP2_D2.1.1_Research-Methodology-to-gather-labour-market-intelligence-and-identify-skills-mismatches_v3.pdf.

Erpenbeck, J., von Rosenstiel, L., Grote, S., & Sauter, W. (2017). *Handbuch Kompetenzmessung: Erkennen, verstehen und bewerten von Kompetenzen in der betrieblichen, pädagogischen und psychologischen Praxis* (3rd ed.). Schäffer-Poeschel.

ESCO. (2022). *Competence.* https://ec.europa.eu/esco/portal/escopedia/Competence.

European Commission. (2022). *Commission kick-starts work on the European Year of Skills.*

Huber, L. (2016). „Studium Generale" oder „Schlüsselqualifikationen"?: Ein Orientierungsversuch im Feld der Hochschulbildung. In U. Konnertz & S. Mühleisen (Eds.), *Bildung und Schlüsselqualifikationen: Zur Rolle der Schlüsselqualifikationen an den Universitäten* (pp. 101–122). Peter Lang.

Huber, L. (2019). „Bildung durch Wissenschaft" als Qualität des Studiums. *Das Hochschulwesen, 67*(6), 154–159.

International Labour Organization. (2017). *Skill needs anticipation: Systems and approaches.: Analysis of stakeholder survey on skill needs assessment and anticipation.* Geneva.

NSDC. (2020). *Global skill gap report: Assessing overseas opportunities for skilled manpower from India.* https://skillsip.nsdcindia.org/sites/default/files/kps-document/Global%20Skill%20Gap%20Report%2021April2020.pdf. Accessed 9 Jan 2023.

OECD. (2018). *The future of education and skills: Education 2030.* https://www.oecd.org/education/2030/E2030%20Position%20Paper%20(05.04.2018).pdf.

OECD. (2019). *OECD skills strategy 2019: Skills to shape a better future.* https://www.oecd-ilibrary.org/docserver/9789264313835-en.pdf?expires=1673340365&id=id&accname=ocid56029192&checksum=4631D141B8717D5D3890C8FDDE1C3706. Accessed 10 Jan 2023.

OECD. (2021). *OECD skills outlook 2021: Lerning for life.* https://www.oecd-ilibrary.org/docserver/0ae365b4-en.pdf?expires=1673340542&id=id&accname=ocid56029192&checksum=B14744308AB7D4644198D1B92E365799. Accessed 10 Jan 2023.

Samochowiec, J. (2020). *Future Skills: Four scenarios for the world of tomorrow.* https://www.gdi.ch/sites/default/files/documents/2020-05/2020_e_future-skills_jacobsfoundation_summary.pdf. Accessed 27 Febr 2022.

Schlaeger, J., & Tenorth, H.-E. (2020). *Bildung durch Wissenschaft.* Berliner Wissenschafts-Verlag.

Schoon, I. (2018). *Conceptualising learner agency: A socio-ecological developmental approach* (LLAKES Research Paper 64). https://www.llakes.ac.uk/wp-content/uploads/2021/03/LLAKES-Research-Paper-64-Schoon-I.pdf. Accessed 1 April 2022.

Stifterverband, & McKinsey (2018). *Future Skills: Welche Kompetenzen in Deutschland fehlen.* https://www.stifterverband.org/medien/future-skills-welche-kompetenzen-in-deutschland-fehlen.

Wild, S., Deuer, E., & Pohlenz, P. (2018). Studienerfolgsverständnis von hauptamtlichen Lehrkräften im Studienbereich Wirtschaft der Dualen Hochschule Baden-Württemberg (DHBW) – Ein Typisierungsversuch. *Zeitschrift für Evaluation – ZfEv, 17*(2), 269–288.

World Economic Forum. (2017). *The future of jobs and skills in Africa: Preparing the region for the fourth industrial revolution.* https://www3.weforum.org/docs/WEF_EGW_FOJ_Africa.pdf. Accessed 10 Jan 2023.

World Economic Forum. (2020). *The future of jobs report 2020.* http://www3.weforum.org/docs/WEF_Future_of_Jobs_2020.pdf.

Marina Brunner is an academic researcher at the Karlsruhe Institute of Technology (KIT Karlsruhe) at the Chair of Innovation and Technology Management. She completed her bachelor's degree in marketing communication and advertising at Pforzheim University, and her master's degree in digital business at OTH Amberg-Weiden. She worked on several Erasmus+ projects related to Future Skills in Higher Education.

Prof. Dr. phil. habil. Ulf-Daniel Ehlers is an internationally renowned Professor for Educational Management and Lifelong Learning at the Baden-Wuerttemberg Cooperative State University (DHBW) Karlsruhe which he headed as Vice-President between 2011 and 2017.

Open Access This chapter is licensed under the terms of the Creative Commons Attribution 4.0 International License (http://creativecommons.org/licenses/by/4.0/), which permits use, sharing, adaptation, distribution and reproduction in any medium or format, as long as you give appropriate credit to the original author(s) and the source, provide a link to the Creative Commons license and indicate if changes were made.

The images or other third party material in this chapter are included in the chapter's Creative Commons license, unless indicated otherwise in a credit line to the material. If material is not included in the chapter's Creative Commons license and your intended use is not permitted by statutory regulation or exceeds the permitted use, you will need to obtain permission directly from the copyright holder.

Future Higher Education in New Zealand: Creating a Universal Learning Community for Future Skills

30

Stephen Marshall

Abstract

Skills challenges for the future embody major challenges for a national system of education. One is the ability of skills-development mechanisms to scale well beyond the limits of the existing models while also reducing dramatically the associated costs of development and operation for providers, and the costs of participation and achievement demonstration for learners. A second is that of being responsive to a rapidly changing environment, evolving existing structures to meet new needs. This chapter explores the New Zealand context for these challenges. A future-facing model, responding to these challenges and using inspiration from the New Zealand Māori concept of 'Ako', is presented. Described as 'microlearning', this model is proposed as an alternative for Future Skills development that avoids the pitfalls of credentialised approaches. The potential for microlearning for Future Skills development in regulated professionals is suggested as a starting point for initial exploration of this new model.

S. Marshall (✉)
Director of Centre for Academic Development, Victoria University of Wellington, Wellington, New Zealand
e-mail: stephen.marshall@vuw.ac.nz

© The Author(s) 2024
U.-D. Ehlers and L. Eigbrecht (eds.), *Creating the University of the Future*, Zukunft der Hochschulbildung - Future Higher Education,
https://doi.org/10.1007/978-3-658-42948-5_30

30.1 Introduction

"The effects of schooling, the way it alters a man's capacity and will to do things, depends not only on what he learns, or the way he learns it, but also on why he learns it. That is at the basis of the distinction between schooling which is education, and schooling which is only qualification, a mere process of certificating — or 'credentialling'." (Dore, 1976, p. 8)

Setting aside the (serious and ongoing) casual sexism, Dore's statement defines the challenge facing the evolving higher education systems of every country. Each generation needs to create a university that responds to its needs (Geiger, 2011) and that prepares each generation for the future needs of society. Historically, the degree, and higher education generally, have been considered as necessities for progress and success individually and for communities as a whole. This has evolved over time in many countries, New Zealand in particular, to create a dominating expectation that people start life with a degree (Carnevale et al., 2012; Marginson, 2016c), but also a separation or disconnection from the life that they subsequently lead and the way that their education supports their future success. This can lead to what Dore has defined as the "diploma disease" (Dore, 1976) which speaks to the disconnect between the acquisition of educational qualifications and the application of that education and skill in other contexts.

The diploma disease is apparent where qualifications are needed to gain employment but where the workplace culture prevents any autonomy or initiative in the application of the worker's skills (Sennett, 1998), a process described as "digital Taylorism" in recognition of the role that this plays in sustaining models of low-value employment (Brown et al., 2011, p. 72). The problems that can arise from the disconnection between education and the enaction of skills has been evident for more than fifty years:

"An 'inflation' of educational credentials of this kind involves social waste in two dimensions. First, it absorbs excess real resources into the screening process: the lengthened obstacle course is unlikely to be the most profitable way of testing for the qualities desired, because its costs are not borne by the employers whose demands give the credentials their cash value. Second, social waste will result from disappointed expectations of individuals and from the frustration they experience in having to settle for employment in jobs in which they cannot make full use of their acquired skills." (Hirsch, 1976, p. 51)

The disconnect also illustrates the problem with the assumptions that underpin human capital theory (Becker, 1993; Fitzsimons, 2015; Gillies, 2015) which states that education is a personal investment generating a capital return that is rewarded through increased wages. Human capital theory is the economic rationale used in countries, such as New Zealand, that have systems funded at least in part through private means or through loans attracting significant interest. The separation of education from its impact on skills needs and investment by employers has led Marginson to observe: "Human capital theory and equal opportunity: these are the foundational myths of modern higher education systems" (Marginson, 2016b, p. 16).

In addition to the problem of equitably and sustainably funding the education of adults, skills challenges for the future reflect two other major themes. The first is the ability of skills development mechanisms to scale well beyond the limits of the existing models while also reducing dramatically the associated costs of development and operation for providers, and the costs of participation and achievement demonstration for learners. The second major theme is that of being responsive to a rapidly changing environment where skill expectations are shifting to reflect personal competencies needed to cope with that dynamism (Ehlers, 2020) and also the impact of growing automation and technology use for cognitive activities to grow productivity (New Zealand Productivity Commission [N.Z.P.C.], 2020).

The scaleability of skills mechanisms has been apparent as a major driver for change in tertiary education since the last millennium. Costs of university education have outpaced inflation for decades, making degree education increasingly unaffordable (Fincher & Katsinas, 2017) even as demand for skills grow and productivity growth stalls in many countries, even without the further burden of the COVID pandemic (New Zealand Productivity Commission, 2020). The driver for this cost disconnect between education and the wider economy, also known as the "cost disease" (Archibald & Feldman, 2010; Bowen, 2012), is attributed to the dependence on human faculty and other teachers as the primary mechanism for delivery.

Another factor driving costs arises from the dual nature of qualifications. Historically, qualifications have carried significant social impact, signalling the worth of a potential employee in the same way that a bird uses its plumage, in effect streamlining the identification of skills by employers through the proxy of the qualification (Arrow, 1973; Hussey, 2012; Spence, 1973). The operation of this mechanism is evident in the competition to gain access to top-ranked institutions by students and their families (Golden, 2006). Hirsch (1976) identified the coexistence of a material economy and a positional economy which is evident in education. Material aspects are amenable to investments in productivity that drive down costs and increase availability, desireable features for those interested in growing and sustained skills development, while positional aspects benefit from scarcity and are compromised if they become more widely available, as is seen in the operation of elite international universities.

The remainder of this chapter examines this process as it is being experienced in the New Zealand education system. First a definition of Future Skills aligned to the New Zealand context is provided along with a summary of key features and recent changes to the operation of the adult education system. This is then followed by a description of a model for Future Skills development that is framed as a response to the skills definition and contextual challenges of the New Zealand vocational environment.

30.2 Future Skills Definition and Conception

The New Zealand Government has positioned the future of work as being defined by four major trends: technological progress; demographic change; globalisation; and climate change (Ministry of Business, Innovation and Employment [MBIE], 2019). This frames the thinking about the skills needed as the country responds to these trends, and the investments in systems and institutions to enact policy responses aimed at building Future Skills by individuals.

Five key competencies have been defined by the New Zealand national educational system as essential to the futures of young New Zealanders. Derived from an OECD conception (Hipkins, 2018) these define Future Skills as managing self, relating to others, thinking, participating and contributing, and using language, symbols, and texts.

More recently, the OECD has described a more expansive set (OECD, 2018) which are framed by three areas: cognitive and meta-cognitive skills, social and emotional skills, and practical and physical skills. These conceptions are quite general in their framing and subject to ongoing revision (Hipkins & Vaughn, 2019), reflecting an awareness that the pace of change and complexity of the modern world means that flexibility, resilience, and the ability to learn throughout life are the real Future Skills needed (Buchanan et al., 2018).

These generalized conceptions of Future Skills drawn from international sources also need to be seen in the light of New Zealand's economic, political, social, and educational context. The New Zealand Productivity Commission in a recent report on the future of work (New Zealand Productivity Commission, 2020) noted that the country's weaknesses included:

- Declining school system performance in reading, mathematics and science, with particular issues for Māori and Pasifika students and those from disadvantaged communities generally;
- A lack of business dynamism, poor capital flows and limited investment, characterised as "weak innovation";
- A weakness in business leadership and management capability to drive changes that might benefit from Future Skills; and
- Minimal engagement with emerging technologies, in part reflecting the lack of capital investment, but also a consequence of a general attitude to business that is driven by cost minimisation and low-cost labour.

The challenges facing the country with its current approach to vocational education are also apparent in analysis showing that attainment of vocational qualifications has no significant impact on subsequent earnings for men (as opposed to women for whom there is a significant benefit) (Hyslop et al., 2020).

The New Zealand school education system is not strongly oriented towards vocational outcomes in the way that those of some countries, such as the Netherlands and Germany are (Deissinger, 2015; Iannelli & Smyth, 2017), and instead has a very open and relatively unstructured curriculum with considerable choice in subjects without alignment to vocational needs (Hipkins & Vaughn, 2019).

The Workforce Development Council (WDC) model recently established by the Government is aimed at addressing Future Skills:

> "They will have a forward, strategic view of the Future Skills needs of industries and will help industry achieve greater influence over what and how training is delivered, by influencing government investment, setting skill standards and playing a leadership role across their relevant industries." (Hipkins, 2021, n.p.)

Exactly what these Future Skills needs are however is yet to be defined with the WDCs less than a year old and not as yet producing detailed descriptions of Future Skills. There is also no unifying Future Skills framework in place beyond the generalized statements noted above. It is also worth noting the focus on government investment, bearing in mind that New Zealand has a very high dependence on public funding for its educational system (OECD, 2021). There is no mention of WDCs acting to lift business investment in skills development in any of the framing policies and establishing legislation enacted by the government, their functions are instead to contribute "to a well-functioning labour market system in which the specified industries can access the skills required to meet their current and future needs" (New Zealand Government, 2021, Sect. 7(1)(f)).

In conclusion, Future Skills in the New Zealand context remain ambiguous and, despite the use of the term repeatedly by government agencies, undefined in any meaningful way. The definition that has the most currency, and which is used for this chapter, is based on that of Buchanan et al. (2018) which states the Future Skills needed are flexibility, resilience, and the ability to learn throughout life. The result is a need to operate the national educational system in a way that can operate effectively within ambiguity and rapidly deliver skills to society as the need for them is realised. The next section describes the current state of the New Zealand tertiary education system in order to assess its capacity to respond to this need.

30.3 The New Zealand Tertiary Education System

New Zealand's tertiary education system was historically modelled after that of the United Kingdom, and although heavily influenced by that of Australia, has since evolved to reflect local policy preferences and the growing importance of the Treaty of Waitangi and Māori models. Tertiary education in 2023 is provided by a range of institutions including eight universities, sixteen former institutes of technology and polytechnic (ITPs) operating under a national body Te Pukenga, the National Institute for Skills and Technology, and three indigenous Māori educational institutions which are called wananga. As well as these public organizations, there are several hundred private tertiary education organizations (PTEs) which operate in a wide range of contexts and scales.

A further complexity of the New Zealand tertiary system is the split between the universities, described as the higher education system, and the rest of the institutions. Universities are approved primarily for degree provision with government policies actively discouraging engagement in vocational education. The rest of the tertiary system is intended to focus on vocational education but also offers an extensive range of degrees, many with very little vocational alignment.

As in many countries, the New Zealand tertiary system has been subject to significant and ongoing change (Crawford, 2016; Department of Education & Training, 2015). The New Zealand ITP sector was given degree-granting status in 1990 which saw their focus shift away from direct service of local employers and communities to a more generalized model that mimicked many of the features of the University system and saw extensive duplication of offerings driven primarily by financial rather than educational or Future Skills outcomes. Despite the intention that this change would lift the level of skills and education in New Zealand, and even after enacting policies to increase access by removing some student fees (Hipkins, 2017), it continued to perpetuate historically situated structural inequities of access and outcome (Strathdee & Cooper, 2017) and its poor performance resulted in recent major restructuring. Symptoms of structural failure were evident in the sector when it became apparent that the majority of Institutes of Technology and Polytechnic were operating significant deficits in 2018 and projections of annual sector wide shortfalls of nearly NZ$300 million by 2020 were predicated (Tertiary Education Commission [T.E.C.], 2018). The reasons for this are complex and included sustained underfunding by the government in an attempt to manage costs as well as excessive and wasteful competition through application of a highly marketized model of operation (Tertiary Education Commission, 2018).

The problems facing the vocational parts of the New Zealand tertiary sector led to the publication in 2019 of a cabinet paper that noted (Hipkins, 2019, p. 10) the "weak governance and management capability in parts of the sector". The inability of sector leaders to place their organizations within a wider public-good framework consistent with its use of public funding and the purposes identified by the Education Act (New Zealand Government, 2020) was also identified by the Productivity Commission (New Zealand Productivity Commission, 2017) in their extensive review of the tertiary system. In the cabinet paper the Minister of Education announced that the problems facing the sector were so severe that he proposed (Hipkins, 2019, p. 1):

> "I seek Cabinet's agreement to consult on proposals for a comprehensive reform of New Zealand's vocational education system. The proposed reforms will:
> 1.1. redefine the roles of education providers and Industry Training Organisations, (ITOs) and extend industry and employers' leadership role across all vocational education through new Industry Skills Bodies
> 1.2. create a New Zealand Institute of Skills & Technology, bringing together our public Institutes of Technology and Polytechnics (ITPs) as a single entity, and
> 1.3. create a unified vocational education funding system, removing barriers to collaboration and flexibility, ensuring a sustainable network of provision, and supporting the wider reforms."

This resulted in drastic restructuring by Ministerial mandate of the vocational education system in New Zealand (Hipkins, 2019). All of the public vocational providers were combined into a single entity, Te Pūkenga, with a centralized governance and management supported by local community and employers through a fix of committees and governance mechanisms. This was done to address a perceived gap in the national capacity to provide skilled workers for the economy and address sustained inequality with the Māori and Pacific communities; however the challenges are far more complex than a simplified supply chain model.

The framing of the challenges facing the sector in the Cabinet Paper (Hipkins, 2019, p. 1) reflects an awareness of the Future Skills needs facing the country:

> "Vocational education can help to ensure that all New Zealanders have the skills, knowledge and capability to adapt and succeed in a world of rapid economic, social and technological change. It can improve people's resilience, employment security and life outcomes, and reduce social inequities, as the trends driving the Future of Work mean they will likely change jobs and careers frequently over their working lives."

The cabinet paper, however, fails to acknowledge the important role that employers have played in creating this situation. Instead the Minister states that a major driver for improvement will result from a shift in leadership to this group (Hipkins, 2019, p. 6):

> "Employers and industry need to be given, and must take on, a greater leadership role across the entire vocational education system"

The changes to the provision of vocational education currently being enacted are unlikely to change the calculus resulting in employer disengagement from the responsibility for contributing to Future Skills development. Instead, they reflect an ongoing application of the flawed ideology (Marginson, 2016a; Wolf, 2004) of human capital theory (Becker, 1993; Fitzsimons, 2015; Gillies, 2015) that perpetuates a model of investment where the costs fall on the public, the benefits are captured by private interests and the worker is typically unable to see a return on their efforts reflected in improvements in their wages.

The tertiary education system in New Zealand has only in recent decades recognized a general role in skills development for employment (Jung, 2021). This started in the 1980s with an awareness of professional skills needs in the context of specific employment related outcomes and then expanded to the generic skills and attributes needed in workplaces beyond the specific professions (Adelman, 2009; Barrie, 2006; Barrie et al., 2009; Spronken-Smith et al., 2015). In the first decades of the millennium this has expanded to a systematised measurement of employment outcomes and performance management systems (Shah et al., 2015) which are used to frame government funding differentials for qualifications (Tertiary Education Commission, 2023) and immigration policies (New Zealand Immigration, 2023).

The context for skills in New Zealand is framed by the intersecting challenges identified in the introduction. The first challenge is the financial model that is enacted by the system. This includes the funding of education as well as the impact of education on individual financial outcomes. OECD data on spending on tertiary education (OECD, 2021) show that New Zealand education is disproportionately funded from the public resources (53% of spending) in comparison to countries such as Australia (35%) and the United Kingdom (29%), particularly when the impact of government-operated student loans are included as these compromise a significant proportion of the expenditure treated as household by the OECD reporting. Policies such as the fees-free for first year at University and for all of the fees of a vocational qualification (Hipkins, 2017; Hipkins et al., 2020) also obscure the actual funding situation and the extent to which it is publically funded rather than invested in by employers and industries by failing to explicity treat these as subsidies for those groups when reporting the government spending.

This financial environment is a consequence of New Zealand's highly marketized neoliberal public policy environment (Larner & Le Heron, 2005; Lewis & Shore, 2019; Martens & Starke, 2008; Wheelahan & Moodie, 2017). This has arisen from a massive period of reform in the 1980s and 1990s where New Zealand's public sector, including the universities and ITPs, underwent reforms that saw increasing competition, and marketization. This has been described as "one of the most aggressive and extensive applications of neo-liberal market policies in the English-speaking world" (Robinson, 2006, p. 42). This saw education reframed from a public good to a private benefit and students expected to pay fees that have increased from the 1990s on average 13% per annum (Healey & Gunby, 2012). The structural inequality this perpetuates (Strathdee & Cooper, 2017) is evident in the New Zealand Treasury (1987) analysis showing that gaining qualifications does not result in individuals earning more (Tumen et al., 2015) and the impact is also apparent in recent declines in participation apparent in the enrolment figures prior to the COVID pandemic (Education Counts, 2022).

The financial stresses are further exacerbated by the longitudinal data reported by the OECD which show that, despite the public rhetoric regarding skill shortages, private investment in tertiary education has remained unchanged over the last decade and is very low as a proportion of GDP in comparison with other similar economies (OECD, 2021). The current models of funding education are highly dependent on declining levels of public wealth, with the risks criticized while industries and employers adopt a typically passive approach to sustaining their workforce. The public role as funder in effect subsidises the employer through policies such as the Targeted Training and Apprenticeship Fund, which pays all of the fees associated with apprenticeships and vocational training in a range of industries (Tertiary Education Commission, 2020), and the direct wage subsidies paid to employers (Hipkins et al., 2020). A combined investment of over NZ$700 million was allocated in the 2020 budget.

Globally, economies are seeing a growing divide between highly skilled employment and very low skilled service roles (Bialik, 2010; Coelli et al., 2012). In New Zealand, this has been emphasized by the dependence of the economy on migration at both ends of the skills continuum. Immigration into New Zealand has been responsible for approximately half the workforce growth for the last decade with net migration of between 40 and 80 thousand working age adults annually from countries other than Australia (New Zealand Productivity Commission, 2021). The New Zealand Productivity Commission observe that "'Buying' skills through immigration is sometimes quicker and easier for employers than 'making' the skills New Zealand needs by training people, especially when feedback mechanisms between the domestic education system and employers are weak" (New Zealand Society of Anaesthesists, 2021, pp. 2–3, referring to NZPC, 2017).

Describing immigration as having a de-facto strategy reflects the absence of any actual strategy with priorities purposefully articulated by the government (New Zealand Productivity Commission, 2021, p. 13). Policy is developed under a very unclearly stated "national interest" mandate under the Immigration Act 2009. New Zealand has been criticised for following a de-facto strategy framed by low wages, limited investment in infrastructure to increase productivity, and an over-dependence on low-value migration to remediate the impact of the first two factors (Hickey, 2021). The result has included a significant growth in large numbers of people employed in low skills employment. The problem with addressing this is that the impact on these low skilled migrants would most likely be mass unemployment, not investment in their skill development, particularly given the issues already evident that were noted above.

NZPC (2021) observe that there are systematic relationships between the immigration settings driven by skills shortage, and the education systems. They note (New Zealand Productivity Commission, 2021, p. 27) that the current policy settings "may weaken accountabilities on employers to train and develop local workers", a passive observation that reflects the limited evidence collected by their enquiry and by agencies normally on direct investment by employers. The deflection of responsibility away from employers to substantially invest in skills development is a further illustration of the neoliberal market model dominating New Zealand under both major political parties (left and right of centre) noted above and was evident in the framing of the Te Pukenga restructuring which failed to address employer responsibility for investment (see below).

The dramatic impact that the COVID pandemic has had on migration calls into question the sustainability of this model of outsourced skills development at least in the short term. Closed borders have seen unemployment drop to very low levels (StatsNZ, 2022b) and many employers struggling to attract skilled staff without having to pay a significant premium (StatsNZ, 2022a). The disruptions are likely to continue for some years and should be seen as an opportunity to consider alternative strategies, if only to provide options and resilience in the operation of the national economy.

In summary, New Zealand faces a number of challenges in its engagement with Future Skills needs:

- An ill-defined conception of Future Skills that prevents any focused development in advance of need;
- Low investment by key private sector stakeholders directly in Future Skills identification and development;
- Low returns on investment in qualifications for individuals discouraging participation and creating a drain on capability through outward migration;
- Low capital investment in technologies to realise the productivity benefits of current and Future Skills; and
- Overdependence on an underperforming and underfunded public education system.

Overlaying all of these is a fixation on a model of education defined by formal qualifications and their regulation by government agencies rather than on development of human capabilities and knowledge for the future. This is sustained by the self-interest of employers who act in many countries to influence the qualification system both directly through investment (in some countries) and employment, and indirectly through political influence on government funding mechanisms and educational policies (Marshall, 2018a). The impact of this has been seen in the attempts to reconceive the university in new forms including the university of technology, the enterprise university, and the entrepreneurial university (Clark, 1998; Fayolle & Redford, 2014; Marginson & Considine, 2000). Despite these attempts, increasingly the degree is being challenged as being disconnected from the needs of society as it grapples with its Future Skills development needs (Calonge et al., 2019; Dlabajová & Nekov, 2017; Ehlers, 2020; Kinash & Crane, 2015; Zaber et al., 2019). This has seen disengagement by employers cited (Ernst & Young, 2015) although such observations are not necessarily consistent with the evidence from employment data and employer research suggesting that the situation is more complex than it might appear on the surface (Gallagher, 2016).

The next section presents a mechanism for responding to this wicked problem and responding to the complexity it embodies through a focus on the power of communities and social engagement to motivate a shift towards Future Skills development.

30.4 The Universal Learning Community: a Laboratory for Future Skills Development

More than fifty years ago, the state of California enacted the Californian Master Plan under the leadership of Clark Kerr (Marginson, 2016b). This plan was guided by the desire to see public investment in tertiary education having a positive impact on reducing social inequality. The plan used a centralized coordination of activities to maximise scale and efficiency and to leverage collective power in negotiations with suppliers and other stakeholders and prioritisation of expensive and constrained resources such that they had the greatest impact on the public good. This was a plan for an age where education and skills development occurred at the start of adult life and where centralized management and control was normalized both in public life and in the operation of businesses. In many respects, this plan reflects the observations and predictions of sociologist Martin Trow who created the conception of mass education (Trow, 1973) to describe the behaviours and expectations made of an education system when its scale and impact grows beyond the historically framed elite model of the early university. Mass education systems are typified by the impact that education has on society, particularly the economy, and the need for a large-scale workforce delivering a clearly defined set of skills to an industrialised economy efficiently and at low cost. These drivers create the context for a regulated bureaucracy and systems aimed at maximizing the economic efficiency and impact of education (Marshall, 2018b).

In contemplating Future Skills needs, the Government has acknowledged that centralised control and education at one stage of life no longer meet our needs and that a more contextualised and lifelong approach to skills development is needed for the future (Ministry of Business, Innovation and Employment, 2019). The current framing of skills development in New Zealand is firmly anchored in the mass education sensibilities of a previous millennium. The Future Skills identified as important to New Zealand are defined in response to a dynamic world and the consequent need for continuous development of the individual. This leads to the conclusion that the role of the formal degree qualification for school leavers is a starting point for a lifetime of learning. Future Skills development depends on systems that empower learning limited only by the energy and interests of the learners. Instead of a curriculum defined in detail in advance generically for all, skills education should respond to individual needs at a point in time, with objectives that they are responsible for defining, and achieved outcomes that represent value to themselves, peers, their employer and the communities they participate in.

Skills development responding to needs implies a context for those needs, which suggests that in-place learning in employment and community contexts is important. This leads to the proposal that skills learning for employment is a workplace activity that needs to be recognized as such and done as paid work, not an activity that occurs elsewhere with costs and outcomes separated from the employer. It also implies that skills development takes place in a community of employees, all learning simultaneously but not synchronously, as experience, roles, and skills will vary. Finally it implies that the measures of success need to be those that are valued directly by those involved, often through accepted measures of productivity, rather than abstract proxies supplied by credentials—micro or macro.

We need to revisit the challenge of educating adults over their lifetime from first principles. Rather than framing skills development as a problem of qualification provision defined by models that draw on the epistemology of the industrial age, it needs to be seen as an opportunity to identify new learning modalities that use post-industrial concepts. This takes the framing into the space that Trow described as universal education (Trow, 2010). Here, the participation in education is routine and experienced by essentially everyone in society according to their needs and interests. Qualifications in a universal space are at still useful as a marker of important transitions but the primary focus shifts to the enablement of lifelong learning.

This leads us to a new conception for Future Skills development—the universal learning community. A feature of this model is its framing as a social network drawing on the human need for connection and meaning through our membership of groups and communities. Although technology is a potentially important enabler of changes in work, particularly in professional contexts (Susskind & Susskind, 2022), it is not the defining feature of the universal learning community.

The Implication of the community model within a workplace or industry is that the different skills and experiences will see participants engaging with each other to support each others' learning. The resulting experience can be expressed through the New Zealand Māori term "Ako" which captures the relationship between learning and teaching as one of reciprocity, i.e., that in teaching someone, learning also occurs for the teacher (Hemara, 2000). Historically, Ako was experienced in the Māori culture in a very tightly controlled manner respecting the worldview, customs, and spirituality of that culture (Mead, 2003). The features of the Ako conception translated into the context of the modern New Zealand bi-cultural society are (Marshall, 2014, p. 57):

- The design of education in the form of relationships between people who are not equals but treat each other with respect.
- The work of the participants is structured by a set of implicit and explicit cultural norms and expectations independent of the subject being studied.
- Learning is active, and the act of learning stimulates and provokes a pedagogical response from the teacher that facilitates deeper learning by both the learner and the teacher.
- The learner and the teacher are participants in a larger community that supports and sustains them and which values both of their contributions to the life of that community.

Finally, the Ako conception reshapes expectations regarding curriculum, shifting it from the structured form enacted in mass education in qualification frameworks to a more fluid framework negotiated by the participants collectively in real time. This is not a completely informal experience: "Ako requires all participants respect each other, respect the systems that sustain their learning, and explicitly participate in a community of shared endeavor" (Marshall, 2014, p. 67). These differences are summarised in Fig. 30.1.

A natural laboratory for the exploration of the universal learning community for Future Skills development is evident in the regulated professions where these features are already present. These groups, including the military, police, emergency, and health care, already recognize the value of practice networks, distributed leadership and continuous professional development. The shift needed to start implementing a new model with such groups is thus relatively subtle.

Currently their continuous professional development is framed by the compliance requirements imposed on individuals to maintain their professional certifications under the regulatory environment operating in a mass model of education. The focus inevitably is on the efficiency of the compliance mechanism rather than the efficacy of the learning mechanism under this model, and the resulting burdens of compliance reduce responsiveness to meeting Future Skills needs which by their nature are not fully evident in the contemporary workplace.

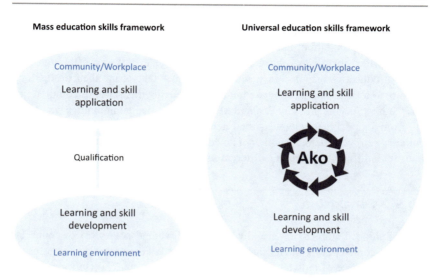

Fig. 30.1 Mass and universal education skills frameworks

Networking with colleagues is separate, often undervalued by employers, and limited in many cases to individual mentoring, occasional seminars, and social events. If the focus shifted to using professional networking as the context for experiencing and engaging in development, with recognition given to those participants who enable regular networking connections, with formal development an adjunct, then the opportunity arises to have a system that can evolve rapidly in the face of emerging changes in the practices and knowledge of the profession.

Modern off the shelf collaboration tools, now a common feature of the COVID workplace, provide all of the necessary infrastructure needed to enable work in this new model to be educationally recognized. Rather than providing training, content, and assessment activities, the role of educators becomes one of enablers, participants in the universal learning community, rather than outsiders operating in disconnected learning environments. The shift in pedagogical approach from certifier to mentor is linked to the skills of professional reflection, evidence-based practice, and self-analysis. The record of learning is no longer the responsibility of the education provider, but rather that of the learner and is evident in their portfolio of work and the recognition it achieves from colleagues as evidence of the cognitive and meta-cognitive skills, social and emotional skills, and practical and physical skills of the learner and their capacity to manage the ongoing learning they are taking in light of Future Skills needs (Scully et al., 2018).

The professions listed above have an advantage in this space through their ethos of collective responsibility and shared values that define their professional identity to a large extent. They are not alone in having this sense of common purpose, others such as the New Zealand Māori and Pasifika communities could benefit from a model that empowers their definition of success from within their own cultures, setting aside the features of an educational system created to solve problems for a different culture in a different time and place.

30.5 Conclusion

By definition, Future Skills are always prospective and somewhat disconnected from the contemporary environment. They reflect beliefs and aspirations for the future experience of individuals, communities, and nations. The Universal Learning Community model provides a sustainable mechanism for supporting individuals as the Future Skills needed for their lives start to emerge as possibilities that are then translated into tangible needs for themselves, their community, and for society.

A major advantage of the model is that it addresses the disconnect between those defining possible Future Skills and those who will enact these in their own communities. Top-down mass models of education reflect the expectations and systems of an earlier industrial society which is rapidly being seen as failing to meet the emerging needs of the millennium and changing values with regard to wealth creation, inequality, sustainability, and our collective and individual place in a global society. The model is also very strongly aligned to the conception of Learning Cities and its objective to "create and reinforce individual empowerment and social cohesion, economic and cultural prosperity, and sustainable development" (UNESCO Institute for Lifelong Learning, 2015, p. 9). The Learning City is defined (p. 9) as mobilizing its resources in every sector to:

- promote inclusive learning from basic to higher education;
- revitalize learning in families and communities;
- facilitate learning for and in the workplace;
- extend the use of modern learning technologies;
- enhance quality and excellence in learning; and
- foster a culture of learning throughout life.

The universal learning community outlined in this chapter is a means by which universities can contribute to this vision, placing themselves in a key leadership role within the living city. The implication for those leading higher education institutions is to recognize the importance of developing organisational capabilities for enacting learning in contexts other than those of the established university campus and classroom. The COVID-19 pandemic has been recognized by some leaders as stimulating positive changes in organisational decision making, flexibility and capacity to enact new learning models (PwC, 2020) and this can be used to further explore new partnerships for the operation of emergent universal learning communities. A step on that pathway can be the use of work-integrated learning or internships but only if these are recognized for the Ako they enable, and not merely seen as being in service of the certification of qualifications.

For individual faculty, the importance of anchoring their scholarship in the wider community cannot be overstated. Those in disciplines associated with professional groups will already be aware of the importance of sustaining their place in the profession, but here also there is a need to act to build networks and connections, not to merely analyse and document.

The model of skill development proposed here strips out the qualification systems and replaces them with a focus on the learner as an agent for their own and others' skill development—"microlearning" if you will. This has the virtue of not requiring abandonment of existing approaches before it is enacted. Formal degrees and established training and skills models can co-exist with microlearning and complement each other. In all likelihood, degrees or similar qualifications will remain an important transition into complex areas of work requiring a broad and deep knowledge of a field. The microlearning model enacted through a universal learning community offers a means by which that foundation can be sustained throughout a life. It can be experienced within a community rather than requiring costly periods away with all of the associated disruptions and disconnections from the context that learning is intended to be used within. By shifting the focus from the credential to the learning, the skills development experience can be framed and reframed continuously to meet current and future needs.

The remaining challenge lies with employers who must invest in creating the environment that enables microlearning, rather than continuing to see Future Skills development as a problem for others to solve for them. Here, the professions need to act to sustain themselves by using their influence over employers and leaders in different industries to create universal learning communities within workplaces. Peter Drucker is said to have observed that "The best way to predict the future is to create it", analogously then, the best way to have the skills needed for the future is to create the environment where those skills are themselves created.

> **Future Skills in Practice: Our Recommendations**
> - Future Skills need to be understood in terms of a context that leads to their identification, development and application.
> - Qualifications need to be understood as important enablers and starting points for learning but insufficient in meeting the needs of individuals and societies for Future Skills.
> - Higher education institutions need to develop systems, capabilities and experience with learning in communities and professional settings beyond the traditional academic campus and classroom.
> - Higher education faculty need to develop the relationships and capabilities needed to associate their scholarship with the wider community.

References

Adelman, C. (2009). *The Bologna process for U.S. eyes: Re-learning higher education in the age of convergence*. Institute for Higher Education Policy.

Archibald, R. B., & Feldman, D. H. (2010). *Why does college cost so much?* Oxford University Press.

Arrow, K. J. (1973). Higher Education as a Filter. *Journal of Public Economics, 2*(3), 193–216.

Barrie, S. C. (2006). What do we mean by the generic attributes of graduates? *Higher Education, 51*(2), 215–241.

Barrie, S. C., Hughes, C., & Smith, C. (2009). *The national graduate attributes project: Integration and assessment of graduate attributes in curriculum*. Australian Learning and Teaching Council.

Becker, G. S. (1993). *Human capital: A theoretical and empirical analysis with special reference to education* (3rd ed.). The University of Chicago Press.

Bialik, C. (2010, September 4). Seven careers in a lifetime? Think twice, researchers say. *The Wall Street Journal.* https://www.wsj.com/articles/SB10001424052748704206804575468162805877990.

Bowen, W. G. (2012). *The 'cost disease' in higher education: Is technology the answer?.* Stanford University.

Brown, P., Lauder, H., Ashton, D., & D. (2011). *The global auction: The broken promises of education, jobs, and incomes*. Oxford University Press.

Buchanan, J., Ryan, R., Anderson, M., Calvo, R., Glozier, N., & Peter, S. (2018). *Preparing for the best and worst of times: Future frontiers analytical report*. Sydney.

Calonge, D. S., Shah, M. A., Riggs, K., & Connor, M. (2019). MOOCs and upskilling in Australia: A qualitative literature study. *Cogent Education, 6*(1), 1687392. https://doi.org/10.1080/2331186X.2019.1687392.

Carnevale, A. P., Jayasundera, T., & Cheah, B. (2012). *The college advantage: Weathering the economic storm.* Georgetown Public Policy Unit.

Clark, B. (1998). *Creating entrepreneurial universities: Organizational pathways to transformation.* IAU and Pergamon Press.

Coelli, M., Tabasso, D., & Zakirova, R. (2012). *Studying beyond age 25: Who does it and what do they gain?.*

Crawford, R. (2016). *History of tertiary education reforms in New Zealand* (Research Note 2016/1). https://www.productivity.govt.nz/assets/Documents/65759a16ed/History-of-tertiary-education-reforms.pdf.

Deissinger, T. (2015). The German dual vocational education and training system as 'good practice'? *Local Economy, 30*(5), 557–567. https://doi.org/10.1177/0269094215589311.

Department of Education and Training. (2015). *Higher education funding in Australia.* Department of Education and Training.

Dlabajová, M., & Nekov, M. (Eds.) (2017). *Report on a new skills agenda for Europe (2017/2002(INI)).*

Dore, R. (1976). *The diploma disease: Education, qualification and development.* George Allen and Unwin.

Education Counts. (2022). *Tertiary summary tables.* https://www.educationcounts.govt.nz/statistics/summary_tables.

Ehlers, U.-D. (2020). *Future skills: The future of learning and higher education.*

Ernst and Young. (2015). EY transforms its recruitment selection process for graduates, undergraduates and school leavers. http://www.ey.com/UK/en/Newsroom/News-releases/15-08-03—EY-transforms-its-recruitment-selectionprocess-for-graduates-undergraduates-and-school-leavers.

Fayolle, A., & Redford, D. T. (Eds.). (2014). *Handbook on the entrepreneurial university.* Edward Elgar Publishing Limited.

Fincher, M., & Katsinas, S. (2017). Testing the limits of the price elasticity of potential students at colleges and universities: Has the increased direct cost to the student begun to drive down higher education enrolment? *Journal of Higher Education Policy and Management, 39*, 31–39. https://doi.org/10.1080/1360080X.2016.1211975.

Fitzsimons, P. (2015). Human capital theory and education. In M. A. Peters (Ed.), *Encyclopedia of educational philosophy and theory* (pp. 1–4). Springer.

Gallagher, S. R. (2016). *The future of university credentials: New developments at the intersection of higher education and hiring.* Harvard Education Press.

Geiger, R. (2011). The ten generations of American higher education. In P. G. Altbach, P. J. Gumport, & R. O. Berdahl (Eds.), *Higher education in the twentyfirst century: Social, political, and economic challenges* (3rd ed., pp. 37–68). Johns Hopkins University Press.

Gillies, D. (2015). Human capital theory in education. In M. A. Peters (Ed.), *Encyclopedia of educational philosophy and theory* (pp. 1–5). Springer.

Golden, D. (2006). *The price of admission: How America's ruling class buys its way into elite colleges—and who gets left outside the gates.* Random House.

Healey, N., & Gunby, P. (2012). The impact of recent government tertiary education policies on access to higher education in New Zealand. *Journal of Educational Leadership, Policy and Practice, 27*(1), 29–45.

Hemara, W. (2000). *Māori pedagogies: A view from the literature.* NZCER Press.

Hickey, B. (2021). Dawn chorus: How populous should New Zealand be? The Kaka. *The Kaka by Bernard Hickey.* https://thekaka.substack.com/p/dawn-chorus-how-populous-should-nz.

Hipkins, C. (2017). Making tertiary education and training affordable for all. *Cabinet Paper.*

Hipkins, C. (2019). Consulting on proposals for vocational education system reform. Wellington: Ministry of Education. https://conversation.education.govt.nz/assets/Uploads/28-2019-01-28-Cabinet-Paper-Consulting-on-Proposals-for-Vocational-Education-System-Reform-plus-annexes-1-4.pdf.

Hipkins, C. (2021). *Industry leadership for our training system becomes reality: Ministerial press release.* https://www.beehive.govt.nz/release/industry-leadership-our-training-system-becomes-reality

Hipkins, C., Sepuloni, C., O'Connor, D., & Jackson, W. (2020). *Free trades training to support New Zealanders into work.* https://www.beehive.govt.nz/release/free-trades-training-support-new-zealanders-work.

Hipkins, R. (2018). *How the key competencies were developed: The evidence base.* Wellington. https://www.nzcer.org.nz/system/files/Paper%201%20Evidence%20base_final.pdf.

Hipkins, R., & Vaughn, K. (2019). *Subject choice for the future of work: Insights from research literature.* Wellington. https://www.productivity.govt.nz/assets/Documents/3d0d213c1e/Insights-from-research-literature-NZCER.pdf.

Hirsch, F. (1976). *Social limits to growth.* Harvard University Press.

Hussey, A. (2012). Human capital augmentation versus the signaling value of MBA education. *Economics of Education Review, 31*(4), 442–451.

Hyslop, D., Le, T., & Riggs, L. (2020). *Returns to adult education and training in New Zealand* (Motu Working Paper 20–03). Wellington. https://www.productivity.govt.nz/assets/Documents/cbd511f006/Returns-to-adult-education-and-training-in-NZ.pdf.

Iannelli, C., & Smyth, E. (2017). Curriculum choices and school-to-work transitions among upper-secondary school-leavers in Scotland and Ireland. *Journal of Education and Work, 30*(7), 731–740. https://doi.org/10.1080/13639080.2017.1383093.

Jung, J. (2021). Working to learn and learning to work: Research on higher education and the world of work. *Higher Education Research and Development, 41*(1), 92–106. https://doi.org/10.1080/07294360.2021.2002274.

Kinash, S., & Crane, L. (2015). Enhancing graduate employability of the 21st century learner. In D. Churchill, Chiu, Thomas K. F., & N. J. Gu (Eds.), *Proceedings of the international mobile learning festival 2015*: *Mobile learning MOOCs and 21st century learning* (pp. 148–171)

Larner, W., & Le Heron, R. (2005). Neo-Liberalizing Spaces and Subjectivities: Reinventing New Zealand Universities. *Organization, 12*(6), 843–862. https://doi.org/10.1177/1350508405057473.

Lewis, N., & Shore, C. (2019). From unbundling to market making: Reimagining, reassembling and reinventing the public university. *Globalisation, Societies and Education, 17*, 11–27. https://doi.org/10.1080/14767724.2018.1524287.

Marginson, S. (2016a). *Higher education and the common good*. Melbourne University Press.

Marginson, S. (2016b). *The dream is over: The crisis of Clark Kerr's California idea of higher education*. University of California Press.

Marginson, S. (2016c). The worldwide trend to high participation higher education: Dynamics of social stratification in inclusive systems. *Higher Education, 72*, 413–434. https://doi.org/10.1007/s10734-016-0016-x.

Marginson, S., & Considine, M. (2000). *The enterprise university: Power, governance and reinvention in Australia*. Cambridge University Press.

Marshall, S. (2014). Open educational curricula interpreted through the Māori concept of Ako. In M. Gosper & D. Ifenthaler (Eds.), *Curriculum models for the 21st century: Using learning technologies in higher education* (pp. 55–70). Springer.

Marshall, S. (2018a). Internal and external stakeholders in higher education. In S. Marshall (Ed.), *Shaping the university of the future: Using technology to catalyse change in university learning and teaching* (pp. 77–102). Springer.

Marshall, S. (2018b). The Scale and Scope of Higher Education. In S. Marshall (Ed.), *Shaping the university of the future: Using technology to catalyse change in university learning and teaching* (pp. 47–76). Springer.

Martens, K., & Starke, P. (2008). Small country, big business? New Zealand as education exporter. *Comparative Education, 44*(1), 3–19. https://doi.org/10.1080/03050060701809367.

Mead, H. M. (2003). *Tikanga Māori: Living by Māori values*. Huia Publishers.

Ministry of Business, Innovation and Employment. (2019). *Future of work tripartite forum strategic assessment: Priorities for New Zealand's future of work*. Wellington. https://www.treasury.govt.nz/sites/default/files/2019-11/fow-forum-aug-4204590.pdf.

New Zealand Government. (2020). *Education and training act 2020*

New Zealand Government. (2021). *Education (Hanga-Aro-Rau manufacturing, engineering, and logistics workforce development council) Order 2021*.

New Zealand Immigration. (2023). *Skills shortage list checker*. https://skillshortages.immigration.govt.nz.

New Zealand Productivity Commission. (2017). *New models of tertiary education: Final report*. Wellington. https://www.productivity.govt.nz/assets/Documents/2d561fce14/Final-report-Tertiary-Education.pdf.

New Zealand Productivity Commission. (2020). *Technological change and the future of work: Final report*. Wellington. https://www.productivity.govt.nz/assets/Documents/0634858491/Final-report_Technological-change-and-the-future-of-work.pdf.

New Zealand Productivity Commission. (2021). *Immigration—Fit for the future: Preliminary findings and recommendations*. Wellington. http://www.productivity.govt.nz/inquiries/immigration-settings.

New Zealand Society of Anaesthesists. (2021). Immigration—Fit for the Future. https://www.productivity.govt.nz/assets/Submission-Documents/immigration-settings/DR-158-New-Zealand-Society-of-Anaesthetists.pdf. Accessed 25 June 2023.

OECD. (2018). *The future of education and skills: Education 2030*. https://www.oecd.org/education/2030/E2030%20Position%20Paper%20(05.04.2018).pdf.

OECD. (2021). *Education at a glance 2021*. OECD Publishing.

PwC. (2020). *COVID-19 recovery and improvement: Overcoming the challenges and locking-in the benefits: A perspective from senior finance leaders in the NHS*. https://www.

pwc.co.uk/healthcare/assets/documents/covid-19-overcoming-challenges-and-locking-in-benefits.pdf.

Robinson, D. (2006). *The status of higher education teaching personnel in Australia, Canada, New Zealand, the United Kingdom, and the United States: Report prepared for education international*. https://www.caut.ca/docs/reports/the-status-of-higher-education-teaching-personnel-in-australia-canada-new-zealand-the-united-kingdom-and-the-united-states-report-prepared-for-education-international-(mar-2006).pdf.

Scully, D., O'Leary, M., & Brown, M. (2018). *The learning portfolio in higher education: A game of snakes and ladders*. Dublin

Sennett, R. (1998). *The corrosion of character*. Norton.

Shah, M., Grebennikov, L., & Nair, C. S. (2015). A decade of study on employer feedback on the quality of university graduates. *Quality Assurance in Education, 23*(3), 262–278.

Spence, M. (1973). Job market signaling. *Quarterly Journal of Economics, 87*(3), 355–374.

Spronken-Smith, R., C., M., A., F., S., S., N., J., M., et al. (2015). Evaluating engagement with graduate outcomes across higher education institutions in Aotearoa/New Zealand. *Higher Education Research & Development, 34*(5), 1014–1030. https://doi.org/10.1080/07294360.2015.1011098.

StatsNZ. (2022). *Annual wage inflation rises to 3.4 percent*. https://www.stats.govt.nz/news/annual-wage-inflation-rises-to-3-4-percent/.

StatsNZ. (2022). *Unemployment rate at 3.3 percent*. https://www.stats.govt.nz/news/unemployment-rate-at-3-3-percent.

Strathdee, R., & Cooper, G. (2017). Ethnicity, vocational education and training and the competition for advancement through education in New Zealand. *Journal of Vocational Education & Training, 69*(3), 371–389. https://doi.org/10.1080/13636820.2017.1300595.

Susskind, R., & Susskind, D. (2022). *The future of the professions: How technology will transform the work of human experts* (Updated). Oxford University Press USA—OSO.

Tertiary Education Commission. (2018). *ITP Roadmap 2020: Sector financial modelling*. Wellington. https://www.tec.govt.nz/assets/Publications-and-others/784c6ab31f/ITP-Roadmap-2020-Sector-Financial-Modelling-report.pdf.

Tertiary Education Commission. (2020). *Targeted Training and Apprenticeship Fund (free trades training)*. https://www.tec.govt.nz/funding/funding-and-performance/funding/fund-finder/targeted-training-and-apprenticeship-fund/. Accessed 7 April 2023.

Tertiary Education Commission. (2023). *2023 funding rates—Unified Funding System*. https://www.tec.govt.nz/rove/a-unified-funding-system-2/ufs-2023-funding-rates-2/.

The Treasury New Zealand. (1987). *Government management: Brief to the incoming government 1987*. Wellington.

Trow, M. (1973). *Problems in the transition from élite to mass higher education*. Carnegie Commission on Higher Education.

Trow, M. (2010). *Twentieth-century higher education: Elite to mass to universal*. The John Hopkins University Press.

Tumen, S., Crichton, S., & Dixon, S. (2015). *The impact of tertiary study on the labour market outcomes of low-qualified school leavers* (Working Paper 15/07). Wellington.

UNESCO Institute for Lifelong Learning. (2015). *UNESCO Global Network of Learning Cities: Guiding Documents*. Hamburg. https://uil.unesco.org/fileadmin/keydocuments/LifelongLearning/learning-cities/en-unesco-global-network-of-learning-cities-guiding-documents.pdf.

Wheelahan, L., & Moodie, G. (2017). Vocational education qualifications' roles in pathways to work in liberal market economies. *Journal of Vocational Education & Training, 69*(1), 10–27. https://doi.org/10.1080/13636820.2016.1275031.

Wolf, A. (2004). Education and economic performance: Simplistic theories and their policy consequences. *Oxford Review of Economic Policy, 20*(2), 315–334.

Zaber, M. A., Karoly, L. A., & Whipkey, K. (2019). *Reimagining the workforce development and employment system for the 21st century and beyond* (research report). https://www.rand.org/pubs/research_reports/RR2768.html.

Professor Stephen Marshall (PFHEA) is Director at the Victoria University of Wellington Centre for Academic Development. Stephen leads Victoria University's Digital Vision and Strategy for Learning and Teaching initiatives and researches in the areas of organizational change in higher education, quality, benchmarking, plagiarism and academic integrity, intellectual property, and the development of educational policy and strategy supporting and encouraging the effective use of technology. He is co-creator of the internationally recognized and applied e-learning maturity model (eMM, http://e-learning.geek.nz/emm/) and author of the 2018 Springer book "Shaping the University of the Future: Using Technology to Catalyze Change in University Learning and Teaching".

Open Access This chapter is licensed under the terms of the Creative Commons Attribution 4.0 International License (http://creativecommons.org/licenses/by/4.0/), which permits use, sharing, adaptation, distribution and reproduction in any medium or format, as long as you give appropriate credit to the original author(s) and the source, provide a link to the Creative Commons license and indicate if changes were made.

The images or other third party material in this chapter are included in the chapter's Creative Commons license, unless indicated otherwise in a credit line to the material. If material is not included in the chapter's Creative Commons license and your intended use is not permitted by statutory regulation or exceeds the permitted use, you will need to obtain permission directly from the copyright holder.

Printed in the United States
by Baker & Taylor Publisher Services